GORDON WRIGHT

Professor of History, Stanford University

ADVISORY EDITOR TO DODD, MEAD & COMPANY

AN AGE OF CONTROVERSY:

Discussion Problems in

Twentieth-Century European History

AN AGE OF CONTROVERSY:

Discussion Problems in
Twentieth-Century European History

GORDON WRIGHT *and*
ARTHUR MEJIA, JR.

STANFORD UNIVERSITY

10 53

DODD, MEAD & COMPANY
New York · Toronto · 1969

Library of Congress Catalog Card Number: 63-10255

Tenth Printing

Printed in the United States of America

PREFACE

To single out the twentieth century as "an age of controversy" is perhaps to betray a certain naïveté about the course of human affairs. Such a label, like the even commoner term "age of transition," applies in some degree to every period in modern history. The really exceptional thing would be an age of noncontroversy—as, for example, that unique "era of good feeling" in United States history of which we used to speak, before we learned that it, too, was a myth.

Yet perhaps the twentieth century deserves the description more than most. For one thing, it has been a time of almost constant stress, upheaval, readjustment; and when revolutionary changes in institutions, ideas, and power relationships are in progress, those changes are likely to generate unusually intense argument. Furthermore, we are still too close to the events of the period to sort out the historians' rival judgments of them with any certainty. It is true that the mere passage of time is not enough to make historians arrive at a common orthodoxy; but time does give their debates a kind of patterned and formalized character, like the steps in a minuet. Historians' debates about our own era, on the other hand, retain much of the passion of remembered events, and much of the distorted focus of a wide-screen movie seen from the second row. If these debates possess the cadence of any dance step, it is certainly not the minuet. Sometimes one suspects that it may be closer to rock-and-roll.

How to attack the study of a period so close behind us, so complex and so filled with controversy, is a chronic problem. The survey textbook and the series of interpretive lectures provide the usual framework in American universities. Reading in specialized monographs, in a volume of "source readings," and in a problem book or two may furnish additional depth and breadth. These are valid devices, but even when combined they are not likely to convey the full complexity of the age, or the controversial nature of most judgments of it.

This volume is designed to provide that extra dimension. It is no substitute for a textbook, or for a set of interpretive lectures; its purpose is to supplement them by providing students with some significant problems for discussion. The problems we have chosen vary widely, both in the kinds of issues they raise and in the nature of the reading selections upon which they rest. It might have been possible to standardize them more rigorously, in length and tone as well as in content; but the cost of standardizing seemed too high. Problems in history cannot be chopped up like cordwood into neat units of equal length and thermal value. Some of them have inspired more printed controversy than others; some of them require more elucidation than others.

It will be noted that the volume is not made up of "source selections" in the normal sense of that term. The editors have no quarrel with those historians who urge the value of reading primary materials—eyewitness accounts, treaty texts, diplomatic documents, and so on. They believe, however, that there may be another kind of value in setting two or more secondary accounts side by side, and requiring students to weigh one against another. In this fashion, the nature of historical writing as a set of subjective judgments about the past comes out much more clearly, and the truth is no longer "what the book says." Several different historians, confronted with exactly the same documentary sources of information, may arrive at sharply different conclusions. This is an often-frustrating fact, but it may as well be learned early. It does not follow, of course, that one man's judgments are as sound, as accurate, as honest as another's. Total relativism is the trap into which the unwary or cynical student of historical variability may slip. There are ways to judge the motives and methods of different historians, just as one learns to judge the credibility and the perceptiveness of witnesses in a court of law, or of acquaintances in everyday life. One purpose of student discussion of these materials in a modern history course ought to be to develop some standards of judgment, some tests by which any work of history may be read with greater penetration and a more critical sense. To furnish some guidance in this enterprise, but without dictating a conclusion, would seem to be the natural function of the instructor.

Although a few good single-problem books exist for the period of twentieth-century Europe, there is no serviceable multiproblem book to accompany a course of a full quarter's or semester's duration. The fifteen topics in this volume are intended to provide weekly supplementary readings and discussion materials for such a course. The editors believe that they can be used in a variety of ways—though they are designed specifically for weekly small-group discussions, preceded in each case by two or three related lectures. This was the system utilized at Stanford University in 1962 when some of the problems were given a trial run. The editors are grateful to the students who served as guinea pigs in the experiment, and who made a number of cogent suggestions for improvement (some of which have been incorporated into the printed version).

Our thanks are due to Dr. F. E. Terman, Provost of Stanford University, who provided funds to prepare the initial experiment in the use of these problem materials; and to the following authors and relatives of authors who generously granted permission to reprint portions of their work: Mr. F. R. Allemann, Prof. Rudolf Allers, M. Raymond Aron, Prof. Daniel Bell, M. Georges Bonnet, Prof. Crane Brinton, Prof. Henry Steele Commager, Mr. C. A. R. Crosland, Mr. R. H. S. Crossman, Dr. M. M. Drachkovitch, Mr. Paul Einzig, Prof. Alfred Kazin, Mrs. Inge Neumann Marcuse, Dr. Margaret Mead, Prof. O. Hobart Mowrer, Lady Namier, Mr. Herman Phleger, Dr. Hermann Rauschning, Lord Robbins, Mr. A. L. Rowse, Prof. Bernadotte E. Schmitt, and Dr. Rudolph

A. Winnacker. We are grateful also to the editors of the following periodicals who have authorized us to reprint passages from articles: *Atlantic Monthly, The Current Digest of the Soviet Press, Encounter, Foreign Affairs, History Today, International Affairs, The New Leader, The New Statesman and Nation, The New York Times, The New Yorker, Political Science Quarterly, Quarterly Review, Review of Politics, Saturday Review, Twentieth Century, Virginia Quarterly Review, World Politics.* The Council of the Historical Association in London, and the administrative authorities of the University of Leeds, graciously consented to allow the use of pamphlet materials issued by them. Finally, we wish to acknowledge the kindness of the following publishing firms which permitted us to include passages from books bearing their imprint: Appleton-Century-Crofts; Atheneum Publishers; Clarendon Press; Coward Mc-Cann; Crown Publishers; Dodd, Mead & Co.; Doubleday and Co.; Droz et Cie.; Duell, Sloan & Pearce; The Free Press of Glencoe; Grove Press; Librairie Hachette; Harcourt, Brace and World; Harper and Row; Harvard University Press; Holt, Rinehart and Winston; Houghton Mifflin Co.; International Publishers; Alfred A. Knopf; Little, Brown and Co.; The Macmillan Co.; Oxford University Press; Frederick A. Praeger; Princeton University Press; Random House; Henry Regnery Co.; Viking Press. We are indebted to Professor Donald G. Rohr of Brown University for a number of cogent suggestions and criticisms, and to Mrs. Genia Graves of Dodd, Mead & Co. for seeing the manuscript through the press and arranging for publishers' permissions.

The original footnotes which appeared in some of the books and articles cited have been omitted. A few explanatory footnotes have been inserted by the editors.

G. W.
A. M., Jr.

CONTENTS

I.

TRANSITION TO THE TWENTIETH CENTURY

Few contrasts in modern history are more striking than that between the Europe of the nineteenth century and the Europe of the twentieth. The nineteenth century, viewed in retrospect, now appears to us as an unparalleled period of peace, progress, and hope. From 1815 to 1914, Europe experienced an unprecedented ninety-nine years without a general war. In almost every realm there was steady advance—in material production, technology, ease and comfort of living, literacy, the practice of constitutional government. The world, under unchallenged European leadership, seemed to be moving toward a kind of automatic, self-balancing economic system, with few barriers to the flow of goods, capital, or people. Psychologically, it was an age of optimism and confidence, of faith in an unlimited destiny for man.

No one born into the mid-twentieth century needs to be provided with a catalog of the differences between that age and his own. Since 1914 (which is often regarded as the true breaking point between the nineteenth and twentieth centuries) Europeans have almost constantly been fighting a war, or recovering from a war, or preparing themselves for a new war. Indeed, the French critic Raymond Aron calls our time an age of chain wars, in which each conflict creates more issues than it settles, and thus serves as catalyst or trigger for its bigger and better successor. Since 1914, the old quasi-automatic world economic system has given way to chronic instability and inflation. And in the psychological realm, the dominant mood has come to be marked by doubt, pessimism, even despair. Someone has observed that if one compares the outlook of late nineteenth-century western man with that of his mid-twentieth-century successor, one finds evidence of the most rapid mental revolution in human history.

It is tempting to suppose that the disastrous war of 1914–18—still "the Great War" to many Europeans—was responsible for destroying the comfortable and optimistic nineteenth-century world. Some scholars have advanced this thesis, and have described August 1914 as "the crucial turning point in modern western history," or as the date when modern history gave way (as ancient and medieval times once did) to a new era that might be labeled "the Fourth Epoch" or "the postmodern age." In its simplest and most extreme form, such a thesis might suggest

1

that a healthy and stable western world was shaken down by a war which might have been avoided, and which left a heritage of chronic instability and violence.

There is another point of view that finds the roots of twentieth-century disorder in the more distant past—either in the rise of secularism from the Renaissance onward (as some Catholic moralists have argued), or in the Enlightenment with its allegedly overrationalistic view of man (as some conservatives contend), or in that very nineteenth century which seems in retrospect to have been so progressive and confident. No doubt we have been too much inclined to stress the differences between the nineteenth and twentieth centuries, and thus to overlook the traits that they may have in common or the impact of the one upon the other. "During certain periods of history," observes Gerhard Masur, "the stabilizing forces prevail over the dynamic forces; during others the process is thrown into reverse. The nineteenth century saw the static energies give way to revolutionary tidal waves which are still surging up in our time." [1] Certainly the nineteenth century's change and flux went deep enough to undermine most of Europe's old institutions and to prepare the way for upheaval as a possible alternative to ordered progress.

"Sometime around 1890," writes the historian H. Stuart Hughes, "the intellectual revolution of our time apparently began." [2] That revolution, whose nature and significance appear more clearly to us than they did to contemporaries, seems to have originated out of two parallel challenges to the dominant world-view of the age. One challenge was external: it represented an attack on scientistic rationalism by men who stood outside that dominant current of ideas and who disliked everything about it. The second challenge was internal: it amounted to a process of questioning and re-examining, conducted by men who stood within the scientistic-rationalistic tradition itself.

The external challenge, mainly esthetic in nature, had been anticipated even before 1890 by such sensitive thinkers as the Russian novelist Fedor Dostoevsky and the German philosopher-essayist Friedrich Nietzsche. Theirs was a kind of emotional revulsion against what they regarded as the crass materialism, the stiflingly narrow rationalism, the worship of science, the faith in progress that had become the orthodoxy of the age. It was carried forward by schools of artists and writers of neoromantic temper, who raised the banner of art for art's sake and reasserted the role of the emotions as the proper guide to truth and beauty. Many of them became declared disciples of Nietzsche; in most central and western European countries, a dedicated coterie of Nietzscheans was active by 1914.

Far more important than this external attack was the parallel challenge that originated within the scientistic-rationalistic mood itself. Even before 1890, the dominant faith in inevitable progress through science and reason (so well expressed by its quasi-official spokesman Herbert Spencer) was being confronted by an attitude of pessimistic determinism that viewed man as caught in the grip of powerful elemental forces, as a helpless product of heredity and environment, rather than as master of his own fate through enlightened rational action. Such a viewpoint, shaped in part by a kind of corrupted Darwinism, emerged most clearly in fictional form—notably in the grim, oppressive novels of Emile Zola.

This new current of thought disturbed some reflective scholars who clung to the faith that man ought to be able to shape his own destiny through science and reason. Products themselves of the scientistic-rationalistic age, trained in its methods, they set out to use those methods in an effort to deepen their understanding of man

[1] Gerhard Masur, *Prophets of Yesterday* (New York: Macmillan, 1961), p. 38.
[2] H. Stuart Hughes, *An Essay for our Times* (New York: Knopf, 1949), p. 15.

and society, and thus to reassert the validity of the orthodox world-view. Some of them—like Sigmund Freud and Ivan Pavlov—were psychologists, concerned primarily with problems of individual behavior. Others—like Gustave Le Bon, Gaetano Mosca, Vilfredo Pareto, Robert Michels, Max Weber—were sociologists, concerned with the activities of men in groups. Whatever their purposes, their discoveries tended to have a common impact: they cast a blinding new light on man's non-rational side, on the subconscious motivation of much of human behavior, on the tendency of small elites to dominate every sort of social or political group, on the frequent contrast between appearance and reality in human affairs. The net effect was to shake the foundations of some of the nineteenth century's most cherished beliefs.

It is true that these new conceptions, essentially antirationalistic and antiequalitarian in nature, had not seriously weakened the hold of scientistic-rationalistic orthodoxy by 1914. Most Europeans remained confident, hopeful, convinced that science and reason could ensure progress. Perhaps the new thought would never have affected more than a limited avant-garde had it not been for the disintegrative impact of the Great War. Or perhaps the orthodox nineteenth-century view would have been swept away in any case, since scientific investigation had now proved it to be based on shaky foundations, on a set of half-truths about the nature of man and society. Or perhaps, without the shattering effect of the war and its aftermath, the valid parts of the nineteenth-century world-view might have been blended with the new insights of the innovators of 1890–1914.

These are some of the questions that might be worth discussing as one examines the post-1890 revolution in ideas, "the intellectual seedbed of our times." The reading selections in Chapter I, unlike those in later chapters, have not been chosen to represent contrasting points of view about the topic. What they do provide is a series of thoughtful interpretive judgments about the period 1890–1914 as a transitional epoch from nineteenth to twentieth century. Thus they may serve as backdrop, or springboard, to later discussion problems—particularly to those which will be designed, at the end of the volume, to stimulate thought about the Freudian impact upon our age and about the past half-century viewed as an historical epoch.

1.

The mid-century mark—January 1, 1950—brought forth a rash of articles in which historians and others sought to assess the character and significance of the past fifty years. One of the most lucid essays of the sort is that of Henry Steele Commager, professor of history at Amherst College and widely known as author and lecturer in the field of United States history. In the first section of his essay, Mr. Commager draws a sharp contrast between our times and the optimistic, complacent Victorian Era, and attempts to set forth the reasons for the repudiation of the Victorian synthesis just after 1900.

COMMAGER: 1900–1950: From Victorian to Atomic Age *

The twentieth century opened with Queen Victoria still on her throne. Already she had given her name to an era, and already men were beginning to

* From Henry Steele Commager, "1900–1950: From Victorian to Atomic Age," in *The New York Times Magazine*, Dec. 25, 1949, pp. 3–7. Reprinted by permission of Professor Commager and *The New York Times*.

pronounce that era the best, the most prosperous, and the most enlightened in history, forgetting or ignoring the poverty and misery, the cruelty, oppression and wars, that had stained its history. "Whatever may be thought of the nineteenth century," wrote the editor of the new World's Work, "when it can be seen in the perspective of universal history, it seems the best time to live that has so far come." It was the age of peace, plenty and contentment; it was the age of confidence; it was the age of progress.

And as men looked back over the years since the defeat of Napoleon at Waterloo they had some reason for pride in the past, and for confidence in the future. The nineteenth century had seen the abolition of slavery throughout the English-speaking world, and the end of serfdom in Russia. It had seen the emergence of the backward peoples of the world, the development of a more benevolent imperialism, the growth of justice and the acknowledgment of international law. Science had at last come into its own, and science promised the conquest of disease and of want and the creation of a world incomparably richer than any that men had known in the past.

The standard of living had been raised everywhere, and there were no material wants that science and technology could not supply. Popular education had spread throughout the Western world, and universal education was about to be realized. The ravages of the industrial revolution, it was felt, were being overcome, and industry tamed; everywhere reformers were busy christianizing the social order, and among the "dark Satanic mills" men were building a new Jerusalem.

Not only had the Victorian Era created what appeared to be general prosperity, it had created a new international order and brought about an era of peace. It was a bit awkward to insist upon the dawn of peace, to be sure, what with the Chinese-Japanese war, the Spanish-American war, the Boer War, and half a dozen minor wars in Africa, all in the decade of the Nineties, but men could argue, at least, that there had been no general war since Napoleon, and that wars seemed, now, to be banished to the fringes of western civilization. And throughout the western world there was free movement of men, money and goods—an achievement the full significance of which only a later generation would appreciate.

The nineteenth century had been a century of mounting nationalism, and of imperialism, but both, now, it seemed, were tempered and tamed. A balance of power had been achieved, and nations no longer needed to struggle for their places in the sun, while great new powers like the United States and Japan could advance without necessarily infringing on other nations.

The naked imperialism of the bad old days was giving way to an enlightened imperialism. The imperialism of the white man's burden had its philosophers in Benjamin Kidd and Josiah Strong, and its poet laureate in Rudyard Kipling, and, what was more, it seemed to be justifying itself by its good works in the backward areas of the earth. The British Empire stood as a vindication of imperialism. It was the empire on which the sun never set; of it men could repeat the proud boast of Horace Walpole after the great triumphs of 1763:

"Burn your Greek and Roman books, histories of little people." And Britain had learned her lesson; the empire was gradually being transformed into a commonwealth of nations, bound together by common ideals and loyalties, stronger by far than when it was held together by force.

The nineteenth century had seen, too, enormous strides toward democracy. It was not merely that suffrage was extended more widely—even to women in some more enlightened countries—but that the principle of popular government was acknowledged everywhere in the western world, and the machinery for making democracy effective was rapidly being perfected. The United States had led the way, and the triumph of the North in the Civil War had gone far to vindicate democracy in the Old World. In the last quarter of the century democracy had come on with a rush in many European countries—notably Germany, which was inaugurating experiments in social reform, in Scandinavia and Britain and France, and in the British dominions. As the nineteenth century melted into the twentieth, liberals could congratulate themselves that the long struggle for democracy was all but won and could look forward confidently to the spread of democratic rule everywhere on the globe.

And along with democracy went humanitarianism and reform. There was little doubt in the minds of contemporaries that the forces of righteousness were triumphing over the forces of evil. The enlightened social conscience was at work in every field and in every country, improving the lot of the laborer, championing the welfare of women and children, eliminating poverty and slums, eradicating disease, spreading education, lifting up the backward peoples, caring for the dangerous and the perishing classes, realizing the teachings of Christianity.

Not only had the nineteenth century achieved such progress as men could scarcely imagine, it had vindicated the philosophy of progress. That philosophy had been formulated in the eighteenth century, but its formulation was on the basis of philosophy now discarded. The nineteenth century had furnished a new and sounder scientific foundation for the doctrine of progress and, what was more, it had found a scientist-philosopher who proved that progress was a scientific fact. This was Herbert Spencer, who—so it was asserted by his rapt contemporaries—boasted the most capacious intellect of all time, and whose genius surpassed that of Aristotle and Newton, as the telegraph surpassed the carrier pigeon. Spencer succeeded in bringing all human phenomena within the framework of scientific laws and of proving that evolution implacably imposed progress on man. "Progress," he wrote, "is not an accident but a necessity. . . . Always toward perfection is the mighty movement—toward a complete development and a more unmixed good."

Then, gradually, a haze drew over the bright Victorian skies. One by one the buoyant hopes of the Victorians were doomed to disappointment. Within less than half a century prosperity gave way to ruin, universal peace to universal war, certainty to fear, security to insecurity, the ideal of progress to the doubt of survival. Never before in history had such bright hopes been so ruthlessly shattered; never had the philosophical temper undergone so profound a change. "My generation," wrote the philosopher James H. Tufts, "has seen the passing of systems of thought which had reigned since Augustus. The conception of the world as a kingdom ruled by God subject to His laws and their penalties . . . has dissolved. The sanctions of our inherited morality have gone. Principles and standards which had stood for nearly two thousand years are questioned."

They were not only questioned; they were repudiated. Philosophically the Spencerian faith in evolutionary progress was already giving way to scientific determinism. The new world of physics, chemistry and biology that science was unveiling was illimitable, impersonal and amoral. Matter, which had once seemed unimpeachable, lost its solidity and became but a complex of electrical reactions, "a wave of probability undulating into nothingness." Mind which had once seemed to distinguish man from all other creatures here below, was seen as indistinguishable from matter. God, Providence, Design, First Causes and Final Ends, all evaporated.

As the telescope and mathematics disclosed a universe so vast that it defied computation except in thousands of millions of light years and reduced the earth to a grain of pollen floating in illimitable space; as the microscope discovered a universe surging about each atom; as biology found the source of life in a series of apparently fortuitous chemical reactions; as the psychologists reduced the most profound thoughts of man, his highest flights of genius, to merely chemical impulses and uncontrollable reactions—the cosmic system familiar to the Victorians in which man possessed a soul, found meaning in life, and was sure of progress and of destiny, slipped quietly away.

Henry Adams, the most profound of all American interpreters of the new day, tells us that after 1900

he found himself in a land where no one had ever penetrated before; where order was an accidental relation obnoxious to nature; artificial compulsion imposed on motion; against which every free energy of the universe revolted; and which . . . resolved itself back into anarchy at last. He could not deny that the law of the new multiverse explained much that had been most obscure, especially the persistently fiendish treatment of man by man; the perpetual effort of society to establish law and the perpetual revolt of society against the law it had established; the perpetual building up of authority by force and the perpetual appeal to force to overthrow it; the perpetual symbolism of a higher law, and the perpetual relapse to a lower one; the perpetual victory of the principles of freedom, and their perpetual conversion into principles of power.

He himself came to the conclusion that mankind was like a clock that was running down, and that history would exhaust itself in another generation or two.

More important—certainly more consequential in conduct—was the teaching of the new psychology, especially that associated with Freud. The new psychology broke down the boundaries between the normal and the abnormal, revealing the unconscious origins of most impulses. Over these impulses man had no control. To Plato the doctrine "that there was no knowing and no use in seeking to know" was but idle fancy, but the new psychological school embraced idle fancy enthusiastically. The new psychology gave a powerful impulse toward irresponsibility and irrationality, and the twentieth century may yet be remembered not as the age of reason but as the age of unreason. Reason, normality, and morality were rejected not so much because they were wrong as because the concepts themselves had been drained of meaning.

It is the misfortune of every philosophy and every science to be vulgarized, and it was not, perhaps, the fault of the new physicists or the new psychologists, that their versions of the nature of man and the relation of man to the universe struck almost mortal blows at authority of all kinds—the authority of law, of morality and of reason. Yet the convulsions that overtook the world in the generation after 1914 and especially in the years after 1930—the rejection of law, the abandonment of morals, the ruthless destruction of life—were not unconnected with these new philosophical and scientific ideas.

Other developments in science, technology, philosophy and even in economy, accelerated the flight from reason and from responsibility. Of these the most obvious was the growing secularization of life, the decline of the influence and authority of the church and of religion. Secularism was no new phenomenon, but it may be doubted whether at any time for three hundred years religion had meant so little to Western man as it meant in the first half of the twentieth century. The decline of faith weakened the sanctions of moral conduct, and it was no accident that the two great powers that specifically repudiated religion, Germany and Russia, were those guilty of the most diabolical affronts to the dignity of man.

The decline of religious faith was, to be sure, as much a symptom as a cause. It was part of the general decline of authority, of the passing of the absolute in fields of thought. It was reflected in literature, art, music, in the social sciences, as in politics and morals. Where in such countries as Britain and the United States, however, this breakdown of authority led to self-expression, experimentation and liberation, in countries without strong traditions of individualism and freedom of thought, such as Germany, Italy and Russia, it led to a frantic search for new authority—even the authority of force.

Science, technology, urbanization and corporate growth all made their contributions to irresponsibility. Science came to seem too much for men, and for the first time since the emergence of modern science, men felt themselves unable to control what they had discovered. As Adams said, with the new science he had "entered a universe where all the old roads ran about in every direction, overrunning, dividing, subdividing, stopping abruptly, vanishing slowly, with sidepaths that led nowhere and sequences that could not be proved." Technology was often dehumanizing, transferring the center of gravity from the individual to the machine. The corporate device was, by its nature, artificial; it concentrated power but dissipated authority: natural man could never wholly escape moral considerations, but a purely artificial man could. The shift from country to city meant, among other things, a removal from the long discipline of nature—of the farm and of animals, of small communities—to the impersonal atmosphere of city and factory.

Soon it was a truism that science had outrun social science, and it was notable that Comte and Spencer had no successors. That science saved millions of lives, enabled millions of others to live who could not otherwise have been supported, released energies, provided leisure, enhanced man's enjoyment of life, could not for a moment be doubted. That it would be put to evil as well as to beneficent uses was no new idea. What was new was the fear that Adams expressed, that "science is to wreck us, and that we are like monkeys monkeying around with a loaded shell." The generation that lived in the shadow of atomic and bacteriological warfare was not one that could take the beneficence of science for granted. . . .

2.

Only in the last decade have intellectual historians begun to make a serious attempt to comprehend and explain the contemporary era in western culture. H. Stuart Hughes's *Consciousness and Society,* which examines the era from 1890 to 1930, is a pioneering work that has already achieved rank as the classic in the field. Mr. Hughes, who is professor of history at Harvard, is concerned with what he calls "the reorientation of European social thought" in the twentieth century; he attempts to portray the emergence and development, in the period 1890–1930, of the ideas that would come to inspire the "governing elites" of the western world in the era after 1930. The selections that follow provide a brilliant analysis of the first generation of positivist rebels against positivism (during the 1890's), and of their immediate successors, whom Hughes describes as "the generation of 1905."

HUGHES: Consciousness and Society *

There are certain periods in history in which a number of advanced thinkers, usually working independently one of another, have proposed views on human conduct so different from those commonly accepted at the time—and yet so manifestly interrelated—that together they seem to constitute an intellectual revolution. The decade of the 1890's was one of such periods. In this decade and the one immediately succeeding it, the basic assumptions of eighteenth- and nineteenth-century social thought underwent a critical review from which there emerged the new assumptions characteristic of our own time. "A revolution of such magnitude in the prevailing empirical interpretations of human society is hardly to be found occurring within the short space of a generation, unless one goes back to about the sixteenth century. What is to account for it?"

Nearly all students of the last years of the nineteenth century have sensed in some form or other a profound psychological change. Yet they have differed markedly in the way in which they have expressed their understanding of it.

* From H. Stuart Hughes, *Consciousness and Society* (New York: Alfred A. Knopf, 1958), pp. 33–37, 63–66, 336–44. Copyright 1958 by H. Stuart Hughes. Reprinted by permission of Alfred A. Knopf, Inc.

In the older, more aesthetically oriented interpretations (we may think of Henry Adams), the 1890's figured as the *fin de siècle:* it was a period of over-ripeness, of perverse and mannered decadence—the end of an era. We need not stop to ask ourselves how much of this was simply an artistic and literary pose. For our present purposes, it is irrelevant: the *fin de siècle* is a backdrop, nothing more.

Somewhere between an aesthetic and a more intellectual interpretation, we might be tempted to characterize the new attitude as neo-romanticism or neo-mysticism. This formulation has considerable plausibility. Unquestionably the turn toward the subjective that we find in so much of the imaginative and speculative writing of the quarter-century between 1890 and the First World War recalls the aspirations of the original Romanticists. It is not difficult to think of writers who in the 1890's or early 1900's felt that they were reaching back over a half-century gap to restore to honor those values of the imagination that their immediate predecessors had scorned and neglected. It was writers such as these who established the cult of Dostoyevsky and Nietzsche as the literary heralds of the new era. There is a pathetic paradox in the fact that the year of Nietzsche's madness—1889—coincides with the time at which his work, after two decades of public neglect, first began to find wide acceptance. Again and again in the course of the present study we shall find one or another social thinker elaborating more rigorously and systematically the suggestions with regard to unconscious strivings and heroic minorities which Nietzsche had thrown out in fragmentary form.

Yet to call Nietzsche a neo-romantic is surely misleading. Any such char-acterization does less than justice to the critical and Socratic elements in his thought. And when it is applied to the social thinkers of the early twentieth century, it fits only a very few—and these are minor figures like Péguy and Jung. The truly great either were hostile to what they took to be neo-romantic tendencies or, like Freud and Weber, sought to curb the romanticism they discovered within themselves. Durkheim was perhaps the most categorical of his contemporaries in protesting against what he called a "renascent mysticism," but he was not an isolated case. It was rather the "mystic" Bergson (whom Durk-heim may have been aiming at) who was less typical. Indeed, of the major new doctrines of the period, the Bergsonian metaphysics was unique in having frankly mystical aspects—and even this doctrine was couched so far as possible in acceptable philosophic terminology. It was on the "lower" levels of thought, rather—on the level of semipopular agitation—that the neo-romantic tendencies were to have their greatest effect. And it was here that their application to politics eventually produced that "betrayal of the intellectuals" which Julien Benda assailed with such telling effect three decades later.

If not "romanticism," will "irrationalism" serve as a general description? It is neat, it is frequently used, and it at least begins to suggest the real concerns of early twentieth-century social thought. Unquestionably the major intellectual innovators of the 1890's were profoundly interested in the problem of irra-tional motivation in human conduct. They were obsessed, almost intoxicated, with a rediscovery of the nonlogical, the uncivilized, the inexplicable. But to call them "irrationalists" is to fall into a dangerous ambiguity. It suggests a tolerance or even a preference for the realms of the unconscious. The reverse was actually the case. The social thinkers of the 1890's were concerned with the irrational only to exorcise it. By probing into it, they sought ways to tame it, to canalize it for constructive human purposes. Even Sorel, who has often been held up as the supreme irrationalist, had as his life's goal the enunciation of a political formula that would fit the new world of industrial logic and the machine.

Sorel, Pareto, Durkheim, Freud—all thought of themselves as engineers or technicians, men of science or medicine. It is obviously absurd to call them irrationalists in any but the most restricted sense. As a substitute, the formula "anti-intellectualist" has sometimes been employed. This characterization is both flexible and comprehensive. It suggests the revulsion from ideology and the *a priori,* from the abstract thought of the century and a half preceding, which served to unite writers otherwise so far apart as Durkheim and Sorel. It recalls the influence and prestige of William James—an influence at the same time comparable, opposed, and complementary to that of Nietzsche. "Anti-intellectualism," then, is virtually equivalent to Jamesian pragmatism. It offers a satisfactory common denominator for grouping a large proportion of the intellectual innovations of the 1890's.

Yet it is at the same time too broad and too narrow. It fails to take account of the unrepentant abstraction and intellectualism in the thought of Benedetto Croce—or, to take quite a different example, the later elaboration by Max Weber of social theory in terms of "ideal types." It suggests, moreover, that the turn from the principles of the Enlightenment was more complete and decisive than was actually the case. The main attack against the intellectual heritage of the past was in fact on a narrower front. It was directed primarily against what the writers of 1890's chose to call "positivism." By this they did not mean simply the rather quaint doctrines associated with the name of Auguste Comte, who had originally coined the term. Nor did they mean the social philosophy of Herbert Spencer, which was the guise in which positivist thinking was most apparent in their own time. They used the word in a looser sense to characterize the whole tendency to discuss human behavior in terms of analogies drawn from natural science. In reacting against it, the innovators of the 1890's felt that they were rejecting the most pervasive intellectual tenet of their time. They believed that they were casting off a spiritual yoke that the preceding quarter-century had laid upon them.

As a preliminary characterization, to speak of the innovations of the 1890's as a revolt against positivism comes closest to what the writers in question actually thought that they were about. Yet even this last formula has its pitfalls. We must be on guard against the tendency of someone like Croce to use positivism as a philosophic catch-all, to embrace under this epithet every doctrine for which he had a dislike. We must not forget the number of influential thinkers of the period—men like Durkheim and Mosca—who remained essentially in the positivist tradition. And, finally, we must take proper account of the others, like Freud, who continued to use mechanistic language drawn from the natural sciences long after their discoveries had burst the framework of their inherited vocabulary. . . .

. . . We may outline in preliminary and schematic form the major ideas that were initially stated in the 1890's, preparatory to their fuller elaboration in the first decade of the twentieth century.

1. Most basic, perhaps, and the key to all the others was the new interest in the problem of consciousness and the role of the unconscious. It was the problem implicit in the title of Bergson's first book, the *Essay on the Immediate Data of Consciousness*. In it he had tried to distinguish between a "superficial psychic life" to which the scientific logic of space and number could properly be applied, and a life in the "depths of consciousness" in which "the deep-seated self" followed a logic of its own: he had come to the conclusion that the world of dreams might offer a clue to this secret and unexplored realm. "In order to recover this fundamental self," he had added, "a vigorous effort of analysis is necessary." A decade later, and proceeding from a philosophic and professional preparation almost totally in contrast to that of Bergson, Freud began to carry out the program that the former had outlined. Freud's first major work, *The Interpretation of Dreams,* built on his own "vigorous effort" of self-analysis a theory of unconscious motivation to which the life of dreams offered the key.

2. Closely related to the problem of consciousness was the question of the meaning of time and duration in psychology, philosophy, literature, and history. It was the problem to which Bergson was to return again and again in an effort to define the nature of subjective existence as opposed to the schematic order that the natural sciences had imposed on the external world. It represented one aspect of the task that Croce had set himself in trying to establish the qualitative and methodological differences between the realm of history and the realm of science. In somewhat different form it was the problem with which the natural scientists were themselves contending in postulating a universe that no longer strictly conformed to the laws of Newtonian physics. Finally it was the dilemma that obsessed the novelists of the first two decades of the new century—Alain-Fournier, Proust, Thomas Mann—the tormenting question of how to recapture the immediacy of past experience in language that in ordinary usage could reproduce no more than the fragmentized reality of an existence that the logical memory had already stored away in neat compartments.

3. Beyond and embracing the questions of consciousness and time, there loomed the further problem of the nature of knowledge in what Wilhelm Dilthey had called the "sciences of the mind." In the early 1880's Dilthey had attempted to establish rules that would separate the areas in which the human mind strove for some kind of internal comprehension from the realm of external and purely conventional symbols devised by natural science. A decade later Croce had resumed the task, with his first important essay, *"La storia ridotta sotto il concetto generale dell'arte."* Croce soon abandoned the simple

solution of including history among the arts. But his conviction of the radical subjectivity of historical knowledge remained. By 1900 it was apparent to the more imaginative of Croce's contemporaries that the nineteenth-century program of building an edifice of historical and sociological knowledge by patient accumulation and painstaking verification no longer sufficed. By such means it would prove forever impossible to penetrate beneath the surface of human experience. One had, rather, a choice between the exercise of the sympathetic intuition postulated in Croce's neo-idealistic theory of history, and the creation of useful fictions, as Max Weber was later to elaborate them, as models for critical understanding.

4. If the knowledge of human affairs, then, rested on such tentative foundations, the whole basis of political discussion had been radically altered. No longer could one remain content with the easy assurances of the rationalistic ideologies inherited from the century and a half preceding—liberal, democratic, or socialist as the case might be. The task was rather to penetrate behind the fictions of political action, behind what Sorel called the "myths," Pareto the "derivations," and Mosca the "political formulas" of the time. Behind these convenient façades, one could postulate the existence of the actual wielders of power, the creative minorities, the political elites. The discussion of politics, then, had been pushed back from the front of the stage to the wings—from the rhetoric of public discussion to the manipulation of half-conscious sentiments.

Such, indeed, is the most general characterization we may give to the new intellectual concerns of the 1890's. They had displaced the axis of social thought from the apparent and objectively verifiable to the only partially conscious area of unexplained motivation. In this sense the new doctrines were manifestly subjective. Psychological process had replaced external reality as the most pressing topic for investigation. It was no longer what actually existed that seemed most important: it was what men thought existed. And what they felt on the unconscious level had become rather more interesting than what they had consciously rationalized. Or—to formulate the change in still more radical terms—since it had apparently been proved impossible to arrive at any sure knowledge of human behavior—if one must rely on flashes of subjective intuition or on the creation of convenient fictions—then the mind had indeed been freed from the bonds of positivist method: it was at liberty to speculate, to imagine, to create. At one stroke, the realm of human understanding had been drastically reduced and immensely broadened. The possibilities of social thought stretched out to infinity. It was perhaps this that Freud had in mind when in 1896 he spoke of "metapsychology"—the definition of the origin and nature of humanity—as his "ideal and problem child," his most challenging task for the future. . . .

In the present chapter . . . we shall be dealing with figures who were closer to the popular world of discourse than were the giants of the generation of the 1890's—slightly younger men in nearly every case, essayists or imaginative writers whose rhythms of thought accorded better with the temper of the general educated public than did the austere lucubrations of the philosophers and social scientists whom we have been considering up to now. We shall be tracing one of the fashions in which the diffusion of the older men's ideas started. The less rigorous writers of a half generation younger than the great intellectual innovators—who, however, still thought of themselves as direct participants in the decisive experience of their elders—served as an initial line of transmission to the true popularizers of the generation following.

Meantime these younger writers were themselves the senior members of the new age group that was coming to maturity in the early twentieth century. In this capacity, they acted as connecting links with the generation that has up to now occupied our attention. Born in the 1870's, men like Péguy and Hesse, Proust and Mann, could mediate between their elders who had been born in the late 1850's and the 1860's and their immediate juniors, born in the 1880's, who were just reaching manhood in the first decade of the twentieth century. This new generation has yet to be described. It falls outside the sphere of our study, consisting as it does of those whose major period of productivity came after the First World War and, in a number of cases, still continues today. But we need to outline its salient characteristics if we are to understand how it happened that by the outbreak of the war so many of the generation of the 1890's felt themselves to be losing touch with their own spiritual descendants. . . .

In the retrospect of the war itself, the year 1905 most clearly offered the watershed. It marked the first time for a quarter-century that all Europe seemed astir. The revolution in Russia had come as the first major social disturbance since the Paris Commune of 1871—and for a moment the Socialist parties of France and Germany, Austria and Italy, had faced the embarrassing prospect that they might be obliged to give reality to the Marxist professions that had gradually been transformed into little more than a litany for the faithful. The revolutionary danger soon passed. But the effects of the other decisive event of the year—the First Moroccan Crisis—were not to be eradicated so quickly. From 1905 on, one diplomatic crisis followed on another in regular succession. The shock of Tangiers—as Péguy put it—"within the space of . . . two hours" introduced a new epoch in his own life, as it did in the history of his country and of the world. For the next decade the youth of Europe lived and breathed in an atmosphere of impending war.

It was this prospect of war service which most sharply marked off the new generation from those who had reached intellectual maturity in the 1890's. By 1905, men like Freud and Weber, Durkheim and Bergson, Mosca and Croce, were already getting too old for front-line duty. Of them, Weber alone put on a uniform during the war, and even he was not permitted to engage in actual combat. The war, when it came, was not *their* war: it was their sons' war. For them the decisive experience had been the intellectual renewal of the 1890's—or perhaps, in the case of the French, the defense of Captain Dreyfus. For the generation of their sons the great event was obviously the war itself. Here we find a dramatic instance of the contrasting experiences that serve to demarcate one age group from another in intellectual history.

Living as it did in a state of nearly constant war alert, the new generation was more impatient than that of its fathers. It respected its elders: in this it differed from the conventional image of a younger generation. But it was looking for something more arresting and dogmatic than its seniors had provided. It admired the discoveries they had made—but it understood these discoveries in cruder fashion. Where the writers of the 1890's had restricted themselves to a questioning of the potentialities of reason, the young men of 1905 became frank irrationalists or even anti-rationalists. This crucial distinction, which so often remains blurred in the history of ideas in our century, was largely a matter of contrasting age groups. The younger men were no longer satisfied with the urbane detachment of their elders. Everywhere they were in search of an ideal and a faith.

Thus in Germany they began to apply the teachings of Nietzsche in the sense of direct action, and thought of themselves as that "first generation of fighters and dragon-slayers" whom he had called on to establish the "Reich of Youth." One of Nietzsche's self-styled disciples—Stefan George—became their poet; from George they learned to regard themselves as a new spiritual aristocracy, with a lofty if ill-defined mission. The newly formed youth groups gave them an organizational outlet and an intoxicating sense of physical and spiritual liberation. Ten months before the outbreak of the war, in October 1913, representatives of the Free German Youth assembled on the Hohen Meissner hill in central Germany and drew up a melodramatic pledge to "take united action . . . under any and all circumstances . . . for the sake of . . . inner freedom." It was young people of this sort that Weber encountered four years later, when, at a gathering at Burg Lauenstein in Thuringia, he declined to serve as the prophet for whom they longed.

In Italy the years between the turn of the century and the First World War brought into prominence new writers, new reviews, and new political organizations. The reaction from positivism that in Croce's case had expressed itself in rational and measured form, with the younger generation became a kind of spiritual explosion. Nationalism in politics, dynamism and "Futurism" in literature, above all the example—both artistic and personal—of the flamboyant word-magician Gabriele D'Annunzio, marked the changed temper of Italian youth. It was not until the review *La Voce* was founded in Florence in 1908, that some of the new writers were able to collaborate with their elders in reconciling a moderate type of nationalism with the older liberal tradition.

From his scholarly eminence, Croce watched the growing effervescence with a sympathy tinged with fatherly reproach—much as the elderly Goethe was alternately flattered and embarrassed at the honor paid him by the German Romanticists. This excited stirring, he implied, would be all to the good, if it were properly controlled and moderated. For D'Annunzio, however, he had only words of reproof. It was quite wrong, he insisted, to couple their names in any way: "D'Annunzianism in the proper sense" belonged to the generation that had "grown up since 1890"; he himself and the poet of youth were "spiritually of two different races."

Though here and there D'Annunzio's art won my admiration, I never felt even a fleeting and sentimental agreement with the ethics which he suggested or preached outright. . . . I cannot remember that I ever for a single moment lost my hold on the distinction between sensuous refinement and spiritual fineness, erotic flight and moral elevation, sham heroism and stern duty.

It was in France, however, that the cleavage between generations was most self-consciously delineated, and it is from here that we shall chiefly draw the literary evidences of a changed temper. In France after the turn of the century, as in Germany a decade earlier, the young people began to declare themselves Nietzscheans. André Gide's *The Immoralist*, published in 1902, is an early example. Subsequently, still younger writers like Alain-Fournier were to recognize the influence, either explicit or unconscious, of Nietzsche on their own thought. But in France the Nietzscheans were only a minority. It was Bergson, rather, who ranked as the tutelary deity of the new generation. After 1905 the educated youth of France became militantly "Bergsonian."

The young people seized hold of Bergson with avidity and interpreted him according to their own tastes. They read into his teaching the notion of direct-action politics—usually of the Right—which was distinctly in contrast with his own convictions, and of dogmatic religion, on which his personal position still remained obscure. As so often has happened in the history of ideas, the originator of the doctrine lost control of his own creation: his disciples escaped from his tutelary guidance. For the half-decade before the First World War, "Bergsonism" was living a life of its own, almost independent of its founder.

It was a curious phenomenon, this new generation in which the sons were more conservative than the fathers. The latter had done battle for the innocence of Dreyfus and fought the power of the "reactionaries" and the clergy. Their children were as likely as not to embrace the neo-royalism of Charles Maurras and the *Action Française*, or the milder version of conservative nationalism preached by the novelist Maurice Barrès. At the Ecole Normale Supérieure the influence of Lucien Herr, the librarian, and of Jean Jaurès, the great Socialist alumnus, began to wane; Léon Blum—who three decades later was to be prime minister of France, but who at this period still ranked only as a brilliant lawyer and a rather precious *littérateur*—was one of the last of their great converts. And, to the more critical of the younger minds, Blum seemed rather superficial; he still took Jaurès's rolling periods seriously.

Another reason for the declining influence of Socialism—and of Left politics in general—among the educated youth of France, had been the exploitation of the Dreyfusard victory. Beginning in 1901, the triumphant Radicals had inaugurated a policy of ideological revenge. Freemasons were encouraged to spy on Army officers of clerical inclinations, and there began the systematic suppression of religious orders and teaching establishments that culminated in 1905 in the separation of Church and State. As the monks and nuns emigrated abroad, as weeping children were forced out of schoolrooms by armed soldiery, "the great pity of the churches of France" (to use Barrès's phrase) began to disturb the consciences even of those who had hitherto been neutral in religious matters.

And to some of these, the support that Jaurès was giving to the anti-clerical campaign seemed like a kind of apostasy. Taking full advantage of his privileged status as an intellectual in politics, Jaurès threw "an oratorical and poetic veil over the dirty business" by giving it an "appearance of lofty philosophical reason that to the naive" made it "appear sublime." Others, however, like Péguy or even Proust, could not stomach the fact that "the same people who had turned the country upside down in order that it should not be said that in France a man had suffered on account of his race and his religion," were now "expelling the teaching orders and declaring war on everything religious." As the Jewish journalist Bernard Lazare put it, the fact that the clericals had plagued people like himself for years was no reason to turn around and do the same to them.

In 1900, in intellectual circles, it had been bad form to be a practicing Catholic. By 1910, while the majority still consisted of unbelievers—philosophical positivists for the most part—a growing minority of the sensitive and discriminating spirits were returning to the faith in which they had been baptized. A few great conversions had served as examples—the poet Paul Claudel from the elders, the philosopher Jacques Maritain in the younger generation. It was the latter who was to appeal in vain with the anti-clerical wife of Péguy to ease her husband's torments of conscience by letting her children be baptized.

In 1905 only three or four students at Normale openly professed their religious faith. By 1912 there were perhaps forty—a third of the student body. The great institution that had so long ranked as "a citadel of bantering agnosticism" was gradually being penetrated by the new spirit. And the same thing was going on in other educational centers and other intellectual circles. This changed attitude toward things religious has been admirably documented by André Gide's younger friend and literary associate, Roger Martin du Gard. In his novel *Jean Barois,* published in 1913, Martin du Gard traced the spiritual pilgrimage of his own generation. With an acute sense for the nuances of religious scruple, he depicted the slow transformation of a child's tender, naive piety into a "Modernist" interpretation of dogma in a symbolic sense. But in the case of the fictitious Jean Barois, as with so many of his actual contemporaries, Catholic "Modernism" could be only an uneasy compromise: the Pope himself was to condemn it. Beyond it lay an aggressive irreligion of a materialist and positivist type, and beyond that in turn a final reconciliation with the Church. In this intellectual progression, Martin du Gard's protagonist seemed typical of the new century. But for religiously minded readers the book had a disconcerting backtwist: Jean Barois's return to Catholicism was denied the character of conscious and responsible choice—it was the despairing product of sickness, personal misery, and fear of death.

Thus Jean Barois is still a transition figure, hovering in unhappy self-division between the skepticism of the older liberal faiths and the dogmatisms of the future. When as a middle-aged man he is faced with two university students come to enlighten him on the new tendencies among French youth, he finds that they are speaking an unfamiliar and rather frightening language. He is repelled by their denigration of science and their cult of force. To him they represent a mere "reaction": in their own eyes they are the bearers of spiritual renewal.

With this contrast, we touch the central ambiguity in the generation of 1905. In France—and the same was true in Germany—during the years just before the outbreak of the war there reigned among the youth a spirit that combined respect for authority with the cult of spontaneous creation. Depending on where they have chosen to lay their emphasis, historians of the epoch have judged it very differently. On the one hand, they have found in it a threatening proto-fascist atmosphere, on the other hand a renaissance of culture and of living brutally cut off at its start. This was the generation of French and Germans of whom the best were to perish in battle—or so, at least, their contemporaries saw it. And the tragic irony of the matter was that they greeted the outbreak of the slaughter with enthusiasm. The more bellicose felt at last within their grasp the life of action for which they had longed. The more reflective welcomed it as a deliverance from unfruitful anticipation: "Better that war should come," they repeated, "than to go on with this perpetual waiting. . . ."

3.

Hans Barth is a Swiss scholar who spent almost twenty years as editor of the *Neue Zürcher Zeitung* before becoming professor of philosophy at the University of Zurich in 1946. He has published a number of books on modern philosophical problems, particularly as they relate to politics. His essay entitled "The Decline of Liberal Values since 1914" focuses briefly but incisively on several thinkers of the pre-1914 generation whose ideas, in Mr. Barth's judgment, did much to undermine the traditional liberal doctrines of the nineteenth century.

BARTH: The Decline of Liberal Values Since 1914 *

Liberal ideas and liberal values were most obstinately and maliciously attacked by various political philosophies at the end of the nineteenth and the beginning of the twentieth centuries. The revolutionary changes that these philosophies strove for can be summed up under four headings. They attempted first of all, in accordance with Schopenhauer's metaphysics of the will, to replace the primacy of reason over the will. Secondly, under the influence of Gaetano Mosca and Vilfredo Pareto, the traditional theory of systems of government—monarchy, aristocracy and democracy—was superseded by the doctrine of the ruling class as the determining principle of all forms of government. And thirdly, Georges Sorel, powerfully influenced by the philosophies of Nietzsche and Bergson, rehabilitated force and made an apology for the political myth as the instrument for activating the modern masses. Fourthly and finally, sociology in its early phase—especially in Auguste Comte—maintained that, properly speaking, mankind existed but not the individual, since the latter is indebted to society for all

* From Hans Barth, "The Decline of Liberal Values Since 1914," *Confluence*, Volume 5 (1957), pp. 362–66. Reprinted by permission of the editors of *Confluence*.

his intellectual insights and technical implements. This amounted to an enormous devaluation of man in favor of society. For although the notion that the individual must always be granted primacy over the group is in no sense liberal, nonetheless the belief that the community attains its true meaning only if independent, free individuals are united in a self-determined legal system must be regarded as essential to liberalism.

Arthur Schopenhauer unleashed an enormous wave of irrationalism. His philosophy was an attack upon the central tenet of Western rationalism that man is a being originally endowed with reason. Schopenhauer made the intellect an instrument of the will to life, a tool which this will had created for itself in order to attain its objectives. True cognition does not lie within the original province of the intellect, whose destiny lies primarily in aiding the will to attain the goals that the latter sets for itself. If the true nature of man is manifested in the insatiable, alogical and antilogical will, whose sole purpose is self-assertion and destruction of any opposing will, then understanding and reason exert no power that can react upon the will. Reason is no longer the distinguishing criterion of human nature.

It was Nietzsche who radicalized Schopenhauer's position and taught that all intellectual activities should be conceived of as biological functions. By replacing the will to life as a metaphysical principle by the will to power, Nietzsche was able to argue that man's entire intellectual and spiritual life and all its creations—law and ethics, art and religion—must be understood as nothing but metamorphoses and sublimations of the original will to power. Interpreting his metaphysical principle logically, Nietzsche concluded that cognition was a means of acquiring power. The consequences for political philosophy of the metaphysics of the will to power can easily be surmised. The crucial question becomes: how can the problem of agreement be envisaged on these terms? What is the significance of the commandments and prohibitions of ethics and religion? What meaning is to be given to the idea of law and justice? There can be no agreement that results from a reasonable controversy that seeks to determine the truth, because adversaries always constitute different power quanta, and the more intense will to power is always the decisive factor, *i.e.,* it is always "right." Religious and ethical rules are merely conventions that the strong enforce upon the weak. What we consider just—what is meant to serve as a criterion for the legal order—is nothing but a fixing of the will to power.

In a similar manner, the elite theory of Mosca and Pareto contributed to the abuse of the idea of justice. They argued that the distinguishing feature of a political order is the fact that a minority, the ruling class, monopolizes the means of coercion and of force, and justifies its mastery by an ideology which the majority more or less voluntarily accepts. This domination by the elite results in a considerable devaluation of conventional political structures, and leads to indifference to the principles which must be acknowledged if the State is to function smoothly. The decline of the old political philosophy clears the way for Caesarism and the dictatorship of the one-party state, which has at its disposal the two elements that must belong and do belong to the State—a ruling class and an ideology. According to Pareto, since man seeks to make his actions appear moral or logical, the battle of ideas plays an important part in the struggle for social power. Ideas do not have a purpose or value in themselves, but they become tools in the struggle for power. The group attempting to gain control, accordingly, pretends only to strive for the attainment of universal human values, such as justice, freedom and welfare. These ideals, however, are merely a means of concealing the elite's own interests in order to gain the support of the greatest possible number of followers. But the decisive factor for the ruling class is the exclusive possession of economic and political power. Whether we are dealing with a struggle between religious attitudes and cults, between legal and political philosophies, or between ethical systems and traditions—at the bottom of these intellectual conflicts there is always and everywhere the struggle between classes and elites. The battles that take place in the world of the mind, and which appear to be controversies between rationally justified or justifiable opinions and values, are, in Pareto's analysis, unmasked as pure forms of the social struggle for power, as "forms of class warfare," as he puts it.

The influence exerted by the highly educated one-time civil engineer Georges Sorel on contemporary political thought can hardly be over-estimated. Nor is he to be exonerated of the charge of having developed a political philosophy that opened the door to all kinds of abuse. Sorel lightened the conscience of men who wanted to use force in social and political controversies. He took from Bergson the idea that human understanding is always incommensurate with life and is therefore never in a position to give it direction, meaning and purpose. These can be provided only by what Sorel calls a social myth. In this myth are embodied the strongest instinctive tendencies of a people, a party or a class. By means of myths, the enormous latent energies of the amorphous masses can be actuated toward a goal that the myth presents in a mysteriously ambiguous and fascinatingly attractive manner, permitting people to guess its content rather than to understand it. Any debate about the realization of its content in the course of history is rejected as completely meaningless by Sorel. The appeal to feeling and instinct takes place without any regard for a preliminary analysis. Attempts at understanding must be altogether eliminated, because, as an instrument of critical judgment, understanding inhibits action. The myth appeals to the sense of sacrifice and the readiness for combat of the social stratum or the nation from which it originates. It has a genuinely moral mission; it awakens the bellicose virtues—abnegation, discipline, single-minded concentration of all energies toward a single task. Since the myth cannot and must not be proved "right" or "useful" by reason, it approaches the character of an illusion. Sorel has often emphasized that men live more by illusions about themselves and about things and their relationships than by a real awareness of events. The last and highest function of the myth is the appeal to force, to *action directe*.

To be sure, Sorel believed that the use of force was not synonymous with terrorism and despotism. But he could not prevent his doctrine of the social myth from being used in practice to justify the unlimited application of power. If the social myth was not to be corrected by reason, it could too easily be misused as an exceedingly effective psychological tool whereby all intellectual controversies about truth and falsity could be proved meaningless. It cannot be denied that Sorel wanted the social myth used in a moral way. But the totally amoral use of the myth could not be prevented. Where could a moral criterion be found, when reason was completely excluded and the entire appeal was to passions, feelings and instincts?

In his essay "Of the First Principles of Government" Hume writes: "Nothing appears more surprising to those, who consider human affairs with a philosophical eye, than the easiness with which the many are governed by the few; and the implicit submission, with which men resign their own sentiments and passions to those of their rulers. When we inquire by what means this wonder is effected, we shall find, that, as Force is always on the side of the governed, the governors have nothing to support them but opinion. It is therefore, on opinion only that government is founded, and this maxim extends to the most despotic and most military governments, as well as to the most free and most popular." In these words of Hume lies a challenge to make the maximum effort to have good and reasonable opinions determine the actions of men. . . .

4.

Gerhard Masur, professor of history at Sweet Briar College, was born and educated in Berlin. After a decade of teaching in his native city, he emigrated to South America in 1936 and headed the language department in the Higher Normal School at Bogota for almost ten years. He has taught at Sweet Briar since 1947. His most recent book, *Prophets of Yesterday*, is subtitled "Studies in European Culture 1890–1914"; his purpose is ". . . to describe the prevailing trends in the period . . . [in order] to give full understanding to the complex structure of the intellectual life of the early twentieth century." Mr. Masur describes his book as a venture into cultural rather than intellectual history; even more than Hughes's *Consciousness and Society*, it ranges widely into the realms of literature, the arts, and pure philosophy. The bulk of the selection reprinted below is taken from Mr. Masur's introductory chapter, wherein he sets the stage for "the profound transition which took place between 1890 and 1914." Two briefer excerpts offer suggestive insights into the esthetic revolt of the so-called neoromantics, and into the changing character of science as a factor in European culture.

MASUR: Prophets of Yesterday *

In the early morning darkness of April 15, 1912, R. M. S. *Titanic,* the largest ship the world had ever known, struck an iceberg in the North Atlantic and went to the bottom with a loss of 1,500 lives. The catastrophe moved the Western world deeply. In a dim and half-conscious way it was felt that the event forecasted greater dangers which would shake the very foundations of European

* From Gerhard Masur, *Prophets of Yesterday* (New York: Macmillan, 1961), pp. 1–2, 3–6, 34–37, 209–10. Copyright 1961 by Gerhard Masur. Reprinted by permission of The Macmillan Company.

civilization. It seemed to reveal the *hubris* of Western man, who prided himself
on having attained control of the forces of nature both within and around him
and who now learned, overnight, that he might become the victim of inner com-
pulsions which could smash his arrogance to bits.

The observer who in the mid-twentieth century tries to comprehend the powers
which sweep his life toward unexplored shores will inevitably be struck by the
contrast between the period which followed 1914 and the preceding age of security in which his parents spent their days. But from experience he knows that
the discrepancy between the present and the past is always more apparent than
real, that every age has been formed in the womb of time, and that the laws of
heredity apply to civilizations as they apply to individuals. Just as we see today
that the Renaissance and the Reformation were prepared by the emotions and
the ideas of the late Middle Ages, that the tremendous outburst of the French
Revolution was nurtured by the thought of the "effeminate eighteenth century,"
so are we compelled to look to the past century for the wellsprings of our own
complexities. That such sources exist we may take for granted, but it is the role
of the historian to point to those causes which produced the cleavage between the
late nineteenth century and our own and which transformed the controlled
transitions of former ages into the infinite dynamic of the present. It is his business to define what is characteristically new in our troubled time as well as
what still links it to the tradition of Western culture. . . .

By 1914 Europe stood in a relation to the rest of mankind never before achieved
by any other civilization. She was the hub of the world, or, as Mazzini expressed
it in 1848, she was "the lever that moved the world." Her unparalleled position
was not alone the result of imperialism and capitalistic enterprise; it was based
on cultural foundations truly unique in the history of mankind.

In its powerful expansion to the most remote corners of the earth European
civilization had acquired an ecumenical character. No other culture had gone
so far; all had been content or resigned to remain within geographical boundaries, however broad these may have been. If they claimed superiority for their
own way of life, they did not, or could not, undergo the test of imposing their
cultural pattern on all people and all nations. Europe itself had not in any earlier
period made the attempt to assert the global validity of its cultural life. European
expansion had, it is true, reached distant shores and had, as in the New World,
established settlements oriented toward Western values and ideals in government and religion, art, and society, but these enterprises had been scattered over
the face of the globe and were no more than Western islands in an ocean of
alien life.

Not until the eighteenth century did Europe embark on her more temerarious
adventure. It was then that the secularization of thought reached a density permitting philosophers to design schemes for humanity on a world-wide scale.
Kant, Lessing, Condorcet, Thomas Paine, and Bentham were among the first
whose thoughts aimed at the whole of the human race.

It was not, however, accidental that Europe was the only civilization to develop cultural molds sufficiently ample to accommodate the whole earth. During

its long history Europe had been the recipient of three great heritages which indicated the part it was to play in nineteenth century history. Greece had taught the universal validity of a truth which all men could perceive; Rome had given the idea of a law universally valid for all men; Christianity had bestowed the ideal of human brotherhood and the belief in one God whose essence is love and ultimate redemption. The philosophy of the Enlightenment was the fusion of these tenets; their crystallization was belief in the perfectibility of man and the progress of humankind through the steady advance of reason. Carl Becker has called this eschatology the heavenly city of the eighteenth century.

The century following confirmed this faith in reason by the extraordinary triumphs that rational thought and empirical observation scored in all fields of scientific endeavor. In geology, biology, and medicine, in history, economics, and jurisprudence, the advancement of reason brought fruits beyond all expectation. While the world of supernatural commands grew dim, man's natural universe increased in perspectives—rich, tantalizing, confusing, and many times contradictory. Navigating on a boundless sea of reality, reason was, more than ever, man's rudder and progress was "the golden harbor" where he hoped to drop sail.

Nor was it a coincidence that European civilization produced the phenomenon of the Industrial Revolution at the same time. Mankind had displayed inventive genius in other ages, but never with the onrushing intensity with which new devices were now introduced in the economic process. Industrial and agrarian production began to rely more and more on science for the solutions of all problems in output, transportation, and distribution. Scientific discoveries in turn opened up new avenues to economic success. The story is well known. The power loom, the steam engine, and the use of chemical fertilizer marked only the beginnings of this "permanent revolution" that has affected the lives of all peoples more deeply than any other historical event.

The nineteenth century carried the products of the Industrial Revolution into countries and continents that had enjoyed autochthony for thousands of years. While scientists and entrepreneurs of the Old World were busy planning and discovering improved methods of production, merchants and salesmen began to penetrate nations which had been sealed to Western trade. These were the foot soldiers who carried out the orders drawn up in laboratories and workshops by a general staff of scientific minds. The steady trickle of goods became a mighty stream. Soon the surface of the globe was inundated by new types of transportation—steamships, railroads, streetcars, and automobiles; by new ways of communication—telegraph, telephones, cables, and the wireless. Together they facilitated the arrival of manufactured goods, and in turn, assured the shipping of raw material on which Europe depended for her survival.

One could, of course, argue that the capitalist expansion did not in reality produce a transformation of the non-European world, that all it did was to cover these people with a veneer of cheap consumer goods which endangered the time honored production of the non-Europeans and jeopardized their deep-rooted customs and habits. Those who adhere to the German distinction between culture and civilization will also insist that the Industrial Revolution did not

carry the best or the most intrinsic European thought overseas, but only a conglomeration of conveniences. But is not this argument fallacious? The ecumenical character of European culture in the nineteenth century is the direct
result of its belief in the universality of scientific truth, valid under every sky.
Western technology is the consequence of this belief, and the Industrial Revolution is, finally, the practical application of technological victories. It is based on
the trinity of science, labor, and capital.

It is true that when Western technology conquered the earth from pole to pole
it came in contact with civilizations radically different from its own. Religious institutions, everyday habits, social customs were opposed to those of the West.
Clashes were inevitable and led to developments of tremendous significance
in Japan, China, India, Persia, Turkey, and Mexico. It soon became apparent
that these countries could absorb Western technology without embracing Western rationalism, which is the spinal cord bracing European control over nature.
In such wise did Europe in the nineteenth century forge the weapons for its
own defeat in the twentieth. Technology, though a creation of the West, was by
no means a monopoly of the West. It was not the carefully guarded secret of a
priest-caste, but the open findings of scientific brains, openly deduced. Just as it
was employed to enforce European control, so could it be utilized to destroy it.

For the student of contemporary history few processes have been quite as stirring as this. During a single century Europe has toppled from unprecedented
heights to political collapse. But the munitions for her defeat were produced in
her own arsenal, and even in her humbling by the non-European world the
triumphs of the Western spirit are many and obvious. At the turn of the century
few Europeans seem to have been apprehensive either of war or of defeat. It
was a general assumption that the privileged position of the European countries
would be maintained ad infinitum. It is only we who have come to know how
really frail and precarious was their position. . . .

The historian who tries to profile these fateful decades finds it easy to fall into
Hegelian terms. There seems to be a true dialectic at work, where every position
becomes its opposite, yet preserves some of its original elements and carries it
forth to new evolutionary stages. The carefully balanced compromise of constitutional monarchy gave way to radical forms of popular government, either
equalitarian or totalitarian. The balance of power deteriorated into the setting up
of superpowers of continental dimensions. The century of peace and prosperity
gave birth to an era of exaggerated unemployment and protracted war. A period
bursting with humanitarian sentiments, in arms for every good cause, was followed by a recrudescence of barbarism. Total war led humanity to the brink of
self-destruction. The general feeling of security and optimism was replaced by
deep-rooted anxiety. But, as we have seen, the seeds that in so short a time could
produce the gigantic transformation, were nurtured in the different segments of
European civilization. It is only natural that those who knew the world in the
days before 1914 think of it as a gilded age and believe, to rephrase Talleyrand,
that those who were not alive before 1914 will never know how sweet life can be.
It was a glorious era—provided you were born on the right side of the tracks.

I am here reminded of my grandfather, a general practitioner in Berlin. Sometimes he found it difficult to decide on a vacation spot. With the trunks ready and the suitcases packed, he still remained uncertain and would say to the coachman, "Johann, drive me to a nice station." And thus Johann would decide where the old gentleman should go: to Baden-Baden, Merano, the Engadine, Ostende. There were indeed no obstacles for a traveler in those days. He was not required to carry a passport, let alone a visa. All he needed in the way of identification was a letter of credit or a sufficient number of those golden coins which everyone could lawfully carry in his purse. Wherever he went he would find that comfort to which he thought himself entitled and the goods to which he was accustomed. In Paris, in Vienna, in London or Berlin he could attend the favorite upper-class form of entertainment, the operetta. Those were the days of Lehar, Oskar Straus, of Gilbert and Sullivan, of light folly that glossed over the cracks and rifts in society. Many of the leading personalities of this period appear to us now in the reflected glow of musical comedies: the Kaiser, Prince Bülow, Boulanger, Edward VII. But the relationship between this surface frivolity and the underlying tensions was in general disregarded. The warnings of the great prophets, Nietzsche, Dostoevski, Kierkegaard, Burckhardt went unheeded.

From time to time the sound of a shot would shatter the over-all confidence and would send a shiver along the spine of the bourgeois age. There were occurrences of terrorism and violence which no one paused to comprehend. Isolated individuals, influenced by Nechayev's and Bakunin's theory that the state is evil and that terror is the only weapon against it, used political murder as their tool. A wave of political crimes such as Europe had not before seen swept the land. Alexander II was assassinated in Russia, King Humbert in Italy; the Empress of Austria was stabbed to death, Spanish and Russian prime ministers became the victims of terrorism and presidents of France and the United States were no exception. But though these murders produced a feeling of horror in Western society, the stout shell of overconfidence did not break. With the exception of the anarchists no group was willing to identify itself with violent and irresponsible acts—least of all organized labor which condemned and abhorred terrorism. After each assassination the people settled back into their old routines convinced that such acts could originate only in the lunatic fringe of society and that, once the guilty were safely put away, there was really nothing to fear.

Nevertheless, terrorism as a political means was no casual or short-term visitant. Again, paradoxically, it had been born in the very century that had tried so hard to eliminate violence from all walks of life. The extremists found it a convenient instrument for the disruption of a social structure that resisted more civilized methods of persuasion. Terrorism was first put into practice on the home front, but in 1914 it emerged on the international scene. The Serbian nationalists who shot the Austrian archduke in Sarajevo on June 28, 1914, adopted political murder as the mechanism most suitable to their aims. The war then made violence a daily occurrence. Thus we find the thread of continuity linking the two centuries even where they seem diametrically opposed.

There are few spectacles in the history of civilization comparable to this picture of Europe, basking in fruitful opulence under the autumn sun of its glory, ripe for the slaughter. The crusading spirit which had borne her forth on her journey of discovery and expansion in 1492 was a distant memory. In those days the white man had controlled 9 per cent of the earth's surface; by 1914 he had subjugated 85 per cent of it. Nor was this latter-day Europe any longer the country that Novalis had identified with Christendom. Europe in 1914 was essentially a secular, rationalistic, and mechanistic civilization; at one and the same time beneficent and Machiavellian, humanitarian and feral, with a rule which extended from Siberia to Tierra del Fuego and from Transvaal to Singapore. No outside power was strong enough to challenge her; her destruction was brought to maturity within her own confines.

Together with so many of my contemporaries, I have been, over a long period of years, deeply perplexed by the profound transition which took place between 1890 and 1914. The war-guilt clause of the Versailles Treaty has led to a thorough search in all European archives for the arsonists who ignited the great conflagration. Diplomatic events and economic causes have been exhaustively studied, but the cultural trends have not received the same close scrutiny. The cultural evolution of a period is not simply the super-structure of the socioeconomic infrastructure that Marx would have us accept. Neither does it exist independently of its sociological setting. The political and economic situation does not produce culture automatically, but it conditions its forms and actions, favoring the appearance of certain features and excluding or harassing others. The interests of society, as Max Weber says, are the great rails on which humanity moves, but the ideas throw the switches. . . .

The last two decades of the nineteenth century witnessed the crystallization of a movement that embraced many of the ideas advanced during the long period since the death of Goethe. It has been referred to as the esthetic movement, neoromanticism, or art for art's sake, but these are merely surface characterizations which fail to reveal the essence.

"We, we!" wrote Hugo von Hofmannsthal in 1895. "I know only too well that I am not talking of the whole great generation. I talk of a few thousand people, dispersed in the great cities of Europe. . . . Nevertheless, these two or three thousand people have a certain significance . . . they are not necessarily the head or the heart of the generation; they are its conscience." Hofmannsthal thus sensed, not only the intimate kinship of this new group which was about to occupy the European scene, but, going further, calls it the conscience of the age. It was indeed a generation of which he spoke, if we take the word in its recently defined sense, that is, as a group born in a certain time span which determines both its inheritance and its living environment, a group which, because of its historical position, is confronted with identical or parallel problems, even though the solutions offered by its individual members may differ widely. By this definition the group that we are to consider was in every way a generation.

Its representatives were born between 1850 and 1880, roughly speaking; Wilde in 1854, Barrès in 1862, d'Annunzio in 1864, Stefan George in 1868, Gide in 1869, and Hofmannsthal in 1874, to mention only the figures of universal renown.

By 1880, when the older members of this generation began to assert themselves, naturalism had reached its zenith. In reality, this movement was little more than the application of positivism to the world of the arts, an attempt to compel the imagination to surrender to natural laws, whether mechanical or biological. Emile Zola was its chief exponent. While the subject matter of literature had vastly enlarged its scope under the influence of the naturalistic movement, the creative impulse of the artist had been sold for a "mess of facts." Yet the victory of naturalistic ideology was not complete, nor was it ever undisputed.

Romanticism as a legacy of the Pre-Raphaelites lived on in England. Schopenhauer's concept of the arts continued to be a decisive element in Wagner and in Nietzsche. Against the mechanistic enslavement of the soul, Paul Bourget in his novels and the "Essais de psychologie contemporaine" proclaimed understanding through self-analysis, symptom of that greater revolution in the realm of psychology soon to come. And from the solitary protest of Baudelaire against the vulgarity of his century stems a new literary movement devoted to pure form and symbolic expression.

However, the naturalists seemed to have the "Zeitgeist" on their side. By 1880 the tide of industrial progress had engulfed all Europe and was rapidly reaching out toward distant shores. The gaslight cities of the period with their revolting slums and the equally revolting elegance of their suburbs seemed in accord with an art that was respectively argumentative and descriptive; its intellectual appeal was directed toward the proletariat or the bourgeoisie.

But there were some who refused to conform, and a new elite began to proclaim its otherness. "We, who are born at the close of this wonderful age, are at once too cultural and too critical, too intellectually subtle and too curious of exquisite pleasures, to accept any speculations about life in exchange for life itself. . . . Metaphysics does not satisfy our temperaments, and religious ecstasy is out of date. The world through which the academic philosopher becomes 'the spectator of all time and of all existence' is not really an ideal world, but simply a world of abstract ideas. When we enter it, we starve amidst the chill mathematics of thought. The courts of the city of God are not open to us now. . . . It is enough that our fathers believed. They have exhausted the faith-faculty of the species. Their legacy to us is the scepticism of which they were afraid." Thus did Oscar Wilde challenge the beliefs of both his fathers and his brothers.

[The Danish physicist] Niels Bohr remarked once that "we are both spectators and actors in the great drama of existence." The tragic part that modern science has played in this drama consists in having shattered man's natural environment by a series of intellectual explosions which make it almost impossible to reconcile the double role we are obliged to play in life.

We would transgress the limitations imposed upon the historian, were we to imply that the crisis in the exact sciences was simply one more symptom of the underlying crisis in European civilization. But it is hard to overlook certain schizophrenic features which we have found in many other manifestations of

Western culture just prior to 1914. There is a similarity between the situation in the cultural sciences and the situation in the exact sciences. At a time when the egocentricity of the Human Studies gave way to historicism, value-relativity, and sociological typology, when, in a word, the European culture had lost its naive feeling of superiority in regard to other civilizations, a similar process broke the husk that had sheltered the exact sciences. In biology, physics, chemistry, new ideas were introduced that replaced the familiar universe of stability and unfailing forces by an amorphous continuum without any fixed architecture, constantly subject to change and distortion.

Deliberately divorced from metaphysics or philosophy, science no longer furnished men with foundations on which to build or with guideposts that directed his steps. If one were to ask whether science had performed this service in other times the answer would have to be in the affirmative. Science was perhaps never a controlling force in European life, but in the long period from 1500 to 1900 it had been a compass by which the European mind had charted its course. It is worthy of note that in the decade that preceded the Great War, natural scientists and cultural scientists had abandoned the hope of retrieving their directional position in human affairs. Both Weber and Dilthey told us that historical knowledge cannot decide the struggle between conflicting values. Planck confessed that "science is not qualified to decide this question. . . ."

5.

One outgrowth of the intellectual revolution that began in the 1890's was the emergence of new philosophic outlooks, new ways of viewing man's place in the world. Among these new world-views, existentialism has probably had the widest impact, especially since the second world war. William Barrett, professor of philosophy at New York University, has provided us with a remarkably thoughtful and literate analysis of existentialism in his book *Irrational Man*. The brief passage that follows summarizes the existentialists' view of the transition between the nineteenth and twentieth centuries. It will serve also to anticipate the readings in Chapter XV, "A Half-Century in Perspective," and thus to link together the first and last discussion problems in this book.

BARRETT: Irrational Man *

The First World War was the beginning of the end of the bourgeois civilization of Europe. Of course, ends often take long in being accomplished, and capitalism is still hanging on by the skin of its teeth in the Western countries. Our point here, however, has to do not with the mere economic organization of society, but with the concrete and total fact of the civilization itself, with all its values and attitudes, spoken and unspoken. It would be superficial to take the outbreak of that war, as Marxists do, as signifying merely the bankruptcy of capitalism, its inability to function further without crisis and bloodshed. August 1914 was a much more total *human* debacle than that, and the words that catch it are those of the novelist Henry James, exclaiming with shocked horror, "To have to take it all now for what the treacherous years were all the while making for and *meaning* is too tragic for any words." As an American, James had experienced to the full the enchantment and refinement of European civilization; it had been a central theme in nearly all his writing, and here in this momentary outburst there rises to his mind the awful vision of all Europe's elegance and beauty being mere gaudy decoration over the face of a human abyss. August 1914 was a debacle for European man as a whole and not merely for the wicked conspiracy of financiers, militarists, and politicians. The period from 1870 to 1914 has been aptly described by one historian as the generation of materialism; the principal countries of Europe had become unified as nations, prosperity was in the air, and the bourgeois contemplated with self-satisfaction an epoch of vast material progress and political stability. August 1914 shattered the foundations of that human world. It revealed that the apparent stability, security, and material progress of society had rested, like everything human, upon the void. European man came face to face with himself as a stranger. When he ceased to be contained and sheltered within a stable social and political environment, he saw that his rational and enlightened philosophy could no longer console him with the assurance that it satisfactorily answered the question What is man? . . .

Thus with the modern period, man—to recapitulate—has entered upon a secular phase of his history. He entered it with exuberance over the prospect of increased power he would have over the world around him. But in this world, in which his dreams of power were often more than fulfilled, he found himself for the first time *homeless*. Science stripped nature of its human forms and presented man with a universe that was neutral, alien, in its vastness and force, to his human purposes. Religion, before this phase set in, had been a structure that encompassed man's life, providing him with a system of images and symbols by which he could express his own aspirations toward psychic wholeness. With the loss of this containing framework man became not only a dispossessed but a fragmentary being.

In society, as in the spiritual world, secular goals have come to predominate; the rational organization of the economy has increased human power over nature, and politically also society has become more rational, utilitarian, democratic, with a resulting material wealth and progress. The men of the Enlightenment foresaw no end to this triumphant expansion of reason into all the areas of social life. But here too reason has foundered upon its opposite, upon the surd and unpredictable realities—wars, economic crises and dislocations, political upheavals among the masses. Moreover, man's feeling of homelessness, of alienation has been intensified in the midst of a bureaucratized, impersonal mass society. He has come to feel himself an outsider even within his own human society. He is trebly alienated: a stranger to God, to nature, and to the gigantic social apparatus that supplies his material wants.

But the worst and final form of alienation, toward which indeed the others tend, is man's alienation from his own self. In a society that requires of man only that he perform competently his own particular social function, man becomes identified with this function, and the rest of his being is allowed to subsist as best it can—usually to be dropped below the surface of consciousness and forgotten. . . .

II.

THE ORIGINS OF THE FIRST WORLD WAR

The disputes concerning the responsibility for the outbreak of the first world war provide an exceedingly valuable source of enlightenment for the student of history. Not only have great efforts been made to trace most of the ills and horrors of the twentieth century back to the blows which western society received from the coming of war in 1914, but these disputes are an excellent illustration of the principal theme of this book, that though the facts of any issue are the *sine qua non,* they do not speak for themselves; one's conclusion depends upon one's interpretation, and the slightest variation in interpretation can deflect the entire line of argument and the entire range of conclusions.

In the allied countries the earliest interpretations of the causes for the outbreak of the war, as one might suspect, were little but war propaganda. One of the best examples of this was Henry Morgenthau's *Secrets of the Bosphorus.* Lurid and dramatic, it recounted how the "greatest of human tragedies was hatched by the Kaiser and his imperial crew" at the Potsdam conference of July 5, 1914, and how this momentous secret was revealed to Morgenthau by an important German diplomat, who seemed "rather proud of the whole performance; proud that Germany had gone about the matter in so methodical and far-seeing a way." [1] However, a strong reaction came very quickly, a number of factors being responsible. Feelings of guilt over the alleged unfairness of the Versailles Treaty in general, and of the war-guilt clause in particular, played a part; cynicism and war-weariness, in part a reaction against the extreme Germanophobia cultivated during the war, and in part a reaction against the horror of war itself, were also significant; moreover, the publication of prewar diplomatic documents showed how incomplete and "doctored" much of the allied wartime propaganda had been. Especially significant in this latter regard was Germany's publication, beginning in 1922, of extensive selections from its diplomatic documents; other countries responded with selections from their own archives, and the final result was an unusually large body of original material from which historians could draw. Some of them went to what now seems the other

---

[1] Henry Morgenthau, *Secrets of the Bosphorus* (London: Hutchinson, 1918), p. 55. It is interesting to compare Sidney B. Fay's account of the Potsdam Conference with Morgenthau's: See *The Origins of the World War* (New York: Macmillan, 1929), II, Chapter IV. See also, for a more recent interpretation which is less favorable to Germany than Fay's, Luigi Albertini, *The Origins of the War of 1914,* translated from the Italian by Isabella M. Massey (London: Oxford University Press, 1953), II, 178–80.

extreme, and insisted that the French and the Russian governments desired the war; others tried hard to balance the responsibilities and thus to achieve a degree of "objectivity"; others refused to revise their original conceptions at all, and, like R. C. K. Ensor,[2] held firmly to the theory that Germany plotted for war in 1914. Since the second world war, one may see some reversion to the stress on German responsibility. Much emphasis is now being placed on the role the military played in Wilhelmine Germany; scholars like the German Gerhart Ritter [3] and the American Gordon A. Craig [4] point out that the military, with its entrée to the Kaiser's court, with the sway it held over much of the German upper and middle classes, and with its rigid strategy and lack of political sense, contributed greatly to the coming of war, and was even eager for war; by overriding and dominating the diplomats and the civilian ministers, it made negotiations and restraint exceedingly difficult in 1914. An outstanding example of the German military's ability to change national policy, without regard for the dangers involved and without consideration for the opinions of others, was the conversion, in 1909, of the alliance with Austria from one which was purely defensive in nature to one which contemplated offensive action as well; Bismarck had feared the consequences of such a change, and 1914 showed his fears to have been well founded.[5]

The questions which arise in any discussion of the responsibilities for the outbreak of the first world war are numerous and intriguing, and still stimulate much controversy. Many of the issues revolve around the question of Serbian complicity: to what degree was the government in Belgrade aware of the plot to assassinate the Archduke; if it was aware of the plot, did it encourage the assassins, directly or indirectly? Other questions concern the mobilizations and their timing: in 1914 did mobilization mean war; did the Russian mobilization set in motion a reaction which inevitably terminated in war, or would the subsequent mobilizations have come about independently of the Russian action? One might also consider if there was ever a chance of localizing the war, and if the attempts to do so were sincere; or if, on the other hand, Europe was so closely meshed, economically, technically, and diplomatically, that there was no chance of localizing the conflict, and if all the apparent attempts to do so were merely propagandistic in intent.

Especially interesting are the problems of Austrian responsibility and of the role of "the balance of power." Austrian statesmen sincerely believed, and were probably correct in believing, that nationalism, especially among the Slavs, would soon prove fatal to the Empire. To what lengths can a nation justifiably go to protect its existence; was Austria entitled to run the risk of involving all Europe in a war to save itself? Can one blame the Austrian statesmen for having acted as they did? As to the balance of power, was it, as so many have asserted, responsible for the war? Were all the great powers so tied to, and so afraid of offending, their allies that in a crisis they felt obliged to offer them unqualified support, regardless of the result? Was Germany afraid of alienating Austria, by urging moderation over an issue which involved Austria's survival; was France afraid of alienating Russia, by urging moderation over an issue which involved Russia's status as a great power? Or did the balance of power fail because some nations violated its rules: would peace have been preserved had England offered unqualified support to France and

[2] See his *England 1870–1914* (Oxford: Clarendon Press, 1936), pp. 469–71, 481–83.
[3] In his *Staatskunst und Kriegshandwerk: das Problem des "Militarismus" in Deutschland*, Vol. II: *Die Hauptmachte Europas und das wilhelmische Reich* (Munich: Oldenbourg, 1960).
[4] In his *The Politics of the Prussian Army, 1640–1945* (Oxford: Clarendon Press, 1955).
[5] *Ibid.*, pp. 288–91.

Russia, and had therefore maintained the balance—or was England's potential role already discounted in German military strategy? Is the role of Italy worth considering? All this raises the basic question: at what point is war most apt to come in a balance of power situation; is peace in the greatest danger when the power blocs are approximately equal in strength, or when the balance is not being evenly maintained, and when one bloc has a convincing superiority over the other; or is war most apt to come when the balance is in flux, the various nations being unsure of their relative strengths? What was the state of the balance of power in 1914?

It has often been asserted that history has few if any lessons to teach, and that the most one can hope for is a vague type of "understanding." Today, in the age of nuclear weapons and world-wide ideological conflict, it is strongly maintained by many people that history cannot offer even this vague understanding, "because everything is so totally different now." Yet, in the immediate origins of the first world war, perhaps some "lessons" for today can be found, for it may be that in mid-1914 the failure to keep the peace resulted from the inability of the governmental, and especially the diplomatic, machinery to function effectively in a moment of crisis. Professor Craig has written that although "historians are in general agreement that the responsibility for the First World War was not exclusively German, . . . yet, thanks to the soldiers, it seemed to be exclusively German to a large part of the western world in 1914. . . . In the fateful summer of 1914 there was . . . none of that co-ordination of political and military strategy which is desirable when a nation goes to war. The technicians were too naive to understand the necessity of such co-ordination." [6] A. J. P. Taylor tells us that "Berchtold, the Austrian Foreign Minister, overwhelmed in July 1914 with contradictory telegrams from Bethmann [the German Chancellor] and Moltke, the German Chief of Staff, [Bethmann's urging restraint and negotiation, Moltke's urging immediate action against Serbia and pledging German support for such action] passed the best verdict on German politics: 'What a joke! Who does rule in Berlin then?' " Mr. Taylor's own comment is: "What a joke! No one ruled in Berlin." [7] It is important for the student to think about the naïveté of those technicians and to consider why it has been said that "no one" ruled in Berlin. Is there always a point in the development of a crisis when the "escalation" has gone so far that there can be no turning back, either because of pride or because of technology? If everyone does not know exactly where that point is, is there danger that it can be passed by accident? If "no one" rules, will "the point of no return," the point at which coordination breaks down, the point at which the technicians take over and the negotiations stop, be lower in the range of "escalation"? It was doubtless very difficult for Tsar Nicholas to decline to mobilize his armies when at every moment his generals were arguing that, were mobilization postponed, they could no longer be responsible for the safety of his empire.

Finally, it is profitable to speculate about the types of material that are most appropriate in a chapter such as this. Is purely diplomatic history, the record of "what one clerk said to another clerk," [8] as G. M. Young once described it, of any particular significance? Do accounts based mainly on diplomatic documents really reflect anything of value; are they even partially accurate reflections of what was being thought

---

[6] *Ibid.*, pp. 294–95.

[7] *The Course of German History* (London: Hamish Hamilton, 1945), pp. 163–64.

[8] Quoted in A. J. P. Taylor, *The Struggle for Mastery in Europe* (Oxford: Clarendon Press, 1954), p. 574.

and decided in the highest places? Should not one always be concerned with the "deep and underlying" factors, ranging from the level of education and the circulation of newspapers to the dominant movements and isms, all of which are the real determinants of events? And even if one is inclined to look for "answers" by means of diplomatic history, should not the concentration be on the "long-range," on shifting power balances and on social, economic, and technological irritants to international concord, rather than on the details of the final and hurried slide into disaster? Or, on the other hand, will a detailed study of the documents of one sad segment of diplomatic endeavor reveal something, which would otherwise be lost to view, of the mechanics and the mentality which went to make up that uniquely European creation, the "polite, discreet, pacific, and on the whole sincere diplomacy," in which "words counted, and even whispers," and which was designed to keep the nations and the empires of the day "lapped in the accumulated treasures of the long peace," and "glittering and clanking in their panoply," while securely "fitted and fastened . . . into an immense cantilever"? Certainly, "the old world in its sunset was fair to see." [9]

1.

It did not take very long for interpretation of the responsibility for the outbreak of the war to go a complete circle; within less than a decade after the Armistice an American historian, Harry Elmer Barnes, was contending that the French and the Russians, rather than the Austrians and the Germans, desired, and even planned for, general war. Mr. Barnes, who has taught at Clark University and Smith and Amherst Colleges, has served as an editorial writer for the Scripps-Howard newspapers and has written extensively in various fields of social science. His version of events caused violent controversy in the interwar period; it continues to be accepted by some scholars in our day.

BARNES: The Genesis of the World War [*]

We may here briefly summarize the general situation in what may be regarded as a brief statement of the revisionist point of view as it appears to the present writer. The general European system after 1870, based as it was upon nationalism, militarism, secret alliances, and imperialistic aims, naturally inclined Europe toward war. The system does not, however, explain why war came in 1914, as the same general European situation had been prevailing for many years prior to that time, though certain problems had become more acute in the years immediately preceding the World War, particularly in the Near East and Morocco.

The Franco-Russian alliance concluded by 1894 was transformed into an offensive organization following 1912 through the cooperation of Izvolski and Poincaré. Both recognized that the chief objects of Russian and French foreign policy, the seizure of the Straits and the return of Alsace-Lorraine could be real-

[9] Winston S. Churchill, *The World Crisis, 1911–1914* (New York: Scribner's, 1924), p. 199.

[*] From Harry Elmer Barnes, *The Genesis of the World War* (New York: Alfred A. Knopf, 1926), pp. 651–59. Copyright 1926, 1927 by Alfred A. Knopf, Inc.; reprinted by permission of the publishers.

ized only through a general European war. From 1912–14 their joint plans involved a manipulation of the Balkan situation in such a fashion as to be able to take advantage of any crisis likely to provoke a European war, an arrangement to get England so involved that she would be bound to come in on the side of France and Russia, and a great increase in military preparations in France and Russia.

It was decided that Serbia would be the most favorable area in which to create the desired incident in the Balkans. In the early spring of 1914 prominent officers in the Serbian General Staff laid a plot for the assassination of the Archduke, Franz Ferdinand. The Serbian civil government was aware of the plot for at least a month before its execution, but made no adequate effort to stop the plot or to warn Austria. Prominent Russians were also aware of the plot, but the degree of the complicity of Russia is as yet uncertain.

When the assassination came, the French and Russians recognized that the impending clash between Austria and Serbia would constitute a highly appropriate episode over which to bring about the desired conflict. The year 1914 was a particularly desirable year for the Entente because there was imminent danger that England might develop more happy relations with Germany, and that the French Radicals might be able to secure the repeal of the French Army Bill. Poincaré went to St. Petersburg, and, before knowing the terms of the Austrian ultimatum, renewed his pledge of two years earlier to support Russia in a war over the Balkans, and indicated that the probable Austro-Serbian conflict would meet the conditions demanded by the French in supporting Russia in intervention in the Balkans.

The Franco-Russian procedure in 1914 was to indicate a show of conciliation and concessions on the part of Serbia, and apparent Franco-Russian willingness to settle the dispute through diplomacy, while secret Franco-Russian military preparations were to be carried on which would ultimately make a diplomatic settlement quite impossible. Hence, Russia urged Serbia not to declare war on Austria, and, to insure a sufficiently conciliatory Serbian reply to Austria the Serbian response to the Austrian ultimatum was drafted in outline in the French Foreign Office. Russia did not desire to have Serbia precipitate matters prematurely by a declaration of war on Austria, because this would have affected European opinion, particularly English opinion, unfavorably and would also have brought about military activities altogether too rapidly for Russia, whose mobilization over a vast area would necessarily be slow as compared with that of Austria and Germany.

On the 24th of July, the moment Russia and France learned of the terms of Austrian ultimatum to Serbia, they began that dual program of a diplomatic barrage combined with secret military preparations which had made a European war inevitable by the afternoon of July 30th. Russia sent a diplomatic message to Serbia counselling moderation, but at the same time decided upon the mobilization of the four great military districts of Central and Southern Russia as well as of the Russian fleets. Russian money in Germany and Austria was also called in.

On the same day Viviani telegraphed to the French Foreign Office that the Austro-Serbian situation was likely to develop serious European complications, and the French troops in Morocco were ordered home. Both countries began systematic military preparations for war on the 26th of July. By the 29th the time had come when Russian military preparations had gone far enough to warrant a general mobilization, and the Tsar was persuaded to consent to this order. A telegram from the Kaiser, however, induced him to revoke the order, but the next day Sazonov and the army officials once more extracted from the Tsar his reluctant consent to the order for general mobilization. The French and the Russians had understood for a generation that once Russian general mobilization was ordered there would be no way of preventing a general European war. General Dobrorolski has told us with great candor that the Russian authorities in 1914 fully realized that a European war was *on* as soon as the mobilization order had been sent out of the general telegraph office in St. Petersburg late in the afternoon of July 30th.

The French authorities had been thoroughly informed as to the nature and progress of the Russian military preparations, but they made no effort to restrain them, though the French well knew that these military activities were bound to render a European war inevitable. They actually urged the Russians to speed up their military preparations, but to be more secretive about them, so as not to alienate England or provoke Germany to counter-mobilization. On the night of July 31st the French government went still further and openly decided for war, handing this information to Izvolski about midnight of the 31st. France was, thus, the first country to declare itself for war in the European crisis of 1914.

The Austrian statesmen in 1914 decided that the time had come when it would be necessary to control the Serbian menace, and they consciously planned an ultimatum to Serbia of such severity that it would be practically impossible for Serbia to concede all of these demands. The plan, then, was to make a show of diplomacy but to move toward certain war. This program was much like that of France and Russia, save for the fact that *Austria desired to provoke nothing but a local punitive war while the plans of France and Russia envisaged a general European conflict.* This is the most important point to be borne in the mind when estimating the relative war guilt of Austria as against that of France and Russia.

Germany, formerly friendly to Serbia, was alarmed by the assassination of the Archduke and the resulting menace to her chief ally. Germany therefore agreed to stand behind Austria in the plan of the latter to execute her program of punishing Serbia. The answer of the Serbians to the Austrian ultimatum, however, impressed the Kaiser as satisfactory, and from that time on he was opposed to further military activity on the part of Austria against Serbia.

In cooperation with Sir Edward Grey, Germany began on the 27th of July to urge upon Austria direct negotiations with Russia and the mediation of her dispute with Serbia. Austria at first refused to listen to this advice and declared war upon Serbia on the 28th. Germany then became alarmed at the rumored Russian military preparations and vigorously pressed Austria for a diplomatic settlement of the dispute. Austria did not give way and consent to this until the 31st of July, which was too late to avert a general European war because the Russian mobilization was then in full swing. Germany endeavored without success to secure the suspension of military activities by Russia, and then, after unexpected hesitation and deliberation, declared war upon Russia.

The Russian general mobilization, undertaken with the full connivance of the French, was ordered at a time when diplomatic negotiations were moving rapidly toward a satisfactory settlement of the major problems in the crisis. Hence, the Russian general mobilization not only initiated military hostilities, but was also the sole reason for the failure of diplomatic efforts.

England was for peace provided France was not drawn into the conflict, but was determined to come into the War in case France was involved. As France decided from the beginning to stand with Russia for war, and as England refused to attempt to restrain either France or Russia, England was inevitably drawn away from her encouragement of the German efforts towards a diplomatic settlement of the crisis and into the support of the military aggression of France and Russia. She made her decision to enter the War after Germany had offered to keep out of Belgium and to refrain from attacking France if England would remain neutral. In fact, Germany even suggested that she might guarantee the integrity of France and the French colonies in the event of war if England would promise neutrality. The Belgian issue in England was a pure subterfuge, exploited by Grey to inflame British opinion against Germany and to secure British support of the war policy of Sir Edward Grey. . . .

In estimating the order of guilt of the various countries we may safely say that the only direct and immediate responsibility for the World War falls upon Serbia, France and Russia, with the guilt about equally distributed. Next in order—far below France and Russia—would come Austria, though she never desired a general European war. Finally, we should place Germany and England as tied for last place, both being opposed to war in the 1914 crisis. Probably the German public was somewhat more favorable to military activities than the English people, but . . . the Kaiser made much more strenuous efforts to preserve the peace of Europe in 1914 than did Sir Edward Grey. . . .

2.

Not all "revisionists" were so extreme in their views as Harry Elmer Barnes. Sidney B. Fay's *The Origins of the World War* has become the most widely accepted and the most durable of the revisionist arguments. Mr. Fay (now retired) was an eminent specialist in the history of seventeenth- and eighteenth-century Prussia; he taught at Dartmouth, Smith, and Harvard, and in 1946 served as president of the American Historical Association. After having read Mr. Fay's summation of the relative responsibilities of the European nations for the outbreak of the war, one should reconsider the arguments advanced by Mr. Barnes, and should try to decide on what issues—if any—the revisionists agree.

FAY: The Origins of the World War *

One may . . . sum up very briefly the most salient facts in regard to each country.

Serbia felt a natural and justifiable impulse to do what so many other countries had done in the nineteenth century—to bring under one national Government all the discontented Serb people. She had liberated those under Turkish rule; the next step was to liberate those under Hapsburg rule. She looked to Russia for assistance, and had been encouraged to expect that she would receive it. After the assassination, Mr. Pashitch took no steps to discover and bring to justice Serbians in Belgrade who had been implicated in the plot. One of them, Ciganovitch, was even assisted to disappear. Mr. Pashitch waited to see what evidence the Austrian authorities could find. When Austria demanded cooperation of Austrian officials in discovering, though not in trying, implicated Serbians, the Serbian Government made a very conciliatory but negative reply. They expected that the reply would not be regarded as satisfactory, and, even before it was given, ordered the mobilization of the Serbian army. Serbia did not want war, but believed it would be forced upon her. That Mr. Pashitch was aware of the plot three weeks before it was executed, failed to take effective steps to prevent the assassins from crossing over from Serbia to Bosnia, and then failed to give Austria any warning or information which might have averted the fatal crime, were facts unknown to Austria in July, 1914; they cannot therefore be regarded as in any way justifying Austria's conduct; but they are part of Serbia's responsibility, and a very serious part.

Austria was more responsible for the immediate origin of the war than any other Power. Yet from her own point of view she was acting in self-defence—not against an immediate military attack, but against the corroding Greater Serbia and Jugoslav agitation which her leaders believed threatened her very existence. No State can be expected to sit with folded arms and await dismemberment at the hands of its neighbors. Russia was believed to be intriguing with Serbia and Rumania against the Dual Monarchy. The assassination of the heir to the throne, as a result of a plot prepared in Belgrade, demanded severe retribution; otherwise Austria would be regarded as incapable of action, "worm-eaten" as the Serbian Press expressed it, would sink in prestige, and hasten her own downfall. To avert this Berchtold determined to crush Serbia with war. He deliberately framed the ultimatum with the expectation and hope that it would be rejected. He hurriedly declared war against Serbia in order to forestall all efforts at mediation. He refused even to answer his own ally's urgent requests to come to an understanding with Russia, on the basis of a military occupation of Belgrade as a pledge that Serbia would carry out the promises in her reply to the ultimatum. Berchtold gambled on a "local" war with Serbia only, believing that he could rattle the German sword; but rather than abandon his war with Serbia he was ready to drag the rest of Europe into war.

* From Sidney B. Fay, *The Origins of the World War* (New York: Macmillan, 1929), II, 550–58 Copyright 1928 and 1930 by The Macmillan Company. Reprinted by permission of the publisher

It is very questionable whether Berchtold's obstinate determination to diminish Serbia and destroy her as a Balkan factor was, after all, the right method, even if he had succeeded in keeping the war "localized" and in temporarily strengthening the Dual Monarchy. Supposing that Russia in 1914, because of military unpreparedness or lack of support, had been ready to tolerate the execution of Berchtold's designs, it is quite certain that she would have aimed within the next two or three years at wiping out this second humiliation, which was so much more damaging to her prestige than that of 1908–09. In two or three years, when her great program of military reform was finally completed, Russia would certainly have found a pretext to reverse the balance in the Balkans in her own favor again. A further consequence of Berchtold's policy, even if successful, would have been the still closer consolidation of the Triple Entente, with the possible addition of Italy. And, finally, a partially dismembered Serbia would have become a still greater source of unrest and danger to the peace of Europe than heretofore. Serbian nationalism, like Polish nationalism, would have been intensified by partition. Austrian power and prestige would not have been so greatly increased as to be able to meet these new dangers. Berchtold's plan was a mere temporary improvement, but could not be a final solution of the Austro-Serbian antagonism. Franz Ferdinand and many others recognized this, and so long as he lived, no step in this fatal direction had been taken. It was the tragic fate of Austria that the only man who might have had the power and ability to develop Austria along sound lines became the innocent victim of the crime which was the occasion of the World War and so of her ultimate disruption.

Germany did not plot a European War, did not want one, and made genuine, though too belated efforts, to avert one. She was the victim of her alliance with Austria and of her own folly. Austria was her only dependable ally, Italy and Rumania having become nothing but allies in name. She could not throw her over, as otherwise she would stand isolated between Russia, where Panslavism and armaments were growing stronger every year, and France, where Alsace-Lorraine, Delcasse's fall, and Agadir were not forgotten. Therefore, Bethmann felt bound to accede to Berchtold's request for support and gave him a free hand to deal with Serbia; he also hoped and expected to "localize" the Austro-Serbian conflict. Germany then gave grounds to the Entente for suspecting the sincerity of her peaceful intentions by her denial of any foreknowledge of the ultimatum, by her support and justification of it when it was published, and by her refusal of Sir Edward Grey's conference proposal. However, Germany by no means had Austria so completely under her thumb as the Entente Powers and many writers have assumed. It is true that Berchtold would hardly have embarked on his gambler's policy unless he had been assured that Germany would fulfil the obligations of the alliance, and to this extent Germany must share the great responsibility of Austria. But when Bethmann realized that Russia was likely to intervene, that England might not remain neutral, and that there was danger of a world war of which Germany and Austria would appear to be the instigators, he tried to call a halt on Austria, but it was too late. He pressed mediation proposals on Vienna, but Berchtold was insensible to the pressure, and the Entente

Powers did not believe in the sincerity of his pressure, especially as they produced no results.

Germany's geographical position between France and Russia, and her inferiority in number of troops, had made necessary the plan of crushing the French army quickly at first and then turning against Russia. This was only possible, in the opinion of her strategists, by marching through Belgium, as it was generally anticipated by military men, that she would do in case of a European War. On July 29, after Austria had declared war on Serbia, and after the Tsar had assented to general mobilization in Russia (though this was not known in Berlin and was later postponed for a day owing to the Kaiser's telegram to the Tsar), Bethmann took the precaution of sending to the German Minister in Brussels a sealed envelope. The Minister was not to open it except on further instructions. It contained the later demand for the passage of the German army through Belgium. This does not mean, however, that Germany had decided for war. In fact, Bethmann was one of the last of the statesmen to abandon hope of peace and to consent to the mobilization of his country's army. General mobilization of the continental armies took place in the following order: Serbia, Russia, Austria, France, and Germany. General mobilization by a Great Power was commonly interpreted by military men in every country, though perhaps not by Sir Edward Grey, the Tsar, and some civilian officials, as meaning that the country was on the point of making war—that the military machine had begun to move and would not be stopped. Hence, when Germany learned of the Russian general mobilization, she sent ultimatums to St. Petersburg and Paris, warning that German mobilization would follow unless Russia suspended hers within twelve hours, and asking what would be the attitude of France. The answers being unsatisfactory, Germany then mobilized and declared war. It was the hasty Russian general mobilization, assented to on July 29 and ordered on July 30, while Germany was still trying to bring Austria to accept mediation proposals, which finally rendered the European war inevitable.

Russia was partly responsible for the Austro-Serbian conflict because of the frequent encouragement which she had given at Belgrade—that Serbian national unity would be ultimately achieved with Russian assistance at Austrian expense. This had led the Belgrade Cabinet to hope for Russian support in case of a war with Austria, and the hope did not prove vain in July, 1914. Before this, to be sure, in the Bosnian Crisis and during the Balkan Wars, Russia had put restraint upon Serbia, because Russia, exhausted by the efforts of the Russo-Japanese War, was not yet ready for a European struggle with the Teutonic Powers. But in 1914 her armaments, though not yet completed, had made such progress that the militarists were confident of success, if they had French and British support. In the spring of 1914, the Minister of War, Sukhomlinov, had published an article in a Russian newspaper, though without signing his name, to the effect, "Russia is ready, France must be ready also." Austria was convinced that Russia would ultimately aid Serbia, unless the Serbian danger were dealt with energetically after the Archduke's murder; she knew that Russia was growing stronger every year; but she doubted whether the Tsar's armaments had yet reached the point at which Russia would dare to intervene; she would therefore run less risk of Russian intervention and a European War if she used the Archduke's assassination as an excuse for weakening Serbia, than if she should postpone action until the future.

Russia's responsibility lay also in the secret preparatory military measures which she was making at the same time that she was carrying on diplomatic negotiations. These alarmed Germany and Austria. But it was primarily Russia's general mobilization, made when Germany was trying to bring Austria to a settlement, which precipitated the final catastrophe, causing Germany to mobilize and declare war.

The part of France is less clear than that of the other Great Powers, because she has not yet made a full publication of her documents. To be sure, M. Poincaré, in the fourth volume of his memoirs, had made a skilful and elaborate plea, to prove *"La France innocente."* But he is not convincing. It is quite clear that on his visit to Russia he assured the Tsar's Government that France would support her as an ally in preventing Austria from humiliating or crushing Serbia. Paléologue renewed these assurances in a way to encourage Russia to take a strong hand. He did not attempt to restrain Russia from military measures which he knew would call forth German counter-measures and cause war. Nor did he keep his Government promptly and fully informed of the military steps which were being taken at St. Petersburg. President Poincaré, upon his return to France, made efforts for peace, but his great preoccupation was to minimize French and Russian preparatory measures and emphasize those of Germany, in order to secure the certainty of British support in a struggle which he now regarded as inevitable.

Sir Edward Grey made many sincere proposals for preserving peace; they all failed owing partly, but not exclusively, to Germany's attitude. Sir Edward could probably have prevented war if he had done either of two things. If, early in the crisis, he had acceded to the urging of France and Russia and given a strong warning to Germany that, in a European War, England would take the side of the Franco-Russian Alliance, this would probably have led Bethmann to exert an earlier and more effective pressure on Austria; and it would perhaps thereby have prevented the Austrian declaration of war on Serbia, and brought to a successful issue the "direct conversations" between Vienna and St. Petersburg. Or, if Sir Edward Grey had listened to German urging, and warned France and Russia early in the crisis, that if they became involved in War, England would remain neutral probably Russia would have hesitated with her mobilizations, and France would probably have exerted a restraining influence at St. Petersburg. But Sir Edward Grey could not say that England would take the side of France and Russia, because he had a Cabinet nearly evenly divided, and he was not sure, early in the crisis, that public opinion in England would back him up in war against Germany. He could resign, and he says in his memoirs that he would have resigned, but that would have been no comfort or aid to France, who had come confidently to count upon British support. He was determined to say and do nothing which might encourage her with a hope which he could not fulfil. Therefore, in spite of the pleadings of the French, he refused to give them definite assurances until the probable German determination to go through Belgium made it clear that the Cabinet, and Parliament, and British public opinion would follow his lead in war on Germany. On the other hand, he was unwilling to heed the German pleadings that he exercise restraint at Paris and St. Petersburg, because he did not wish to endanger the Anglo-Russian Entente and the solidarity of the Triple Entente, because he felt a moral obligation to France, growing out of the Anglo-French military and naval conversations of the past years, and because he suspected that Germany was backing Austria up in an unjustifiable course and that Prussian militarists had taken the direction of affairs at Berlin out of the hands of Herr von Bethmann-Hollweg and the civilian authorities.

Italy exerted relatively little influence on the crisis in either direction.

Belgium had done nothing in any way to justify the demand which Germany made upon her. With commendable prudence, at the very first news of the ominous Austrian ultimatum, she had foreseen the danger to which she might be exposed. She had accordingly instructed her representatives abroad as to the statements which they were to make in case Belgium should decide very suddenly to mobilize to protect her neutrality. On July 29, she placed her army upon "a strengthened war footing," but did not order complete mobilization until two days later, when Austria, Russia, and Germany had already done so, and war appeared inevitable. Even after being confronted with the terrible German ultimatum, at 7 p.m. on August 2, she did not at once invite the assistance of English and French troops to aid her in the defense of her soil and her neutrality against a certain German assault; it was not until German troops had actually violated her territory, on August 4, that she appealed for the assistance of the Powers which had guaranteed her neutrality. Belgium was the innocent victim of German strategic necessity. Though the German violation of Belgium was of enormous influence in forming public opinion as to the responsibility for the War after hostilities began, it was not a cause of the War, except in so far as it made it easier for Sir Edward Grey to bring England into it.

In the forty years following the Franco-Prussian War, . . . there developed a system of alliances which divided Europe into two hostile groups. This hostility was accentuated by the increase of armaments, economic rivalry, nationalist ambitions and antagonisms, and newspaper incitement. But it is very doubtful whether all these dangerous tendencies would have actually led to war had it not been for the assassination of Franz Ferdinand. That was the factor which consolidated the elements of hostility and started the rapid and complicated succession of events which culminated in a World War, and for that factor Serbian nationalism was primarily responsible.

But the verdict of the Versailles Treaty that Germany and her allies were responsible for the War, in view of the evidence now available, is historically unsound. It should therefore be revised. However, because of the popular feeling widespread in some of the Entente countries, it is doubtful whether a formal and legal revision is as yet practicable. There must first come a further revision by historical scholars, and through them of public opinion.

3.

A. J. P. Taylor has been called the *enfant terrible* of the British academic world for his outspoken opinions and his indifference to the attacks of professional colleagues. He is a fellow of Magdalen College, Oxford, and has written extensively in the fields of Austrian and German history; he has also achieved a measure of fame usually denied to those in the academic world by his television appearances on the BBC. The following selection is taken from a book which will eventually form one volume in a series on the history of Europe since 1789. While reading it, one should consider whether any of the foregoing "revisionist" arguments survive in Mr. Taylor's version, or whether his arguments mark a return to a prerevisionist position.

TAYLOR: The Struggle for Mastery in Europe *

On 4 August the long Bismarckian peace ended. It had lasted more than a generation. Men had come to regard peace as normal; when it ended, they looked for some profound cause. Yet the immediate cause was a good deal simpler than on other occasions. Where, for instance, lay the precise responsibility for the Crimean war, and when did that war become inevitable? In 1914 there could be no doubt. Austria-Hungary had failed to solve her national problems. She blamed Serbia for the South Slav discontent; it would be far truer to say that this discontent involved Serbia, against her will, in Habsburg affairs. In July 1914 the Habsburg statesmen took the easy course of violence against Serbia, as their predecessors had taken it (though with more justification) against Sardinia in 1859. Berchtold launched war in 1914, as consciously as Buol launched it in 1859 or Gramont in 1870. There was this difference, Buol counted on support from Germany; he would not have persisted in a resolute line if it had not been for the repeated encouragements which came from Berlin. The Germans did not fix on war for August 1914, but they welcomed it when the occasion offered. They could win it now; they were more doubtful later. Hence they surrendered easily to the dictates of a military time-table. Austria-Hungary was growing weaker; Germany believed herself at the height of her strength. They decided on war from opposite motives; and the two decisions together caused a general European war.

The Powers of the Triple Entente all entered the war to defend themselves. The Russians fought to preserve the free passage of the Straits, on which their economic life depended; France for the sake of the Triple Entente, which she believed, rightly, alone guaranteed her survival as a Great Power. The British fought for the independence of sovereign states and, more remotely, to prevent

* From A. J. P. Taylor, *The Struggle for Mastery in Europe 1848–1918* (Oxford: Clarendon Press, 1954), pp. 526–31. Reprinted by permission of The Clarendon Press.

a German domination of the Continent. It is sometimes said that the war was caused by the system of alliances or, more vaguely, by the Balance of Power. This is a generalization without reality. None of the Powers acted according to the letter of their commitments, though no doubt they might have done so if they had not anticipated them. Germany was pledged to go to war if Russia attacked Austria-Hungary. Instead, she declared war before Russia took any action; and Austria-Hungary only broke with Russia, grudgingly enough, a week afterwards. France was pledged to attack Germany, if the latter attacked Russia. Instead she was faced with a German demand for unconditional neutrality and would have had to accept war even had there been no Franco-Russian alliance, unless she was prepared to abdicate as a Great Power. Great Britain had a moral obligation to stand by France and a rather stronger one to defend her Channel coast. But she went to war for the sake of Belgium and would have done so, even if there had been no Anglo-French entente and no exchange of letters between Grey and Cambon in November 1912. Only then, the British intervention would have been even less effective than it was.

As to the Balance of Power, it would be truer to say that the war was caused by its breakdown rather than by its existence. There had been a real European Balance in the first decade of the Franco-Russian alliance; and peace had followed from it. The Balance broke down when Russia was weakened by the war with Japan; and Germany got in the habit of trying to get her way by threats. This ended with the Agadir crisis. Russia began to recover her strength, France her nerve. Both insisted on being treated as equals, as they had been in Bismarck's time. The Germans resented this and resolved to end it by war, if they could end it no other way. They feared that the Balance was being re-created. Their fears were exaggerated. Certainly, Russia would have been a more formidable Power by 1917, if her military plans had been carried through and if she had escaped internal disturbance—two formidable hypotheses. But it is unlikely that the three-year service would have been maintained in France; and, in any case, the Russians might well have used their strength against Great Britain in Asia rather than to attack Germany, if they had been left alone. In fact, peace must have brought Germany the mastery of Europe within a few years. This was prevented by the habit of her diplomacy and, still more, by the mental outlook of her people. They had trained themselves psychologically for aggression.

The German military plans played a vital part. The other Great Powers thought in terms of defending themselves. No Frenchman thought seriously of recovering Alsace and Lorraine; and the struggle of Slav and Teuton in the Balkans was very great nonsense so far as most Russians were concerned. The German generals wanted a decisive victory for its own sake. Though they complained of "encirclement," it was German policy that had created this encirclement. Absurdly enough, the Germans created their own problem when they annexed Alsace and Lorraine in 1871. They wanted an impregnable frontier; and they got one, as was shown in August 1914, when a small German force held its own there against the bulk of the French army. After 1871 the

Germans could easily have fought Russia and stood on the defensive in the west; this was indeed the strategical plan of the elder Moltke. It was not a strategy which guaranteed final, decisive victory; and Schlieffen therefore rejected it. In 1892, he insisted that France must be defeated first; ten years later he drew the further inevitable conclusion that the German armies must go through Belgium. If the strategy of the elder Moltke had been adhered to with all its political consequences, it would have been very difficult to persuade French and British opinion to go to the assistance of Russia; instead, it appeared in 1914 that Russia was coming to the assistance of France and even of Great Britain. Schlieffen first created the Franco-Russian alliance; and then ensured that Great Britain would enter the war as well. The Germans complained that the war could not be "localized" in 1914; Schlieffen's strategy prevented it. He would be content with nothing less than total victory; therefore he exposed Germany to total defeat.

There is a deeper explanation still. No one in 1914 took the dangers of war seriously except on a purely military plane. Though all, except a few fighting men, abhorred its bloodshed, none expected a social catastrophe. In the days of Metternich, and even afterwards, statesmen had feared that war would produce "revolution"—and revolutionaries had sometimes advocated it for that very reason. Now they were inclined to think that war would stave off their social and political problems. In France it produced the "sacred union"; in Germany William II was able to say: "I do not see parties any more; I see only Germans." All thought that war could be fitted into the existing framework of civilization, as the wars of 1866 and 1870 had been. Indeed, these wars had been followed by stabler currencies, freer trade, and more constitutional governments. War was expected to interrupt the even tenor of civilian life only while it lasted. Grey expressed this outlook in extreme form, when he said in the house of commons on 3 August: "if we are engaged in war, we shall suffer but little more than we shall suffer if we stand aside"; and by suffering he meant only the interruption of British trade with the continent of Europe. No country made serious economic preparations for war. In England the cry was raised of "business as usual" to mitigate the unemployment which war was expected to cause. The Germans so little understood the implications of total war that they abstained from invading Holland in August 1914, so as to be able to trade freely with the rest of the world.

The Balkan wars had taught a deceptive lesson. Everyone supposed that decisive battles would be fought at once, and a dictated peace would follow. The Germans expected to take Paris; the French expected to break through in Lorraine. The Russian "steam-roller" would reach Berlin; more important from the Russian point of view, their armies would cross the Carpathians and take Budapest. Even the Austrians expected to "crush" Serbia. The British expected to destroy the German fleet in an immediate naval engagement and then to establish a close blockade of the German coast; apart from that, they had no military plans, except to applaud the victories of their allies and perhaps to profit from them.

None of these things happened. The French armies failed to make headway in Lorraine and suffered enormous casualties. The Germans marched through Belgium and saw from afar the Eiffel Tower. On 6 September they were halted on the Marne and driven back in defeat. But though the French won the battle of the Marne, they could not exploit their victory; the Germans were neither destroyed nor even expelled from French soil. By November there was a line of trenches running from Switzerland to the sea. The Russians invaded east Prussia; they were catastrophically defeated at Tannenberg on 27 August, and their armies in Galicia failed to reach the Carpathians. The Austrians occupied Belgrade, from which the Serbs had withdrawn; they were driven out again in November, and Serbian forces entered southern Hungary. The German fleet remained in harbour; and the British fleet was similarly imprisoned in order to balance it. Everywhere siege warfare superseded decisive battles. The machine-gun and the spade changed the course of European history. Policy had been silenced by the first great clash; but in the autumn of 1914 diplomacy was renewed. All the Powers sought to consolidate their alliances; to enlist new allies; and, more feebly, to shake the opposing coalition. . . .

4.

When L. C. B. Seaman's *From Vienna to Versailles* appeared in 1956 it was well received by reviewers; many scholars acclaimed it as an outstanding first book for the young, Cambridge-trained London schoolmaster. Mr. Seaman, quite like A. J. P. Taylor, is outspoken and often original; whether one agrees or not with his contentions, there is no doubt that they are provocative. The following selection represents a point of view far removed from that of Mr. Barnes; perhaps it marks a decline in historical "objectivity," inspired by prejudice left over from the second world war; or perhaps it marks an increasing awareness of the importance of social and political factors ignored by earlier historians. At any rate, few will deny that Mr. Seaman's arguments make interesting reading.

seaman: From Vienna to Versailles *

. . . In a very real sense the most important cause of the war of 1914 was not the succession of crises, not the Balkan wars, nor even the Austrian ultimatum to Belgrade, but the complete, though unobserved, collapse of the German system of government.

Bismarck's Reich . . . was of a character similar to that of Napoleon III's Empire. It depended for its efficient operation on the personal domination either of the German Chancellor or the German Emperor. There was no effective co-ordinating machinery between the various civilian departments and the army and the navy, and no real responsibility to the Reichstag; the system depended for its coherent direction upon the personality, while Bismarck held

* From L. C. B. Seaman, *From Vienna to Versailles* (New York: Coward-McCann, 1956), pp. 167–72. Reprinted by permission of Coward-McCann, Inc.

office, of the Chancellor. When William II dropped Bismarck his intention was to exercise this power of direction and coordination himself. This was quite possible and perfectly constitutional, since Bismarck had always claimed to be the servant of the Emperor. In practice, under Bismarck's successors, there was a sort of indeterminate condominium between Emperor and Chancellor, with William striking the attitudes and the Chancellors endeavouring to combine the tasks of managing the Emperor and of manipulating the political blocs in the Reichstag. But in 1908 William was compelled to abdicate his claim to be the All-Highest in fact, and henceforth was so only as a fiction. The occasion of his relegation was the blunder of his celebrated *Daily Telegraph* interview; though the real causes were not unconnected with the jealousy felt by the army leaders at the Emperor's hysterical passion for building a navy. Thereafter a coherent German policy was possible only if the Chancellor was a dominating personality with a clear head and precise aims; or if the Chancellor had become a Prime Minister of a cabinet constitutionally dependent on the Reichstag. But in 1909, Bülow having failed to maintain a majority in the Reichstag, William used the event as an opportunity to dismiss him (though this lack of a majority did not require the Chancellor's resignation). By universal consent Bethman-Hollweg [sic] who was appointed to succeed Bülow had no personal qualifications for controlling policy at all. Like Lichnowsky in London, and the many Germans who in 1913 protested against the savagery of the army's treatment of the civilian population in Saverne, in Alsace, Bethman-Hollweg belonged to the category known as "good" Germans. These were men, however, who did not possess and did not know how to acquire power, to use Shelley's words about good people in general, to do more than "weep barren tears."

Amid the collapse of authority caused by this combination of an Emperor without power, a Chancellor without power and a Parliament without power, the army became the only coherent force in Germany. What had never been true under Bismarck had come true now. There was now no authority in Germany but that of the men of blood and iron, and they alone would make the great decisions of the day because nobody else was capable of making decisions. The Bismarckian system had been stood on its head. Under him the army waited upon a diplomacy that in turn served a clearly conceived policy. Now there was neither diplomacy nor policy. Consequently the issue of peace or war would be decided by the army; and on the only basis on which an army could be expected to make decisions—that of simple military calculation as to what was the most militarily favourable moment to fight. And it would not be a war for any purpose beyond that of achieving victory, for what is to be done with victory when it is won is not a soldier's business. Thus Germany had no war aim except victory.

The German authorities also differed from those of the other great powers in having fewer problems of internal morale to hamper them. It was only in Germany that there was any general feeling in favour of a policy of aggression before the war started. It is true that there were anti-militarist groups in Germany, but to transform their pressure into effective restraint upon the government was impossible since there was almost literally no government to restrain and only a shadow of a parliament by which to restrain it. Hence the only action by which the "good" Germans could stop war was by direct action— a general strike or a revolution. And what could not happen at the outset of war even in demoralized Russia or the racially divided Dual Monarchy could certainly not happen in Germany. As it turned out, the moment war began the "good" Germans hastily dried their tears and got down to business.

The idea that the Germans were more aggressive in the early years of the twentieth century than other peoples was sometimes discounted in later years because it was claimed that there are no "scientific" (i.e. biological) grounds for asserting that any national group is more aggressive than any other, or indeed for asserting that such distinctions as race or nation "really" exist at all. But to try to study national characteristics by reference to biology is to appeal to the wrong science. National character is the product not of biology but of history; chromosomes have nothing to do with it. The Germans were unaggressive before the creation of Bismarck's Reich because they had no history of aggression behind them and no state machinery through which to make aggression effective. But by 1914 they had the machinery, and they had as their sole historic tradition a record of a successful exercise of power unparalleled in the records of European civilization. With no resources other than a relatively small army directed by his own resolute will, Bismarck had created his artificial Empire in defiance of all reasonable calculation. Neither in economic nor military strength, nor in population, had Prussia or the North German Confederation been notably superior either to Austria or to France in the 1860's. Yet the miracle had been wrought, by a few brief decisive strokes that had changed the course of destiny. Blinded by its success and flattered by its sole author, who told them that this was the German Empire of their dreams when all it was was Bismarck's Empire, the Germans appropriated the miracle to themselves as if they had wrought it through their own efforts, when the truth was that Bismarck had wrought it upon them and in spite of them. Henceforth, what had been the triumph of Bismarck's will became the triumph of the German will; and that this German will to power was irresistible became the fundamental myth of the German people, the ground which nourished all their thinking as a nation. The myth of swift, world-defying success was the more compelling because it was their only myth. It was the only German history there was. Into the history of every other nation had been written the record of defeats as well as victories, of hesitancy as well as adventurousness, of disasters as well as triumphs. This was true even of the history of Prussia, as Bismarck never forgot; but it was not true of Bismarck's Reich. Its history was only of success and therefore its national character could think only in terms of success, achieved easily and swiftly by an irresistible display of force, sometimes by the mere threat of force.

Finally, the historical tradition of the Reich knew no principle other than that of the exercise of power for its own sake. The very phrases *Weltpolitik* and

Flottenpolitik reveal in their purposelessness that the Reich had no aim but to be powerful for the sake of being powerful. To have an aim implies a readiness not merely to take action but also to limit action to what is essential to the achievement of the aim. To have a principle necessarily involves the exercise of restraint whenever action threatens to contradict the principle. Thus, all the other powers could point to specific ambitions which they would like to satisfy. France could point to Alsace-Lorraine; Russia could point to Constantinople; England to the defence of the seas and her empire; Austria-Hungary to the destruction of Serbia. But nothing could satisfy the Germans, because they had no aims to satisfy; and nothing could satisfy the principles Germany stood for, since Germany did not stand for any. Thus diplomacy could not settle Germany's problems, because there were no problems that could be solved. There was only blind incoherent force, with which nobody could negotiate because it had no co-ordinating brain or directing intelligence. The Germans stampeded into the war, the mindless and purposeless victims of their own monstrous history.

5.

Marxists are among the few people who harbor no doubts concerning the causes of the coming of war in 1914. Economic factors are seen as decisive here, as in every important historical episode. The following passage is taken from the "official" history of the Bolshevik party, and is a clear and concise statement of the communist point of view. It is interesting to speculate whether the Marxist approach may not have considerable merit; are not economic factors at the base of most of men's actions; does not economic determinism find considerable support in even the most devoutly capitalist circles in the United States? Or is the Marxist approach ludicrously oversimplified, an example of an attempt to make history serve ideology?

History of the Communist Party of the Soviet Union *

Long before the actual outbreak of the war the Bolsheviks, headed by Lenin, had foreseen that it was inevitable. At International Socialist congresses Lenin had put forward proposals the purpose of which was to determine a revolutionary line of conduct for the Socialists in the event of war.

Lenin had pointed out that war is an inevitable concomitant of capitalism. Plunder of foreign territory, seizure and spoliation of colonies and the capture of new markets had many times already served as causes of wars of conquest waged by capitalist states. For capitalist countries war is just as natural and legitimate a condition of things as the exploitation of the working class.

Wars became inevitable particularly when, at the end of the nineteenth century and the beginning of the twentieth century, capitalism definitely entered the highest and last stage of its development—imperialism. Under imperialism

* From *History of the Communist Party of the Soviet Union* (*Bolsheviks*) (Moscow: Foreign Languages Publishing House, 1945), pp. 160–62, 180.

the powerful capitalist associations (monopolies) and the banks acquired a dominant position in the life of the capitalist states. Finance capital became master in the capitalist states. Finance capital demanded new markets, the seizure of new colonies, new fields for the export of capital, new sources of raw material.

But by the end of the nineteenth century the whole territory of the globe had already been divided up among the capitalist states. Yet in the era of imperialism the development of capitalism proceeds extremely unevenly and by leaps: some countries, which previously held a foremost position, now develop their industry at a relatively slow rate, while others, which were formerly backward, overtake and outstrip them by rapid leaps. The relative economic and military strength of the imperialist states was undergoing a change. There arose a striving for a redivision of the world, and the struggle for this redivision made imperialist war inevitable. The war of 1914 was a war for the redivision of the world and of spheres of influence. All the imperialist states had long been preparing for it. The imperialists of all countries were responsible for the war.

But in particular, preparations for this war were made by Germany and Austria, on the one hand, and by France and Great Britain, as well as by Russia, which was dependent on the two latter, on the other. The Triple Entente, an alliance of Great Britain, France and Russia, was formed in 1907. Germany, Austria-Hungary and Italy formed another imperialist alliance. But on the outbreak of the war of 1914 Italy left this alliance and later joined the Entente. Germany and Austria-Hungary were supported by Bulgaria and Turkey.

Germany prepared for the imperialist war with the design of taking away colonies from Great Britain and France, and the Ukraine, Poland and the Baltic Provinces from Russia. By building the Baghdad railway, Germany created a menace to Britain's domination in the Near East. Great Britain feared the growth of Germany's naval armaments.

Tsarist Russia strove for the partition of Turkey and dreamed of seizing Constantinople and the straits leading from the Black Sea to the Mediterranean (the Dardanelles). The plans of the tsarist government also included the seizure of Galicia, a part of Austria-Hungary.

Great Britain strove by means of war to smash its dangerous competitor—Germany—whose goods before the war were steadily driving British goods out of the world markets. In addition, Great Britain intended to seize Mesopotamia and Palestine from Turkey and to secure a firm foothold in Egypt.

The French capitalists strove to take away from Germany the Saar Basin and Alsace-Lorraine, two rich coal and iron regions, the latter of which Germany had seized from France in the war of 1870-71.

Thus the imperialist war was brought about by profound antagonisms between two groups of capitalist states.

This rapacious war for the redivision of the world affected the interests of all the imperialist countries, with the result that Japan, the United States and a number of other countries were subsequently drawn into it.

The war became a world war.

The bourgeoisie kept the preparations for imperialist war a profound secret from their people. When the war broke out each imperialist government endeavoured to prove that it had not attacked its neighbours, but had been attacked by them. The bourgeoisie deceived the people, concealing the true aims of the war and its imperialist, annexationist character. Each imperialist government declared that it was waging war in defence of its country. . . .

The war would not have been so destructive, and perhaps would not even have assumed such dimensions, if the parties of the Second International had not betrayed the cause of the working class, if they had not violated the antiwar decisions of the congresses of the Second International, if they had dared to act and to rouse the working class against their imperialist governments, against the warmongers.

The Bolshevik Party was the only proletarian party which remained faithful to the cause of Socialism and internationalism and which organized civil war against its own imperialist government. All the other parties of the Second International, being tied to the bourgeoisie through their leaders, found themselves under the sway of imperialism and deserted to the side of the imperialists. . . .

6.

Pierre Renouvin, one of France's most distinguished historians, is a professor at the University of Paris. He is an authority on diplomatic history, and among his many works is an antirevisionist study of the events of July 1914, *The Immediate Origins of the World War,* written in the 1920's. In the following selection from a more recent book he presents an interpretation which is notable for its breadth and balance and for its refusal to denounce and accuse. It presents a particularly vivid contrast to the simplicity of the Marxist argument. M. Renouvin's analysis ought to inspire reflection on the role of economic factors in diplomacy, on the importance of individual statesmanship, and on the question of the "inevitability" of the conflict.

RENOUVIN: Histoire des relations internationales *

In an over-all view of these years that mark the apogee of Europe and the first signs of its decline, diplomatic conflicts take on their proper significance only within the framework of economic and social change. Vast scope and accelerated speed of industrial development; rapid development of finance capitalism; tensions between social classes; broad movement of transatlantic emigration; spread of primary education; power of the daily press, and also— let us not forget—increase in military obligations and costs: all these aspects of a transformed world lend a new appearance to international relations. We

* From Pierre Renouvin, *Histoire des relations internationales* (Paris: Hachette, 1955), Vol. VI, pp. 377-84. Translated by the editors. Reprinted by permission of Librairie Hachette.

must try to evaluate, therefore, the respective influence of these underlying causes and of diplomatic initiatives. . . .

The role of individual initiatives, always important in diplomatic action, appears quite different when one compares the "Bismarckian period" with the period that followed it.

Before 1890, how can one study this aspect of history without focusing on the deeds or the designs of that statesman on whom all the others—Disraeli and Gladstone, Jules Ferry, Gorchakov—kept their eyes steadily fixed? In the diplomatic correspondence, nothing is more striking than this constant presence of the German chancellor or of his shadow: what will Bismarck think, and what is he planning to do? No doubt this master of diplomacy had his blind spots: he had little comprehension of economic questions; he took a dim view of colonial expansion; he failed to recognize, in Posen and Alsace, the strength of nationalist protest. But he retained his gift of seeing through his adversary, his faculty of long-range political foresight, and his incomparable virtuosity. The uneasiness that he inspired among his partners as well as among his opponents spread outward into public opinion as well. "Bismarckianism" was a reality of collective psychology and, in consequence, constitutes an indispensable element in the study of that epoch.

After the fall of the Chancellor, the scene changes completely. William II, for want of finding "his Bismarck"—but if he had found one, would William have tolerated him for long?—was forced to fall back on "supporting actors," or at most on brilliant diplomats. Were the other European governments any better off? The epoch was poor in statesmen. In some cases, a disturbing instability of character—that of an Izvolsky or a Berchtold—or a mediocrity that even contemporaries could detect; in other instances, the routine honesty of a high-ranking bureaucrat who adequately managed day-to-day affairs without looking beyond them; or again, a man too clearly marked by parliamentary life, one who pursued "diplomatic victories" even when those victories were useless or dangerous. No doubt some men of conspicuous qualities emerge from this greyness: Salisbury's finesse and Raymond Poincaré's firmness of spirit stand out, for example. Yet even those leaders whose achievements were most important and whose programs went beyond the usual horizon—Joseph Chamberlain, Delcassé, Aehrenthal—demonstrated strength of will and audacity rather than long-range foresight.

Along with these ministers, what sort of men collaborated in the shaping of foreign policy?

In all of the major states, the ranks of career diplomacy contained many men whose professional conscience, whose shrewdness in gathering political information, whose dexterity as negotiators were excellent, and whose opinions got a hearing. But only in the case of France were the principal ambassadors, during the first years of the twentieth century, men of sufficient character and personal authority to become, at moments of serious tension, advisers to their government and even, at times, what one might describe as "mentors." In no country did diplomatic agents exceed their instructions with more tranquil assurance than in autocratic Russia. An examination of this diplomatic world remains indispensable for an understanding of political action; certainly it allows one to comprehend the outlook of a closed social milieu which, in many cases, tended to neglect deeper trends and to believe that the intentions or the maneuvers of chancelleries were the center of interest in international relations. An awareness of this fact is a necessary element in explaining history.

The high military and naval personnel of the period deserve no less attention, if one reflects on the need for harmonizing the orientation of foreign policy with the quality of the armed forces. It is certainly not useless to observe that in democratic and parliamentary countries each government, between 1900 and 1914, unceasingly supervised the plans of its general staff, perhaps for the simple reason that it secretly distrusted the military leaders—while, on the other hand, the German general staff was freer in its action, freer also to succumb to the temptation of profiting by its superiority in armaments.

The fact remains, nevertheless, that in the development of international "tensions" during the early years of the twentieth century, individual actions had far less importance than in the period 1850–1870. . . . In the "Old Continent," the actions of statesmen seem to have been dominated by conditions that they may not have perceived clearly, and that they certainly felt themselves unable to control. Even in the final crisis, although certain "choices" made by the various governments appear to have been decisive, how can one study these choices without taking account of the deeper forces?

The action of economic and financial factors was unceasingly demonstrated: it was guided especially by the influence of private interests and by the quest for profits; but it also took into account the nation's interests insofar as the citizens of a given state, despite the social conflicts that divided them, were conscious of their solidarity in confronting other nations. These factors were a powerful motive force in Europe's expansion into other continents and, therefore, in the jealousies and rivalries that resulted: competition among the great powers of Europe for the conquest of new markets or reserves of raw materials, and for the "control" of land or sea routes of communication, weighed almost constantly upon political relationships. These same factors played an essential role in Europe itself, in the development of war potential and in determining the relative level of armed forces, while at the same time they created suspicion and hostility between certain great states—Germany and England particularly. Germany, when it demanded its "place in the sun," was responding to imperious economic necessity. "In seeking to plug up every outlet of a boiler," noted Jules Cambon in 1913, "doesn't one risk an explosion, and shouldn't one avoid constant antagonism to an inevitable expansion?" This rise in economic power also exerted its influence on national psychology or on the psychology of social classes. In that mood of superiority which marked the German people from the Bismarckian era, and which began to affect the United States at the end of the nineteenth century, industrial achievements played an important part. Finally, the attitude of a social group toward questions of foreign policy is sometimes shaped by its economic and its class interests.

All this confirms the value of the "economic explanation." But should one neglect the factors that correct or limit it?

Rivalries among the various colonial imperialisms often reached the critical point where the adversaries seemed to have said their "final word"; and yet conflicts did not always follow threats: the question of Afghanistan was settled in 1885 by an Anglo-Russian compromise; the English cabinet, despite the importance of Far Eastern markets for the British economy, abandoned Port Arthur to Russia in 1898; and the French government, however eager to re-open the "Egyptian question," retreated at the moment of Fashoda rather than face an armed conflict. At bottom, governments and peoples were conscious that these clashes of material interests were not worth a war, at least a "great war."

Competition between national economies seems to have been no more decisive. In the tension between France and Germany, and in the Russo-German difficulties, economic interests undoubtedly played a role, but a secondary role, so far as one can judge on the basis of research to date. And in the "typical example"—the Anglo-German trade rivalry—what do we see? Did English business circles, even those that were most directly affected by German competition, think of destroying this competition by force of arms? There is no sign that this was the case; and the mood of the financiers of the City, hostile in July 1914 to a policy of armed intervention on the continent, suggests a negative response. Did the German heavy industrialists, in order to avert possible but future dangers, have any interest in making war on Russia, their best European source of supply, and on Great Britain, their best customer? Did they need to resort to force in order to open new foreign markets, when the prosperity of their enterprises in 1914 was in no way threatened in the immediate future, and when they had an opportunity to broaden their outlets in Asia Minor and Africa by agreements made with Great Britain? It must be said that the proofs are lacking.

No doubt competition between material interests helped shape the collective consciousness, intensify the atmosphere of mutual distrust and reinforce the "desire for power"; therefore it increased the risks of general war, but it does not seem to have been the direct cause of its outbreak. . . .

Historical explanation can be no simpler than the behavior of human groups. When it isolates one aspect of this behavior, it denatures that behavior, for between the drives of material interests and the impulsion of nationalism, there is a reciprocal influence. In 1914, the character of the relationships among states or peoples would surely have been much different if the world's economic life had not undergone profound changes during the preceding half-century. But was the European war the necessary result of this clash of material interests? In fact, the conflict broke out only at the moment when there was a violent clash of political aims: concerns for security, or desires for power. No doubt economic interests may have had a place within these aims; governments and peoples were not unaware of the material advantages that would result from such successes. But it was not this calculation that determined their acceptance or their choice. The decisive impulse was provided by national sentiment and bursts of passion.

7.

Bernadotte E. Schmitt is one of America's most respected historians. A former Rhodes scholar, he took a first in modern history at Oxford, and later became a professor of history at the University of Chicago. He has been editor of *The Journal of Modern History* and president of the American Historical Association. After the second world war he became one of the American editors-in-chief of the series called *Documents on German Foreign Policy, 1918–1945*, made up of materials from the captured German foreign office archives. Many of his historical studies have been devoted to the diplomacy of the decade preceding 1914, and his *The Coming of the War, 1914* (1930) is considered by many scholars to be the most thorough study of the subject. The following selection is drawn from a recent pamphlet, and is designed to provide the reader with the distillation of the views of an eminent scholar; although Mr. Schmitt endeavors to be impartial, do his views lean more to the revisionist or the antirevisionist side?

SCHMITT: The Origins of the First World War *

The First World War broke out suddenly and unexpectedly in midsummer 1914, following the murder of the Archduke Francis Ferdinand of Habsburg, heir to the throne of Austria-Hungary, at Sarayevo, in Bosnia, on 28 June. Since no war involving the European great powers with each other had occurred since 1871, the possibility of a general war seemed increasingly remote, at least to the man in the street. At the moment, the international atmosphere was calmer than it had been for some time, for while some Balkan problems were threatening to become difficult, there was nothing unusual about that, nothing so dangerous as the questions that had been settled peacefully in the winter of 1912–1913. Another crisis would, it was assumed, be resolved by another compromise. Statesmen everywhere professed their devotion to peace and more or less sincerely believed their professions. Only a few persons in any country were psychologically prepared for the catastrophe which in the last two weeks of July 1914 plunged Europe into war. To be sure, there were prophets who had made predictions in English, French, German, Italian, and Russian of impending disaster, all written in the ten or fifteen years before 1914, but, truth to tell, they aroused little attention and only a handful of experts believed these Cassandras.

The belief was widespread, on the contrary, that modern governments were

* From Bernadotte E. Schmitt, *The Origins of the First World War* (London: The Historical Association, 1958), pp. 3–6, 7–16, 17–26. Reprinted by permission of the author and the Council of the Historical Association.

much too enlightened to go to war. A great sensation was produced in 1911 by a book called *The Great Illusion,* by Norman Angell, an American who had lived most of his life in Europe. Angell asserted bluntly that wars did not pay. He did not say, as was sometimes alleged, that for economic reasons governments would not go to war, but he put it to them that if they did, they would lose much more than they could gain, for the complicated mechanism of modern business would be thrown out of gear and economic ruin would result for the victors as well as for the vanquished. Angell's arguments were by no means universally accepted and more than one formal refutation was offered. Nevertheless, the view was often expressed that if governments did try to go to war, financiers would stop them; while still others, chiefly socialists, hoped that the workers would not respond to the order of mobilization. But when on 23 July Austria-Hungary in a formidable note accused its small neighbour Serbia of responsibility for the death of the Archduke and made demands that seemed to portend military action, it was instantly recognized that here was no ordinary crisis which might be overcome by negotiation, but that the whole constellation of European power was at stake. Illusions vanished overnight, and millions who before Sarayevo had had no thought of war accepted it as something which could not be avoided.

Once the shock of war had been absorbed, men asked themselves how it had happened, both the intermediate antecedents and the underlying causes. A popular explanation was that the war had grown out of economic jealousies and rival imperialisms. Cited in proof were the trade competition between Germany and Great Britain for a generation before 1914; the conflicting colonial ambitions of the European powers which had more than once led to the "brink" (to use the term adopted forty years later); and the intrigues of high finance for concessions in Asia, Africa and the Near East, concessions for loans, railways, canals and other profitable enterprises. This interpretation was automatic for socialists, who derived their ideas from Karl Marx, but it was not exclusive with them, for an English radical, H. N. Brailsford, on the very eve of the war published a well-known book entitled *The War of Steel and Gold,* which said much the same thing.

Economic interests and rivalries undoubtedly had much to do with poisoning international relations in the forty-three years from the Treaty of Frankfort in 1871 to the outbreak of war in 1914. Thus, the Austro-Serbian dispute, which in 1914 was to provide the spark for the explosion, became serious only when Austria sought to control Serbia by means of "pig wars" and harsh commercial treaties. On the colonial side, there were sharp conflicts between Britain and Russia in Persia and the Far East, between France and Italy in Tunisia, between France and Germany in Morocco, between France and Britain in Egypt and Siam, between Britain and Germany in South Africa. More than once war threatened to break out. Likewise, the most famous project of financial imperialism, the Bagdad railway, involved Britain, France, Germany and Russia in long years of bitter wrangling. These disputes about colonies and the competition for concessions had much to do with the building up of large navies by the western powers, for sea power seemed necessary to guard overseas interests.

Yet economic interests, in the ordinary sense of that term, had little to do, directly at least, with the outbreak of war in August 1914. The most conspicuous trade rivalry of the pre-war years, the competition between Britain and Germany, was ceasing to be a cause of tension because the two countries were developing their markets in different parts of the world, Britain more and more with its own Empire, Germany more and more on the continent of Europe. In July 1914 the loudest protests against war were made by the businessmen in Germany and Britain, who foresaw clearly what war would do to them.

On the colonial side, to the credit of much-abused secret diplomacy, the great powers succeeded in partitioning Africa without recourse to war. To be sure, the British fought the Boers in South Africa, and British, French, Germans and Italians fought native peoples in Africa, but they did not fight each other. In the spring of 1914 Britain and Germany, sixteen years after they had begun to negotiate, were ready to sign an agreement providing for the ultimate disposition of the Portuguese colonies. Also at this time the western powers arrived at a compromise respecting the Bagdad railway and had divided the Ottoman Empire in Asia into spheres of economic influence for the laudable purpose of avoiding war over the Ottoman succession. Thus by 1914 the economic rivalries that were so troublesome in the first decade of the century had been in large measure adjusted, and they played no part in the hectic negotiations that preceded the war. Finally, it is to be noted that in 1914 the ruling groups in European governments were not men who thought in terms of business and economic advantage. They were usually members of the hereditary aristocracy, who thought in terms of strategy and military power and national prestige and who, in the crisis of 1914, paid little heed to the wails of businessmen.

The primary cause of the war was the conflict between political frontiers and the distribution of peoples, the denial of what is commonly called the right of self-determination (although this term was not ordinarily used before 1914). In 1914, from the Rhine eastwards, political frontiers, as determined by the Congress of Vienna a century before and by the wars of the nineteenth century, everywhere cut across well-recognized lines of nationality. To begin with, Germany held Alsace-Lorraine, taken from France in 1871, where the majority of the population resented having been annexed to Germany, disliked German rule, and wished to return to France. Austria-Hungary contained eleven different racial groups, nine of which were kept in greater or less submission by a ruling clique of the other two (Germans, Magyars). In the Balkans, racial and political frontiers rarely coincided. Finally, the western portion of the Russian Empire was made up of non-Russian regions represented today by Finland, the Baltic States, and Poland. Poland was the most notorious case, for it was still divided between the Austrian, German and Russian empires which had partitioned it in the eighteenth century. . . .

From 1872 to 1913, . . . rigorous competition in the building up of armies went on, every government spending as much money as it could persuade its people to pay or its national economy would support. (Germany bore this cost easily, but for Italy the burden was ruinous), without, however, any corresponding increase in security being felt. In fact, the proportionate strength of the various armies was not greatly different in 1914 from what it had been in 1872, but the feeling of insecurity was much greater than it had been forty years earlier. The memoirs of General Ludendorff, the most famous German soldier of the war, are eloquent on this point. . . .

It was because of the increasing feeling of insecurity that European governments, one after another, sought to strengthen their respective positions by concluding alliances with other governments having similar interests. Germany enjoys the doubtful honour of launching this system of alliances, as it does in the matter of conscript armies, for it was Bismarck, the German chancellor, who in 1879 made an alliance with Austria-Hungary and in 1882 engineered a second alliance, the Triple Alliance between Germany, Austria-Hungary and Italy. These alliances marked a turning-point in the history of Europe. There had often been alliances in the past, but they were usually concluded for specific purposes and were dissolved when the aim was accomplished. These Bismarckian alliances were destined to be permanent, the Austro-German treaty lasting until it was dissolved by military defeat in October 1918, the Triple Alliance surviving until 1915. Since the principle and the practice of the balance of power were as old as European history, it was to be expected that sooner or later a counterpoise should be created to the Triple Alliance. Bismarck succeeded in staving this off by very clever diplomacy (first by a Three Emperors' League from 1881 to 1887 and then by a "reinsurance" treaty with Russia from 1887 to 1890) which kept France isolated; but after his fall in 1890, his complicated system was discarded by his successor, and in the early 'nineties a Franco-Russian alliance—which had been Bismarck's nightmare—came into being. One combination dominated the centre of Europe, the other possessed the periphery.

Both of these continental alliances were originally strictly defensive, providing for the maintenance of the *status quo* and for assistance only if one party were attacked. Gradually, however, each alliance was transformed. The Triple Alliance was modified to permit changes in the *status quo* in the Balkans, in Africa and even in Europe, for the Italo-German treaty signed in conjunction with the second treaty of the Alliance concluded in 1887 contained a promise by Germany to support, in certain conditions, Italian claims to Nice and Savoy (which had been ceded to France in 1860 as payment for French assistance in the war of unification). Likewise, the Franco-Russian alliance was modified in 1899 to provide for "the maintenance of the balance of power," the words being meant to take care of the situation which would arise when the Habsburg state went to pieces, as it was confidently expected to do when the Emperor Francis Joseph died. Finally, in 1909, the Austro-German alliance was given a new twist when the chief of the German general staff, by an exchange of letters with his Austro-Hungarian opposite number, promised that if Austria invaded Serbia and in consequence Russia intervened on behalf of Serbia, Germany would go to the assistance of Austria-Hungary, a promise that Bismarck had consistently refused to give, for he insisted that Austria must not provoke Russia. Thus the alliances ceased to be the guarantors of the *status quo,* and might instead become instruments of aggression. The terms of the several treaties and commitments were not published, but each side came to suspect the other of sinister intentions.

Down to the turn of the century, Great Britain did not join either of the continental groups, preferring a policy of "splendid isolation." The two groups, although directed against each other, were often more concerned, in the 'nineties, with diplomatic action against Great Britain, and stood, as it were, side by side, rather than face to face. In 1898 and again in 1901, Britain tried to come to an agreement with Germany, but the German terms proved too high: Britain was asked to join the Triple Alliance, which it was unwilling to do because it was reluctant to underwrite the shaky Habsburg state. The German chancellor of the day, Count Bülow, was sure that in the end Britain would come to heel and stood on his terms. When in 1904 Britain adjusted its many old disputes with France and in 1907 compromised its differences with Russia in the Middle East, Germany found itself confronted by a Triple Entente which had been deemed impossible. Europe was not mentioned in any of the several agreements, but the British, French and Russian governments were all suspicious of Germany, and by settling their own differences they ensured themselves free hands in dealing with Germany. Nevertheless, for years after the formation of the Entente, Germany held on to a policy based on the premise of irreconcilable hostility between Britain and the Franco-Russian Alliance.

At the beginning of the twentieth century, Germany was the most restless nation in Europe. Its population, its industry, its foreign trade were growing more rapidly than those of any other country, and its future seemed brilliant, at least to other countries. But the Germans themselves were not so sure. As they looked at the world around them, they observed that Britain and France had secured control, in one form or another, of the most desirable parts of Africa, held large possessions in Asia, and ruled the ocean lanes from innumerable islands in the seven seas, which provided naval bases and coaling stations. In comparison, the German colonies in Africa and Asia and the German islands in the Pacific were pitifully inadequate. Even the colonial nations of the past, Spain, Portugal, the Netherlands, were better off than Germany. In the current view colonial possessions were considered necessary for an industrial nation, in order to supply raw materials needed in industry and to furnish markets for manufactured goods and opportunities for the investment of capital, and Germany, not having rich, productive and populous colonies, felt discriminated against. So there arose a tremendous agitation and a loud cry for "a place in the sun," and along with it, the charge was heard that Germany's rivals, principally Britain and France, were standing in the way of

Germany's acquiring what was its just due. The Pan-German League, a small but noisy and influential association, proclaimed what needed to be done in Europe to achieve the unification of the German people, and innumerable books and pamphlets set forth in considerable detail what was wanted elsewhere in the world. Since these programmes were to be realized at the expense of other nations and the view was often expressed that if necessary Germany would use force to accomplish its ends, it was not surprising that the countries most affected should draw together, as Britain, France and Russia did in the Triple Entente.

The German government never associated itself with the specific demands of the expansionist agitation, but it resorted to methods of diplomacy which gave great offence. Thus, it took advantage of the Boer War in South Africa to force concessions from Britain in Samoa; it used the opportunity offered by the Russo-Japanese war to secure a tariff treaty from Russia that was unduly advantageous to Germany; and when Russia, France's ally, was being defeated in the Far East, Germany compelled France to get rid of its foreign minister and to change its policy in Morocco. The resistance which Britain, France and Russia offered to this policy, which they regarded as blackmail, was denounced by Germany as "encirclement," and Germany reacted to it by giving unqualified support to the action of Austria-Hungary when that power proclaimed the annexation of Bosnia in 1908, which caused great irritation in Russia.

In addition, the German government, from 1900 onwards, began the construction of a navy which was intended to be second only to that of Great Britain. This was a pet project of the Emperor William II, and he declined all suggestions from Britain for a limitation of naval armaments. The faster the German fleet grew, the more alarmed the British became, the closer they drew to the French and the Russians—and the more the Germans complained of "encirclement." As the years passed, the more clearly did Europe appear to be divided between the Triple Alliance and the Triple Entente.

Actually, things were not so simple. In 1902 Italy made a secret agreement with France by which it promised to remain neutral if France went to war with Germany in consequence of a German attack on Russia. In 1909 Italy concluded a secret agreement with Russia by which both parties recognized each other's interests in the Balkans and promised support for each other's policies. Thus the Triple Alliance was for some years a broken reed. But in the Balkan wars of 1912–1913 Italy worked with Austria-Hungary to establish an independent Albania, and in the winter of 1913–1914 negotiated new military and naval conventions with Germany and Austria-Hungary which seemed to bring the wavering ally back into the fold. The chief of the German general staff, General von Moltke, became convinced that Italy's loyalty was "not open to doubt" and he acted on that assumption in the crisis of July 1914.

The Triple Entente never became so closely-knit as the Triple Alliance, for the British Government refused to commit itself to go to the help of France, in spite of French arguments that an Anglo-French alliance would be the most effective means of discouraging Germany from going to war. The most that

Britain would concede was a promise, made in 1912, that if either Britain or France had grave reason to expect attack by a third party or a threat to the general peace, they would consult with each other and if they should decide to take common action, they would put into effect the plans which their general staffs had drawn up.

These plans, elaborated from 1906 on, provided for the sending of a British army of 160,000 troops to fight in France alongside the French army, and for the deploying of the French navy in the Mediterranean while the British fleet guarded the North Sea and the Channel. The French had to be satisfied (as of course they were not!) with this "half-alliance," which left the British free to decide whether to intervene—a freedom of which they took full advantage in 1914.

Anglo-Russian relations never reached the degree of intimacy of those between Britain and France. Russian interests in the Near East were not regarded in Britain as something Britain might have to fight for, and Russian activity in Persia was much disliked. In the spring of 1914 the Russian foreign minister, Sazonov, proposed that the Triple Entente should be converted into a Triple Alliance, but this was rejected by the British foreign secretary, Sir Edward Grey. Grey agreed, however, to the Russians being informed of the Anglo-French notes exchanged in 1912 and to the opening of conversations between the British and Russian admiralties, so that, as he said to the German ambassador, although Britain was not allied with France and Russia, it "did from time to time talk with them as intimately as allies."

Thus in July 1914 the two groups, Triple Alliance and Triple Entente, were at long last ranged face to face, three on each side. Was war the inevitable consequence of this schism of Europe? At the moment there was no immediate prospect of it. Relations between Britain and Germany had improved considerably since 1912. An informal agreement had been reached for the construction of battleships in the ratio of 16:10. During the crisis of the Balkan wars (1912–1913) Britain and Germany had co-operated to restrain Russia and Austria respectively, and in 1914 they had negotiated and were ready to sign two agreements regarding the future of the Portuguese colonies and settling their differences about the Bagdad railway. This led the British to expect that in the event of another Balkan crisis they could count on German help to deal with it; on the other hand, the Germans drew the conclusion that Britain would no longer necessarily take the side of France in the event of war.

After the great crises of 1905–1911 over Morocco, during which Germany seemed ready for war with France, the relations between those two countries had also taken a turn for the better. In February 1914, an agreement was reached concerning railway schemes and spheres of economic interest in Turkey, and the president of the Republic, Poincaré, who was later to be denounced as a war-monger, breaking a tradition of forty years, had dined at the German embassy. If Alsace-Lorraine had not been forgotten, there was practically no sentiment for a "war of revenge" (as the German ambassador recognized), and the elections of May 1914 gave a majority to the parties of the Left, who wished to abolish the three-years' military service restored in 1913.

In the midsummer of 1914, then, neither Anglo-German nor Franco-German relations involved any threat to peace. On the other hand, there was plenty of explosive material lying around in the Near East. At the end of 1913 such tension was produced between Russia and Germany by the despatch of a German military mission to Constantinople for the rehabilitation of the Turkish army that Sazonov toyed with the idea of seizing the Straits by force (an idea rejected by his colleagues and the Russian general staff); a compromise was patched up, but public opinion in both countries remained excited. Austria and Italy were intriguing against each other in Albania, Bulgaria was sullenly nursing its defeat the year before at the hands of Serbia, Greece and Romania, Greece and Turkey were at loggerheads about certain islands in the Ægean. As it happened, however, the spark that touched off the explosion was a completely unexpected incident, the murder of the Archduke Francis Ferdinand of Habsburg at Sarayevo on 28 June.

The tragedy at Sarayevo was the culmination of an antagonism between Austria-Hungary and Serbia that had been growing for a generation. In 1859, the Habsburgs had faced the question of Italian unification, and had been driven out of Italy; in 1866 they faced the same problem in Germany, and with the same result. From 1903, when the pro-Austrian king of Serbia, Alexander Obrenovich, was assassinated, they were confronted with the Yugoslav problem. At the beginning of the century, the Yugoslavs were widely disunited in Austria, Hungary, Bosnia, Serbia, Montenegro and Turkey. In the decade before 1914 it became evident that a national movement was gaining headway because of the rather shabby treatment of the Yugoslavs within the Habsburg monarchy, and one of two things seemed likely to happen: either Austria-Hungary must bring the Yugoslavs outside the Monarchy (those in Serbia, Montenegro and Turkey) under Habsburg rule, or the Serbs, the most energetic group among the Yugoslavs and the only one possessing an independent state, would detach their kinsmen from Habsburg rule and establish a unified independent Yugoslav state. If Habsburg experience with the Italians and the Germans provided any guide, the second contingency was the more likely.

Naturally the ruling groups in Austria-Hungary favoured the first course. The military party, led by the chief of the general staff, General Conrad von Hötzendorf, made no secret of its desire for war against Serbia, which would lead to direct annexation of the troublesome little neighbour. The political leadership was more cautious, thinking in terms of a customs union or a change of dynasty, which might be accomplished by diplomacy, but it was just as eager as the soldiers to put an end to Serbian independence and thus extinguish the restlessness of its Yugoslav peoples. The first step in this direction was the annexation of Bosnia–Herzegovina, two provinces with a mixed population of Serbs and Croats which had been under Habsburg administration since 1878 but were nominally still parts of the Ottoman Empire. This action precipitated a six months' crisis (October 1908–March 1909), which almost ended in an Austrian attack on Serbia and was settled only after Germany had sent a near-ultimatum to Russia requiring the cabinet of St. Petersburg to recognize the annexation without reference to a European conference. The Russian foreign minister of the time, Izvolsky, accused his Austro-Hungarian opposite number, Aehrenthal, of tricking him, and he bitterly resented the intervention of Germany at the last minute. The echoes of this conflict had not died away in 1914.

In the plans of the Austro-Hungarian government to deal with the Yugoslav problem, the Archduke Francis Ferdinand played a peculiar role. He had come to the conclusion that the existing Dual system, by which the Germans ruled in Austria, the Magyars in Hungary, although both were minorities, was driving the Monarchy to destruction, and he hated the Magyar clique and was determined to clip its power. He proposed to solve the Yugoslav problem by granting to the Yugoslavs within the Monarchy full autonomy (which would destroy the Dual system) and then bring Serbia into some kind of connection with the Monarchy. Whether Francis Ferdinand would have been able to accomplish this is anybody's guess. He was a rather hot-headed, bigoted, avaricious man who was heartily disliked by the great majority of his future subjects, and any attempt to carry out his plan, had he lived to succeed his uncle Francis Joseph, would have met with determined resistance by the Germans and Magyars. But his violent death at the hands of a man of Serbian race (who, however, was a Habsburg subject) provided the forward party with an excuse for action against Serbia that was too tempting to be neglected.

The full circumstances of the crime at Sarayevo have never been cleared up. That the conspirators were fitted out with arms in Belgrade and secretly passed across the frontier into Bosnia became known in 1914 and was used by the Austro-Hungarian government as justification for the demands made on Serbia. But precisely who inspired the crime, how much the Serbian government knew about the plot in advance, what steps it took to prevent the crime's execution —either by warning Vienna or by attempting to stop the assassins from crossing into Bosnia, whether also the authorities in Sarayevo took proper precautions to protect the heir to the throne, are questions to which precise answers are still not possible. Actually the answers do not really matter, for an official sent from Vienna to Sarayevo reported that the responsibility of the Serbian government was not established; yet Austro-Hungarian policy could hardly have been more drastic if Serbian official complicity had been proved.

The situation in 1914 cannot, however, be judged exclusively in terms of Austro-Serbian relations, for Serbia, a small nation of 5,000,000 people, occupied a key position in Europe. Romania was the ally of Austria-Hungary; Bulgaria was anxious to be taken into the Triple Alliance; in Turkey German influence was stronger than that of any other power. If Serbia were brought under Austrian control, then German-Austrian influence would prevail from Berlin to Bagdad. If, on the other hand, Serbia were maintained as an independent state, a wedge would be driven into the German-Austrian-Turkish combination, and Constantinople would be susceptible to Russian, French and British pressure. So the crisis of July 1914 was concerned with more than the question whether, as Austria-Hungary demanded, Austrian officials should go into Serbia and investigate the *minutiae* of the crime at Sarayevo. The fundamental issue was a test of strength between the Triple Alliance and the Triple Entente, the outcome of which would affect the balance of power in Europe for an incalculable time to come. . . .

The Austro-Hungarian government quickly decided that the heaven-sent opportunity for a reckoning with Serbia should not be lost. But since action against Serbia was likely to bring about the intervention of Russia, it was essential for the cabinet of Vienna to know what Germany would do in such a situation. To be sure, the German general staff had declared in 1909, during the Bosnian crisis, that Russian intervention on behalf of Serbia would cause Germany to mobilize, which, in German terminology, was the prelude to war. But, during the crisis of the Balkan wars of 1912–1913, the German government had consistently restrained the war party in Vienna, and furthermore, the German Emperor, William II, was supposed to entertain considerable partiality for Serbia. In order to discover the state of mind of Berlin, the Austro-Hungarian foreign minister, Count Berchtold, sent both an official note and a private emissary to the German capital; also Francis Joseph wrote a letter to William II. The letter stated that Austria-Hungary must aim at "the isolation and diminution of Serbia," which must be "eliminated as a political factor in the Balkans." The emissary, Berchtold's *chef de cabinet,* Count Hoyos, explained that the Austrian plan was to "march into Serbia" without any warning and to partition Serbia between the Monarchy, Albania and Bulgaria.

Only two weeks before, the German chancellor, Bethmann Hollweg, had said that in the event of a new crisis arising in the Balkans, "whether . . . it would come to a general European conflagration would depend exclusively on the attitude of Germany and England." But when Hoyos appeared in the German capital on 5 July, this caution was laid aside. The Austrian plan to invade and partition Serbia was cordially received by the German Emperor and the German government, and immediate action was urged on the cabinet of Vienna. Because a royal personage had been murdered, William II professed to believe that Tsar Nicholas II would be loath to go to the help of Serbia, but if he did, Germany was ready to support its ally and to wage war against Russia and France. This decision was not a matter of Germany putting its head into a noose (as is sometimes asserted) and signing away its freedom of action; both emperor and government knew exactly what they were doing. They made their decision on the assumption that Great Britain would remain neutral (in spite of the fact that the German ambassador in London, Prince Lichnowsky, had been reporting for eighteen months that in the event of war between Germany and France, Britain would join France). The general staff was confident that Germany and Austria-Hungary could defeat Russia and France, and, assuming war to be inevitable, it now welcomed the prospect of war, for victory would be easier in 1914 than later, when French and Russian military plans would be nearer completion. Some conservative elements in Germany looked upon war as a good means of dealing with the menace of socialism, which seemed to be steadily increasing. The emperor and the chancellor took their decision without reference to the foreign minister, a cautious man who happened to be away on his honeymoon and who had hitherto worked to restrain Austria, and without any formal consultation of the highest authorities of the German Empire; furthermore, the decision was taken instantly, without reflection. William II and Bethmann accepted the risk of war with unbelievable nonchalance; it was they who put the system of European alliances to the test. Without this German action, it is unlikely that a European war would have broken out in the summer of 1914.

For twenty-odd years German policy had vacillated between East and West. From 1890 to 1914, that is, the period after the fall of Bismarck during which William II was the ruler of Germany, the German government pursued its policy of expansion in both directions. Admiral Tirpitz and the navy people thought Britain the enemy and concentrated on building a fleet, although the more they built the more they alarmed Britain. The general staff thought in terms of French enmity and demanded as much money as possible for the army. Business men were divided, some wishing to go into Africa, others into the Near East. Neither the emperor nor any of his chancellors could make up their minds where the fundamental interest of Germany lay; in one sense, they thought that Germany was strong enough to move in both directions. In 1914, however, they were seriously concerned about the stability of Austria-Hungary, the one sure ally, and they persuaded themselves that only a successful military demonstration against Serbia could stop the process of Habsburg decay. The decision of July 1914 to support Austria-Hungary against Russia, in the calculation that Britain would remain neutral, may be interpreted as meaning that the long indecision had, at least for the moment, been resolved by a decision to go East.

The Austro-Hungarian government could now act. But because of the opposition of the Hungarian premier, Count Tisza, the plan to "march into Serbia" without warning was abandoned. At a ministerial council held on 7 July, in its place a forty-eight hour ultimatum was decided upon which theoretically would provide Serbia with a chance to submit. Actually, seven supposedly unacceptable demands were included, in order to ensure the rejection of the ultimatum and thus pave the way for military action. In the minds of the Austro-Hungarian ministers the treatment to be meted out to Serbia after the war included "rectifications of frontier" for the benefit of the Monarchy, while other parts of its territory were to be apportioned to other Balkan states; what was left might be attached to the Monarchy by a military convention to be signed by a new dynasty. These designs were of course not mentioned when the Austro-Hungarian government assured the other powers that it did not intend to take Serbian territory for itself.

The ultimatum was presented to the Serbian government on 23 July. It contained ten demands, the most important of which required Serbia to admit Austrian officials into Serbia for the suppression of the agitation against the Monarchy and to take action against the persons involved in the murder of Sarayevo. Outside of Austria and Germany, the ultimatum was regarded as a monstrous document which no independent state could accept. To the intense surprise and annoyance of Vienna, the Serbian reply, delivered a few minutes before the expiry of the ultimatum on 25 July, was conciliatory and to a large extent appeared to accept the Austrian demands, as was later stated by both William II and Bethmann Hollweg. Nevertheless, diplomatic relations were broken off, partial mobilization of the Austrian army was ordered, and on 28 July war was declared against Serbia. The military chiefs would have preferred to wait until mobilization had been completed, but insistent German pressure forced immediate action, which began with the bombardment of the Serbian capital on 29 July.

This action precipitated the intervention of Russia. For generations the principal Russian interest in the Near East had been the question of the Straits: how to break through the barrier of the Bosphorus and the Dardanelles and secure free access to the Mediterranean for Russian merchantmen and men-of-war. Although various plans for accomplishing this had been devised since 1798, no plan existed in 1914, for the Russian generals had rejected a suggestion of the foreign minister for seizing the Straits. The other facet of Russia's Near Eastern policy was the defence of the Slav peoples of the Balkans against Turkish misrule or German pressure. Ever since the Bosnian crisis of 1908, Serbia had looked to Russia for help against Austrian action, but Russia was weak after the war against Japan and the abortive revolution of 1905, so successive foreign ministers kept putting off the importunate Serbs with promises for the future. The Russian government probably did not want war in 1914, for its army was still in process of reorganization and revolutionary symptoms were again in evidence, but, this time, it had to help Serbia or see that country be crushed by Austria. The German argument that the Austro-Serbian conflict could be "localized" was completely unrealistic, all the more so since the Austrian assurances of disinterestedness were equivocal. The Russian foreign minister, Sazonov, vainly tried to get the terms of the Austrian ultimatum modified; at the same time, by ordering partial mobilization, he sought to make clear that if Austria attacked Serbia, Russia would act. This calculation misfired for two reasons. First, the news of the partial Russian mobilization did not deter Vienna and Berlin from the course they had charted. Second, the Russian general staff was aghast (it had not been consulted!) for it had no plan for a partial mobilization, so the generals persuaded first Sazonov and then the Tsar that partial mobilization was impracticable and general mobilization inevitable. The Tsar wavered, giving his consent on 29 July and then withdrawing it; but on 30 July he agreed, and on 31 July the order was published.

Russian general mobilization was ordered in the sure knowledge that it would be followed by German mobilization, which, according to the German view, "meant war." In a sense, then, Russia "willed the war," as the Germans were fond of saying; the Italian historian Albertini thinks that the mobilization was premature, for by 30 July Sir Edward Grey had come forward with an idea that might have led to compromise and peace. But inasmuch as Austria had attacked Serbia, and Germany had forbidden even the Russian partial mobilization, Russia, as the Russian government saw it, had to mobilize or abdicate as a great power. The Tsar promised that his armies would not attack so long as negotiations continued—but these assurances seemed as flimsy to Germany as the Austrian assurances about the integrity of Serbia did to Russia.

From the beginning of the crisis precipitated by the Austrian ultimatum to Serbia, Germany had declined to restrain its ally and had urged it to act quickly. But by 28 July, the day on which Austria declared war on Serbia, the German Emperor had had a change of heart. Reversing his attitude of 5 July when he urged immediate action, he now sensed that the conciliatory Serbian reply had removed "every reason for war"; he therefore suggested that Austria should stop with the occupation of Belgrade and offer to negotiate. On the following day it began to seem likely that, contrary to German calculations, Britain would be drawn into the war. So the German government shifted its ground and advised Vienna to accept a British proposal, practically identical with that of William II, that after occupying Belgrade, it should offer to negotiate. Before the Austrian government had replied, rumours of Russian mobilization began to reach Berlin. The chief of the general staff, Moltke, now pressed for war (as is admitted by the two most objective German students of the crisis). On the evening of 30 July he persuaded the chancellor to relax the pressure on Berchtold to accept Grey's proposal, and he himself telegraphed to Conrad urging rejection of this proposal and promising full German support if war resulted. Vienna did as Moltke desired and ordered Austrian general mobilization—before news had been received of the Russian general mobilization.

When the official news of the Russian general mobilization reached Berlin on the morning of 31 July, Moltke, with the help of William II, secured the consent of Bethmann, who had been holding out against the pressure of the generals, to the proclamation of a "state of danger of war," which was the necessary preliminary to formal mobilization, the order for which was issued on the following day, 1 August. Whether, without the intervention of Moltke, Austria would have accepted the British proposal, whether a compromise with Russia could have been worked out, no one can say; but it is clear that the interference of Moltke prevented any last-minute attempt to keep the peace.

Because Germany expected to have to fight a two-front war against Russia and France, the general staff had persuaded itself that the only chance of victory lay in a headlong attack on France that was expected to defeat the French in six weeks, after which the German armies would be transferred to the eastern front to meet the more slowly mobilizing Russians. In 1914 there was no plan for an attack first on Russia and a defensive action against France. Yet in 1914 Germany had no quarrel with France. In order to have an excuse for attacking France, the German general staff had to make the Russian mobilization a *casus belli* and then ask France if it would remain neutral; since France would, because of its alliance with Russia, reply in the negative, Germany would then have justification for war against France. But the Prussian minister of war, Falkenhayn, was of the opinion that Germany could wait for several days before responding to the Russian general mobilization; Moltke, however, was so eager for war that the German government did not wait to see if Grey's efforts for peace might be successful.

Germany declared war on Russia on 1 August, which enabled the Russian government to say that it had been attacked while it was ready and anxious to negotiate. The German action required France, according to the Franco-Russian treaty of alliance, to attack Germany, but the French government, in reply to the German ultimatum, instead of replying that it would march with Russia (as expected and desired by Germany), said that it would consult its interests. This reply did not stop the German armies from invading France, and on 3 August Germany declared war on France, alleging, wrongly, that French planes had bombarded Nuremberg. Thus France also appeared to be the victim of brutal aggression, a circumstance of great value to France in consolidating sentiment at home and winning help abroad.

France played little part in the crisis of 1914. It had no direct interest in Serbia, but it was the ally of Russia, and if it did not support Russia in this crisis, the alliance would be broken and France would be left isolated. It happened that at the moment when the Austrian ultimatum was presented in Belgrade, the president of the Republic, Poincaré, and the president of the council of ministers, Viviani, were paying a state visit to Russia, and they gave the Tsar and his ministers the assurance that France would support Russia in resisting Austria-Hungary and Germany, an assurance that certainly strengthened the determination of Sazonov. During the crisis, the French government advised its ally to do nothing that would provide Germany with an excuse for war, but it did not object to any step taken by Russia. This attitude was firmly supported by all shades of French public opinion, and the government did not feel it necessary to reveal the secret terms of the alliance. It will be noted that both Germany and France supported their allies on an issue—Serbia—not of direct concern to themselves, and thus it was that a quarrel between Austria-Hungary and Serbia became transformed, in the interests of the balance of power, into a general European war.

The role of Great Britain was not easy. The crisis found the Liberal government facing the prospect of civil war in Ireland over the question of Home Rule, which may have helped to convince the German government that Britain would remain neutral. Actually in view of the European situation, the Irish controversy was adjourned, and both the Irish parties supported the government in its efforts to preserve peace. Grey made various proposals for delay, discussion and compromise, all of which were rejected by Austria-Hungary and Germany.

Britain was urged by Germany to accept the principle that the Austro-Serbian conflict should be localized, in other words, to proclaim its neutrality, and by Russia and France to declare its solidarity with them as the only means of stopping Germany from war. Grey, together with the prime minister,

Asquith, and some other members of the cabinet, believed that Russia could not be expected to stand aside and abandon Serbia, and Grey, attaching great importance to British relations with Russia, refused to exert pressure on Russia to do so or to advise Russia against mobilization; they also believed that an Austro-German victory in the approaching struggle would establish a German ascendancy in Europe which would be dangerous for Britain. On the other hand, they could not announce British solidarity with Russia and France because this would have been rejected by the majority of the cabinet and no doubt by both parliament and the country. At the moment, even the limited commitment of 1912 made to France . . . was still secret, as were also the military and naval conversations begun in 1906. Whatever Grey and his group might desire, and they were sure that in its own interests Britain must range itself with France, the temper of the country, at the beginning of the crisis, was predominantly for abstention from the war that seemed likely. Grey privately told the German ambassador that, in the event of war, Britain would be drawn in, but he apparently did not inform the cabinet that he had done so. It was not until Germany had declared war on Russia and sent an ultimatum to France that a promise was given that Britain would defend the northern coast of France against German attack, and even this was made dependent upon the approval of parliament and could be given only because the Conservative opposition promised to support it. As Germany promised not to attack the French coast, the British promise might never have been put to the test had Germany not violated the neutrality of Belgium.

This changed the situation immediately, for the German action persuaded cabinet, parliament and country of the necessity for Britain to join the war. Grey was later reproached for not making clear to Germany much earlier than he did that the violation of Belgium would be a *casus belli*. This would probably have been useless. The German general staff had only *one* plan for fighting the war, a plan which involved going through Belgium, and Moltke was not alarmed by the prospect of British intervention, which he expected; he was confident that his armies would defeat the French before British help arrived or, if the British did manage to land a small army, that it would be easily beaten. It is quite true, as Germans have often asserted, that for Grey the German violation of Belgium was not the reason for British participation in the war, which he advocated on general grounds, but it is equally true that without the Belgian issue, the British government could probably not have persuaded the British people to accept intervention in the war in August 1914.

Ever since 1914 the question has been endlessly debated whether a clear-cut declaration of British solidarity with France and Russia would have prevented the war, but there is no agreement among the publicists, diplomatists and historians who have written on this question. All that can be said with any assurance is that Grey thought it impossible to make such a declaration and never asked it of the cabinet. Mindful of this controversy, the British government of 1939 did make such a declaration, but it did not stop Hitler from making war on Poland.

Italy, the sixth great power, disapproved of the Austrian action from the beginning. In the light of its own history, it did not think it possible for Habsburg power to suppress the Yugoslav national movement by force; but if it did succeed, Italian interests in the Adriatic would be prejudiced. Furthermore, Italy was unwilling to expose its long coastline to the British fleet. The Italian government therefore took advantage of the failure of Austria, in violation of Article VII of the treaty of the Triple Alliance, to inform its ally in advance of its intended action and to arrange compensation, to declare that Germany and Austria were waging a war of aggression and to proclaim its neutrality—which permitted France to withdraw troops from the Italian frontier and send them against Germany.

Previous international crises were long-drawn-out affairs—Morocco 1905, 1911; Near East, 1908–1909, 1912–1913—during which diplomacy had time to function. In 1914 only thirteen days elapsed from the presentation of the Austrian ultimatum on 23 July to the declaration of war against Germany by Great Britain on 4 August. Austria-Hungary and Germany hoped to force the other powers into accepting their violent programme. To meet this situation, which clearly caught them by surprise, Russia, France and Britain were forced to improvise, with not too happy results. Sazonov and Grey kept making new suggestions almost daily, before their previous proposals had made the rounds of the chanceries and been considered, so that the diplomatic situation grew more and more confused. The confusion reached its height on 1 August, when Germany declared war on Russia, at the very moment when both Austria and Russia seemed at last to be willing to negotiate. A little time was needed to determine what the situation was in fact, but the military men, thinking in terms of mobilization time-tables, had begun to take over from the diplomatists. The three emperors, Francis Joseph, Nicholas II, William II, all hesitated long before they consented to the irrevocable measures of mobilization and declaration of war; unhappily, the first was almost senile, the second a weak character, the third volatile and impetuous. Also, among the numerous men who had to make decisions, there was no outstanding personality—no Cavour, Bismarck or Disraeli—who could dominate the situation.

From 1871 to 1914 the peace of Europe was maintained by the combination of alliances and armaments. In the crises before 1914 governments did not take the plunge because they were not ready for war, were not assured of support from their allies, or did not consider the issue worth fighting for. In 1914 what was at stake was the balance of power in Europe for an indefinite time ahead, and the governments were nearer ready for war than they had been in any previous crisis. Austria-Hungary and Germany insisted on a military solution of the Serbian problem, and clearly wished to upset the *status quo;* Russia, France and Britain were ready to tolerate a diplomatic humiliation of Serbia but not its military subjugation, and while they were not committed to the *status quo,* they were unwilling to see it altered without their consent. Thus the alliances, which had originally served the cause of peace, when put to the final test, almost mechanically operated to convert a local conflict into a general war.

Likewise the great armaments helped to keep the peace—so long as they were not used. But as soon as one power, in order to reinforce its diplomacy, began to mobilize, its action made military men everywhere jittery, for no general staff was willing to allow a rival to get a start. "Once the dice were set rolling," as the German chancellor said, nothing could stop them.

8.

Many Americans stoutly maintain that history is nothing but a "cultural" subject, something for the dilettante, and something for the student who is not sure what he wants to make of his life; after one announces that he is study- ing history, very often the reply is "Fine, but what do you want to *do* with it?" It may be that history's "cultural" value alone is great enough to justify its retention in college curricula; but on the more "practical" level, some people insist on pushing ahead with attempts to find useful lessons. Herman Kahn, a physicist by training, has been with the RAND Corporation since 1948, and is an expert on the relationship between weapons and strategy; he has been a consultant to the Atomic Energy Commission and to the Office of Civil Defense Mobilization. In his book, *On Thermonuclear War,* Mr. Kahn has arrived at conclusions which some readers consider exceedingly valu- able and realistic, and which others regard as cynical, dangerous, and inac- curate. Whether one agrees with his broader conclusions or not, it is interesting to note that Mr. Kahn has supported them by a study of the origins of the first world war, and has found many parallels between our own time and July 1914.

KAHN: On Thermonuclear War *

The most interesting thing about World War I in addition to its technology and tactics is the prewar situation, the manner in which the war got started. The last really big European war had ended in 1815 with the defeat of Napoleon. The last moderately large war in Europe, the Franco-Prussian, had terminated in 1871. The next forty-three years, until 1914, were for the European continent years of almost complete peace, marred only by small wars between relatively unimportant Balkan nations and a relatively innocuous war between the Russians and the Turks in 1877. That is, Europe had had about a century of relative peace and almost half a century of almost com- plete peace. The thought of war had grown unreal to the governments in- volved. They got used to making threats to go to war, either directly or by implication, and they even got used to getting their way when they made these threats strong enough. There were a number of crises which made

* From Herman Kahn, *On Thermonuclear War* (Princeton: Princeton University Press, 1960), pp. 357–60, 361–62, 368–70. Reprinted by permission of the Princeton University Press.

newspaper headlines and scared both governments and people, but after a while even these became unreal and the armies were thought of more as pieces in a game played by diplomats (called "let's find a formula") than as tools to be used. Even though the two sides snarled ferociously at each other, one side was always expected to give way graciously, or ungraciously, before it came to a trial of arms. Both consciously and unconsciously, all the top decision makers were afraid of being involved in a large war. In spite of the optimistic calculations of some of the military, there was a feeling in all the governments that the war would be big and that it was too risky an activity to engage in unless the odds were overwhelmingly in one's favor, and none of the nations felt the odds were sufficiently high in 1914. Therefore, *just because neither side really wanted war, one side or the other would presumably withdraw before things got out of hand.*

As far as I know, just about all modern historians agree on this thesis—that none of the top statesmen or the rulers and very few, if any, of the soldiers wanted a world war in 1914 (though some wanted a war somewhat later, after certain preparations had been made), and only the Serbs and the Austrians wanted even a small war. And yet war came. How did it happen?

The British historian A. J. P. Taylor described the prewar situation in an article in *The Observer.* . . .

The statesmen of Europe with one accord accepted the theory of "the deterrent": the more strongly and firmly they threatened, the more likely they were both to preserve the peace of Europe and get their way. . . .

. . . The German rulers were firmly wedded to the theory of the deterrent. A resolve to go to war, loudly proclaimed; and the other side would give way. In Jagow's words: "The more boldness Austria displays, the more strongly we support her, the more likely Russia is to keep quiet." Those who condemn the German policy should reflect that Sir Edward Grey did the opposite from the Germans: he failed to make his position clear in advance. And for this he has often been saddled with responsibility for the war. . . .

The amateur strategist, devising actions without inquiring whether they were technically possible, was a recurring theme in July 1914. . . . It was no doubt the penalty for forty years of peace, years in which armies and campaigns had been weapons of diplomacy, not of war.

The most striking feature of the July crisis was the total lack of contact in every country between the political and military leaders. Military plans were at their most rigid in the railway age; yet no statesman had the slightest idea what the timetables involved. Their sensations, when diplomacy collapsed, were those of a train passenger who sees the express thundering through the station at which he intended to alight.

As Taylor says, World War I was a railroad war. It was a war for which the general staffs of the four great continental powers had spent decades planning meticulous timetables. The war plans were literally cast in concrete in the sense that governments built railroads according to the requirements of the war plan. One could look at a nation's railroads and get a very accurate idea of what its war plans were. All nations except Britain had very large numbers of trained reserves available that were quite different from the kind of manpower we refer to as reserves today; the 1914 conscripts were prepared to be mobilized into fighting armies. As soon as they were called to the colors, most of them could march into battle on an equal footing with the best professional troops available. This ability to increase one's force by a large factor and in a very short period of time gave a disastrous instability to the situation, because it promised to give the nation that mobilized first a crucial advantage.

As General Boisdeffre, the assistant chief of the French General Staff explained to Tsar Nicholas:

The mobilization is the declaration of war. To mobilize is to oblige one's neighbor to do the same. . . . Otherwise, to leave a million men on one's frontier, without doing the same simultaneously, is to deprive oneself of all possibility of moving later; it is placing oneself in a situation of an individual who, with a pistol in his pocket, should let his neighbor put a weapon to his forehead without drawing his own.

While the Tsar answered that that was his understanding also, his general staff in 1912 decided that the belief that "the proclamation of mobilization is equivalent to the declaration of war," had serious disadvantages for the Russians, since it took them so long to mobilize. Therefore, they formally annulled the rule and instructed the Foreign Office, "It will be advantageous to complete concentration without beginning hostilities, in order not to deprive the enemy irrevocably of the hope that war can still be avoided. Our measures for this must be masked by clever diplomatic negotiations, in order to lull to sleep as much as possible the enemy's fears."

While the above is a perfectly reasonable "military requirement," since it is very valuable to be able to steal a march on the enemy, it is not a reasonable diplomatic requirement. The Foreign Office felt that the enemy was just not going to be fooled by soothing words while the Russians prepared to draw (rather noisily) their pistols. As a matter of fact the Russian Foreign Office was wrong; they did succeed, in the crisis of July 1914, in holding off a German mobilization for about a week while the Russians went through preparatory moves. They did this not by being superlatively clever, but by not knowing themselves what they really intended to do and managing to transmit this confusion to the Germans. The Germans had not prepared any temporizing measures; unlike the other nations they had no plans to mobilize and then hold, but only plans to mobilize and attack. From the precrisis viewpoint of the German General Staff this was not a serious disadvantage, since they felt that it would be a military disaster to hold off and let the Russians complete their mobilization; but in the event itself, the government could not make the decision for war. As long as the situation was ambiguous, it was not willing to make an irrevocable step, and no temporizing measures had been prepared, so the German government did nothing while its enemies stole a march on it. As we know, when war finally came the Germans were not able to meet their schedule, but it is possible that if they had not allowed the Russians to steal this march, they might have met the original timetable and won World War I according to plan. The trouble was that the Russians attacked East Prussia in the second week of the war in such strength that Von Moltke got frightened and detached two army corps from the crucial right wing of the German offensive against the French and sent them East to reinforce the German army in Prussia. It is widely believed that if he had not done this the Germans might have won the battle of the Marne and defeated France, though it is clear that troop fatigue, logistic problems, and possibly some poor tactical decisions played an important role. The final irony occurred when the Germans succeeded in defeating the Russian attack before the two army corps reached the Eastern front. . . .

Thus it turned out that the German plan for protecting themselves by quick countermeasures failed. There were many reasons for this failure. We have mentioned the first and most important, the Germans' failure to react quickly. This is, of course, the standard problem in dealing with any situation in which there might be false alarms and in which the reaction to a false alarm is costly. One may be unwilling to react. Countries are usually reluctant to go to war except at a time and manner of their own choosing, and as long as there is any chance of peace they usually feel obligated to discount the signals they are getting; because they do not want to be premature, they accept the risk of giving the enemy precious time until the threat becomes unambiguous.

A second reason that the timing of the German plan was thrown off was that the Russians turned out to be somewhat better at mobilizing than expected. In addition to mobilizing faster than the experts thought they could, the Russians attacked before being fully prepared. Either out of enlightened self-interest or possibly from loyalty to their alliance they were determined to create a diversion that would help the French, even if it meant attacking prematurely and risking a disaster (which it did). This, too, is a standard problem. Whenever a plan depends on a very precise estimate of either the enemy's capability or his willingness to run risks, it is automatically unreliable.

Like the Germans, the Russians had a rather rigid war plan. All their thinking had been devoted to the problem of how to attack Germany and Austria together, and they had not considered any other kind of large war. In particular, they had made no plans for attacking just Austria-Hungary. The Russian government found, to its surprise and consternation, that it could not even carry out a partial mobilization for the purpose of threatening Austria without threatening the Germans by troop movements on their frontier and at the same time leaving themselves helpless before a German mobilization or attack, because they could not reverse their movements. The rigidities and pressures toward pre-emptive action contained in the Russian and German war plans proved disastrous in the events that followed. In much the same way, careless and rigid plans today by either the Russians or the Americans to use certain kinds of quick reaction as a defense might be disastrous.

Many people realized then that the basic situation was unstable and that a chain of events could erupt into a conflagration, but I think relatively few people took the possibility seriously; that is, few of the decision makers "cared" until events had gone too far. The possibility of war by miscalculation was too hypothetical; the civilians tended to leave such matters to the military and the military tended to take a narrow professional view of the risks. The fact that the hypothetical situation could be predicted made it seem even more impossible that it would happen. People do not deliberately walk off cliffs; they believe that only hidden cliffs are dangerous. Only it did not prove to be really like that. . . .

The more historians examine World War I, the more it seems to be clear that this was a war none of the responsible governments wanted, a war set in motion by relatively trivial circumstances, a motion which, given the state of the world, could not be stopped. It is quite possible that if there had been a really great statesman in a responsible position the war could have been averted. But there was no such statesman, and so the automatic machinery that had been set in motion ground on to its inevitable conclusion.

Because the whole concept of a war by accident or a miscalculation is so important, and because there seem to be many valid analogies between July 1914 and almost any crisis month in the 1960–1975 period, I should like, at the risk of belaboring the obvious, to list some of the analogies:

1. The need to meet or even beat the enemy's mobilization timetable has a number of similarities to many current quick reaction schemes. We have today, even more than in 1914, the possibility of setting into motion a series of self-confirming signals generated by reactions and counteractions taken on almost sheerly technical grounds without much reference to further developments in policy. There is also the opposite problem (which paradoxically can occur simultaneously). The dangerous counteractions may not be adequate countermeasures, because the signals which are setting them off are disguised as peacetime training maneuvers, as moderate measures undertaken to reduce vulnerability, or as bargaining threats to bluff the opponent into acquiescence.

2. The need to have a quick victory or stalemate to prevent a situation in which both sides lost. It is interesting to note that Schlieffen recognized this and suggested that if the initial campaign against the French failed, the Germans should try for a negotiated peace. Unfortunately for the moderates, the consequences of not terminating hostilities were not recognized by the decision makers; the desire for victory and "the honor of the battlefield" was too strong.

3. The rigidity of the war plans. In 1914 this occurred because they were so complicated that the general staffs felt that they could not draw up more than one. This single war plan was then made even more rigid because it depended on such detailed railroad schedules. In 196X there is a fair chance that the war plan will be handled by a high-speed computer—if we have not made a real effort, nothing could be more rigid. While there will be doubtless be opportunities for human intervention, events may move so quickly that these opportunities may be formal rather than of real effect. It is also likely that there will be only one plan because some planners find it hard to take seriously the

thought of a number of different situations. They want to examine and plan for only the most obvious one, and ignore the others.

4. As in 1914, in 196X the various governments, having seen the world go through so many false alarms and crises, will have become blasé. Most people today, in and out of government, find it difficult to believe that any sane decision maker would deliberately initiate a thermonuclear war, no matter how tense the crisis. Therefore, temptation for both sides to take firm (and incompatible) positions is likely to become irresistible.

5. Even more than in 1914, governments in our day are likely to be ignorant of the technical details of war and the tactical measures that can or cannot (or, more important, must or must not) be taken in various specialized situations. In peacetime the study and preparation of these measures will be relegated to military staffs as being narrow and technical. As a result they may be considered in a narrow and technical way. In 196X the ignorance of major decision makers is likely to be more profound than in 1914, because at that time the ignorance was related mainly to disuse; there was no philosophical and doctrinaire position that war was "unthinkable." The study of the strategy and tactics of the actual fighting as opposed to deterrence was considered an eminently practical and respectable subject. Today, on the contrary, it is almost impossible to get people interested in the tactics and strategy of thermonuclear war. It is now believed that only the prewar moves are of interest, and even these are not too important because deterrence is supposed to be so close to "automatic." Also, war is technically more complex today than in 1914, and the technological situation changes rapidly.

6. The year 196X should have at least as many chances for decision makers to make mistakes due to having been under physical and emotional strain and pressures for quick reaction. The issues are bigger, crises develop faster, and the time for reaction may be less.

7. Probably the most important similarity between 1914 and 196X is the ease with which small powers and allies may be able to manipulate the major powers for their own ends. Instead of Serbia and Austria, we can think of China and almost any Asiatic power; West Germany and East Germany; France and the Middle East; and so on. On the other hand, the military situation is such that allies are both more firmly tied and less important to the United States and the Soviet Union than they once were to Germany, Russia, France, and England. With the possible exception of the Soviet Union's relations to China (Khrushchev's announced policy to support the Chinese in the Formosa dispute), neither country really has to sign "blank checks" to hold its allies.

There are, of course, major differences between 1914 and today. On the stabilizing side, the most important difference is that the thermonuclear balance of terror is much more effective than the 1914 fear of defeat or revolution. However, for that reason, the balance of terror is also more likely to be strained since blackmail, firm positions, reckless actions, and sheer ignorance of the details all look safer. *It is reasonably likely that the passage of time will see a gradual growth in the willingness of all parties to be both provoking and careless about their actual capabilities.*

The other differences seem to be mostly on the destabilizing side and make the balance more precarious. Today, because both sides are in effect permanently mobilized, it may be possible to strike without giving any internal or external advance signals. In addition, there are now so many ways to destroy a nation or its armed forces that the danger of unconventional attacks or the exploitation of unconventional effects is ever-present. . . . Sometimes these unconventional attacks, while seeming to be bizarre or reckless, are still more calculable than was a 1914 offensive. Even with the most careful mutual and unilateral arrangements, the possibility of accidents or errors by relatively minor officials, setting off a disastrous chain of events, will exist. In addition, measures designed to limit this last possibility will themselves create new vulnerabilities of either a physical or psychological sort. Lastly and most important, the fear of future instability caused by an insufficiently controlled arms race is so great and growing that it may create pressures for preventive war or other destabilizing moves.

III.

THE RISE AND
DECLINE OF
OVERSEAS EMPIRE

It is often asserted that the single most important fact of the last half-century is the relative decline of European power in the world. In 1914 the nations of Europe controlled virtually all of Africa and Asia, and their economic and military power could not be contested; today, nearly all the peoples of those continents have gained independence, and Europe has seemingly been thrown back on its own resources. In this chapter, two interrelated problems are presented: first, how can one account for the tremendous burst of energy in the latter half of the nineteenth century and in the opening years of the twentieth century which was responsible for the spread of European control over so much of the earth; second, how can one account for the equally sudden decline of European power in the middle of the twentieth century, and what does this decline foretell about Europe's future?

As to the first problem, in recent years the attempts to find reasons for the phenomenon of European expansion have grown far more elaborate and far more subtle than they used to be. No longer will the simple answers provided by Marxism suffice; the economic aspects of imperialism, however important they may have been, do not provide an adequate explanation in themselves.[1] For example, one scholar, Hannah Arendt, has set forth a theory centered on the existence of a tacit alliance between the upper classes and "the mob." She maintains that although nationalism and imperialism are logically incompatible, they were bridged by "tribal nationalism" and by outright racism, and that imperialism provided the way in which the ruling groups saved their nations from class warfare by turning the attention of the mob from its sad plight at home to adventure and glory abroad; through imperialism, she argues, the nation as a whole was given a common interest.[2] Another scholar, Joseph Schumpeter, contends that imperialism is atavistic in character: capitalism was not responsible for imperialist impulses—the explanation

[1] It is instructive to compare the writings of the Marxists with more recent interpretations of the economic background of imperialism; see, for instance, Mark Blaug, "Economic Imperialism Revisited," *The Yale Review*, Vol. 50 (Spring 1961), pp. 335-49.
[2] See *The Origins of Totalitarianism*, second edition (New York: Meridian Books, 1958), especially Chapter 5.

for imperialism lies "in the vital needs of situations that molded peoples and classes into warriors . . . and in . . . psychological dispositions and social structures acquired in the dim past."[3] Some observers maintain that the so-called age of imperialism in the later nineteenth century was only superficially different from the prior years: European control had been spreading for decades, and the only change was that it now became convenient, for various reasons, to rely on direct political control of many of the newly acquired regions rather than on the indirect methods which had previously been adequate.[4] It may be that many of these newly developed theories, which are largely dependent on psychological arguments, indicate as much about the period in which they were developed as they do about the period they discuss.

The second problem presented in this chapter—the rapid disintegration of imperialism in the last two decades—is echoed almost daily in the popular press. New African and Asian nations emerge with disconcerting frequency, the once "great powers" seem to shrink in world importance, and American officials worry over the effects of their close association with the former "imperialistic" states of Europe. For the first time in modern history China, with its gigantic population, is entering world politics on a large scale, and may eventually wield power equal to that of all the European nations combined. Does the end of imperialism, then, mean the end of Europe as a really significant part of the world? Or is such a conclusion short-sighted and superficial; has Europe's importance always lain in its own natural and human resources rather than in its domination of vast underdeveloped continents? Should it not be argued that the decline in European "power" represents a decline in political control only; that the "Europeanization" of the world is in fact continuing, and at an ever-increasing pace? The decline of colonialism, one might assert, is not the result of the resurgence of long-suppressed civilizations, but of the demands of largely Europeanized native leaders to be as independent as the Europeans themselves. "Freedom," "self-determination," "nationalism," and so on, are surely all European products—now, to be sure, being turned against European political control, but representing at the same time an increasing commitment to western civilization and ideals. Where, indeed, would the nations of Africa and Asia be today, economically, socially, and politically, had it not been for European imperialism? Have not its benefits balanced or even outweighed its admitted defects?[5] In fact, is it not true that the only civilization now possessed by many of the newly freed peoples is that of Europe, their own having long since disappeared or having been resuscitated today merely as a propagandistic device for manipulating the masses?[6]

Imperialism has commonly been regarded as a western European phenomenon, and its harshest critics have been found in the United States and the Soviet Union. Yet these two anti-imperialistic nations have been increasingly inclined to point accusing

[3] *Imperialism and Social Classes,* translated from the German by Heinz Norden (New York: Meridian Books, 1955), pp. 64 *et seq.*

[4] J. Gallagher and R. Robinson, "The Imperialism of Free Trade," *The Economic History Review,* VI (August, 1953), 1–15.

[5] See, for a justification of British imperialism, Sir Alan Burns, *In Defence of Colonies* (London: George Allen and Unwin, 1957).

[6] An interesting recent article argues forcefully that "Today, in its struggle with the Communist powers, the West, notwithstanding a stereotype to the contrary, is the beneficiary of cultural linkages it forged with the colonial peoples during its long years of imperial rule." William G. Carleton, "Leninism and the Legacy of Western Imperialism," *The Yale Review,* Vol. 51 (Summer 1962), p. 518.

fingers at each other, and to charge that imperialism, far from disintegrating, has merely taken on a new form. Moreover, some critics contend that the nineteenth-century continental expansion of both the United States and Russia was in fact no less imperialistic than the overseas expansion of the European powers; that to ignore this fact is to succumb to "the salt-water fallacy." Other critics argue that only since the decay of Europe's power have the Americans (or the Soviets) stepped in as heirs to the older imperialism, which they carry forward in more sophisticated or more brutal fashion. An attempt to compare or contrast Europe's overseas expansion with more recent American and Soviet activities in Asia, Africa, and Latin America may help to clarify both the nature and the long-range significance of imperialism in its European form.

The rise and fall of modern imperialism has taken place within a remarkably short span of time. Whether this cycle represents the sudden flowering and the equally sudden collapse of European greatness the student must decide for himself; but in doing so he might consider imperialism's impact on the modern world as a unifying force. One contemporary historian has noted that the first world war, whatever its destructive impact, "generated an awareness of the global interdependence of all countries and all nations." [7] It may be that here, as in so many other respects, the first world war turns out to be the decisive event of the twentieth century.

1.

John Atkinson Hobson (1858–1940) was a pioneer in the study of the phenomenon of imperialism. One noted scholar, William L. Langer, regards his book as "perhaps the best yet written on the subject" and thinks that the most divergent theories can be traced back to his writings. Hobson was also an economist of controversial views; he attacked the pure and classical economics of men like Alfred Marshall, and asserted that economic theory should be bound to ethical problems and to questions of social welfare. Of particular interest in the following selection is Hobson's view of the impact of imperialism on a democratic society.

HOBSON: Imperialism: a Study *

Over-production in the sense of an excessive manufacturing plant, and surplus capital which could not find sound investments within the country, forced Great Britain, Germany, Holland, France to place larger and larger portions of their economic resources outside the area of their present political domain, and then stimulate a policy of political expansion so as to take in the new areas. The economic sources of this movement are laid bare by periodic trade-depressions due to an inability of producers to find adequate and profitable markets for what they can produce. The Majority Report of the Commission upon the Depression of Trade in 1885 put the matter in a nutshell. "That, owing to the nature of the times, the demand for our commodities does not

[7] Gerhard Masur, *Prophets of Yesterday*, p. 412.

* From J. A. Hobson, *Imperialism: a Study* (London: George Allen and Unwin Ltd., 1938; first printed 1905), pp. 80–81, 130, 150–52, 196–98, 204–5, 214, 217–22. Reprinted by permission of The Macmillan Company, New York.

increase at the same rate as formerly; that our capacity for production is consequently in excess of our requirements, and could be considerably increased at short notice; that this is due partly to the competition of the capital which is being steadily accumulated in the country." The Minority Report straightly imputed the condition of affairs to "over-production." Germany was in the early 1900's suffering severely from what is called a glut of capital and of manufacturing power: she had to have new markets; her Consuls all over the world were "hustling" for trade; trading settlements were forced upon Asia Minor; in East and West Africa, in China and elsewhere the German Empire was impelled to a policy of colonization and protectorates as outlets for German commercial energy.

Every improvement of methods of production, every concentration of ownership and control, seems to accentuate the tendency. As one nation after another enters the machine economy and adopts advanced industrial methods, it becomes more difficult for its manufacturers, merchants, and financiers to dispose profitably of their economic resources, and they are tempted more and more to use their Governments in order to secure for their particular use some distant undeveloped country by annexation and protection.

The process, we may be told, is inevitable, and so it seems upon a superficial inspection. Everywhere appear excessive powers of production, excessive capital in search of investment. It is admitted by all business men that the growth of the powers of production in their country exceeds the growth in consumption, that more goods can be produced than can be sold at a profit, and that more capital exists than can find remunerative investment.

It is this economic condition of affairs that forms the taproot of Imperialism. . . .

Imperialism—whether it consists in a further policy of expansion or in the rigorous maintenance of all those vast tropical lands which have been earmarked as British spheres of influence—implies militarism now and ruinous wars in the future. This truth is now for the first time brought sharply and nakedly before the mind of the nation. The kingdoms of the earth are to be ours on condition that we fall down and worship Moloch. . . .

. . . It remains to point out how the spirit of Imperialism poisons the springs of democracy in the mind and character of the people. As our free self-governing colonies have furnished hope, encouragement, and leading to the popular aspirations in Great Britain, not merely by practical successes in the arts of popular government, but by the wafting of a spirit of freedom and equality, so our despotically ruled dependencies have ever served to damage the character of our people by feeding the habits of snobbish subservience, the admiration of wealth and rank, the corrupt survivals of the inequalities of feudalism. This process began with the advent of the East Indian nabob and the West Indian planter into English society and politics, bringing back with his plunders of the slave trade and the gains of corrupt and extortionate officialism the acts of vulgar ostentation, domineering demeanour and corrupting largesse to dazzle and degrade the life of our people. Cobden, writing in 1860 of our

Indian Empire, put this pithy question: "Is it not just possible that we may become corrupted at home by the reaction of arbitrary political maxims in the East upon our domestic politics, just as Greece and Rome were demoralised by their contact with Asia?"

Not merely is the reaction possible, it is inevitable. As the despotic portion of our Empire has grown in area, a larger and larger number of men, trained in the temper and methods of autocracy as soldiers and civil officials in our Crown colonies, protectorates and Indian Empire, reinforced by numbers of merchants, planters, engineers, and overseers, whose lives have been those of a superior caste living an artificial life removed from all the healthy restraints of ordinary European society, have returned to this country, bringing back the characters, sentiments, and ideas imposed by this foreign environment. The South and South-West of England is richly sprinkled with these men, many of them wealthy, most of them endowed with leisure, men openly contemptuous of democracy, devoted to material luxury, social display, and the shallower arts of intellectual life. The wealthier among them discover political ambitions, introducing into our Houses of Parliament the coarsest and most selfish spirit of "Imperialism," using their imperial experience and connexions to push profitable companies and concessions for their private benefits, and posing as authorities so as to keep the yoke of Imperialism firmly fixed upon the shoulders of the "nigger." The South African millionaire is the brand most in evidence: his methods are the most barefaced, and his success, social and political, the most redoubtable. But the practices which are writ large in Rhodes, Beit, and their parliamentary confederates are widespread on a smaller scale; the South of England is full of men of local influence in politics and society whose character has been formed in our despotic Empire, and whose incomes are chiefly derived from the maintenance and furtherance of this despotic rule. Not a few enter our local councils, or take posts in our constabulary or our prisons: everywhere they stand for coercion and for resistance to reform. Could the incomes expended in the Home Countries and other large districts of Southern Britain be traced to their sources, it would be found that they were in large measure wrung from the enforced toil of vast multitudes of black, brown, or yellow natives, by arts not differing essentially from those which supported in idleness and luxury imperial Rome.

It is, indeed, a nemesis of Imperialism that the arts and crafts of tyranny, acquired and exercised in our unfree Empire, should be turned against our liberties at home. Those who have felt surprise at the total disregard or the open contempt displayed by the aristocracy and the plutocracy of this land for infringements of the liberties of the subject and for the abrogation of constitutional rights and usages have not taken sufficiently into account the steady reflux of this poison of irresponsible autocracy from our "unfree, intolerant, aggressive" Empire.

The political effects, actual and necessary, of the new Imperialism, as illustrated in the case of the greatest of imperialist Powers, may be thus summarised. It is a constant menace to peace, by furnishing continual temptations to further

aggression upon lands occupied by lower races and by embroiling our nation with other nations of rival imperial ambitions; to the sharp peril of war it adds the chronic danger and degradation of militarism, which not merely wastes the current physical and moral resources of the nations, but checks the very course of civilization. It consumes to an illimitable and incalculable extent the financial resources of a nation by military preparation, stopping the expenditure of the current income of the State upon productive public projects and burdening posterity with heavy loads of debt. Absorbing the public money, time, interest and energy on costly and unprofitable work of territorial aggrandisement, it thus wastes those energies of public life in the governing classes and the nations which are needed for internal reforms and for the cultivation of the arts of material and intellectual progress at home. Finally, the spirit, the policy, and the methods of Imperialism are hostile to the institutions of popular self-government, favouring forms of political tyranny and social authority which are the deadly enemies of effective liberty and equality.
. . .

There exists in a considerable though not a large proportion of the British nation a genuine desire to spread Christianity among the heathen, to diminish the cruelty and other sufferings which they believe exist in countries less fortunate than their own, and to do good work about the world in the cause of humanity. Most of the churches contain a small body of men and women deeply, even passionately, interested in such work, and a much larger number whose sympathy, though weaker, is quite genuine. Ill-trained for the most part in psychology and history, these people believe that religion and other arts of civilization are portable commodities which it is our duty to convey to the backward nations, and that a certain amount of compulsion is justified in pressing their benefits upon people too ignorant at once to recognize them.

Is it surprising that the selfish forces which direct Imperialism should utilize the protective colours of these disinterested movements? . . .

So Leopold, King of the Belgians, claimed for his government of the Congo —"Our only programme is that of the moral and material regeneration of the country." It is difficult to set any limit upon the capacity of men to deceive themselves as to the relative strength and worth of the motives which affect them: politicians, in particular, acquire so strong a habit of setting their projects in the most favourable light that they soon convince themselves that the finest result which they think may conceivably accrue from any policy is the actual motive of that policy. As for the public, it is only natural that it should be deceived. All the purer and more elevated adjuncts of Imperialism are kept to the fore by religious and philanthropic agencies: patriotism appeals to the general lust of power within a people by suggestions of nobler uses, adopting the forms of self-sacrifice to cover domination and the love of adventure. So Christianity becomes "imperialist" to the Archbishop of Canterbury, a "going out to all the world to preach the gospel"; trade becomes "imperialist" in the eyes of merchants seeking a world market.

It is precisely in this falsification of the real import of motives that the gravest vice and the most signal peril of Imperialism reside. . . .

Yet it is quite evident that sincere men are prepared to support the use of political and military force in order to open fields for missionary enterprise, and that the missionary, who is by turns trader, soldier, and politician, seems a most desirable instrument of civilization.

How close in motive and in conduct this combination really is may be thus illustrated from the history of the Soudan.

Detachments of officers and men from every regiment, British and Egyptian, were conveyed across the Nile in the gunboats to take part in the Gordon memorial service, and to witness the hoisting of the British flag on the ruins of Khartoum. . . . Surrounded by the soldiers he had directed with terrible and glorious effect, the successful general ordered the flags to be hoisted. . . . The officers saluted, the men presented arms, and the band played the Egyptian National Anthem and our own. Then the Sirdar called for three cheers for Her Majesty. . . . The memorial service followed, and the solemn words of the English Prayer Book were read in that distant garden. . . . The bands played their dirge and Gordon's favourite hymn, "Abide With Me"; a gunboat on the river crashed out the salute. . . . The Highlanders played a long lament, and thus the ceremony was duly fulfilled. Nine thousand of those who would have prevented it lay dead on the plain of Omdurman. Other thousands were scattered in the wilderness, or crawled wounded to the river for water.

While the writer of this passage [Winston Churchill] omits the final touch, the deliberate shooting of wounded crawlers by troops under British commanders, the picture is profoundly suggestive, with its strange amalgam of the British flag, "Abide with Me," and the avenging of Gordon. . . .

The sporting and military aspects of Imperialism form, therefore, a very powerful basis of popular appeal. The desire to pursue and kill either big game or other men can only be satisfied by expansion and militarism. . . .

Most serious of all is the persistent attempt to seize the school system for Imperialism masquerading as patriotism. To capture the childhood of the country, to mechanize its free play into the routine of military drill, to cultivate the savage survivals of combativeness, to poison its early understanding of history by false ideals and pseudo-heroes, and by a consequent disparagement and neglect of the really vital and elevating lessons of the past, to establish a "geocentric" view of the moral universe in which the interests of humanity are subordinated to that of the "country" (and so, by easy, early, natural inference, that of the "country" to that of the "self"), to feed the always overweening pride of race at an age when self-confidence most commonly prevails, and by necessary implication to disparage other nations, so starting children in the world with false measures of value and an unwillingness to learn from foreign sources—to fasten this base insularity of mind and morals upon the little children of a nation and to call it patriotism is as foul an abuse of education as it is possible to conceive. Yet the power of Church and State over primary education is being bent consistently to this purpose, while the blend of clericalism and autocratic academicism which dominates the secondary education of this country pours its enthusiasm into the same evil channel. Finally, our centres of highest culture, the universities, are in peril of a new perversion from the path of free inquiry and expression, which is the true path of intellectual life. . . .

The interference with intellectual liberty is seldom direct, seldom personal, though both in the United States and Canada some instances of the crudest heresy-hunting have occurred. The real danger consists in the appointment rather than in the dismissal of teachers, in the determination of what subjects shall be taught, what relative attention shall be given to each subject, and what text-books and other apparatus of instruction shall be used. The subservience to rank and money, even in our older English universities, has been evinced so nakedly, and the demands for monetary aid in developing new faculties necessarily looms so large in academic eyes, that the danger here indicated is an ever-growing one. It is not so much the weight of the "dead hand" that is to be feared as that of the living: a college so unfortunate as to harbour teachers who, in handling vital issues of politics or economics, teach truths deeply and obviously antagonistic to the interests of the classes from whom financial aid was sought, would be committing suicide. . . .

The area of danger is, of course, far wider than Imperialism, covering the whole field of vested interests. But, if the analysis of previous chapters is correct, Imperialism stands as a first defence of these interests: for the financial and speculative classes it means a pushing of their private businesses at the public expense, for the export manufacturers and merchants a forcible enlargement of foreign markets and a related policy of Protection, for the official and professional classes large openings of honourable and lucrative employment, for the Church it represents the temper and practice of authority and the assertion of spiritual control over vast multitudes of lower people, for the political oligarchy it means the only effective diversion of the forces of democracy and the opening of great public careers in the showy work of empire-making. . . .

For these business politicians biology and sociology weave thin convenient theories of a race struggle for the subjugation of the inferior peoples, in order that we, the Anglo-Saxon, may take their lands and live upon their labours; while economics buttresses the argument by representing our work in conquering and ruling them as our share in the division of labour among nations, and history devises reasons why the lessons of past empire do not apply to ours while social ethics paints the motive of "Imperialism" as the desire to bear the "burden" of educating and elevating races of "children." Thus are the "cultured" or semi-cultured classes indoctrinated with the intellectual and moral grandeur of Imperialism. For the masses there is a cruder appeal to hero-worship and sensational glory, adventure and the sporting spirit: current history falsified in coarse flaring colours, for the direct stimulation of the combative instincts. But while various methods are employed, some delicate and indirect, others coarse and flamboyant, the operation everywhere resolves itself into an incitation and direction of the brute lusts of human domination which are everywhere latent in civilized humanity, for the pursuance of a policy fraught with material gain to a minority of co-operative vested interests which usurp the title of the commonwealth.

2.

Lenin's *Imperialism* was written in the spring of 1916 in Zurich, and has become the classic statement of the Marxist position on "the highest stage of capitalism." Dogmatic in tone, it leaves little room for noneconomic explanations of imperialism; economic conditions compelled the capitalists to divide the world; those who stress any other factors confuse form with content and thus sink into sophistry. In reading the following selection it is important to try to see where Lenin was blinded by his own propaganda, and where he made valid points which are still significant to any student of history. It may be useful to ask, too, whether Hobson and Lenin approached imperialism with the same bias toward economic determinism. Or was there a deep-rooted English empiricism in Hobson that set him apart from Marxist dogma?

LENIN: Imperialism, the Highest Stage of Capitalism *

. . . Imperialism emerged as the development and direct continuation of the fundamental attributes of capitalism in general. But capitalism only became capitalist imperialism at a definite and very high stage of its development, when certain of its fundamental attributes began to be transformed into their opposites, when the features of a period of transition from capitalism to a higher social and economic system began to take shape and reveal themselves all along the line. Economically, the main thing in this process is the substitution of capitalist monopolies for capitalist free competition. Free competition is the fundamental attribute of capitalism, and of commodity production generally. Monopoly is exactly the opposite of free competition; but we have seen the latter being transformed into monopoly before our very eyes, creating large-scale industry and eliminating small industry, replacing large-scale industry by still larger-scale industry, finally leading to such a concentration of production and capital that monopoly has been and is the result: cartels, syndicates and trusts, and merging with them, the capital of a dozen or so banks manipulating thousands of millions. At the same time monopoly, which has grown out of free competition, does not abolish the latter, but exists over it and alongside of it, and thereby gives rise to a number of very acute, intense antagonisms, friction and conflicts. Monopoly is the transition from capitalism to a higher system.

If it were necessary to give the briefest possible definition of imperialism we should have to say that imperialism is the monopoly stage of capitalism. Such a definition would include what is most important, for, on the one hand, finance capital is the bank capital of a few big monopolist banks, merged with

* From V. I. Lenin, *Imperialism, the Highest Stage of Capitalism* (New York: International Publishers, 1939), pp. 88–89, 123–25, 126. Reprinted by permission of International Publishers.

the capital of the monopolist combines of manufacturers; and, on the other hand, the division of the world is the transition from a colonial policy which has extended without hindrance to territories unoccupied by any capitalist power, to a colonial policy of monopolistic possession of the territory of the world which has been completely divided up.

But very brief definitions, although convenient, for they sum up the main points, are nevertheless inadequate, because very important features of the phenomenon that has to be defined have to be especially deduced. And so, without forgetting the conditional and relative value of all definitions, which can never include all the concatenations of a phenomenon in its complete development, we must give a definition of imperialism that will embrace the following five essential features:

1) The concentration of production and capital developed to such a high stage that it created monopolies which play a decisive role in economic life.

2) The merging of bank capital with industrial capital, and the creation, on the basis of this "finance capital," of a "financial oligarchy."

3) The export of capital, which has become extremely important, as distinguished from the export of commodities.

4) The formation of international capitalist monopolies which share the world among themselves.

5) The territorial division of the whole world among the greatest capitalist powers is completed.

Imperialism is capitalism in that stage of development in which the dominance of monopolies and finance capital has established itself; in which the export of capital has acquired pronounced importance; in which the division of the world among the international trusts has begun; in which the division of all territories of the globe among the great capitalist powers has been completed. . . .

[Therefore] the economic quintessence of imperialism is monopoly capitalism. This very fact determines its place in history, for monopoly that grew up on the basis of free competition, and precisely out of free competition, is the transition from the capitalist system to a higher social-economic order. We must take special note of the four principal forms of monopoly, or the four principal manifestations of monopoly capitalism, which are characteristic of the epoch under review.

Firstly, monopoly arose out of the concentration of production at a very advanced stage of development. This refers to the monopolist capitalist combines, cartels, syndicates and trusts. We have seen the important part that these play in modern economic life. At the beginning of the twentieth century, monopolies acquired complete supremacy in the advanced countries. And although the first steps towards the formation of the cartels were first taken by countries enjoying the protection of high tariffs (Germany, America), Great Britain, with her system of free trade, was not far behind in revealing the same basic phenomenon, namely, the birth of monopoly out of the concentration of production.

Secondly, monopolies have accelerated the capture of the most important sources of raw materials, especially for the coal and iron industries, which are the basic and most highly cartelised industries in capitalist society. The monopoly of the most important sources of raw materials has enormously increased the power of big capital, and has sharpened the antagonism between cartelised and non-cartelised industry.

Thirdly, monopoly has sprung from the banks. The banks have developed from modest intermediary enterprises into the monopolists of finance capital. Some three or five of the biggest banks in each of the foremost capitalist countries have achieved the "personal union" of industrial and bank capital, and have concentrated in their hands the disposal of thousands upon thousands of millions which form the greater part of the capital and income of entire countries. A financial oligarchy, which throws a close net of relations of dependence over all the economic and political institutions of contemporary bourgeois society without exception—such is the most striking manfestation of this monopoly.

Fourthly, monopoly has grown out of colonial policy. To the numerous "old" motives of colonial policy, finance capital has added the struggle for the sources of raw materials, for the export of capital, for "spheres of influence," *i.e.,* for spheres for profitable deals, concessions, monopolist profits and so on; in fine, for economic territory in general. When the colonies of the European powers in Africa, for instance, comprised only one-tenth of that territory (as was the case in 1876), colonial policy was able to develop by methods other than those of monopoly—by the "free grabbing" of territories, so to speak. But when nine-tenths of Africa had been seized (approximately by 1900), when the whole world had been divided up, there was inevitably ushered in a period of colonial monopoly and, consequently, a period of particularly intense struggle for the division and the redivision of the world.

The extent to which monopolist capital has intensified all the contradictions of capitalism is generally known. It is sufficient to mention the high cost of living and the oppression of the cartels. This intensification of contradictions constitutes the most powerful driving force of the transitional period of history, which began from the time of the definite victory of world finance capital.

Monopolies, oligarchy, the striving for domination instead of the striving for liberty, the exploitation of an increasing number of small or weak nations by an extremely small group of the richest or most powerful nations—all these have given birth to those distinctive characteristics of imperialism which compel us to define it as parasitic or decaying capitalism. More and more prominently there emerges, as one of the tendencies of imperialism, the creation of the "bondholding" (rentier) state, the usurer state, in which the bourgeoisie lives on the proceeds of capital exports and by "clipping coupons." It would be a mistake to believe that this tendency to decay precludes the possibility of rapid growth of capitalism. It does not. In the epoch of imperialism, certain branches of industry, certain strata of the bourgeoisie and certain countries betray, to a more or less degree, one or other of these tendencies. On the whole, capitalism is growing far more rapidly than before. But this growth is not only becoming more and more uneven in general; its unevenness also manifests itself, in particular, in the decay of the countries which are richest in capital (such as England). . . .

The receipt of high monopoly profits by the capitalists in one of the numerous branches of industry, in one of numerous countries, etc., makes it economically possible for them to corrupt certain sections of the working class, and for a time a fairly considerable minority, and win them to the side of the bourgeoisie of a given industry or nation against all the others. The intensification of antagonisms between imperialist nations for the division of the world increases this striving. And so there is created that bond between imperialism and opportunism, which revealed itself first and most clearly in England, owing to the fact that certain features of imperialist development were observable there much earlier than in other countries. . . .

From all that has been said in this book on the economic nature of imperialism, it follows that we must define it as capitalism in transition, or, more precisely, as moribund capitalism. . . .

3.

William L. Langer has been a professor of history at Harvard University for over thirty years; he has also had wide experience in government service, having served with the OSS during the war, and later with the State Department and the CIA. He is a past president of the American Historical Association. The following selection is one of the most penetrating commentaries that has ever been written on the subject of imperialism, for, although it concentrates on the British experience, it is of relevance to the state of the entire western world in the late nineteenth century. Whether one finds its analysis accurate depends upon one's approach to the study of history; some readers will think that it mistakes surface manifestations for fundamental causes; others will think that it gives a more accurate account than can be derived from the writings of those committed to a single-cause explanation.

LANGER: The Diplomacy of Imperialism *

The tide of European control has already turned and we are living now in an age of retreat and retirement. The tremendous outburst of expansion and the almost complete victory of Europe was, therefore, crowded into a couple of generations, the peak of the movement being reached in the last decade of the 19th and the first decade of the 20th centuries. During that score of years the competition in the acquisition of territory and the struggle for influence and control was the most important factor in the international relations of Europe. We cannot avoid giving it some special attention.

* William L. Langer, *The Diplomacy of Imperialism 1890–1902* (New York: Alfred A. Knopf, 1935), I, 67–76, 80–88, 90–96. Reprinted by permission of Alfred A. Knopf, Inc. Copyright 1935 by the Bureau of International Research of Harvard University.

Imperialism is a word which is now in bad repute, partly because of a psychological reaction to what it was supposed to stand for, partly because it is generally used in so loose a sense that it means nothing to the historian or the political scientist. As everyone knows, the term was originally connected with the word *Imperator,* and was frequently associated with the ideas of dictatorial power, highly centralized government, arbitrary methods of administration, and in general with the ideas of Caesarism and Bonapartism. In this sense it is now almost obsolete. For our purposes it may be taken to mean simply the rule or control, political or economic, direct or indirect, of one state, nation or people over other similar groups, or perhaps one might better say the disposition, urge or striving to establish such rule or control.

Taken in this sense, imperialism is probably as old as recorded history. One writer has taken his discussion of it back to the Assyrians and the Egyptians, and admirable studies have been made of both Greek and Roman imperialism. The medieval and earlier modern period has perhaps been somewhat neglected by students, but there has been a wealth of critical writing on the imperialism of recent times. Indeed, the socialists of the Neo-Marxian school have made a specialty of the subject and have linked imperialism with capitalism as an object of condemnation. This is not the place to consider the purely theoretical side of the problem. The historian, in fact, is apt to feel that the abstractions of the political scientist are of little help in reconstructing or understanding the past. Suffice it to say, then, that there is no agreement among those who have analyzed imperialism as to what the motives are that impel a state or people to expand its territory or control. The liberal-bourgeois writers, who generally deny that there is any natural or necessary connexion between capitalism and imperialism, are apt to stress considerations of prestige, the desire for security, the striving towards national self-sufficiency, the tendency towards the organization of ever larger social units, or the urge of deeply-rooted ethical sentiments as the impelling motives underlying the desire for expansion. Professor Schumpeter has advanced the ingenious and persuasive argument that imperialism is really nothing but an atavism, a belated outcropping of a primitive disposition towards aggression for the sake of aggression and of domination for the sake of domination, without any specific object or limit. Another recent student of the problem ends by rejecting all previous explanations and reduces imperialism to an expression of the honor motif which is so potent a force in the social group as in the individual.

The Marxian interpretation, which makes practically all imperialism economic, does not go back to Marx himself, who appears to have had no definite theory on the subject. It was, as a matter of fact, first propounded by thoroughly bourgeois writers in the United States and England, starting perhaps with Charles A. Conant and going down to the remarkable book of J. A. Hobson. It was then adopted and developed by socialist writers like Karl Kautsky, Otto Bauer, Rudolf Hilferding, Rosa Luxemburg and others, till now it has become enshrined in the works of Lenin and lesser communist prophets. Writers of this persuasion regard imperialism as the expression of a need for new markets for the surplus products of industrialism, as a search for raw materials and for cheap labor. Futhermore, they argue that it is an inevitable phase in the evolution of capitalism, a phase in which surplus capital, accumulated by the system of production, is obliged by the ever diminishing returns at home to find new outlets for investment abroad. Imperialism begins with the export of producers' goods and capital; when the last outlets for surplus capital have been taken up by capitalistic countries, the whole economic-social system is bound to die of congestion.

With all this mass of theoretical, not to say speculative writing, it is curious that almost no attempt has been made to analyze a concrete example of imperialist action in the period of high capitalism. Tenney Frank seems to have been driven to his study of Roman imperialism by his dissatisfaction with generalizations and formulas that drifted further and further from the ascertained facts. His conclusions are startling enough: the Roman Empire, in many ways the prototype of all later empires, appears to have grown up in spite of the Romans. "It is safe to say that the idea of universal power never occurred to any Roman before the Punic War." "Specific accidents . . . led the nation unwittingly from one contest to another until to her own surprise Rome was mistress of the Mediterranean world." "Pompey seems to be the first general frankly sent out for the purpose of extending Rome's boundaries," and Caesar was the first candid imperialist in Rome. These are some of the conclusions reached by a scholar working with the facts alone. They seem to bear out the contention of Sir John Seeley that the British apparently "conquered and peopled half the world in a fit of absence of mind." This was a reference to the growth of the Empire in the 17th and 18th centuries, but it might be that an examination of the imperialism of the late 19th century would bear out the conclusions of these writers who have analyzed the earlier manifestations of imperialism. . . .

If you are willing to define the word imperialism loosely enough and to make it synonymous with love of country, patriotism, sense of nationality, etc., you can trace it back to Shakespeare or even Chaucer. In the 19th century there was an unbroken line of literary men, from Carlyle and Kingsley through Ruskin to Tennyson, who sang the praises of Britain, gloried in her command of the sea and exulted in her imperial mission. Since this literary strain was nothing new, we need not stop to discuss it in any detail. We may start by recalling the fact that in the period from 1840 to 1870 interest in the colonies reached its nadir in England. It was indeed the climax of anti-imperialism.

It has been shown over and over again that this attitude was the direct reflection of England's industrial supremacy in the mid-century. England was in very fact, at that time, the workshop that clothed the world. She had something of a monopoly not only of the continental market but of the world market. Nothing more natural, then, than that she should have fallen under the sway of Manchester doctrine, that she should have become the great exponent of the principle of free trade, of laisser faire, of retrenchment and reform at home and good will and peace abroad. The Englishman at that time had no desire to expand the responsibilities of government—he did not want to rule, he wanted to trade. In this scheme of things there was no place for empire or expansion. Cobden, Gladstone and the other leaders of the school may not actually have worked for the dissolution of the Empire, but they expected the Empire to disintegrate, they were willing to aid the process by the extension of self-government, and they envisaged the ultimate dissolution of existing ties without misgiving and without regret.

With the year 1870 a distinct change becomes noticeable in the English attitude. Disraeli, in his famous Crystal Palace speech of 1872, sounded a new note of imperialism. With him, to be sure, the maintenance of the Empire was largely a question of prestige; the Empire was a proof of "the commanding spirit of these islands," a valuable make-weight in the councils of Europe. His policy in the years 1874–1880 was essentially concerned with questions of power and security, all pointed at the protection of the routes to India and the safe-guarding of the great Indian Empire itself. Disraeli never showed any genuine interest in Britain's self-governing colonies, and revealed no deep understanding of the needs of England in the economic sense. It is probably safe to say that his imperialist attitude was inspired directly by the changes that had taken place on the Continent. The triumph of the principle of nationality and the emergence of a powerful German Empire called forth a corresponding feeling of national pride among the English and resulted in a new appreciation of the Empire which was, at bottom, not at all in keeping with Manchester doctrine.

The new pride in the Empire was reflected in the epoch-making books of Sir Charles Dilke (*Greater Britain,* 1870), Sir John Seeley (*The Expansion of England,* 1883) and J. A. Froude (*Oceana,* 1885). The writings of these men are so well known and their influence has been so generally recognized that there would be no point in reviewing them at length. It is important to note, though, that they were concerned with the Empire as it was, and not so much with the expansion of the Empire. Seeley, indeed, warned his audience that "when a State advances beyond the limits of the nationality, its power becomes precarious and artificial." G. P. Gooch, writing at the end of the century, remarked quite truly that if Seeley were still alive he would be classed as a Little Englander.

Contemporaneous with this historical teaching was the activity of the Imperial Federation League, founded in 1884 for the purpose of furthering the integration of the Empire through constitutional and other devices. For a full decade the League was the chief embodiment of the imperial movement. It enjoyed the enthusiastic support of many prominent political and intellectual leaders and Lord Rosebery once declared that its object, imperial federation, was the "dominant passion" of his life. But the agitation for imperial federation had only an indirect bearing upon international affairs, and we cannot, for that reason, afford the space required for a detailed analysis. Movements toward expansion of empire are often accompanied by a striving towards integration and concentration of forces within the existing state, and therefore the project for federation was not without its significance. It will suffice, however, to call attention to this aspect of it.

The movement for imperial federation enjoyed the support of Liberals as well as Conservatives. The Liberals, in fact, had been responsible for the granting of self-government to the colonies and had thus made possible the idea of a free union of the white colonies and the mother-country. But there was a further reason for their adoption of the new slogan. By the beginning of the last decades of the century the economic situation of England was no longer what it had been in the middle of the century. Dozens of books and hundreds of articles, many of them loaded with a crushing burden of statistical matter, have been written on the theme of England's decline and approaching fall. We need not struggle through this welter of evidence, much of which was incomplete and distorted, and little of which was rightly understood. The main facts are fairly clear.

During the years of her economic ascendancy England had undoubtedly helped to equip the other nations of the Continent with the means of production which enabled them ultimately to set upon their own, take over their home markets for themselves and eventually to enter into competition in the world market. The temporary settlement of the great national questions in the years just before 1870 unquestionably released a good deal of energy for economic and especially industrial activity. The English themselves were surprised at the beneficial results for German business of the *Zollverein* and the political unification of the many German states. By the middle of the 1880's Germany was already becoming an important industrial power. Like most of the continental states she had thrown over the ideas of free trade, had adopted a protective tariff and had thrived under the new system. German goods had already begun to find their way into unprotected England, to say nothing of the British colonies, which, incidentally, were also erecting tariff barriers against the mother country. A parliamentary commission of 1886 had to listen to many complaints about German competition: in every quarter of the globe, said the final report of the commission, "the perseverance and enterprise of the Germans are making themselves felt. In actual production of commodities we have few, if any, advantages over them; and in a knowledge of the markets of the world, a desire to accommodate themselves to local tastes and idiosyncrasies, a determination to obtain a footing wherever they can, and a tenacity in maintaining it, they appear to be gaining upon us."

Now the situation was aggravated, as the Englishman saw it, by the general depression during all but the closing years of the last quarter of the century. It was a period during which exports were declining while imports were rising in value; prices were generally falling, the population was steadily increasing, and unemployment, though not appalling when measured by present-day conditions, was felt to be a real problem. It is, to be sure, a relatively simple matter to show that the situation was not as black as contemporaries believed. The declining value of exports was at least in part to be explained by the steady fall in prices, while the growth of imports was due in no small measure to the increasing capital investment abroad, the interest on which had to be paid in goods.

England's real economic difficulty in this period, though few contemporaries recognized the fact, arose not so much from the decrease of exports or from the growing disparity between exports and imports, as from the steady accumulation of capital and the ever more pressing need for opportunities for profitable investment. Throughout the early 19th century England's available capital had grown along with her productive powers. She was, prior to 1850, almost the only source for funds and in those times she poured money onto the Continent in the form of government loans, railway loans and to some extent industrial investments. After 1850 France and then Germany began to appear as lending countries, but England was still far in advance of any competitor. Despite the so-called depression and the prevalence of unemployment, which at times reached almost 10% of the trade unionists, there was a pretty steady and at times very striking rise in savings bank deposits. The floating capital of Great Britain rose from about $7,300,000,000 in 1860 to $21,000,000,000 in 1896. The discount rate, while fluctuating, tended to drop and reached its lowest point in the mid-nineties, when the bank rate was 2% and the market rate rarely much above 1%.

Under the circumstances it was inevitable that capital should flow abroad in an ever stronger stream. Less money was being invested on the Continent, but tremendous sums went into railway loans to the United States, to Latin America and to Australia. The foreign investment of Great Britain has been put at nearly $6,000,000,000 in 1875 and at not much less than $10,000,000,000 in 1900. At the turn of the century the interest on the foreign investment was not far from $500,000,000 per annum, while the clear profit from foreign trade came to hardly a fifth of that figure. One half to two thirds of all new capital was going abroad. "The necessity of sending capital abroad to obtain profitable returns is the salient economic lesson of the closing days of the 19th century," wrote an American economist. "England could not remain the workshop of the world; she is fast becoming its creditor, its mortgagee, its landlord," remarked a contemporary British writer, who continued: "The fact is, the trade of the world, as well as its soil, if we do not foolishly disturb it, or meddle with it from unwarrantable jealousy, is becoming more and more one, and becoming more and more British, in whatever country it is going on and under whatever flag it sails."

The Neo-Marxians, following the lead of these discerning bourgeois writers, have insisted on the close connexion between this accumulation of capital and the growth of imperialism. "The inexorable progress of economic tendencies has made expansion the inevitable policy of states which would survive in the future," declared Conant. "It is not too much to say that the modern foreign policy of Great Britain is primarily a struggle for profitable markets of investment. . . . Imperialism is the endeavour of the great controllers of industry to broaden the channel for the flow of their surplus wealth by seeking foreign markets and foreign investments to take off the goods and capital they cannot sell or use at home," according to J. A. Hobson. But just what necessary connexion is there between these two phenomena?

It should be noted at the outset that the export of British capital developed at a remarkably rapid rate in the days when anti-imperialism reached its climax. In 1875 it was already more than half what it was in 1900. This would suggest that the accumulation of capital and the creation of a surplus have no necessary connexion with territorial expansion. In the hey-day of free trade and Manchester doctrine the British did not hesitate to export their surplus to continental countries and above all to the United States, where they could not possibly have had any political or territorial aspirations. Indeed, we know that such aspirations were unreservedly rejected by the Cobdenites.

It does not follow from this, however, that the movement for expansion in the last quarter of the century was not conditioned by the need for fields of investment, because in the interval new factors had been introduced into the situation. The continental nations had gradually become equipped with the means of production, they were no longer spending immense amounts of money on the conduct of expensive wars, they were frankly embarking upon a policy of industrial development and were scrapping the doctrine of free trade in order to secure the necessary protection. By the middle of the eighties France was already in a position to export large amounts of capital and Germany was invading the British preserves with her goods. Furthermore, French economists and statesmen, followed somewhat reluctantly by the Germans, decided that for future safety they must have colonies. On the Continent the advocates of colonial expansion were inspired in part, no doubt, by the British example. It was thought that the British had grown great through their foreign possessions. The French and Germans placed a much higher estimate upon the value of the British Empire than did the British themselves. But for the rest it was generally held, following the teachings of the great French economist, Leroy-Beaulieu, that colonies were a *sine qua non* of national greatness. Jules Ferry, the founder of the second French Empire, never tired of stressing the need not only for new markets, but for new fields of investment: "Colonies are for rich countries one of the most lucrative methods of investing capital. . . . I say that France, which is glutted with capital and which has exported considerable quantities, has an interest in looking at this side of the colonial question. . . . It is the same question as that of outlets for our manufactures."

What the French and Germans did, then, was to enter the colonial field and begin to take over territory in Africa and Asia, territories which they then surrounded by tariff walls. The impression this new departure made upon the English was as profound as it was natural. "There is nothing," says a well-known British historian of colonial policy, "which causes men to put so high a value on their own possessions as the observing that they are being coveted by their neighbours. The scramble for colonies among the continental nations has had the good effect at least of determining the English not to be left behind in the race for empire." So what we observe in the eighties is not only a revaluation of the existing Empire, but a demand for a *Zollverein* between its component parts. There is a rising agitation for "fair trade" as opposed to free trade, an eagerness to build up some sort of wall of preferential treatment around the immense domains already under British rule.

It was but a natural step from imperial federation to a policy of expansion. As business men the English would undoubtedly have preferred to continue as before, with the whole world as a market and no very serious competitor. But now, with the setting aside of large parts of the unclaimed world as French and German colonies, there was an obvious danger that the British market would be steadily restricted. Hence the emergence and sudden flowering of the movement for expansion. The English felt that they had to take over large blocks of territory, if only to prevent them from falling into the hands of exclusive rivals. Economic control was no longer possible, it seemed, without political control.

The English, being a commercially-minded people, thought almost exclusively in terms of markets and they discussed the situation primarily in terms of exports. It did little good to argue that trade does not follow the flag, but the price list; that the trade with the colonies was only a third of the total trade of England; that France, Germany, and the United States, all protectionist states and all rivals of Britain, were still England's best customers. It did no good either to point out to the Englishman his own short-comings, his easy-going business methods, his lack of interest in small orders, his unwillingness to adapt his goods to the peculiar needs of the customer, his inadequate technical training, etc. Frederick Greenwood accused his countrymen of positive levity. They pursued what he called a "skim-and-skip" system, taking the cream off a market, leaving the rest to competitors and then rushing off with a loud clamor in search of new markets.

The fact remains, then, that during the eighties there was increasing alarm about the future. The economic situation brought with it a general revision of economic theory. In the last quarter of the century there was a pronounced decline in the popularity of the Manchester teaching. Cobdenism had lost its attractiveness for many. Economists and political writers began to point out the fundamental fallacy in the free trade doctrine. It had been assumed that the whole world would gradually adopt the free trade system, but in reality the reverse had proved to be the case. England had equipped other nations to be her competitors, and now, with the English market wide open, they were pouring their products into what ought to be a British preserve. Cobden, wrote H. E. Egerton, had preached that England's chief concern with foreign nations was to trade with them, but it had turned out that the chief concern of foreign nations was *not* to trade with England. Cobden, said other critics, had looked forward to the spread of the new commercial spirit, which would make for general world prosperity and world peace. Yet what Europe had witnessed was a long series of wars. The keynote of the new Europe was not the development of internationalism, but the dominance of a spirit of militarism and bloated armaments. In short, Manchester doctrine had been belied by the facts.

It was an outworn theory to be thrown into the discard. Birmingham and Manchester itself were said to have turned against it and at the London meeting of the Cobden Club in 1897 only thirteen members were present. . . .

Perhaps the most remarkable feature of late Victorian imperialism was its popularity with the lower classes. The political leaders of the movement never tired of pointing out the advantages of expansion for the workingman. "You must remember," said Chamberlain in a speech in 1895, "that, speaking generally, the great cure for this difficulty of want of employment is to find new markets." . . .

Rhodes was, if anything, more outspoken: "The mechanic has woke up to the fact that unless he keeps the markets of the world he will be starved. The 'three acres and a cow' idea has been found to be humbug, and the workingman has found out that he must keep the world and the trade of the world if he is to live, and that if the world is shut to him he is done."

Now it has frequently been asserted by opponents of imperialism that the ignorant public was misled and deluded by false promises made by financiers, industrialists, armaments manufacturers, stock speculators and politicians, into supporting a movement which, in the last count, worked to its detriment by halting the necessary work of social reform. It is always difficult to determine what is cause and what is effect in a case like this, but it does appear, from a study of such imperial crises as the Kruger telegram episode, the Port Arthur affair, the Fashoda crisis, etc., that the public was more excited than the government. There is surely some room for argument that popular pressure was more important in the growth of imperialism than was the action of the ruling classes. It must be recalled, for example, that the rise of imperialism was contemporaneous with the extension of the suffrage in 1867 and 1884 and that it fell in the period when the effects of universal education were just beginning to make themselves felt. It was noted at the time that "power and dominion rather than freedom and independence are the ideas that appeal to the imagination of the masses."

Both Masterman and Hobson, as well as other writers, recognized the danger. The workingmen, it was pointed out, had never had much use for Manchester liberalism with all its teaching of non-interference by the state in economic affairs. They expressed themselves as soon as the extended suffrage gave them a chance. Instead of working for peace and social reform they deserted the Liberal party, put the Conservatives in power, neglected reform and backed imperialism. The new urban proletariat, says Masterman, was narrow-chested but voluble and excitable, and sought stimulus in drink, gambling and conflict at home and abroad. The half-literate slum-dweller demanded fiercer excitement: "more chops, bloody ones, with gristle." . . .

This popular thirst for excitement and pageantry was undoubtedly nourished by the great Jubilee celebrations of 1887 and 1897, with their tremendous display of pomp and power. The South African War at first was a wonderful outlet for the spirit of adventure and conflict. Mafeking Night of June 1900, with its unbridled rioting and its appalling vulgarity, shocked people who were not otherwise prudish or Victorian. But by that time the public had been nourished for fully a decade by a sensational newspaper press and by a literature of brutality which we cannot afford to leave out of account. In approaching the problem we are at once confronted by the question whether the press and literature of imperialism brutalized the people or whether the emergence of an unrefined, uncultured reading public called forth the type of literature which was so popular in the last years of the century. Surely there was an interaction of the two, but in the last count it is, I think, fairly clear that it was the demand that created the supply. Walter Bagehot believed that ages as well as nations have a character, and held that this *Zeitgeist* ultimately finds expression through some writer, frequently not a genius, who produces something a bit more congenial to the minds about him. Thereupon other writers "catch the words that are in the air, and the rhythm which comes to them they do not know from whence."

It was such a "tidal mood of mankind" which carried Kipling to unprecedented literary success in the decade following 1890. Edmund Gosse, in one of his essays, has remarked upon the fact that in the early eighties there was still a pronounced dislike for any narrative literature which exalted the boisterous part of human nature. Literature was expected to be idyllic or reflective, and even historical writing was diverted to the unromantic, arid field of institutional study. The success of Stevenson's *Treasure Island* in 1883 may be taken to mark the turn of the tide, which by 1886 had risen so high that Rider Haggard's *King Solomon's Mines* sold five thousand copies in the first two months. His other African yarns, with their "colonial butcheries," were hardly less successful. Englishmen began to develop an interest in what Bismarck once called their "sporting wars," and in their colonial heroes. Mahan's glorification of British sea power and his warm appreciation of Nelson found a deep response. Books on the accomplishments of British rule in the far corners of the earth rivalled stories of adventure and war in popularity. . . .

Kipling fitted perfectly into this setting. From the time of the appearance of his first book in England (1890), his popularity increased so rapidly that by the end of the century it could be fairly said that no other writer of his time had so profoundly swayed the English mind. His influence, wrote Edmund Gosse, was "simply prodigious"; "his breath has stirred the veins not of hundreds of men, nor of thousands, but of a cluster of nations." Kipling stands revealed, wrote W. T. Stead at the time of Kipling's illness, "as the man who most of all has impressed the popular mind, fired the popular imagination, interpreted the popular consciousness." More than any other writer he reflected the diverse ideas that went under the general term of imperialism. In his *Barrack-Room Ballads* and his army stories he stimulated interest in British activity over-seas and at the same time appealed to the fighting instincts of the race. Hostile critics accused him of exalting brutality and of giving a libelous picture of the British soldier. In his books, they said, he gave "a picture of unmitigated barbarism, drunken, swearing, coarse-minded, vulgar hooliganism, fit for low drinking-dens and gin-palaces." "The voice we hear is always the voice of the soldier whose God is a cockney 'Gawd' and who is ignorant of the aspirate in either Heaven or Hell." There was, they said, in all his works the tacit assumption that the conquered natives were merely made to be fought with, conquered and ruled. They were viewed "merely as a huge mass of raw, brown, naked humanity to be manipulated by the civil and military officials for the arcane purposes of the great Indian Empire." They objected to his preaching contempt for individual rights, his glorifying of the soldier, his cult of the silent strong man and his idealizing of discipline and obedience.

These criticisms, however justified, must not blind us to the fact that in the eyes of his admirers Kipling was the man who saved the Empire, that, more perhaps than any other one man, he roused "the sleeping nerve centres of Imperialism." In the larger sense his popularity merely reflects the impatience of the average Englishman with Ruskin and Browning societies, with pre-Raphaelite poetry, to say nothing of the decadents, Wilde, Beardsley, Dowson and the rest. The young Englishman, it has been said, yawned and longed to go out and shoot something he could understand. Hence the host of literary followers of Kipling, the "literary rough-riders" the exponents of a literature of energy and of action, the now forgotten writers of "blood-stained fiction." . . .

The development of a cheap, popular newspaper press ran parallel to the rise of the literature of action. The attempt to give the rank and file of the population something more palatable than the dignified old newspapers of the ruling classes was made by William T. Stead and John Morley and the whole group gathered about the *Pall Mall Gazette* in the early eighties. But this "new" journalism was soon overshadowed by the "popular" journalism of which Alfred Harmsworth was the prophet. It was in 1894 that Harmsworth bought the *Evening News* and in May 1896 that he began the publication of the *Daily Mail,* the first halfpenny morning paper to attain larger success. He was convinced that the general public had no interest in the long and forbidding columns of parliamentary debates and court reports that were so characteristic of the older papers. His idea was to let people decide what they wanted and then give them just that, attractively presented in bold headlines and striking type.

It did not take Harmsworth and his collaborators long to realize that what the public wanted was general news of an exciting kind. "We realized," says one of his closest associates, "that one of the greatest forces, almost untapped, at the disposal of the Press was the depth and volume of public interest in Imperial questions." So Harmsworth, who was an admirer of Chamberlain, came out vigorously for imperialism. When the *Daily Mail* was founded the announcement was made that it would stand first and foremost

for the power, the supremacy and the greatness of the British Empire. . . . The *Daily Mail* is the embodiment and mouthpiece of the imperial idea. Those who launched this journal had one definite aim in view . . . to be the articulate voice of British progress and domination. We believe in England. We know that the advance of the Union Jack means protection for weaker races, justice for the oppressed, liberty for the down-trodden. Our Empire has not exhausted itself.

The success of the Harmsworth papers literally startled thoughtful people. The *Daily Mail* had an average daily sale of over 200,000 copies in the first year. By 1901 it reached the unheard of figure of 1,000,000. So great in fact was the success of this type of journalism that even the best-established of the older papers were obliged to follow the same line, at least to a certain extent. The *Manchester Guardian* was a striking exception, but even the *Times* became vigorously imperialistic, until it could be said of it that it differed from the *Mail* only in price, quality of paper and volume of news. It showed the same spread-eagleism, the same contempt for moral ideals, the same unquestioning confidence in the efficacy of force.

Journalists of the Harmsworth type created for themselves a tremendous personal power, and the fact could not remain hidden for very long. . . . Lord Salisbury, who began by saying that Harmsworth had invented a paper for those who could read but could not think, and another for those who could see but could not read, ended by becoming completely discouraged by the turn which had been given journalism:

The diplomacy of nations is now conducted quite as much in the letters of special correspondents, as in the despatches of the Foreign Office [he wrote to Canon MacColl in 1901]. The result is that there is a raw state of irritation between the upper classes in the two countries, which makes any advance on the part of either Government quite impracticable.

The tone of realism, not to say ruthlessness and brutality, that was so striking a characteristic of imperialism was due in a measure to the general cast of sociological thought prevailing at that time. A large number of contemporary writers remarked upon the tremendous vogue of Darwinian theories of social evolution. The phrases *struggle for existence* and *survival of the fittest* carried everything before them in the nineties. One critic has asserted that the vogue of this doctrine was "the primary intellectual cause of the reaction."

It has often been pointed out that Darwin himself made no effort to apply the principles of organic evolution to the study of the social structure, and that many of the ideas supposedly taken from his writings were ideas for which he could not justly be held responsible. That is, of course, the fate of every great thinker. The historian, however, is obliged to study the impact of ideas, whatever their true origins or their scientific validity. In the matter of Darwinian influence it may be noted that before the publication of the *Descent of Man* in 1872 a theory of social evolution had been worked out by Spencer and the effort had been made by Walter Bagehot to apply the idea of organic evolution and natural selection to the study of social organization. In Bagehot's brilliant essay, *Physics and Politics,* may be found, at least in embryo, the argument as it was elaborated by others later on:

In every particular state of the world, those nations which are strongest tend to prevail over the others; and in certain marked peculiarities the strongest tend to be the best.

The strongest nation has always been conquering the weaker.

The majority of groups which win and conquer are better than the majority of those which fail and perish, and thus the first world grew better and was improved.

. . . In England the biological or "natural history" conception of social and international relations was, if anything, more in vogue than on the Continent. . . . Perhaps the classic formulation of this entire viewpoint . . . was that given by Professor Karl Pearson in his essay of 1900 entitled *National Life from the Standpoint of Science*. In this he says:

History shows me one way, and one way only, in which a state of civilisation has been produced, namely, the struggle of race with race, and the survival of the physically and mentally fitter race.

This dependence of progress on the survival of the fitter race, terribly black as it may seem to some of you, gives the struggle for existence its redeeming features; it is the fiery crucible out of which comes the finer metal. You may hope for a time when the sword shall be turned into the ploughshare, when American and German and English traders shall no longer compete in the markets of the world for raw materials, for their food supply, when the white man and the dark shall share the soil between them, and each till it as he lists. But, believe me, when that day comes mankind will no longer progress; there will be nothing to check the fertility of inferior stock; the relentless law of heredity will not be controlled and guided by natural selection. Man will stagnate. . . .

The path of progress is strewn with the wreck of nations; traces are everywhere to be seen of the hecatombs of inferior races, and of victims who found not the narrow way to the greater perfection. Yet these dead peoples are, in very truth, the stepping stones on which mankind has arisen to the higher intellectual and deeper emotional life of to-day.

. . . The biological conception of the struggle for existence and the survival of the fittest led not only to the glorification of the struggle but to the general acceptance of the ideas of race superiority, destiny and divine ordination. There was, in the last decade of the century, a widespread idea that the tendency of social development was toward larger and larger units and that ultimately the world would be divided between the three or four fittest nations. "It seems to me," said Chamberlain in 1897, "that the tendency of the time is to throw all power into the hands of the greater Empires, and the minor kingdoms—those which are non-progressive—seem to be destined to fall into a secondary and subordinate place." Or, to quote a speech of 1902: "The future is with the great Empires, and there is no greater Empire than the British Empire."

This last sentence will serve admirably to lead us to the all-important idealistic aspect of British imperialism. Not a few writers, of course, would deny that there was any such thing. For them the fine sentiments of the British are nothing but pure hypocrisy. Perhaps the classic formulation of this viewpoint is given by Bernard Shaw, in his *Man of Destiny,* from which a rather long quotation may not be amiss:

Every Englishman is born with a certain miraculous power that makes him master of the world. When he wants a thing he never tells himself that he wants it. He waits patiently till there comes into his head, no one knows how, the burning conviction that it is his moral and religious duty to conquer those who have the thing he wants. Then he becomes irresistible. Like the aristocrat he does what pleases him and grabs what he wants; like the shopkeeper he pursues his purpose with the industry and steadfastness that comes from strong religious conviction and deep sense of moral responsibility. He is never at a loss for an effective moral attitude. As the great champion of freedom and independence, he conquers half the world and calls it Colonization. When he wants a new market for his adulterated Manchester goods, he sends a missionary to teach the natives the gospel of peace. The natives kill the missionary; he flies to arms in defense of Christianity; fights for it, conquers for it; and takes the market as a reward from heaven. . . . There is nothing so bad or so good that you will not find an Englishman doing it; but you will never find an Englishman in the wrong. He does everything on principle. He fights you on patriotic principles, he robs you on business principles, he enslaves you on imperialistic principles, he bullies you on manly principles, he supports his King on loyal principles, he cuts off his King's head on republican principles. His watchword is always duty; and he never forgets that the nation which lets its duty get on the opposite side of its interest is lost.

Call the Englishman's faith in his mission rationalization of more sordid motives if you like, but I doubt if you can honestly speak of hypocrisy. No one could deny the sincerity and high purpose of the missionary and aborigines protection societies which were so deeply interested in the spread of the gospel and the improvement of the "backward" races. No one could deny that the English, themselves the champions of the ideas of liberty and good government, had given their white colonies self-government and had maintained a sentimental bond with these colonies which was unprecedented in the history of modern expansion. So long as they kept to the policy of free trade they could argue with much force that they kept the territories under their rule open to the enterprise of the world and did not demand a monopolistic position for themselves. In short, they had been more successful than all others in making colonies profitable and contented. Their huge Empire was a standing proof of their fitness to rule, consequently the extension of the Empire would be a boon to those peoples that were taken over, even if they were brought in by force. They did not claim to be infallible, and they admitted that on occasion they were brutal and rough, but they were convinced that it was all for the best in the end. . . .

The British, then, were convinced that they were the patricians of the human race, and that they had been called upon to fulfil a certain duty, to carry the White Man's Burden, if we may borrow the name of Kipling's classic formulation of the idea. They are not, they think, imperialists because they want to be, but because they are called upon to be, because they must be:

Why are we Imperialists? As well ask the owner of an estate why he is a land-lord. We have inherited Empire and intend to do our duty by the many peoples in cluded in it. . . . We are Imperialists in response to the compelling influences of our destiny. We are not grouped with nations "vacant of our glorious gains." We are the heirs of the ages, with all the great prerogatives and solemn obligations which attach to this high privilege. We are, and shall be, Imperialists because we cannot help it. . . .

The whole conception of the mission and burden of empire presupposes some sort of superhuman force intervening in the affairs of mankind. If England has been particularly fitted for empire there must be some divine purpose in it all. In the eyes of some, evolution and the survival of the fittest was simply the working of the divine will. Rhodes was a firm believer in this doctrine. "The perfecting of the fittest species among the animals, or of races among men, and then the conferring upon the perfected species or race the title-deeds of the future; that seemed to Mr. Rhodes, through his Darwinian spectacles, the way in which God is governing His world, has governed it and will continue to govern it, so far as we can foresee the future," says Rhodes' close friend and admirer, William Stead. . . . Lord Rosebery was lost in adoration when he contemplated the handiwork of God:

How marvellous it all is! Built not by saints and angels, but the work of men's hands; cemented with men's honest blood and with a world of tears, welded by the best brains of centuries past; not without the taint and reproach incidental to all human work, but constructed on the whole with pure and splendid purpose. Human, and yet not wholly human—for the most heedless and the most cynical must see the finger of the Divine. . . . Do we not hail in this less the energy and fortune of a race than the supreme direction of the Almighty? Shall we not, while we adore the blessing, acknowledge the responsibility? (Inaugural address as rector of Glasgow University, November 16, 1900).

The logical conclusion from all this is that any interference with the progress of British imperialism is an attempt to counteract the will of God. H. D. Traill spoke of the complacent belief of the Englishman that he had a sort of roving commission from above to carry the blessings of good government to all the races of the world which were either too undeveloped or too effete to provide it for themselves:

Any interference with him in the execution of this commission may be justly resented and resisted by him, not only on personal and self-interested grounds, but as a perverse attempt to obstruct the manifest designs of Providence. . . .

This brings us back to the use of force and the inevitability of conflict. The circle is closed, and the line of argumentation is complete from the theory of evolution through the doctrine of the Divine mission back again to the struggle for existence and the survival of the fittest. There we may leave the discussion of British imperialism in the late-Victorian period. It is hard to theorize about it and of the many explanations that have been offered no single one is entirely satisfactory. At bottom the movement was probably as much economic as anything else. It resulted from the tremendously enhanced productive powers of European industry and the break-down of the monopolistic position of England through the appearance of competitors. The feeling that new markets must be secured was very widespread and the need for new fields of investment, though not much discussed at the time, was probably even more important. These needs, however, had been met in the past without any corresponding expansion of territory. It was the embarkation of France, Germany, and other countries on the course of empire that brought the British to the conviction that only political control could adequately safeguard markets.

But this economic side, whatever its importance, must not be allowed to obscure the other factors. Psychologically speaking, I imagine, the prevalence of evolutionary teaching was perhaps crucial. It not only justified competition and struggle but introduced an element of ruthlessness and immorality that was most characteristic of the whole movement. The rise of a popular electorate, quite without culture and only semiliterate, underlined the crudity of the expansionist movement. It called forth a cheap newspaper press and a raw literature of action. In the larger sense, I suppose, it is perfectly true that the industrial system, which was tending more and more toward the mechanization of humanity, made inevitable the yearning for escape and action. Just as, at this very time, people were beginning to seek an outlet for physical urges, even if only vicariously by attendance at huge sporting events, so they tried to find some expression for the combative instincts of the race through the encouragement of aggressive action and adventure abroad. At the same time the religious strain was too strong in the English to be left out of account entirely. The profound conviction of their superiority as a governing race, of their divine mission to improve the world, was not only a rationalization of other motives, it was in itself a primary moving force.

Now this elaborate analysis of British imperialism must not be taken to imply that the British alone were imperialistic. I have examined their case in particular not only because they were, of all peoples, the most imperially minded, but because the political and economic structure of Britain of itself brought the imperial movement to its most perfect flower. The other nations also were imperialistic. Indeed, the main theme in the history of international relations in this period is the clash of imperialisms. These others, too, were convinced of their mission:

In every nation of Europe from England and France to Russia and Turkey, in almost every nation in the world from the Americans to the Chinese and the Finns, the same whisper from below the threshold sounds incessantly in men's ears. "We are the pick and flower of nations; the only nation that is really generous and brave and just. We are above all things qualified for governing others; we know how to keep them exactly in their place without weakness and without cruelty. . . . The excellence of our rule abroad is proved in black and white by the books of our explorers, our missionaries, our administrators and our soldiers, who all agree that our yoke is a pure blessing to those who bear it."

And so, if you have followed and analyzed the classic example of modern imperialism you are in a position to understand the others and to grasp the problems presented by the conflict between them. For in the larger sense the story is more than the story of rivalry between European imperialisms; it is the story of European aggression and advance in the non-European parts of the world.

4.

Raymond Aron, professor of sociology at the University of Paris, is one of France's most distinguished scholars and journalists. In the following lecture, he provides a stimulating discussion of the background of imperialism and of its role in the cold war. Not only should M. Aron's analysis cause one to reconsider the preceding selections, but it should also cause one to reflect on the West's chances of wresting a propaganda advantage from the Soviet Union in the present battle for the allegiance of the formerly colonial peoples of Africa and Asia.

ARON: Imperialism and Colonialism *

. . . It is clear that a *colony*—and in particular, the type of colony which divers European States chose to carve out for themselves in Africa during the latter years of the nineteenth century—is indisputably a specially brutal form of imperialism. European colonists assumed the right of governing and administering African populations, with no other justification for their usurpation than the self-ascribed and (to them) self-evident superiority of their own civilisation over that of the negro races who, only a few decades earlier, had lived under the constant threat of slavery and deportation. If the colonies of Central Africa represent the authentic expression of the colonial spirit, colonialism is only an extreme manifestation of imperialism—a form which encourages and thrives upon a sense of inequality between the conquering and the subject peoples.

On the other hand, it has by now become traditional—even in scientific studies on the subject—to place these two distinct concepts in close proximity. Three works in particular, in my own opinion, have powerfully contributed to the forging of this link: the book entitled *Imperialism,* by Hobson, the English economist, which deals with the expansionist policies of different European States in Africa towards the end of the last century; Lenin's *Imperialism, the Final Stage of Capitalism,* which, in the authentic Marxist tradition, borrows its ideas from the English economists, systematises them, and deduces from the result a thoroughgoing condemnation of the whole capitalist economy; and, finally, the book called *The Diplomacy of Imperialism,* by the American historian William Langer, which is a study of the period which saw the race for colonies in Africa.

Today, in 1959, we have travelled no little distance along the road to *decolonisation.* The European empires in Asia have melted away. The various "zones" of European influence in the Middle East have vanished, leaving the

* Raymond Aron, *Imperialism and Colonialism* (Leeds: The University, 1959), pp. 3-7, 12-14, 16-18. Reprinted by permission of the University of Leeds.

arena free for a struggle between conflicting nationalisms and ideologies—Arab, Soviet, American. In Africa, which was the last major area to be submerged by the rising tide of imperialism, the now ebbing influence of Europe has brought to the surface a number of States whose avowed intention it is to fashion themselves upon the European pattern. The moment is propitious, therefore, to examine the various theories which are currently in vogue.

Is it true, for instance, that the spirit of imperialism normally finds expression through the establishment of colonies, in the specific sense which the term implies among the negro populations of Africa south of the Sahara? Is it true that the African colonies were merely a symptom of internal conflicts raging within the capitalist system itself, the inevitable by-products of the demands of a market economy? Is it true that the disappearance of colonialism must necessarily entail the collapse of imperialism? Or, on the other hand, is it not conceivable that imperialism may survive not only the disappearance of the colonies themselves, but likewise the elimination of those economic motives, by which it is commonly sought to explain the very fact and existence of colonialism?

The economic interpretation of colonial imperialism has always struck me —perhaps because I am a Frenchman—as being dubious in the extreme. Indeed, if we may single out a specific instance of colonial expansion which, at first sight, seems to make the materialist explanation of such phenomena sound like arrant nonsense, this instance is surely that of France under the Third Republic. *Why* should France have seen fit to annex, in Asia no less than in Africa, such vast agglomerations of territory and inhabitants, when she had at home a stationary population already threatened with decline by a low birth-rate, and when her industrialisation was proceeding at a feeble pace compared with that of her neighbours? It would be futile to hunt for "compelling reasons of economic necessity" to explain those military and naval expeditions which planted the *tricolore* at Saigon or Tunis, at Rabat or Brazzaville.

The national economy of France was starved neither of raw materials (which she could purchase from abroad without the slightest strain on her currency), nor of market outlets for those manufactured articles, which her industry was as yet incapable of mass-producing. In point of fact, France had only one surplus commodity to deal with: a surplus of capital savings, which her thrifty citizens were only too eager to invest abroad, either on their own initiative, or else at the prompting of the government. But, out of a total of forty to fifty thousand million francs thus exported in the form of investments, less than 10 per cent had, by 1914, found its way into the territories of the French Empire. French capital investment, which principally took the form of European loans, was used as an instrument of diplomacy, and served to cement various political alliances—notably, the Franco-Russian *entente*. The justification of such a policy, assuming one to be needed, is to be found in the victory of the Marne: had it not been for the railways built with money obtained by loan from French investors, the Russian offensive in East Prussia would, in all likelihood, have proved an impossibility. It was thanks to this offensive that two German army-corps were transferred away from the Western Front; without it, they would certainly have been available on the Marne, and might well have given a very different outcome to the battle.

If, instead of prating about "monopoly capitalism" which carried little decisive weight in France, and which, in any case, took no interest in Africa, we could only manage to take a straightforward, unprejudiced look at the growth of the French Empire, we should discover that the actual sequence of events in itself provides a solution to the mystery—a solution which may perhaps seem superficial, but which at least has the virtue of inherent probability. Initially, it was the fact of French sovereignty in Algeria—acquired by accident in the nineteenth century—which filled the breast of authority with anxious doubts concerning its Tunisian and Moroccan frontiers, and consequently urged those responsible, in plain self-defence, to set up Protectorates, first over Tunis, later over Morocco. In Tunisia, the French were apprehensive of being forestalled by the Italians; moreover, in the years which followed the defeat of 1870, France stood urgently in need of some victory to constitute a symbol of national recovery, and to set the seal of finality upon her revival. In the early years of the twentieth century, Morocco presented a picture not dissimilar from that which had been offered by Tunis a quarter of a century earlier. The army, moreover, put forward the same type of argument: the strategic positions occupied by France could never be deemed secure, so long as there remained a single patch of North African soil outside the dominion of the French flag.

Meanwhile, there was a further operative cause to be taken into account, whose influence was decisive in Equatorial Africa: namely, the fact that each and every European State was not a whit less perturbed to see the establishment of a rival on any given territory than it was anxious to gain a foothold for itself. In Germany, where public opinion was more reluctant than elsewhere to accede to the spirit of colonial imperialism, the country was finally won over, not so much by the profits which might be expected to accrue from the actual fact of conquest, as by the jealous bitterness inspired by the conquests of other nations.

In the particular case of France, the driving impulse behind those in whose hands lay the initiative seems to have been, in North Africa, the military logic of Algerian security, and in Equatorial Africa, the pioneering spirit of adventure and exploration. This double motive-force was strengthened, in metropolitan France, by the humiliation of the recent defeat, and by a passionate longing for compensation. France was resolved to prove to herself that even the disasters of that terrible year, 1870, still left pages to be written in the glorious book of history. As a consequence, she proceeded to carve out an African Empire which was, economically speaking, entirely superfluous, and in which "monopoly capitalism" took a minimum of interest, at least up to the crisis of 1929, in which year the advantages of a protected market first became apparent. . . .

Against this interpretation of the facts (which I have attempted elsewhere to expound in greater detail, and with fuller evidence) there are two possible arguments which may be advanced. The first is the economic type of argument, which, even in France, the protagonists of an imperialist or expansionist policy have always been eager to exploit. Jules Ferry, in those great speeches of his, was wont to invoke a whole disordered host of arguments drawn from the doctrine of "economic necessity"—necessity for bases, for markets, for raw materials. The facts in this case are not open to doubt, and the historian feels no compulsion to suspect the leader of the "Colonialist Party," either of having sold himself to sordid commercial interests, or of hypocrisy. Jules Ferry was an honest man speaking in all sincerity a language which was the fashion in his day. Had he confessed to any quest for power and glory, he would have been guilty of an anachronism no less glaring than that of Louis XIV, had this latter monarch thought fit to talk in terms of raw materials and supply-lines. Marxist historians have a tendency to believe that all statesmen choose to dazzle their listeners with visions of power and glory, whilst all the time, in reality, they are motivated by an unavowable passion for economic gain. In this particular instance, I suspect that the contrary is true: the statesmen of the time were exploiting an economic argument—frigid, passionless, but rationally acceptable to their contemporaries—in order to disguise their dreams of political grandeur—dreams which found their expression in the sight of the banners of France floating proudly over Saigon or Rabat.

The second objection maintains that it was primarily *private* interests which provided the spur to colonial annexations, and which profited from the results; and in this assertion there resides a certain element of truth. Even if private interests—or, to use the more accurate English expression, *sectional* interests—were not the prime movers of the actual annexation, they arose directly out of it, and, once brought into being, were prepared to put up a dogged resistance against the first signs of interference. At bottom—and this was Hobson's thesis—it was not that capitalism as such *demanded* imperialist expansion, but rather, so he asserted, that *individual* capitalists, having first discovered in the colonies a source of abnormal profit, then proceeded to exploit the State and to invoke grandiose ideals in order to conserve their privileges and to exclude competitors. Hobson concluded, not without some justification, that the major powers were dooming themselves to an inevitable and universally fatal conflict, by their violation of the rules of legitimate competition, and by the manner in which they were straining their ingenuity in every case to exclude all industrial and commercial rivals through the exercise of the privileges of sovereignty.

This argument, beyond a doubt, contains a certain element of truth—a far greater element than the theory advanced by Lenin, which, in the accepted Marxist tradition, prefers an inexorable dialectic, over-riding all individual considerations, to any solution which takes into account the actions of *particular* men and of *particular* interests. The cause-and-effect relationship between "monopoly capitalism" and the partition of Africa has no real existence outside the imagination of the doctrinaires. High finance scarcely wasted a thought on Black Africa, and made no appeal for military protection in those territories which it was exploiting for profit. Even Hobson's moderate theory calls for correction. The relationship between "private economic interests" and political intervention may, on occasion, prove to be the very reverse of what Hobson suggests. Indeed, as E. Staley has amply demonstrated in his well-known study, *War and the Private Investor,* in certain instances the initiative came directly from the politicians, who would urge a given bank or business concern to cultivate interests in some distant territory, in order that the State might later possess, should the need arise, a valid case for intervention, to be exploited not so much against the claims of the native populations (whose feelings in the matter carried no weight whatsoever in the minds of those contemporary diplomats who were accustomed to dictate their destiny), as against those of rival European Chancelleries. Such, as I see it, were the facts of the case in the affair of the Bank of Italy in Tripolitania.

The partition of Africa in the closing years of the last century was the consequence—indeed, the inverse picture—of the general state of peace which reigned on the Old Continent. South of the Sahara, the cost of the conquest was negligible. Even in North Africa, France experienced at least as much difficulty in wresting the consent of the Concert of European Nations to her acquisitions as in overcoming the armed resistance of the Berbers or of the Arabs. Africa was considered as an *object,* rather than as a subject of history; and the partition of the Black Continent was the last prize at stake to be disputed by the traditional rivalry of the Greater European Powers. . . .

The last great colonial empire which exists in the world today is undoubtedly that which was originally conquered by Tsarist Russia, and which the Bolshevik Party has managed to preserve intact by re-baptising it the *Union of Soviet Socialist Republics.* The populations of Central Asia belong neither to the same race nor to the same creed as their rulers in Moscow, and some of them cherish memories of a glorious past. If the West chooses to denounce Russian "colonialism," there is no shortage of arguments ready to hand. Yet, without necessarily entering the warring world of propaganda, it is perfectly legitimate to engage upon a study—as Professor Kolarz has already done—of *Russia and her Colonies.*

This first point being once made clear, the significant question arises in the mind almost unbidden: *why* is it that the Russian Empire has offered such stubborn resistance alike to the spirit of the age and to the stirrings of nationalism, whereas the Empires of Europe have collapsed utterly before the onslaught of these same historical forces, no less in Asia than in Africa? I make no claims to offer the full and final solution to so vast a problem in the space of a few moments; none the less, it is not hard to grasp one or two of the more salient factors which explain the provisional stability of the Russian Empire.

To start with, the geographical structure of this Empire is radically different from that of its late European rivals. The Russian Empire comprises one single, unbroken continental land-mass; Russian expansion followed *land-*routes, and, in the majority of cases, civilian settlers, whether peasants or townsfolk, followed or even preceded the troops. In his book entitled *Asia and the Western Dominance,* Mr. Pannikar, who today is Indian Ambassador in Paris, explains that, in the eyes of the peoples of Asia, the British, the Dutch, the French, the Portuguese and the Spaniards were all considered to be "imperialistic" because each arrived by sea, and because each group of invaders exploited the superiority of their warships in order to establish themselves in the land and to usurp its government. By contrast, the Russians, who were merely following in a reverse direction the routes so often used earlier by the horsemen of Asia, seemed consequently far less "foreign" and far less "imperialistic." Whether or not we accept the accuracy of this popular impression is immaterial; the fact remains that the single-continent unity of the Russian Empire has proved more propitious to stability than has the geographical dispersion of the others. That the Queen of England could ever have been crowned Empress of India was, and must always remain, one of the great paradoxes of history.

Considered as a conquering people, the Russians seem to have possessed two outstanding virtues: they had comparatively little sense of racial distinction, and they early established and subsequently maintained a tradition of imperial citizenship open to all the colonial peoples. To these characteristics, the Bolsheviks have more recently adjoined the twin practices of cultural autonomy and of rigorous centralisation. On the one hand, the so-called "national" languages are accepted and encouraged, although a knowledge of Russian proper is becoming year by year more essential to all citizens of the USSR who aspire to any kind of career. On the other hand, in flagrant contrast to this policy of cultural autonomy, the central government is fierce and merciless in its repression of the faintest stirrings of *"bourgeois nationalism."* Where exactly lies the borderline between this flower of "national cultural autonomy," which the Bolsheviks are forever fostering with such glamour and publicity, and this weed known as "bourgeois nationalism," which they are forever most brutally detecting and uprooting? No-one may say with certainty; or rather, they alone can trace its hourly-shifting position who wield the supreme power, and who therefore can establish this ticklish frontier to suit their current whim and pleasure.

Finally, the difference in standards of living between one region and another within the Empire has never been so great as that, say, between Great Britain and India, between the average Parisian and the average Algerian, between the native of Provence and the native of Guinea. The Russo-Soviet Empire is a single economic unit, and has always been treated as such by the Muscovite State, whereas neither the British nor the French Empire has ever constituted a single economic unit, nor was it possible so to treat it. Thanks to the technique of the "Economic Plans" the distribution of investments has been so organised that the Soviet Empire, in spite of the vast diversity which distinguishes its different regions, has avoided any tendency to split up into a prosperous metropolitan nucleus surrounded by under-developed provinces.

It should be added that the absence of political liberty, together with the monopoly exercised by the State over all organs of press and publicity, prevents the outside world from hearing any protests which may arise from the colonially subject peoples, while at the same time it makes it impossible to draw up any accurate balance-sheet of credit and debit, or to calculate the advantages and disadvantages which the indigenous population may reap from the ascendancy of Greater Russia. Suffice it to record the fact that the strongest argument against any unconditional condemnation of colonialism as such is provided for us ready-minted by the extreme sectarians of anti-colonialist propaganda: for if indeed, in the Soviet Union, the administration of the Muslim populations of Central Asia by the Representatives of the People of Greater Russia is "consistent with historical trends" and therefore to be applauded, is it not an inescapable consequence that whether colonialism, in any individual case, is judged to be either tolerable or abominable, must depend in every instance upon the character and the conduct of both colonisers and colonised?

In any case, outside the frontiers of the Soviet Union, colonialism, ideologically suspect to Russia and America alike, has come already to be a rare phenomenon. The same is by no means true of imperialism, at least in its subtler forms: forms employed by the strong to dominate the weak. Admittedly, present circumstances exclude the classical manifestations of imperialism. There are no more uninhabited or sparsely-inhabited territories to be had for the asking by incoming settlers. No-one talks any longer about the "white man's burden"; one and all, the governments of the world proclaim the doctrine that all races and all peoples are equal, and at the General Assembly of the United Nations, one vote is as good as another: Haiti or the Yemen count as one with India or the United States. The one exception is the Soviet Union, which, by a stroke of fortune in the mêlée of war-time diplomatic bargaining, managed to secure for herself three separate votes (the Ukraine and Byelorussia being reckoned as independent States) . . . .

In the battle of slogans, in the context of the war of rival propagandas now being waged with the Soviet Union, we of the West are by no means ill-provided with fact or argument. The only colonial Empire still surviving intact today is that which Tsarist Russia once constructed, and which Lenin himself, before taking power, denounced. Even in Europe, the Soviet Union is busy introducing new forms of imperial domination, well-concealed beneath a smoke-screen of liberal epithets; she is profiting even now from the advance of her armies to propagate her institutions, and she is merciless in the extirpation of all stirrings or revolt against the so-called communist national parties.

However, we must not forget that the quarrels of history are never resolved by some impartial arbiter, whose verdict is based upon the intrinsic merit of the respective briefs. Officially, the Soviets stand before the world as liberators; unofficially, they contrast the disintegration of the Empires of Europe with the stability of their own. The tide of Europe is ebbing; does this fact constitute a *defeat*? Does it mark, as the school history-books would have us believe, the beginning of the end?

Of all questions, this perhaps, is the most vital; and the understanding which we Europeans are to gain concerning our own ultimate destiny must depend upon the answer which we give to it. What is the significance of this current phase of imperial and colonial *disengagement?* Is it the final stage, by which Europe is to fulfil her destiny as the bringer of freedom? Or is it simply the collapse of the old imperial powers, and the imminent threat for Europe of a return to weakness and provincialism? In my opinion, the reply has not yet been vouchsafed us; history itself will provide the final answer.

In terms of economics, the disbanding of the Empires is no loss to their respective European capitals. The modern metropolis has no need to exercise sovereign rights in order to keep up commercial relationships. A State which attempted to maintain its sovereign rights by force of arms against the tide of popular revolt would find itself faced with overwhelming losses, and then indeed would have experienced an overwhelming defeat (the example of France in Indo-China is ample evidence of the truth of this assertion.)

Politically speaking, neither Great Britain nor France nor Holland has proved capable of putting forward an ideological system powerful enough to cement the fabric of an Empire. Each nationality in turn is confronted by the alternative, either of assimilating its colonies altogether, or else of transferring its rights of sovereignty to them as independent States. France alone, in her North African Empire, has shown some disposition to assimilate her erstwhile colonies. The ultimate creation of a series of new, independent States was the logical outcome of the whole colonial enterprise of Western Europe—with this qualification, that the final timing and manner of the operation lies outside the scope of any general law.

In every instance, the newly-liberated peoples have shown themselves more eager to *adapt* than to reject the divers economic and political institutions which the Europeans had brought with them. Each new nation is anxious to build itself an industrial society comparable to that whose model was first presented to them by the colonists. And the final verdict of history concerning the achievement of European civilisation in its world wide missionary venture is destined, in the long run, to depend upon the greater or lesser degree of success with which these many peoples now tackle the problems of industrialisation and of modernisation. Today, the races of Europe have the opportunity of establishing relations on an equal footing, and for the benefit of all, with their sometime colonial subjects. *Power* is not the only manifestation of greatness.

Writers of the nineteenth century used to believe that the truly decisive contests in human history were those where class rushed headlong against class; they were apprehensive of a class-struggle, whose violence was fated to annihilate whole communities, to put an end to peace and to destroy prosperity. We in our day are tempted to believe that the prospect of class-warfare is less terrifying than that of conflict between races and ideologies. In regions where two communities of different racial origins exist side by side, how is peace to be enjoined, or re-established? In continents where rival ideologies clash head on, how are the fanatics to be persuaded that social organisation knows no absolute or definitive truth, and that the real "imperialist"—he who bears the responsibility for those fatal dissensions by which humanity is destroyed—is the man who claims the right to impose *his* truth upon all others?

Let us lift our eyes over and beyond the tragedies which darken the present. Industrial society, based on science and technology, is in the process of becoming a universal condition of life. It sets before mankind an opportunity without precedent, reveals the possibility of a peaceful existence devoid of slavery and devoid of exploitation. To-morrow, perhaps, man may grow aware of this common purpose imposed by the process of history; and who knows but that he may perchance take that which is now but a common aim of material fulfilment, and transmute it at last into a genuine unity of the spirit?

5.

John Strachey is one of the most controversial politicians of recent British history. Although educated at those most conservative institutions of English learning, Eton and Magdalen College, Oxford, he moved to the extreme left in the 1930's, resigned from the Labour party, and, in *The Coming Struggle for Power* (1932) showed himself to be one of Britain's ablest young Marxists. In recent years, however, he has moved back to the center of the political stage, and served under Clement Attlee as Minister of Food and then as Secretary of State for War in the postwar Labour governments. Whether he is still a good Marxist or whether he has succumbed to British relativism one can perhaps determine from the following selection. In the early chapters of the book from which the following selection is taken, Mr. Strachey argues that empires are far more apt to be a liability than an asset to their owners.

STRACHEY: The End of Empire *

Much of the . . . evidence of the irrelevance of imperial possessions to a nation's standard of life rests upon the assumption that the British and other empires either have been, or are being, liquidated. But it may be suggested that this assumption is false: that nothing of the sort has taken place: that behind the political changes involved on paper, in this or that act of independence, the exploitation of the native peoples by the British and other imperialists goes on, only now in a different way. This, we may be told, is the simple and sufficient explanation of why the terms of trade have not turned against Britain as her empire has (apparently) dissolved, and in general of why our standard of life has not suffered.

This is essentially the communist account of the matter. It is for example the main argument used by Mr. R. P. Dutt, a principal exponent of Marxist-Leninist views in the English language . . . [and by] Professor Paul Baran, that unique phenomenon, a Marxist working at an American university. . . .

Mr. Dutt duly puts forward the Leninist thesis that the whole British economic and social system rests upon imperialist exploitation and that in particular any increase in the standard of life of any section of the British people, which, he reluctantly implies, may have taken place, is the result of the further degradation of many millions of primary producers in a continuing British empire. Mr. Dutt sweeps aside the blank contradiction for this view which arises from the simultaneous achievement of independence by nine-tenths of the inhabitants of the former British empire and the existence of terms of trade considerably better for Britain than in her empire's heyday. He simply denies that any dissolution of the British Empire has occurred. India, Pakistan, Ceylon and Burma, he holds, were just as much British colonies when he wrote in 1953 as ever they had been. Britain, he alleges, can and does exploit their populations just as grossly as ever. Nothing has changed: or rather, nothing has changed in the substance of the imperialist relationship; there has merely been a change in the form and method by which exploitation is carried on.

The test adopted in these pages of whether or not a particular country is a colony, *de facto* or *de jure,* of another is the simple one of where effective *sovereignty* lies. Can or cannot some foreign country impose its will without war or the threat of war upon the country in question? Of course we must not be misled by whether or not the official forms of colonisation have been established. It would be formalistic in the extreme to deny that the Egypt of Cromer was a British colony because that absolute ruler of the country was called "British Agent and Consul-General" instead of Governor, as in most other colonies. Nor can it be denied that there are borderline cases. Was or was not Iraq between 1918 and 1958 a British colony? On the whole up till 1945 she was. For if we apply the simple test of war-making, we find that in the second World War, Iraq was used by British forces and the anti-British revolt of Rashid Ali unhesitatingly put down by British troops. On the other hand, after 1945 the British hold on the country was visibly relaxing and a considerable measure of self-determination was achieved even under the Nuri régime, although British troops (the R.A.F.) remained in occupation. Full independence was clearly achieved in the revolution of 1958 and British troops left. And the same transition over roughly the same period took place in Egypt. Again it can be very plausibly argued that some of the "banana republics," as they are contemptuously called, in Central America are effectively American colonies, even though they have never been, for long, occupied by American troops. For as was recently demonstrated in the case of Guatemala, the State Department exercises a veto over the kinds of government which they may elect.

Nevertheless, and although each case must be examined on its merits, it will not usually be difficult to apply the above test of whether a country is *effectively* sovereign over itself or not. To return to the great case of India, for example, can the British Government to-day decide, as up till 1947 it undoubtedly could do, the height of India's tariffs, her rates of income tax, her foreign trade and payments policy, her economic policy in general and, surest test of all, whether or not India shall go to war in any given situation? By this obvious test India is to-day as unequivocally independent as she was unequivocally a colony up till 1947. It was, as a matter of fact, this very issue of the right to decide on peace or war which brought matters to a head. With remarkable folly the British Government of 1939 caused the Government of India to declare war on Germany without any attempt at consultation with the Indian people. This was one of the factors which caused the final determination of almost all politically conscious Indians to be rid of British rule. And the fact is that they are rid of it. No one can possibly pretend that a British Government could to-day declare war on India's behalf.

Mr. Dutt, of course, makes much of the fact that India, Pakistan and Ceylon have chosen to remain part of the British Commonwealth. He does not put it like that. For him Britain "imposed the Mountbatten settlement," including partition, upon the unwilling peoples of India and Pakistan, who were striving to make a united revolutionary republic. It does not disturb Mr. Dutt that this allegation of an imposed settlement is in flat contradiction to another of his allegations, in which there is much more truth. This second allegation is that there was nothing else which Britain could do after 1945 than to come to terms with the Asian nationalist movements. This is basically correct. The real credit which may be claimed for the British Government of the day is not that it magnanimously "gave" India her freedom, when it need not have done so, but that it appreciated the necessity of recognising Indian independence instead of fighting futilely against it. For, if we had not recognized this necessity, we should inevitably . . . have ruined both India and Britain. And, after all, this recognition was no small achievement. I am aware of no other important instance of imperial authorities recognising such a necessity when they encountered it. It was Frederick Engels who cited the Hegelian maxim that freedom was the recognition of necessity. If so, the British Government's recognition of the necessity of Indian independence in 1947 was one of the most truly free acts in history. The truth is that in 1947 Britain had neither the capacity nor the intention of continuing to govern the sub-continent herself or of compelling the Indians and Pakistanis either to remain within the Commonwealth or to partition the peninsula.

Professor Baran . . . takes the same view as Mr. Dutt but he expresses it in more general terms. He assumes without question that imperialism, mainly on the part of Britain and America, is still in full swing, and that the fact that in the last fourteen years Britain has relinquished, and America has not acquired, political sovereignty over the greater part of the non-communist pre-industrial world, is largely irrelevant. He assumes, rather than argues, that Britain and above all America, are continuing to exploit the pre-industrial peoples just as atrociously as ever.

His view appears to be that the imperial powers have succeeded in setting up in most of their ex-colonies, and for that matter in other pre-industrial countries also, what he calls "comprador governments." These governments are run, he writes, by the native merchants and other business men who have large and close commercial relations with the major firms of the imperialist powers, and they run their pre-industrial countries strictly in the interests of the imperial powers, either arresting development entirely or distorting it to a fatal degree. Usually, he writes, they only permit development in (i) the extraction of raw materials for the imperialists (ii) in light consumer industries and (iii) in agriculture. They prevent development in the basic heavy industries. In return the imperialist powers heartily support such "comprador régimes." It is true that Professor Baran occasionally notices that some of the governments of the non-communist pre-industrial world do not fit into this description, in particular the Indian Government. He calls these "New Deal type governments" and credits them with rather better intentions, but not with much else. In general he too is evidently convinced that no undeveloped or pre-industrial society which has not become communist has really escaped from imperialist exploitation.

What are we to say of this communist thesis, put forward in the more plausible version of Professor Baran? No impartial observer would wish to deny that it is possible to carry on the imperialist control and exploitation of an undeveloped country without retaining it as, or making it into, a direct and formal colony. . . . Of course it is possible to rule and exploit people in this way. Every experienced imperialist will tell Professor Baran, however, that such indirect rule and exploitation is by no means the same thing as possession of the country in question as a direct colony. Once an even nominally sovereign local government is established, forces are invariably set in motion which tend in the direction of genuine independence. Imperialist control can go on, often for some time, but it becomes more and more precarious. To say that the advent of even partial political independence makes no difference is a grotesque oversimplification.

Again Professor Baran represents the Western powers as determined to prevent the development of the pre-industrial nations at all costs. He writes:

Western big business heavily engaged in raw materials exploitation leaves no stone unturned to obstruct the evolution of social and political conditions in underdeveloped countries that might be conducive to their economic development. It uses its tremendous power to prop up the backward areas' comprador administrations, to disrupt and corrupt the social and political movements that oppose them, and to overthrow whatever progressive governments may rise to power and refuse to do the bidding of their imperialist overlords. Where and when its own impressive resources do not suffice to keep matters under control, or where and when the costs of the operations involved can be shifted to their home countries' national governments—or nowadays to international agencies such as the International Bank for Reconstruction and Development—the diplomatic, financial and, if need be, military facilities of the imperialist power are rapidly and efficiently mobilized to help private enterprise in distress to do the required job. . . .

This is carrying overstatement to the point of falsification. It is entirely true that there are examples in which Western power has been used (though usually with greater folly than success) to prop up reactionary governments in the pre-industrial world. Moreover, the Western powers could and should be arraigned for failing whole-heartedly to support with adequate funds the development of the pre-industrial world. But, after all, for the first time in history, a good deal of money has been actually given by the rich countries to the poor countries for the express purpose of development. It is perverse to make no distinction between say, the monies provided under the Colombo Plan, or the American Point Four programme and traditional imperialist investment for profit by private enterprise. And it is equally perverse to assume that, say, £50 million lent by Russia to India to build a steel works is an act of the purest philanthropy, while £50 million lent by Britain to India to build another steel works, is an act of imperialist exploitation. Again it is true that there is a tendency for the Western powers, for selfish reasons, to try to bias development in the direction of extractive and consumer goods industries, and towards agriculture, to the prejudice of heavy industry. But after all, there is something to be said for some development, at least, taking one or other of these forms. It is not true that all the profits of the extractive industries go to foreigners. (. . . the Arab oil states have now got hold of half of them.) Consumer industries are very useful to consumers, and concentration upon agricultural development does not *necessarily* mean being kept as hewers of wood and drawers of water for the imperialists. It *may* do so—as for example in the East Indies under the Dutch. But it may not, if the pre-industrial country's government is both independent and capable. The cardinal example of this is New Zealand, which by reason of, precisely, a heavy concentration upon agricultural development with some development of consumer industries, was actually able for one year at least (1956) to raise the per capita income of her people to the highest in the world, exceeding that of the United States themselves by a narrow margin. (And if she could not retain that world leadership, she yet maintains very great prosperity.)

Thus the whole question is far more complex than communist and Marxist writers are willing to admit. It is quite true that the dissolution of imperial sovereignty over most of the undeveloped world is no proof that its exploitation for the benefit of the highly developed countries has ceased. But it is a prerequisite for it ceasing.

6.

The most significant development of our time, some people believe, is not the development of atomic power or the rise of Communism, but the world revolution produced by the new self-assertiveness of Africa and Asia. Here is one of the unforeseen but crucially important by-products of the imperialist age. Perhaps it is a mark of Lenin's genius that he was one of the first to foresee this development, and to propose to use it for his purposes. One of the best studies of the colonized peoples' reactions to imperialism, especially in the period of decolonization, is Rupert Emerson's *From Empire to Nation* (significantly subtitled "The Rise to Self-Assertion of Asian and African Peoples"). Mr. Emerson has taught international relations at Harvard University for twenty-five years, and has specialized in the area of Southeast Asia. His comments ought to stimulate discussion on the significance of the imperialist episode in modern history, and on its probable after-effects both on the course of the cold war and on Europe's relations with the so-called "third world" of neutralist nations.

EMERSON: From Empire to Nation *

A great era of human history has come to a close—the era of Western domination over the rest of mankind. In many respects that era is too near to us, too much a part of our daily lives, whether we be of the West or of the East, to make possible the kind of objective and dispassionate evaluation which would be desirable. To undertake to be the historian of several hundred years hence or that always shrewd and penetrating visitor from Mars is a risky business. A plausible case can, however, be made for the proposition that the future will look back upon the overseas imperialism of recent centuries, less in terms of its sins of oppression, exploitation, and discrimination, than as the instrument by which the spiritual, scientific, and material revolution which began in Western Europe with the Renaissance was spread to the rest of the world. To broaden this proposition as widely as does a recent analyst of British rule in India who contends that imperialism throughout the ages has been "the main process by which civilization has been diffused" is to leap unduly far. The importance of more peaceful and egalitarian processes of cultural diffusion need not be minimized in order to identify the positive role which imperialism has played.

To assert that imperialism has served through the ages as a great diffuser of civilization is not to imply that every imperialism played the role of bringing a higher civilization to a people at a lower level. Imperialism, by definition, involves the domination of one people over another, of a stronger over a weaker community; yet it would be grossly improper to assume a universal identification of greater strength with loftier culture. Few today would back the optimistic claim of Walter Bagehot in the first flush of evolutionary doctrine, not only that the strongest nations tend to prevail over the others, but also that "in certain marked peculiarities the strongest tend to be the best," and his further, more elaborate, claim that: "Conquest is the premium given by nature to those national characters which their natural customs have made most fit to win in war, and in many most material respects those winning characters are really the best characters. The characters which do win in war are the characters which we should wish to win in war." The general superiority of Roman civilization to that of the bulk of the peoples whom Rome overran would not be open to much question, but Rome also overran Greece and was itself later overrun by the barbarians from the north, and the Mongol hordes imposed themselves on China. The diffusion of civilization through imperialism is by no means always a one-way affair. In the contemporary scene, Nazi imperialism would find few supporters as the vehicle for the advance of civilization.

In the case of the overseas imperialism of modern times, the peoples of Western Europe have carried with them the civilization of the revolution which they were experiencing, driven or inspired by the force of the revolution itself and increasingly endowed by it with the necessary greater strength. This is, of course, in no way to suggest that it was the deliberate intent of the builders of empire to fulfill the *mission civilisatrice* of which they occasionally boasted and by which their apologists justified their actions. Only in the rarest instances, if ever, do states or statesmen, embarking on imperial expansion, appear to have been swayed by the desire to do good for their fellow, but alien, man. Missionary zeal of one stamp or another has rarely been wholly absent, but the desire for power and profit, the rivalry of states and peoples, and perhaps even a sense of insecurity, have all been more constant factors in imperialism. The question of intent is, however, in the long run of less consequence than the actual impact of what was done. Even the resolution to hold back the peoples who were overrun by denying them access to the languages and instrumentalities of European civilization could do no more than delay the impact. It was only by staying firmly at home that the Europeans could fail to spread their new outlooks and techniques, and staying at home was the one thing which seemed quite impossible. The imperialist explicitly out for the profit, strategic advantage, or glory of his own people was likely to be as radical a transformer of the native society on which he impinged as the avowed missionary or modernizer. As one of the Soviet leaders phrased it, "Imperialism itself is the stimulator of revolutions." . . .

It was an . . . inevitable concomitant of the Western supremacy in power that the peoples who came under the sway of the white man should soon yearn to possess the secrets and the sources of his power for themselves. If only for the purpose of survival, it became necessary for any non-white people which sought to maintain its identity to achieve some mastery of the ideas and techniques, the institutions and instruments, which had enabled the imperial conquerors to take over the world. This sense of an otherwise impending doom led the Japanese to undertake their uniquely successful effort to pull themselves into the modern world by their own bootstraps, rather than to allow themselves to be pulled into it by alien force. In face of the inability of any of the non-European societies to produce a countervailing strength from within themselves, the alternatives were sharply drawn: either to seek out and adopt those things from which the white man derived his power or to accept a subordination to which there was no foreseeable end and which might involve disintegration as well.

In fact, the matter was only rarely reduced to these harsh and oversimple terms because, in addition to the drive for survival, there was an almost universal tendency within a newly rising leadership to accept the conquering

Western civilization as superior and in itself desirable. If the first reaction of the peoples on whom the West imposed itself was generally a xenophobic defense of the existing order, the next phase was likely to be a swing in the direction of an uncritical self-humiliation and acceptance of alien superiority. The third phase, in the fashion of the Hegelian dialectic, was a nationalist synthesis in which there was an assertion or reassertion of a community with pride in itself and in its past but still looking, at least as far as its leaders were concerned, in the direction of Westernization and modernization. Those leaders were, almost without exception, men who had achieved substantial acquaintance with the West.

The most obvious element to be sought after by the non-European peoples was the duplication of the immense material advance which the West had made for the purposes of both peace and war. Increasingly this advance was seen to embrace, not only the new gadgets of all varieties which the West introduced, but also the scientific outlook from which they sprang, an outlook resting upon a revolutionary rationalism which undercut old ways of life and thought. The nineteenth-century efforts of the Ottoman Empire and of Mohammed Ali in Egypt to take over from the West only its military instruments and techniques were soon demonstrated to be futile. The new modes of transportation and communication, modern medicine, hygiene, and sanitation, and the achievement of higher standards of living through a basic reorganization of economic life, came to be adopted as goals which the non-European societies now set for themselves. Colonial governments came to be damned not so much because they had ruthlessly upset the old order of things—although they were damned for that too—as because they had so inadequately carried through the work of industrializing ancient societies and dragooning them into the modern world.

Education on Western lines for both the elite and the masses was eagerly sought. This education plus economic and other pressures brought a swing toward acceptance of individualism and a far greater measure of egalitarianism in social and political life. The Indian caste system was undermined by the conditions of factory work and of travel on train and bus, and the African chief became subject to the control of councils elected by commoners. There grew up a sense that the introduction of Western-style parliamentary democracy symbolized the attainment of political maturity—save for those who sought salvation in Moscow's brand of Westernization. Although a scattering few like Gandhi declined to acknowledge the West as a model, much the more usual reaction was to seek salvation by entering voluntarily into the new world, both spiritual and material, which had been opened up. All this is by no means to suggest that the traditional cultures were totally repudiated by Indians and Indonesians, Iraqi and Nigerians, but the non-European peoples in general, or at least the leading and vocal elements among them, have very largely acquiesced in the notion of the superiority of Western civilization which the white man so confidently held in the nineteenth century. . . .

At least for the last century or so the rooting out of what were, in Western eyes, gross offences against human rights and decency has been generally accepted as one of the major responsibilities of colonial administrations. Western conceptions of the dignity and equality of man, slow enough to become living reality at home, moved ahead at a snail's pace in the lands under imperial control. Consciously or unconsciously, however, the Western administrator brought these conceptions with them in their mental baggage and in the institutions which they introduced. The barriers were not only in the bad will or the shortcomings of the Western rulers but also in the traditions and social structure of the peoples upon whom they had thrust themselves. The boasted equality of Islam could not hide vast actual inequality; the caste system of Hinduism was explicitly based on a pattern of absolute superiority and inferiority; and slavery, in one or another guise, was an almost universal institution.

In terms of political practicality the means to implement the desire of the colonial administrator to promote equality or check oppression and arbitrary exaction were likely to be meager at best. At home the conceptions of the philosophers had behind them the demands of increasingly powerful groups and classes for recognition as equal human beings. In the colonies, however, the administrators were an isolated and alien handful of men operating in the setting of an apathetic and often hostile social climate. To produce gold, coffee, or rubber or to build jails or roads is a far easier assignment than to transform the inner social structure of old and close-knit communities.

In another dimension lay the gnawing problem as to the right of the alien to cut into the fabric of the society whose destiny he had undertaken to control. Some things, such as cannibalism, Hindu widow-burning, or the cruder variants of slavery, constituted such outrageous violations of the fundamental Western code that they might, as particulars, properly be attacked; but to cut deeper raised an ethical issue of fundamental importance as well as a fear that the whole cloth might disintegrate. The administrator soon became aware that he was damned if he did and damned if he didn't: to undertake the reform of the society was wantonly to impose alien idiosyncrasies on a rounded and living culture, whereas to refrain was to protect the very backwardness which had justified intervention in the first place.

Colonialism at its extreme best brought no new heaven on earth nor did it produce any approximation of the advances which had been made in the metropolitan countries, but it undoubtedly worked to adapt the administrative structure of the societies on which it impinged to the requirements of the modern world. However adequate the indigenous political systems were to their traditional tasks, they were normally as inadequate to meet the new pressures as the governments of medieval Europe would have been. With occasional exceptions the dependent peoples have been given more rationalized and efficient administrations in the present century than they had known before. This was particularly true of the central colonial governments and of areas brought under direct Western rule. Even in territories, such as West Africa or Malaya, where the indirect rule so highly esteemed by the British maintained the position of traditional authorities, the trend was fairly constantly in the direction of curbing arbitrary personal power and regularizing the transaction of public business. The lowliest were raised somewhat in status, and the ever revolutionary doctrine of equality began its work. Institutionally the latter found expression in the movement toward equality before an objective and impartial law.

. . . Whether one looks at Indonesia, Iraq, or Sierra Leone, it is evident that the gulf between the unlettered mass and the Westernized leaders who challenged the colonial systems renders suspect the claim of this latter elite to represent the people. Certainly from the standpoint of the conscientious colonial administrator—especially if his native bent led him neither to humility nor to the role of the teacher—it was a very painful thing to hand over the intricate machinery which he had laboriously built to people whom he did not trust or judge competent or representative. Benevolent paternalism no less than lust for power or profit can render the transition to independence exceedingly difficult. . . .

. . . Winston Churchill in 1931 condemned the Indian National Congress as possessing neither the numbers, the strength, nor the virtue of the Indian people: "They merely represent those Indians who have acquired a veneer of Western civilization, and have read all those books about democracy which Europe is now beginning increasingly to discard. . . . To transfer that responsibility to this highly artificial and restricted oligarchy of Indian politicians . . . would be an act of cowardice, desertion and dishonor."

A counterattack upon the nationalists as unrepresentative of the people for whom they claim to speak is thus a standard feature of the defense put forward by beleaguered colonial authorities, who also contend that nationalist victory is likely to mean no real advance toward meeting popular needs and aspirations. It can, indeed, be argued that the achievement of independence does no more by itself than to answer the demand for independence. . . .

[But] the simple truth is that, once a certain stage of development is passed, colonial peoples will not accept good government as a substitute for self-government. Their own version of what they want coincides with the answer given to Lord John Russell in 1854 when he suggested that if the Italians would only keep quiet Austria would be more humane and grant them more privileges than they could secure by insurrection. To this proposition Daniel Manin, defender of Venice, replied: "We do not ask that Austria be humane and liberal in Italy—which, after all, would be impossible for her even if she desired; *we ask her to get out*. We have no concern with her humanity and her liberalism; we wish to be masters in our own house."

In point of fact, good government, far from being a substitute for self-government, appears to be one of the prime keys to the emergence of clamorous political demands. It is not the most down-trodden who rise in their wrath, but those who had made a good start on the path of advance: "A population that rebels is a population that is looking up, that has begun to hope and to feel its strength."

If one would devise an equation to serve as a guide to the circumstances under which colonial nationalism is most likely to appear, two major variables would need to be taken into account.

In the first place, the greater the disruption of the old society under the impact of the intruding Western forces—assuming that that disruption takes the form of a development of modern enterprise and administration and not merely the suppression of the native population—the speedier and more complete the assertion of nationalism is likely to be. Those countries which have experienced the largest measure of Westernizing change are the most restive under colonialism, and the elements of their population which have been most drastically divorced from the close-knit pattern of their traditional society are the most susceptible to the appeal of nationalism.

In the second place, the appearance of a Westernized elite is an indispensable part of the movement toward nationalism. It is this elite—the new intelligentsia and the professional men—which translates to the local scene the nationalist experience and ideology of the West and serves as the crystallizing center for the inchoate disaffections of the mass. . . .

Paradoxical as it may seem, colonial nationalism is far less a response to oppression or neglect than to the widened horizons opened up by progressive colonial governments. The concurrent spread of nationalism and of free institutions in the Philippines can be cited as an obvious example. Equally striking is the contrast between developments in British and French West Africa and other African territories. The earlier appearance and wider sweep of nationalism in British India as compared with the Netherlands Indies is surely not unrelated to the greater freedom and political advance of the former. . . .

It is not the Indian princes, Malay Sultans, or African chiefs who have typically taken the lead in the nationalism of their countries. The quarrel between the native ruler and his entourage, often sustained by the colonial administration, and the newly rising Westernized middle class elements has become a commonplace of the literature dealing with colonial problems. When E. M. Forster served in the court of Dewas Senior in India in 1921, he reported: "There is no anti-English feeling. It is Gandhi whom they dread and hate." Even where, as in Morocco and Uganda, traditional rulers have become symbols of nationalist aspirations, the formulation and driving force of nationalism has rested in the main with the new middle class schooled in the West. Furthermore, the position which the upper class Western-trained elite attained in the new type of political activity appeared to derive more from their personal abilities and from their mastery of the ideas and techniques of the West than from their inherited traditional status, although the latter might also contribute to their prestige. Certainly their nationalist associates were likely to be men drawn from the lower ranks of society who had been able to rise through missionary or other education or to amass wealth from the new types of enterprise.

Of the Indian nationalist movement Nehru has said that "the backbone and leadership were always supplied by the middle classes," even though the direct action struggles were based on the masses and especially the peasantry. Finding the middle class an inchoate group, too much tied up with property and at the top allied with British imperialism, he still asserted that "paradoxically, it is only from the middle class intellectuals that revolutionary leadership comes."

Any sample of the leading figures in the nationalist movements would demonstrate the immense preponderance of men who went through the processes of Western education and who may decently be assigned to the middle class. . . .

The strength of the West was something to be studied and copied, and a major component of that strength was the existence of integrated nations. For Asians and Africans who underwent a Western type of education at home or abroad, this lesson was sharply emphasized by the body of doctrine which was thrust upon them. Since it was an age of nationalism in the West the achievement and maintenance of national unity and independence were central themes of the literature, history, and political tradition to which they were exposed. The praise of freedom and equality, and of the patriots who fought for national honor and integrity were basic assumptions of their new intellectual milieu. The writings of Rousseau, Burke, Fichte, and Mazzini, or their intellectual descendants became familiar to them and exercised among them the influence which they had first exercised in the West itself. They came to an acquaintance with the great figures of American independence, with Cavour, Garibaldi, and Bismarck, and with the new doctrines of social Darwinism, not to mention the later nationalist vehemence of Hitler and Mussolini. The academic fare which was laid before them and the climate of ideas and expectations in which they came to live formulated for them their own grievances and aspirations and pointed the paths they might follow. Though the differences were great—as, for example, between Catholic missionary schooling in French Africa, the Sorbonne, the London School of Economics, Oxford, and Lincoln University in Pennsylvania—common elements of the Western tradition still pointed in the same direction. In the more recent phase a variant strand of Western thought and political action has made its impact through the revolutionary doctrines of Marx, Lenin, Stalin, and their followers. . . .

Conclusions that make sense for peoples who have had relatively elaborate experience of nationalism may be completely out of order for newcomers to the national era, standing on the other side of what might be called the Bandung Conference divide. The West, having sown its own national wild oats in the past, is now sometimes inclined to look with a combination of dismay and superior wisdom on the upstart countries which assert an allegedly anachronistic desire to follow the same course. With Indochina gone and much of Africa slipping away, the French have been especially insistent that this is supposed to be a century of interdependence and not of national separatisms. "Nationalism," Foreign Minister Christian Pineau told the General Assembly in the 1957 debate on Algeria, "whatever some of you may think of it, is no longer a sign of progress."

However great the disenchantment of Europe with nationalism, the colonial nationalist is little likely to be persuaded by an argument so easily identifiable with the interest of the West in maintaining some facsimile of its older relationships in a world swiftly sliding out of its grasp. He is, furthermore, exposed to the vulgar temptation of suggesting that if the relinquishment of national sovereignty is really as good as it is made out to be, why have not the Western powers made more venturesome use of it for themselves before urging it upon their overseas clients. Even if it be conceded that nationalism fails to furnish the foundations for an acceptable world order and has outlived its usefulness for the advanced, thoroughly "nationalized," countries of the West—a point which many in the West would vigorously dispute—it has by no means exhausted its contribution to the development of the non-Western peoples. Nationalism, I have contended in earlier pages, has a chronology of its own derived not from the calendar but from the stages of the gradually spreading impact of the revolution which originated in Western Europe. It appears to have an essential role to play for peoples undergoing the kind of social and psychological transformation which that revolution imposes on them. One can plausibly argue that in the different but related stages of the cycle in which Asia and Africa are now engaged nationalism intrudes itself not only with an aura of inevitability but also as the bearer of positive goods.

Such a view carries with it no implication that everything ticketed with a nationalist label should be taken as desirable. The profoundly evil potentialities of nationalism have been amply demonstrated in the West by Fascism, Nazism, and many less globally disastrous movements. There is no reason to assume that its Asian and African variants are less likely to plunge into intolerable excesses. Japan's imperialism, the slaughter accompanying the partition of India, and the pretensions of Mossadegh, Nasser, and other Middle Eastern leaders are clues enough to the directions in which Asian nationalism can turn. Renan's idealized version of the nation as a soul and a spiritual principle is not wholly devoid of meaning, but it needs to be balanced by the harsh reality of national politics and prejudice and by taking into account the many millions whose poverty and ignorance exclude them from any effective share in the nation. . . .

Colonialism has in many respects changed its spots of late, but the basic fact remains that, as a system, it involves the assertion of alien supremacy and the denial of the right and ability of peoples to manage their own affairs. Colonialism created not only the conditions which made nationalism possible, but also, as a complex of relationships subordinating "natives" to expatriate officials and employers, the conditions which made it an appropriate response for those who would regain their self-esteem. At least until the most recent times the white man who went out to any of the imperial domains assumed automatically the privileged position which the imperial order assigned him and which the people of the country were obligated to respect. Writing of Indochina, Paul Mus referred to the "colonial axiom" that the first of the Annamites should come after the last of the French. The assumption that colonial status is degrading was illuminated by the comment of the President of Burma, look-ing back to his days at Cambridge, that while Japanese, Chinese, and Siamese students were accepted as equals, "Indian and Burmese students were merely tolerated, if not treated with open contempt."

Where this principle is explicitly linked to race—as in South Africa's apartheid, the legislation and practices of Southern Rhodesia, or the white taunt in Kenya that the Kikuyu came down from the trees only fifty years ago—the humiliation which is inflicted runs so deep as to be almost beyond repair. What is involved is no longer an accidental or historically conditioned backwardness which may be overcome, but a charge of inherent inferiority against a race as a whole. To make matters worse this charge is often brought most vigorously by white settlers who have taken over the land and preroga-tives of the people whom they condemn and who in this fashion seek to justify their position to themselves and to the world at large. The colonial peoples were not slow to point out that the racialism of empire ran very close to that of the Nazis which the imperial democracies were denouncing, and Nehru contended that the whole ideology of British rule in India was that of "the herrenvolk and the master race."

Even for the French, who have boasted their freedom from Anglo-Saxon race prejudice, racialism has been by no means wholly absent. While it is open to question that Algeria could under any conditions have been successfully assimilated to France, the overt assumption, particularly of the *colons,* that the Moslems were an inferior breed which must be kept in its place made the spread of nationalism an inevitability. The transition of Ferhat Abbas from his reliance on France and his denial of the existence of an Algerian nation in 1936 to nationalist leadership in 1943 coincided with growing disbelief in the possibility of achieving other than subordination to France. Despite brave French pronouncements and much new legislation the postwar years only worked to confirm the disbelief.

Imperial arrogance and racial discrimination have been the prime sources of the vehemence of Asian and African nationalism. Tragically they have also given currency to the conviction that the West, despite its pretensions of having reformed, continues to live by a double standard which justifies acting toward non-white peoples in a fashion that would not be tolerated for the white man. Thus, the United States is accused of seeing it as fitting to drop atom bombs on Asians but not on Europeans, and the West in general of being deeply concerned with sufferings inflicted on white men but casually indifferent to far more widespread sufferings of men of darker shades. As one sample among many, the whole complex of suspicions and resentments boiled to the surface in the speech of the Lebanese delegate on the Hungarian question in the General Assembly on November 21, 1956. With somewhat curious but characteristic disregard of other contemporary UN actions, he asked whether French and British bombs were less deadly than those of the Soviet, and why the fate of Arab refugees in the Gaza strip was ignored while attention was showered on the Hungarian refugees:

Are Egyptian lives, Algerian lives, Cypriote lives and the lives of other subjected peoples worth less in the scales of the United Nations than the lives being lost in Hungary? . . . For when the rights of a European or a Westerner are affected, even though it be at the hands of another European, the whole world becomes indignant. But when the rights of an African or an Asian are at stake, the United Nations' conception of man becomes so different that one is led to believe that contrary to the principles of the Charter, man is not the same everywhere.

Whether or not it is justified by the objective imperial record, the plain fact remains that this attitude is generally shared by those who have been on the receiving end of imperialism. Propaganda has, of course, made the most of all the points it could score in this domain, but the significant element is not that propaganda has whipped sentiment up, but that peoples have been conditioned by their experience to be immediately responsive to appeals couched in such terms. "We have gone forward to build a strong Egypt. We go forward towards political and economic independence," said President Nasser in his speech of July 26, 1956, announcing the nationalization of the Suez Canal Company. "But, whenever we look behind, we do so to destroy the traces of the past, the traces of slavery, exploitation, and domination."

The contributions which nationalism can make are presumably most significant for peoples still in process of establishing their freedom, but even for the older-established nations it retains not only charms but also virtues. The retreat from nationalism in France in the period of the outbreak of World War II was far from presenting a pretty spectacle. Apart from such general contentions as that the nations remain vital centers of free and creative diversity in a world threatened by drab uniformity, more specific claims can be put forward. It is, after all, largely to nationalism that the West looks for a shattering of the Soviet empire, welcoming every nationalist gesture of the Yugoslavs or Poles, Hungarians or Ukrainians, and hoping for the appearance of a Tito among the Chinese. A resurgent nationalism inspired the resistance movements of the European countries overrun by Hitler. Churchill led a Britain whose young men had forgotten that they would not fight for King and Country. There is a ring of authenticity to the comment of the *New Yorker's* London correspondent on the British reaction to Eden's decision to attack Egypt in October 1956: "There has been, too, an undoubted profound psychological pleasure throughout England in seeing, as you hear people say, 'the old lion wag its tail again'; and the fact that the old lion was wagging this much-docked appendage with no directives from a ringmaster in Washington was certainly balm to national feelings." Nationalism can give a lift to the spirits of even the oldest of nations, although, as in the British case, it may also leave some bad effects for the morning after. . . .

At this uncertain point in history no definitive answer can be given to the question whether the nationalism of Asia and Africa will turn out to be a blind alley, leading nowhere except to ultimate disaster, or the path leading toward internationalism which nineteenth-century liberalism proclaimed nationalism to be. Gunnar Myrdal opened an attractive prospect with his comment that

"Only when all these underprivileged nations, with their great multitude of peoples with different racial features, color of skin, religions, folklores, and cultural heritages, have risen to equality of opportunity will the world become integrated." But it remains a wide-open gamble whether freedom and equality will, in fact, be turned toward the end of world integration.

IV.

THE TREATY OF VERSAILLES

The Versailles treaty has been a subject for dispute since it was signed; indeed, the conference which drew it up was under attack even before it completed its work. Whatever the merits or defects of the treaty itself, it was a factor of tremendous importance in the history of the interwar years, in both diplomatic history and in the history of individual nations. As the selections below indicate, it provided a magnificent propaganda weapon for Adolf Hitler; as will be indicated in the discussion of the Munich pact, it provides at least a partial explanation of British policy in 1938. From the readings, it will often seem that the Versailles treaty, like the Magna Carta, is less important for what it was than for what it was believed to be.

The treaty should stimulate one to consider the merits of idealism in action. Did idealism, working through the Fourteen Points, provide a splendid opening for the revisionists, when the Fourteen Points proved too high-minded to put into operation? Did idealism, by lifting men like Harold Nicolson to heights of moral fervor, bring about a dangerous reaction in the direction of cynicism? Did rigid moral principles, when confronted with the inevitable need for compromise, bring about undesirable results which could have been easily avoided by a little frank self-interest and healthy, openly expressed hypocrisy? Or, on the other hand, is idealism, even when compromised, better than an attitude of revenge, and better than campaigning on a platform calling for the hanging of the Kaiser? Is idealism the necessary first step on the road to a just world order? It may be that the answers to these questions depend on the flexibility of the individual administering the idealism, on how shrewdly he can twist the absolute, and on how well he can seemingly reconcile the irreconcilable.

Since the first world war was the war to end all war, and since the peace treaty was intended to confirm that happy fact, it is not surprising that the reactions were bitter when all did not turn out as expected. But before one criticizes, one should contemplate alternatives. How, for example, could the peacemakers have prevented the political disintegration of the Danube valley? Could Woodrow Wilson have been a more effective advocate of moderation from Washington than he was over the negotiating tables of Paris? Should the old "balance of power" system have been restored; could it have been restored? Would the presence of representatives from Germany at the conference have soothed the Germans at home, or would the result have been even greater bitterness and frustration? Was the reparations settlement levied against the defeated powers cruel and unjust, was it simply the device adopted in 1919 to bring home to the Germans the reality of their defeat, just as the Nuremberg Trials were used as retribution a generation later? Or was it a valid charge on Germany, made necessary by the great war damage sustained in northern France? Was it not proper that Germany should pay at least part of the expense of the restoration and rehabilitation made necessary by the fighting? But was the reparations settlement effectively presented, or did it provide Germany with the opportunity to discredit the entire treaty, including the rather lenient political settlement which stood in such contrast to he terms imposed on Russia by the imperial government at Brest-Litovsk? Could it be that there were too many experts, with too many alternatives, at Paris in 1919?

Excepting perhaps only the matter of reparations, the war-guilt clause, Article 231, is the most controversial aspect of the treaty. Whether the clause was justified by history, one may have decided on the basis of the readings in Chapter II. But the psychological factor should also be considered. If the Allies intended to encourage the formation of a "new" Germany, and a "new" Austria, would it not have been more politic to omit references to war guilt? After all, in 1919 the Emperor was gone, and Germany was a democratic republic; but were all the other important "power elites" of Imperial Germany gone too? And as a matter of general policy, is it wise to make a defeated nation admit guilt; is an Article 231 a manifestation of the total war, of the war of absolutes, which has come to mark the twentieth century?

Many historians think that the treaty of Versailles set the style for a new era in diplomacy; that the relations of the great powers were no longer to be guided by trained, experienced, and polished diplomats, who were nurtured in the traditions of the old aristocracies, who were motivated by a loyalty to the European system as a whole, and who felt themselves to be members of a noble profession which embraced honorable men from all countries. From 1919 on, ambassadors and ministers were to become nothing more than agents of their governments, rather than men who played an important and independent role in guiding policy. The pomp and glamour of the prewar world, which were often more than merely decorative, were to dissolve in a democratic age; foreign ministers, and even prime ministers and presidents, henceforth began to conduct negotiations once reserved for the professional diplomat, so that the ups and downs of partisan politics, rather than the enduring interests of a nation, were reflected in the conduct of diplomacy. No longer can diplomacy be secret, but it must now be accompanied by the publicity which inevitably results from the arrivals and departures of heads of state and chiefs of government; moreover, after the propaganda communiqués have been issued, there may be little elbow-room left for negotiation, negotiation during which expectations of wondrous settlements are not raised, and during which positions can be shifted and modified without loss of face and without national humiliation. On the other hand, it may be that the countervailing merits of "democratic diplomacy" are as great as, or greater than, the merits of the "old diplomacy"; perhaps Versailles did not really mark a turning point in diplomatic practice, which continued much the same as before; these are questions for individual judgment.

At times, one is tempted to wonder whether any kind of treaty at all had much chance of ensuring a century of peace, in the manner of the Vienna settlement of 1815. One may examine the Versailles treaty as a whole, or one may consider its political and economic aspects separately, but from whatever angle it is surveyed, the tremendous problems which confronted the men in Paris in 1919 are obvious. Whether more inspired statesmanship could have resolved them, or whether the problems were manifestations of the permanent dilemmas of the twentieth-century world, is something which it is well to contemplate.

1.

Adolf Hitler was an exceedingly shrewd man; he had the knack of using his opponent's arguments for his own benefit. In doing so, of course, he was not bothered by problems of morality or historical accuracy, for, in his mind, such problems of bourgeois ethics should never be allowed to stand in the way of the ultimate ends of the Nazi movement. In the following selection from *Mein Kampf* there will be little discussion of the actual merits or demerits of the Versailles treaty; that is quite appropriate, for to Hitler the issues themselves were not of importance. It was the idea, or what the French might call the *mystique,* which mattered. Nowhere can one find a better example of the conscious projection of a false image than in Adolf Hitler's discussion of the treaties of Brest-Litovsk and Versailles.

HITLER: Mein Kampf *

In this period the Festsaal of the Munich Hofbräuhaus assumed an almost sacred significance for us National Socialists. Every week a meeting, almost always in this room, and each time the hall better filled and the people more devoted. Beginning with the "War Guilt," which at that time nobody bothered about, and the "Peace Treaties," nearly everything was taken up that seemed agitationally expedient or ideologically necessary. Especially to the peace treaties themselves the greatest attention was given. What prophecies the young movement kept making to the great masses! And nearly all of which have now been realized! Today it is easy to speak or write about these things. But in those days a public mass meeting, attended, not by bourgeois shopkeepers, but by incited proletarians, and dealing with the topic, "The Peace Treaty of Versailles," was taken as an attack on the Republic and a sign of a reactionary if not monarchistic attitude. At the very first sentence containing a criticism of Versailles, you had the stereotyped cry flung at you: "What about Brest-Litovsk?" "And Brest-Litovsk?" The masses roared this again and again, until gradually they grew hoarse or the speaker finally gave up his attempt to convince them. You felt like dashing your head against the wall in despair over such people! They did not want to hear or understand that Versailles was a shame and a disgrace, and not even that this dictated peace was an unprecedented pillaging of our people. The destructive work of the Marxists and the poison of enemy propaganda had deprived the people of any sense. And yet we had not even the right to complain! For how immeasurably great was the blame on another side! What had the bourgeoisie done to put a halt to

* From Adolf Hitler, *Mein Kampf* (Boston: Houghton Mifflin, 1962), pp. 463–64, 466–68. Reprinted by permission of Houghton Mifflin Company.

this frightful disintegration, to oppose it and open the way to truth by a better and more thorough enlightenment? Nothing, and again nothing. In those days I saw them nowhere, all the great folkish apostles of today. Perhaps they spoke in little clubs, at teatables, or in circles of like-minded people, but where they should have been, among the wolves, they did not venture; except if there was a chance to howl with the pack. . . .

In those days I learned something important in a short time, *to strike the weapon of reply out of the enemy's hand myself.* We soon noticed that our opponents, especially their discussion speakers, stepped forward with a definite "repertory" in which constantly recurring objections to our assertions were raised, so that the uniformity of this procedure pointed to a conscious, unified schooling. And that was indeed the case. Here we had an opportunity to become acquainted with the incredible discipline of our adversaries' propaganda, and it is still my pride today to have found the means, not only to render this propaganda ineffective, but in the end to strike its makers with their own weapon. Two years later I was a master of this art.

In every single speech it was important to realize clearly in advance the presumable content and form of the objections to be expected in the discussion, and to pull every one of them apart in the speech itself. Here it was expedient to cite the possible objections ourselves at the outset and demonstrate their untenability; thus, the listener, even if he had come stuffed full of the objections he had been taught, but otherwise with an honest heart, was more easily won over when we disposed of the doubts that had been imprinted on his memory. The stuff that had been drummed into him was automatically refuted and his attention drawn more and more to the speech.

This is the reason why, right after my first lecture on the "Peace Treaty of Versailles," which I had delivered to the troops while still a so-called "educator," I changed the lecture and now spoke of the "Peace Treaties of Brest-Litovsk and Versailles." For after a short time, in fact, in the course of the discussion about this first speech of mine, I was able to ascertain that the people really knew nothing at all about the peace treaty of Brest-Litovsk, but that the adroit propaganda of their parties had succeeded in representing this very treaty as one of the most shameful acts of rape in the world. The persistence with which this lie was presented over and over to the great masses accounted for the fact that millions of Germans regarded the peace treaty of Versailles as nothing more than just retribution for the crime committed by us at Brest-Litovsk, thus viewing any real struggle against Versailles as an injustice and sometimes remaining in the sincerest moral indignation. And this among other things was why the shameless and monstrous word *"reparations"* was able to make itself at home in Germany. This vile hypocrisy really seemed to millions of our incited national comrades an accomplishment of higher justice. Dreadful, but it was so. The best proof of this was offered by the propaganda I initiated against the peace treaty of Versailles, which I introduced by some enlightenment regarding the treaty of Brest-Litovsk. I contrasted the two peace treaties, compared them point for point, showed the actual boundless humanity of the one treaty compared to the inhuman cruelty of the second, and the result was telling. At that time I spoke on this theme at meetings of two thousand people, and often I was struck by the glances of three thousand six hundred hostile eyes. And three hours later I had before me a surging mass full of the holiest indignation and boundless wrath. Again a great lie had been torn out of the hearts and brains of a crowd numbering thousands, and a truth implanted in its place.

I considered these two lectures on "The True Causes of the World War" and on "The Peace Treaties of Brest-Litovsk and Versailles," the most important of all, and so I repeated and repeated them dozens of times, always renewing the form, until, on this point at least, a certain clear and unified conception became current among the people from among whom the movement gathered its first members.

2.

The Versailles treaty bred disillusionment among many young Anglo-American idealists, Harold Nicolson among them. His book, *Peacemaking 1919,* is based on his own recollections as an expert attached to the British delegation in Paris; it gives one an unusually sensitive picture of the atmosphere of Paris during the days following the conclusion of the war. The frustrations, the antagonisms, and the loathing of Germany—the latter intensified by the torpedoing of the *Leinster* a few days before the armistice—are clearly pictured. One can also sense the ill-will which existed between the various cliques of experts, the clashes of personal pride, and the bitterness of having one's long-considered advice ignored. Like many others, Mr. Nicolson found himself, not participating in a triumph of idealism on the highest level, but spending much time on minor issues involving what seemed to him sordid compromise. Harold Nicolson is the son of one of Britain's most influential diplomats, the late Lord Carnock (Sir Arthur Nicolson). He served in the diplomatic corps for some time himself, and has achieved considerable fame through his political career and through his writings, which include biographies of French literary figures and prominent Englishmen.

NICOLSON: Peacemaking 1919 *

The purpose of this book is . . . not so much to formulate a record of events, as to catch, before it evaporates, the unhealthy and unhappy atmosphere of the Peace Conference; to convey some impression of that gradual drift, away from our early peaks of aspiration towards the low countries where figures laboured hurriedly together in a gathering fog. I apprehend that unless the pressure (the actual inevitability) of this atmosphere is realised as a determining factor in itself, the historian may approach the Conference with wisdom after the event, and may concentrate, in critical tranquility, upon apportioning

* From Harold Nicolson, *Peacemaking 1919* (London: Constable and Co. Ltd., 1933), pp. 185–89. Reprinted by permission of Harcourt, Brace and World, Inc.

praise and blame. I do not think, however, that any useful description of the Paris Conference can be conveyed in terms of ethical, as distinct from technical, values.

The Conference may, as Mr. Winston Churchill has said, have been "a turbulent collision of embarrassed demagogues." . . . Yet in spite of this, many durable, and some useful things were accomplished. Many evil things were avoided. None the less, there were few of us who were not disappointed: and in some of us the Conference inculcated a mood of durable disbelief—a conviction that human nature can, like a glacier, move but an inch or two in every thousand years.

I wish . . . to summarise some, at least, of what might be called the psychological factors (or were they symptoms?) of failure; to comment upon the gradual deterioration of our state of mind; to indicate our "change of heart"; and to ascribe, if possible, this decline of thought and feeling to some tangible causes. The historian, with every justification, will come to the conclusion that we were very stupid men. I think we were. Yet I also think that the factor of stupidity is inseparable from all human affairs. It is too often disregarded as an inevitable concomitant of human behaviour; it is too often employed merely as a term of personal affront.

What, in the first place, was the nature of this moral and intellectual deterioration? I can speak with assurance only of my own change of heart, yet I believe that the mutations through which I passed were shared by many others, and that my own loss of idealism coincided with a similar loss of idealism on the part of those (and they were many) who had come to the Conference fired by the same certitudes as myself. Our change of heart can be stated as follows. We came to Paris confident that the new order was about to be established; we left it convinced that the new order had merely fouled the old. We arrived as fervent apprentices in the school of President Wilson: we left as renegades. I wish to suggest, . . . (and without bitterness), that this unhappy diminution of standard was very largely the fault (or one might say with greater fairness "the misfortune") of democratic diplomacy.

We arrived determined that a Peace of justice and wisdom should be negotiated: we left it, conscious that the Treaties imposed upon our enemies were neither just nor wise. To those who desire to measure for themselves the width of the gulf which sundered intention from practice I should recommend a perusal of the several Notes addressed to the Supreme Council by the German Delegation at Versailles. An excellent summary and confrontation of these Notes is furnished by Professor Hazeltine in Volume II of Temperley's *History of the Peace Conference*. It is impossible to read the German criticism without deriving the impression that the Paris Peace Conference was guilty of disguising an Imperialistic peace under the surplice of Wilsonism, that seldom in the history of man has such vindictiveness cloaked itself in such unctuous sophistry. Hypocrisy was the predominant and unescapable result. Yet was this hypocrisy wholly conscious, wholly deliberate? I do not think so. I certainly agree that the sanctimonious pharisaism of the Treaties is their gravest fault. Yet was there any conscious dissimulation? In some cases (such as the article forbidding Austria to join with Germany) a deliberately evasive form of words was consciously employed. Yet in most cases, hypocrisy *just happened*. How did it happen? The fact that, as the Conference progressed, we were scarcely conscious of our own falsity, may indicate that some deterioration of moral awareness had taken place. We did not realise what we were doing. We did not realise how far we were drifting from our original basis. We were exhausted and overworked. We kept on mumbling our old formulas in the hope that they still bore some relation to our actions. There were few moments when we said to ourselves "This is unjust": there were many moments when we said to ourselves "Better a bad treaty to-day, than a good treaty four months hence." In the dust of controversy, in the rattle of time-pressure, we lost all contact with our guiding stars. In interludes the dust would settle, the machine would stop, and we would observe, with tired regret, that these stars were themselves fading pale against the sky. *"Il faut aboutir"* ["It must be finished"] they shouted at us: and we returned to the din and dimness of our compromises. We still desired ardently to maintain our principles intact: it was only in the after-vacancy that we realised that they remained for us only in the form of empty words: it was then, and then only, that we faced the fact that the falsity of our position had led us into being false. It was by then far too late.

The above is not written in any desire to defend our state of mind. I am examining only: I am not defending. My contention is that this dimming of our moral awareness constituted the most regrettable and perhaps the only interesting element in our deterioration. I wish to explain how it occurred that in the dust of incessant argument, amid the by-paths of unceasing detail, we strayed away from the main avenues of our intention: and how it was unconsciously, rather than consciously, that we boasted, on arrival, to have come the way we meant.

The point is, I think, of some importance. If future generations come to believe that the Paris Conference was, in every single point, deliberately and exceptionally hypocritical, they will (when they also come to attend Congresses) be less on their guard against the tired falsity which is inseparable from any attempt to adjust high general principles to low practical detail. In every discussion between sovereign States claiming equality with each other, decisions can only be taken by a unanimous and not by a majority vote. This inevitable curse of unanimity leads to the no less inevitable curse of compromise. All compromises have an element of falsity, but when they have to be referred back to governing principles or generalisations a double falsity is introduced. I do not deny the ghastly hypocrisy of the Paris Treaties: I contend only that this hypocrisy was not, in every case, conscious or deliberate; that it was not, in every case, humanly avoidable; and that similar hypocrisy may not, in every case, be humanly avoidable in the future.

3.

Etienne Mantoux was educated at the University of Paris and the Ecole des Sciences Politiques; he also studied at the London School of Economics. He was killed in action during the last days of the war, in April 1945, after having participated in the liberation of Paris. In the following passages from his book, *The Carthaginian Peace,* he takes issue with the late Lord Keynes himself, and attacks the premise that the economic clauses of the Versailles treaty were "one of the most outrageous acts of a cruel victor in civilized history"; rather, M. Mantoux argues that Lord Keynes' predictions were far too pessimistic, and sees the political aspects of the treaty as having been far more significant. Not only should the reader carefully examine the contentions set forth below, but he should also ask himself whether the economic and political aspects of the treaty can be separated for purposes of analysis.

MANTOUX: The Carthaginian Peace *

[Lord Keynes'] *The Economic Consequences of the Peace* appeared in London in December 1919. It contained a vehement indictment of the Peace Treaty, and accused its authors of perjury, imbecility, and mass murder. The book became at once a best seller in Great Britain and in the United States. It was soon to be a classic of the English language; and its felicity of expression was certainly remarkable.

"Paris," wrote Mr. Keynes, "was a nightmare, and everyone there was morbid. . . ." Its atmosphere was "hot and poisoned," its halls "treacherous" . . . Paris was a "morass." The European statesmen of the Conference were "subtle and dangerous spellbinders . . . ," the "subtlest sophisters and most hypocritical draftsmen"; what inspired them was "debauchery of thought and speech . . . ," "greed, sentiment, prejudice and deception. . . ." Their labours were "empty and arid intrigue," "the dreams of designing diplomats," "the unveracities of politicians," "endless controversy and intrigue," "contorted, miserable, utterly unsatisfactory to all parties." President Wilson was "a blind and deaf Don Quixote"; he was "playing blind man's bluff" in the party; he ended in "collapse" and "extraordinary betrayal." The Treaty was clothed with "insincerity," with "an apparatus of self-deception," with "a web of Jesuitical exegesis," which were to distinguish it "from all its historical predecessors." Its provisions were "dishonourable," "ridiculous and injurious," "abhorrent and detestable"; they revealed "imbecile greed," "senseless greed overreaching itself," "oppression and rapine." For the Treaty "reduced Germany to servitude." It refused Germany "even a modicum of prosperity, at least for a generation to come"; it "perpetuated its economic ruin"; year by year, if it were enforced, "Germany must be kept impoverished and her children starved and crippled." Thus the Peace, that would "sow the decay of the whole civilized life of

* From Etienne Mantoux, *The Carthaginian Peace* (New York: Charles Scribner's Sons, 1952), pp. 5, 162–63, 187–88. Reprinted by permission of Mme Paul Mantoux.

Europe," was "one of the most outrageous acts of a cruel victor in civilized history. . . ."

Mr. Keynes predicted that the Treaty, if it was carried into effect, "must impair yet further, when it might have restored, the delicate, complicated organisation, already shaken and broken by war, through which alone the European peoples can employ themselves and live." Europe would be threatened with "a long, silent process of semi-starvation, and of a gradual, steady lowering of the standards of life and comfort." Ten years after the Treaty, European production was well above its pre-war level, and European standards of living had never been higher.

He predicted that the iron output of Europe would decline as a consequence of the Treaty. In the ten years that followed the Treaty, the iron output of Europe, which had fallen considerably during the War, increased almost continuously. In 1929, Europe produced 10 per cent more iron than in the record year 1913, and would no doubt have produced still more had not the producers combined to restrict output for fear of injuring prices by overproduction.

He predicted that the iron and steel output of Germany would diminish. By 1927, Germany produced nearly 30 per cent more iron and 38 per cent more steel than in the record year 1913, within the same territorial limits.

He predicted that the efficiency of the German coal-mining industry lowered by the War, would remain low as a consequence of the Peace. By 1925, the efficiency of labour, which had dropped seriously in the meantime, was already higher, in the Ruhr coal industries, than in 1913; in 1927 it was higher by nearly 20 per cent; and in 1929 by more than 30 per cent.

He predicted that a pre-war level of output could not be expected in the German coal industry. In 1920, 1921, and 1922, coal output was well above the average level of the five years preceding the war, within the same territorial limits. It fell sharply in 1923, and was slightly below pre-war average in 1924. It was above that average in 1925; and in 1926, it was already higher than in the record year 1913.

He predicted that Germany "cannot export coal in the near future, . . . if she is to continue as an industrial nation." In the first year following the Treaty, Germany exported (net) 15 million tons of coal; and in 1926 she exported (net) 35 million tons, or *twice* the amount of the average (1909–13) pre-war exports of *all* her pre-war territories.

He predicted that the German mercantile marine "cannot be restored for many years to come on a scale adequate to meet the requirements of her own commerce." The total German tonnage was a little above 5 millions in 1913. It was reduced in 1920 to 673,000; but in 1924 it already approached 3 million tons; in 1930 it was well above 4 million, and German liners were the wonder of the transatlantic world.

He predicted that "after what she has suffered in the war and by the Peace," Germany's annual savings would "fall far short of what they were before." The monthly increase in German savings bank deposits was 84 million in 1913; in 1925 it had become 103 million; and in 1928 it was nearly 210 million.

He predicted that Germany's annual surplus would be reduced to less than 2 million marks. In 1925, the net accumulation of domestic capital was estimated at 6.4 milliards, and in 1927 at 7.6 milliards.

He predicted that in the next thirty years, Germany could not possibly be expected to pay more than 2 milliard marks a year in Reparation. In the six years preceding September 1939, Germany, by Hitler's showing, had spent each year on rearmament alone about seven times as much. . . .

The present book was never intended as an apologia for the Treaty of Versailles; but while the economic defects of that settlement were, for the most part, illusory or exaggerated, the present writer shares the opinion of those who have maintained that the political defects were the really decisive ones. It may have been a mistake, from the economic point of view, to allow or even encourage the break-up of the Danubian Monarchy into several sovereign states; but these states were always free, had they found it to their interest, to organize themselves into some sort of economic federation, and in so far as they failed to do this, the economic loss thus caused has been sustained primarily by themselves. How much more serious to the rest of the world, on the other hand, have been the *political* consequences of the division of Central and South-Eastern Europe! There, as has in fact frequently been pointed out, lay the cardinal vice of the system—in the constitution of a Europe where a strong and centralized Germany of some 70 millions remained surrounded by a string of small states, who had to rely for the preservation of their independence upon the assistance of faraway Powers; to put it shortly, in the failure, and one might almost say in the deliberate failure, to establish a true *balance of power*. For Wilson himself, intent though he was upon the rejection of this type of diplomatic system, had foreseen that the Europe which he had thus left, largely by his own doing, was not one that could be expected to stand by itself—that without the support of *outside* Powers, Germany would yet have her will upon it. "All the nations that Germany meant to crush and reduce to the status of tools in her own hands have been redeemed by this war," he had explained, "and given the guarantee of the strongest nations of the world that nobody shall invade their liberty again. If you do not want to give them that guarantee, then you make it certain that . . . the attempt will be made again, and if another war starts like this one, are you going to keep out of it?" Now the League of Nations was designed to ensure precisely this kind of support. But the Powers concerned proved themselves unwilling, undecided, or unprepared to face their responsibilities in time. The truth is, that the spirit in which the League had been conceived presumed too much of them. As has been well said, "it was not the League that failed, but the nations." And if Wilson was guilty of one illusion, that illusion was mankind. . . .

4.

L. C. B. Seaman's opinions about the Versailles treaty are quite as positive as his judgments about the origins of the Great War. There is little doubt that the following selection, covering as it does just about every issue that arises in a discussion of the Peace Conference, will arouse great hostility in many readers. That, however, is one of the reasons for its inclusion here. Mr. Seaman's judgments, sometimes shrewd, sometimes a little extreme, should stimulate all but the most listless and bored into either vigorous attack or enthusiastic defense. Of course, it may be that Mr. Seaman is right about some issues and wrong about others.

SEAMAN: From Vienna to Versailles *

From January 1917 until the late spring of 1918, the allies and President Wilson between them proceeded to dangle before the eyes of a world struggling in the toils of a seemingly endless war the intoxicating prospect of a heaven on earth at the end of it all. Wilson was inspired by that deep sense of conviction which is the unique possession of those who combine profound idealism with profounder ignorance. The British and French supported him as an act of diplomacy and public relations. It is easy to be cynical about this but the difficulty was that the allies could only get Wilson's help by uttering phrases of the sort that he himself delighted to utter. In addition, people had the right to expect a better world as a result of their suffering, and the statesmen had a moral duty to try to give it to them. The trouble was that Wilson's exalted unawareness of realities was not matched by serious statesmanship among the French and the English. Clemenceau merely wanted revenge, and Lloyd George, though he understood people with intuitive genius, understood foreign affairs hardly at all, and was not much better informed about Europe than Wilson. A statesmanlike synthesis between idealism and the facts of the European situation was therefore not forthcoming, and it is perhaps not too harsh to say that diplomatic history from 1918 to 1920 is concerned with a chaos compounded of ignorance and smooth opportunism. The English badly wanted to moderate Wilson's idealism; but what they did seems to have been to support it in public, while manoeuvring against it in secret. The result was to discredit the peace settlement, not because its terms were bad, but because they failed to conform to a series of wildly exaggerated promises that ought never to have been made.

Wilson viewed the war in much the same way as the left wing in England had viewed it in 1914 and was again beginning to view it under the influence of the heady slogans of the Russian Revolution. As far as Wilson was concerned, Germany's crime was adequately defined as that of having violated the territory of small nations; and all that the war was for was the restoration of these small nations to their former status. There was nothing greatly wrong with the state system in Europe in 1914 as such; and Wilson would have liked it restored with only minor changes. The future would be looked after by removing what were to be considered the "real" causes of war. Among these were

* From L. C. B. Seaman, *From Vienna to Versailles* (New York: Coward-McCann, 1956), pp. 189–91, 192–95, 196–202, 204–11. Reprinted by permission of Coward-McCann, Inc.

Prussian militarism, the abolition of which would at once transform Germany into a liberal and pacific democracy; secret treaties, regardless of the fact that few important treaties were really very secret and that no treaty, secret or otherwise, was invoked by any of the contestants in 1914; and—very confusingly indeed since they could hardly exist together—the principle of the balance of power and something dramatically called "international anarchy." All were to be abolished by general disarmament, beginning with the Germans, and by the creation of a League of Nations which, by waving the fairy wand of universal brotherhood among nations, would enable everyone to live happily ever afterwards. . . .

The trouble with this amiable nonsense was that it impressed itself on the minds of everybody at the time except the Germans. The Germans ignored it; and only when they were at last faced with the prospect of total defeat did they suddenly proclaim that they had been offered a "just" peace which would not injure their greatness. The point was that by the end of 1918 the Germans had forfeited any right to appeal to these principles, because to all intents and purposes they had rejected the Fourteen Points. They had preferred instead to answer them with an all-out drive for total victory. The German reply to the Fourteen Points was perfectly clear. It consisted of the treaty of Brest-Litovsk with Russia and that of Bucharest with Roumania. These, coming hard on the heels of Wilson's Fourteen Points and Four Principles, proved beyond doubt that the German idea of "a peace of understanding and conciliation" involved unlimited annexation. The German Reich was not, after all, an organization like other state organizations in Europe. It was a ruthless machine for subjugation and conquest. The German Reich regarded the rest of Europe as populated by racial inferiors, and its aim was the reduction of the other states of Europe to the condition of colonial dependencies.

Wilson's reaction was clear enough, but ignored in Germany and barely noticed even in the history books. In April 1918 he said: "I am ready to discuss a fair and just and honest peace at any time. . . . But the answer when I proposed such a peace [i.e. in January 1918] came from the German commanders in Russia and I cannot mistake the meaning of the answer. I accept the challenge. . . . Germany has once more said that force and force alone shall decide whether justice and peace shall reign in the affairs of men."

. . . Thus the arrogant self-confidence and ruthlessness of the Germans in their dealings with defeated Russia and Roumania, and their repeated insistence that the only peace they were interested in was one which gathered the fruits of victory into their own barns, had knocked most of the generosity out of the heads of allied statesmen long before the Paris conference opened. Both Wilson and the British were now convinced that to achieve a "peace without victory" was, as far as Germany was concerned, out of the question. Even before the armistice the allies had adopted the view that the Fourteen Points were to be open to modification only in a sense favourable to themselves and not at all in a sense favourable to the Germans. The way was therefore clear for Clemenceau when the conference opened. The purpose of the settlement was not at all to try to be fair and just to the Germans, but to impose drastic penalties upon them.

Unfortunately, whereas Wilson's various idealistic pronouncements had received world-wide publicity, the modifications of them decided upon between April and October 1918 had not. Worse still, nothing could deter Wilson from continuing all through the year to utter noble-sounding phrases which implied that the conference would be guided solely by the most exalted precepts. "No peace," he announced as late as September 27th 1918, "shall be obtained by any kind of compromise or abatement of the principles we have avowed." Wilson's historical studies can have taught him but little if he could think in terms like that. The truth was that Wilson suffered from much the same sort of moral megalomania as that which afflicted Alexander I in 1815 and Frederick William IV between 1840 and 1848. Elevated and sonorous phrases were propounded by all of them because such phrases were currently popular and because they were men intoxicated by a sense of their own righteousness and by the opportunity they imagined to be theirs to become the saviours of the world. The label "demagogue" ought not to be restricted to those who, regardless of consequences, appeal to the lowest in the human mind. It ought to be applied sometimes to men like Wilson, who appeal to the highest in men; for to tell humanity that peace and justice are about to be achieved without "any kind of compromise or abatement" is to practise the worst of all forms of deceit.

Wilson made a further resolution, induced by Brest-Litovsk, to strengthen his opinion that the Hohenzollerns must go, and with them, the Prussian "militarists"; Germany must become a democracy. Accordingly, he virtually refused to treat with the German Imperial Government. He would demand "not peace negotiations but surrender" if he had to deal "with the military masters and monarchical autocrats" of Germany, and would sign only with "the veritable representatives of the German people."

This was a blunder. It created the entirely false impression among the Germans that if they overthrew the Hohenzollerns and manufactured democratic institutions they would escape the consequences of defeat. The facts are that the British, and the Americans by now, had already decided on a severe peace, which would not be limited by the Fourteen Points; and they were to be given no chance by the French to go back on that sensible decision. But the Germans did not know this; nor, it seems, did public opinion with the disastrous result that the peace treaty could, not without justice, be regarded as having been brought about by a piece of shameful deceit on the part of the allies.

What made this all the more ironical was the fact that the real act of deceit came from the Germans themselves. The German Revolution of 1918, out of which the Weimar Republic emerged, was an attempt to bamboozle the British and Americans into granting Germany a lenient peace treaty, while at the same time keeping the German army intact, if not in its organization, at the least in its reputation. . . .

The consequence . . . was that only the German army leadership emerged intact from it. The idea that because the Imperial autocrats and militarists started the war it was impossible to sign a peace treaty with them was supremely illogical. They, one would have thought, were just the people with whom it should have been signed. Versailles should have been signed by plenipotentiaries representing Ludendorff rather than by shadow creatures representing Ebert, who stood for nothing real in Germany at all. For, obscured by these shadowy creatures, the army leaders survived, undefeated in the hour of defeat, and unsullied by the slightest association with the document that registered that defeat.

Moreover—and the point is vital—so little had been changed by the absurd policy of trying to compel the Germans to be democratic by allied fiat that it was nothing but the sheer lack of an army to fight with that prevented the Germans from resuming the war as soon as the treaty terms were presented to them. The army leaders meanwhile remained the real force behind the scenes in Germany and the real representatives of German opinion. They could now say, and not without a show of truth, that they had been tricked, if not into defeat, at any rate into the Treaty of Versailles.

Thus the failure of the allies to insist on the real nature of the German menace until after Wilson had issued his Fourteen Points was a major disaster. For while the Fourteen Points and Four Principles and Wilson's subsequent high-sounding elaborations of them were disseminated far and wide, the allied recovery of a sense of realities after Brest-Litovsk was not. This was to lead to that undermining of their faith in their own cause which almost led to England and France losing the Second World War before it had started. Worse still, the misguided attempt to make the Germans democrats by compulsion created in the Germans the impression that they could escape the consequences of their responsibility for the war, and of their defeat. They who in the event of victory would have conceded it to nobody were themselves to be treated with justice: and the existence of the Fourteen Points enabled them to go on insisting subsequently that they "ought" to have had justice and that they were an innocent people deceived by the allies into laying down arms on terms which the allies had no intention of carrying out. So it came to be accepted that the Germans were in a sad plight, not because they had started and then lost a war, but because the wicked allies had cheated them in 1918.

The impression was reinforced by the decision to exclude the Germans from the negotiation of the treaty terms. Their presence would have greatly prolonged those negotiations; but the presentation of the terms in the form of what amounted to a comprehensive ultimatum to a people much less capable of free choice even than the Serbs in 1914 gave the Germans yet another chance to evade the full realization of the fact that they had lost the war. It might still have been possible to bring it home to them if they had been compelled to admit it point by point at the conference table. Instead they could henceforth, and with a show of justification, speak of the treaty as a *"diktat."* It was, as has been said, of paramount importance that accredited German representatives should themselves have been brought to an admission of defeat; instead, that salutary confession was never made by the Germans at all. They were foolishly allowed to go on record as helpless martyrs protesting vainly against other people's injustice, instead of as repentant criminals who freely admitted both their guilt and their acceptance of its consequences.

As it was, the German claim that the terms of Versailles could be summed up in the sentence "L'Allemagne renonce à son existence" must be regarded as one of the bad jokes of recent history. By 1925, German steel production was twice that of Great Britain and while the latter's industrial production in that year was only ninety-two per cent of the 1914 figure the corresponding figure for Germany was 117. For a country that had renounced its existence, Germany did very well indeed in the fifteen years after 1919, despite its losses in that year and the later inflation and depression. The territorial settlement imposed on the Germans was not in fact particularly severe. The return of Alsace-Lorraine to France was inevitable and only the Germans would have expected anything else; and the other cessions to Belgium, Czechoslovakia and Denmark were not crippling. It is worth recalling that the only standard of comparison by which the Versailles treaty can be properly judged is that of the Germans' own treaty with the Russians at Brest-Litovsk. This the Germans regarded as a peace based on "understanding and conciliation," yet it deprived Russia of thirty-four per cent of her population, fifty-four per cent of her industrial undertakings and eighty-nine per cent of her coal mines. Nor was the cession of territory to the new Poland at all the tragedy the Germans insisted it was. While it might be good for historians in general to be a little less partisan in their treatment of the Polish problem, it is requisite that they accept as fundamental the proposition that Poles had as much right to a national existence and to the economic necessities of that existence as the Germans. This the Germans never accepted; and much sympathy was sought and obtained by them on account of the separation of East Prussia from the rest of the Reich by the Polish corridor. But there was nothing in the least unnatural about this. It was a mere matter of geography. It was not the fault of the Poles or the allies but of the Germans themselves that East Prussia was where it was, on the further side of Poland, and it was no more contrary to justice than the fact that an Englishman who wished to travel overland to Gibraltar had to cross the territory of France and Spain. Nor was the loss of the German colonial empire a serious blow. It made far less difference to the Germans than the disappearance of their colonial empire would have made to the French; and the Germans would certainly have taken over the French colonies had the allies been defeated. Finally, there was nothing at all vindictive about either the demilitarization of the Rhineland or the fifteen-year cession of the Saar to the French.

Of all the various objections to the disarmament and reparations clauses, the most serious was that they could not be enforced. It was also a mistake to imply that German disarmament was to be connected with general disarmament. The real reason for the disarmament clauses was that it was hoped they would make Germany powerless. Instead, it was indicated that the object was to enable the other powers to disarm. This they did not do, and the fact provided more nourishment for the belligerent self-pity of the Germans. Thus the allies got nothing out of the disarmament clauses except a general reputation for hypocrisy. As for the celebrated "war guilt" clause, inserted to justify reparations, it is difficult to see what were the value of the objections to it. It imputed "sole" responsibility not to Germany, but to "Germany and her allies." Whether this was intended to mean that Germany and her allies were responsible legally, practically, or morally does not really matter. In whatever sense the word "responsibility" is taken, to apply it to Germany and her allies was merely to state historical fact. The clause naturally stimulated a number of historians inside and outside Germany to try to prove that the war was really the fault of the French or the Russians, or Sir Edward Grey, or armament manufacturers or the balance of power and so forth; but by now there is no need to take such attempts seriously.

The problem of Austria-Hungary is often regarded as a quite separate issue from that of Germany, but was in fact inseparable from it. It has been seen that the dissolution of the Dual Monarchy was not envisaged when the war began, though wartime diplomacy made it probable: it is not even precisely specified in the Fourteen Points. It has been alleged also that but for Wilson's energetic encouragement of the principle of self-determination it might have held together. This is perhaps not only to under-estimate the strength of the Czechoslovak and Jugoslav liberation movements, but to ignore the fact that the course of the war had reduced the Bismarckian division of Germany into one state governed from Berlin and another governed from Vienna to a palpable fiction. The events of the war faced Europe with a solid German-Magyar power bloc stretching from the Baltic to the Balkans and directly controlled by Berlin. It is difficult to see how Austria-Hungary could have been preserved after 1919 and yet kept free from control by Berlin. For the simple fact was that only if Austria-Hungary was entirely freed from Berlin could it be anything other than what it had been from 1908 to 1918—a means for the maintenance of German domination throughout south-east Europe and a permanent jumping-off ground for the penetration of Turkey and Asia Minor. A German *imperium* from Berlin to Bagdad was implicit in any scheme for the maintenance of the Habsburg Monarchy after 1919; and in applying the principle of self-determination to the Slavs and the Roumanians the peace treaties did in fact create a state system which, while it lasted, prevented that *imperium* from reviving. A great Poland, a great Roumania and a great Serbia rechristened Jugoslavia, together with Czechoslovakia, effectively cut off Germany from Russia, from the Balkans and from Turkey, reduced the Magyars to impotence, and Austria to its ancient status as a German outpost amid a world of Slavs. The refusal to allow Austria, even when shorn of its non-German provinces, to unite with the German Reich called forth much sympathy among the many critics of the 1919 settlement. Yet it was to miss the whole significance of the war to imagine that either peace or justice would have been served by making Austria a part of the Reich. Berlin's influence would then stretch directly via

Vienna and (inevitably) via Budapest to the borders of Transylvania; it would have loomed over almost the entire northern frontier of Jugoslavia; and would have condemned Czechoslovakia to encirclement by its ancient German and Magyar enemies from the very day of its birth.

Seen in this light, the peace treaties of 1919 have a clear justification as an attempt to contain the German Reich by the liberation of the Slavs, and the peasants of Transylvania. The cause both of peace and justice was served in eastern Europe by the treaties; and better served than they had been for centuries. It was not the Versailles system but the success of the Germans in wrecking it in 1938 and 1939 that caused the Second World War. The real German grievance against the settlement was not that it was a *"diktat"* or that they had been cheated by President Wilson. It was chiefly that it prevented them from dominating and exploiting the valleys of the Vistula and the Danube and kept them away from the approaches to Asia Minor and the Ukraine, and because it emphatically asserted that in south-eastern Europe the Slavs had as much right to an independent existence as the Germans and Magyars. . . .

The real weakness of the Versailles system . . . lies not in the creation of the small states to the east and south of the Germans, but in the absence of any effective means of maintaining and defending their existence. . . .

In resources and manpower, France, when Versailles was really the capital of Europe and not merely the title of a peace treaty, had been the largest civilized state in the western world. Now she was not. The gravest weakness of the Versailles Settlement is therefore that it created a state system which depended exclusively on France to maintain it; for France was not strong enough.

The solution was to follow precedent and maintain in peace the coalition that had won the war; but the military guarantees for France which would alone have made a reality of the Versailles system were not forthcoming from either England or the United States. The consequence was that France was committed to that neurotic search for "security" in the 1920's which so irritated her friends but was an inevitable consequence of the fact that the peace treaties imposed on France duties that were too great for her.

For England, France was, by 1919, what she had been in 1856—the loyal ally who had done too well out of the war. . . . As the peace conference ended, the British had resumed that unawareness of realities which had characterized them in 1914. They had reverted to their former belief in the innate superiority of Germans over Frenchmen and Slavs. . . .

The truth was that the British did not much like the principle of self-determination. Although an acceptable slogan for encouraging the dissolution of the enemy from within, and for justifying the war to those many Americans still susceptible to phrases about *"entente* imperialism" it was a very dangerous slogan to the ears of an Imperial War Cabinet in London. Refusals to grant self-determination to Ireland, to India, to Egypt and to the Boers either had been or were about to be major issues in British politics. Once established as the sole principle of political justice it could mean the division of the empire into a series of independent sovereignties. . . .

It is thus not true that the east European states provided an inadequate bulwark against Germany. They were a quite adequate device for preventing that German domination of the non-Germans which had for so long been the characteristic feature of east European history. Nor is it a fair criticism of the settlement to say that these states were a temptation to the Germans to make a war. It was not their weakness but that of the wartime allies that proved the real incitement to the Germans. Equally irrelevant is the argument that their existence was in some way artificial because it depended on the weakness of Russia after 1917. There is much to be said for the view that it was a strong Russia rather than a weak Russia that better served their security. Certainly, while Germany was the only potential threat to them, a strong Russia was as necessary a guarantee of their safety as a strong France backed by Great Britain and the United States.

. . . It is relevant to notice how much harm was done by the setting up of the League of Nations in 1919. The peace could be preserved only by the great powers who had so arduously earned it. Only an alliance of Great Britain, the United States, France and Russia to defend the treaties by force of arms could keep Germany within bounds, as the facts eventually proved. But the first three powers were afraid of Bolshevism, and were themselves regarded by the Russians as nothing more than imperialist interventionists; the United States wanted to go on pretending that Europe did not exist; the British wanted German markets for their goods, and resented the power and the ruthlessness of the French. A League of Nations which excluded Germany, from which the United States and Russia excluded themselves, and in which the British pursued one policy and the French an entirely different one, had the disastrous effect of presenting a war-weary public opinion with the mere shadow of collective security. Worse still, it was a shadow just substantial enough to prevent people from realizing that if the machinery had been there, raucous voices would still have been raised in condemnation of it as "Great Power domination" or as "return to the balance of power." In a famous, but coolly-received phrase, Neville Chamberlain was later to say that it was "midsummer madness" to suppose that the League of Nations could protect anyone from aggression. Unfortunately the words had been true from the day of the League's foundation. No lesson was writ larger over the history of the nineteenth century than the simple one that just as only great powers could start wars, only the great powers could prevent them. The League of Nations was a failure because that lesson was ignored.

5.

Even though the following selection looks at the treaty of Versailles from an American point of view, it provides one of the most effective rebuttals to the critics of Versailles. Mr. Birdsall, a former professor of history at Williams College who later entered government service, may be too sympathetic to Woodrow Wilson to suit the tastes of some readers; others may deplore his lack of respect for "the methods of social psychology" and the "remote, detached, and scientific" approach to the study of history; but his book remains an unusually balanced and rational treatment of the problems faced by the Allied statesmen in 1919.

BIRDSALL: Versailles Twenty Years After *

The intellectual nihilism of the twenty years since Versailles has destroyed faith in the Wilsonian program at Paris. By misrepresenting the character of the treaty, the motives that inspired it, above all by denial of any genuine American stake in European settlement, it has provided the strongest moral force by which Hitler "softens" his victims before striking them down with physical force. The disillusioned liberal has been the unwitting ally of the cynical advocate of physical force as the only conceivable basis for world politics.

In such an atmosphere, any constructive effort like Wilson's is bound to appear silly and unrealistic. The romantic liberal must see the immediate realization of his hopes or turn on the author of his hopes with charges of betrayal, and those who have thoroughly cynical reasons for opposing a new order will welcome the charges. The statesman who labors for the best constructive results obtainable in a chaotic world starts under the terrible handicap of a war on two fronts: against cynical opposition, and equally against his sentimental and perfectionist supporters. At Paris the situation was complicated by the fact that the American Delegation contained not merely representatives of the Simon-pure liberal school, but advocates of the opposition itself, not in any cynical sense, but because they were so profoundly impressed with political realities as they existed that instinctively they thought in terms of compromise beyond the limits of any real necessity.

In this welter of conflicting viewpoints it has recently become fashionable to eschew all standards of judgment and to resort to the methods of social psychology in describing the mêlée. The result has the pleasingly remote, detached, and scientific atmosphere of a study in anthropology. It becomes a study in abstraction and determinism, and involves no issues or principles with which any reader need concern himself. It is both the realistic and the scientific method applied to the writing of history, and it reinforces the intellectual nihilism of the disillusioned liberal.

Is it really scientific in taking account of all the data within the particular field of its concern? The only thing this method leaves out is the set of standards and principles which men themselves accepted as the basis upon which they agreed to work, and thereby accepted as the standards by which they might legitimately be judged. The only element which gives coherence

* From Paul Birdsall, *Versailles: Twenty Years After* (New York: Reynal and Hitchcock, 1941), pp. 289–95. Copyright 1941 by Paul Birdsall. Reprinted by permission of Harcourt, Brace and World, Inc.

and significance to the study of the Paris Peace Conference is the set of principles with reference to which it acted, the degree to which it embodied them in the treaties, the extent to which it departed from them, and the reasons—personal and political—for the result. No account which ignores or pre-judges that frame of reference can claim to be scientific.

To assume at the outset that the Fourteen Points were unreal and impractical, incapable of being translated into concrete terms of peace, ignores the simple fact that they constituted a legal contract between the Allied and Associated Powers and Germany to govern the terms of peace. It is just as unrealistic to impugn the intelligence and integrity of the Peace Commissioners who took the contract seriously in the first place as to denounce them all indiscriminately as hypocrites who systematically violated principles in which they never believed, or as fools who could not recognize the violation of a principle when they committed it. The contract was there as the basis of all their efforts. It was a reasonably ascertainable contract, the details of application admittedly difficult, but by no means so impossible as many writers have alleged. It is quite as possible to distinguish between the degrees of good faith and intelligence brought to the task by the different national delegations at Paris, as it is possible to distinguish the degrees of intelligence and good faith within the personnel of any one of these delegations. Such treatment must, obviously, take account of the real political pressures upon men by national tradition and public opinion. To ignore the necessity of reasonable compromise in political affairs is just as fatal to realism as to assume that, all politics being of the essence of compromise, there are no rules at all and no standards of judgments but those of immediate political success.

It is an extraordinary fact that as yet there has been no balanced interpretation of Peace Conference diplomacy to take the measure of all the factors involved. When a penetrating critic like Harold Nicolson undertakes to recall the discussion to a firm basis of reality by emphasizing the fundamental conflict of principle, he does so only to go off the deep end of romantic-liberal disillusionment, and produces a spiritual autobiography of his loss of faith in Wilson. In his reaction against the prophets and dreamers of the world, he embraces the realists who at least know the rules of the balance of power in Europe—for example, Eyre Crowe of the British Foreign Office and Colonel House, "the best diplomatic brain America has yet produced."

The issue of realism at Paris is mainly the question of the short-term as against the long-range view. The pressures of national demands, made effective and menacing through diplomatic strategy in the League of Nations Commission, made immediate and pressing by the danger of delay in pacifying a turbulent and disintegrating Europe, necessitated a degree of compromise. The realists of the American Delegation lost their perspective under such pressure and were ready to throw away all their cargo in the scramble for the lifeboats. The cargo consisted of the Fourteen Points, the substance of the Pre-Armistice Agreement, the contract with Germany. Colonel House felt that if the boat were lightened sufficiently, it would still carry the League of

Nations, but Harold Nicolson's description of a general *sauve qui peut* attitude in the later phases of the Peace Conference applies well to elements within the American delegation. In this atmosphere, one concession was an argument for the next.

Mezes could not see why the American delegation should "stand up so much straighter" on the Fiume question against the Italians than in other questions involving other Powers; Colonel House advocated extreme concessions to the Japanese on the ground that, although clearly a violation of principle, it was no worse than many other concessions which had already been made. There was little attempt to discriminate between detail and principle, between the relative merits of national demands, between the varying degrees of diplomatic strength which supported the demands. Above all, there was no thought save for the immediate future—make peace quickly and start the League of Nations. The realism of these men consisted in an abdication of sheer nerve and intelligence.

Naturally, President Wilson looked stiff and unrealistic when viewed through the eyes of such men, at the very time when William Bullitt was resigning from the American Delegation in protest at Wilson's sacrifice of principle, and others were grumbling that the treaty was thoroughly bad. To the former group he seemed rigid and uncompromising, to the latter weak and uncertain in his stand on principle. A careful study of the record reveals an extraordinary consistency in Wilson's fight for his program under overwhelming difficulties, as well as a high degree of political intelligence in translating the abstract principle of his program into concrete details of application.

The President's understanding of the real issues involved in the Saar case was superior to that of his own experts, and that was the only issue where he stood completely alone against everyone in Paris. In the Polish case, he was convinced by the arguments of Lloyd George as to the long-term results of a settlement based on the Polish Commission's report and loyally supported Lloyd George's efforts to modify that settlement in the face of the Polish sympathies of the American experts. He withstood steadfastly Colonel House's pressure to compromise on the Colonial question, the Rhineland, the Saar, the Adriatic. His worst defeats were the Reparations settlement and Shantung; the first occurred while Wilson was ill, when Colonel House abandoned the American program; the second, because of an impregnable political and diplomatic position held by the Japanese.

Throughout the conference Wilson maintained his stand on principle as the only safe guide in a welter of conflicting interests, as the sole safeguard against laying foundations for future conflict. That was the meaning of his attempt to force an admission from Colonel House that the pro-French proposals of the American experts for the Saar valley were a violation of the Fourteen Points. The record for the crucial April period is eloquent testimony to the President's perspective and force, and Fiume is the final symbol. In the nature of the case, Wilson's role—aside from the arduous work in the League of Nations Commission—had to be negative rather than constructive, to concern itself with prevention rather than cure. Consequently the failure of his curative and constructive work, as the result primarily of American refusal to ratify the treaty and enter the League of Nations, has obscured the real nature of his achievement at Paris. It is so much easier to record failures than to carry through the laborious task of assessing a man's work by careful measurement of what he prevented, as well as by study of positive achievements.

Perhaps the most general criticism President Wilson has encountered, at the time and since, has been on the score of his decision to attend the Peace Conference in person. The decision itself was attributed to excessive vanity, and the effect has generally been described as the degradation of the remote and lofty, almost godlike arbiter to a bloody and battered contestant in the European prize ring. The assumption is that Wilson in Washington could have retained his detachment with an ultimate power of decision while delegating the rough-and-tumble of negotiation to Colonel House in Paris. It is interesting that Secretary Lansing and Colonel House, who agreed upon practically nothing else, should have consistently concurred on the unwisdom of the President's coming to Paris. Independently, they tried in advance to prevent it; subsequently, they communed over the misfortune of the event. Yet, in view of Lansing's attitude toward Colonel House, it is difficult to imagine his acquiescing in the Colonel's primacy in Paris. It is possible that each man in the assurance of his own superior wisdom felt confident of exercising greater influence in Wilson's absence.

The present book affords the most positive answer on this point. The record cleary shows that on every major question but that of Reparation, the Treaty of Versailles would have been a worse treaty had Wilson remained in Washington. With all his mistakes, he emerges as the only man of real stature at Paris.

V.

THE EMERGENCE OF TOTALITARIANISM IN RUSSIA

When future generations study the history of our era, remarks one contemporary historian, they may describe it not as the age of democracy but as the age of totalitarianism. A strong case can be made for the thesis that the totalitarian system is the most typical political phenomenon of twentieth-century Europe.

The term is not an easy one to define, however; it has been loosely used, and has often served as a synonym for "fascist," to signify a right-wing, passionately nationalist dictatorship. Political theorists in recent years have pointed out that there can be totalitarianisms of the left as well as the right; that political systems which seem to lie at the two extremes of the spectrum may in fact have many features in common, especially when contrasted with the various forms of "bourgeois" or socialist democracy that share a constitutional structure and a representative base.

What are the distinguishing features of totalitarian systems, whether of the left or of the right? A strong man and a single party: these are the traits that come to mind at once. But these are, to some degree, external traits; other aspects are probably more profound and more important. One of them is the ideal of the state as an all-embracing institution, that leaves no aspect of life outside its control, that permits no "island of separateness" to which men or groups may retreat. Another is the concentration of real power in the hands of a single dominant power-group which destroys or domesticates all other organized groups, leaving them no independent role, no direct share in decision-making, no indirect control over the decision makers. Still a third feature is the peculiar character of the dominant power-elite, which cuts across the old traditional class structure and seeks to destroy that structure together with the traditional institutions supporting it. Its spirit, then, tends to be revolutionary rather than conservative. Finally, totalitarian systems all profess a considerable degree of social radicalism—perhaps sincere, perhaps merely demagogic in inspiration. For all totalitarian systems seek to root themselves in the masses, and are in that sense unlike any autocratic or dictatorial systems of the past, before the so-called mass age.

No loyal citizen of the Soviet Union would accept the label "totalitarian" to describe the system under which he lives; indeed, Soviet leaders claim the term "democracy" as properly their own. Certainly the doctrines of Karl Marx did not embody anything like the totalitarian ideal, despite the ambiguities that permit Marx's professed disciples to find different meanings in his work. Marx, after all, was a man of his era, of the mid–nineteenth century, when democracy was the great ideal, the panacea preached by all social reformers. Never once did Marx consider the possibility that a small elite might dominate the vast majority of citizens, even as a temporary interlude. Even his "dictatorship of the proletariat" phase meant, to Marx, control by the majority, for in his scheme the proletariat would not come to power until it vastly outnumbered the declining classes in society. Yet in the first state to be taken over by Marx's disciples, there promptly emerged the first totalitarian system of the twentieth century.

How did this happen, and why? Some analysts have attributed the responsibility to Josef Stalin, who emerged from the struggle for power after Lenin's death to assert his absolute domination over both party and nation. Stalin's critics see him as a primitive type moved by a taste for brutality and a thirst for personal power; his defenders plead historical necessity, and stress the overwhelming problems involved in dragging a backward "Asiatic" country up into the twentieth century. But there is good reason to ask whether the crucial decisions had not already been taken before Stalin fought his way to the top—whether Lenin rather than Stalin was not in fact the founder of Soviet totalitarianism.

Most of Lenin's defenders are outraged at such a suggestion. They point to the contrast in temperament between Lenin and Stalin, to Lenin's frequent professions of faith in free speech and in the responsiveness of leadership, to Lenin's preference for the methods of discussion and persuasion as the proper way to run the party. If harsher methods had to be adopted temporarily, they insist, that was only because the country he inherited from the tsars was in a state of near-chaos, and because the capitalist world drove him to it by a bigoted policy of intervention. They argue, too, that there were no workable alternatives for Russia save bolshevik rule or a return to tsarist autocracy, and that any methods were justifiable to avert the latter.

Lenin's critics, on the other hand, observe that while Lenin lacked Stalin's primitive brutality, he possessed another trait almost as dangerous: an intense and blind fanaticism, an absolute conviction that he possessed the truth, an inability to comprehend the meaning of compromise. They point out that Lenin's advocacy of such ideals as free speech and responsiveness of leadership was confined for the most part to the years before he seized power, and that his attitude changed once the Bolsheviks were in control. They contend that after the worst of the post-1917 crisis was over, and foreign intervention ended, Lenin refused to consider any real relaxation of the Bolsheviks' grip on the country, or any sharing of power to give the regime a broader popular base. Instead, they say, he destroyed what was left of a political opposition, and wiped out what remained of factionalism within the bolshevik ruling elite itself. These decisions to consolidate a monolithic system, the critics contend, made Lenin the real author of Soviet totalitarianism, and paved the way for the rise of a more brutal and arbitrary leader after Lenin's death.

The questions at issue, then, are these: Should Russia in Lenin's time really be classed as a totalitarian state? If so, how much responsibility for it does Lenin bear? Was he driven unwillingly to such action by domestic and foreign pressure? Were his decisions the logical outgrowth of his fanatical convictions? Was there really no alternative to monolithic rule by the bolshevik elite, short of a return to the tsars? Is there a kind of logic of revolution, a pattern which all great upheavals are likely to follow, and which carries revolutionary leaders along almost in spite of themselves?

1.

That Lenin was one of the most remarkable figures in twentieth-century Europe, and one of the principal shapers of our era, is a view shared by both communist and noncommunist historians. His skill as a revolutionary tactician was amply proved both in 1917 and in the critical years of civil war that followed. One of Lenin's warmest admirers and defenders is the Oxford historian Christopher Hill, who has been a fellow and tutor in modern history at Balliol College since 1938. Mr. Hill is the author of a number of books on the seventeenth-century English revolution; his brief popularized biography of Lenin is his only venture into Russian history. It was written while Mr. Hill was still a member of the British Communist party (from which he resigned in 1957).

HILL: Lenin and the Russian Revolution *

During this period the foundations were laid on which Lenin's successors, in less than two decades, created a great power. Merely looked upon as reconstruction of a devastated country, the work of the Soviet government was prodigious; but it was far more than that. This was a period of trial and error on a gigantic scale, of experimenting with hitherto untested forms of social organization.

There were no precedents, no blue-prints. Marx and Engels had suggested the general principles for the organization of socialist society, both in its final classless (communist) form and during the transitional period of "the dictatorship of the proletariat." But Marx and Engels had tacitly assumed that the socialist revolution would take place in a highly industrialized state, or else virtually simultaneously over the whole of Europe. At first Lenin and his government hoped that the Russian Revolution would be the signal for successful socialist risings in the West. When this hope had faded, they faced the incredibly difficult task of applying the principles of Marxism in a single state, and that a peasant country whose small industrial sector had been shattered by war and civil war.

This point cannot be overemphasized in any estimate of Lenin and the Russian Revolution. We must judge the successes and failures of the Soviet regime not by abstract absolute standards, as those of an ideal socialist state; but as part of an experiment which had unexpectedly to be made in conditions of quite exceptional difficulty, with desperately inadequate resources, material and human, in face of the avowed hostility of almost every other government in the civilized world.

* From Christopher Hill, *Lenin and the Russian Revolution* (New York: The Macmillan Company, 1950), pp. 166-68, 213-14, 216-26, 231-34. Reprinted with the permission of The Macmillan Co. First printed in 1947.

Lenin and his government, then, were trying to apply to a peculiarly Russian situation principles which they held to be universal. Some of Lenin's greatest qualities were brought out by the very difficulties of the situation— his courage, his resourcefulness, his empiricism, his readiness to compromise on anything but essentials, and his remarkably constant grasp of what were essentials, in a period when almost all his foreign critics and even some of his colleagues lost their sense of proportion at one stage or another. As a symbol of this period may be taken the spring evening in 1918 when, as so often happened, the Moscow electricity system failed; and Lenin and Gorky sat together in the Kremlin discussing by candlelight the electrification of the whole country. . . .

Lenin died on January 21st, 1924. Kalinin, the peasant who, as he put it, had climbed with dirty feet into the place of the tsars, wept when he announced the news to the Congress of Soviets. For a week Lenin lay in state, whilst long queues waited for hours in the bitter cold to see him. "The Bolsheviks can organize much," wrote Mr. Duranty to the *New York Times* on January 27th, "but it is not their propaganda which draws these hundreds of thousands to Lenin's feet." From the construction of the mausoleum in the Red Square in which Lenin lies embalmed until its closure during the Nazi-Soviet War there was every day a long procession of simple people who wished to pay their respects to the dead leader. Lenin's body, like those of the saints of the Orthodox Church, has not known corruption. Trotsky, the Westernizing émigré, opposed the suggestion that the corpse should be thus preserved, and it is doubtful whether such a process would have a similar effect in the more sophisticated West of today. But in seventeenth-century England Oliver Cromwell's effigy lay in state for many weeks after his death, "multitudes daily crowding to see this glorious but mournful sight." There can be no doubt that the decision to embalm and exhibit Lenin's corpse responded to a real popular sentiment. His dead body has been seen by millions more than ever saw him alive. . . .

It may be worth summarizing now the personal characteristics in him which in a peculiar way symbolized the Russian Revolution, and for which he is especially remembered today.

First and foremost Lenin symbolizes the Russian Revolution as a movement of the poor and oppressed of the earth who have successfully risen against the great and the powerful. That was and is the most important single fact about the revolution, both in its internal and international effects. "It's a fine thing, the revolution," said a peasant whose holding had increased from eight to eighty-five acres. "Everyone is in favour of it. They don't like the Communist party, but they like the revolution." That was the authentic note of the underdog, which scarcely any first-hand observer of the revolution failed to capture. An old worker who drove John Reed back to Petrograd from Tsarskoye Selo a few days after the October Revolution, "swept the far-gleaming capital with an exultant gesture. 'Mine,' he cried, his face all alight. 'All mine now! My Petrograd.'"

All who met him agreed that Lenin, for all his aristocratic origins and his middle-class upbringing, was very close to the common average Russian. In his campaign against those who in March 1918 wanted to fight a revolutionary war against the Germans, the severest thing Lenin could find to say was that they "look at things from the point of view of the knight, who said as he died, sword in hand, in a beautiful pose: 'Peace is disgraceful, war is honourable!' They argue from the point of view of the aristocrat: I argue from the point of view of the peasant." "There was in him something of kinship with the soil of Russia," said his political opponent, Axelrod; "the most earthly of all who have walked this earth of men," said the poet Mayakovsky. Lenin summed up the period in 1889 when his mother tried to get him to manage the family estates by saying: "My relations with the peasants became abnormal." When he lived in the Kremlin Lenin quite unaffectedly continued to live in the most simple style, sleeping on an iron bedstead in a carpetless room; he did not even consciously dispense with luxuries, but was merely rather irritated when any-one tried to force them upon him. Presents of food which peasants sent in to him during the famine he invariably gave away.

In its feeling for the ordinary man Lenin's thought was fundamentally democratic. Many people before him had expressed the view that genuine democracy was impossible without socialism; but Lenin insisted on the converse, that socialism without democracy was impossible, since "(1) the proletariat cannot achieve the socialist revolution unless it is prepared for this task by the struggle for democracy; (2) victorious socialism cannot retain its victory and lead humanity to the stage when the state withers away unless it estab-lishes complete democracy." Lenin praised the soviets because they represented "democracy for the poor, for the people, not for the rich," and thought of the main function of trade unions in a socialist state as the education of the work-ers in democratic habits.

Lenin summed up his conception of what the revolution meant by reporting a conversation that he had overheard in a railway train. An old woman had said with surprise: "Today you don't need to be afraid of a man with a gun. When I was in the forest a man with a gun met me, but instead of taking away my firewood he helped me to gather some more." Lenin used this remark to illustrate the change in the basis of the state, the fact that its power was now used to protect the masses of the population. Under tsarism it had been used against them.

He returned to the same point in a later speech, though here he is thinking more of the liberating effect of the revolution on things of the mind: "Hitherto the whole creative genius of the human intellect has laboured only to give the advantages of technique and civilization to the few, and to deprive the rest of the most elementary necessities—education and free development. But now all the marvels of technique, all the conquests of civilization, are the property of the whole people, and henceforth human intellect and genius will never be twisted into a means of oppression, a means of exploitation. We know this: surely it is worth striving with all our might to fulfil this stupendous historic task? The workers will carry out this titanic historic labour, for there are vast revolutionary powers slumbering in them, vast powers of renovation and regeneration."

Lenin's style of speaking seems to have had the same characteristics of straightforwardness and simplicity as his arguments. He was not a great orator, in the sense in which Kerensky and Trotsky were. All observers agree that he dominated his audiences by sheer force of intellect and personality: "I came out into the street feeling as if I had been beaten over the head with a flail," said a political opponent. Lenin dispensed with gesticulation, oratorical tricks and flourishes, flattery of his audience or appeals to their emotions. "His words always brought to my mind the cold glitter of steel shavings," wrote Gorky; Clara Zetkin said he threw out sentences "like unhewn blocks of granite." "What a professor lost to the world!" said the great historian Kovalevsky. All his speeches got down at once to hard thinking, and as soon as he had made his points he stopped, often abruptly. In his maturer years his self-confidence was supreme, because based on a deep analysis of the facts, and he spoke with a breathless urgency and conviction which swept all before it. Morally, the oratorical spell-binder Trotsky "was as incapable of standing against Lenin as a flea would be against an elephant," observed Bruce Lockhart.

Lenin possessed a second quality which symbolizes the achievements of the revolution as a whole. It is the quality which on Maurice Baring's first visit to Russia most impressed him as typical of the ordinary Russian—humaneness. The attempt to overthrow the Bolsheviks after the revolution produced cruelties indeed; but the revolutionary process abolished a regime of despair and created a new world of hope. "Children, these hands cannot write," said an old peasant in 1918, holding up his worn and calloused hands to a group of school-children; "they cannot write because the only thing the tsar wanted them for was to plough. But you, children of a new Russia, you can learn to write. Oh that I might begin again as a child in the new Russia!"

These were the new things which affected popular judgment. Murder and sudden death, alas, had been familiar enough for centuries in Russian history. Gorky, who on many occasions in the hard times of civil war intervened with Lenin on behalf of suspected intellectuals, and never met with a refusal, says of him: "I have never met anyone in Russia, the country where the inevitability of suffering is preached as the general road to salvation, nor do I know of anyone who hated, loathed and despised all unhappiness, grief and suffering as Lenin did." Lenin once said to Gorky, after enjoying a Beethoven sonata: "But I can't listen to music too often. It affects your nerves, makes you want to say stupid, nice things, and stroke the heads of people who could create such beauty while living in this vile hell. And now you mustn't stroke anyone's head—you might get your hand bitten off. You have to hit them on the head, without mercy, although our ideal is not to use force against anyone. H'm, h'm, our duty is infernally hard."

He told the sculptress Claire Sheridan that her allegorical figure of Victory was not to his taste because it was too beautiful: victory was not like that.

("I'm not criticizing you," he added mildly; "only please don't touch me up."
Like Cromwell, he wanted to be represented warts and all.)

Hatred of tyranny and oppression because of their degrading effects on
oppressors and oppressed alike was the moral force behind Lenin's loathing
for tsarism, for any system of economic exploitation or national subjugation.
Yet in 1916 he did not forget to remind Poles and Finns, "who now justly hate
the Great Russians for the executioner's role they are playing, that it is not
wise to extend this hatred to the *socialist* workers and to a socialist Russia;
that economic interests as well as the instinct and the consciousness of internationalism and democracy demand the speediest establishment of intimacy
among and amalgamation of all nations in a socialist society."

In September 1919, when Soviet Russia was still involved in desperate war,
Lenin was talking to women about their "actual position of inferiority because
all the housework is thrust upon them, . . . the most unproductive, most
barbarous and most arduous work," which "is extremely petty and contains
nothing that facilitates the development of women." To Clara Zetkin Lenin
spoke angrily of "the calm acquiescence of men who see how women grow
worn out in petty, monstrous household work, their strength and time dissipated and wasted, their minds growing narrow and stale, their hearts beating
slowly, their wills weakened." He advanced it as a further argument in favour
of collective agriculture that "small peasant economy means small separate
households, with the women chained to them." And he called on women
themselves to take the lead in establishing the communal institutions which
would help to liberate them from their burden and make them free and equal
citizens.

A small enough beginning; but it is such small and concrete beginnings that
are recollected, as was Lenin's speech to school-teachers extolling the dignity
of the part they had to play in the creation of a socialist society, and ending
up by saying it was "most, most, most important of all to improve their
material position." In pre-revolutionary society the position of the teacher had
been so lowly that without that postscript the rest would have been mere
verbiage. One of the few non-political occasions on which Lenin is recorded
to have lost his temper was with a father who said it did a healthy child no
harm to get tired. Lenin, who had got off his bicycle to help the child up a
steep hill, said furiously, "People like you should not be allowed to have
children at all."

Thirdly, Lenin stands for all those qualities going to make the Russian
Revolution—purposefulness, realism, common sense, will-power, pugnacity—
which were most conspicuously lacking in the pre-revolutionary intelligentsia
satirized by Chekhov. At the London Congress of 1903 a political opponent
complained to Lenin, "How oppressive the atmosphere is at our Congress!
This bitter fighting, this agitation one against the other, this biting controversy,
this uncomradely behaviour!" "What a splendid thing our Congress is!" Lenin
replied. "A free and open struggle. Opinions stated. Shades of disagreement
made clear. Groups have taken shape. Hands have been raised. A decision has

been taken. A stage has been passed. Forward! That's the stuff for me! That's life! That's something different from the endless, tedious logic-chopping of your intellectuals, which doesn't stop because the question has been settled, but because they are too tired to talk any more. . . ." After this Congress Lenin stood out almost alone of the leading émigrés against all five of his old editorial colleagues on *Iskra,* persons much older than himself, great names in the Russian revolutionary movement. Unperturbed, and relying on support from inside Russia, he wrote *One Step Forward, Two Steps Back,* in which he proclaimed, "It would be criminal cowardice to doubt even for a moment the inevitable and complete triumph of the principles of revolutionary Social-Democracy, of proletarian organization and party discipline." What, as the Menshevik Dan asked, are you to do with a man like that? For such self-confidence there is only one justification: success.

Fourteen years later, in June 1917, the Menshevik leader Tseretelli, full of ministerial dignity and grandeur, proclaimed at the First Congress of Soviets that there was not a single party in Russia which would agree to take over sole power. "Oh yes there is," called out Lenin from the back of the hall. "Our party is prepared at any moment to take over the entire power." They laughed then, but Lenin knew exactly what the possibilities were. He disliked nothing more than revolutionaries who, instead of soberly calculating the realities of any given situation, resorted to "the vigorous waving of small red flags." "To wage a socialist revolutionary war without railways would be the most sinister treachery," he told the romantic supporters of Trotsky during the Brest-Litovsk negotiations. "I am absolutely horrified," he had written to the party leaders in Russia in 1905, "that people can go on talking about bombs for more than six months without making a single one." "Insurrection is an art," Lenin proclaimed on every appropriate occasion, an art which he studied with his usual thoroughness. The tactics of October—the seizure of the telephone exchange and General Post Office, of bridges, railway stations and the power station, and above all the maintenance of a vigorous offensive—were based on the conclusions which Lenin had arrived at after studying the revolution of 1905 and the military textbooks of the Geneva libraries. . . .

Finally, there is Lenin the Russian patriot. We are coming to appreciate the patriotic aspect of the Russian Revolution more nowadays, but it is one of which Soviet citizens have always been conscious. The revolution freed Russia from foreign domination and exploitation, gave her an independent foreign policy, defeated the foreign invader, and through manifold sufferings created the powerful U.S.S.R. of today. As early as 1931 Prince Mirsky found that patriotic acceptance of Soviet policy brought the émigrés to a closer study of the Russian Revolution and its leader, and led him to conclude that it was impossible to accept the October Revolution without accepting Lenin's ideas. The Russian Revolution was Lenin's revolution.

For all his years of exile and his internationalism, Lenin was no cosmopolitan. He had a very special affection for and pride in Russian literature, especially Chernishevsky and Tolstoy. Lenin's own Russian prose is a model of efficiency and straightforwardness. His writings contain no fireworks about patriotism, because there were too many of them on the other side of the barricades. But he was ready on occasion to "crawl on his belly in the mud" if the interests of Russia and the revolution required it, as when he went in person to the German Embassy to apologize for the assassination of Count Mirbach, whom a Socialist Revolutionary had killed in the hope of embroiling the Soviet government with Germany.

Above all Lenin is identified with the economic and political reconstruction of the U.S.S.R., with the building of socialism. His wife said after his death: "Let not your deep, abounding grief be expressed in outward honours for Lenin's personality. Monuments to his name and sumptuous ceremonies—all that in his life he valued so little, found them all so tiresome. Remember how much poverty and lack of order yet exist in our country. If you want to honour Lenin's name, build crèches, children's homes, schools, libraries, hospitals, sanatoria, and above all try so to act that by you his will be done."

I have tried to suggest how in dealing with all the major problems which faced the Bolsheviks Lenin stood for the application of Marxism to the specifically Russian historical situation. His greatness lies in that he perfectly represented the point of intersection of the old and the new, the Russian and the Western, the peasant and the socialist. Unlike the pro-German tsarist court, the French-speaking aristocracy, the Anglophil Cadets, unlike even the Westernizing intellectuals in the revolutionary movement—the Mensheviks and Trotsky —Lenin knew the Russian peoples and valued their traditions. So he was able to carry the masses with him. But on the other hand, unlike the Slavophils and the Narodniks, he did not despise the achievements of Western science and thought. When a code of Soviet laws was being drafted Lenin wrote to the official concerned: "Get hold immediately of all the literature there is and consider the experience of the west European countries. But don't stop there (that is the most important of all). Don't be satisfied with 'Europe' but go further. . . . Don't miss the smallest chance of intensifying state interference in private property relations."

It was because of his Marxism that Lenin was able to succeed where the Narodnik terrorist Zhelyabov had failed, in "giving history a shove." To the old fatalistic Russia, with its philosophies of passivity and suffering, the revolution brought the tremendous hope that men might control their own destinies.

With Gorky, the greatest contemporary Russian man of letters, who was also his intimate friend, Lenin often during his last illness discussed the meaning of the revolution which had been his life's work. Gorky records a remark from one of these conversations which might form Lenin's epitaph. Speaking of the rising Soviet generation, Lenin said, "These will have much happier lives than we had. They will not experience much that we lived through. There will not be so much cruelty in their lives. . . . And yet I don't envy them. Our generation achieved something of amazing significance for history. The cruelty, which the conditions of our life made necessary, will be understood and vindicated. Everything will be understood, everything."

2.

Not all historians are prepared to excuse or to justify Lenin's decisions during the chaotic years from 1917 to 1921. One of his most vigorous and perceptive critics is Leonard Schapiro, Reader in Russian Government and Politics at the University of London. Mr. Schapiro first stated his case against Lenin in a brief article published in 1951 in the British periodical *History Today;* since that time, he has buttressed it in two remarkable books entitled *The Origins of the Communist Autocracy* and *The Communist Party of the Soviet Union.* A greater man than Lenin, Schapiro argues, would have struck out on a different path in 1921; by choosing to build a monolithic state, Lenin opened the way to Stalin. "He was a great revolutionary," concludes Schapiro, "but not a statesman."

SCHAPIRO: The Russian Revolution *

While it was easy for the Bolsheviks to seize power, it seemed at the outset that they would have the greatest difficulty in retaining it. Yet the hesitation and disunity of their opponents assured them of victory in the end. The attitude of the army was the first question upon which much turned. Though demoralized by weariness and by desertions, there were still more than sufficient units in the field to sweep the Bolsheviks from their insecure power, had prompt and decisive action been taken. No such immediate attempt was made. The troops, where they were not pro-Bolshevik, preferred a policy of neutrality to the possibility of civil war. The officers, in the first few critical days, were not prepared to come to the aid of the Provisional Government, which they distrusted little less than they detested the Bolsheviks. They may have hoped that, if the Bolsheviks got rid of the Provisional Government, they could then in turn sweep away the Bolsheviks. If so, they miscalculated their strength. Within a few months of the Bolshevik revolution, however, they succeeded in rallying a volunteer army in the interior of Russia to wage civil war. They were supported by a legion of Czechs, who in a clash with the Bolsheviks in May of 1918, fired the first shots. They also received some support from the Allied Powers, who were anxious to restore an Eastern front in the campaign with Germany. This front had been eliminated when Lenin proposed an armistice immediately after seizing power. The Allies now hoped that the Russian armies would overthrow the Bolsheviks and carry on the war with Germany. For over two years, until the end of 1920, various anti-Bolshevik armies struggled against the new Bolshevik Red Army, and were all defeated. Their defeat was not entirely due to the valour of the Red Army, important as this factor was. Trotsky attributed the victory of the Bolsheviks mainly to the political ineptitude of the White Commanders. Their policy of restoring the land to the dispossessed landlords in the territories which they reconquered, and their

*From Leonard Schapiro, "The Russian Revolution," in *History Today* (London: August, 1951), pp. 10-13. Reprinted by permission of the author and of the editors of *History Today.*

methods of dictatorship, which yielded in no respect to those of the Bolsheviks, swung the balance of peasant support to the side of the Bolsheviks, as the lesser of two evils. Trotsky, as the chief architect and organizer of the Red Army throughout the civil war, was in the best position to judge. The Allied intervention, at no time sufficient to turn the scales, also served to rally national feeling in the country against the invader.

The political opposition, following on the Bolshevik *coup d'état,* presents the more interesting problem. Lenin before long had to face certain difficulties inside his own party. Ostensibly power had been seized in the name of the All-Russian Congress of Soviets, a body upon which the Bolsheviks and their supporters had a bare majority and in which the socialist parties were strongly represented. There had been nothing in Lenin's utterances to suggest that a one-party dictatorship was to be established, nor that the ordinary freedoms of speech and press were to be promptly suppressed. When forced, in November 1917, under the threat of a general strike by the union of railwaymen, to go through the motions of attempting to form a coalition with the socialist parties, Lenin astounded his followers by explaining to them in private conclave that he was merely playing for time. The simple railwaymen were in the end placated by a coalition with the dissident left wing of the Socialist Revolutionaries, whose views at the time were identical with those of the Bolsheviks. The impact of Lenin's duplicity on his party, together with the suppression of some socialist as well as of the liberal newspapers, led to a short-lived party crisis and to a number of resignations from the Bolshevik leadership. There was another minor crisis in January 1918 when Lenin decided to disperse the Constituent Assembly after one day's session. There was a major crisis in March 1918 when Lenin insisted on signing peace with Germany, on Germany's terms. He had repeatedly promised—before seizing power—that, if Germany refused the Bolshevik conditions of "democratic" peace, i.e. peace without annexations of territory or peoples, he would launch a revolutionary war. This revolutionary war, or popular rising against the imperialist invaders, was designed to kindle revolution in Germany and throughout Europe. With this promise now thrown to the winds, a serious revolt against Lenin spread through the Bolshevik party. Lenin weathered all these crises without difficulty. His personal authority over his party far outweighed that of any other leader. His opponents within the party understood only too well that their personal chances of survival, if they broke with him, were slight. Those who had resigned soon petitioned for reinstatement, and dissident groups acknowledged their error. Throughout the civil war the common peril cemented the Bolshevik party.

The Liberals were immediately outlawed after the seizure of power and played little part in subsequent events. Some perished in prison, many escaped. A group of them survived in hiding long enough to help to organize a plot for the forcible overthrow of the Bolsheviks. The plot was uncovered and many dozens paid with their lives. The socialists in the main repudiated the violent seizure of power, though groups on the extreme left of each of the two parties were willing to make common cause with the Bolsheviks. This collaboration was uneasy from the start and short-lived. As for the main body of the two big socialist parties, each adopted a very different policy.

The Socialist Revolutionaries, for all their antagonism to the Bolsheviks, hesitated to take up arms. At one time they hoped that the Constituent Assembly would restore them to their rightful position. Even when it became plain that this Assembly's existence was likely to be short-lived, they could not bring themselves to resort to force in its defence, though there were several regiments in the capital prepared to support them if they gave the order. Only when peace with Germany was signed by Russia did they decide to resort to arms, justifying the civil war as a continuation of the war against Germany, in whose interests they now believed the Bolsheviks to be acting. They joined the Czech legionaries and set up new provisional governments, on the Volga, in Siberia and elsewhere. Yet this resistance was brief. Before long the socialist governments had been swept away by more resolute White military dictatorships. Allied victory over Germany no longer made it possible to justify the civil war as a war primarily directed against Germany. The Socialist Revolutionaries were thus faced with the prospect of fighting Bolshevism under the banner of the White generals, and the great majority of them refused to do so. Some capitulated to the Bolsheviks; others escaped abroad to form an *émigré* party. Only individuals and individual groups continued the fight. It was such individual extremists also who were responsible for the risings, assassinations and the attempt on the life of Lenin in the summer and autumn of 1918, which were used to justify the official inauguration by the Bolsheviks of the so-called Red Terror in September 1918.

An entirely different policy was adopted by the Mensheviks. They chose from the outset to play the part of a legal opposition. Their aim was by political action in the Soviets and in the trade unions, and by written and spoken propaganda to turn the Bolsheviks from the method of dictatorship to a system of democracy, or at any rate democracy for all socialist parties. It was no easy task. Although officially outlawed for only a short period—from June to November 1918—they were confronted with a much more formidable campaign of illegal persecution. Their newspapers were suppressed, their activities interrupted by frequent arrests, and their chance of success in elections frustrated by every form of violence and chicanery. Yet, in spite of these difficulties, the Mensheviks achieved remarkable success. It is not possible to measure their success in election figures, since elections were rigged and were no indication of opinion. But by the end of 1920 the Mensheviks had the support of majorities in a number of important trade unions, and a wide following among the workers. What was more serious from the point of view of the Bolshevik leaders, their unceasing advocacy of democracy in trade union and soviet elections, of the elementary freedoms, and of some rudiments of legality in government, were beginning to find a responsive echo within the Bolshevik party itself.

The end of the civil war had brought a change in the temper of the Bolshevik rank and file. With victory achieved, they were growing resentful of the

dictatorship of the Central Committee over the party. They resented the privileges of the party bureaucrats. They demanded the right to voice their criticism
without fear of reprisals and to elect their own local party and trade union
organizations without nomination from the centre. When, in March 1921, the
sailors of the naval base of Kronstadt mutinied and demanded free elections,
free speech and an end to party dictatorship and administrative terror, they
were supported by up to half the local Bolsheviks. Of the remainder, the
majority remained neutral.

Faced with this situation, there were two alternatives open to Lenin. One
was to yield to the demand for moderation and for some semblance of liberty.
This would have revived some of the waning enthusiasm which the revolution
had once evoked, and it would have allowed the development in Russia of
the elements of order and self-reliance which the country had always lacked.
But this course would have entailed the loss by the Bolsheviks of their monopoly
of power, since they must inevitably have shared it at any rate with the
Mensheviks. The other alternative, which Lenin adopted, was to launch Russia
on the path which she has since pursued. The Mensheviks and the socialist
revolutionaries still at large were eliminated from the political scene by arrests,
which no longer, as hitherto, proved temporary. Opposition groups within the
Bolshevik party were proscribed. Comparatively moderate men like Preobra-
zhensky and Krestinsky were removed from the party secretariat. A new party
apparatus was set up, with Molotov in charge, soon to be succeeded by his
patron, Stalin. Before long it became evident that the function of this party
apparatus was to secure submission and implicit obedience, to eliminate criticism and to ensure complete control by the Central Committee over all party
activity throughout the country. Lenin had started the modern form of the
one party state on its path. At the same time, by limited concessions to free
enterprise he lulled the violent opposition of the peasantry to the Bolshevik
policy of forcible food-requisitioning. These also made possible the revival of
Russian industry, which had almost reached collapse. The Mensheviks had
for some time been advocating just such a policy. It was not a coincidence that
the initiation of it by Lenin was accompanied by their elimination from the
political scene. In order to adopt their policy without admitting them to a
share in the government, he muzzled them forever.

Lenin justified the eclipse of his socialist political opponents by an appeal to
the argument of self-preservation. He argued that the Mensheviks and the
Socialist Revolutionaries were, wittingly or unwittingly, agents of the White
Guards, of the imperialists, or of the secret services of foreign powers. This
argument might appear more convincing if the elimination of Lenin's socialist
opponents had taken place during the course of the civil war, when there was
a serious threat that the Bolsheviks might yet be defeated. For the fact is that
the socialist opposition was tolerated to some extent during the civil war, and
only exterminated when the threat from the White Armies and from Allied
intervention no longer existed. Lenin's argument has often been reiterated and
is still to be met with. For example, Mr. E. H. Carr, after a short sketch of

the socialist opposition between 1917 and 1921 in the recently published first volume of his *The Bolshevik Revolution,* concludes: "If it was true that the Bolshevik regime was not prepared after the first few months to tolerate an organized opposition, it was equally true that no opposition was prepared to remain within legal limits. The premise of dictatorship was common to both sides of the argument." This assertion is not altogether true even of the Socialist Revolutionaries. It is true only in that they resorted to arms against the Bolshevik regime after the Constituent Assembly, in which they had gained a majority, was dispersed by force; and that some individuals within the party were prepared to co-operate with the White Armies in order to bring about the displacement of the Bolshevik dictatorship by a military dictatorship. It is wholly untrue of the Mensheviks, the most important political opposition. If the history of the rise to power of the Bolsheviks is to be seen in the light of historical fact, then it is time that these ghosts of Lenin's propaganda were laid once and for all. Lenin's "legal" opponents failed because, although they had the moral authority, they were not prepared to use Lenin's methods in order to defeat him. Conversely, his opponents in the field, the White Armies, while fully prepared to use Lenin's own methods against him, failed because they lacked the moral authority to reinforce their arms.

It remains to consider why Lenin's opponents within the Bolshevik party accepted his new political policy. For no major Bolshevik leader was prepared to head those who opposed Lenin. It is significant that there was no open support for the Kronstadt mutineers within the Bolshevik party anywhere outside Kronstadt. Some of the Bolshevik leaders, such as Karl Radek, a future victim of Stalin's purges, saw that the weapon now being forged could some day be turned against themselves. Trotsky, who a few years later was to lead an opposition against Stalin on this very issue of inner party freedom, fully supported Lenin in 1921. There were two main reasons for this submission. In the first place, no one fully grasped the real nature of the apparatus of control which was being created. The knowledge that their own monopoly of power was in jeopardy, the panic induced by the grim reality of the Kronstadt mutiny, in progress while the party congress which passed the fateful new resolutions was in session—all contributed to obscure the issue. Some may have had apprehensions. But no one saw the simple truth that, if unlimited and uncontrolled power is put into the hands of one small group, the inevitable result must be loss of all freedom for all except the strongest and least scrupulous member of that group. But the main reason was the ascendancy which Lenin's personality had won over the party. The spirit which underlay the Bolshevik revolution was the spirit of surrender. The liberals and socialists had surrendered rather than face squarely the issues which confronted them. The Bolsheviks had, in turn, surrendered their will and judgment to Lenin when he led the *coup d'état* of November 1917. They surrendered again when the promises of freedom, of revolutionary war, of the workers' state, were successively shattered. It was too late for them to draw back now.

Thus Lenin's blind rejection of compromise and his bid for sole power both made the Bolshevik revolution and, in the course of time, destroyed what it stood for. According to Trotsky's accounts, Lenin died disappointed with what he had created. This may well be true, for there is some independent evidence of serious dissension in 1922 between Lenin and the new masters of Russia, Stalin and Zinoviev, eighteen months before Lenin's death, but after illness had removed him from active control of affairs. Few men in history can have made a greater mark on the fate of their country, and few men have thrown away a greater opportunity. In 1917, with his country reduced to chaos by irresolute leadership, Lenin had the courage to seize power into his own hands. One can criticize his methods, while allowing due praise to his resolution. But in 1921, when wisdom, vision, compromise and moderation might have given Russia the beginnings of normal democratic development, he failed. His one lasting achievement remains that of having created an instrument of state tyranny, which in time completed the work he began—the elimination of moderation, tolerance, freedom and responsibility from the political life of his country.

3.

The most detailed analysis of the Leninist and Stalinist periods is the multi-volume *History of Soviet Russia* by the British scholar Edward Hallett Carr. Mr. Carr has had a varied career: twenty years (1916–1936) in the British diplomatic service, five years (1941–1946) as assistant editor of *The Times,* plus periods of teaching at the University College of Wales and Oxford. Since 1955 he has been a fellow of Trinity College, Cambridge. Mr. Carr has based his history of Soviet Russia on a minute analysis of contemporary Russian sources, and has sought to maintain an aloof value-free objectivity in examining those sources. Some of his critics have alleged that this technique leads him to accept the Soviet viewpoint somewhat uncritically; other critics charge him with a kind of amoral and deterministic view of history—the view that what happened was almost bound to happen.

CARR: History of Soviet Russia *

The term "dictatorship of the proletariat" applied by the Bolsheviks to the regime established by them in Russia after the October revolution, carried no specific constitutional implications. It defined the ruling class, but was neutral about the form of government through which that class exercised power. There was no opposition in this sense between dictatorship and representative government: the "dictatorship of the bourgeoisie," which was the antithesis of the dictatorship of the proletariat, was generally exercised through the medium of representative government. The emotional overtones of the word "dictatorship" as associated with the rule of the few or of one man were absent from the

* From E. H. Carr, *History of Soviet Russia: The Bolshevik Revolution 1917–1923* (London: Macmillan, 1950), Vol. 1, pp. 151–43, 164–68, 176–79, 184–87. Copyright 1950 by the Macmillan Company. Reprinted by permission of the publisher.

minds of Marxists who used the phrase. On the contrary, the dictatorship of the proletariat would be the first regime in history in which power would be exercised by the class constituting a majority of the population—a condition to be satisfied in Russia by drawing the mass of the peasantry into alliance with the industrial proletariat. Moreover, since the dictatorship of the proletariat was the rule of the vast majority, it would require, once the bourgeoisie was struck down, less compulsion to maintain it than any previous order of society. Far from being a rule of violence, it would pave the way for the disappearance of the use of violence as a social sanction, i.e. for dying away of the state.

Nothing in the first days of the revolution shattered this idealistic and optimistic mood. The almost effortless success of the Petrograd coup of October 25, 1917, seemed to show that it indeed had behind it the vast majority of the population. The boast of the Bolsheviks that the revolution itself cost remarkably few lives, and that most of these were lost in attempts by their opponents to wrest the victory from them when it had already been won, was justified. By one of those acts of generosity which often attend the first hours of a revolution, the young officer cadets captured at the Winter Palace were allowed to go free on promising not to "take up arms against the people any more." Krasnov, the "white" general who helped Kerensky to organize his futile counter-offensive from Gatchina and was captured there, was released on parole—which he broke a few weeks later to participate in the civil war in the south; and that this clemency was no accidental freak is shown by a statement of Lenin ten days after the Bolshevik victory: "We are reproached with using terror. But such terror as was used by the French revolutionaries who guillotined unarmed people we do not use and, I hope, shall not use. . . . When we have made arrests we have said: 'We will let you go if you will sign a paper promising not to commit acts of sabotage.' And such signatures are given." The members of the Provisional Government who had been arrested and lodged in Peter-and-Paul fortress on the day of the revolution were quickly released and subjected only to a nominal form of supervision, which did not prevent them from conspiring actively against the new regime. Capital levies or forced loans extracted more or less at haphazard from the bourgeoisie, or such incidents as that of the threat to send fifteen wealthy Kharkov capitalists down the Donetz mines if they did not provide a million rubles to pay the Kharkov workers, were evidence not so much of calculated ferocity as of the dilemma of inexperienced and determined men trying to create a workable administrative machine out of non-existent or recalcitrant material. In the desperate chaos of the first weeks of the revolution the new rulers had little time for concerted action or even for consistent thinking and planning; almost every step taken by them was either a reaction to some pressing emergency or a reprisal for some action or threatened action against them. In seeking to ride the storm they were themselves driven before it. Many cases of mob violence occurred in the cities and throughout the country. Many brutalities and atrocities were committed by revolutionaries as well as by their adversaries. But no regular executions either by summary judgment or by normal judicial process appear to have taken place in the first three months of the regime. The first legislative act of the second All-Russian Congress of Soviets on the day after the revolution had been to abolish the death penalty at the front, where it had been restored by Kerensky in September 1917 under military pressure after its total abolition at the time of the February revolution. The revolutionary tradition of opposition to the death sentence weakened and collapsed only after the outbreak of the civil war and open insurrection against the Soviet regime. . . .

The situation was . . . exceedingly tense when the fifth All-Russian Congress of Soviets met in Moscow at a critical moment in history on July 4, 1918. Of the 1132 delegates with voting powers, the Bolsheviks accounted for 745, the Left SRs for 352, the remainder representing various small fractions. The proceedings at once developed into a duel between the two major parties. The peasant issue was raised, but was less in evidence than indignation at the suppression of rival parties and at the use of the death penalty. The sharpest protests of all were heard against the Brest-Litovsk treaty and the subservience of the Soviet Government to Germany; and the most animated clashes of the congress occurred over Trotsky's insistence that it would be madness to tolerate any attack on the German forces in the Ukraine. On July 6, 1918, apparently in the hope of forcing a breach, two Left SRs assassinated the German ambassador, Mirbach. The murder was planned by SR members of the Cheka [the secret police], and the assassins gained admittance to the ambassador by producing papers purporting to have been signed by Dzerzhinsky. This coup was followed by an attempt to seize power in Moscow and by insurrections in various provincial centres, of which that at Yaroslav was the most serious. Savinkov, the well-known SR terrorist, afterwards claimed to have been financed by funds supplied through the French military attaché in Moscow.

Faced with treason on this large scale at a moment when allied forces were landing in Murmansk and Vladiovostok, when the Czech legions had begun open hostilities against the Bolsheviks, and when the threat of war was looming on all sides, the Soviet Government was under no temptation to resort to half measures. The rising in Moscow was quickly put down. Most of the Left SR delegates to the fifth All-Russian Congress of Soviets were arrested, including Spiridonova, who admitted that Mirbach's assassins had acted on her instructions; thirteen of them who had been members of the Cheka were shot. Several newspapers were suppressed. After three days of confusion the congress resumed its sittings and, having expressed approval of the actions of the goverment, passed a cautiously worded resolution to the effect that "in so far as certain sections of the Left SR party associate themselves with the attempt to involve Russia in war through the murder of Mirbach and the rising against Soviet power, these organizations can have no place in the Soviets of Workers' and Peasants' Deputies." The concluding act of the congress on July 10, 1918, was to approve the constitution of the RSFSR, which thus came into force at the darkest and most dangerous moment in the history of the republic, when the open revolt of the last considerable independent party had driven the regime a long step further on the road to the one-party state.

Accounts of punitive measures taken by the Cheka are nearly always fragmentary and unreliable. But some authentic information exists of the reprisals which followed the suppression of the wide-spread provincial revolts of the summer of 1918. The insurgents in Yaroslav held out for a fortnight, and 350 were shot when the city was finally taken. In the neighbouring town of Murom, where the revolt collapsed at once, 10 leaders were shot and a levy of a million rubles imposed on the bourgeoisie. In Nizhny-Novgorod, 700 "officers and gendarmes" were arrested, and the local Cheka "broke up the white-guard organization . . . by arresting almost its entire membership and shooting part of it." On the night of July 16–17, 1918, the former Tsar and his family were shot in Ekaterinburg by order of the Ural regional Soviet. When the Czechs captured the town ten days later, the Ural regional Cheka moved to Vyatka, where it arrested more than 400 persons and shot 35 who were "involved in counter-revolutionary plots." When a *"kulak* rising" occurred in August 1918 in Penza, Lenin himself telegraphed instructions "to put into effect an unsparing mass terror against *kulaks,* priests, and white guards, and to confine suspects in a camp outside the city," and recommended the taking of hostages who would "answer with their life" for prompt and accurate deliveries of grain. These bald records undoubtedly conceal horrors and brutalities committed both in the heat of battle and in cold blood and common to all parties, though specific accounts of them rarely carry conviction. Such occurrences, as well as the multiplication, exaggeration and sheer invention of them by opponents, are the invariable concomitants of war and revolution waged with the fanatical desperation which marked the struggle unleashed in Russia by the events of October 1917.

The sanctions thus applied were frankly described by their authors as "terror" and justified as measures of war. "The Soviet power must guarantee its rear" ran a resolution adopted by VTsIK [the All-Russian Central Executive Committee] on July 29, 1918, after speeches by Lenin and Trotsky, "by putting the bourgeoisie under supervision and carrying out mass terror against it." And Dzerzhinsky said in a press interview at this time:

The Cheka is not a court. The Cheka is *the defence of the revolution* as the Red Army is; as in the civil war the Red Army cannot stop to ask whether it may harm particular individuals, but must take into account only one thing, the victory of the revolution over the bourgeoisie, so the Cheka must defend the revolution and conquer the enemy even if its sword falls occasionally on the heads of the innocent.

But the culmination of the terror was provoked by a further recourse of the SRs to the method of political assassination—this time against the Bolsheviks. Volodarsky, a Bolshevik leader famous in his day as a mob orator, had been killed in Petrograd in June 1918. On August 30, 1918, Uritsky was also assassinated in Petrograd, and Lenin seriously wounded in Moscow. All these assaults could be traced to SRs of one faction or another. The indignation and the fear caused by them put fresh weapons into the hands of the Cheka. Next day the British representative in Moscow was arrested on a charge of British complicity in counter-revolutionary plots, and the British naval attaché was killed in an attack on the British embassy in Petrograd. On September 2, 1918, VTsIK adopted a resolution on the murder of Uritsky and the assault on Lenin which concluded:

All counter-revolutionaries and all who inspired them will be held responsible for every attempt on workers of the Soviet Government and upholders of the ideals of the socialist revolution. To the white terror of the enemies of the Workers' and Peasants' Government the workers and peasants will reply by a mass red terror against the bourgeoisie and its agents.

More than a coincidence of date recalls the Paris terror of September 2, 1792, when, following on the Duke of Brunswick's proclamation threatening foreign intervention and ruthless repression of the revolution, mass reprisals started in Paris in which 3000 aristocrats are said to have perished. In both revolutions this date marked the turning-point after which the terror, hitherto sporadic and unorganized, became a deliberate instrument of policy. . . .

The first months of 1921 brought the most serious internal crisis in Soviet history since the summer of 1918. The end of the civil war revealed the full extent of the losses and destruction which it had entailed and removed the restraints of loyalty which war commonly imposes; discontent with the regime became, for the first time outside political circles, widespread and vocal, extending both to peasants and to factory workers; the Kronstadt mutiny of the beginning of March 1921, was its expression and its symbol. At the tenth party congress in the same month, which approved the New Economic Policy (NEP), party discipline was tightened up to meet the emergency. The toleration of dissentient minorities outside the party became all the more anomalous. No formal decree similar to that of June 1918 was issued. But Lenin himself seems to have given the signal. In a pamphlet in defence of NEP published in May 1921 he wrote:

As for the non-party people who are nothing else but Mensheviks and SRs dressed up in modern, Kronstadt, non-party attire, we shall either keep them safely in prison or send them to Martov in Berlin for the free enjoyment of all the amenities of free democracy and for free exchange of ideas with Chernov, Milyukov and the Georgian Mensheviks.

According to a Menshevik source, the result of this hint was immediate:

Repressions against social democrats began all over Russia. The only way to avoid persecution was to write a statement to the Bolshevik newspaper renouncing any connexion with the Social-Democratic Party. Many complied; but many also were banished to Solovki, to Suzdal, Siberia, Turkestan and so forth.

Martyrs seem to have been few. No obstacles were placed in the way of the departure of the Menshevik leaders for Berlin, where in the spring of 1921 an important Menshevik centre was established with a Menshevik weekly journal, *Sotsialisticheskii Vestnik*. The rank and file for the most part made their submission or abandoned political activity. There is, however, a certain irony in the fact that the extinction of organized political opposition to Bolshevism from without coincided with the development of the most important organized opposition within the party since the days of Brest-Litovsk. Sharp differences of opinion continued to exist. But they were now concentrated within the party. The party had drawn into itself the whole political life of the country. Its internal affairs were henceforth the political history of the nation.

It is, however, once more significant of the flexibility of Soviet policy, and of its empiricism in the choice of means, that this same spring and summer of 1921, which saw the virtual extinction of all independent parties in Soviet Russia, should have witnessed the two most serious attempts made to bring about an understanding between the Soviet power and the survivors of the bourgeois intelligentsia remaining on Soviet soil. On the Soviet side, NEP was the symptom of a willingness to compromise which might be supposed to have its political counterpart; on the other side, many of those Russians hitherto hostile to the Soviet power, whether in Russia or already in emigration, saw in NEP a surrender of the hitherto uncompromising principles of Bolshevism which might pave the way for a partial reconciliation. In April 1921 a proposal was put forward for a joint public meeting to be followed by a banquet between representatives of the Soviet Government and of the bourgeois intelligentsia, at which the official spokesmen were to explain the significance of NEP and the spokesman of the intelligentsia to welcome the change in policy. The plan broke down owing to the intransigence of the representatives of the intelligentsia who were unwilling to commit themselves to any public blessing of Soviet action. At the end of June 1921 news of the catastrophic famine threatening the eastern provinces of European Russia began to reach Moscow; and a group of public men and intellectuals approached the Soviet authorities with proposals for an appeal to foreign countries for help. The magnitude of the impending disaster and the belief that a conciliatory gesture would favourably impress foreign opinion made the Soviet Government amenable to the project. A decree of July 21, 1921, set up an All-Russian Committee for Aid to the Hungry consisting of some sixty persons. These included Kamenev, the president of the committee, Rykov, Lunacharsky, Krasin, Maxim Gorky and a few other Bolsheviks, two former ministers of the Provisional Government, Kishkin and Prokopovich, some prominent Kadets and a large number of non-party intellectuals. It was to draw funds from voluntary contributions and from a state subsidy, to collect supplies both in Russia and abroad, and to see to their distribution.

Such a committee was unique in the history of the Soviet regime, and the difficulties inherent in it were quickly revealed. The *émigré* Russian press hailed the step as proof that the Soviet regime was in desperate straits and no longer able to maintain itself without bourgeois support; the British representative, newly arrived in Moscow, entered into relations with the committee over the head of the Soviet Government; and foreign governments showed an obvious inclination to treat it as an alternative government which might succeed to power once the Soviet regime was overthrown. The committee in fact did little but collect information and make publicity at home and abroad. On August 20, 1921, the Soviet Government concluded an agreement with Hoover's American Relief Administration (ARA) for the organization of famine relief. This success made the continued existence of the committee, from the Soviet point of view, not only superfluous, but dangerous; for ARA clearly hoped to use the relief programme to weaken the position of the Soviet government and would seek as far as possible to deal with the predominantly bourgeois committee rather than with the Bolshevik authorities. At an earlier stage plans had been made for delegates of the committee to proceed to London and other foreign countries to solicit aid. This was now out of the question. The Soviet Government informed the committee that its work in Moscow was complete, and that its members should take their place in the organization of relief in the stricken region. When the majority of the committee refused to accept this decision and insisted on the plan of sending delegates abroad, it was formally dissolved by a decree of August 27, 1921, and its leading bourgeois members arrested. Thus ended the first and last attempt at cooperation between the Soviet regime and the surviving elements of the old order. It illustrated both the intensity of the mutual animosity between them and the way in which any independent force in Soviet Russia became, or could be plausibly suspected of becoming, a focus of foreign intervention against the regime. . . .

The tendency to concentrate power at the centre of any large organization, and the necessity of concentration as a condition of efficient working, has been a commonplace of modern political parties. Parties, like the anarchists, which resisted it condemned themselves to political sterility; other parties were, on the whole, successful in proportion to their willingness to accept the discipline of a strong central authority and management. This fact has disturbing implications for parties purporting to be organized on democratic lines. All organized political parties—and particularly parties representing the masses, where the rank and file is widely separated from the leaders by the intellectual and technical qualifications required for leadership—have tended, however democratic the principles on which they rest, to develop in the direction of a closed oligarchy of leaders. A sociologist [Robert Michels] whose material was derived mainly from study of the German Social-Democratic Party and the Italian Socialist Party before 1914 has diagnosed the symptoms:

In every social relation nature itself creates domination and dependence. Thus every party organization represents a powerful oligarchy resting on democratic feet. Everywhere are electors and elected. But everywhere, too, is the power of the elected leadership over the electing masses. The oligarchic structure of the building conceals the democratic foundation.

When the Bolsheviks became a mass party after 1917 this process set in rapidly. It was no doubt accelerated by the traditions of secrecy and discipline established in the party before 1917, by the special position which it gradually achieved after 1917 as a monopoly party in the state, and perhaps also by the political backwardness and inexperience of the Russian workers in comparison with their western counterparts. But the perspective will be seriously distorted if the process is regarded as peculiarly Russian or peculiarly Bolshevik. It was common, in greater or less degree, to all political parties of the first half of the twentieth century.

The evolution of a revolutionary party into a governmental party has been a feature of all victorious revolutions, and produces some consequences so familiar that they may be called stereotyped. The party, turning from the task of destruction to that of administration, discovers the virtues of law and order and of submission to the rightful authority of the revolutionary power; and it is attacked from the Left by those who wish to carry on the revolution in the name of former revolutionary principles which the government of the revolution is now alleged to be betraying. This pattern was followed in the history of the Russian revolution. But another and more distinctive feature resulted from the new interaction of party and state. The association between party and state directly involved the party in every national crisis, and transformed every call for national unity and national leadership into a call for party unity and loyalty to the party leader. To close the ranks was, for the party as for the nation, the natural reaction to the national danger. Nor was it possible to separate Lenin the party leader from Lenin the leader of the nation. The ascendancy which he exercised was one of moral authority rather than of external power. But it helped to establish in the party, as well as in the state, a tradition of personal leadership which it was difficult to shake off.

. . . [Another] important change was the acquisition by the party of what was in effect a political monopoly in Soviet territory. No political theory denies to a political party the right to impose rigid conditions, whether of conduct or of creed, on its members and to exclude those who fail to comply. This right, however, had hitherto presupposed that the individual had the option of changing his party allegiance, and that some alternative party had a comparable opportunity of influencing public affairs. Before the revolution dissenting Bolsheviks could, and did, become Mensheviks or join other parties or political groups. In the first months after the revolution this fluidity of membership between the surviving parties—Bolsheviks and Mensheviks, Left and Right SRs—was still to some extent operative. The Bolsheviks were the ruling party, but still one of several parties. But after the summer of 1918 other political parties existed only in sufferance, their status becoming more and more precarious; and from 1921 onwards they virtually disappeared. Resignation or expulsion from the sole remaining party henceforth normally meant—to say the least—exclusion from any legal form of political activity. Thus disputes within the party were liable to grow increasingly bitter both because there was no other channel through which dissentient opinions could be expressed and because such opinions could now plausibly be attributed to former Mensheviks or SRs who had entered the party for insincere or interested motives. It became easy and natural to treat dissent as disloyalty. In the one-party state conceptions of party unity and party discipline developed hitherto unsuspected implications.

4.

The comparative anatomy of revolutions is a subject of perennial interest. Isaac Deutscher, in his biography of Josef Stalin, makes a brief excursion into this realm, and seeks to lay out a basic pattern of revolution. He is particularly concerned to show how and why the initial harmony between the revolutionary party and the masses breaks down, and what happens when the party faces the crucial choice between compromise and dictatorship. Mr. Deutscher was born in Poland, where he worked as a journalist from 1924 to 1939. After emigrating to England, he joined the staffs of *The Economist* and *The Observer;* since 1949 he has written and lectured extensively on Russia. Mr. Deutscher was a member of the Polish Communist party until 1932, when he was expelled for anti-Stalinist deviationism. Some of his critics find in his writings a strong surviving remnant of historical determinism, the product perhaps of his early Marxian training.

DEUTSCHER: Stalin: A Political Biography *

The October upheaval—a mild, bloodless event—was followed by a cruel civil war and foreign intervention which lasted nearly three years. The new revolutionary state formed itself less under the influence of ideas preached by the Bolsheviks when they seized power than under the harsh exigencies of civil war. Events compelled the party of the revolution to give up some of its aspirations, hopes, and illusions in order to save the essential framework of the revolution. In the process, the party itself, its leaders and followers, underwent a profound spiritual and political change.

One broad aspect of that change has been common to all revolutions so far. Each great revolution begins with a phenomenal outburst of popular energy, impatience, anger, and hope. Each ends in the weariness, exhaustion, and disillusionment of the revolutionary people. In the first phase the party that gives the fullest expression to the popular mood outdoes its rivals, gains the confidence of the masses, and rises to power. Even the most revolutionary party is sometimes not revolutionary enough in the eyes of the most extreme section of the people. It is driven forward by the swelling tide to overcome all the obstacles in its way and to challenge all conservative powers. Then comes the inevitable trial of civil war. The revolutionary party is still marching in step with the majority of the nation. It is acutely conscious of its unity with the people and of a profound harmony between its own objectives and the people's wishes and desires. It can call upon the mass of the nation for ever-growing efforts and sacrifices; and it is sure of the response. In this, the heroic phase, the revolutionary party is in a very real sense democratic, even though it treats its foes with dictatorial relentlessness and observes no strict constitutional precept. The leaders implicitly trust their vast plebeian following; and their policy rests on that trust. They are willing and even eager to submit their policies to open debate and to accept the popular verdict. Though they aspire to lead the masses, they also allow themselves to be led.

This happy relationship between the party of the revolution, whether it be called Independent, Jacobin, or Bolshevik, and the mass of the people does not last long. It hardly survives the civil war. Many of the devoted and energetic supporters of the new order perish in the civil war. Others rise from their modest and unpretentious existence to power and often also to privilege. The party of the revolution emerges triumphant, with tremendous pride and self-confidence, but also with inner weariness and enervation. The weariness of the people is even deeper. The country, ravaged by civil war and intervention, has sunk into a misery that may be worse than that against which the people had risen in revolt. In 1920 Russia suffered worse hunger and privation than in 1917. The ruthlessness of the new rulers, a ruthlessness dictated by circumstances and the needs of self-preservation, provokes a reaction. The reaction may be strongest among those who have previously urged the party to pursue the course that has made that ruthlessness inevitable.

The anti-climax of the revolution is there. The leaders are unable to keep their early promises. They have destroyed the old order; but they are unable to satisfy the daily needs of the people. To be sure, the revolution has created the basis for a higher organization of society and for progress in a not very remote future. This will justify it in the eyes of posterity. But the fruits of revolution ripen slowly; and of immediate moment are the miseries of the first post-revolutionary years. It is in their shadow that the new state takes on its shape, a shape that reveals the chasm between the revolutionary party and the people. This is the real tragedy which overtakes the party of the revolution. If its action is to be dictated by the mood of the people, it will presently have to efface itself, or at least to relinquish power. But no revolutionary government can abdicate after a victorious civil war, because the only real pretenders to power are the still considerable remnants of the defeated counter-revolution. Abdication would be suicide. It would entail, too, a reversal of the vast work of the revolution by which society has been transformed but which has not yet been consolidated. The political mechanics of a regime around which all the passions of revolution and counter-revolution have been let loose has no feature like those political revolving doors provided by any stable parliamentary order, through which governments come or go more or less politely without chopping off one another's heads. The party of the revolution knows no retreat. It has been driven to its present pass largely through obeying the will of that same people by which it is now deserted. It will go on doing what it considers to be its duty, without paying much heed to the voice of the people. In the end it will muzzle and stifle that voice.

At first the party of the revolution is by no means clearly aware of all the implications of the new phase. It has assumed office as a government of the people, by the people, and for the people. It now forfeits at least one of its honourable attributes—it ceases to be government by the people. The whole party may still hope that its discord with the mood of the country is transient; and that honest exertion in one direction or another will allow it to fire anew the imagination of the people and to recapture the recent heroic past. But the chasm is growing wider and deeper. The rulers acquire the habits of arbitrary government and themselves come to be governed by their own habits. What had hopefully begun as a great, warm-hearted popular venture gradually degenerates into a narrow and cold autocracy. In the transition, the party of the revolution is split between those who have promoted the new outlook, or made peace with it, and those who have not. Some of its leaders point in alarm to the divorce between the revolution and the people. Others justify the conduct of the party on the ground that the divorce is irremediable. Still others, the actual rulers, deny the fact of the divorce itself: for to admit it would be to widen further the gap between the rulers and the ruled. Some cry in alarm that the revolution has been betrayed, for in their eyes government by the people is the very essence of revolution—without it there can be no government for the people. The rulers find justification for themselves in the conviction that whatever they do will ultimately serve the interests of the broad mass of the nation; and indeed they do, on the whole, use their power to consolidate most of the economic and social conquests of the revolution. Amid charges and counter-charges, the heads of the revolutionary leaders begin to roll and the power of the post-revolutionary state towers hugely over the society it governs.

In this broad scheme of revolutionary development much must seem simplified and confused. Historical truth consists less in the broad generalizations than in the complex sequence of events, different in each revolution. Some features which appear only dimly in the picture of one revolution are very clear and distinct in that of another. Processes, for instance, by which Jacobinism was consumed and destroyed within a few months, have developed in Bolshevism slowly, over whole decades; and their results, too, have in many respects been vastly different. But what is important in this context is the general trend of events; and this has been common to all great revolutions so far. It is in this broad perspective that the metamorphosis of triumphant Bolshevism, and Stalin's own fortunes, can best be understood. . . .

In March 1921 the restive mood of the country suddenly flared up in the rising of Kronstadt which coincided with the tenth Congress of the party. "This was the flash," said Lenin, "which lit up reality better than anything else." There was a bitter irony in the fact that the scene of the rising was Kronstadt, the Bolshevik stronghold of 1917. White Guards sympathizers, Anarchists, and even Bolsheviks fought side by side against the Red troops which, on Tukhachevsky's orders, rushed across the frozen surface of the Bay of Finland to suppress the rising. A measure of the alarm that the rising caused in the ruling party can be seen in the fact that on receiving the news about the outbreak the Congress of the party interrupted its debates and sent most of its delegates to participate in the storming of Kronstadt. At no critical moment of the civil war had there been any comparable panic.

The insurgents of Kronstadt demanded an end to the dictatorship of the

Bolshevik party and the restitution of genuine government by Soviets such as the Bolsheviks had promised to establish. They also demanded an end to economic and political oppression. Some of the leaders were Anarchists and left Communists; and their watchwords were borrowed from the slogans of the Bolsheviks in the early days of the revolution. Yet, in spite of its extreme left colouring, the rising stirred new hope in the ranks of the defeated counter-revolution. The dictatorship had reached a point, familiar from other revolutions, when, having defeated the adherents of the *ancien régime* it drove Right and Left, conservatives and revolutionaries, into a common bitter opposition. For a while, the shadow of the tumbrils which amid the rejoicing of the Parisian plebs and aristocracy carried Robespierre to the guillotine must have appeared before Lenin's eyes.

The rising was defeated, and from it Lenin drew the following conclusion: ". . . we had advanced too far . . . we had not secured a sufficient base . . . the masses had sensed what we ourselves could not as yet consciously formulate . . . namely, that the direct transition to purely Socialist distribution, was beyond our strength, and that, unless we proved able to retreat and to confine ourselves to easier tasks, we would be threatened with disaster." The system of War Communism was scrapped and replaced by the so-called New Economic Policy. . . .

Almost simultaneously another, less conspicuous, act was carried out in the political field, an act the implications of which were hardly clear to its authors. While the economic dictatorship was radically relaxed, the political dictatorship was tightened. During the later stages of the civil war the parties of the opposition, Mensheviks and Social Revolutionaries, were finally suppressed. The next step was to forbid the formation of any opposition groups inside the ruling party itself. Unknowingly, almost gropingly, Bolshevism now reached the threshold of what was later to be called the totalitarian state. It is necessary to stop here for a moment to contemplate once again the outlook of Bolshevism and to analyse the impulses and the motives of its leaders in order to obtain a clue both to the further evolution of the Soviets and to Stalin's subsequent ascendancy. . . .

The idea that a single party should rule the Soviets was not at all inherent in the Bolshevik programme. Still less so was the idea that only a single party should be allowed to exist. The proscription of the other parties, wrote Trotsky, was "obviously in conflict with the spirit of Soviet democracy" and "the leaders of Bolshevism regarded [it] not as a principle but as an episodic act of self-defence." For a party with such a record of free and uninhibited inner controversy, the ban on internal opposition groups was a most drastic departure from its own time-honoured custom. The party was now at loggerheads with its own nature, it contradicted itself while it was trying to assert itself.

Towards the end of the civil war Bolshevism was in conflict with the classes that had supported it. The discontent of peasants and workers was voiced by Mensheviks, Social Revolutionaries, and Anarchists, whose criticisms of the Bolsheviks were now as convincing and effective as they had been ineffective between 1917 and 1919. If the mechanism of Soviet democracy had been allowed to function, if the Soviets had been freely elected and free to elect the Government, they would almost certainly have swept the Bolsheviks out of office and returned to power the same parties on whom they had previously turned their backs. The Bolsheviks were determined to forestall this. To their mind the revolution was safe only if the party of the revolution was in power. All their recent experience confirmed them in that view. The revolution had conquered in spite of and against all the doubts, hesitations, and obstructiveness of the Mensheviks and the Social Revolutionaries. The moderate Socialists had not the pluck and the fibre to wage a civil war. Their return to power could, in the Bolshevik view, be no more than an episode ending in the return of the White Guards and the restoration of the *ancien régime*. True enough, from weariness and exhaustion, the masses were now inclined to back Mensheviks or Anarchists; but should the masses be allowed to jeopardize the whole work of the revolution? Should the Soviets be given back their freedom of action when they were almost certain to use it for their own undoing? This was a situation in which, in Dante's words, "the people shouted: 'Death to our life! Life to our death!' "; and most of the Bolshevik leaders refused to listen.

Yet, while the mouthpieces of popular discontent were removed or silenced, the discontent was not. Nor could the conflicting interests of the various classes, especially those of the peasants, be conjured out of existence by the repression of their spokesmen. Now the mind of the ruling party itself, of that lonely victor on the political battlefield, began to be invaded by moods of frustration and discontent. Now this and now that section of the party began to air familiar grievances and complaints. The cleavages existing in the country threatened to cleave the ruling party itself and it had now to be kept together with iron bands. The sensitiveness of the party had to be blunted, its sight dimmed, and its hearing dulled in order to make its mind immune from undesirable influences. The need for all this seemed to become even more urgent in connexion with the reforms of the N.E.P. Capitalist groups and interests were allowed new scope in the economic domain; but no party was left to represent them in the political field. It was only natural that they should seek channels of expression, and that they should seek them amid the only political party left in existence. Only absolute insulation could prevent the party from splitting into a number of hostile parties.

The task Bolshevism now set itself, however, was little different from squaring a circle. To save the revolution's conquests it had to suppress the spontaneous rhythm of the country's political life. But in doing so, the party was mutilating its own body and mind. From now on its members would fear to express opinions which might, on analysis, be found to reflect "the pressure of alien classes." Only the highest authority could decide which view was Bolshevik and proletarian and which was not. Matters of ideology became mysteriously elusive; and the Politbureau became the sole repository of revolutionary wisdom. Most leaders were gradually losing touch with the feeling of their followers since the traffic of ideas moved only one way—from the Politbureau downwards. The party was gradually to transform itself into a bureaucratic machine. It was true enough that concern for the revolution compelled Bolshevism to take the road chosen by the tenth congress; but it was also true that as it moved along that road Bolshevism was losing more and more of its original self. In order to save the revolution the party ceased to be a free association of independent, critically minded, and courageous revolutionaries. The bulk of it submitted to the ever more powerful party machine. It saw no other solution. Those who handled the levers of the machine and were most intimately associated with it, those to whose upbringing and temperament the new bureaucratic outlook was most congenial, automatically became the leaders of the new era. The administrator began to elbow out the ideologue, the bureaucrat and committee-man eliminated the idealist. Who could be favoured by this evolution and who could favour it more strongly than Stalin, the committee-man *par excellence,* the committee-man writ large?

The trend of events did not very rapidly become apparent. It developed gradually, in contradictory zigzags, always at odds with the inertia of earlier habits. Nor was the cleavage between administrator and idealist hard and fast. There was no lack of idealism in the administrators; and the ideologues at first willingly surrendered to the bureaucrats or even vied with them in fostering the new discipline. Thus, in the debate over the trade unions, the ideologue Trotsky so overreached himself in promoting bureaucratic aspirations that he shocked even the staunchest bureaucrats and incurred considerable unpopularity. In Lenin the different characters were almost perfectly blended. That is why he was so ideally suited to preside over the transition of his party from one stage to the other. For the time being his moral authority enforced a temporary and shaky compromise on the conflicting tendencies, a compromise that was bound to break down after his death. But even in his lifetime the weight of the bureaucratic caucus grew steadily, if imperceptibly, with every month that passed by; and so did Stalin's role inside the caucus.

VI.

THE FIRST APPEASEMENT ERA: LOCARNO

The Locarno pact was regarded by many Europeans at the time of its signing as marking the dawn of an era of goodwill, and as the final reconciliation of the principal contestants of the first world war. Although this viewpoint may seem naïve today, it did not seem naïve in 1925, and there can be little question that in the mid-1920's the world was in need of some good news.

It should be recalled that the Locarno pact was concluded after a long series of disappointments. The United States had declined to join the League of Nations, various draft agreements and protocols designed to bring some measure of security against a resurgent Germany had failed to obtain the necessary ratifications, and the bitterness of the war seemed to be lingering on, especially, it appeared to many observers, because of the French occupation of the Ruhr in 1923 and the runaway German inflation. But with the Locarno pact, peace and concord seemed to be assured at long last; perhaps the memories of the war could now be buried. At any rate, expectations were raised, and Briand, Austen Chamberlain, and Stresemann shared the Nobel Peace Prize for their roles in negotiating Locarno.

In a consideration of the Locarno era, it is well to look ahead, and to see it in the light of what was to come. Was Locarno an example of appeasement which worked, and which stands in contrast to Munich? Does it help to justify those later statesmen who thought appeasement might work a second time, or does it simply provide another example of the German leaders' skill in taking advantage of the credulity and war-weariness of the western powers? Did the Germans, or the French, concede anything, or gain anything, of importance by the Locarno pact? Did Locarno mark a significant turning point in British foreign policy, or was it just another manifestation of Britain's desire to keep its continental commitments to the minimum—even in regard to France? Was the unwillingness of the British to concern themselves with eastern Europe, and thus to consider an "eastern Locarno," an indication of the attitude they would adopt in 1938 toward Czechoslovakia, an attitude that, in 1925, as well as later, was just what the Germans were seeking? Indeed, was not the policy of the West, as shown by Locarno as well as by Munich, clearly one of protecting itself by turning German ambitions against the Bolsheviks? Did Stresemann's efforts immediately after Locarno to maintain friendly relations with the Soviet Union show Germany's hypocrisy in its dealings with the West and foreshadow the Nazi-Soviet Pact of 1939? Or was Stresemann doing all he could, in the face of considerable opposition at home, to reduce world tensions, and to enable Germany to re-enter the community of nations as an equal, with its vital interests protected and guaranteed? It has been argued that Locarno provided the one great opportunity to establish the Weimar Republic more firmly, but that the West's delays in completing the evacuation of the Rhineland and in achieving a final solution of the reparations problem caused the opportunity to be lost: "a rapid and generous redress of the justified German grievances might have prevented the rise of the nationalist tide in the early thirties." [1] On the other hand, Locarno may have been intended by the Germans to act as a smoke screen: it has been argued that Stresemann was, despite his reputation as a man of peace and as an early leader in the move toward European unification, influential in the secret and illegal rearmament of Germany.[2]

It is essential to consider the foundations on which European diplomacy rested in the 1920's, in order to appreciate fully the importance of the Locarno pact. The attempts of the French to maintain, or to establish, hegemony in Europe by means of alliances with the small nations of eastern Europe have often been criticized as a policy far beyond the capabilities of a nation gravely weakened by war. But before one is unduly hard on the French, it is well to consider the failure of the Anglo-Saxon powers to help France gain a sense of security and to police the continent; did France have any alternative to a system of eastern European alliances? Could any European "system" which excluded the Soviet Union (and the United States) operate successfully? What was the role, and what were the possibilities, of the League of Nations? Did the difficulties of Europe in the 1920's indicate that an era had ended, that Europe's economy and political system were no longer capable of providing the foundation for a rational balance among competing interests, and that the vacuums of power left by the collapse of the great empires of central and eastern Europe could be filled only at the expense of what was left of the "old order?" It may be that all of this marked the beginning of the end of the era of the "nation-state," and the beginning of the age of the continental power, just as an earlier period had marked the decline of the "city-state."

Whatever the reasons, Locarno did not provide the basis for a lasting peace. Whether this was because of the pact itself or was because of the reservations of the powers which signed the pact, or whether Locarno was a hopeful start toward peace, killed in youth because of factors beyond the control of those who conceived it, is the central question toward which discussion ought to be directed.

1.

Arnold Wolfers was born in Switzerland, and after a varied and distinguished career, which included several years of teaching in Berlin and wartime government service in Washington, retired as Sterling Professor of International Relations at Yale in 1957. He is presently director of the Johns Hopkins Cen-

[1] Felix G. Hirsch, "Locarno—25 Years After," *The Contemporary Review*, 178 (November, 1950), p. 285.

[2] Hans W. Gatzke, *Stresemann and the Rearmament of Germany* (Baltimore: Johns Hopkins Press, 1954).

ter of Foreign Policy Research. In the following selection he provides an excellent introduction to the study of the diplomacy of the interwar years. After reading Mr. Wolfers' comments, one should be clearly aware of the extent of the friction which developed between Britain and France in respect to Germany, and one may well wonder which of the two powers was more bound by prejudices inherited from the past, and which of the two showed the greater foresight.

WOLFERS: Britain and France Between Two Wars *

Stresemann has been accused of having deceived Briand. Was he not simply advising Germany to "lie low" so that she might gain time to prepare for the great attack on the treaty? However, it is unnecessary to postulate an interpretation so unfavorable to Stresemann's sincerity in his dealings with Briand. Germany inaugurated the policy of *rapprochement* with what she regarded as great sacrifices. By the treaty signed at Locarno she waived her claims to Alsace and Lorraine; she put her signature to an agreement that provided for the permanent demilitarization of the Rhineland; she promised not to use force to change the boundaries of Germany in the east. Stresemann assumed that this, together with a willingness on the part of Germany to fulfill her current treaty obligations, should be enough gradually to allay France's fears and suspicions of her neighbor. Once she learned to feel secure at the side of Germany, France would come to realize that it was to her own advantage and to that of her continental allies to accept the German point of view and promote revision of some of the most unjust and untenable provisions of the Versailles settlement. Reconciliation was thus to pave the way toward peaceful change.

It is hard to believe that so shrewd a statesman as Briand could have been under any illusions as to the German feelings about Versailles, at least at the time the policy of *rapprochement* was inaugurated. But what he apparently hoped for was that time would work in favor of France. If the German Republic were given time to consolidate, and if the German people regained prosperity through economic collaboration with France, would they not realize that they could live and prosper without changing the order of Versailles? Would they not then prefer to abide by the *status quo* rather than risk their own welfare by creating new trouble and perhaps plunging Europe into a new war? Briand's plans for European confederation and economic agreements, proposed during the same period, would lessen the importance of boundaries and thus eliminate the main incentive for territorial revision. *Rapprochement* would reconcile Germany with the *status quo*.

The effects of this basic Franco-German misunderstanding, the *"équivoque"* of Locarno (as Millerand, one of Briand's ardent opponents, repeatedly called

* From Arnold Wolfers, *Britain and France Between Two Wars* (New York: Harcourt, Brace and Co., 1940), pp. 64–65, 236–40, 257–61, 380–83. Reprinted by permission of Harcourt, Brace and World.

it), were bound in time to make themselves felt. Impatience grew on both sides and in both countries strengthened the nationalists, who were hostile to the Locarno policy and who were soon able to declare triumphantly that the promises were not being fulfilled. Germany was waiting for evidence that her "good behavior" and her voluntary acceptance of certain essential clauses of the Treaty of Versailles were going to bear fruit in the form of substantial concessions. The French, meanwhile, were waiting for Germany to show her gratitude for having been spared further threats and intimidations and to cease raising new claims every time one had been satisfied. It is not surprising that under these circumstances *rapprochement* should have ended in dismal failure. . . .

Britain was constantly trying to keep France from provoking Germany. As Lloyd George put it, "A nation which is exasperated by incessant provocation will not reckon the cost. . . ." It was one of her basic assumptions that the pacification of Germany and of the Continent depended upon France's not taking any action or continuing any policy which would give Germany legitimate reasons for feeling provoked. The result was that practically any move France undertook to enforce the treaty or to preserve her preponderance was open to the interpretation of provocativeness. Britain was taking it upon herself to be the judge of the psychological effects of French policy. The clash between Clemenceau and Lloyd George at Versailles on this very question gives some indication of how Frenchmen must have resented this attitude of Britain, though few of them dared to declare themselves as plainly as Clemenceau. Germany's resentment and dissatisfaction, he said, did not depend upon what France and her continental allies did in the future. By destroying Germany's position as a world power, by taking her colonies, destroying her navy, and seizing her capital holdings abroad, the British themselves had provoked Germany and laid the foundation for German dissatisfaction. Germany would never allow herself to be compensated for her loss of world power and prestige by mere concessions on the Continent. According to this view, Germany was provoked to revolt by the war spoils that Britain had taken, and it was therefore unfair and highly hypocritical to demand that the French, the Poles, or any other continental country make concessions to Germany and risk their own security for the sake of mitigating the evil effects of a German state of dissatisfaction to which the British themselves had contributed so largely.

One of the thorniest problems of British "psychological policy" was how to make the French desist from further provocation. There were some who believed that the best solution would be for Britain to give France more security. She would then, they asserted, become less nervous and therefore less aggressive. "The provocative policy inspired by her present uncertainty will tend to diminish," said a Foreign Office memorandum, if, by a British guarantee "France will know that her ultimate security is regarded as of direct interest to the British Empire." Lloyd George, in supporting a promise of assistance to France, declared, "You have to give to France the feeling that she is not isolated and that she is not left alone. . . . Give confidence and you give calmness, and calmness of judgment in the present disturbed state of the world is vital to wise decisions." . . .

Others argued that the very opposite course was the one to be followed. The more secure France came to feel, they claimed, the less willing would she be to make concessions. Her attitude and that of her Central European allies would be stiffened; the redress of grievances would become even more difficult. Therefore, Britain should keep France sufficiently apprehensive and insecure so that she would be willing to yield to justified German demands for adjustment. . . .

Britain never made up her mind which of these two apparently contradictory psychological theories to adopt. It seemed wiser to apply them alternately according to the circumstances, that is, to resort to the old device of using sugar and whip at the same time, in this case the sugar of security and the whip of pressure. . . .

The original incentive which led to . . . [Locarno] was . . . the French demand for more security. The initiative for this particular pact was taken by Germany. However, once the pact was signed, the most permanent and broad approval was that given by the British. Briand and Sresemann, the negotiators of the treaty for their respective countries, as well as their followers, of course praised the agreement. In both France and Germany, nevertheless, there was an outburst of violent nationalist criticism.

The French Rightists . . . regarded Locarno as a poor substitute for a straightforward Franco-British alliance. They resented the fact that France was being treated on no more than equal terms with Germany. Above all they feared the effect of the limitation of Britain's commitments to the Rhine which was a blow to the French policy of indivisible defense on Germany's western and eastern borders.

The German Nationalists were in an uproar because, according to them, Germany had not been treated as an equal. It was she, they said, who had to make all the sacrifices. She was accepting voluntarily not only the reincorporation of Alsace and Lorraine into France, but the unilateral demilitarization of wide sections of German territory. What was she receiving in return? Would Britain ever protect Germany against a French attack?

No such complaint was raised by Britain's traditionalists. Locarno not only gave Britain's unavoidable new commitment a form against which there was no objection, but proposed a new order in Western Europe which was in complete accord both with Britain's interests and with ideas that were dear to the traditionalists. This accounts for the fact that many of the features of Locarno, as we shall see, turn up in every British traditionalist plan for a new settlement in Western Europe even down to the final period before the new war. The British Conservatives clung to the pact as a model with an unusual degree of consistency.

The Locarno Treaty was not an alliance. It was not directed against any one country; it was fundamentally an agreement between one-time opponents who would normally have been expected to enter into alliances against one another.

"It is the distinction between an alliance of certain Powers against another Power or group of Powers and a mutual guarantee of the peaceful settlement of disputes between a group of Powers interested in a particular area." Therefore, it fulfilled Britain's often-expressed desire to avoid splitting the Continent into rival groups. They knew that "one defensive alliance is apt to call into existence a rival group, and this process might result ultimately in the division of Europe into hostile camps." Military arrangements under these circumstances were out of the question, which had the advantage of making Britain's commitments less rigid and automatic. She retained her freedom to decide on how to fulfill her pledge.

At the same time, the pact differed no less fundamentally from the Geneva Protocol, since Britain's commitment was explicitly limited to a specified geographic region in which Britain had vital interests. This was a decisive victory of traditionalist policy over the collectivist idea of world-wide commitments and "indivisible peace." As Austen Chamberlain himself put it, Britain's obligations were "narrowly circumscribed to the conditions under which we have an actual vital national interest." The *status quo* in Eastern Europe was not given the same guarantee as the *status quo* on the Rhine.

Thus the pitfalls of both forms of commitments that had been suggested earlier were avoided. Britain was not to become a partner to either a bilateral or a general alliance. Like Italy, she was assigned the role of guarantor. Chamberlain stated that Locarno "enabled Britain once again to take her historic part as mediator and peacemaker in the new Europe created by the Great War," and therefore theoretically, at least, she was able to act again as a disinterested party. The French nationalists who attacked Briand for accepting the pact fully understood the consequences if Britain, the one-time war ally, became the guarantor both of France, *"la grande victime,"* and of Germany, "the aggressor." Britain had drawn "the real dividing point between the years of war and the years of peace" by putting an end to any differentiation between victors and vanquished. "We were divided four years ago," said Baldwin in 1928, "into two camps, the victors and the vanquished; that distinction exists no longer. I hope those words will be forgotten."

In fact Locarno did not entirely end British discrimination between France and Germany. Britain, with her frontier on the Rhine, was not really disinterested. France still represented the "friendly power" which protected Channel ports from the potential "hostile force" which might some day cross the Rhine again. There was discrimination within the pact itself since some of its main provisions dealt with the demilitarization of German territory. More discrimination, the German Nationalists pointed out, would come to light if France should ever violate the pact, since nobody, either in Britain or France, could conceive of Britain's taking sides with Germany and fighting against the French.

This does not mean that British commitments to Germany were farcical and of no practical use to her. It was Germany, after all, who had proposed the treaty. Stresemann realized that it would be to the interest of Britain to prevent any situation from arising in which she would have to choose between helping Germany against France or violating her obligations to Germany. She would, therefore, use every means of diplomatic pressure to restrain France from attacking Germany and in particular from repeating her invasion of the Ruhr. Germany's prestige was enhanced by being treated formally, at least, as an equal, and the wind was taken out of the sails of those who were still working for a bilateral Franco-British alliance. British diplomacy had therefore succeeded in giving France additional security without provoking Germany and in lessening the vulnerability of Germany to new acts of French military pressure without thereby destroying the closer "entente" which linked Britain to France. . . .

It would be tempting, in drawing conclusions, to explain the discord between Britain and France by attaching labels to their respective attitudes and thereby deriving some simple formula. The discussions . . . have indicated that France was possessed by a desire to organize preponderant force and prepare coercive measures, while Britain was engaged in establishing a better balance of power and in applying methods of concilation and appeasement. Or it might be affirmed that, while both countries feared a German revolt against the new order of 1919, France hoped to prevent it by making the defenders of the *status quo* strong and invincible, whereas Britain wished to avert the danger by removing what she believed to be its main causes.

Such statements, however, are misleading and unfair to France, since they do not explain why the two countries came to take such divergent views. They give the false impression that France was motivated by some irrational predilection for coercive methods and the strict enforcement of the *status quo,* while Britain, moved by greater generosity or wisdom, preferred gradual adjustments and the redress of grievances. Even if the real conflict had concerned general principles, which it did not, a value-judgment such as this would be open to question. Skeptics could point to the fact that the British collectivists, who were the champions of high moral principles in the conduct of foreign affairs, came much nearer in their views to the French attitude than to the traditional British stand. They, too, were in favor of organizing overwhelming force, only in their abstract terminology it was to be that of the peace-loving nations arrayed against the potential aggressors. They sought just as persistently as the French to reinforce the *status quo* by the threat of coercive means, only they meant not a threat directed specifically against Germany by a group of allies, but the threat of League sanctions against any country using force to attack the established order.

The basic issue underlying the controversy between Britain and France was not a matter of general attitudes, but the concrete political problem of Germany's power and position. How strong could Germany be permitted to become without menacing the vital interests of the two countries? The British and the French disagreed on the answer to this question; this disagreement accounts for most of the discord between them.

France worked on the assumption that for the sake of her security she could not allow any rise of German strength above the limits prescribed for Germany at Versailles. Britain, who was obviously more remote, was not opposed to the restoration to Germany of much of her previous power, but even wished for it. Such a change would be to Britain's advantage, since it would improve the balance of power on the Continent and since, by satisfying the Germans to a reasonable extent, it might prevent a great explosion which would carry Germany beyond permissible limits.

It should, however, be added immediately that Britain made two important reservations, which account for what harmony there was between her and France. While she wanted Germany to strengthen herself, it was not to be at the expense of Britain's vital interests and was not to give Germany domination over Europe. All along, therefore, the British and the French concurred in a desire to protect and stabilize the settlements in Western Europe, in which Britain had a vital interest. Also in 1939, in the face of what Britain regarded as a drive for domination, she and the French joined their efforts to stop the rise and expansion of Germany, and unity was established.

Harmony of opinion in regard to Western Europe meant little, since Germany did not challenge the territorial *status quo* in the West. At least, she was not likely for a long time to seek to increase her power by an attack on France. Rather would she try to accomplish such an increase through changes of the territorial settlements in the East. Even the remilitarization of the Rhineland, which barred French access to Central Europe, was essentially part of a program aimed toward revision in the East. For this reason the Locarno Pact, so highly regarded in Britain, was no more than a temporary solution to the Franco-German and Franco-British conflicts. Because it did not determine what Germany's total strength and position was to be, it was nothing more than a truce.

This explains why the difficulties on the Vistula and the Danube should have come to play so decisive a role. To keep Germany at the level set at Versailles required putting the same obstacles in the way of her rise in the East as in the West. To France, Austrian independence and the territorial integrity of Poland and Czechoslovakia were therefore almost as important as the safety of her own soil. This made her a party to the age-old conflict between Teuton and Slav in Eastern Europe and committed her to the pro-Slav solution that had been formulated in 1919. Since Britain had no objection to a rise of German power, her attitude in regard to those regions ran at cross-purposes to that of France. As far as she was concerned, the East was an ideal place for making concessions to Germany. Not only would they divert German attention from the regions of vital interest in the West, but they might also improve the existing settlement of the Slav-Teuton conflict, a solution in the wisdom, justice, and durability of which Britain had little faith. While France, therefore, opposed concessions to Germany, regardless of what region they affected, and stood for "indivisible peace," Britain made every effort to discriminate between East and West. She tried to limit her own commitments to the Rhine and, if possible, to draw France away from the regions east of Germany.

2.

Stephen Borsody, professor of history at Chatham College, was born in Hungary and educated at Charles University, Prague; he was later a newspaperman in both Prague and Budapest, and until 1947 he served in the Hungarian diplomatic corps. In the following passage, Mr. Borsody argues that the Locarno pact was designed to keep Germany and the Soviet Union apart. Not only should the validity of such an argument be considered, but the student should contemplate the possibility of establishing a durable peace in a Europe which treated the Soviet Union as an outcast. It is also worth pondering whether Locarno may have had any influence on the course of Soviet foreign policy in the 1930's, and after; or whether the Soviets determine their policies on the basis of a "realistic" appraisal of the opportunities of the moment, and not on the basis of suspicions inherited from episodes in the past.

BORSODY: The Triumph of Tyranny *

France's alliances with Poland and the Little Entente, which set up the cordon sanitaire in Central and Eastern Europe, were intended to encircle Germany and to keep the Soviet Union contained. Without ever abandoning this basic purpose of the French alliances in the Middle Zone, Western diplomacy was inclined to play up the Soviet Union in Germany's encirclement and to enlist Germany in Soviet Russia's containment. This European "balance of power" could have worked beautifully if Germany and Russia had co-operated in a system which encircled and contained them respectively; but—hardly surprisingly—neither Germany nor Russia filled its appointed role.

The cordon sanitaire, directed against Germany and Russia, had the logical effect of bringing these "two outcasts" closer to each other. Hans von Seeckt, Chief of the Reichswehr from 1920 to 1926, was the first to draw the logical conclusions from the cordon sanitaire. General Seeckt and the chiefs of staff around him, despite their fervent opposition to communism, were quick to realize that with Russian assistance Germany might be able to break up the French encirclement and defeat the Versailles system. Soviet Russia, though absorbed in fomenting revolution in Germany—chosen by Lenin as the centre of world revolution—was not slow, either, to embrace the cynical rules of old power politics. While hopes of stirring up Bolshevik revolution in industrial Germany were dwindling, Soviet Russia stood ready for old-fashioned, nonideological co-operation with the German generals.

Co-operation between reactionary Prussian militarists and Russian Bolshevik revolutionaries started in the early 'twenties, when, in accordance with secret agreements, Junkers, the great German aircraft builders, began to operate a

* Stephen Borsody, *The Triumph of Tyranny* (New York: The Macmillan Co., 1960), pp. 39–45. Copyright 1960 by C. Stephen Borsody. Reprinted by permission of The Macmillan Company.

factory near Moscow. Shells and presumably also guns were manufactured by Krupp in several Russian factories for export to Germany. A tank factory too was established, near Kazan, with training facilities for German officers.

Some of the facts concerning German-Russian co-operation came to the attention of a shocked group of European diplomats gathered at a conference in Genoa in 1922. Britain had been anxious to push the rehabilitation of trade relations, and it was in the spirit of this policy that all European countries, Germany and Russia included, were invited to Genoa. So far as the West was concerned, the conference ended in failure, due mainly to France's uncompromising attitude. Germany and Russia, however, scored a great success when in near-by Rapallo the Soviet People's Commissar for Foreign Affairs, G. V. Chicherin, and the German Minister of Foreign Affairs, Walter Rathenau, signed a separate economic treaty.

The German-Soviet treaty ended the isolation of the "two outcasts" of Europe. It also awakened the West to the unpleasant reality that the cordon sanitaire paved the way to German-Russian rapprochement. Western diplomacy was called upon to find more effective means for keeping Germany and Russia apart. From the point of view of the simple power politics that dominated European diplomacy, the logical course of action lay in taking a more conciliatory attitude towards both Germany and Russia, or one of the two. Western Europe perceived the necessity of reconciliation, but remained indecisive in face of the alternatives. It was a Central European friend of the West, Eduard Beneš, who pondered the alternatives and declared his preference for a rapprochement with Russia.

During the Second World War Beneš liked to remind Western statesmen that it was he who had urged the diplomatic recognition of the Soviet Union immediately after Rapallo. At that time German-Russian rapprochement had hung like the sword of Damocles over the Middle Zone. There was no doubt in Beneš's mind that, in the interest of strengthening the European status quo, the Western Powers would have to co-operate with Russia against Germany.

Beneš had of course always been willing and eager to co-operate with Germany, as with anybody else, on the basis of the status quo. But he was only too well aware that Germany could never become a guarantor of Czechoslovak frontiers. Russia on the other hand was, in his view, despite the Bolshevik revolution, a potential Slav ally in an anti-German European system. Beneš's pro-Russian thinking may be explained also by the fact that Czechoslovakia shared no common frontiers with Russia, and hence—unlike Poland and Rumania—had no territorial disputes with her, an almost decisive factor in determining international relations in nationalistic Europe. While Beneš was hoping for a rapprochement between the West and Russia, he took an active part in drafting the Geneva Protocol of 1924. The Protocol was intended to provide collective action under the aegis of the League of Nations against the violator of the territorial status quo. But beyond such paper guarantees Beneš was ahead of everyone else in thinking of the Soviet Union—which was not at that time a member of the League of Nations—as a Great Power, capable of strengthening the real forces of security.

General Seeckt wanted to upset the Versailles system with Russia's help. Eduard Beneš hoped to stabilize the peace settlement by improving the relations between Russia and the West. Britain and France had no such set views on this subject. Although France was preoccupied with security, she could not renew her First World War alliance against Germany with a Bolshevik Russia. In addition to an ideological horror of communism, Paris refused even diplomatic recognition of Soviet Russia because of its repudiation of the debts Czarist Russia owed France. London's attitude towards the Soviet Government was also basically negative. But as one keen observer saw it, British and Soviet politics, for all their ideological conflicts, developed in part along parallel lines. For different reasons, from opposite fringes of Europe, both Britain and Russia sought to counteract the domination of the Continent by a single military power —France. Lloyd George made feeble attempts to improve the relations between Britain and Russia. But when he invited the Russians to the Genoa conference, he was criticized for "coquetting with the Bolsheviks." The failure of Genoa was satisfying to those who wanted to have nothing to do with Soviet Russia. The Russo-German Rapallo Treaty, however, caused concern to everybody, including of course those who were anxious to keep the Russians in quarantine.

The Western Powers were eager to undo Rapallo and neutralize Russo-German co-operation. Strengthening the Middle Zone could have furnished a powerful and logical counter-move to Rapallo, but this could have been achieved only by radically changing the policies inside the Middle Zone. Unfortunately, the nations there were all preoccupied with their petty rivalries. Meanwhile France was busy currying favour with those countries in the Middle Zone that had profited from the peace settlement. And Britain's interest was limited to eyeing with suspicion France's manoeuvring in that region.

There was some reason to believe, in 1924, that the relationship between the Soviet Union and the West would follow the course favoured by Beneš. For one thing, the political trend in the West took a swing to the Left. In 1924, when the Labourite Ramsay MacDonald became Prime Minister, Britain recognized the Soviet Government. Official recognition by the French Socialist Government under Edouard Herriot, and by several European states, followed. Interestingly enough, Czechoslovakia was not among the countries that established formal diplomatic relations with the Soviet Union. Although European diplomacy was taking exactly the course Beneš had so favoured, nevertheless the delicacy of Czechoslovakia's position—her anxiety to gain sympathy abroad and to build unity at home—cautioned Beneš to go slowly on such a controversial issue as the formal diplomatic recognition of Soviet Russia. However, Czechoslovakia signed two "provisional treaties" with the Russian and Ukrainian Soviet Republics as early as June 1922, shortly after the German-Soviet Rapallo Treaty.

Changes in Soviet policies contributed to easing the tension between East and West. In domestic affairs the Soviet Union returned, with the so-called New Economic Policy (NEP), to a limited form of free enterprise. In foreign policy the Communist International (Comintern) redrafted its strategy for world revolution following the abortive Communist rising in Germany in October 1923. Thereafter, expectation of the collapse of capitalism was relegated to the background, being replaced by the slogan of coexistence between communism and capitalism. Despite this easing up in Communist revolutionary zeal, the rapprochement between the Soviet Union and the West was of very short duration. After a short *détente,* a new crisis developed, in the autumn of 1924, precipitated by a letter ostensibly written by Gregory Zinoviev, president of the Comintern, to the British Communists, inciting them to revolt. (The authenticity of the letter was denied, however, by the Soviet Government.)

In contrast with the failure to improve Russo-Western relations, there was a change for the better between Germany and the West. In the autumn of 1924 France withdrew her troops from the Ruhr. Following this, Gustav Stresemann, Foreign Minister of Germany, repeated his earlier offer of guarantees for Germany's treaty obligations. Aristide Briand, French Foreign Minister, accepted the German offer. Britain favoured the move. The result was the Locarno Pact of 1925, which mutually guaranteed the German-French and German-Belgian frontiers. Britain and Italy served as guarantors of the pact, pledging aid to the attacked country in case of treaty violation.

The Locarno Pact underscored Germany's Western orientation and improved her relationship with her former enemies, France and Britain; but it did not guarantee Germany's eastern frontiers, due to Germany's own opposition, as well as to British and Italian reluctance to undertake obligations in regard to the Middle Zone. France, however, signed treaties of mutual assistance with Germany's eastern neighbours, Poland and Czechoslovakia, to assure them against German aggression. And Germany concluded arbitration treaties with Poland and Czechoslovakia as a further assurance that she would not use force against them. In spite of these assurances, the sharp distinction which the Locarno Pact made between Germany's western and eastern frontiers was a sign of the equivocal attitude the Western Powers—especially Britain, but even France, the patron of the status quo in the Middle Zone—were inclined to take towards the security problems of Eastern Europe. It was also a disturbing indication that a rapprochement between the West and Germany might leave the nations of the Middle Zone more exposed to Germany's traditional eastward expansion, the ill-fated *Drang nach Osten.* How far Western disengagement could go in regard to the cordon sanitaire was revealed later—in Munich, in 1938, when Germany was appeased at the expense of Czechoslovakia with fatal consequences for the independence of the entire Middle Zone of small nations; and during the Second World War, when Russia was an ally of the Western Powers against Germany, this disengagement of the West from the Middle Zone produced similar results.

France did not succeed in assuaging the fears of her smaller allies over the

Locarno Pact. Only Czechoslovakia, France's most devoted satellite, acclaimed the pact as a means of promoting the continent's general peace. But the true sentiments of France's small allies were voiced by her least enthusiastic satellite, Poland, who was openly critical of the new trend in European politics.

Meanwhile the mutual assistance treaties that France signed with Poland and Czechoslovakia reminded Germany that the danger of encirclement was still the order of the day. Germany reminded the West, too, that the Locarno Pact did not alter her own determination to counteract the threat of encirclement. Almost simultaneously with the Locarno Pact, a new German-Soviet trade treaty was signed. Furthermore, in 1926, the German and Soviet Governments concluded in Berlin a non-aggression treaty, the negotiations for which must have run simultaneously with the Locarno conferences. The German General Staff did not change their attitude towards the Russians either. German military technicians continued, on Russian soil, experiments which under the Versailles Treaty they could not carry out in Germany; in fact they continued "by force of inertia" for some time even after Hitler seized power.

The Locarno Pact was intended to reinforce Russia's containment by luring Germany away from the pro-Soviet course charted in Rapallo. No wonder the Soviet Union did its best to make Locarno unpopular in Germany. "To think that Germany will put up with this state of affairs is to hope for miracles. . . . Locarno, which . . . sanctions the loss by Germany of Silesia, the Corridor and Danzig . . . will share the fate of the old Franco-Prussian treaty, which deprived France of Alsace and Lorraine. . . . Locarno is fraught with a new European war"—such were Stalin's comments on the pact. Meanwhile the Sixth Comintern Congress, in 1928, decided that the era of imperialistic attacks and of preparation for intervention against the Soviet Union must be anticipated. The Communist parties in the capitalistic countries were alerted. The Social Democratic parties were singled out by the Comintern as the arch-enemies of communism and were labelled "Social Fascists." Communists in Germany, following instructions from Moscow, concentrated their attacks upon the Social Democrats, who were engaged in an ever-growing struggle with Hitler's National Socialists. Stalin thus contributed his share to Hitler's victory in Germany; and the West, through its failure to follow up the Locarno Pact with a vigorous policy of European co-operation, contributed its share.

3.

A. J. P. Taylor's book, *The Origins of the Second World War,* has provoked what can only be described as exceedingly bitter controversy. In the following passage from that book, Mr. Taylor discusses the Locarno era in his usual forthright manner. His comments ought to provoke some reflection about the specific virtues and faults of the Locarno pact. Might conceivably the pact have contributed to a lasting peace, or was it nothing but icing on a European order destined to crumble? One might also speculate as to whether Mr. Taylor is unduly kind to any of the principal figures of the 1920's: does he play favorites?

TAYLOR: The Origins of the Second World War *

It would be wrong to suggest that the occupation of the Ruhr was without effect on Germany. Though it taught the French the folly of coercion, it also taught the Germans the folly of resistance. The occupation ended with a surrender by Germany, not by France. Stresemann came to power with the avowed policy of fulfilling the treaty. Of course this did not mean that he accepted the French interpretation of the treaty or that he would acquiesce in the French demands. It meant only that he would defend German interests by negotiations, not by resistance. Stresemann was as determined as the most extreme nationalist to get rid of the whole treaty lock, stock, and barrel: reparations, German disarmament, the occupation of the Rhineland, and the frontier with Poland. But he intended to do this by the persistent pressure of events, not by threats, still less by war. Where other Germans insisted that revision of the treaty was necessary for the revival of German power, Stresemann believed that the revival of German power would inevitably lead to revision of the treaty. There was a great outcry in allied countries against Stresemann after his death when the publication of his papers revealed clearly his intention to destroy the existing treaty-settlement. The outcry was grotesquely unjustified. Given a great Germany—and the Allies had themselves given it by their actions at the end of the war—it was inconceivable that any German could accept the treaty of Versailles as a permanent settlement. The only question was whether the settlement would be revised, and Germany become again the greatest Power in Europe, peacefully or by war. Stresemann wanted to do it peacefully. He thought this the safer, the more certain, and the more lasting way to German predominance. He had been a bellicose nationalist during the war; and even now was no more inclined to peace from moral principle than Bismarck had been. But, like Bismarck, he believed that peace was in Germany's interest; and this belief entitles him to rank with Bismarck as a great German, even as a great European, statesman. Maybe even as a greater. His task was certainly more difficult. For Bismarck had only to maintain an existing settlement; Stresemann had to work towards a new one. It is the measure of his success that, while he lived, Europe moved towards peace and treaty revision at the same time.

This achievement was not due to Stresemann alone. Allied statesmen also contributed their part, foremost among them Ramsay MacDonald, who came to power in 1924; and thereafter, whether in or out of office, set his mark on British foreign policy for the next fifteen years. The MacDonald policy seemed to end in catastrophic failure with the outbreak of the second World war in 1939. His name is now despised; his very existence ignored. Yet MacDonald should be the patron-saint of every contemporary Western politician who favours co-operation with Germany. More than any other British statesman,

* From A. J. P. Taylor, *The Origins of the Second World War* (New York: Atheneum, 1961), pp. 50–58. Copyright 1961 by A. J. P. Taylor. Reprinted by permission of Atheneum Publishers.

MacDonald faced "the German problem" and attempted to solve it. Coercion was futile, as the occupation of the Ruhr had just shown. The alternative of bringing Russia back into Europe as a Great Power was ruled out on both sides during the nineteen-twenties, for good or ill. Only conciliation of Germany remained; and if conciliation were to be practised at all, it should be practised whole-heartedly. MacDonald did not ignore French anxieties. He met them more generously than any other British statesman had done or was to do. He assured Herriot in July 1924 that violation of the Treaty "would lead to the collapse of the permanent foundations on which rests the peace so painfully achieved"; and he promoted at the League of Nations the abortive Geneva Protocol, by which Great Britain, along with the other members of the League, guaranteed every frontier in Europe. But he was thus generous with the French because he thought that their anxieties had no real foundation. Even in August 1914 he had not believed that Germany was a dangerous and aggressive power, bent on the domination of Europe. He certainly did not believe it in 1924. Therefore the promises of the Protocol, which looked "Black . . . and big on paper," were in fact "a harmless drug to soothe nerves." Every problem could be solved by "the strenuous action of good will." The important thing was to launch negotiations. If the French could be lured into negotiating only by promises of security, then the promises should be given, much as a small child is lured into the sea by assurances that the water is warm. The child discovers that the assurances are false; but he gets used to the cold, and soon learns to swim. So it would be in international affairs. Once the French began to conciliate Germany, they would find the process less alarming than they imagined. British policy should urge the French to concede much, and the Germans to ask little. As MacDonald put it some years later: "Let them especially put their demands in such a way that Great Britain could say that she supported both sides."

MacDonald came just at the right time. The French were ready to disentangle themselves from the Ruhr by moderating their demand for reparations; the Germans were ready to make a serious offer on the other side. The temporary settlement of reparations by the Dawes plan, and the wider relaxation of temper between France and Germany which accompanied it, were essentially Mac-Donald's doing. The general election of November 1924 ended the Labour government; but, though MacDonald ceased to direct British foreign policy, he continued to shape it indirectly. The path of conciliation was, from the British point of view, too attractive to be abandoned by any British government. Austen Chamberlain, MacDonald's Conservative successor, specialised in loyalty (if only to atone for his father's activities in the other direction); and in his puzzled way would have liked to renew the offer of a direct alliance with France. British opinion—not Labour only, but Conservative also—was now resolutely against this. Stresemann suggested a way out: a pact of peace between France and Germany, guaranteed by Great Britain and Italy. This was wonderfully attractive to the British. A guarantee against an unnamed "aggressor" offered exactly the even-handed justice to which Grey had aspired before the war and which MacDonald preached now; yet the friends of France like Austen Chamberlain could console themselves that the only conceivable aggressor would be Germany—hence the Anglo-French alliance would be smuggled in unperceived. The proposal was also wonderfully attractive to the Italians who had been treated as poor relations ever since the war and now found themselves elevated to the British level as arbiters between France and Germany. The idea was less attractive to the French. Even though the Rhineland was to remain demilitarised, it would cease to provide France with an open door through which to threaten Germany, once it was placed under an Anglo-Italian guarantee.

But the French too had found the right statesman for the moment. In 1925 Briand returned as French foreign minister. He was a match for Stresemann in diplomatic skill, the equal of MacDonald in high-minded aspiration, and master of all in romantic utterance. Other French statesmen talked "hard" without meaning it. Briand talked "soft," and did not mean that either. The outcome of the Ruhr occupation had shown the futility of the hard way. Briand now had another chance to find security for France in a cloud of words. He deflated Stresemann's moral lead by proposing that Germany should promise to respect all her frontiers, east as well as west. This was an impossible condition for the German government. Most Germans had acquiesced in the loss of Alsace and Lorraine; few of them even raised the question until after the defeat of France in 1940. The frontier with Poland was felt as a grievance by all Germans. It might be tolerated; it could not be confirmed. Stresemann stretched conciliation a long way, in German eyes, when he agreed to conclude treaties of arbitration with Poland and Czechoslovakia. Even so, he added that Germany intended to "revise" her frontiers with these two countries at some time in the future, though of course she would do it peacefully—a favourite phrase of statesmen who are not yet ready to go to war though perhaps, in Stresemann's case, sincere.

Here was a gaping hole in the system of security—an open repudiation by Stresemann of Germany's eastern frontiers. The British would not fill the gap. Austen Chamberlain spoke complacently of the Polish Corridor "for which no British Government ever will or ever can risk the bones of a British grenadier." Briand provided an alternative solution. France reaffirmed her existing alliances with Czechoslovakia and Poland; and the signatories of Locarno agreed that French action under these alliances would not constitute aggression against Germany. In theory France thus remained free to go to the assistance of her Eastern allies across the demilitarised Rhineland without forfeiting British friendship. Her two contradictory systems of diplomacy were reconciled, at any rate on paper. Locarno enshrined the Western alliance with Great Britain, yet preserved the Eastern alliance with the two satellite-states at the same time.

Such was the treaty of Locarno, signed on 1 December 1925. It was the turning-point of the years between the wars. Its signature ended the first World war; its repudiation eleven years later marked the prelude to the second. If the object of an international agreement be to satisfy everyone, Locarno was a

very good treaty indeed. It satisfied the two guarantor Powers. They had rec·
onciled France and Germany and brought peace to Europe without incurring,
as they supposed, anything beyond a moral obligation, a mere form of words.
Neither Great Britain nor Italy ever made any preparations to fulfil their
guarantee. How could they when the "aggressor" would not be known until the
moment for decision arrived? The practical result of the treaty, odd and unforeseen, was to prevent any military co-operation between Great Britain and
France so long as it remained in force. Yet Locarno also satisfied the French.
Germany accepted the loss of Alsace and Lorraine; she agreed to keep the
Rhineland demilitarised; Great Britain and Italy underwrote the German
promise. Any French statesman of 1914 would have been bewildered with
delight at such an achievement. At the same time the French were still free to
operate their eastern alliances and to play a great part in Europe if they wished
to do so. The Germans could be satisfied too. They were firmly protected
against a new occupation of the Ruhr; they were treated as equals, not as the
defeated enemy; and they kept the door open for a revision of their eastern
frontier. A German statesman of 1919, or even of 1923, would have found no
cause for complaint. Locarno was the greatest triumph of "appeasement." Lord
Balfour called it rightly "the symbol and the cause of a great amelioration in
the public feeling of Europe."

Locarno gave to Europe a period of peace and hope. Germany was admitted
to the League of Nations, though after more delay than had been expected.
Stresemann, Chamberlain, and Briand appeared regularly at the League Council. Geneva seemed to be the centre of a revived Europe: the Concert really in
tune at last, and international affairs regulated by discussion instead of by the
jangling of arms. No one in these years lamented the absence of Russia and the
United States—affairs ran more smoothly without them. On the other hand,
no one seriously proposed to turn the Europe of Geneva into either an anti-
American or an anti-Soviet *bloc*. Far from wishing to be independent of the
United States, the European countries were all busy borrowing American
money. A few wild projectors talked of a European crusade against Communism; but there was nothing in it. Europeans had no desire to go on a
crusade against anyone. Apart from this, the Germans wanted to keep friendship with Russia as a card in reserve, a form of reinsurance treaty which might
some day be used against France's eastern alliances. Immediately after the
signing of the treaty of Locarno, Stresemann renewed with the Russians the
agreement made at Rapallo in 1922; and when Germany joined the League,
Stresemann declared that she could not, in her disarmed state, participate in
sanctions—a veiled assertion of neutrality towards Soviet Russia.

A graver flaw in the Locarno-Geneva system than the absence of the United
States and Soviet Russia was the presence of Italy. She had been brought into
the Locarno arrangement solely in order to reinforce the British appearance of
impartiality. No one supposed at this time that Italy could really hold the
balance between Germany and France. This did not matter while Locarno,

like the League, rested on calculation and good-will, not on direct force. Later, when circumstances grew harsher, the memory of Locarno helped to foster the delusion that Italy had real weight to throw into the scales; the Italian leaders themselves were the victims of this delusion. In the Locarno era Italy had a worse defect than lack of strength: she lacked moral standing. The Locarno Powers claimed to represent the great principles for which the war had been fought; and the League claimed to be an association of free peoples. No doubt there was something fraudulent in these claims. No country is ever as free or as high-principled as it makes out to be. But there was something genuine in the claims as well. The Great Britain of Baldwin and MacDonald; the Weimar Republic in Germany; the Third republic in France were truly democratic countries, with freedom of expression, the rule of law, and good intentions towards others. They were entitled to claim that, grouped in the League, they offered the best hope for mankind; and that, broadly speaking, they offered a superior political and social order to that offered by Soviet Russia.

All this became a tawdry pretence when it was extended to the Italy of Mussolini. Fascism never possessed the ruthless drive, let alone the material strength, of National Socialism. Morally it was just as corrupting—or perhaps more so from its very dishonesty. Everything about Fascism was a fraud. The social peril from which it saved Italy was a fraud; the revolution by which it seized power was a fraud; the ability and policy of Mussolini were fraudulent. Fascist rule was corrupt, incompetent, empty; Mussolini himself a vain, blundering boaster without either ideas or aims. Fascist Italy lived in a state of illegality; and Fascist foreign policy repudiated from the outset the principles of Geneva. Yet Ramsay MacDonald wrote cordial letters to Mussolini—at the very moment of Matteoti's murder; Austen Chamberlain and Mussolini exchanged photographs; Winston Churchill extolled Mussolini as the saviour of his country and a great European statesman. How could anyone believe in the sincerity of Western leaders when they flattered Mussolini in this way and accepted him as one of themselves? It is not surprising that the Russian Communists regarded the League and all its works as a capitalist conspiracy—though also not surprising that Soviet Russia and Fascist Italy early established and always maintained cordial international relations. Of course there is always some gap between theory and practice. It is disastrous for both rulers and ruled when the gap becomes too wide. The presence of Fascist Italy at Geneva, the actual presence of Mussolini at Locarno, were the extreme symbols of unreality in the democratic Europe of the League of Nations. The statesmen no longer believed their own phrases; and the peoples followed their example.

Though Stresemann and Briand were both in their different ways sincere, they did not carry their peoples with them; and each justified Locarno in his own country by contradictory arguments which were bound to end in disillusionment. Briand told the French that Locarno was a final settlement, barring the way against further concessions. Stresemann assured the Germans that the purpose of Locarno was to bring further concessions at an ever faster rate.

Briand, the great rhetorician, hoped that a cloud of benevolent phrases would make the Germans forget their grievances. Stresemann, in his patient way, believed that the habit of concession would grow on the French with practice. Both men were disappointed; both were in sight of failure by the time they died. Further concessions were made, but always with ill-will. The Control Commission on German disarmament was withdrawn in 1927. Reparations were revised downwards by the Young plan in 1929, and external control of German finances was abandoned; the occupying forces left the Rhineland in 1930—five years ahead of time. Appeasement was not achieved. On the contrary German resentment was greater at the end than at the beginning. In 1924 German Nationalists sat in the Cabinet and helped to carry the Dawes plan; in 1929 the Young plan was carried only against fierce Nationalist opposition. Stresemann, who had put Germany back among the Great Powers, was harried into the grave.

The German resentment was partly a matter of calculation: the obvious way to obtain more concessions was to condemn each gain as not enough. The Germans had a plausible case. Locarno treated them as equals, freely negotiating an agreed treaty. What justification then could there be for preserving reparations or one-sided German disarmament? The French could think of no logical answer to this argument, yet knew that, if they accepted it, German predominance in Europe must follow. Most contemporaries blamed the French. Englishmen, particularly, agreed more and more with MacDonald that appeasement, once started, should be continued fast and whole-heartedly. Later on, men blamed the Germans for not accepting the defeat of 1918 as final. It is futile to suppose that more concessions, or fewer, would have made much difference. The conflict between France and Germany was bound to go on as long as the illusion persisted that Europe was still the centre of the world. France would seek to preserve the artificial securities of 1919; Germany would strive to restore the natural order of things. Rival states can be frightened into friendship only by the shadow of some greater danger; neither Soviet Russia nor the United States cast this shadow over the Europe of Stresemann and Briand.

4.

Hajo Holborn was born in Berlin, and taught at Heidelberg before becoming a professor of history at Yale; he has also had extensive experience in government service. The following passage from his extremely interesting book, *The Political Collapse of Europe,* causes one to wonder if the 1920's were not the years in which a stable and peaceful Europe could have been established, with a little more luck or with a little more statesmanship. Had the European nations, or at least the western European nations, been willing to cooperate and to constitute themselves into a strong power bloc, might not the horrors of the 1930's and the 1940's have been avoided, and might not the peoples of Europe have achieved long ago what they are struggling to attain today?

HOLBORN: The Political Collapse of Europe *

The Locarno treaties and Germany's entrance into the League have often been described as the apogee of the international system of 1919. In reality Locarno did not create a secure foundation of a European peace. It covered up certain deep cracks that had appeared in the building, but failed to repair the structural weaknesses. It would have been desirable, and in any case unobjectionable, to make concessions to Germany between 1924 and 1930 in such matters as the occupation of the Rhineland and reparations. Probably much more should have been done to enable the young German democracy to develop under favorable conditions. But it was absolutely essential for Britain and France to keep control of any changes in Germany's position in Europe. Any revision of the Versailles Treaty should have been sought by procedures of international law and multilateral agreement and by the determined refusal of unilateral *faits accomplis*. It was a tragic fallacy to believe that eastern Europe could be neglected politically and economically without courting the gravest dangers. Even worse was the unfounded belief that international conflicts would dissolve if the states scuttled their armaments.

. . . The new eastern European states did not possess sufficient unity among themselves. Nor was this lack of unity among them surprising, since they had developed in different directions as borderlands of the historic European community. For a time the Habsburg monarchy had bound the nationalities of the Danube basin together, and this Austria had been a major force in the maintenance of a European order. But once the Turkish pressure subsided and democratic national movements raised their heads, the Habsburg empire was doomed. No doubt, the establishment of some sort of Danubian federation after 1919 would have been desirable for many reasons, but it alone would not have solved the decisive problems of security of the new eastern states. They could have found a solution only within a closely integrated European system, which the League of Nations and the European diplomacy of the interwar period failed to provide.

The fragile nature of the political conditions of Europe was further endangered by the pious hope that international disarmament by itself constituted a means for the creation of greater security. Large sections of the British people entertained this expectation with an almost religious fervor, and America gave their aspirations strong moral support. But in spite of the idealism of these sentiments, which deserved respect, they were utterly incapable of improving the actual political conditions of Europe. There disarmament could only mean the disarmament of the victors and new strength for Germany. In the absence of ready and fully equipped armed forces elsewhere, the superior industrial and manpower resources of Germany were bound to become even higher trumps than they were before. It would even have been preferable to raise the level of

* From Hajo Holborn, *The Political Collapse of Europe* (New York: Alfred A. Knopf, 1951), pp 131–37. Copyright, 1951 by Hajo Holborn. Reprinted by permission of Alfred A. Knopf, Inc.

German armaments by international agreement, rather than demand the curtailment of the French army.

In most cases disarmament was claimed to be the cure of Europe's political ills by the very people who wanted all nations to accept the rule of international law. But they did not admit what is a truism in national life, that unenforceable law becomes a mockery of justice. Who was to protect the eastern states against Germany or against a revived Russia? Who was to defend western Europe, including the Lowlands and Great Britain, against the onrush of a remilitarized Germany, possibly abetted by Russia? Only one lonely European statesman warned the world that the French army was the single stabilizing factor in Europe and that "the sudden weakening of that factor of stability . . . might open floodgates of measureless consequences in Europe at the present time, might break the dyke and 'Let the boundless deep / Down upon far off cities while they dance— / or dream.' "

But the British people were not inclined to listen to Winston Churchill in those years. From 1926 to 1934, first on the Preparatory Commission for the Disarmament Conference, then at the Disarmament Conference itself, which started its sessions in Geneva in 1932, steady pressure was brought on France to decrease her armaments. Even after Hitler's accession to power, Ramsay MacDonald pushed a disarmament plan that would have equalized French and German armed strength. France in British eyes appeared petulant in her insistence upon a system of general security or at least upon international arms inspection as preconditions of a further reduction of armaments. The result of all the disarmament discussions in the interwar period was the further discredit of the peace settlement of 1919 and the psychological preparation of a large segment of world opinion for German rearmament.

Locarno did not lay a safe foundation of a lasting European peace, though it created, at least for a while, closer co-operation between Germany and the two western European powers. The personal relationship established between Sir Austen Chamberlain, Aristide Briand, and Gustav Stresemann gave Europe a kind of unofficial council that tended to stabilize the European scene in spite of continuous German desire for change. Besides, for the time being Germany was in no position to press her claims for revision at the expense of eastern countries. Nevertheless, Great Britain, though she had refused to guarantee the eastern states, feared eastern conflicts. Consequently, British diplomacy chose the easy course and backed the strongest power, France. As late as 1931 British policy supported the French opposition to the Austro-German customs union. Once Germany had become stronger than France the eastern policies of Britain were to be reversed.

By hindsight it is easy to say that the years between 1925 and 1930 were the years in which Europe could have been reconstituted, not as an entirely self-contained political system, but as a strong powerblock in world politics if the beginnings of co-operation between Britain, France and Germany had been carried to a full understanding on all the major issues of Europe. Such a firm understanding among the three powers could also have led to a common program for the strengthening of the eastern European states. Britain, however, was not willing to consider additional commitments in Europe. Perhaps Germany and France could have acted alone, disregarding the British sensitiveness to separate Franco-German co-operation; but Germany felt that France would never voluntarily make those concessions that Germany considered her due and that France was aiming exclusively at bolstering the *status quo*. Briand's proposal for the formation of a European Federal Union, first broached in 1929, was too vague and did not contain special concessions that might have won over Germany. Britain poured cold water on the plan, while Germany at first took a reserved attitude. Later, in March, 1931, the German Government used the idea of a European federation as a cloak for the Austro-German customs union, judged by France to be a unilateral revision of the Paris settlement rather than a step in the direction of a European federation. By then the chance for real understanding was gone.

The five years after 1925 gave Europe a last Indian summer before the blizzard of the world economic crisis struck in 1931. Nobody foresaw that Europe, politically and economically, lived on borrowed time. Once confidence had been restored, Europe showed her vigor. By 1925 most nations of Europe had achieved their prewar production levels, and in the subsequent five years the expansion of European production proceeded at a faster rate than that of American production during the boom period. Most startling was Germany's progress. In 1919 her industrial production was only one third of what it had been in 1913. By 1922 a considerable recovery had taken place in spite of the instability of the German currency, which was not the result of German reparation payments, as is so often asserted, but of the inability of the German Republic to put its finances in order. The decision to meet the French invasion of the Ruhr by passive resistance and to cover the bill by the printing of money led to the German hyper-inflation that was stopped only at the end of 1923, and in that year German industrial production fell again to 40 per cent of the 1913 figure. But in 1924 Germany doubled her output, and by 1927 she had reached her prewar position and resumed her place as the chief industrial country of Europe.

Another aspect of these five years was the ease with which Europe as a whole rebuilt her trading position, even though, while Europe had been at war, the overseas countries, primarily the United States but also other nations such as Japan, had greatly expanded their productive capacity. Higher world production seemed to find a greater world market. It was not recognized that the market conditions were largely the result of the credit expansion caused by American capital looking for profitable investment. The foreign capital issues publicly offered in the United States between 1920 and 1931 amounted to 11.6 billion dollars, of which Europe received 40 per cent, Canada almost 29, and Latin America 22 per cent. In Europe, American capital was augmented by British, Swiss, and Dutch funds. Germany, in the six years between 1924 and 1929 received from all these countries more than 4 billion dollars, about half of these funds coming from the United States and constituting a greater grant of foreign funds than the rest of the world received in those years.

The economic expansion of credit thus made it possible to postpone the adjustment to the structural changes of the world economy produced by the war. For the same reason a realistic financial settlement of the World War could be delayed for many years. The Dawes Plan of 1924 had set up a payment schedule of German reparations without, however, revising the original total sum demanded by the Allies in 1921. The stillborn Young Plan of 1929, announced as the final reparation settlement on the eve of the big crash, once again evaded the most fundamental political problems. Germany, beginning in 1926, paid 10,333 million German marks as reparations, which was a little less than two and a half billion dollars. But the transfer of German funds could not have been made if private American loans had not gone to Germany at the same time. The Allies in turn used these sums to service their American loans or war debts. Winston Churchill called this system "insane."

Once the bubble burst and it dawned upon the world that there had been general overproduction and overinvestment, the American Government preferred virtually to stop all intergovernmental debts, reparations, and inter-Allied obligations in order to save the American private loans that more directly affected the American banking situation. President Hoover proposed in 1931 a holiday of reparation and inter-Allied debt payments. In 1932 at the Conference of Lausanne reparations were actually buried. But at that time Germany was already determined not only to demand a radical revision of the Paris settlement in her favor but to force a full reversal of the historic decisions of World War I.

5.

In May 1953 the British prime minister, Sir Winston Churchill, described Locarno as "the highest point reached between the wars," and told the House of Commons: "I have a feeling that the master thought which animated Locarno might well play its part between Germany and Russia." Sir Winston's suggestion that Locarno might provide a model for the relaxation of cold-war tensions in eastern Europe brought an immediate and angry reaction from Moscow. A *Pravda* editorial declared that Locarno had become a "notorious" word, and denounced the Locarno policy as "one of the important factors which prepared the Second World War," for, said *Pravda*, it had been designed to channel German aggression eastward. Sir Winston's trial balloon may have been quickly punctured, but it did inspire some students of modern history to re-examine the Locarno episode. One of the ablest of these reassessments, by the British scholar George A. Grün, concluded that Locarno ought to stand "much less as a lesson than as a warning."

GRÜN: Locarno: Idea and Reality *

Thirty years ago, in October 1925, the leading statesmen of seven European countries met at Locarno, and after a Conference lasting less than a fortnight,

* George A. Grün, "Locarno: Idea and Reality," *International Affairs*, vol. 31 (1955), pp. 477–85. Reprinted by permission of the editors of *International Affairs*.

were able to put their signatures to a number of documents, which together became known as the Pact or Treaty of Locarno.

After the early post-war years of European strife—which not infrequently threatened to become war—this was the first European Conference which had reached agreement and held out promise for the future. The acclaim of contemporaries was tremendous; and posterity, with few exceptions, has continued to accord praise, and more than that, to the work of Locarno. It has been called the high-water mark of Europe's reconstruction and been described as the moment of transition from war to peace. . . .

"The Locarno spirit," "the Locarno era," terms current in the later nineteen-twenties and still in use in our time were proof that contemporaries, and after them historians, were content to associate the short period in which international relations ran smoothly with the treaties, and the spirit of those treaties. Later, in more troubled times, the hallowed name of Locarno was again invoked. Strenuous, but unsuccessful, efforts were made in the nineteen-thirties to bring about a similar system in Eastern Europe—the so-called "Eastern Locarno." In our own time a British Prime Minister has called for a new Locarno, and expressed his conviction that the principles laid down then were valid as models for the possible solution of the pressing problems of our day.

Were contemporary observers and historians right in seeing in the agreements of 1925 the one real advance in the conduct of international affairs made for a long time? . . .

From the evidence available to contemporaries, it was not difficult to conclude that only wise and moderate statesmanship and a genuine desire to eliminate difficulties could have achieved these results. Locarno was invested with a moral significance transcending the practical importance of the results.

Certainly there was also opposition to the agreements. But, in the prevailing mood it could be dismissed as an uninformed survival of parochial chauvinism, which in many cases it undoubtedly was. The opponents of the idea of Locarno were concerned with the alleged sacrifice made by their respective countries— not with any weakness inherent in the idea itself. In the years after 1925 it could be ignored. The improvement in international relations was so marked and the contrast with the immediate past so startling that no further indication of the achievements of Locarno seemed to be required.

Even now, a generation later, it must be admitted that the idea of Locarno might be considered attractive. Though it failed to stem the trend towards deterioration which set in only a few years after the conclusion of the Pact, this was not considered sufficient reason for invalidating the significance of its fundamental principles. No diplomatic document can claim to have an unlimited life. Locarno could not necessarily be judged by failure to provide for every unforeseeable contingency in the future. The principles and methods then applied can still be extracted and considered as valid models and general precepts for other circumstances.

The justice of this view, which is widely held, must depend on the answers to two questions, one of fact and one of principle. Is the interpretation that

Locarno was a major diplomatic triumph of moderation justified historically? And can the claims made for the universal validity of the principles of Locarno stand up to a realistic analysis which goes beyond the immediate emotional and psychological appeal? . . .

Within the general pattern of European instability, France faced a particular problem. Though apparently the most successful of the victorious Powers, she had not succeeded in imposing upon Europe a pattern which would satisfy her need for protection. The term "security" had assumed a specific meaning for France. The reasons for this . . . were often misinterpreted as a veiled attempt to establish an unchallengeable French hegemony in Europe. In reality the deep-seated feeling of insecurity in France sprang from the fear that Germany, restored to her previous strength, would attempt to reverse the decision of 1918. . . .

Compared with the clear though unachieved purpose of French diplomacy, the aims of Germany are less easily comprehensible. After an initial phase in which diplomacy was subordinated to the concern for her survival, Germany had to face the decision whether to reconcile herself to existing conditions, or whether to attempt, by diplomacy or otherwise, to regain her lost position in Europe. The confused political picture in Germany, which led to an infinitely more marked interaction between internal pressure and foreign policy than elsewhere, has tended to obscure this question. There were advocates of both schools, but it seems clear that the policy of fulfilment was soon abandoned in view of its extreme unpopularity. An analysis of German tactics shows that from an early stage onwards, restoration was the real aim. The difficulties were of course immense; it can however be seen, in retrospect, that German diplomacy, operating under severe restrictions, had become extraordinarily successful. By mobilizing world public opinion, by exploiting skilfully the existing divisions and tensions in Europe, and by adapting her methods to the circumstances of the time, Germany had succeeded in re-establishing her position in international diplomacy in a remarkably short period. . . .

It is against this background that the course of the negotiations which led to Locarno must be seen. The initiative to open talks came from Germany. Her offer to give an undertaking to respect, at least in part, the frontiers as established at Versailles in return for a similar guarantee and for some alleviations in the application of the occupation provisions was startling, and appeared to be a genuine attempt to relax international tensions.

It is, however, important to realize that it coincided with two simultaneous French moves, both with the familiar aim of increasing her own security. One was yet another attempt to strengthen the machinery of the League through the adoption of the Geneva Protocol, and had reached a crucial phase in diplomatic discussions between London and Paris. The other, even more important, was aimed at negotiating a concrete military agreement between France, Britain, and Belgium.

The German offer, therefore, cannot be viewed in isolation; it must be interpreted as countermove, and as such it proved successful. By offering to

Britain an alternative approach in the solution of international problems it stiffened her opposition to the greater commitments in Europe which were urged by France. At the same time the German offer could not reasonably be rejected even by France, whose insistence on tangible guarantees was bound to be met with suspicion and hostility. When the German proposal to enlarge the original frontier guarantee by means of a broad general agreement became known, it was clear that there would be a conflict between two conceptions of security; one vague, but superficially satisfactory, because of its international character, the other—the French—specific, and concrete, but naturally limited by being confined to definite national interests. . . .

The outcome was the Locarno Pact, as we know it. Viewed realistically, it is difficult to call it a compromise: the idea of Locarno represents no less than the defeat of French aspirations and their substitution by an untried, though undoubtedly attractive, conception, the success of which depended on certain assumptions which were by no means true.

For if France eventually accepted Locarno, and even collaborated in making it effective, it was because it was hoped that at any rate the immediate problem of the Franco-German frontier was settled. The assumption here was that by abandoning her insistence on armed security France had already conceded enough to Germany to expect a stabilization of the position. It seems however clear that this did not completely accord with the facts: there are indications that not only the implacable enemies of the Pact in Germany but also some of its highly placed advocates were prepared to treat the German renunciation with that "inner reservation" which came from the correct assessment of the immediate degree of strength at Germany's disposal. In any case, Germany, having established her case in the East by leaving the question open for revision, was entitled to assume that elsewhere, too, the effect of the Pact might lead to revision once the atmosphere of good will had eliminated the opposition to it. These ambiguities in fundamental assumptions remained concealed for some time; they were, however, the essential cause of the eventual failure of the "Locarno spirit" to influence European affairs. Faced in its historical context, the idea of Locarno contrasts unfavourably with the reality; the same contrast also emerges when the theoretical principles underlying it are examined more closely.

This applies particularly to the central concept of Locarno: the flexible guarantee assuring, whichever of two Powers may become the victim of unprovoked aggression by the other, the aid and support of the non-committed neutral outsiders. This may have suited the countries concerned in 1925: it assured France, at any rate in theory, of the eventual support of Britain—an assurance which she had failed to obtain by more direct methods; it was certainly not unpopular in Germany as it conferred upon her a status equal with that of France; and by avoiding the need for immediate strategic decisions it was the only solution acceptable to Britain. In practice, however, such a concept ignores all fundamental essentials of modern strategy. "Assistance"—and even more so "immediate assistance"—stipulated in case of flagrant violation, cannot possibly be improvised in a short space of time. Mobilization of men and allocation of resources have become complex operations requiring detailed planning. Moreover, where the forces of two or more countries are involved, co-ordination of strategy and tactics is essential. This in turn depends on fairly full and frank disclosures of military and technical secrets by Powers to third parties. Such disclosures can only be made in cases where fairly close and genuine political ties already exist, that is to say, when conditions for an alliance already obtain. Yet it was precisely this—the formation of firm alliances, or blocs—which the Pact of Locarno tried to prevent. In this respect, too, the idea of Locarno as a model for the future could hardly be described as realistic.

Locarno was never tried in practice; on the only occasion—the German entry into the Rhineland in 1936—when it might have led to action, the political alignment of forces in Europe was so different from that of 1925 that the application of its provisions could hardly be seriously considered. The significance of the idea of Locarno consisted exclusively in the psychological and emotional effect which it exercised upon a world weary of perpetual conflict. . . . On conscientious reflection it may well appear that the work of Locarno will serve much less as a lesson than as a warning.

VII.

THE GREAT

DEPRESSION

Periods of intense and long-sustained crisis—wars, plagues, and the like—are likely to leave a lasting mark on the generations that experience them. Some historians have even suggested that just as an individual may suffer severe traumatic effects from some shattering personal experience, so a whole society may perhaps reveal a kind of generalized trauma or mass psychosis as a consequence of a severe social upheaval of long duration.

Such a theory is still largely speculative; it rests on little empirical research. Even the psychological impact of the two great wars of the twentieth century cannot be assessed with any accuracy. But if there is any validity at all in such a theory, then perhaps the great depression of the 1930's ought to be classed as one of the traumatic experiences of the modern era. For the depth and breadth of its impact on political life, on ideas, on attitudes, it may have been almost as significant as the great wars themselves.

One of the curious things about the great depression is the meagerness of the retrospective literature about it. On both world wars we have books by the thousand; on the depression, a mere handful of them, and not very good ones at that. Economists of the depression era did expend a good deal of time and energy in examining the causes of the crisis (though they came nowhere near agreement in the matter). But there have been few attempts to study the episode in perspective, to weigh rival theories about its origins, to isolate and then synthesize its short- and long-term consequences.[1] Perhaps that is because economists, who are technically equipped to handle such subjects, are more interested in problems of the immediate present than in those of the past, while historians, who ought to be interested, usually lack the requisite technical training. Besides, historians have been more intrigued by the ways in which various nations and statesmen responded to the depression than by the origins and nature of the episode itself.

Despite the shortcomings of the available reading material, this discussion problem is included here simply because the intrinsic importance of the topic is so great. To omit the great depression in a course on twentieth-century Europe would be as unjustifiable as to omit one of the great wars. And while both the world wars are quite adequately dealt with in every good textbook, the depression usually gets the

[1] J. K. Galbraith's *The Great Crash, 1929* (Boston: Houghton Mifflin Co., 1955) is an exception, but it is confined to the American experience.

sketchiest of textbook treatment. The readings in Chapter VII are therefore intended to be supplementary as well as provocative of discussion.

Some knotty issues are raised by an examination of the great depression. Was it,
at bottom, the consequence of a misguided and impossible attempt by European
and American statesmen after 1918 to restore the nineteenth-century world? Or was
the attempt to restore that world a quite sensible idea—one that might have been
accomplished save for the technical errors committed by statesmen and businessmen
during the 1920's? To what extent were the great war and the peace settlement that
followed it significant factors in producing the disorder that led to an economic
breakdown ten years later? Were the Europeans merely the unfortunate victims of
American shortsightedness and speculative frenzy, culminating in the Wall Street
crash of 1929? Were any sensible remedies for the crisis proposed during the depression years? Did any nations really achieve economic recovery during the depression decade? Was the second world war the almost unavoidable outgrowth of
the great depression?

1.

There is a story (no doubt apocryphal) that when an economist some years
after the great depression sought to list all the theories advanced to explain the
origins of that crisis, he arrived at the astronomical total of almost four hundred—ranging from faulty currency policies to the influence of sunspots. A
shorter and more sensible list of alternative theories, as propounded by contemporaries, is contained in Paul Einzig's brief study *The World Economic
Crisis.* Mr. Einzig, who was educated in Budapest and Paris, has spent forty
years as a correspondent in Paris and London for several leading financial
newspapers. In his spare moments he has published almost fifty books on contemporary economic and financial problems.

EINZIG: The World Economic Crisis 1929–1931 *

It is a commonplace of economic text-books that the function of economic science is to explain and foresee economic phenomena. The view is widely held
that, in the case of the present world economic crisis, economic science has failed
deplorably to fulfil its task. This conception does, however, rather less than justice to the exponents of economic science of our generation. It is true that few
economists, if any, were aware of the coming trouble, and that, even after its
arrival, they were unable to gauge its significance, or to provide an adequate
explanation. The uninitiated public complains—and not altogether without reason—of having been left in the dark as to the causes of the world-wide depression. Many attempts have been made to provide the much-needed explanation,
but none of them carry much conviction. The main reason for this is that most attempts aiming at the explanation of the crisis are partisan, either because those
who put them forward strive to establish or support a theory of their own or

* From Paul Einzig, *The World Economic Crisis 1929–1931* (London: Macmillan, 1932), pp.
23–28. Reprinted by permission of Macmillan and Co., Ltd., and of the author.

because they are too eager to use the facts of the crisis to defend or attack certain political or economic interests.

At the same time, it is beyond question that many of the theories put forward contain a certain percentage of truth; in spite of their one-sidedness, they undoubtedly contribute towards finding the right solution. It is obvious that the present economic crisis is the outcome of the combination of a large number of causes. Those economists who are inclined to overemphasise one single cause in which they are particularly interested may not provide the complete explanation, but certainly contribute towards it. After all, exaggeration is sometimes necessary to draw attention to certain facts which may be overlooked unless they become the subject of controversy. . . .

We propose to enumerate below the principal theories which have been put forward to explain the earlier stages of the present crisis, and to examine them, one by one, in subsequent chapters.

(1) Periodic crises (business cycles).
(2) The necessity to return to the pre-war level.
(3) Overproduction.
(4) Underconsumption.
(5) Monetary causes.
(6) Overcapitalisation.
(7) Overspeculation.
(8) The moral factor.
(9) Coincidence of a number of independent factors.

(1) According to an explanation popular with the pre-war school of economists, there is nothing exceptional or extraordinary in the present crisis. Before the war, there was a crisis on the average every seven or eight years, and nothing that has happened since 1914 has changed this state of affairs. Although the war disorganised economic life throughout the world, it made no difference in the fundamental tendencies which have been responsible for the crises since the beginning of the modern economic system. But for the war, the crisis would most probably have occurred about 1917; as a result of exceptional circumstances, it was postponed till 1920. In less than ten years the business cycle ran its course once more and, after the period of comparative stability and prosperity, produced the crisis that broke loose in 1929.

(2) A section of the representatives of economic thought has always held the opinion that normal conditions could not be regarded as having been attained until the world price level had declined to its pre-war figure. A very large section of the public held the same opinion. Those who remember pre-war conditions would find it difficult to regard any conditions other than those as normal and permanent. During the period of comparative stability between 1922 and 1928 many people were inclined to hold the view that equilibrium had been attained at a price level which was different from the pre-war level. They argued that economic conditions had changed considerably since the war, and that, even

if there had been no war at all, the price level would have probably moved in an upward direction. They failed to convince, however, a large section of both expert and public opinion, who regard the fall of prices as the justification of their belief in the necessity for the return to pre-war prices.

(3) As the immediate cause of the decline of prices was the accumulation of stocks in various branches of production, a natural conclusion is that we are faced with the phenomenon of overproduction. There is no doubt about it that both agricultural and industrial production have increased considerably during the last few years and, in many branches, is in excess of its pre-war figures. The world is suffering, therefore, from acute *embarras de richesse*.

(4) Those who are not satisfied with the superficial explanation of the crisis as a result of the increase of production arrive at the conclusion that the reason why the surplus cannot be absorbed is deficient consumption. It stands to reason that, if the world produces more, its inhabitants should be better off and not worse off than they were before. If this is not the case, there must be something which prevents them from consuming the goods they produce. A great variety of theories are put forward to explain this phenomenon of underconsumption. According to some, the habit of saving is responsible for it; according to another, disequilibrium between the production of capital goods and consumers' goods is the source of the evil.

(5) One of the most popular explanations of the crisis is that the depression and the fall of prices are due to monetary causes. The maldistribution of gold is regarded by many of our leading economists as the root of all evil. It is said that although the world's gold stock available for monetary purposes is larger than before the war, the major part of it is hoarded in two countries, while the rest of the world does not possess an adequate supply to meet its monetary requirements. As a result, the volume of currency and credit based on the gold stock is not sufficient to enable the consumers to buy all the goods that are produced.

(6) The excessive amount of fictitious wealth as represented by the enormous increase of public and private indebtedness in every country is regarded as one of the causes of the present crisis. The productive section of the population in every country has to carry an unbearable burden of deadweight debt in the form of excessive taxation. Relief from these burdens can come either through the depreciation of currencies (which would cause a substantial rise in the prices of the commodities or manufactured goods produced by the debtors) or else through the repudiation of the debts themselves.

(7) In the past most crises were preceded by a frenzy of speculation. As the present crisis was preceded by the Wall Street boom, it is natural that there should be people who should regard overspeculation as the cause which led to the crisis.

(8) According to another explanation, the crisis was due to the lack of confidence on the part of the public, brought about by a series of disappointments suffered during the last few years. In almost every country there have been a number of financial frauds and scandals of great magnitude, and millions of investors suffered heavy losses in consequence. It is not surprising, therefore,

that the public become distrustful and adopt for a time a reserved attitude.

(9) An essentially practical explanation is that the world crisis is the outcome of the coincidence of a number of independent factors, such as the untimely increase of wheat production brought about by the increasing use of tractors, the demonetisation of silver, the suspension of American foreign lending, and, last but not least, Soviet activities. According to this theory, all these factors were completely independent of each other. In themselves they would not have caused much damage, but owing to the unfortunate fact that they happened to coincide, their combined effect was responsible for the crisis.

Our task is to examine how far the causes given by these various theories may have contributed to bring about the crisis. The contradiction between the explanations is more apparent than real; each of them contains some constructive elements which are well worth retaining.

2.

As political leaders groped for solutions to the crisis, leading economists everywhere attempted to offer them guidance by providing *ex post facto* explanations of what had gone wrong. Probably the most influential British economist of the period was John Maynard Keynes of Cambridge University, who combined technical talent with an extraordinary gift for polemic writing. Late in 1930 Keynes addressed himself to the current crisis in an essay entitled "The Great Slump of 1930." The traditional economic system, he argued, was not at fault; rather, ". . . we have involved ourselves in a colossal muddle, having blundered in the control of a delicate machine. . . ." And he added, in another Keynesian metaphor: "The patient does not need rest. He needs exercise." Keynes suggested a degree of governmental economic intervention that startled some of his fellow Liberals; eventually, as the depression dragged on, he was to expand and elaborate this suggestion to such a degree that both his disciples and his critics could speak of a "Keynesian revolution" in the utilization of economics as a policy science.

KEYNES: Essays in Persuasion *

The world has been slow to realise that we are living this year in the shadow of one of the greatest economic catastrophes of modern history. But now that the man in the street has become aware of what is happening, he, not knowing the why and wherefore, is as full to-day of what may prove excessive fears as, previously, when the trouble was first coming on, he was lacking in what would have been a reasonable anxiety. He begins to doubt the future. Is he now awakening from a pleasant dream to face the darkness of facts? Or dropping off into a nightmare which will pass away?

He need not be doubtful. The other was *not* a dream. This *is* a nightmare, which will pass away with the morning. For the resources of Nature and men's

* From John Maynard Keynes, *Essays in Persuasion* (New York: Harcourt, Brace, 1932), pp. 134–37, 140–47. Reprinted by permission of Harcourt, Brace and World.

devices are just as fertile and productive as they were. The rate of our progress towards solving the material problems of life is not less rapid. We are as capable as before of affording for every one a high standard of life—high, I mean, compared with, say, twenty years ago—and will soon learn to afford a standard higher still. We were not previously deceived. But to-day we have involved ourselves in a colossal muddle, having blundered in the control of a delicate machine, the working of which we do not understand. The result is that our possibilities of wealth may run to waste for a time—perhaps for a long time.

I doubt whether I can hope to bring what is in my mind into fully effective touch with the mind of the reader. I shall be saying too much for the layman, too little for the expert. For—though no one will believe it—economics is a technical and difficult subject. It is even becoming a science. However, I will do my best—at the cost of leaving out, because it is too complicated, much that is necessary to a complete understanding of contemporary events.

First of all, the extreme violence of the slump is to be noticed. In the three leading industrial countries of the world—the United States, Great Britain, and Germany—10,000,000 workers stand idle. There is scarcely an important industry anywhere earning enough profit to make it expand—which is the test of progress. At the same time, in the countries of primary production the output of mining and of agriculture is selling, in the case of almost every important commodity, at a price which, for many or for the majority of producers, does not cover its cost. In 1921, when prices fell as heavily, the fall was from a boom level at which producers were making abnormal profits; and there is no example in modern history of so great and rapid a fall of prices from a normal figure as has occurred in the past year. Hence the magnitude of the catastrophe. . . .

We have magneto trouble. How, then, can we start up again? Let us trace events backwards:—

1. Why are workers and plant unemployed? Because industrialists do not expect to be able to sell without loss what would be produced if they were employed.

2. Why cannot industrialists expect to sell without loss? Because prices have fallen more than costs have fallen—indeed, costs have fallen very little.

3. How can it be that prices have fallen more than costs? For costs are what a business man pays out for the production of his commodity, and prices determine what he gets back when he sells it. It is easy to understand how for an individual business or an individual commodity these can be unequal. But surely for the community as a whole the business men get back the same amount as they pay out, since what the business men pay out in the course of production constitutes the incomes of the public which they pay back to the business men in exchange for the products of the latter? For this is what we understand by the normal circle of production, exchange, and consumption.

4. No! Unfortunately this is not so; and here is the root of the trouble. It is not true that what the business men pay out as costs of production necessarily comes back to them as the sale-proceeds of what they produce. It is the characteristic of a boom that their sale-proceeds exceed their costs; and it is the

characteristic of a slump that their costs exceed their sale-proceeds. Moreover, it is a delusion to suppose that they can necessarily restore equilibrium by reducing their total costs, whether it be by restricting their output or cutting rates of remuneration; for the reduction of their outgoings may, by reducing the purchasing power of the earners who are also their customers, diminish their sale-proceeds by a nearly equal amount.

5. How, then, can it be that the total costs of production for the world's business as a whole can be unequal to the total sale-proceeds? Upon what does the inequality depend? I think that I know the answer. But it is too complicated and unfamiliar for me to expound it here satisfactorily. . . . So I must be somewhat perfunctory.

Let us take, first of all, the consumption-goods which come on to the market for sale. Upon what do the profits (or losses) of the producers of such goods depend? The total costs of production, which are the same thing as the community's total earnings looked at from another point of view, are divided in a certain proportion between the cost of consumption-goods and the cost of capital-goods. The incomes of the public, which are again the same thing as the community's total earnings, are also divided in a certain proportion between expenditure on the purchase of consumption-goods and savings. Now if the first proportion is larger than the second, producers of consumption-goods will *lose* money; for their sale proceeds, which are equal to the expenditure of the public on consumption-goods, will be less (as a little thought will show) than what these goods have cost them to produce. If, on the other hand, the second proportion is larger than the first, then the producers of consumption-goods will make exceptional *gains*. It follows that the profits of the producers of consumption-goods can only be restored, either by the public spending a larger proportion of their incomes on such goods (which means saving less), or by a larger proportion of production taking the form of capital-goods (since this means a smaller proportionate output of consumption-goods).

But capital-goods will not be produced on a larger scale unless the producers of such goods are making a profit. So we come to our second question—upon what do the profits of the producers of capital-goods depend? They depend on whether the public prefer to keep their savings liquid in the shape of money or its equivalent or to use them to buy capital-goods or the equivalent. If the public are reluctant to buy the latter, then the producers of capital-goods will make a loss; consequently less capital-goods will be produced; with the result that, for the reasons given above, producers of consumption-goods will also make a loss. In other words, *all* classes of producers will tend to make a loss; and general unemployment will ensue. By this time a vicious circle will be set up, and, as the result of a series of actions and reactions, matters will get worse and worse until something happens to turn the tide.

This is an unduly simplified picture of a complicated phenomenon. But I believe that it contains the essential truth. Many variations and fugal embroideries and orchestrations can be superimposed; but this is the tune.

If, then, I am right, the fundamental cause of the trouble is the lack of new enterprise due to an unsatisfactory market for capital investment. Since trade is international, an insufficient output of new capital-goods in the world as a whole affects the prices of commodities everywhere and hence the profits of producers in all countries alike.

Why is there an insufficient output of new capital-goods in the world as a whole? It is due, in my opinion, to a conjunction of several causes. In the first instance, it was due to the attitude of lenders—for new capital-goods are produced to a large extent with borrowed money. Now it is due to the attitude of borrowers, just as much as to that of lenders.

For several reasons lenders were, and are, asking higher terms for loans than new enterprise can afford. First, the fact, that enterprise could afford high rates for some time after the war whilst war wastage was being made good, accustomed lenders to expect much higher rates than before the war. Second, the existence of political borrowers to meet Treaty obligations, of banking borrowers to support newly restored gold standards, of speculative borrowers to take part in Stock Exchange booms, and, latterly, of distress borrowers to meet the losses which they have incurred through the fall of prices, all of whom were ready if necessary to pay almost any terms, have hitherto enabled lenders to secure from these various classes of borrowers higher rates than it is possible for genuine new enterprise to support. Third, the unsettled state of the world and national investment habits have restricted the countries in which many lenders are prepared to invest on any reasonable terms at all. A large proportion of the globe is, for one reason or another, distrusted by lenders, so that they exact a premium for risk so great as to strangle new enterprise altogether. For the last two years, two out of the three principal creditor nations of the world, namely, France and the United States, have largely withdrawn their resources from the international market for long-term loans.

Meanwhile, the reluctant attitude of lenders has become matched by a hardly less reluctant attitude on the part of borrowers. For the fall of prices has been disastrous to those who have borrowed, and any one who has postponed new enterprise has gained by his delay. Moreover, the risks that frighten lenders frighten borrowers too. Finally, in the United States, the vast scale on which new capital enterprise has been undertaken in the last five years has somewhat exhausted for the time being—at any rate so long as the atmosphere of business depression continues—the profitable opportunities for yet further enterprise. By the middle of 1929 new capital undertakings were already on an inadequate scale in the world as a whole, outside the United States. The culminating blow has been the collapse of new investment inside the United States, which to-day is probably 20 to 30 per cent less than it was in 1928. Thus in certain countries the opportunity for new profitable investment is more limited than it was; whilst in others it is more risky.

A wide gulf, therefore, is set between the ideas of lenders and the ideas of borrowers for the purpose of genuine new capital investment; with the result that the savings of the lenders are being used up in financing business losses and distress borrowers, instead of financing new capital works.

At this moment the slump is probably a little overdone for psychological reasons. A modest upward reaction, therefore, may be due at any time. But there cannot be a real recovery, in my judgement, until the ideas of lenders and the ideas of productive borrowers are brought together again; partly by lenders becoming ready to lend on easier terms and over a wider geographical field, partly by borrowers recovering their good spirits and so becoming readier to borrow.

Seldom in modern history has the gap between the two been so wide and so difficult to bridge. Unless we bend our wills and our intelligences, energised by a conviction that this diagnosis is right, to find a solution along these lines, then, if the diagnosis *is* right, the slump may pass over into a depression, accompanied by a sagging price level, which might last for years, with untold damage to the material wealth and to the social stability of every country alike. Only if we seriously seek a solution, will the optimism of my opening sentences be confirmed—at least for the nearer future.

It is beyond the scope of this essay to indicate lines of future policy. But no one can take the first step except the central banking authorities of the chief creditor countries; nor can any one Central Bank do enough acting in isolation. Resolute action by the Federal Reserve Banks of the United States, the Bank of France, and the Bank of England might do much more than most people, mistaking symptoms or aggravating circumstances for the disease itself, will readily believe. In every way the most effective remedy would be that the Central Banks of these three great creditor nations should join together in a bold scheme to restore confidence to the international long-term loan market; which would serve to revive enterprise and activity everywhere, and to restore prices and profits, so that in due course the wheels of the world's commerce would go round again. And even if France, hugging the supposed security of gold, prefers to stand aside from the adventure of creating new wealth, I am convinced that Great Britain and the United States, like-minded and acting together, could start the machine again within a reasonable time; if, that is to say, they were energised by a confident conviction as to what was wrong. For it is chiefly the lack of this conviction which to-day is paralysing the hands of authority on both sides of the Channel and of the Atlantic.

3.

A more orthodox attempt to explain the crisis, and to suggest appropriate remedies, was offered by another British Liberal, Lionel Robbins. Mr. Robbins, who taught at the University of London from 1929 to 1961, was one of the most influential economists of his generation; in 1959 he was raised to the peerage as Baron Robbins. In the introductory chapter of his book *The Great Depression* (written in 1934), he stressed the virtues of the nineteenth century's quasi-automatic economic system and emphasized the disruptive effects of the Great War. The orthodoxy of his views emerged more clearly in later chapters, where he charged that "socialistic" state intervention in the economic sphere, both during and after the war, had "sapped the essential strength of capitalism." Only a return to the principles of the free market, he argued, could restore stability and prosperity.

ROBBINS: The Great Depression *

1. The object of this Essay is to examine the nature and the causes of the present depression of trade. Its first task, therefore, is to trace the background of the depression and the broad conditions amid which it was generated.

To do this it is necessary to draw the picture on a canvas wider than that which would at first sight seem appropriate to an enterprise of this nature. The onset of the present crisis may perhaps be dated from the autumn of 1929. But its causes and the conditions under which they have operated take their rise long before this date. The body-economic, equally with the body-politic, has been in a state of violent tension ever since the war. We live, not in the fourth, but in the nineteenth, year of the world crisis. If our discussion of the events since 1929 is not to be wholly unrelated to their most significant causes, it must take some account, however brief, of events before that date. 1914 is the beginning of our epoch.

2. For the hundred years which preceded the outbreak of the Great War, the economic system had not at any time shown itself to be in serious danger of grave breakdown. It was a period of unprecedented change. The external conditions of economic activity were in process of continual alteration. In the old world the advent of steam and machinery was changing the nature and the structure of manufacturing industry. In the new, the coming of new modes of transport was opening up vast areas, hitherto undeveloped, both as sources of food supply and raw materials, and as markets for the products of the manufacturing processes. The population of the world, whose normal state there is reason to suppose to have been more or less stationary, was growing rapidly. The aggregation of people into large cities, dependent for the most elementary necessities of life upon supplies produced at the other ends of the earth, proceeded at a rate unknown in any earlier epoch. Yet the economic mechanism was adjusted to this complex of change without anything like the present dislocations, and, year in, year out, turned out what, for a substantial proportion of the increasing population, has been regarded as the basis of an increasing standard of real income. According to the calculations of Sir Josiah Stamp, the level of real incomes in Great Britain in the years before the war was four times as great as in the Napoleonic period.

To say all this is not in the least to contend that the pre-war period was immune from economic difficulties, or that what has come since is to be regarded as spontaneous catastrophe, having no intimate connection with anything that went before. No student of those times is likely to be unaware of the ups and

* From Lionel Robbins, *The Great Depression* (New York: Macmillan, 1936), pp. 1-11. Reprinted by permission of The Macmillan Company, Ltd., and of the author. (Lord Robbins points out that some of the views expressed in his book no longer coincide with his opinions today.)

downs of trade, the recurrent waves of business depression and unemployment, which ruffle the lines of secular development. Nor will he be blind to the increase towards the end of the period in political tendencies which, viewed in the light of more recent developments, can be seen to have been fraught with danger to the stability of the whole system. The Great War itself was the product, not of accident, but of some of these tendencies. Nevertheless, compared with what has come since, the difficulties of those times must be admitted as being of a minor order. During the years for which we have records, the number of unemployed trade-unionists in Great Britain only once rose above 10 per cent. The crises were not such as to disrupt the unity of monetary conditions in the important financial centres. The interventionist and restrictive tendencies of economic policy, although no doubt calculated to retard the increase of productivity, were never such as seriously to threaten to reverse it. There is no need to present the world before the war as a Utopia to point the contrast with what has come after.

3. Into this world there came the catastrophe of war. There is no need at this point to dwell on the intellectual and cultural changes which this catastrophe involved, although for those who are not dominated by a purely materialist conception of history it is arguable that, even in this context, these were the most important changes of all. More germane, however, to the purpose of this survey, are certain more tangible influences.

As an influence on economic activity, the war, and the political changes which followed the war, must be regarded as a vast series of shifts in the fundamental conditions of demand and supply, to which economic activity must be adapted. The needs of war called a huge apparatus of mechanical equipment into being. The resumption of peace rendered it in large part superfluous. The fact of war involved a disruption of the world market. The settlement, which came after, created conditions which aggravated this disruption. The struggle which was to end nationalist friction in fact gave nationalism new scope.

As an influence on subsequent developments, these changes have a double significance. In the first place, they were discontinuous. They therefore involved vast destruction of capital. Secondly, they were restrictive of free economic activity. They therefore involved a reduction in the productivity of the factors of production. For four years, the capital resources of the belligerent countries of the world were devoted to providing offerings to Mars, which either perished in the moment of their production or remained as useless as the pyramids of the Pharaohs, once the occasion for the sacrifice had ceased. The disruption of the world market, consequent on the war and on the peace settlement, meant a restriction of the area within which the division of labour had scope. It meant therefore a limitation of the increase of wealth to which division of labour gives rise.

Concurrently with these structural dislocations, there came a further series of changes no less important in the causation of post-war difficulties. At the same time as the using up of capital and the lowering of productivity were producing conditions demanding readjustment on a scale hitherto unknown in economic history, the economic system was losing its capacity for adaptation. The successful prosecution of war involved, as we have seen, a large and discontinuous alteration of the "set" of the apparatus of production. This alteration was carried through. But the measures which were necessary to bring it about—the centralisation of control of industrial operations—were such as permanently to impair its capacity for further change. The grouping of industrial concerns into great combinations, the authoritarian fixing of wages and prices, the imposition of the habits of collective bargaining, were no doubt measures which would be justified by appeal to the necessities of war. But they carried with them a weakening of the permanent flexibility of the system, whose effects it is difficult to over-estimate. This was a dish of eggs not easy to unscramble.

Here, as with other contrasts between pre-war and post-war conditions, it is important not to exaggerate differences. It is not contended that the pre-war system was entirely flexible, or that the post-war system has shown itself to be incapable of some adaptation. This would be untrue. All that is argued is that the changes introduced by way of groupings which made for cartellisation on the one hand and a greatly increased rigidity of the labour market on the other, were such as to produce an important and far-reaching impairment of what degree of flexibility there was. In the light of well-known facts regarding the rigidity of wages and the prices of cartellised products in the post-war period, this does not seem to be a contention which is open to serious question.

Beyond all this came the break-up of international monetary unity. For forty years before the war, the financial systems of the leading countries of the world had been linked together by the international Gold Standard. For a century, the Gold Standard had been virtually effective. Trade between different national areas took place on the basis of rates of exchange which fluctuated only between very narrow limits. Capital moved from one part of the world to another, if not with the same ease with which it moved within national areas, at least with much the same effects as regards the volume of credit available. The prices of internationally traded commodities moved together in all the important centres. The price and cost structures of the different financial areas maintained a relationship which was seldom seriously out of equilibrium.

The war put an end to all this. Within a few days of the outbreak of hostilities, in each of the belligerent financial centres, measures had been taken which amounted to an actual, if not to a legally acknowledged, abandonment of the Gold Standard. Of the chief financial centres, the United States was the only one to remain on gold. The others not only suspended the rights of effective convertibility; they each, in greater or lesser degree, resorted to the device of inflation as a means of financing the war. The results were as might have been expected. The gold supplies of the world tended more and more to be concentrated in the vaults of the Federal Reserve Banks. Prices rose in the inflating countries in various degrees, according to the measure of the inflation. In the markets for foreign exchange the conditions of supply and demand reflected the internal depreciation. It was the first phase of a period of international disequilibrium from which we have not yet emerged.

4. The conclusion of peace brought no end to this disorder. The inordinate claims of the victors, the crass financial incapacity of the vanquished, the utter budgetary disorder which everywhere in the belligerent countries was the legacy of the policies pursued during the war, led to a further period of monetary chaos. In the United States a brief inflationary boom was followed by collapse, and then a fairly rapid recovery. In Great Britain the boom and the collapse had no such fortunate sequel: a long period of relative stagnation followed. In continental Europe, the confusion was without precedent. It was the era of great inflations. The rouble, the crown and the mark all suffered what was virtually an annihilation of value. The franc and the lira underwent serious depreciation. The results were what was to be expected—severe curtailment of trade, further structural dislocations, capital consumption and the wiping-out of middle-class resources, a further disruption of the basis of the international equilibrium of prices.

5. By the middle of the 'twenties, this intense disorder had come to an end. One by one, budgets were balanced and disordered currencies were restored to some kind of stability. In the spring of 1925, Great Britain and the British dominions returned to the Gold Standard. By the end of the year, of the important countries, only France was still on a fluctuating standard.

There followed a period of good trade—a period, indeed, which in the light of more complete knowledge of the relevant statistics can be seen to have been, for some parts of the world, one of the biggest booms in economic history. Trade revived, incomes rose. Production went ahead by leaps and bounds. International investment was resumed on a scale surpassing even pre-war dimensions. The stock exchanges of the more prosperous centres displayed such strength that speculation for a rise seemed a more certain path to a secure income than all the devices of ancient prudence. It was a period in which the finance ministers of the world, looking forward to years of increasing revenue, felt no hesitation in incurring fresh obligations on the side of expenditure. Men of the type of the late Ivar Kreuger moved rapidly from one capital city to another, arranging without fuss or inconvenience to anybody, what were described as "good constructive loans"—the acolytes of the "new economics." It was in these days that it was said that the trade cycle had become extinct.

Nevertheless, there were certain features of this phase which were such as to distinguish it, if not in kind, at any rate in degree, from other periods of expanding trade. It was pre-eminently an industrial boom. The rise in profitability was essentially a feature of manufacture and raw material producing industry. Throughout the period, the profitability of certain lines of food production was relatively low. In the United States—then as now the centre of the world fluctuation—side by side with extreme prosperity in the manufacturing industries, there existed severe difficulties, and in parts even distress, among the producers of agricultural products. All over the world the relative decline of agriculture was giving rise to severe political strain and desperate attempts, in the shape of pools and restriction schemes, to evade the consequences of technical progress.

Moreover, even in manufacturing industry the boom was not universal. Im-

portant areas of manufacturing production experienced its influence only indirectly. Throughout the boom years in the United States, industrial activity
anywhere in Great Britain could never have been described as more than
moderately good. There were large areas in the North where this description
would have been an exaggeration. In Central Europe, particularly in Austria,
partly as a result of the peace settlement, partly as a result of internal policy,
there was definitely discernible a tendency to capital consumption. In Germany,
the appalling shortage of capital created by the war and the post-war inflation
was partly compensated by large imports of capital. But the business situation
was never normal, and at a much earlier date than elsewhere it became quite
obviously perilous.

At the same time, in the financial centres of the world there existed conditions wholly without parallel in any earlier period of prosperity. The stabilisation of European currencies and the fixing of new parities, after the colossal
fluctuations of the post-war years, had been carried through on the basis of
what very often could only be described as hit-or-miss methods; and although
in some cases the miss was not very great, in others it was considerable. In the
case of Great Britain, the parity chosen was almost certainly too high. In France
there is reason to suppose that the error was in the opposite direction. The result was a most peculiar state of inter-local monetary disequilibrium. The
centres which had returned too high were continually in danger of losing gold;
the centres which had returned too low were almost embarrassed by the gold
they attracted. Now it so happened that the centre which suffered chiefly from
over-valuation was also the chief centre of organised capital export. While the
over-valued exchanges made long-term capital export from London a highly
difficult operation, the relatively high rates, which were necessary to keep gold
from flowing out, were especially tempting to short-term balances. Hence,
throughout the whole of this period there existed in one of the chief financial
centres of the world a lack of balance between long- and short-term investment
which was itself conducive to disequilibrium and latent with dangers of extensive catastrophe, should anything occur to disturb the insecure prosperity
elsewhere.

6. Thus, in spite of the appearance of considerable prosperity and a very real
measure of revival of trade and industry, the period immediately preceding the
slump was not without conditions which might justifiably have given rise to
very grave anxiety. Clearly, if the forces making for prosperity were to slacken,
the ensuing depression was likely to be a depression of more than usual severity.

They did slacken. Looking back, it is possible to discern the beginning of the
depression about the end of 1928, when the flow of American lending to
Germany first began to lose its pace. By the middle of 1929, the evidences of
serious weakening in that part of the world were unmistakeable. In certain raw
material producing centres, too, there were signs of weakness quite early in the
summer.

But the main tide of American speculation continued to flow with un-
diminished strength until the autumn. As early as February the authorities

of the Federal Reserve System had become persuaded that the boom had reached such dimensions that a crash was inevitable. But, in spite of private warnings, rising discount rates, and all kinds of unofficial indications, the rise of stock exchange values continued. Then suddenly there came a crack. The collapse of the Hatry swindles in London caused a sudden tightening of markets there. The rate of interest was advanced to 6-½ per cent. In New York there was a sympathetic movement. On October 23rd the Dow-Jones index of the price of industrial shares in New York dropped about 21 points; during the next six days it fell about 76 points more. Prosperity was at an end. The bottom had dropped out of the market.

7. The depression which followed has dwarfed all preceding movements of a similar nature both in magnitude and in intensity. In 1929 in the United States the index of security prices stood in the neighbourhood of 200–210. In 1932 it had fallen to 30–40. Commodity prices in general fell in the same period by 30–40 per cent; the fall in particular commodity markets was even more catastrophic. Production in the chief manufacturing countries of the world shrank by anything from 30–50 per cent: and the value of world trade in 1932 was only a third of what it was three years before. It has been calculated by the International Labour Office that in 1933, in the world at large, something like 30 million persons were out of work. There have been many depressions in modern economic history but it is safe to say that there has never been anything to compare with this. 1929 to 1933 are the years of the Great Depression.

4.

One notable by-product of the great depression was that it stimulated the interest of young intellectuals in Marxism and fascism—doctrines which claimed to provide substitutes for a decadent liberal capitalism that was allegedly doomed to recurrent and ever-worsening crisis. One of the most talented converts to Marxism in this era was a young Englishman named John Strachey, whose books became best sellers both in Britain and in America. Although Strachey was eventually to repudiate Marxism (and to attain considerable eminence in British political life), his essays of the depression decade were particularly forceful attacks upon all schools of "capitalist" economists, whether "free traders" (Strachey's label for men such as Lionel Robbins) or "national planners" (a category which, according to Strachey, included Keynes).

STRACHEY: The Coming Struggle for Power *

There have arisen today . . . at least two comparatively realistic schools of thought amongst orthodox theorists. For both these schools see clearly and face frankly the present crisis in capitalism. Both admit that the present situation is impossible. But each proposes a remedy which appears to be antithetical to the

* John Strachey, *The Coming Struggle for Power* (New York: Covici-Friede, 1933), pp. 131–32, 135–36, 146–47, 150–51, 200–205. Reprinted by permission of Crown Publishers.

other's. One school proposes to attempt to restore the free market in all its pristine purity: the other proposes to hasten forward the process by which the freedom of the market is being curtailed. We may, perhaps, call the adherents of the school which wishes to re-establish full free market conditions, the "market restorers" or the "free traders," using the words free trade to mean not merely the absence of international tariff barriers but to imply every kind of freedom of exchange. The school which wishes further to curtail the market, we may call "the national planners."

Let us consider first the solutions proposed by the "free traders." Now it is clear that the "free traders" are facing very great practical difficulties. They avowedly wish to revert to a previous condition of affairs. Hence, existing tendencies are dead against them. Their theoretical position, however, is strong (stronger, I shall submit, than that of any other capitalist school). Let us look for a moment at their aims and at the arguments which, they claim, show that their policy offers a solution for capitalism.

They diagnose the malady from which capitalism is suffering as being due to interferences with free exchange. Hence, they believe that the cure is to be found in the abolition of these interferences, and the restoration of the nearest possible approximation to what the economists call "a perfect market" (that is, a market in which the laws of supply and demand work upon price without check) all over the world. They would not claim that such perfect market conditions had, in fact, ever existed. They admit that the new tendencies to interference with freedom of exchange had arisen long before the old restrictions had been dissolved. But this is no reason, they feel, why something much nearer a perfect world market than has ever before existed, should not now be established. For economic science has made great strides. In the outside world the market is becoming, it is true, less and less perfect; but in the brains of the economists it is becoming more and more perfect. And so the "free traders" consider that the time has at length arrived when the perfect market can be established. All that is necessary is that the statesmen of the world shall listen to the advice of the economists. If only they will do so, mankind may be led back from the edge of the abyss into a promised land of economic progress and stability. . . .

It is comprehensible that the economists, having proved to their own satisfaction the theoretical possibility of such a system, sincerely believe that the best interests of humanity will be served by efforts to bring this ideal and perfect market into existence, or, at any rate, to return to a state of things in which its most elementary and essential conditions are not, as they are to-day, universally flouted. For the best of them see and are horrified by the chaos and devastation, the stupendous waste of desperately needed wealth, which is going on around them to-day. And it is natural that they should suppose that all these disasters are a punishment to the nations which have abandoned the one true god—the perfect market—and have worshipped false economic deities. And so they arise like the prophets of old to warn a stiff-necked and hard-hearted generation to return to its forsaken faiths. . . .

. . . The execution of such a programme cannot even be attempted unless some powerful class, or coalition of classes, is solidly behind the attempt. How can the market restorers hope to find such a basis of support? Only by finding a class whose interests would be promoted, whose wealth and power would be aggrandized, by the restoration of the market. Does such a class exist? Surely it must, for if there were no such class at all the very idea of the restoration of the market would hardly have arisen. That class is the remnant of the old middle class of small-scale producers for the market. Naturally, this now disregarded and diminishing class yearns after the days when it was the dominant class in the community. Naturally, its members dream of a sort of small bourgeois restoration in which all their enemies, the big monopolistic capitalists who are crushing them out, the trade unions, which are hampering them, the tariff barriers which hem them in, the recurrent crises which ruin them in the night, shall all be abolished. Nor do their dreams lack verisimilitude. For it is from this particular class that many of the ablest theorists and economists derive. And they can show that compared with the hell which the large-scale imperialistic capitalists are making of the world, the reign of *their* class was, in some ways, comparatively tolerable. . . .

We may estimate then that the real amount of support behind the market restorers is just about enough to conceive of the idea of such a restoration of the market, but is not enough to move a single step towards its accomplishment. This in no way disproves, however, the arguments by which they demonstrate that the only way in which the present capitalist system can be preserved is by the restoration of the market. Their arguments cannot, in fact, be disproved. They remain impeccable.

We arrive at these conclusions. The free traders are able to prove that their solution is the only one; yet they have not the slightest prospect of being able even to attempt to apply it; hence, capitalism cannot in fact be much longer maintained in existence.

It is sad, though it is explicable, and indeed inevitable, that so much talent should be lavished by these able economists on a cause lost these thirty years. Let us erase from our minds for a moment all that has been said of the practical impossibility of restoring the market. And let us envisage the psychological task which would be involved. Let us consider the dying faiths which would have to be revived, the worn-out political watchwords recoined, the strange outdated weapons of social struggle refurbished, if the free trader economists could only by some stroke of magic have their way. In order that the free market might flourish again, that whole system of ideas which reached perhaps its highest point in nineteenth-century Britain, and its very apogee in nineteenth-century Lancashire, would have to be raised from the dead. Out of the Lancashire of to-day, out of the now silent mills, out of the empty weaving sheds, the very machinery of which has been sold off to Allahabad or to Shanghai, would have to emerge, as from the grave, a new generation, with the unquestioning faith of their grandfathers in the principles of democracy, the British Parliamentary system, the Protestant faith, and a total absorption in self-enrichment as a religious duty. Even the ghosts of these ideas do not walk. They are laid for ever. For the epoch of human history and the material conditions which alone gave them life have passed away down the irreversible stream of time. Only the least historically minded men on earth, only English economists, could dream of their resurrection. . . .

Mr. J. M. Keynes . . . is the ablest of the surviving economists of the British capitalist class. . . . In fact, he is more than an economist in the narrow sense of the word. He is, as we have suggested, a major social and political theorist of the English-speaking capitalist class. . . .

In the preface of [*Essays in Persuasion*], Mr. Keynes tells us that he has been a Cassandra "who could never influence the course of events in time." And it is essential that this remark should be kept in mind as one reads Mr. Keynes' various prescriptions for the survival of capitalism. The application of the measures of "intelligent management" which he suggests will ensure, he is convinced, that in about a hundred years' time capitalism will have carried the human race into an era of universal plenty and security. For, needless to say, the thesis which runs through Mr. Keynes' collected papers is the exact antithesis of these pages. We have sought and, it is submitted, discovered, a direct causal connection of a necessary and predictable character, between the inherent characteristics of capitalism and the present disastrous condition of the world; and we have discovered in particular a connection between these characteristics and the recurrence of crises such as that which began in 1931. We submit, further, that it is possible to predict future and far worse consequences from these characteristics of capitalism. Naturally, therefore, we draw the conclusion that the only hope for the dawn of that day when man shall have finally reached . . . a level of civilization at which the economic problem is no longer his chief concern lies in the overthrow of capitalism. For Mr. Keynes himself rightly says that such a level of civilization is now becoming a technical possibility.

Mr. Keynes, on the contrary, finds no causal connection whatever between the character of our economic system and the present condition of affairs. On the contrary, he says . . . that his "central thesis" and his "profound conviction" is that "the Economic Problem, as one may call it for short, the problem of want and poverty and the economic struggle between classes and nations, is nothing but a frightful muddle, a transitory and *unnecessary* muddle."

Mr. Keynes is a most satisfactory writer: he says clearly and forcibly what the other theorists of his class merely mumble and mutter. For example, it is perfectly consistent with the above expression of opinion that he has not the slightest use for the Marxist case. . . . As we read Mr. Keynes' always reasonable, persuasive, and logically, self-consistent pages, we are driven more and more to realize that it is precisely his basic eclecticism, his profound antagonism for the only unitary theory which will account for the political and economic phenomena of the modern world, which renders so academic, so beside the real point, nearly all of his suggestions. Has he never, one cannot help wondering, paused to enquire *why* his *Essays in Persuasion* have been so uniformly unpersuasive: has he never asked *why* he has always been unable "to influence the course of events in time"? . . . Surely, the leaders of capitalism all over the world are not all so foolish or so ill-advised, as to ignore in their desperate need, such hopeful advice; and to rush wilfully upon their own destruction? And yet this is just the hypothesis that Mr. Keynes and all "enlightened" capitalist opinion has to resort to in order to account for the present situation. It is felt that capitalism is a perfectly sound system which by some dreadful mistake the capitalists are themselves now wilfully smashing to pieces.

Nothing could be further from the truth. The leaders of capitalism are not fools: they are for the most part very able men struggling against overwhelming difficulties. There is, in fact, a complete contradiction between our diagnosis of the present situation and that of Mr. Keynes. And this contradiction arises precisely from a basic difference of opinion as to whether there is a causal chain between the historical development of capitalism and the recurrence of crisis and war, or whether their coincidence is, as Mr. Keynes says, "nothing but a frightful muddle." . . . The causal chain which we have attempted to trace has not been exclusively composed of material links. . . . It has involved the view that certain economic and material conditions determine certain mental and psychological points of view: and these mental and psychological points of view, in their turn, determine by reaction further material developments. In the causal chain, each economic link has been followed by a mental and psychological one: it has been a chain of action and reaction between the economic basis and the ideal structure, which has been built on that basis. To instance a few successive links, the growth of large-scale production caused certain consequences in the minds of entrepreneurs which made them strive towards the formation of monopolies. The formation of monopolies in turn caused . . . certain changes in the minds of statesmen which caused them to undertake imperialist adventures. The existence of empires causes certain further tendencies in the minds of the governing class which must sooner or later involve them in war. And no one denies that wars, in their turn, cause marked economic changes. . . .

Thus, the philosophical basis upon which Marxism rests: the view which attributes unity, though not identity, between the material and the ideal, between theory and practice, is not without its practical application. But for Mr. Keynes there is no such unity. Any kind of economic system may be combined with any kind of point of view amongst the men who control it. . . . True, with another part of his mind he knows that capitalism has consequences in the realm of ideas which are "extremely objectionable." He thinks, however, that by subjecting ourselves to these "extremely objectionable" consequences for another hundred years or so, we shall solve our economic problem. Can he not see that even if we could do so, "we" should not be there at all at the end of a hundred years: that these capitalist values, which he himself calls "detestable," would long before then have made us totally unfit for the promised land of economic plenty? Indeed, they would have so degraded—nay they are even now so degrading—the whole race that, far from attaining any promised land of plenty, the race would certainly lose in titanic wars that level of civilization which it has.

This extreme indifference to the real drift of events—this conviction that the crisis in capitalism is not only a "frightful" but a "transitory and unnecessary" muddle, has hitherto allowed Mr. Keynes to believe in a kind of restoration of the world free market. Now, however, he is becoming a little more realistic, and is inclining towards that school of thought . . . which we called "the national planners." And again in this field, his blindness to the political consequences of economic tendencies will for some time yet enable him to plan nationally without ever definitely answering his own question "Am I a liberal?" with a negative. When that moment does come, however, the next question which Mr. Keynes will have to ask himself will be "Am I a fascist?" And the answer will be in the affirmative.

5.

If the great depression brought widespread misery and soul-searching throughout the western world, it reinforced the confidence and hope of capitalism's bitterest critics. Fascist doctrinaires could claim to offer quick and drastic remedies; communist spokesmen could point out that they had foreseen the crisis all along, since it grew naturally out of the contradictions of capitalism. A neat and concise summary of the communist viewpoint was provided by the British Communist party's leading intellectual—R. Palme Dutt, a member of its executive committee since 1922, and editor of the party organ, *The Labour Monthly*. Mr. Dutt's political career began during his undergraduate years at Oxford, when he was expelled from the university for his Marxian activities.

DUTT: World Politics 1918–1936 *

The period of temporary stabilisation—which may well be called the period of illusions of a restored and prosperously advancing capitalism—lasted from 1924 to 1929.

It began with the London Conference and the adoption of the Dawes Plan in 1924, which was regarded as settling the vexed question of reparations on a practical basis ("the standpoint adopted has been that of business and not politics," declared the experts), and opened the way for the economic restoration of capitalism in Germany. This was followed by a flow of American capital and credits into Germany and other European countries, leading to rapid in-

* From R. Palme Dutt, *World Politics 1918–1936* (New York: International Publishers, 1936), pp. 64–72. Reprinted by permission of International Publishers. For a more detailed Marxian analysis of the origins and characteristics of the great depression, see the classic account by the leading Soviet economist Eugen Varga: *The Great Crisis and its Political Consequences* (New York: International Publishers, 1934).

dustrial development and expansion. A series of League of Nations loans assisted the smaller European States. . . .

Production and trade leapt up throughout the world. Between 1925 and 1929 the League of Nations index of the world production of foodstuffs (on the basis of 100 as the average of 1925–9) rose from 98 to 103, of industrial raw materials from 92 to 111, of industrial goods from 92 to 111, and of the volume of world trade from 92 to 111. In those same years the index of German industrial production rose from 87 to 109, of the United States from 95 to 109, of the United Kingdom from 99 to 112, of France from 88 to 114. Profits piled up; capital investments soared; share values soared. The index of the market value of industrial shares rose in the United States from 100 in 1926 to 189 in 1929, in Germany from 93 in 1925 to 126 in 1929, in the United Kingdom from 109 in 1925 to 139 in 1929.

That was one side of the picture—a picture of boom conditions, of a loudly acclaimed prosperity, peace and progress of a supposedly stabilised and reorganised capitalism which was believed to have overcome its contradictions and antagonisms. On this basis was built a host of illusions of "organised capitalism," the "conquest of poverty," the "end of crises," and in general a "new era" of limitless expansion and world peace. Hoover declared in 1928 that "the outlook for the world to-day is for the greatest era of commercial expansion in history," and again that "unemployment in the sense of distress is finally disappearing; we in America to-day are nearer to the final triumph over poverty than ever before in the history of any land." The American Professor N. Carver of Harvard University published a book in 1928 entitled *This Economic World* in which he raised the question "How long will this diffusion of prosperity last?" and answered: "'There is absolutely no reason why the widely diffused prosperity which we are now witnessing should not permanently increase." . . . The special conditions of the American expansion of this period, and the high wages paid to a section of the workers, were regarded as the type of modern capitalism. The view was expressed that capitalism was evolving, with the growing concentration of the great trusts and co-operation of the central banks, to a new type of "organised capitalism" or "ultracapitalism," i.e. to a rational productive organisation of economy on a world scale, eliminating crises and gradually overcoming poverty and unemployment. These views were especially promoted by the reformist leadership of the Labour movements in Europe and America. The theorist of German Social Democracy, Hilferding, stated at the Kiel Congress of his party in 1927, that "we are in the period of capitalism which in the main has overcome the era of free competition and the sway of the blind laws of the market, and we are coming to a capitalist organisation of economy . . . to organised economy," and that "organised capitalism in reality signifies the supersession, in principle, of the capitalist principle of free competition by the Socialist principle of planned production."

These illusions of the period of temporary stabilisation as a supposed new era of a stable and permanently advancing capitalism were shared and expressed, in one form or another, by all the political leaders, the business leaders and the economic theorists of capitalism, as well as by the trade union and Labour reformist leaders and theorists. The Marxists alone at the time correctly analysed the situation and its future outcome.

The reality was indeed different, as the subsequent world economic crisis which began in 1929 rapidly made clear to all. So far from the inner contradictions and antagonisms of capitalism having been overcome, they were intensified by the general crisis of post-war capitalism; and the subsequent world economic crisis exceeded in intensity all that had gone before. The whole basis of the post-war temporary stabilisation was in fact rotten at the root. It did not represent in any sense a return even to the pre-war level of relative stability, but was built on forces which made certain the future collapse. The reasons for this lay both in the particular conditions of the process of partial stabilisation, and in the general conditions of the stage of capitalism that had been reached.

The immediate pillar of the process of capitalist restoration in Europe was the flow of American capital export to Europe, and especially to Germany. This laid the basis for the return to the gold standard, and produced a temporary flush of prosperity and expansion. In reality it concealed a heavier dilemma than that which it was intended to solve.

The United States had emerged from the war a creditor nation in place of its previous debtor position. But it was a creditor nation of a new type. Unlike the United Kingdom, which had since the middle of the nineteenth century combined a rising creditor position with a rising net balance of imports, representing the portion of the overseas tribute which was not reinvested, the United States combined its new creditor position with a large surplus of exports, which was being forced up by every means of highly organised mass production and competitive selling, at the same time as high tariffs were being maintained and increased to exclude imports. From this resulted an obvious contradiction. The impoverished world after the war was in debt to the wealthy American capitalism, and at the same time America was pouring out a surplus of goods on the world, which increased the debt. Europe with an adverse trade balance of four hundred million pounds was needing to pay tribute to America with a favourable trade balance of two hundred million pounds. The result inevitably reflected itself in the flow of gold to America. Between 1913 and 1924 American gold holdings rose from 1,924 million dollars to 4,499 million dollars, or roughly half the gold in the world. The apoplexy of capitalist development had now reached an extreme point. While Europe was struggling with paper inflation and dear credit, the United States was struggling to "immobilise" and "sterilise" its gold in vaults in order to prevent "gold inflation." "Your country has most of the gold in the world; what are you going to do about it?" was the question asked of Ambassador Kellogg by "a distinguished London banker," according to a speech of the former at a farewell banquet in London. His reply was: "Bring the pound sterling to a gold basis and restore the currencies of Europe, and the gold question will settle itself" (*The Times*, January 31st, 1925). But, as subsequent experience has shown, the question did not "settle itself" so easily.

The short-lived "solution" found was the export of American capital to Europe and the world. From the second half of 1924 loans and credits, governmental and industrial, of which the Dawes Loan was only the leading example and signpost, poured into Europe from America. The restoration of Europe was in full swing. The Democratic Left (represented by the MacDonald Government in Britain and the Herriot Government in France) had their brief heyday while the golden chains were being imposed—to be speedily replaced by sterner forces as soon as the exaction of the tribute became the task. The flow of gold was turned. Gold began to pass out again from America to the rest of the world. In the first half of 1924 the net gold import into America was 450 million dollars; in the second half there was a net gold export of 170 millions. The dollar exchange began to climb down closer to sterling. The restoration of the gold standard followed in Britain in 1925.

It was obvious that the whole basis of this restoration was precarious and bound to lead to a future collapse. So long as the flow of American capital export could be maintained, the position could be held. Between 1925 and 1928 the average annual total of American foreign investments amounted to 1,100 million dollars (U.S. Commerce Reports, May 13th, 1929). By 1928 the net interest from foreign investments amounted to 523 million dollars, and the receipts on war debts to 210 millions (it will be noted that the question of reparations and war debts accentuated, but played a secondary rôle in the total tangle), or a total of 733 millions. . . . Thus the new foreign investment exceeded the return in interest and receipts on war debts. It was clear that this situation could not continue for more than a limited period. On the side of Germany the total gross foreign debt mounted up from 2.5 milliard Reichsmarks in 1925 to 25 milliards in 1929. . . . By 1928 the German statistician, Dr. Kuczynski, estimated that of the total German wealth, computed at 50 to 60 thousand million dollars, foreign holdings in one form or another amounted to 13 to 15 thousand millions, or one quarter (New York Nation, November 7th, 1928). As the pyramid of debt mounted up, and the interest was only being paid by new borrowing, each new loan became more precarious, and the prospect drew closer in sight when the flow of new foreign capital would dry up. But once this flow should begin to dry up (as it finally did in 1930), the whole structure would come crashing, unless a vast surplus of exports could have been achieved in the interim period to pay the tribute. At the end of the process of "stabilisation" the original problem recurred in sharpened form.

To meet this situation it was necessary for the European countries, and for Germany in particular, enormously to increase their exports. But in the four years 1925 to 1928 Germany had a net imports surplus of 7,811 million marks. . . . To turn this into an exports surplus sufficient to pay the interest on the foreign debts (even if reparations payments had been completely cancelled) would have made it necessary to flood the world market with German goods. Every effort was made to achieve this aim. A gigantic rationalisation process was carried through, with the aid of the borrowed capital, to equip German industry to pour mass-production goods on the world market. But here the effort broke down against the deeper causes of the world economic crisis.

Every capitalist industrial country in the period of partial stabilisation was enormously increasing its productive power. Each one was seeking to obtain an enlarged share of the world market to absorb its output. At the same time the production of primary materials in the colonial and semi-colonial countries was enormously forced up. For a period the process of expansion could develop through the phase of the boom so long as the actual expansion of production could help to provide the expanding market. But ultimately this expansion of necessity broke against the limits of mass consumption in the conditions of capitalist exploitation. The very process of rationalisation, which extracted a continually increased output from a diminished labour force and with a diminished net return to labour, intensified this contradiction. Already in the beginning of 1928 the Chief of the United States Bureau of Labour Statistics was raising the problem: "The question which everybody was asking in 1927 was: How is the reduced employment going to buy the increased output? Rationalisation spells increased output. The year 1927 did not answer the question, and let us hope that it will be as successfully sidestepped in 1928."

The first signs of the approaching crisis appeared in the accumulation of stocks in primary products. World stocks of primary products, on the basis of 1923–1925 as 100, increased by the end of 1926 to 134, by 1928 to 161, and by 1929 to 192. An agrarian crisis developed in the colonial and semi-colonial countries.

The crash came in 1929. The crash began in the United States and extended to the world. American capitalism, which had been held up as the type of the "new capitalism," and which had been the principal organiser of "stabilisation," became the principal demonstration of capitalist bankruptcy and the immediate agent of disorganisation of world economy. When the crash came, it was all the more extensive, far-reaching and lasting in its effects, both because of the enormous increase in productive power, and because of the economic-political conditions of the general crisis of capitalism already described.

The world economic crisis of 1929 to 1933 was the most devastating economic crisis in capitalist history. It is unnecessary to describe in detail the havoc of this crisis, whose effects, continued into the prolonged depression that has succeeded it, have affected the lives of every human being. Between the peak in the second quarter of 1929 and the lowest point of the crisis in the third quarter of 1932, world industrial production outside the Soviet Union (whose production nearly doubled in the same period), on the basis of the average of 1925–1929 as 100, fell from 113.1 to 65.9, or a fall of 42 per cent. . . . For contrast it is only necessary to note that in any previous pre-war crisis the maximum recorded fall of production was 7 per cent. Between 1929 and 1932 world trade, measured in gold dollars, fell by 65 per cent. The previous maximum drop, in the crisis of 1907–1908, was 7 per cent. Mass unemployment rose to a total estimated at thirty to fifty millions. The League of Nations international index of unemployment rose from 100 in 1929 to 164 in 1930, 235 in 1931, and 291 in 1932, and remained at 274 in 1933 and 221 in 1934.

The period of temporary stabilisation thus ended in the greatest economic crash in history. In the earlier stages the attempt was still made to minimise its significance as a temporary interruption of capitalist progress. The attempt was made to attribute its causes to isolated, incidental factors, and in particular to the working of the vicious system of reparations and war debts. But the aboli-tion of reparations and war debts payments by the Hoover moratorium of 1931, so far from solving the crisis, only laid bare its deeper character. As the deeper effects of the crisis began to operate in 1931–1933, and the prolonged depression ensued, far-reaching economic and political changes followed which have transformed the world situation and shaped the present era.

6.

It is customary to view the great depression as a crisis whose origins were largely economic but whose consequences were largely social and political. The crisis undermined democracies everywhere, and brought men like Adolf Hitler to power. This view has been challenged by David J. Dallin, a Russian-born scholar who lived in exile in western Europe or the United States from 1921 until his death in 1961. The reality, he contends, was quite the reverse: the depression was in large part the outgrowth of political tensions and un-certainties. In fact, ". . . it was Hitlerism that caused the Great Depression." Furthermore, he adds, the slow pace of recovery during the 1930's was also traceable to political conditions: "Hitlerism was casting a gloomy shadow upon the world economy"; "the crisis could be cured only by political medi-cine."

DALLIN: Politics and World-Economy in the Great Depression of 1929–1934 *

In the long history of economic highs and lows, of prosperity and depression, no single change seems to have played so great a political and ideological role as the Depression of 1929–1934. Our generation having lived through that period, cannot gauge its great significance, but future historians (casting a retrospective glance at these years) will probably dwell on the Depression as an astoundingly powerful factor in our psychology as well as on the great number of errors connected with it. . . .

In Germany the Depression developed and deepened during the three years from 1930 to 1932, and Hitler's party derived from it great political profit. There, the struggle was directed against the "Weimar System" and against the Ger-man democratic parties which were unable to cope with the economic disaster. When the Depression reached its climax, Hitler came to power. Soon the wheels started turning, and unemployment steadily decreased. In this uptrend, state and particularly military needs played a decisive part. Until the very outbreak

* From David J. Dallin, "Politics and World-Economy in the Great Depression of 1929–1934," in *The Review of Politics*, VII (1945), pp. 15–24. Reprinted by permission of the editors of *The Review of Politics*.

of the war, the history of the German Depression remained the strongest argument for, and a potent instrument of, the National-Socialist Party against the other parties, particularly against the democratic ones.

Very great influence was exercised by the Depression on the ideology of Soviet Russia. From 1924 on Stalin time and again had written and said that the world prosperity which had set in was temporary and unstable, and that it would be followed by a new big depression. "This is merely a relative stabilization of capitalism," was Stalin's formula. According to his concept, capitalism had fulfilled its mission in past centuries and was now on the decline; growing decrepit, it was no longer able to stimulate the economic life of mankind, and from now on would go zigzag. The depressions in their new universal form, Stalin maintained, were a symptom of "the decay of capitalism." Thus, when a depression broke out at the end of the twenties and persisted into the thirties, it seemed to furnish a splendid confirmation of his judgment. Stalin used to begin all his speeches at party congresses with a detailed analysis of world economy; pointing in particular to England and America, he compared with them Socialist Russia which was almost unaffected by the world depression. At that time Russia was going through the process of collectivization of farms and deportation of the "kulaks"; in 1932-1933 she was visited by a great famine. These events, however, were not an outcome of the economic world disaster.

In schools and universities and in thousands of party lectures these theories of Stalin were assiduously explained and hammered in—theories which foresaw the economic depression, the new international conflicts and the new war "which will represent capitalism's attempt to find a way out of its hopeless situation."

A close study of the origin and history of the Great Depression shows that there is no justification for any of the political inferences that have been drawn from it in various countries. Moreover, the origin of the Depression, its roots and sources cannot be traced either to the economic sphere or to the sphere of domestic policy; neither to the Republican Party in America, nor to the democratic parties in Germany; nor to the capitalist system in general. Unlike the many depressions of the nineteenth and twentieth centuries which came as a result of preceding economic growth, the Great Depression originated in the domain of international politics. It was not so much economy (Depression) that caused political sequels (Hitlerism, war) as it was political events that led to economic depression.

The world prosperity of the middle twenties was based on the general conviction that Europe—and for that matter the whole world—had at last found rest, and that peace was assured for a very long period. This calm assurance brought about intense economic activity. Those who possessed bank accounts looked for a more profitable investment in industry. Shareholders increased their companies' capital, and willingly contributed additional sums. French and other peasants untied the stockings in which gold coins had been kept for ten years and acquired more livestock, land and buildings. Enterprising men sought a vider field for their activity and better prospects in foreign lands, and a stream of foreign, mainly American, capital flowed into Europe. A great deal of time and effort had been needed to clear the clouds from the horizon, but now this aim seemed to have been reached.

This conviction was shared by the entire economic world after the new German attempt at *revanche* was utterly defeated in 1923. . . . It appeared that despite the passive and negative stand of the British government, . . . with Italy inactive and Russia practically non-existent as a great power, France was strong enough to break Germany's will. The inference was that the German menace had vanished, that there was no danger of a new war, and that Europe at long last had reached the path of peaceful development. . . .

The situation within Germany was consolidating, and her war wounds were healing faster than could have been expected. Her industrial output exceeded the volume of 1913; her agriculture and foreign trade prospered.

Foreign capital from England, France, Holland, and particularly from America flowed to Germany and Austria. It flowed in large streams to non-German countries as well, for the certitude prevailed that no political upheavals were to be feared. Parallel with foreign loans granted to municipalities and private persons went the acquisition of German real property and the opening of large credits to German banks from abroad. . . .

In 1929 the situation underwent a speedy change. The extreme currents of German nationalism, suppressed in 1923–1924 and since then reduced to silence, were not quite dead. With Germany recovering her position as a first-rate power and with the international situation growing more favorable to her, Hitlerism once more raised its head. Within the large camp of German nationalism the conservative and the uncompromising trends were engaged in a continuous struggle. Between 1924 and 1929 the big conservative party (Deutschnationale) seemed to be the only serious, though not dangerous, form of German nationalism. Apparently, as soon as the international situation took an aspect more favorable to Germany and a more brazen, aggressive-nationalistic policy became possible, the conservative party found itself confronted with a steadily growing dangerous rival in the form of Hitlerism which by that time had succeeded in uniting the formerly split forces of *revanche*. . . .

It is highly significant that this new growth of militant nationalism occurred not in the years of economic depression, but, on the contrary, during the last stages of prosperity. National Socialism has often been described as the product of despair that took hold of millions, as a result of hunger and unemployment. In later years these factors undoubtedly played a certain role. Yet in Hitlerism there is more reasoning than despair; it is calculating rather than emotional. Had the international situation not changed at the end of the twenties, had it not offered to Hitler new and brilliant prospects, he would have been doomed for the rest of his days to lead a miserable existence as a grumbling leader of an insignificant party.

The essence of this change was that a regenerated Germany was becoming stronger than France. Her metallurgical and chemical industries, her railway system, and whatever could later be turned into war industry steadily outstripped the French economy. The army training, performed in secret and lagging behind the French, still gave every reason to expect the formation of a strong force. No less important was the existing discord among the powers regarding problems of foreign policy. Britain, in constant opposition to France, wished a speedy abrogation of the conditions of the Versailles Treaty, which Germany resented as burdensome and humiliating. The United States virtually took the same stand and helped Germany back out of the reparation payments. France's European allies, Poland and the Little Entente, were weak. As to the Soviet Union, its policy did not basically change; from the outset it continued along the line of neutrality between Germany and France, with all its sympathy on Germany's side, against "the shameful Versailles Treaty." Toward the end of the twenties the formerly united anti-German front showed a number of slits and cracks. . . .

In October 1929 the great crash occurred in the New York stock exchange. Among its causes the events in Germany played a minor role.

True, the American financial world which from 1925 to 1928 had granted large credits to Germany held back in 1929, and some German projects of municipal and other loans did not materialize. Yet the American stock exchange catastrophe was predetermined by the preceding tremendous boom. The increase in the stock values could not continue for ever. A crisis was inevitable.

However, the crisis which affected everybody connected with the stock exchange and stock values did not immediately grow into the Great Depression which is still vivid in our memory. As a matter of fact, the fall from the height of prosperity to the depth of depression at first proceeded slowly.

A close examination of the history of the Depression reveals two periods in its development. The first lasted for about a year, from the autumn of 1929 to the autumn of 1930, the second, from the end of 1930 until the spring of 1933, when the crisis reached its peak. If we set the average value of the United States industrial output in 1923-1925 at 100, its value in the autumn of 1929 amounted to 120, and in the autumn of 1930 to 87. After a continued decrease, at the end of 1932 it hit the low of 59.

A similar development took place in other countries as well. The change became particularly marked in Germany. According to the statistics of obligatory health insurance, the number of workers engaged in German industry in the autumn of 1929 amounted to 18 million. In the autumn of 1930 it dropped to 16 million. From this moment a speedy decrease set in. In the autumn of 1932 there were fewer than twelve million employed, and it was at that moment that the number of unemployed reached 6 million.

If we set the production index for the entire German industry in 1928 at 100, then the autumn of 1929 (beginning of the depression) shows also 100, and the autumn of 1930 85%; yet after this decrease of only 15%, a tremendous fall set in, and the average index for 1932 shows 58%. The turnover of the German retail trade—if we once more put it for 1928 at 100—dropped in the autumn of 1930 to 85, and in the middle of 1932 to 55.

Thus in the first year, the Depression did not exceed the usual and normal limits of crisis, such as had frequently happened before. It seemed reasonable to assume that if the economy was to be ruled by economic laws, the crisis would soon be followed by a new prosperity. It became apparent, however, that political factors are stronger than the economic ones. Bursting into the economic sphere, they turned the developing crisis in another direction.

The political factor which proved decisive was the unexpected and rapid growth in Germany of a party which in reality was a party of war.

. . . In September, 1930 an event occurred which more than anything else prevented the overcoming of the Depression by intrinsic economic forces and which served to protract and deepen it, namely, the sensational elections to the German Reichstag on September 14, 1930. At that election Hitler's small, seemingly insignificant party, which two years earlier (at the elections of May 20, 1928) with great effort had gathered 810,000 votes and had won only 12 seats, now gained 6,400,000 votes and 107 seats. With one stroke the party came to the fore and claimed its right to take the helm. This was a turning point not only in the inner life of Germany, but in the life of the whole world. All foreign governments took alarm. Out of nothing a force was growing up in Germany which promised not the *Erfüllung,* but the violation of the existing treaties, which spoke of peace but meant war, and which obviously did not intend to give any consideration to economic or political obligations, adopting instead a breakthrough policy.

Stability in Europe was obviously vanishing. Germany was becoming a riddle, and all nations were keeping a close watch on the growth of the new party: treaties and agreements with the government of the German republic seemed of no avail since it could be replaced any day by Hitler's government which would repudiate all disagreeable obligations. "If a new treaty with Germany is to be valid," said the French Foreign Minister, Aristide Briand, half earnestly and half in jest, "it needs beside the signature of the German government that of Adolf Hitler." . . .

Meanwhile the long-term principles of Soviet policy and the stability of the Soviet government were becoming ever clearer. Normal diplomatic relations between Moscow and London lasted for only three years, from 1924 to 1927. In 1927 Britain severed them, and though she renewed them in 1929, the relations between the two nations did not improve. The Vatican maintained its stand against atheist Moscow. The great spectacular trials of 1930–1931 in Moscow were intended to prove English and French hostility against Russia and the fact that they were bracing for a war against her, a war allegedly "fixed for the end of 1930." Hinting at England Stalin said in February, 1931, that "war is inevitable with the capitalist powers which are feverishly preparing for an invasion of the USSR."

In contrast to this unfriendliness, fairly good relations existed between the Soviet government and Germany in spite of sporadic quarrels. In July, 1930, Chancellor Brüning suggested the inclusion of Russia in the future superstate union (Briand's plan did not include Russia); the Soviet government promised not to hamper the activity of German concessionaires in Russia, etc.

Was this the appeased, normalized Europe as visualized only a few years earlier by bank announcements and financial newspapers throughout the world?

Capital became apprehensive; the best prospects could not lure it. Foreign capital started withdrawing from Germany and from the rest of Europe. After three, five, or seven years of rosy optimism it began to flow in the opposite direction in the form of bank accounts or gold. Europe and the whole world were seized with growing alarm, and to economic enterprise alarm means paralysis.

Thus the industrial depression developed into a great crisis. During the eight months following the September elections of 1930 in Germany, world economy was hurriedly breaking its ties with that nation, and extra-European nations were severing their trade with Europe. The flight of capital was becoming total. German banks fed from abroad turned bankrupt. The panic was so great that in mid-July, after the bank failure in Vienna, the German government ordered the stock exchange closed. Special laws were enacted in Germany to stop currency and capital from leaving the country. It was only then that the tremendous fall in German stock values began, for the holders were anxious to get rid of them at any price.

The economy is often more sensitive and more responsive to great events than are statesmen and the press. No alarm was yet sounded in the political field; the hope of eluding difficulties and of prevailing upon Hitler's party still lingered. But the economy already sensed the approach of an era of international conflicts, and was timidly withdrawing into its shell.

Meanwhile in Germany the economic disaster exacerbated the political struggle. The number of unemployed, which had already reached millions, steadily increased. The inefficiency and helplessness of the government provided the militant opposition with additional arguments. More brilliant successes won by Hitler soon brought him to the helm. Economic events were naturally reflected in politics. Yet the basic factors of the new development which had taken shape even prior to the Great Depression were of a political or political-psychological nature. With some crudeness and simplification of the situation, it may be said that it was not the Great Depression that called forth Hitlerism, but it was Hitlerism that caused the Great Depression.

7.

After the second world war, American officials and their advisers faced a set of crucial decisions in the field of foreign economic policy, and found it necessary to re-examine the first postwar era for any possible lessons that it might provide. One of the most penetrating reassessments of this kind was written by John H. Williams, who taught economics at Harvard University for almost forty years, served as dean of Harvard's Graduate School of Public Administration for ten years, and acted frequently as a government consultant in matters of international economic policy. In the course of his essay, Mr. Williams reflected on the essential question: ". . . whether this attempt to reconstruct the world as it had been was foredoomed to failure. . . , or whether the new collapse was due to the specific errors committed [in the 1920's]."

WILLIAMS: Economic Lessons of Two World Wars *

The first war produced profound maladjustments in the internal economies of the European countries and in their balances of payment. The United States was converted from a borrowing to a lending country. Germany's international position, by the loss of foreign assets, trade and shipping, was affected in the same kind of way as Britain's after this war. Most of the European countries had international deficits due to shortages of food, raw materials and other goods, internal inflation and the loss of foreign assets; there was the same kind of "dollar shortage" as at present, though on a smaller scale. England did not have a deficit but did suffer a loss of foreign markets and investments that marked the first undermining of her international creditor position, now dramatically completed by the second war.

We had no plans for the transition from war to peace, beyond loans for relief, sales on credit of surplus war stocks, and governmental and bank credits to finance exports; after 1920 our Government withdrew from the financing of external aid and left the field to private lending. We refused to join the League of Nations or to sign the Versailles Peace Treaty. International developments in the twenties were dominated by the controversies over German reparation payments owed to our Allies and the war debts owed by them to us, and by the closely related large-scale outflow of American private capital. I shall not try to tell in detail the story of the reparation payments, the "final" London Settlement of 1921, which broke down within a year and was followed by the French invasion of the Ruhr, hyperinflation in Germany and other parts of Europe, and the complete destruction of the German currency; the Dawes Plan of 1924 and the Young Plan of 1929; the final breakdown in the great depression; or the parallel story of our refusal to recognize the interdependence of the war debts and reparations or accept a feasible settlement, and the final abandonment of the question in the great depression, though we have not yet cancelled our claims.

Granting the impossibility of compressing a decade into a few pages, we can find three outstanding lessons in the twenties. (1) Though food was supplied by relief organizations in the immediate postwar period, no international plan was developed to provide other goods, particularly raw materials, essential for European reconstruction. The problem was not faced as an international issue until the Brussels Conference of October 1922, when the Ter Meulen Plan for raw material credits was presented but failed to materialize. Countries were left to obtain raw materials and other needed goods out of their own financial resources and with their international positions already acutely in deficit. Our exports, initially very large, underwent a severe decline. Wartime controls in Europe, internal and external, broke down, prices rose violently, the foreign

* From John H. Williams, "Economic Lessons of Two World Wars," in *Foreign Affairs*, XXVI (1947), pp. 140–46. Excerpted by special permission from *Foreign Affairs*, October 1947. Copyright by the Council on Foreign Relations, Inc., New York.

exchanges collapsed, tax receipts declined while expenditures increased, the deficits being covered by government demands upon the central banks until government credit collapsed, and monetary inflation undermined not only the power to produce but the social and political fabric of the Continent. (2) The reparation payments and the war debts, superimposed upon the already un-balanced international position, not only greatly intensified the external malad-justments and the internal inflation but for years kept international policy persistently pointed in the wrong direction. (3) The outflow of American capi-tal served as the great counterweight; but I think it must be concluded, as we look back today, that though our capital exports alleviated, and on the surface in the last half of the decade even seemed to have cured, Europe's difficulties, in the end they intensified the maladjustments and contributed greatly to the severity of the world depression of the thirties. But this is a complex subject, and what to conclude for present policy is not an easy task.

As I have indicated, reconstruction in Europe came too late. It did not get under way until inflation had run its course. Though the first of the League loans, which did so much for the smaller countries of central and southeastern Europe, went into effect in Austria in October 1922, German reconstruction was not attempted until 1924 (the Dawes Plan), England resumed the gold standard in 1925, the French budget was balanced and the franc stabilized in 1926–28, and the Polish stabilization came in 1927. These were all parts of the attempt to restore the gold standard, which had broken down in the war, and with the controls removed had given way after the war to international currency chaos and internal inflation. Whether this attempt to reconstruct the world as it had been was foredoomed to failure because a world organization of the gold-standard, multilateral-trade type was no longer workable, or whether the new collapse was due to the specific errors committed—the long delay, the over-valuation involved in restoring the prewar pound (Keynes's "economic con-sequences of Mr. Churchill"), the undervaluation of the franc, the inclusion of reparation payments in the Dawes Plan, American protectionism and the Smoot-Hawley tariff—has been the world's most debated economic question ever since. It provides the key to much of the discussion of Bretton Woods and the International Trade Organization and its Charter.

The twenties were the big decade of American private international invest-ment. It was our first experience and we did it badly. The optimism engendered by our long period of prosperity from 1922 to 1929, the high interest rates ob-tainable, the easy task of salesmanship distorted our vision and put the emphasis on the apparent profits rather than on productivity. The eventual losses have been an almost insurmountable deterrent to further private foreign investment ever since. The conclusion, however, that our capital exports were mistaken is easier to reach now than it was then. The restoration of the gold standard and balanced budgets and the large rebound in European production and trade that accompanied them in the last half of the twenties—and it was in that period that our capital exports were really large—were conditions calculated to invite investment, which in turn further stimulated production and trade. Between 1925 and 1929 the world production of primary products rose by 11 percent, industrial production by about 23 percent and the volume of world trade by about 20 percent.

It is the occurrence of the great depression that makes the record look so bad —and the human propensity to rationalize history after the event. The question really raised is what caused the great depression, how much was it due to domestic developments within the United States (where it began and was most severe), and how much to international maladjustments that had been staved off but in the end were intensified by an extravagant wave of American foreign investment. This is a question that will probably never be settled, though I lean to the view that the causes were more domestic than foreign. It was apparent, however, even in the twenties that our capital exports to Germany were unduly large and in considerable part misdirected. It has been estimated that between 1924 and 1930 Germany borrowed from abroad, mainly from this country, about 30 billion marks. With these loans she was able to make her reparation payments under the Dawes Plan and to rationalize her industries and increase her capacity to pay. There was a body of respectable economic opinion which held that this was a logical way of solving the reparations problem so far as the German end of it was concerned, though it still left unsettled the questions whether other countries were really willing to receive the payments, whether Germany could make net remittances after the capital inflow had diminished, and perhaps above all (and this is a question which has entered into the present postwar discussion of German reparations) whether the rest of the world wanted to see Germany's economic power developed by this process. Between 1924 and 1930, by the aid of these loans, Germany not only built up her industries and paid reparations but increased her gold reserves, built up foreign balances and investments of almost 10 billion marks and, in addition, enjoyed a large surplus of imports despite the fact that she was paying reparations both in money and in kind. She also indulged in many extravagant expenditures at home. As the American capital inflow continued, it became increasingly short-term (roughly half of the whole was short-term), and, when finally the storm broke over Europe in 1931, it was the flight of short-term capital, first from Austria, then from Germany, and finally from London that precipitated the new collapse of the gold standard, drew three-quarters of a billion dollars of gold from our market in the five weeks following England's going off gold in September, and led to a wave of hoarding of gold, internally and externally, round the world which did not end until our bank holiday of February 1933. This was followed by our own experiment of going off gold and devaluing the dollar—a chapter which did not end until the Gold Reserve Act of January 30, 1934.

The great dividing line of the inter-war period is the year 1931. Thereafter, the world increasingly turned its back on the gold standard and multilateral trade. The thirties were a period of greatly restricted international trade and investment. Neither really recovered from the blow of the depression. But the flight of short-term capital to this country continued, accompanied by an absorption of the world's gold on a scale much exceeding even the flight of short-term capital and gold of the early twenties. The first Roosevelt Administration was intensely nationalistic, at least in its early years, and must take its very large share of the blame for the failure of the World Monetary Conference of 1933, which was the last attempt, before the present, to stabilize world conditions of currency and trade by organized international cooperation on multilateral trade and currency lines.

The broad fact about the thirties was the turning away from multilateral trade and the search for internal stability and security even at the expense of international trade. We watched it go through its various phases, the leaning toward autarchy, the depreciation of currencies that ended only in a vicious circle, the spread of restrictive trade and currency devices—bilateral clearing agreements, quotas and other direct import controls, exchange controls. One of the large issues in economic thinking is whether the events and the policies of the thirties, including our own, were inevitable against the earlier background, and whether—looking not merely at the depression and what may have caused it but at the whole sweep of change in world organization and relationships which many, especially in Europe, trace back even before the First World War—the meaning is that the nineteenth century kind of world has disappeared, and we have been making the mistake repeatedly of vainly trying to set it up again. It is clear that in the beginning the whole movement was involuntary and defensive; it grew perforce out of the contraction of trade in the depression, the panic flights of short-term capital, and, as the Hitler menace grew and war approached, out of political insecurity. But deeper-seated forces have also been suggested, such as a growing lack of balance in the world between agriculture and industry and the cumulative advantage of the United States in world trade, based on our comparative self-sufficiency, rapid technological progress, and the strong foreign demand for our consumer durable goods and capital goods. It is perhaps these broader considerations that have given currency to the phrase "chronic dollar shortage."

One final circumstance to be mentioned is Secretary Hull's attempt to combat the tide by his trade treaties. The restrictive trade and currency practices of the thirties were frankly discriminatory. They represented an attempt to balance accounts between individual countries, a method which obviously gives much freer play than multilateral trade for protecting the internal economy against external strains, and is the logical counterpart of the movement toward internal economic planning. The Reciprocal Trade Agreements Act of 1934 was an attempt at compromise along lines now being carried forward in the discussions of the International Trade Organization and its Charter. As a step toward restoring multilateral trade, it sanctioned bilateral trade agreements based on the principle of nondiscrimination, which was a reassertion of the most-favored-nation principle that had previously characterized our tariff policy.

As we look back over the inter-war period, it seems clear that the generalization often made that the wave of nationalism following the war wrecked the peace needs elaboration. The chief mistake, which certainly was nationalistic, was our refusal to join the League of Nations, which Wilson hoped would overcome the imperfections of the peace treaty. Much of the bargaining among the European countries at the peace table was nationalistic and paved the way for our isolationism. But the failure to organize the transition from war to a normal state of peace was probably due to ignorance. The world had never had such a war and was slow to appreciate what conversion to peace involved. The attempts to collect reparations and war debts were understandable, and perhaps we had to go through those experiences to find out their economic consequences. The attempt at reconstruction, though much too late and involving many mistakes, was nevertheless, in its broad outline, the kind of attempt that most of us, at least in this country, would want to make again. The depression presents the most difficulty; I can only repeat that I think it was primarily of American domestic origin, though with many complicating international circumstances. It brought down the whole house of cards, and the possibility of its recurrence is probably today the chief holdback round the world against the kind of world economic organization we would like to recreate. The real period of nationalism, so far as trade and currency are concerned, was the thirties, and, looking to the longer future, it raises the hardest questions that our postwar planning has to face.

VIII.
THE ORIGINS OF NAZISM

The great depression shook, but did not destroy, the old and deep-rooted democratic systems of western and northern Europe. It both shook and destroyed German democracy; and more important still, it substituted the most effective right-wing totalitarian system of our age.

In this episode we confront one of the most crucial and complex problems in twentieth-century history: how did a gangster movement like Adolf Hitler's manage to get power, and hold power, in a nation of advanced culture like Germany, and how did it manage to win the loyal devotion of the great bulk of the German people? Was his movement peculiarly German, the natural culmination of old and powerful currents in the German cultural and psychological heritage? Or was it (as many German historians insist) essentially un-German in nature, representing a contradiction of all the dominant strains in Germany's past, an unlucky sidetrack in German history rather than the main line?

If one takes this latter position—that it *ought not* to have happened in Germany —then one immediately faces the sensitive question, why *did* it happen there? The answers tend to sort themselves out into two main categories. In the first camp are those who see the interwar Germans as the victims of a peculiar set of circumstances, for most of which they themselves were not responsible. Except for the unlucky concatenation of all these circumstances, it is argued, the rise of a Nazi system would have been as unlikely in Germany as in any other western nation. In the second camp are those who contend that Hitlerism was not a fluke, an aberration, but rather a symptom of a malady that is endemic throughout the western world in our age. That malady, they suggest, is produced by the decay of capitalism, or by the inner contradictions of the mass age, when the common man finds himself baffled by the complexities of a technical civilization. It is a sickness that breaks out in virulent totalitarian form in any nation whose resistance against the infection happens to be lowered. If this point of view is valid, then every western nation was potentially susceptible to something like Hitlerism, and the fact that the Germans succumbed should not really be held against them. The western attitude ought to have been, rather, an attitude of Christian humility: "there, but for the grace of God, go we."

One fact is clear beyond doubt: that few Germans were seriously tempted by the Nazi movement until the depression struck. In 1928, the party won only 12 seats in the Reichstag; by 1932, the figure had risen to 230. Still, other countries felt the depression's impact almost as severely, yet did not turn to the same desperate solution. Economic stress alone cannot explain Hitler's success; to the depression there must be added one or several other contributing factors. But which factors? On this point, opinions still differ; and they have tended to go through a series of changes since 1933.

In the early years after Hitler's accession, it was common to explain his rise as the product of a simple combination: the depression plus the treaty of Versailles. Both the German people and Hitler himself (so ran the argument) wanted nothing more than economic recovery and a slashing away of the bonds that had hamstrung Germany since the iniquitous peace settlement.

The Marxians, however, had a different answer from the outset; and as Hitlerism in practice revealed itself as something more than a device to secure economic recovery and international justice, the Marxian explanation began to win wider support. It viewed fascism as the natural and even inevitable last stage of capitalism, emerging in those countries where the capitalist class was most desperate. Such was the case in Germany, contended the Marxians; big business and its henchmen, threatened by collapse and hysterical at the rise of the Marxian left, chose to put Hitler into power as its tool. One Marxian sympathizer defined fascism as "capitalism with a gun in a hurry"; and some Marxians believed for a time that fascism might serve a useful purpose as "the ice-breaker for Communism."

This simple explanation of Nazism as a narrowly class-bound phenomenon gave way during and after the second world war to an equally simplified thesis that Hitlerism was only a new form of German viciousness, the product of the nation's paranoid tendencies. This paranoia in turn was traced to one or several factors in the German cultural heritage: the authoritarian family structure, or the corrupting doctrines of Luther, or deep immersion in romanticism.

More recently, the trend appears to have run back toward broader explanations of a psychological or sociological nature—explanations that see totalitarianism not as a peculiarly German phenomenon, but as a potential threat to any contemporary society. Sometimes the stress is on the nature and limitations of man—on his inability to bear the responsibilities of freedom and his urge to escape from that freedom. Sometimes the emphasis is on social tensions, on a new kind of class conflict—the revolt of the so-called Hitler-class, of the little man, caught between powerful organized capital and organized labor, seeking a mythology to restore his ego and prestige. Sometimes the explanation is sought in an alleged disintegration of the old class structure—in the emergence of uprooted elements, "marginal men," who have lost their stable position in society and who are desperate enough for any solution.

It is not easy to pick one's way through these tangled thickets, to select one simple explanation or to fuse together the relevant parts of several explanations to form a coherent and logical whole. To do so, the historian must rely even more than is usually the case on the insights provided to him by the psychologists and the sociologists; and he must, in addition, take a hard look at what is peculiarly German in modern Germany's cultural and political heritage. Finally, he must pay some special attention to the man who created and embodied Nazism: to the charismatic role of Adolf Hitler himself.

1.

Soon after the end of the second world war, UNESCO adopted a resolution calling for a thorough study, by an international team of scholars, of the underlying causes of Nazism and fascism. One of the purposes of this enterprise was ". . . to make possible the identification of similar movements in the future, from the first moment of their appearance." [1] But the massive book which emerged from the labors of this team, however valuable its individual contributions, hardly bore out the initial hope. For the twenty-seven authors varied widely in their conclusions, and covered almost the whole range of possible explanations. The selections by Vermeil and Ritter that follow will illustrate this heterogeneity.

Edmond Vermeil, professor of history at the Sorbonne, has devoted a lifetime to the study of modern German intellectual and cultural history. His introductory essay in the UNESCO volume, like his earlier works, argues that Nazism was deeply rooted in the German cultural tradition.

VERMEIL: The Origin, Nature and Development of German Nationalist Ideology *

At various periods of their history, and particularly in the nineteenth century, the Germans have believed with a desperate conviction, born either of their internal divisions and weaknesses or, on the contrary, of the idea of a sovereign and invincible power, that they have a divine mission, that Germany has been singled out by Providence. By virtue of a superior right and sustained by Prussian arms, the Germanic community, they have thought, must prevail over its neighbours as it prevails over its own members, over their many activities, and over the means by which its pre-eminence can be assured. . . .

This irrational and fervent faith is the outcome of a historical development which, throughout the centuries, gives the German imagination, with its combination of fanatical nationalism and preoccupation with internal cohesion, precedents which it can never forget and on which it builds up limitless aspirations.

Hence the constant references to the struggles between the Teutons and the Romans, to the legendary fame of Arminius, and above all to the migrations. The Germans dislike the word "barbarian" as applied to the great invasions. Herder launched a violent attack on Voltaire for describing the invaders as "savages." Long before the Romantics he saw in them the saviours of medieval Europe. It was Herder who evolved the thesis that the Teutons brought youth and virility to a declining and corrupt world. Herder believed that the Teutons

---

[1] From the introduction to *The Third Reich* (New York: Praeger, 1955), p. xiii.

* From Edmond Vermeil, "The Origin, Nature and Development of German Nationalist Ideology in the 19th and 20th Centuries," in *The Third Reich* (New York: Praeger, 1955), pp. 6, 110–11. Reprinted by permission of Frederick A. Praeger, Inc.

had a divine mission. He naturally linked up their emergence with that of Christianity. Klopstock, and later on the Romantics, confidently followed the same line of argument. One need only read Fichte or Fr. Schlegel to find confirmation of this. . . .

This tradition [of "elated nationalism" or pan-Germanism] seems to me to have arisen from four sources, from four basic components which, in the nineteenth and twentieth centuries, develop and expand, particularly under Wilhelm II, with growing clarity and force: (1) a philosophical and religious type of Pangermanism, which insists on Germany's predestination and divine mission; (2) a coherent series of pseudoscientific arguments culled from geography, history, biology, or anthropology, which attempt to define the so-called "living-space" that the Reich needs and the so-called "racial cohesion" that it must acquire; (3) a plan of continental conquest and expansion; (4) finally a so-called "world" political programme, the final aim of which is the creation of a colonial Empire that will supplement or replace colonial Empires already existing.

One may well wonder, of course, to what extent this vast symposium can be —or even must be—identified with the mentality of the German public throughout the two centuries in question. Ideas are born, more often than not, in the minds of individual thinkers. But, when they are stimulated by social upheavals, widespread collective crises, or sudden, far-reaching changes, they rapidly filter down to the masses. Even a historian of the eminence of Fr. Meinecke was not afraid to admit in his recent work *The German Catastrophe* (1946) that fanatical nationalism in the pre-1914 years wrought havoc in the ranks of the German *bourgeoisie,* an aggressive, ambitious nationalism that treated Socialism and the demands of the workers with scorn and gravitated more and more towards the "national revolution" I have tried to define. . . .

But one can, in all fairness, admit that up to 1914 the popular masses had not been entirely won over to Pangermanism, although its most natural and most effective breeding-grounds were the primary Confessional schools, the high schools, the universities, and, above all, the barracks. Pangermanism, as it developed under Wilhelm II from 1890 to 1914, became a mass-movement with Hitler in 1919 only when the single Party was first set up. The neo-nationalism of the intellectuals in the Weimar period had an importance all of its own.

But, from 1929 and the great social crisis onwards, the Nazi tidal wave carries everything before it. The Nazi doctrine, with the help of anti-Semitism, revives and popularises the current themes of the Pangermanic tradition. If it is guilty of any originality at all, it is in using anti-Semitism as a jumping-off ground for its attack on Western humanism and for its active policy in Germany, and also in giving the continental programme priority over the colonial programme.

Hitler could never have established the totalitarian dictatorship he did establish in January 1933 if his Party, so to speak under the mantle of the Weimar Republic, had not revived the essential themes of Pangermanic imperialism, reinforcing them with an extremely powerful propaganda machine, and if, on the other hand, the Schachts, von Seeckts, and Stresemanns had not reorganized industry and the banking system, the army and foreign policy. This dual effort is the really significant feature of the Weimar episode, and throws a revealing light not only on the past, but also on the future of the German Reich.

2.

In sharp rebuttal to Vermeil's theory, Gerhard Ritter contends that the historical origins of Hitlerism were to be found outside Germany, and that Nazi doctrines clashed sharply with the true German cultural tradition. Ritter, now retired as professor of modern history at the University of Freiburg, is one of the most distinguished and prolific of contemporary German historians.

RITTER: The Historical Foundations of the Rise of National Socialism *

It is a very great mistake to believe that the modern function of leader of the people is in any way the heritage and continuation of the old, monarchic power of the princes. Neither Frederick the Great, Bismarck, nor Wilhelm II were the historical precursors of Adolf Hitler. His precursors were the demagogues and Caesars of modern history, from Danton to Lenin and Mussolini. It is also erroneous to see in the fanatical enthusiasm which millions of men felt for Hitler between 1930–1933 a continuation of the traditional veneration of Germans for their ancient princely houses. . . .

Hitler's party was, on the contrary, composed of numerous uprooted individuals whose mentality was revolutionary, who all consciously desired a new order, and who were convinced that their *Führer* was superior to any earlier leader. The characteristic of the Hitlerian movement which most strongly attracted the masses was its modernity, the fact that it was contemporary (facts which were brought out by the very far-flung technical apparatus used to gain support for the Party). Hitler's obscure, popular origins added to this attraction, and seemed an assurance that he could have nothing in common with the hated right-wing reactionaries—the great Junker landowners, the officer class, and the great capitalists—even if he was sometimes obliged by force of circumstances to co-operate with people like Ludendorff and Hugenberg. Ludendorff himself declared himself opposed to Junker and capitalist prejudice, and a public-spirited friend of the people. Hitler and his supporters always contended that the electoral alliance established between the National-Socialists, the Stahlhelm group, and Hugenberg's party—the "Harzburg front" of 1931—was nothing more than a tactical agreement, for Hitler detested "all reaction." And when he opened negotiations with the big industrialists once more, being short of money and desirous of rapid success, Otto Strasser and the Schwarze Front, the most

---

* From Gerhard Ritter, "The Historical Foundations of the Rise of National-Socialism," in *The Third Reich* (New York: Praeger, 1955), pp. 399–400, 412–16. Reprinted by permission of Frederick A. Praeger, Inc.

convinced revolutionary elements in the Party, deserted the cause and started an open rebellion. Later he was to seize every opportunity of condemning the "selfishness" of the capitalist class and stating how much his policy favoured the workers.

In any case, he did not wish to be a conservative, either socially or politically; he wished to be a revolutionary. But what did this revolution imply? What was the difference between his dictatorship and that of other modern dictators? What was specifically German in it, what could be only explained by specifically German historical events?

If the situation is simplified somewhat, one can answer that *Volksführer* Hitler's mission in history was to accomplish that which the Emperor and his Government had been unable to accomplish in the First World War: to weld the nation into a closed, warlike community under the leadership of a really popular *Führer,* respected by all. . . .

Great care should be exercised in making use of literary evidence in order to show that the German mind had propensities which made it particularly accessible to *National-Socialist doctrines.*

These doctrines, tirelessly hawked round by Hitler, were based on the racial superiority of the German people, thanks to its Nordic-Germanic elements, over all non-Germanic peoples, and hence the German claim to dominate others. This doctrine of a "people of German lords," which was transformed into incredible methods of violence during the Second World War, made the National-Socialist regime (and also the name of Germany) detested by the whole world. It is thought to be Hitler's distinctive (and very evil) mark on the one-party state, as opposed to the one-party states of Italy and Russia.

Whence came this doctrine? Was it widespread in Germany before Hitler's day, or did he himself develop it? Up to the present time precise scientific research on Hitler's intellectual origins has scarcely begun. But it is clear that his theory of a "people of lords" is not based either on the general racial theories of biologists and ethnologists, or on that branch of the biological theory of races which is applied to history (Gobineau, Schemann, or Chamberlain), with, moreover, the unanimous contradiction of German historians. Similarly German and Austrian anti-Semitism, which changed its character in these two countries as in others from a purely denominational movement to a purely racial one, cannot be regarded as being the basis of the "people of lords" doctrine.

It is true that such theories were to be found in small, isolated groups of people, composed of fanatical germanophile racial theorists with occultist tendencies, whose writings were regarded in pre-1914 Germany as wildly eccentric, and that the young Hitler apparently studied them with enthusiasm. Apparently a group of his friends and future adherents belonged to a group of this kind in Munich after 1919 (among them Hess and Rosenberg)—the "Thule Society" (*Thule Gesellschaft*), which was connected with an older "Germanic order," violently anti-semite, founded in 1912. The obscure writings of this racialist society, which partly followed in the wake of the Pangerman movement, contained by 1914 numerous ideas which are similar to the later National-Socialist racial writings. Up to the present time the way in which these writings, anti-semite pamphlets and books of all kinds, Nietzsche's works and the cult of Wagner may have influenced Hitler's thought has not been sufficiently examined. He read a great deal, and had had no formal intellectual education. Innumerable combinations were therefore possible. The history of Hitler's intellectual background certainly bears little relation to the general intellectual history of Germany.

It is more related to the history of his own country, Austria. The domestic history of the Hapsburg state is surely one of the decisive factors, not of Hitler's rapid rise to power, but of his political theories. The unusual situation of the Danubian state, with its numerous peoples, made the national consciousness of the Germans there particularly excitable and assertive. For many centuries they had really been "a people of lords," and were now deposed by non-Germanic peoples. The nationalist struggle embraced all classes of people, including the working classes, so that a connection between nationalism and Socialism was possible in Austria, and National-Socialist parties sprang up well before Hitler's arrival. Here lay the roots not only of the partisan spirit of Hitlerian nationalism, but also of his racial pride as regards the Slavonic peoples—the unceasing and ever more acrid disputes between Austrian Germans and Czechs and Poles, the constant fear of Pan-Slavs and Russian imperialism. The "cultural superiority" of Germanism in the face of the Slavonic races was a battle-cry which was continually raised. There were, no doubt, similar conflicts in the German states which bordered on Poland; but a nationalist born in the Reich would never turn his energies to these, instead of to the traditional rivalry with the West, with the "hereditary enemy," France, nor dream of a great campaign against Russia in alliance with England, so that a large German colony might be established on Russian soil—a dream which Hitler tried desperately to make a reality in 1941–42.

In this respect, therefore, the historical origins of Hitlerism are to be found outside the Reich. It is impossible to state that there was in Germany a traditional hatred for the Slavs which was the basis of an anti-Russian policy. Only the Poles were hated, not the Russians, and that only after Germany's bitter post-war experiences.

Hitler's racial doctrines had much less scope in Germany than in Austria, as a result of natural and historical circumstances. The German people were, indeed, flattered to hear themselves continually declared a people of born lords, and that the Germanic-Nordic race was superior to all others. But when the causes of Hitler's great electoral successes are examined, his racial doctrines cannot be regarded as very important. In any case, the most profound secrets of this doctrine, as expounded by Rosenberg in the form of a muddled mystique, were incomprehensible to the masses. What was the race, and "racial patrimony?" Was it a physical or an intellectual phenomenon? What is the difference between race and nationality? Throughout the reign of National-Socialism most Germans never knew the answers to these questions. Mass sentiment saw no difference between the nationalists' praise of the German people and praise of the race of Germanic lords.

The appeal to instincts of hatred for the Jews had much more practical effect. These instincts were stronger in Germany than in Western European countries, but less strong than in the countries of Eastern Europe. These instincts had, by 1914, already been made use of in politics, but anti-semite groups had not been able to last for long. In the period after the war, hatred of the Jews had been aroused once again by numerous disagreeable incidents, principally the migration of Jews from the East—a circumstance which favoured National-Socialism. Most educated people continued to regard politically active anti-Semitism as a plebeian affair; but Hitler's anti-semite agitation at first had a powerful effect on the lower middle class. When, under the Third Reich, he passed from words to action on a huge scale, it is true to say that his popularity diminished rather than increased.

The most effective of all National-Socialist theories was undoubtedly the doctrine of the struggle for *Lebensraum,* of all creatures' eternal struggle for existence, and of the natural law of the strongest. This was not invented by Hitler, but came from Darwinian theories which had been influencing the political literature of Europe for many years, and which caused disturbing symptoms in the writings of other countries too.

Why did the theory of a people without room (*Volk ohne Raum*) have so great a success in Germany? There is no point in discussing this at length. The geographical situation, the natural vitality of the nation, and the strong pressure of an expanding population are sufficient to explain it. But it is certain that Hitler would never have dared make his warlike plans for conquest known to the public earlier than 1933, for fear of destroying all the electoral success of his party. A war of conquest was certainly not a slogan for elections.

All this raises serious doubts as to whether the National-Socialist racial doctrines, their *Weltanschauung,* won the masses over to Hitler's side. This conception of the world remained until the collapse of the Third Reich, an idea which was much talked of and little understood, which innumerable lessons were to instil into the German people, but which never became really popular (as the fate of most of the party's publications shows). The masses did not hail Hitler as the prophet of a new conception of the world, but as a man in whom they could put their trust, and they expected him to bring about a new unity within the nation through which deliverance from the internal and external troubles of the post-war period would be attained.

The most powerful element in his advent (which continued to act even during the Second World War) was his gift of radiating confidence in the future—an indomitable confidence in the principle "where there's a will there's a way." This confidence was due to his fanatical faith in himself and in his mission, a faith that doubts and self-criticism scarcely touched. This was what assured him political superiority over so many highly cultured politicians in the Weimar Republic, who were, however, tormented by doubts and problems. The sentimental feeling that the victory of this man would put an end to these gnawing problems and that speedy action would then begin certainly won him a great many supporters.

His indomitable confidence in himself was closely connected with his belief that he represented the true will of the people. Therein lay his strength, but also the danger which was to be fatal to him. Since his confidence in himself laid low all criticism, it became idolatry. If one rises up as a superman, one becomes inhuman. By challenging all the world to take up arms against him, he became the victim of his own inhumanity.

It may perhaps be legitimate to point out that the danger which became visible in Hitler did not end with his fall; not because his supporters have not entirely disappeared, and nationalists even less so; but mainly because it seems as if there is today a dangerous want of proportion between the indomitable self-confidence of the heads of totalitarian states whose instinct for power goes straight to the point, and the mentality of the free Western world, which is tormented by innumerable doubts and even by outbursts of nihilism.

3.

Professor Ritter suggests that the western world in our time is susceptible to "outbursts of nihilism." It is this theory of National Socialism as an essentially nihilistic movement that was forcefully advanced by Hermann Rauschning in the first of several books about Nazism published just before the outbreak of the second world war. Rauschning wrote from direct experience; an old-style conservative, he had joined the National Socialist party and had become an intimate of Hitler's. Two years after the Nazis took power, Rauschning went into disillusioned exile, settling eventually in the United States. The new Nazi elite, he insisted, believed in nothing save power and action, action for its own sake; its talent lay solely in the cynical manipulation of the masses.

RAUSCHNING: The Revolution of Nihilism *

Irreconcilable opposites were harnessed together in the German revolution of 1933, with the result not of mutual stimulation but of mutual paralysis. . . . The Conservative, national elements thought they had created a political machine; what they had really done was to deliver themselves up to a revolutionary power whose creed was action for action's sake and whose tactics were the destruction and undermining of all that is of value in the existing order. . . .

What matters politically to-day is not the rise of National Socialism as a philosophy. Its roots lie certainly in the racial ideas of the pan-Germans of Austria and Germany, in their rabid anti-Semitism, their hatred of the Habsburgs. . . . [But] the crucial fact is that the revolution has progressed far beyond its racialist origins and is now using this doctrinal armory of its youth, in

* From Hermann Rauschning, *The Revolution of Nihilism: Warning to the West* (New York: Alliance Book Corporation, 1939), pp. 12–13, 15–16, 18–19, 22–23. Reprinted by permission of Dr. Hermann Rauschning.

so far as it retains any of it, merely as a necessary element in propaganda. Racialism is its make-believe; the reality is the revolutionary extremism revealed not in its philosophy but in its tactics. . . . The movement attracted all those people who wanted a radical change in the existing conditions—the most primitive and the most obvious of revolutionary cravings. . . .

A sharp distinction must be drawn in National Socialism between this genuinely irrational revolutionary passion, affecting not only the mass of followers but the leaders themselves, and the very deliberate, utterly cold and calculating pursuit of power and dominance by the controlling group. We may generalize: The doctrine is meant for the masses. It is *not* a part of the real motive forces of the revolution. It is an instrument for the control of the masses. The elite, the leaders, stand above the doctrine. They make use of it in furtherance of their purposes. . . .

This irrational element in National Socialism is the actual source of its strength. It is the reliance on it that accounts for its "sleep-walker's immunity" in the face of one practical problem after another. It explains why it was possible for National Socialism to attain power almost without the slightest tangible idea of what it was going to do. . . . An open mind and no program at all— that is what enabled National Socialism to win through in its own way with its practical problems. Its strength lay in incessant activity and in embarking on anything so long as it kept things moving. . . .

If there is one thing that does not and cannot exist among the National Socialist elite, it is a genuine sense of social solidarity with the propertyless classes of the nation. One may count on finding just the opposite, and it is easily discernible in Hitler himself—an unconcealed contempt of the crowd, the common people, the mob: they are there not to be served but to be used.

National Socialism is action pure and simple, dynamics *in vacuo,* revolution at a variable tempo, ready to be changed at any moment. . . .

4.

Although Franz Neumann's *Behemoth* was written more than twenty years ago, it remains one of the most perceptive and provocative analyses of National Socialism as a sociopolitical system. In the early chapters, Neumann advanced a complex explanation of the factors that contributed to the rise of Nazism. Among the principal factors, in his judgment, were the shortsightedness of working-class leadership (the Socialist party and the trade unions) and the overwhelming power of German monopoly capital. Neumann's interpretation, which is essentially that of an economic determinist, reflects his Marxian (but noncommunist) outlook. During the seven years that preceded Hitler's accession to power, Neumann served as legal adviser to certain trade unions in Berlin, and lectured at the School for Politics there. He then emigrated to Great Britain, took advanced degrees at the University of London, and moved on to the United States in 1936. From 1947 until his death in 1954, he served as professor of government at Columbia University.

NEUMANN: Behemoth: The Structure and Practice of National Socialism *

The Social Democratic party and the trade unions . . . could have swung the great masses of the people over to democracy; not only the workers but also the middle classes, the section of the population that suffered most from the process of monopolization.

Other strata reacted to the complex post-war and post-revolution situation exactly as one would have expected. The big estate owners pursued a reactionary policy in every field. Monopolistic industry hated and fought the trade unions and the political system that gave the unions their status. The army used every available means to strengthen chauvinistic nationalism in order to restore itself to its former greatness. The judiciary invariably sided with the right and the civil services supported counter-revolutionary movements. Yet the Social Democracy was unable to organize either the whole of the working class or the middle classes. It lost sections of the former and never won a real foothold with the latter. The Social Democrats lacked a consistent theory, competent leadership, and freedom of action. Unwittingly, they strengthened the monopolistic trends in German industry, and, placing complete reliance on formalistic legality, they were unable to root out the reactionary elements in the judiciary and civil service or limit the army to its proper constitutional role.

The strong man of the Social Democratic party, Otto Braun, Prussian prime minister until 20 June 1932 when he was deposed by the Hindenburg-Papen *coup d'état,* attributes the failure of the party and Hitler's successful seizure of power to a combination of Versailles and Moscow. This defence is neither accurate nor particularly skilful. The Versailles Treaty naturally furnished excellent propaganda material against democracy in general and against the Social Democratic party in particular, and the Communist party unquestionably made inroads among Social Democrats. Neither was primarily responsible for the fall of the Republic, however. Besides, what if Versailles and Moscow had been the two major factors in the making of National Socialism? Would it not have been the task of a great democratic leadership to make the democracy work in spite of and against Moscow and Versailles? That the Social Democratic party failed remains the crucial fact, regardless of any official explanation. It failed because it did not see that the central problem was the imperialism of German monopoly capital, becoming ever more urgent with the continued growth of the process of monopolization. The more monopoly grew, the more incompatible it became with the political democracy.

One of Thorstein Veblen's many great contributions was to draw attention to those specific characteristics of German imperialism that arose from its position as a late-comer in the struggle for the world market.

* From Franz Neumann, *Behemoth: The Structure and Practice of National Socialism* (New York: Oxford University Press, 1942), pp. 13–15, 29–30, 33–34. Reprinted by permission of Mrs. Inge S. Marcuse.

The German captains of industry who came to take the discretional management in the new era were fortunate enough not to have matriculated from the training school of a county town based on a retail business in speculative real estate and political jobbery. . . . They came under the selective test for fitness in the aggressive conduct of industrial enterprise. . . . The country being at the same time in the main . . . not committed to antiquated sites and routes for its industrial plants, the men who exercised discretion were free to choose with an eye single to the mechanized expediency of locations. . . . Having no obsolescent equipment and no out of date trade connections to cloud the issue, they were also free to take over the processes at their best and highest efficiency.

The efficient and powerfully organized German system of our time was born under the stimulus of a series of factors brought into the forefront by the First World War. The inflation of the early '20s permitted unscrupulous entrepreneurs to build up giant economic empires at the expense of the middle and working classes. The prototype was the Stinnes empire and it is at least symbolic that Hugo Stinnes was the most inveterate enemy of democracy and of Rathenau's foreign policy. Foreign loans that flowed into Germany after 1924 gave German industry the liquid capital needed to rationalize and enlarge their plants. Even the huge social-welfare program promoted by the Social Democracy indirectly strengthened the centralization and concentration of industry, since big business could far more easily assume the burden than the small or middle entrepreneur. Trusts, combines, and cartels covered the whole economy with a network of authoritarian organizations. Employers' organizations controlled the labor market, and big business lobbies aimed at placing the legislative, administrative, and judicial machinery at the service of monopoly capital.

In Germany there was never anything like the popular anti-monopoly movement of the United States under Theodore Roosevelt and Woodrow Wilson. Industry and finance were of course firmly convinced that the cartel and trust represented the highest forms of economic organization. The independent middle class was not articulate in its opposition, except against department stores and chains. Though the middle class belonged to powerful pressure groups, like the Federal Union of German Industries, big business leaders were invariably their spokesmen.

Labor was not at all hostile to the process of trustification. The Communists regarded monopoly as an inevitable stage in the development of capitalism and hence considered it futile to fight capital concentration rather than the system itself. Ironically enough, the policy of the reformist wing of the labor movement was not significantly different in effect. The Social Democrats and the trade unions also regarded concentration as inevitable, and, they added, as a higher form of capitalist organization. . . .

The Social Democracy and the trade unions were completely helpless against the many-sided attacks on the Weimar democracy. . . . The Social Democratic party was trapped in contradictions. Though it still claimed to be a Marxian party, its policy had long been one of pure gradualism. It never mustered the courage to drop one or the other, traditional ideology or reformist policy. A radical break with tradition and the abandonment of Marxism would have de-livered thousands of adherents into the Communist camp. To have abandoned gradualism for a revolutionary policy, on the other hand, would have required cutting the many links binding the party to the existing state. The Socialists therefore retained this ambiguous position and they could not create a demo-cratic consciousness. The Weimar constitution, attacked on the right by Na-tionalists, National Socialists, and reactionary liberals, and on the left by the Communists, remained merely a transitory phenomenon for the Social Demo-crats, a first step to a greater and better future. And a transitory scheme cannot arouse much enthusiasm.

Even before the beginning of the great depression, therefore, the ideological, economic, social, and political systems were no longer functioning properly. Whatever appearance of successful operation they may have given was based primarily on toleration by the anti-democratic forces and on the fictitious pros-perity made possible by foreign loans. The depression uncovered and deepened the petrification of the traditional social and political structure. The social con-tracts on which that structure was founded broke down. The Democratic party disappeared; the Catholic Center shifted to the right; and the Social Democrats and Communists devoted far more energy to fighting each other than to the struggle against the growing threat of National Socialism. . . .

The National Socialist German Workers Party was without an ideology, com-posed of the most diverse social strata but never hesitating to take in the dregs of every section, supported by the army, the judiciary, and parts of the civil service, financed by industry, utilizing the anti-capitalist sentiments of the masses and yet careful never to estrange the influential moneyed groups. Terror and propaganda seized upon the weak spots in the Weimar democracy; and from 1930 to 1933 Weimar was merely one large weak spot. . . .

The Weimar democracy . . . had to rebuild an impoverished and exhausted country in which class antagonisms had become polarized. It attempted to merge three elements: the heritage of the past (especially the civil service), parliamentary democracy modeled after Western European and American pat-terns, and a pluralistic collectivism, the incorporation of the powerful social and economic organizations directly into the political system. What it actually pro-duced, however, were sharpened social antagonisms, the breakdown of volun-tary collaboration, the destruction of parliamentary institutions, the suspension of political liberties, the growth of a ruling bureaucracy, and the renaissance of the army as a decisive political factor.

Why?

In an impoverished, yet highly industrialized, country, pluralism could work only under the following different conditions. In the first place, it could rebuild Germany with foreign assistance, expanding its markets by peaceful means to the level of its high industrial capacity. The Weimar Republic's foreign policy tended in this direction. By joining the concert of the Western European powers the Weimar government hoped to obtain concessions. The attempt failed. It was supported neither by German industry and large landowners nor by the

Western powers. The year 1932 found Germany in a catastrophic political, economic, and social crisis.

The system could also operate if the ruling groups made concessions voluntarily or under compulsion by the state. That would have led to a better life for the mass of the German workers and security for the middle classses at the expense of the profits and power of big business. German industry was decidedly not amenable, however, and the state sided with it more and more.

The third possibility was the transformation into a socialist state, and that had become completely unrealistic in 1932 since the Social Democratic party was socialist only in name.

The crisis of 1932 demonstrated that political democracy alone without a fuller utilization of the potentialities inherent in Germany's industrial system, that is, without the abolition of unemployment and an improvement in living standards, remained a hollow shell.

The fourth choice was the return to imperialist expansion. Imperialist ventures could not be organized within the traditional democratic form, however, for there would have been too serious an opposition. Nor could it take the form of restoration of the monarchy. An industrial society that has passed through a democratic phase cannot exclude the masses from consideration. Expansionism therefore took the form of National Socialism, a totalitarian dictatorship that has been able to transform some of its victims into supporters and to organize the entire country into an armed camp under iron discipline.

5.

According to the noted Oxford historian A. J. P. Taylor, National Socialism had its nihilistic, "gangster" side; but by a curious paradox, it was only half-nihilistic. It represented also, according to Mr. Taylor, the natural culmination of modern German history; it embodied, in certain ways, just what every class of Germans really wanted. The book from which the following selection was taken was written shortly after the end of the second world war—a fact that may bear some relationship to the severity of its judgments.

TAYLOR: The Course of German History *

There was nothing mysterious in Hitler's victory; the mystery is rather that it had been so long delayed. The delay was caused by the tragic incompatibility of German wishes. The rootless and irresponsible, the young and the violent embraced the opportunity of licensed gangsterdom on a heroic scale; but most Germans wanted the recovery of German power, yet disliked the brutality and lawlessness of the National Socialists, by which alone they could attain their wish. Thus Brüning was the nominee of the Reichswehr and the enemy of the republic, the harbinger both of dictatorship and of German rearmament. Yet he hated the paganism and barbarity of the National Socialists and would have

* From A. J. P. Taylor, *The Course of German History* (New York: Coward-McCann, 1946), pp. 211–14. Copyright 1946 by A. J. P. Taylor. Reprinted by permission of Coward-McCann, Inc.

done anything against them—except breaking with the generals. Schleicher, in
control of the Reichswehr, was obsessed with German military recovery; yet he
contemplated an alliance with the trade unions against the National Socialists
and, subsequently, paid for his opposition with his life. The generals, the judges,
the civil servants, the professional classes, wanted what only Hitler could offer
—German mastery of Europe. But they did not want to pay the price. Hence
the delay in the National Socialist rise to power; hence their failure to win a
clear majority of votes even at the general election in March 1933. The great
majority of German people wanted German domination abroad and the rule of
law at home, irreconcilables which they had sought to reconcile ever since 1871,
or rather ever since the struggles against Poles, Czechs, and Danes in 1848.

In January 1933 the German upper classes imagined that they had taken
Hitler prisoner. They were mistaken. They soon found that they were in the
position of a factory owner who employs a gang of roughs to break up a strike:
he deplores the violence, is sorry for his workpeople who are being beaten up,
and intensely dislikes the bad manners of the gangster leader whom he has
called in. All the same, he pays the price and discovers, soon enough, that if he
does not pay the price (later, even if he does) he will be shot in the back. The
gangster chief sits in the managing director's office, smokes his cigars, finally
takes over the concern himself. Such was the experience of the owning classes
in Germany after 1933. The first act of the new dictators won the game. When
the terror of their private armies looked like failing, the National Socialists set
fire to the Reichstag, proclaimed the discovery of a Communist plot, and so
suspended the rule of law in Germany. The Reichstag fire, burning away the
pretentious home of German sham-constitutionalism, was the unexpected push
by which the old order in Germany, hesitating on the brink, was induced to
take the plunge into gangster rule. The new Reichstag, still, despite the outlaw-
ing of the Communists, with no clear National Socialist majority, met under
open terror. Hitler asked for an Enabling Bill, to make him legal dictator. He
was supported by the "national" parties, and the Centre, faithful to its lack of
principles to the last, also voted for Hitler's dictatorship, in the hope of protecting the position of the Roman Catholic Church; impotent to oppose, they
deceived themselves with the prospect of a promise from Hitler, which was in
fact never given. Only the Social Democrats were loyal to the republic which
they had failed to defend and by a final gesture, impotent but noble, voted
unitedly against the bill. But even the Social Democrats went on to show the
fatal weakness which had destroyed German liberties. When in May 1933 the
Reichstag was recalled to approve Hitler's foreign policy, the Social Democrats
did not repeat their brave act: some abstained, most voted with the National
Socialists. This was an absurdity. If Germany intended to undo the system of
Versailles, she must organize for war, and she could organize for war only on
a totalitarian basis. Only by renouncing foreign ambitions could Germany become a democracy; and as even the Social Democrats refused to make this
renunciation the victory of the National Socialists was inevitable.

This is the explanation of the paradox of the "Third Reich." It was a system founded on terror, unworkable without the secret police and the concentration camp; but it was also a system which represented the deepest wishes of the German people. In fact it was the only system of German government ever created by German initiative. The old empire had been imposed by the arms of Austria and France; the German Confederation by the armies of Austria and Prussia. The Hohenzollern empire was made by the victories of Prussia, the Weimar republic by the victories of the Allies. But the "Third Reich" rested solely on German force and German impulse; it owed nothing to alien forces. It was a tyranny imposed upon the German people by themselves. Every class disliked the barbarism or the tension of National Socialism; yet it was essential to the attainment of their ends. This is most obvious in the case of the old "governing classes." The Junker landowners wished to prevent the expropriation of the great estates and the exposure of the scandals of the *Osthilfe;*[1] the army officers wanted a mass army, heavily equipped; the industrialists needed an economic monopoly of all Europe if their great concerns were to survive. Yet many Junkers had an old fashioned Lutheran respectability; many army officers knew that world conquest was beyond Germany's strength; many industrialists, such as Thyssen, who had financed the National Socialists, were pious and simple in their private lives. But all were prisoners of the inescapable fact that if the expansion of German power were for a moment arrested, their position would be destroyed.

But the National Socialist dictatorship had a deeper foundation. Many, perhaps most, Germans were reluctant to make the sacrifices demanded by rearmament and total war; but they desired the prize which only total war would give. They desired to undo the verdict of 1918; not merely to end reparations or to cancel the "war guilt" clause, but to repudiate the equality with the peoples of eastern Europe which had then been forced upon them. During the preceding eighty years the Germans had sacrificed to the Reich all their liberties; they demanded as reward the enslavement of others. No German recognized the Czechs or Poles as equals. Therefore every German desired the achievement which only total war could give. By no other means could the Reich be held together. It had been made by conquest and for conquest; if it ever gave up its career of conquest, it would dissolve. Patriotic duty compelled even the best of Germans to support a policy which was leading Germany to disaster.

This implacable logic of circumstance doomed to failure every attempt to arrest the advance of National Socialist "totalitarianism." The institutions which had been too much for Bismarck, the conflicting political forces which had for so long pulled Germany this way and that, were all overborne. The political parties were abolished in the summer of 1933; the trade unions were taken over without the semblance of a struggle; the states, last relics of particularism, were wiped out of existence. Nuremberg, proudest of Free Cities, became the meeting place of the annual National Socialist demonstration; and Bavaria, most separatist of states, the very heart of the National Socialist movement. Only the

[1] The *Osthilfe* scandals involved the alleged misuse of government funds granted to the large east German landowners during the Weimar period.

Roman Catholic Church attempted to resist; and, though it was defeated, yet its defeat was perhaps a little less thorough than that of every other organization in Germany. Roman Catholics accepted Hitler's course of policy, and none ever protested against any of the barbarities of German conquest; but they were allowed to remain Roman Catholics. In this record of subjection, the National Socialist programme was no exception. Where it clashed with the claims of total war, it too was disregarded. The destruction of "interest slavery," liberation from "monopoly capitalism," a new social order, these turned out to mean nothing at all; and even when war raged, the profits of the German capitalists were less controlled than in any other belligerent country. Still a Socialist element, in the German sense, remained. What German Socialists and German workers had objected to in capitalism was not so much inequality of incomes, as freedom of enterprise and the freedom of action which comes with the secure ownership of property. This freedom the German capitalists lost as completely as if they had been expropriated: they could not conduct their undertakings ("enterprises" no longer) according to their own wishes and were no more free to choose their course than the most degraded worker driven into the factory by hunger. Capitalism had deprived the industrial workers of their freedom, or so they thought. National Socialism was their revenge; it deprived the capitalists of freedom also.

6.

One of the most powerful institutions in pre-Nazi Germany was the professional army. Although it was cut back sharply in size after 1919, and was apparently subjected to civilian control, it retained much of its traditional prestige and functioned as a kind of autonomous force within the Weimar Republic. One of the most remarkable studies of the political role of the German army in modern times is Gordon A. Craig's *Politics of the Prussian Army*. Professor Craig, who was educated at Princeton and Oxford, teaches modern history at Stanford University. In the brief selection that follows, he argues succinctly that the military establishment played a significant role in Hitler's accession to power.

CRAIG: The Politics of the Prussian Army *

The five years that followed the introduction of the Dawes Plan in 1924 were good years for Germany and were marked by economic prosperity and growing political stability. Hopes that the gains of this brief period might lead to the consolidation of the Weimar Republic were dispelled, however, by the repercussions of the stock market crash in the United States at the end of 1929. In the months that followed that event, all of the ills that had plagued Germany in 1923 were revived, and in more virulent forms. Political extremism grew in direct proportion to economic misery, and the republic was menaced now by a

* From Gordon A. Craig, *The Politics of the Prussian Army 1640–1945* (New York: Oxford University Press, 1955), pp. 427–28, xviii–xix. Copyright 1955 by Gordon A. Craig and reprinted by permission of the publishers.

reinvigorated Communist party on the one hand and, on the other, by a National Socialist movement which commanded mass support on a national scale. In the face of this threat from left and right, the moderate parties showed no ability to co-operate. The so-called Great Coalition of 1928 was in full disintegration by the end of 1929; and the subsequent period was marked by a deplorable spectacle of intramural feuding and parliamentary bankruptcy. Under the double stress of its economic and its political troubles, the Reich in the early 1930's seemed to be on the point of disintegration or total collapse.

To this danger the German army could not be expected to remain indifferent in view of the fact that its leaders had grown accustomed to regarding themselves as the protectors of the Reich and the best-qualified interpreters of its essential interests. In the long series of crises which filled the years 1930-32, the military establishment, therefore, played an important role. Indeed, there is no period in German history in which representatives of the army intervened more frequently and more directly in the internal politics of the country: but, it must be added, there is no period in which the results of this intervention were more unfortunate. In their desire to end a political situation which threatened to degenerate into complete anarchy, the military chiefs rashly took upon themselves tasks of political negotiation and party manipulation for which they were not qualified. At the start they justified this activity by claiming that it was necessary to prevent the victory of the extremist parties; but, when their experiments proved unsuccessful, they looked with increasing approval to one of those parties and, in the end, concurred in its accession to power. There were doubtless many reasons for Adolf Hitler's elevation to the chancellorship in January 1933; but, in the last analysis, that event proved the validity of the maxim *exercitus facit imperatorem* [the army makes the emperor]. . . .

The most dangerous enemies of the republic realized that they could not hope to overthrow it unless they secured at least the sympathetic neutrality of the army; and Hitler for one was guided by that knowledge in all phases of his policy before 1933. Hitler set out deliberately to play upon the dissatisfaction which existed within the army, and while his promises of a restored and expanded military establishment gradually enticed the bulk of the junior officers to his support, his charges that the republican regime lacked national spirit and failed adequately to defend the interests of the state found a sympathetic response in the hearts of the officer corps in general. Thus the fateful political change of 30 January 1933 was supported, at least tacitly, by the army; and within eighteen months the best-known military journal in Germany was writing: "In the new state of Adolf Hitler, the *Wehrmacht* is no foreign body as it was after the November revolt of 1918. Today it is a part of the organic community and shares in the common distribution of the nation's work; and it follows Adolf Hitler as the Fuehrer of the people with full confidence and with devotion to its great national task."

In the light of what followed the "revolution" of 1933, these words have a somewhat ironical ring. For the professional officer corps the Hitler period was marked by a long series of humiliations, beginning with the murder of Generals von Schleicher and von Bredow in 1934, made evident to the whole world in the disgraceful dismissal of General von Fritsch in 1938, and ending with the cavalier treatment accorded to professional officers during the campaigns of the Second World War. For more than a century the army had successfully defended its autonomous position in the state, beating off all attempts to impose constitutional restraints upon it and, by these very tactics, frustrating Germany's progress toward democracy. Yet in 1933, when it assented to Hitler's seizure of power, it encompassed its own, as well as Germany's, ruin. Within five years Hitler had accomplished what the liberals of 1848 and 1862 and the republicans and socialists of 1918 had sought to accomplish in vain: he had completely subordinated the army to his own control. And within the space of another two years he had driven it into a war which all responsible German soldiers dreaded —as events were to show, with reason.

7.

A professional army cannot play a significant political role in an advanced society unless that society is broadly sympathetic to the army's aims. Professor J. J. Schokking of the University of Cologne argues, in the following selection, that a militaristic outlook continued to pervade much of German society after the Weimar Republic was established. The Nazis, he suggests, took advantage of this heritage, and set out to make themselves "the nucleus of the militarized people."

SCHOKKING: Nazism's Way to Success *

With the fall of the army in 1918, the whole structure of Wilhelmian Germany broke asunder. There was no alternative to replace it—at least not immediately. The mere act of founding the Republic—a rather external, a purely constitutional change—was not enough. In order to establish a stable democracy Germany would have had to be reorganized from top to bottom. It required a new social integration, on the basis of democratic principles and usages. The remnants of the Prussian tradition, as well as the effects of the queer, ambivalent propaganda for popular militarism, which had supplemented this tradition in the preceding decades, had to be wiped out. Intentions to do so were not absent, nor was there a lack of men who had the will and the capacity to reframe Germany along democratic lines. In order to succeed, however, they needed freedom from foreign pressures, the immediate prospect of economic recovery and of increasing prosperity, and, most of all, they needed time. None of these conditions was granted to them.

One of the most pernicious effects of the sudden collapse of Germany was that all groups and individuals for whom militarism had become the guiding ideology and the only possible way of life, felt themselves deprived of their

* From J. J. Schokking, "Nazism's Way to Success," in *The Third Reich* (New York: Praeger, 1955), pp. 485–87. Reprinted by permission of Frederick A. Praeger, Inc.

beliefs, their community, their nation. They rejected the Republic, not so much because they were against the replacement of monarchical institutions by republican ones, as because it represented in their eyes a society which was strange to them and in which they could have no share—a victory of forces which had thrown them back on their own mental and material resources, to manage as best as they could as scattered and isolated individuals. In the great majority of cases those resources were very small or did not exist at all.

Now that the social fabric which had satisfied their wants of sociability had fallen to pieces, many ex-officers and soldiers, hoping to escape the loneliness they were unable to face and somehow to gain a substitute for the lost footholds in life, and also thereby to find an occupation and material support, sought refuge in the several Free Corps, which at the end of the war and in the first post-war years were formed all over Germany. These were fighting units, operating haphazardly under self-appointed leaders. Marching against the Reds in Germany and on Germany's eastern border, resisting the Poles, stimulating local revolts in the Ruhr and elsewhere, they were inspired by the social and political aspirations of the past that had disappeared, and were ever animated by an outright hostility towards the Republic. Otherwise they followed the precepts of their militarist training, which somehow forbade soldiers to intervene constructively in politics or to pursue a positive policy of their own. The inner contradiction of this mental situation was a cause of utter frustration. Despite their tenacity, audacity, and ruthlessness, the Free Corps came to nothing.

National-Socialism was a different movement from the outset. Though born of the same deceptions and urges which led to the creation of the Free Corps, National-Socialism chose another approach.

It did not confine its appeal to demobilised officers and soldiers, but extended it to all militaristically-minded Germans, whatever they were or had been. In the course of time, after the Free Corps had disbanded, many of their former members were to become Nazism's fiercest enemies, while others took the opposite course and found a lasting home under the Nazi roof. In any case among the high echelons of the Nazi hierarchy the proportion of Free Corps veterans was gradually to become very numerous. From their side, however, the Nazis undertook nothing to continue the Free Corps tradition of segregation, but consistently tried to penetrate into all sections of German society.

Moreover, Nazism understood that under the changed conditions a revival of militarism could not be brought about by copying the Wilhelmian methods. It sensed that the spell of the Prussian tradition had to be broken and that a new, more radical, and more exclusively popular orientation was wanted. Nazism realised that the militarism prevalent before World War I had been closely connected with the social and political texture of Imperial Germany. Being aware of the fact that this had been destroyed beyond repair, Nazism foresaw the possibilities of socialising militarism and of creating a powerful nation-in-arms, an armed society, a people living by war and for war. As slogans these notions had already been used by militarist propaganda under the Kaiser, but the will to accept the full consequences of them was absent then. Such a will implied the necessity of throwing overboard all technical inhibitions, all endeavors to direct the socio-political institutions in consonance with the dictates of justice and rationality, and indeed all other doctrines and theories. Instead, the demands of expediency, resulting from total mobilisation for total war, had alone to prevail.

To National-Socialism politics meant the struggle for "naked power" by all means promising rapid success.

The Nazis viewed themselves as the nucleus of the militarised people in the process of becoming, as the military "counter-society" that had one day to take the place of the Weimar Republic and of all other states in which Germans lived. They thought that they had only to increase their numbers and strength in order to reach their political aims. The movement was instrumental to the new German militarism and its quest for power. That in this development the Weimar Republic had to disappear was taken for granted. To reach their ends, however, it was not necessary, in the first instance, to fight it with physical means. For the Nazis a private army had its advantages; it was in a way indispensable, but it could be really effective only if the movement gave priority to the political aim and in pursuit of that knew how to profit from the opportunities which were offered by the Weimar democracy. In contradistinction to the Free Corps, the Nazis discovered that democracy could be wrecked by constant abuse of its liberties. By instinct, rather than by calculation, they knew that once militarist tendencies were developed to the utmost in German society their movement would automatically sweep away the Weimar Republic, and eventually the other European States within whose frontiers Germans were living.

8.

The aberrant behavior of many Nazi leaders, and of certain broader segments of the German population during the Nazi era, has led a number of psychologists to apply their specialized knowledge to an examination of this segment of contemporary history. Some of these scholars have claimed to find a special paranoiac streak in modern German society; others have concluded that the Germans share their aberrant tendencies with most other western societies. One of the most remarkable treatises of this sort is that of Zevedei Barbu, a Rumanian-born scholar who teaches social psychology at the University of Glasgow. Barbu contrasts the "cardinal socio-psychological concepts" of democracy with those of Nazism and communism, and contends that adherents to both of the latter systems reveal strongly pathological tendencies of related but not identical kinds. In seeking to isolate the factors that contributed to the rise of Nazism in Germany, Barbu stresses the importance of widespread frustration and insecurity, and the role of a *"déclassé"* (unclassed) social group whose personalities have become "sociopathic." As he makes his case, Barbu briefly sketches the related theses of several other scholars: e.g., Dr. R. M. Bricker, Erich Fromm, and G. M. Gilbert (who served as prison psychologist during the Nuremberg Trials).

BARBU: Democracy and Dictatorship *

During the period of the rise of Nazism the German nation lived in unique conditions of stress and insecurity. The defeat of 1918 is usually mentioned as the starting point in the development of this situation. Quick structural changes such as the downfall of the monarchy, the collapse of the army, the appearance of new political parties are also important contributing factors. A series of inner contradictions and tensions within German society in the post-war period are in our opinion more important than the defeat itself, or the downfall of the Empire, for the understanding of this specific condition of stress and insecurity. Many demobilized soldiers and dismissed officers refused to go home and integrate themselves with the new conditions of life. They formed special military organizations, *Freikorps,* offering their protection to peasants threatened by raids of starving townsfolk, and to landlords from the eastern territories. And though the early Weimar regime used them in its struggle against the Communists, they became a menace to authority and security in the state by their independence and mercenary spirit. But, apart from the activities of the *Freikorps,* there were many other sources of instability and insecurity in the Weimar Republic. The Social Democrats were confused. Their manoeuvres between a strong Communist movement, deeply rooted in the German working classes, and the anti-Communist feelings of other classes and of the army in particular, resulted in a complete lack of orientation and of a programme. In this way, an inefficient government increased even more the frustration of the population. To this should be added a series of revolutionary attempts and Communist uprisings. Thus, the whole social atmosphere was loaded with tension, anxiety, and a spirit of brutality. The political parties took on a military character, each of them possessing fighting organizations.

The frustrating effects of economic crises, of unemployment, and particularly of the inflations of 1924 and 1929 are so well known that there is no need to enter into details. A word should be said about the contribution of the international scene to the situation of stress of the German group. Loss of colonies and national territories, military occupation of the Ruhr district all intensified the insecurity. To all of this should be added the tensions caused in Bavaria— the birthplace of Nazism—by a series of separatist movements.

What are the most important psychological effects of this exceptional situation of stress? Perhaps the loss of the frame of reference for the behaviour of both groups and individual is the most comprehensive symptom of this. The collapse of old institutions followed by a relatively long period of instability weakened and destroyed in many individuals the sense of discrimination and orientation in social life in particular. Since nothing remained unshaken, and certainly nothing unshakable, people swung from a state of naivety to one of

* From Zevedei Barbu, *Democracy and Dictatorship, Their Psychology and Patterns of Life* (New York: Grove Press, 1956), pp. 124-34, 144-45, 156-59, 169-70. Copyright 1956 by Grove Press. Reprinted by permission of the publishers.

desperate incredulity. All opinions were equally good, or all equally meaningless. They lived in a *Meinungschaos* [chaos of opinions] which produced in them apathy and complete detachment, and at the same time anxiety and readiness to do something, to do anything.

This state of mind affected, consciously or unconsciously, most individual members of German society. But the main problem for the social psychologist as well as for the political scientist is not the extension of this state of mind, but rather why a movement of the right, Hitler's movement, presented itself as the best answer to it. Why could not Socialism or Communism play this role, for both exploited the feelings of frustration and insecurity in the masses, and both promised a stable social order? The answer to these questions is, in essence, simple. The Nazis offered to the people the quickest and the most radical way of relief from a situation of stress and insecurity. While the Socialists kept on talking vaguely in the name of peace and democracy, while the Communists promised a narrow class policy, the Nazis attacked the Versailles Treaty, promised economic autarky and employment. While the Socialists tied up the destiny of Germany with that of European democracy, and the Communists with that of Soviet Russia, the Nazis stirred up the feeling of pride of a heroic nation which is not only the master of its own destiny, but is called upon to master the world.

In principle there could be no competition with this kind of language addressed to a group in a condition of stress. It gave immediate outlets for the feeling of guilt and for the need of aggression, and provided a solution to the need for security in the near future. The Socialists and Communists were doomed to failure since the Nazis provided for the deeper and more immediate needs of the masses. They spoke about dignity to the humiliated, about power to the defeated, about the organic stability of human society to people who were experiencing the ruin and disintegration of age-old institutions. The society they spoke of was not an idea, and not of the future, as was that propounded by the Communists, but of the past, of the glorious German past.

There are two main means by which the Nazi leaders assured their success. The first consists of a specific mental quality found in most of these leaders which can be called compulsive determination. As will be shown later, Hitler and other Nazi leaders belong to a specific mental type with strong tendencies towards over-simplification. Their rare ability to find solutions to any kind of problem, the radical and solemn tone in which they announced their decisions, even the most absurd and banal ones, constituted a particular attraction for people living in a chaotic world. The second means is of a more complex nature than the first; it even contradicts it. The Nazis displayed also a remarkable lack of a fixed programme of government, a certain disengagement with regard to any precise policy. To know the state of mind of the masses and to satisfy it by hazy and fantastic prospects was their first tactical principle. Thus they can be described as masters of subjective methods in politics. This resulted, on the political plane, in demagoguery, and on the economic plane, in a fluid and compromising scheme usually known as the two-front economic policy. Since the former characteristic is well known we reserve a few words for the latter.

Precarious though it was, the Nazi economic order rested mainly on Hitler's ability to play on the contradiction between two groups of interests, the industrialists and Junkers on the one hand, and the workers on the other. From the very beginning Hitler spoke with two voices. With one he addressed the economically upper classes, emphasizing the Nazi repudiation of any class programme in the economic field. In the language of these classes this meant that no revolutionary methods were to be used against them. . . . With the other voice he addressed the working classes, preaching a new type of socialism. . . .

The socialistic flavour of the Nazi economic order was ostentatiously advertised by a certain check put on free enterprise by the system of compulsory cartels and by other forms of State control. But at the same time the spirit of private initiative and profits was generally encouraged. The State itself created by its aggressive policy large scope for the expansion of big monopolies. The alliance between the State and big monopolies was an obvious fact, although its terms were never explicit, for the State showed great concern for the well-being of the masses and found devices—temporary of course—to reduce unemployment, to raise wages, etc.

One of the sources of Hitler's success in this difficult enterprise consisted in the simple fact that he never regarded the industrialists or the industrial workers as belonging to two constitutive interest groups, but rather as members of the German nation undergoing conditions of stress. He looked at their frustrations and insecurity rather than at their group or class interest. The common factor in all classes was insecurity. To the industrialists he showed the danger of Communism and of international competition. These dangers were real enough to make the capitalists prefer the Nazi order in which they were simply transformed into managers of their own enterprises. With the workers Hitler exploited their fears of exploitation and unemployment, and above all their equalitarian aspirations, by denouncing material equality as "extrinsic and mechanical" and by wilfully diverting "the gaze of the masses" from material to spiritual things.

There was a bit of everything in the Nazi economic order. With the middle classes and peasantry the Nazis entertained their prejudices against Communism and their respect for private ownership. From this point of view one can say that the Nazis tried to please everybody. That is why it is hard to maintain that the movement had a class character. Though our reasons are different we nevertheless agree with [the economist Ludwig] von Mises when he writes: "The German entrepreneurs and businessmen contributed their share to the triumph of Nazism, but so did all other strata of the nation." In the following section we shall see who were the first and most reliable people to form the movement. . . .

It would be true to say that, sociologically, Nazism, as a political and spiritual movement, represents a cross-section of the German nation during the inter-war period. It answered a state of frustration and insecurity widespread in all strata of the population during this period. It would also be right to infer from this that the cadres, and particularly the leadership of the party, were made up of individuals and groups who suffered more than others from frustration and insecurity.

The core of the party was formed by socially nondescript people, frustrated in their efforts to achieve a certain status in their society, the prototype of whom is Hitler. The demobilized soldiers and officers, former members of the *Freikorps,* formed an important Nazi group. Goering and Röhm are typical. Unemployed youngsters, émigrés, and students also found a point of attraction in the movement. To this is added a number of intellectuals frustrated in their aspirations, as Goebbels was, or incapable of adjusting themselves to the cultural climate of their time and consequently escaping into the mythical world of the past, like those belonging to the Thule Society of Munich. From the historically constituted classes Nazism attracted in the first place the peripheral elements. From the working class it attracted "the flotsam, the strugglers living on the fringe of their own class, the workers of odd jobs, and the unemployed." In the upper classes the party appealed in particular to aristocrats who identified themselves with a highly inadequate concept of their own class; they joined the party in order to remake the position once held by the Junkers in Imperial Germany. Peasants who were by their aspirations above their group, or by their poverty below it, were also attracted to the movement.

All the individuals and groups mentioned above have one trait in common: they all can be called déclassés, that is, people who failed completely or partly to integrate themselves with one of the institutionalized forms of their society. They also suffer from lack of social attachment. In this way the déclassés can, by analogy with psychopathic personality, be described as sociopathic personalities. As the psychopathics are liable to all forms of delinquency, so are the sociopathics liable to political delinquency in particular, that is, they are breakers of the political order of their own society. More will be said later about the connexion between psychopathic and sociopathic personality. For the moment we consider the sociopathic personality in itself. It should be mentioned in the first place that industrial society has a great capacity for creating sociopathic groups. Its fluid character and its rapid growth are among the main causes of this phenomenon. The impersonal character of this society and the mechanical type of integration required by it have also contributed to this. The situation of post-war Germany is characteristic from this point of view. The instability of that period forms an additional factor contributing to the creation of non-integrated individuals and groups.

The Nazi movement can be considered as the meeting point of all individuals and groups with an unstable social status; it evolved as a result of the disrupting processes taking place in the post-war period. It is, therefore, the classless element, rather than a particular social class, that should first be considered in order to understand Nazism. As opposed to any socialist party—obviously a class party—and to any democratic party normally based on a particular social group, Nazism represents in its structure the entire nation on a reduced scale. This is one of the first factors determining its totalitarian character. . . .

Few psychologists interested in the origins of Nazism could escape the temptation of using the concept of national character. Most of them deal at large with the "famous" and "perennial" Germanic aggression, with the Germanic mysticism, ethnocentrism, authoritarian family, etc. Though far from expressing a definite opinion on this point, we feel that the concept of the national character is too much of a theoretical construct. Examples of aggression, collective or individual, can easily be found in every nation. Consequently, we started to trace the origins of Nazism in a collective state of mind historically limited to the inter-war period. This is the state of mind created in a group of individuals and groups belonging to the German nation as they are expressed at mystical inclinations, group-centrism and aggression are normally involved in the behaviour of a group living under such conditions. To us the problem of the German national character is secondary as a determining factor in the rise of Nazism. Thus one can speak about various mental features of various individuals and groups belonging to the German nation as they are expressed at the cultural level. Here are included the family system, old customs and traditions, philosophies supporting aggression—Nietzsche for instance—totalitarian views (Hegel), mysticism (Schelling), etc. All these were skilfully used by Nazi leaders as cultural symbols to express a state of mind existing in themselves and in the masses. (But so also were used a series of other ideologies—racial and socialistic—which are not entirely German products.) In this way the Nazi way of life became articulated at the cultural level. The next chapter will deal with this aspect of Nazism. . . .

The *Weltanschauung* of Nazism rests on the assumption of the irrationality of human nature. Human action, and human will in general, is guided by instincts, intuition and feelings. Will has its end in itself, and it reaches its purposes more adequately if not embarrassed by reasoning. Though doubting the ability and power of reason, Nazis are neither sceptics nor nihilists. According to their convictions, will and feeling provide human knowledge and action with a greater degree of certainty than reason. Human action, though basically irrational, leads by itself to order, to a new type of order. For, while the fundamental category of rational order is that of equality, and agreement between equals, the order springing from the irrational factors of the human mind rests on the feeling of "distance" (Nietzsche); it expresses itself as power hierarchy. Man's most important virtue consists in the fact that he can impose his will by force, and fears force at the same time. This human quality becomes the main feature of the Nazi way of life. Man's wisdom is shown in his ability to discover the leader and to let himself be ruled by him. Needless to say, this wisdom is by no means the work of reason. For will and affection guide the people towards the choice of their leader, rather than reason. The leader himself would very seldom, if at all, use reason to get the consent of the people. His strongest weapons consist in his power and its capacity to fascinate and to dominate.

As to the nature of society, Nazism is radically opposed to the rationalist conception of the Enlightenment. Social organization, whatever its size and ends, cannot be subject to debate and "contract." One of the great faults of the nineteenth century was to create and foster the belief that society could be organized rationally by discussions and programmes. As a result society has gradually become the prey of the corrupting reason of the politicians. The truth is that society is founded on irrational factors, its essence lying in the primitive emotional bonds which unite a group of individuals and which cannot be changed by reasoning. Society is a mystery of nature . . . which reveals itself only in symbolic forms and in words loaded with emotional forces, in myths, in the action of the group, or finally in the personality of the leader. It is on no account a matter of reasoning. . . .

The Italian Fascists, Gentile in particular, rightly invoke the name of Hegel when defining the totalitarian character of Fascist society. The pattern of such society is ultimately given by the Hegelian "concrete Idea," that is, the Idea which has reached the stage of its full realization. At this stage the contradiction between ideal and real, universal and particular, potential and actual, totality and multiplicity, is superseded. The Idea lives adequately in its concrete forms of manifestation, and these forms represent adequately the Idea, or the whole, they belong to. On the social plane, this means that society as a whole or pattern is realized in each of its members, and that the life of each individual is a particular case in the life of its society. Consequently society is not merely a concept, or a general term for a multiplicity of individuals, but exists in the same way as the individual himself. It has a will of its own, the work of which is seen in all integrating and coercive forces holding the individuals together and leading them towards common ends. Hegel himself gives several examples of society as being concrete in its existence. The State, "the people" as "organic totality," a great personality (Napoleon) are the most important of them. . . .

In Nazism the "totality" is created by irrational factors exclusively. The main totalitarian category is that of *Das Volk*. For Nazism also the State is a means. "It is a basic principle, therefore, that the State represents not an end but a means. . . . Its purpose is in the maintenance and advancement of a community of human beings with common physical and spiritual characteristics." The bonds between the individual and "the people" are fundamentally emotional. The way in which the totalitarian reality of Nazi society is expressed suggests the presence of a magic and symbolic form of thinking. Words like "Fatherland," "German," etc. were loaded with such an emotional power that the mere perception of them created in individuals the feeling that they all are one. The Rumanian Fascists used to symbolize their "totality" by a tiny bag of Rumanian soil which they carried with them as a talisman; whenever the bag was shown by one of them, there was no sacrifice in the world a *legionar* would not make for his country.

"The people" as a manifestation of the totalitarian reality is, however, not

specific to Nazism. The two specific forms of the Nazi totalitarian reality are:
A. "Race," B. The Leader.

A. "Race" constitutes the most accurate form of totalitarian reality. "Race" is the voice of the group in the individual. This is the basic assumption on which the Nazi leaders had developed their own ideas about the Germanic Race. The purity of the race came first, for the purer the race the stronger its binding forces over the individual. Purity in the racial character means first of all superiority, in the sense that the totalitarian reality is more adequately represented. Consequently Nazis appealed to those racial theories which demonstrated the superiority of the Germanic Race on the ground of its purity. . . . On the psychological level they had systematically worked for the creation of strong positive in-group and negative out-group feelings in the members of their own society. . . .

B. The totalitarian reality is manifested also through the personality of the *Führer*. The *Führer* is first of all a charismatic figure, the *geniale momentum* of the German nation. He is "the bearer of the people's will. . . ."

In conclusion, the unifying forces of Nazi society, whatever their name, are irrational. Consequently, they do not allow any deliberation concerning the conforming behaviour of the individual. The individual's mind cannot be divided about their acceptance. Nor can the members of the group divide themselves into *pro* and *contra* and follow the decision of the majority. With regard to the interests of the group as expressed by the *Führer,* there cannot be partial or gradual consent, but unavoidable unanimity. The formula is all or nothing. . . .

The perspective of individual freedom opened up by the Renaissance and the Reformation has, according to [Erich] Fromm, reached a critical point in our era. The thirst for freedom arose in modern man as a reaction from medieval society; it grew up in step with the dissolution of the primary bonds characteristic of the medieval community, and in step with the weakening of the integrating forces of religion. But, as Fromm notices, if some results of this wide process led to modern democracy, some others led to social disintegration. Modern society has not supplied the individual with integrating values strong enough to compensate for the loss of the bonds of the medieval community. Thus, in many contemporary societies, the need for freedom has gradually become aimless. The individual is free to realize himself, feeling, at the same time, that there is nothing outside to give sense to his life, and thus to separate his freedom from vacuum and nothingness. Here Fromm rightly points out that as long as freedom meant freedom *from,* . . . the experience of freedom in modern man had a full meaning. The moment of crisis is marked by the projection of the experience of freedom into the future, as freedom *for*. To this type of freedom modern society has failed to give a satisfactory answer. The main symptom of this crisis is shown in the insecurity, loneliness and fear of personal responsibility unavoidably implied in the experience of freedom in contemporary society. . . .

The direction in which the crisis of freedom is solved, suggests the Dostoevskian formula outlined in *The Grand Inquisitor* (Brothers Karamazov), escape from freedom into security by an indiscriminate acceptance of external authority.

Nazism is, according to Fromm, one of the historical forms of this escape from freedom. The individual escapes the burdens of freedom and responsibility by his unconditional surrender to a despot and by his uncritical acceptance of a body of secular beliefs and myths arranged for him by an authoritarian regime. . . .

There is no doubt that Nazism is partly determined by the fear of freedom and responsibility in contemporary men and by its positive aspect as an escape into authoritarianism. Fromm's only mistake is that he lays too great a stress on the importance of this process in the psycho-genesis of Nazism. Consequently he completely fails to see an opposite process to that described by him as "fear of Freedom." This is the type of integration produced by modern society which is—as [the French sociologist] E. Durkheim suggests—a counterbalancing process to the disintegration and specialization inherent in large-scale organizations. We can talk therefore about excessive integration, and responsibility existing in contemporary man side by side with excessive freedom and lack of responsibility. Paradoxically enough, this process has also contributed to the rise of Nazism. This has happened in two main ways: On the psychological level it has gradually led to the annihilation of the individual's personality by the weakening of his critical mind. On the social plane it has gradually created a type of civilization whose main characteristics consist in a high degree of inter-individual dependence—a factory type of society. This made it all the easier for the Nazi leaders to create a highly integrated society. . . .

Can one explain the origins of the pathological aspects of Nazism only by the presence of certain psychopathological traits in the Nazi leaders, or has one to resort, for the solution of this problem, to certain qualities of contemporary German society and culture? One is on safe ground when talking about the presence of psychopathological traits in Hitler and other Nazi leaders from the simple fact that a certain amount of empirical evidence is available. In his study [the American psychologist G. M.] Gilbert made use of reliable psychological methods. But when trying to analyse the pathological elements involved in the German culture-pattern, during the period preceding Nazism, one can hardly rely on any systematic research, psychological or anthropological. In this case the psychologist's only choice is to give his own interpretation to a series of historical facts selected by him as symptomatic for the mental structure of the German group during the period under consideration. The hypothetical elements have to be very strong indeed. And yet, this hypothesis seems to be necessary. For Hitler's paranoia or Goering's narcissistic traits, symptomatic as they were, could hardly create a series of psychopathological trends in the Nazi group, or in the German group, had they met indifferent or hostile surroundings. The fact is that they built themselves on elements found already in German society and culture.

In what follows we describe some of the main aspects of contemporary German society and culture which disclose the existence of certain abnormal and pathological traits in the individuals belonging to this society and culture.

1. The concept most accurately covering the main pathological symptoms shown by German society during and immediately preceding Nazism is that of a sociopathic group. As in the case of sociopathic personality, the sociopathic character of the group is motivated by a basic insecurity, and, as in the case of psychopathic personality again, the acting out of the feeling of insecurity leads to a morbid urge for self-assertion of the group. Hence the authoritarian character of its organization, its policy based on force, and its anti-social behaviour.

Insecurity can be considered as the main cause of German society's failure to adjust itself to twentieth-century democratic civilization; it prevented the German group from projecting its aspirations on the values created by this civilization. This basic insecurity destroyed the frame of reference for the aspirations of the German group.

The lack of an adequate frame of reference has a particular sociological importance, which in the case of Nazism has received too little attention. This is the group trait that can explain to a great extent the importance played by the *déclassés* and psychopathic personalities of the Nazi movement. For it is this sociological category and this personality type that can more successfully crystallize the various mental factors in a group with a lost frame of reference. Its disorientation, its fears and revolt against a hostile environment, and finally its urge to escape into adventure, all these find their highest expression in that type of personality and group described by us as sociopathic.

We hasten to say that we cannot describe the whole of the twentieth [-century] German society as having a well-defined sociopathic structure. Its general state of insecurity and its incapacity to integrate with European democratic civilization can be considered only as a fertile ground in which a sociopathic structure could develop. . . .

. . . 2. Some people . . . see certain specific psychotic features in German culture. R. Brickner, among others, speaks of a paranoiac German culture, wondering whether this is curable or not. The paranoiac symptoms most frequently referred to are self-centeredness, self-glorification, and obsessional forms of aggression. Gilbert takes up this point, and sensing the difficulty involved in the application of clinical concepts to culture-pattern and group behaviour, reformulates the whole problem in new terms. Thus, he distinguishes between "clinical" and cultural pseudo-paranoia, only the latter being characteristic of German society. This means that one can find certain paranoiac trends in the German group, although its members—with the exception of a few Nazi leaders—cannot be classified as cases of clinical paranoia. The members of the Nazi group, and of the German group as a whole, behaved as if they were paranoiacs, for their personalities were directed by their culture. Their perceptions, emotions and thoughts were conditioned by a process of cultural learning to such an extent that they showed signs of delusional behaviour. In the totalitarian State created by Nazism—Gilbert concludes—the national behaviour resembles paranoia, i.e., behaviour based on systematized delusions (innate superiority) and aggression. . . .

3. Compulsion is also connected with Nazism. It is seen in the rigidity and repetitiveness of behaviour-pattern such as saluting, mechanically executing meaningless orders, and generally speaking, in the German fondness for discipline. Gilbert is again of the opinion that the compulsive traits in the Nazi group cannot be regarded as compulsive behaviour in a clinical sense, but as cultural pseudo-compulsion. The Nazi regime had intensified the militaristic character of German culture to such an extent that the individual carried on the group behaviour rituals with little possibility of resistance. There was no scale of values to put a check to his rigid loyalty to the group. He would exterminate people *en masse* to satisfy this loyalty. Cultural pseudo-compulsion consists, therefore, in the culturally conditioned tendency of the individual "to carry to the extreme the repetition of group behaviour rituals." Gilbert makes clear that the individuals themselves showed no signs of clinical compulsive behaviour. . . .

. . . As we have already shown, the Nazi personality is easily inclined to take on stereotyped modes of reaction, and to mould his emotionality according to the pattern of the group, to think with "official" ideas, to avoid personal responsibility, and on the whole to reduce his behaviour to a few clichés offered by his own group. "Think for yourself" does not apply in this case.

Deep analysis reveals a certain connexion between insecurity and lack of individuation. According to this view, insecurity is reflected first of all on the emotional pattern of personality. The insecurity produced in the child by his parents' behaviour—mother-separation, negligence, and other factors determining instability in the environment—prevents the child from acquiring a unilinear sense of values in life. The first layer of ambiguity in the world of values is determined by the internalization of the parental figures. For they are internalized as good and bad figures, according to their behaviour, at the same time. The other elements of the environment being themselves in a state of instability cannot help the child to escape from this primary ambivalence. Many psychoanalysts interpret the spirit of conformity and group identification in the authoritarian personality as defences against this fundamental ambivalence. In this way, the values of one's own group become the criterion of good and right, while those of the out-group become the criterion of bad and wrong. The basic ambivalence is solved by a rigid distinction between good and bad at the conscious level.

Yet, in spite of all this rigid social integration, the Nazi personality suffers from lack of integration. For the inner integration of this personality is weak. His weak ego, his lack of self-reliance, cause him to form a conventional superego. Thus he sticks desperately to conventional opinions because he has neither the initiative nor the courage to form his own; he adheres mechanically to the prejudices of his group because he fears his anti-social and anarchic tendencies; he identifies himself with the group in order to maintain his precarious mental balance. The ideas he holds, the feelings he displays and the prejudices he fanatically defends are shields against himself. They act as external forces and the individual has no power to transform them into an internal structure. The moment an idea becomes his own—not supported by external authority—its sense becomes ambiguous, and consequently the individual would be no longer sure of its validity. That is why this type of personality is afraid to individualize his behaviour.

9.

Whether individuals have much to do with the shaping of history is a perennially debated issue. In various deterministic systems of thought (of which economic determinism is the most widely diffused in our day), not much room is left for autonomous individual action; leaders merely respond to powerful undercurrents, and are the playthings of "broad historical forces." Yet there continue to be some impenitent believers in the role of the individual in history; they contend that, occasionally at least, "event-making men" may be brought to the surface in the flow of history, and may redirect that flow.[1] Was Adolf Hitler one of these "event-making" men? Many of his foreign critics scoffed at any such idea during his lifetime; they made scathing references to "that Austrian housepainter," or even remarked (as did the French foreign minister in 1937) that "Hitler remains at Berchtesgaden most of the time playing pinochle with his cook, his butler and his chauffeur while Goebbels sits in Berlin and directs Germany's destinies." [2]

To write a full-scale biography of Hitler so soon after the event is an audacious enterprise. Fortunately, it has been undertaken by one of the ablest British historians of our generation, Alan Bullock of St. Catherine's, Oxford. Mr. Bullock makes a persuasive case for the thesis that Hitler's distorted genius had much to do with bringing Nazism to power.

BULLOCK: Hitler: A Study in Tyranny *

. . . The foundation of Hitler's success was his own energy and ability as a political leader. . . . Hitler's genius as a politician lay in his unequalled grasp of what could be done by propaganda, and his flair for seeing how to do it. He had to learn in a hard school, on his feet night after night, arguing his case in every kind of hall, from the smoke-filled back room of a beer-cellar to the huge auditorium of the *Zirkus Krone;* often, in the early days, in the face of opposition, indifference or amused contempt; learning to hold his audience's attention, to win them over; most important of all, learning to read the minds of his audiences, finding the sensitive spots on which to hammer. "He could play like a virtuoso on the well-tempered piano of lower middle-class hearts," says

[1] A remarkable study of the role of the individual in history is Sidney Hook's *The Hero in History: a Study in Limitation and Possibility* (Boston: Beacon Press, 1955).

[2] United States, Department of State, *Foreign Relations of the United States, 1937* (Washington: Government Printing Office, 1954), I, 118.

* From Alan Bullock, *Hitler: A Study in Tyranny* (New York: Harper, 1952), pp. 61–64, 340–49, 356, 361–62, 351–53. Reprinted by permission of Harper and Row.

Dr. Schacht. Behind that virtuosity lay years of experience as an agitator and mob orator. Hitler came to know Germany and the German people at first hand as few of Germany's other leaders ever had. By the time he came to power in 1933 there were few towns of any size in the Reich where he had not spoken. Here was one great advantage Hitler had over nearly all the politicians with whom he had to deal, his immense practical experience of politics, not in the Chancellery or the Reichstag, but in the street, the level at which elections are won, the level at which any politician must be effective if he is to carry a mass vote with him.

Hitler was the greatest demagogue in history. Those who add "only a demagogue" fail to appreciate the nature of political power in an age of mass politics. As he himself said: "To be a leader, means to be able to move masses."

The lessons which Hitler drew from the activities of the Austrian Social Democrats and Lueger's Christian Socialists were now tried out in Munich. Success was far from being automatic. Hitler made mistakes and had much to learn before he could persuade people to take him seriously, even on the small stage of Bavarian politics. By 1923 he was still only a provincial politician, who had not yet made any impact on national politics, and the end of 1923 saw the collapse of his movement in a fiasco. But Hitler learned from his mistakes, and by the time he came to write *Mein Kampf* in the middle of the 1920s he was able to set down quite clearly what he was trying to do, and what were the conditions of success. The pages in *Mein Kampf* in which he discusses the technique of mass propaganda and political leadership stand out in brilliant contrast with the turgid attempts to explain his entirely unoriginal political ideas.

The first and most important principle for political action laid down by Hitler is: Go to the masses. "The movement must avoid everything which may lessen or weaken its power of influencing the masses . . . because of the simple fact that no great idea, no matter how sublime or exalted, can be realized in practice without the effective power which resides in the popular masses."

Since the masses [wrote Hitler] have only a poor acquaintance with abstract ideas, their reactions lie more in the domain of the feelings, where the roots of their positive as well as their negative attitudes are implanted. . . . The emotional grounds of their attitude furnish the reason for their extraordinary stability. It is always more difficult to fight against faith than against knowledge. And the driving force which has brought about the most tremendous revolutions on this earth has never been a body of scientific teaching which has gained power over the masses, but always a devotion which has inspired them, and often a kind of hysteria which has urged them into action. Whoever wishes to win over the masses must know the key that will open the door to their hearts. It is not objectivity, which is a feckless attitude, but a determined will, backed up by power where necessary.

Hitler is quite open in explaining how this is to be achieved. "The receptive powers of the masses are very restricted, and their understanding is feeble. On the other hand, they quickly forget. Such being the case, all effective propaganda must be confined to a few bare necessities and then must be expressed in a few stereotyped formulas." Hitler had nothing but scorn for the intellectuals who are always looking for something new. "Only constant repetition will finally succeed in imprinting an idea on the memory of a crowd." For the same reason it is better to stick to a programme even when certain points in it become out of date: "As soon as one point is removed from the sphere of dogmatic certainty, the discussion will not simply result in a new and better formulation, but may easily lead to endless debates and general confusion."

When you lie, tell big lies. This is what the Jews do, working on the principle "which is quite true in itself, that in the big lie there is always a certain force of credibility; because the broad masses of a nation are always more easily corrupted in the deeper strata of their emotional nature than consciously or voluntarily, and thus in the primitive simplicity of their minds they more readily fall victims to the big lie than the small lie, since they themselves often tell small lies in little matters, but would be ashamed to resort to large-scale falsehoods. It would never come into their heads to fabricate colossal untruths and they would not believe that others could have the impudence to distort the truth so infamously. . . . The grossly impudent lie always leaves traces behind it, even after it has been nailed down."

Above all, never hesitate, never qualify what you say, never concede an inch to the other side, paint all your contrasts in black and white. This is the "very first condition which has to be fulfilled in every kind of propaganda: a systematically one-sided attitude towards every problem that has to be dealt with. . . . When they see an uncompromising onslaught against an adversary, the people have at all times taken this as proof that right is on the side of the active aggressor; but if the aggressor should go only halfway and fail to push home his success . . . the people will look upon this as a sign that he is uncertain of the justice of his own cause."

Vehemence, passion, fanaticism, these are "the great magnetic forces which alone attract the great masses; for these masses always respond to the compelling force which emanates from absolute faith in the ideas put forward, combined with an indomitable zest to fight for and defend them. . . . The doom of a nation can be averted only by a storm of glowing passion; but only those who are passionate themselves can arouse passion in others."

Hitler showed a marked preference for the spoken over the written word. "The force which ever set in motion the great historical avalanches of religious and political movements is the magic power of the spoken word. The broad masses of a population are more amenable to the appeal of rhetoric than to any other force." The employment of verbal violence, the repetition of such words as "smash," "force," "ruthless," "hatred," was deliberate. Hitler's gestures and the emotional character of his speaking, lashing himself up to a pitch of near-hysteria in which he would scream and spit out his resentment, had the same effect on an audience. Many descriptions have been given of the way in which he succeeded in communicating passion to his listeners, so that men groaned or hissed and women sobbed involuntarily, if only to relieve the tension, caught up in the spell of powerful emotions of hatred and exaltation, from which all restraint had been removed. . . .

Hitler always showed a distrust of argument and criticism. Unable to argue coolly himself, since his early days in Vienna his one resort had been to shout his opponent down. The questioning of his assumptions or of his facts rattled him and threw him out of his stride less because of any intellectual inferiority than because words, and even facts, were to him not a means of rational communication and logical analysis, but devices for manipulating emotion. The introduction of intellectual processes of criticism and analysis marked the intrusion of hostile elements which disturbed the exercise of this power. Hence Hitler's hatred of the intellectual: in the masses "instinct is supreme and from instinct comes faith. . . . While the healthy common folk instinctively close their ranks to form a community of the people, the intellectuals run this way and that, like hens in a poultry-yard. With them it is impossible to make history; they cannot be used as elements supporting a community."

For the same reason Hitler rated the spoken above the written word: "False ideas and ignorance may be set aside by means of instruction, but emotional resistance never can. Nothing but an appeal to hidden forces will be effective here. And that appeal can scarcely be made by any writer. Only the orator can hope to make it."

As an orator Hitler had obvious faults. The timbre of his voice was harsh, very different from the beautiful quality of Goebbels. He spoke at too great length; was often repetitive and verbose; lacked lucidity and frequently lost himself in cloudy phrases. These shortcomings, however, mattered little beside the extraordinary impression of force, the immediacy of passion, the intensity of hatred, fury and menace conveyed by the sound of the voice alone without regard to what he said.

One of the secrets of his mastery over a great audience was his instinctive sensitivity to the mood of a crowd, a flair for divining the hidden passions, resentments and longings in their minds. In *Mein Kampf* he says of the orator: "He will always follow the lead of the great masses in such a way that from the living emotion of his hearers the apt word which he needs will be suggested to him and in its turn this will go straight to the hearts of his hearers."

One of his most bitter critics, Otto Strasser, wrote:

Hitler responds to the vibration of the human heart with the delicacy of a seismograph, or perhaps of a wireless receiving set, enabling him, with a certainty with which no conscious gift could endow him, to act as a loudspeaker proclaiming the most secret desires, the least admissible instincts, the sufferings and personal revolts of a whole nation. . . . I have been asked many times what is the secret of Hitler's extraordinary power as a speaker. I can only attribute it to his uncanny intuition, which infallibly diagnoses the ills from which his audience is suffering. If he tries to bolster up his argument with theories or quotations from books he has only imperfectly understood, he scarcely rises above a very poor mediocrity. But let him throw away his crutches and step out boldly, speaking as the spirit moves him, and he is promptly transformed into one of the greatest speakers of the century. . . . Adolf Hitler enters a hall. He sniffs the air. For a minute he gropes, feels his way, senses the atmosphere. Suddenly he bursts forth. His words go like an arrow to their target, he touches each private wound on the raw, liberating the mass unconscious, expressing its innermost aspirations, telling it what it most wants to hear.

Hitler's power to bewitch an audience has been likened to the occult arts of the African medicine-man or the Asiatic Shaman; others have compared it to the sensitivity of a medium and the magnetism of a hypnotist.

The extravagant conversations recorded by Hermann Rauschning for the period 1932–1934, and by Dr. Henry Picker at the Fuehrer's H.Q. for the period 1941–1942, reveal Hitler in another favourite role, that of visionary and prophet. As the French Ambassador, André Francois-Poncet noted, there was in Hitler much of King Ludwig II of Bavaria. The fabulous dreams of a vast empire embracing all Europe and half Asia; the geopolitical fantasies of intercontinental wars and alliances; the plans for breeding an *élite,* biologically pre-selected, and founding a new Order to guard the Holy Grail of pure blood; the design for reducing whole nations to slavery—all these are the fruits of a crude, disordered, but fertile imagination soaked in the German romanticism of the late nineteenth century, a caricature of Wagner, Nietzsche and Schopenhauer. This was the mood in which Hitler indulged, talking far into the night, in his house on the Obersalzberg, surrounded by the remote peaks and silent forests of the Bavarian Alps; or in the Eyrie he had built six thousand feet up on the Kehlstein, above the Berghof, approached only by a mountain road blasted through the rock and a lift guarded by doors of bronze. It was also the mood in which he and Himmler drew up the blueprints and issued the orders for the construction of that New Order which was to replace the disintegrating liberal bourgeois world of the nineteenth century. After the outbreak of the war and the conquest of the greater part of Europe, all practical restraint upon Hitler's translation of his fantasies into brutal reality was removed. The S.S. extermination squads, the *Einsatzkommandos,* with their gas-vans and death camps; the planned elimination of the Jewish race; the treatment of the Poles and Russians, the Slav *Untermenschen* (sub-humans); these, too, were the fruits of Hitler's imagination.

All this combines to create a picture of which the best description is Hitler's own famous sentence: "I go the way that Providence dictates with the assurance of a sleepwalker." The former French Ambassador speaks of him as "a man possessed"; Hermann Rauschning writes: "Dostoevsky might well have invented him, with the morbid derangement and the pseudo-creativeness of his hysteria"; one of the Defence Counsel at the Nuremberg Trials, Dr. Dix, quoted a passage from Goethe's *Dichtung und Wahrheit* describing the Demoniac and applied this very aptly to Hitler. With Hitler, indeed, one is uncomfortably aware of never being far from the realm of the irrational.

But this is only half the truth about Hitler, for the baffling problem about this strange figure is to determine the degree to which he was swept along by a genuine belief in his own inspiration and the degree to which he deliberately exploited the irrational side of human nature, both in himself and others, with a shrewd calculation. For it is salutary to recall, before accepting the Hitler-Myth at anything like its face value, that it was Hitler who invented the myth, assiduously cultivating and manipulating it for his own ends. So long as he did this he was brilliantly successful; it was when he began to believe in his own magic, and accept the myth of himself as true, that his flair faltered.

So much has been made of the charismatic nature of Hitler's leadership that it is easy to forget the astute and cynical politician in him. It is this mixture of calculation and fanaticism, with the difficulty of telling where one ends and the other begins, which is the peculiar characteristic of Hitler's personality: to ignore or underestimate either element is to present a distorted picture. . . .

The link between the different sides of Hitler's character was his extraordinary capacity for self-dramatization. "This so-called *Wahnsystem,* or capacity for self-delusion," Sir Nevile Henderson, the British Ambassador, wrote, "was a regular part of his technique. It helped him both to work up his own passions and to make his people believe anything that he might thing good for them." Again and again one is struck by the way in which, having once decided rationally on a course of action, Hitler would whip himself into a passion which enabled him to bear down all opposition, and provided him with the motive power to enforce his will on others. The most obvious instance of this is the synthetic fury, which he could assume or discard at will, over the treatment of German minorities abroad. When it was a question of refusing to listen to the bitter complaints of the Germans in the South Tyrol, or of uprooting the German inhabitants of the Baltic States, he sacrificed them to the needs of his Italian and Russian alliances with indifference. So long as good relations with Poland were necessary to his foreign policy he showed little interest in Poland's German minority. But when it suited his purpose to make the "intolerable wrongs" of the Austrian Nazis, or the Germans in Czechoslovakia and Poland, a ground for action against these states, he worked himself into a frenzy of indignation, with the result—immediate and calculated—that London and Paris, in their anxiety for peace, exerted increased pressure on Prague or Warsaw to show restraint and make further concessions to the German demands.

One of Hitler's most habitual devices was to place himself on the defensive, to accuse those who opposed or obstructed him of aggression and malice, and to pass rapidly from a tone of outraged innocence to the full thunders of moral indignation. It was always the other side who were to blame, and in turn he denounced the Communists, the Jews, the Republican Government, or the Czechs, the Poles, and the Bolsheviks for their "intolerable" behaviour which forced him to take drastic action in self-defence.

Hitler in a rage appeared to lose all control of himself. His face became mottled and swollen with fury, he screamed at the top of his voice, spitting out a stream of abuse, waving his arms wildly and drumming on the table or the wall with his fists. As suddenly as he had begun he would stop, smooth down his hair, straighten his collar and resume a more normal voice.

This skilful and deliberate exploitation of his own temperament extended to other moods than anger. When he wanted to persuade or win someone over he could display great charm. Until the last days of his life he retained an uncanny gift of personal magnetism which defies analysis, but which many who met him have described. This was connected with the curious power of his eyes, which are persistently said to have had some sort of hypnotic quality. Similarly, when he wanted to frighten or shock, he showed himself a master of brutal and threatening language, as in the celebrated interviews with Schuschnigg and President Hacha.

Yet another variation in his roles was the impression of concentrated willpower and intelligence, the leader in complete command of the situation and with a knowledge of the facts which dazzled the generals or ministers summoned to receive his orders. To sustain this part he drew on his remarkable memory, which enabled him to reel off complicated orders of battle, technical specifications and long lists of names and dates without a moment's hesitation. Hitler cultivated his gift of memory assiduously. The fact that subsequently the details and figures which he cited were often found to contain inaccuracies did not matter: it was the immediate effect at which he aimed. The swiftness of the transition from one mood to another was startling: one moment his eyes would be filled with tears and pleading, the next blazing with fury, or glazed with the faraway look of the visionary.

Hitler, in fact, was a consummate actor, with the actor's and orator's facility for absorbing himself in a role and convincing himself of the truth of what he was saying at the time he said it. In his early years he was often awkward and unconvincing, but with practice the part became second nature to him, and with the immense prestige of success behind him, and the resources of a powerful state at his command, there were few who could resist the impression of the piercing eyes, the Napoleonic pose and the "historic" personality.

Hitler had the gift of all great politicians for grasping the possibilities of a situation more swiftly than his opponents. He saw, as no other politician did, how to play on the grievances and resentments of the German people, as later he was to play on French and British fear of war and fear of Communism. His insistence upon preserving the forms of legality in the struggle for power showed a brilliant understanding of the way to disarm opposition, just as the way in which he undermined the independence of the German Army showed his grasp of the weaknesses of the German Officer Corps.

A German word, *Fingerspitzgefühl*—"finger-tip feeling"—which was often applied to Hitler, well describes his sense of opportunity and timing.

No matter what you attempt [Hitler told Rauschning on one occasion], if an idea is not yet mature you will not be able to realize it. Then there is only one thing to do: have patience, wait, try again, wait again. In the subconscious, the work goes on. It matures, sometimes it dies. Unless I have the inner, incorruptible conviction: *this is the solution,* I do nothing. Not even if the whole Party tries to drive me into action.

Hitler knew how to wait in 1932, when his insistence on holding out until he could secure the Chancellorship appeared to court disaster. Foreign policy provides another instance. In 1939 he showed great patience while waiting for the situation to develop after direct negotiations with Poland had broken down and while the Western Powers were seeking to reach a settlement with Soviet Russia. Clear enough about his objectives, he contrived to keep his plans flexible. The date he fixed for the invasion of Czechoslovakia, 1 October, 1938, is one of the few instances in which Hitler committed himself to a definite time-table, out of fury at the way the Czechs had scored off him on 28 May. Much more characteristic was his action in the case of the annexation of Austria and the occupation of Prague, where he made the final decision on the spur of the moment.

Until he was convinced that the right moment had come Hitler would find a hundred excuses for procrastination. His hesitation in such cases was notorious: his refusal to make up his mind to stand as a Presidential candidate in 1932, and his attempt to defer taking action against Roehm and the S.A. in 1934, are two obvious examples. Once he had made up his mind to move, however, he would act boldly, taking considerable risks, as in the reoccupation of the Rhineland in 1936, or the invasion of Norway and Denmark just before the major campaign in the west.

Surprise was a favourite gambit of Hitler's, in politics, diplomacy and war: he gauged the psychological effect of sudden, unexpected hammer blows in paralysing opposition. An illustration of his appreciation of the value of surprise and quick decision, even when on the defensive, is the second presidential campaign of 1932. It had taken Goebbels weeks to persuade Hitler to stand for the Presidency at all. The defeat in the first ballot brought Goebbels to despair; but Hitler, now that he had committed himself, with great presence of mind dictated the announcement that he would stand a second time and got it on to the streets almost before the country had learned of his defeat. In war the psychological effect of the *blitzkrieg* was just as important in Hitler's eyes as the strategic: it gave the impression that the German military machine was more than life-size, that it possessed some virtue of invincibility against which ordinary men could not defend themselves.

No regime in history has ever paid such careful attention to psychological factors in politics. Hitler was a master of mass emotion. To attend one of his big meetings was to go through an emotional experience, not to listen to an argument or a programme. Yet nothing was left to chance on these occasions. Every device for heightening the emotional intensity, every trick of the theatre was used. The Nuremberg rallies held every year in September were masterpieces of theatrical art, with the most carefully devised effects. "I had spent six years in St. Petersburg before the war in the best days of the old Russian ballet," wrote Sir Nevile Henderson, "but for grandiose beauty I have never seen a ballet to compare with it." To see the films of the Nuremberg rallies even today is to be recaptured by the hypnotic effect of thousands of men marching in perfect order, the music of the massed bands, the forest of standards and flags, the vast perspectives of the stadium, the smoking torches, the dome of searchlights. The sense of power, of force and unity was irresistible, and all converged with a mounting crescendo of excitement on the supreme moment when the Fuehrer himself made his entry. Paradoxically, the man who was most affected by such spectacles was their originator, Hitler himself, and, as Rosenberg remarks in his memoirs, they played an indispensable part in the process of self-intoxication.

Hitler had grasped as no one before him what could be done with a combination of propaganda and terrorism. For the complement to the attractive power of the great spectacles was the compulsive power of the Gestapo, the S.S. and the concentration camp, heightened once again by skilful propaganda. Hitler was helped in this not only by his own perception of the sources of power in a modern urbanized mass-society, but also by possession of the technical means to manipulate them. This was a point well made by Albert Speer, Hitler's highly intelligent Minister for Armaments and War Production, in the final speech he made at his trial after the war.

Hitler's dictatorship [Speer told the court] differed in one fundamental point from all its predecessors in history. His was the first dictatorship in the present period of modern technical development, a dictatorship which made complete use of all technical means for the domination of its own country.

Through technical devices like the radio and the loudspeaker, eighty million people were deprived of independent thought. It was thereby possible to subject them to the will of one man. . . .

Earlier dictators needed highly qualified assistants, even at the lowest level, men who could think and act independently. The totalitarian system in the period of modern technical development can dispense with them; the means of communication alone make it possible to mechanize the lower leadership. As a result of this there arises the new type of the uncritical recipient of orders. . . . Another result was the far-reaching supervision of the citizens of the State and the maintenance of a high degree of secrecy for criminal acts.

The nightmare of many a man that one day nations could be dominated by technical means was all but realized in Hitler's totalitarian system.

In making use of the formidable power which was thus placed in his hands Hitler had one supreme, and fortunately rare, advantage: he had neither scruples nor inhibitions. He was a man without roots, with neither home nor family; a man who admitted no loyalties, was bound by no traditions, and felt respect neither for God nor man. Throughout his career Hitler showed himself prepared to seize any advantage that was to be gained by lying, cunning, treachery and unscrupulousness. He demanded the sacrifice of millions of German lives for the sacred cause of Germany, but in the last year of the war was ready to destroy Germany rather than surrender his power or admit defeat.

Wary and secretive, he entertained a universal distrust. He admitted no one to his counsels. He never let down his guard, or gave himself away. This is reflected in the almost total absence of any correspondence apart from official letters such as those he wrote to Mussolini. Hitler rarely committed himself to paper. "He never," Schacht wrote, "let slip an unconsidered word. He never said what he did not intend to say and he never blurted out a secret. Everything was the result of cold calculation."

While he was in Landsberg gaol, as long ago as 1924, Hitler had preserved his position in the Party by allowing rivalries to develop among the other leaders, and he continued to apply the same principle of "divide and rule" after he became Chancellor. There was always more than one office operating in any field. A dozen different agencies quarrelled over the direction of propaganda, of economic policy and the intelligence services. Before 1938 Hitler continually went behind the back of the Foreign Office to make use of Ribbentrop's special bureau or to get information through Party channels. The dualism of Party and State organizations, each with one or more divisions for the same function, was deliberate. In the end this reduced efficiency, but it strengthened Hitler's position by allowing him to play off one department against another. For the same reason Hitler put an end to regular cabinet meetings and insisted on dealing with ministers singly, so that they could not combine against him. "I have an old principle," he told Ludecke: "only to say what must be said to him who must know it, and only when he must know it." Only the Fuehrer kept all the threads in his hand and saw the whole design. If ever a man exercised absolute power it was Adolf Hitler.

He had a particular and inveterate distrust of experts. He refused to be impressed by the complexity of problems, insisting until it became monotonous that if only the will was there any problem could be solved. Schacht, to whose advice he refused to listen and whose admiration was reluctant, says of him: "Hitler often did find astonishingly simple solutions for problems which had seemed to others insoluble. He had a genius for invention. . . . His solutions were often brutal, but almost always effective." In an interview with a French correspondent early in 1936 Hitler himself claimed this power of simplification as his greatest gift:

It has been said that I owe my success to the fact that I have created a *mystique*. . . . or more simply that I have been lucky. Well, I will tell you what has carried me to the position I have reached. Our political problems appeared complicated. The German people could make nothing of them. In these circumstances they preferred to leave it to the professional politicians to get them out of this confused mess. I, on the other hand, simplified the problems and reduced them to the simplest terms. The masses realized this and followed me.

The crudest of Hitler's simplifications was the most effective: in almost any situation, he believed, force or the threat of force would settle matters—and in an astonishingly large number of cases he proved right. . . .

Hitler had been brought up as a Catholic and was impressed by the organization and power of the Church. Its hierarchical structure, its skill in dealing with human nature and the unalterable character of its Creed, were all features from which he claimed to have learned. For the Protestant clergy he felt only contempt: "They are insignificant little people, submissive as dogs, and they sweat with embarrassment when you talk to them. They have neither a religion they can take seriously nor a great position to defend like Rome." It was "the great position" of the Church that he respected, the fact that it had lasted for so many centuries; towards its teaching he showed the sharpest hostility. In Hitler's eyes Christianity was a religion fit only for slaves; its ethics he detested, and he mocked all talk of a life after death. Death was the end: such immortality as man could achieve was in the race and history. From political considerations he restrained his anti-clericalism, seeing clearly the dangers of strengthening the Church by persecution. Once the war was over, he promised himself, he would root out and destroy the influence of the Christian Churches in Germany, but until then he was a good deal more cautious than some of his followers, like Rosenberg and Bormann, in attacking the Church publicly.

Earnest efforts to establish self-conscious pagan rites roused his scorn and ridicule. Nor has any evidence appeared to substantiate the belief that he resorted to astrology. His secretary says categorically that he had nothing but contempt for such practices, although faith in the stars was certainly common among some of his followers like Himmler. The truth is that Hitler was a complete materialist, without understanding of either the spiritual side of human life or its emotional, affective side. Emotion to him was the raw material of power. The pursuit of power cast its harsh shadow like a blight over the whole of his life. . . .

Hitler was no fool. The element of calculation in his actions would never have been possible had he not possessed considerable intellectual powers. Reason, however, was the slave, not the master, of the passions, a faculty for discovering means, not for criticizing ends. He combined a technical virtuosity with the coarseness and ignorance of a moral illiterate.

The adjective "uneducated" can be applied to him in more than a formal sense. He refused to criticize, or allow others to criticize, his assumptions. He read and listened, not to learn, but to acquire information and find additional support for prejudices and opinions already fixed in his mind; his reading, like his thinking, was entirely pragmatic, never speculative.

Hitler delighted in amassing facts with which to impress his listeners, but cared little for the accuracy of his information, provided it suited his purpose. In the same way he used figures purely with an eye to effect. The idea of objective science or the disinterested search for truth he dismissed as out-of-date liberal prejudices. He claimed to have read widely in history, but his conversation and speeches show only a superficial knowledge of it, habitually distorted to fit his argument. Any of the quotations he used he might have got at second-hand. He liked to regard himself as a prophet and seems to have been genuinely unaware of the extent of his own unoriginality. He knew no foreign languages, and the imaginative and speculative world of European literature was closed to him. One of his secretaries recalls that his library contained not a single classic of literature, indeed not a single book reflecting humane tastes. His reading, she adds, was limited to technical works and books of information, together with newspapers of which he had been an avid reader from his early days in Vienna.

The hostility Hitler showed towards freedom of thought or discussion represented a personal dislike quite as much as a political expedient. On occasion he could be a good listener and derived much information from questioning those who visited him, but he was intolerant of disagreement or even interruption once he had begun to speak himself. The habits of despotism extended from political to personal life, and he became accustomed to have his opinions on any subject accepted as the *ex-cathedra* pronouncements of an oracle, no matter how ignorant and ill-founded they might be. . . .

A hundred years before Hitler became Chancellor, Hegel, in a famous course of lectures at the University of Berlin, had pointed to the role of "World-historical individuals" as the agents by which "the Will of the World Spirit," the plan of Providence is carried out.

They may all be called Heroes, in as much as they have derived their purposes and their vocation, not from the calm regular course of things, sanctioned by the existing order; but from a concealed fount, from that inner Spirit, still hidden beneath the surface, which impinges on the outer world as on a shell and bursts it into pieces. (Such were Alexander, Caesar, Napoleon.) They were practical, political men. But at the same time they were thinking men, who had an insight into the requirements of the time—what was ripe for development. This was the very Truth for their age, for their world. . . . It was theirs to know this nascent principle, the necessary, directly sequent step in progress, which their world was to take to make this their aim, and to expend their energy in promoting it. World-historical men— the Heroes of an epoch—must therefore be recognized as its clearsighted ones: *their* deeds, *their* words are the best of their time.

To the objection that the activity of such individuals frequently flies in the face of morality, and involves great sufferings for others, Hegel replied:

World History occupies a higher ground than that on which morality has properly its position, which is personal character and the conscience of individuals. . . . Moral claims which are irrelevant must not be brought into collision with world-historical deeds and their accomplishment. The litany of private virtues—modesty, humility, philanthropy and forbearance—must not be raised against them. So mighty a form [he adds elsewhere] must trample down many an innocent flower, crush to pieces many an object in its path.

It may well be questioned whether Hitler ever read Hegel, but like so many other passages in nineteenth-century German literature—in Nietzsche, in Schopenhauer, in Wagner—it finds an echo in Hitler's belief about himself. Cynical though he was, Hitler's cynicism stopped short of his own person: he came to believe that he was a man with a mission, marked out by Providence, and therefore exempt from the ordinary canons of human conduct.

Hitler probably held some such belief about himself from an early period. It was clear enough in the speech he made at his trial in 1924, and after he came out of prison those near him noticed that he began to hold aloof, to set a barrier between himself and his followers. After he came to power it became more noticeable. It was in March, 1936, that he made the famous assertion already quoted: "I go the way that Providence dictates with the assurance of a sleep-walker." In 1937 he told an audience at Wurzburg:

However weak the individual may be when compared with the omnipotence and the Will of Providence, yet at the moment when he acts as Providence would have him act he becomes immeasurably strong. Then there streams down upon him that force which has marked all greatness in the world's history. And when I look back only on the five years which lie behind us, then I feel that I am justified in saying: That has not been the work of man alone.

Just before the occupation of Austria, in February, 1938, he declared in the Reichstag:

Above all, a man who feels it his duty at such an hour to assume the leadership of his people is not responsible to the laws of parliamentary usage or to a particular democratic conception, but solely to the mission placed upon him. And anyone who interferes with this mission is an enemy of the people.

It was in this sense of mission that Hitler, a man who believed neither in God nor in conscience ("a Jewish invention, a blemish like circumcision"), found both justification and absolution. He was the Siegfried come to reawaken Germany to greatness, for whom morality, suffering and "the litany of private virtues" were irrelevant. It was by such dreams that he sustained the ruthlessness and determination of his will. So long as this sense of mission was balanced by the cynical calculations of the politician, it represented a source of strength, but success was fatal. When half Europe lay at his feet and all need of restraint was removed, Hitler abandoned himself entirely to megalomania. He became convinced of his own infallibility. But when he began to look to the image he had created to work miracles of its own accord—instead of exploiting it—his gifts deteriorated and his intuition deluded him. Ironically, failure sprang from the same capacity which brought him success, his power of self-dramatization, his ability to convince himself. His belief in his power to work miracles kept him going when the more sceptical Mussolini faltered. Hitler played out his "world-historical" role to the bitter end. But it was this same belief which curtained him in illusion and blinded him to what was actually happening, leading him into that arrogant overestimate of his own genius, which brought him to defeat. The sin which Hitler committed was that which the ancient Greeks called *hybris,* the sin of overweening pride, of believing himself to be more than a man. If ever a man was destroyed by the image he had created it was Adolf Hitler. . . .

IX.

STALIN'S PURGES

Even in an era like ours when both fiction and reality are strongly marked by excess and violence, there are certain episodes that almost surpass the limits of human comprehension. Among these episodes are Hitler's "Final Solution"—the liquidation of several million Jews during the second world war—and Stalin's Great Purge —the liquidation of uncounted Soviet citizens during the years 1935–38. Whether mass murder on such a colossal scale reflects the true nature of the age may be open to dispute; at least it has no precedent in modern western civilization. In any case, the student of twentieth-century history will have missed one grim aspect of the period if he ignores or forgets the evidence of a resurgent barbarism.

Although the full story of the Great Purge was not known outside the Soviet Union at the time (and is still not known today in its entirety), the general course of events could not be concealed. In a few cases, indeed, the Soviet government publicized its actions in the form of "show trials" of alleged saboteurs and traitors. The vast majority of those purged, however, were arrested, tried and punished without public trial; full authority to act had been delegated by the Kremlin to the secret police (then called the NKVD, or People's Commissariat of Internal Affairs).

Foreign observers who sought some explanation for the Great Purge arrived at a variety of conclusions. Some of them held that Stalin's police had uncovered evidence of seditious activity by a widespread anti-Stalinist opposition, whose inspirer was the exiled Leon Trotsky. The United States ambassador to Moscow, Joseph E. Davies (who attended some of the show trials), believed that this was the case, and argued that Stalin was merely liquidating a potential fifth column that might endanger Soviet security in time of war. Others believed that the domestic opposition, though it existed, was largely unorganized and constituted no real threat to the regime; they surmised that Stalin was seeking to avenge himself on those rivals within the party who had opposed and criticized him during his rise to power and his ruthless enforcement of the first five-year plan. But all attempts at sensible explanation were made difficult by the fantastic nature of the accusations made during the show trials, by the even more fantastic confessions of most of the defendants, and by the growing tendency of the purge to reach out into almost every cranny of Soviet society. Then, inexplicably, during 1938, the process slowed and stopped; the purgers themselves were purged, and a kind of uneasy normalcy was restored.

For a decade or more, students of Soviet history had to content themselves with the impressionistic judgments of foreign journalists and diplomats who had lived through the purge period, or with the official account provided by Soviet historians, or with such remarkable imaginative reconstructions as that of the Hungarian-born former Communist Arthur Koestler in his novel Darkness at Noon. Occasionally the memoirs of Soviet defectors or of one of the rare purge victims who was released (notably Alexander Weissberg's *The Accused*) provided shafts of light into the darkness. More recently, a new generation of highly trained western specialists in Soviet affairs has sought to re-examine both the events and the meaning of the Great Purge, and to ask whether such an episode represents a macabre aberration, traceable to the psychotic impulses of a dictator, or whether it may be considered a natural and logical product of a totalitarian system, a device that is essential to maintain a monopoly of power in the hands of a small elite. And in 1956, the new Kremlin leadership contributed to the discussion by dramatically charging Stalin with full responsibility for the Great Purge, and by describing that episode not as a painful necessity but as an unmitigated disaster for the Soviet Union.

1.

In 1938 an official *History of the Communist Party of the Soviet Union* was published in Moscow. Of anonymous authorship, it was generally assumed to be the collective work of a commission of Soviet historians. After the second world war, its authorship began to be attributed to Stalin himself; indeed, plans were made to include the volume in a complete edition of Stalin's collected works. New postwar editions appeared, both in Russian and in translation, but the content was altered very little. Until several years after Stalin's death, the official Soviet version of the Great Purge continued to be the account that Stalin had written (or approved) just as the purge was ending in 1938.

History of the Communist Party of the Soviet Union *

The achievements of Socialism in our country were a cause of rejoicing not only to the Party, and not only to the workers and collective farmers, but also to our Soviet intelligentsia, and to all honest citizens of the Soviet Union.

But they were no cause of rejoicing to the remnants of the defeated exploiting classes; on the contrary, they only enraged them the more as time went on.

They infuriated the lickspittles of the defeated classes—the puny remnants of the following of Bukharin and Trotsky.

These gentry were guided in their evaluation of the achievements of the workers and collective farmers not by the interests of the people, who applauded every such achievement, but by the interests of their own wretched and putrid faction, which had lost all contact with the realities of life. Since the achievements of Socialism in our country meant the victory of the policy of the Party and the utter bankruptcy of their own policy, these gentry, instead of admitting the obvious facts and joining the common cause, began to revenge themselves on the Party and the people for their own failure, for their own bankruptcy; they began to resort to foul play and sabotage against the cause of the workers and collective farmers, to blow up pits, set fire to fac-

* From *History of the Communist Party of the Soviet Union* (*Bolsheviks*) (Moscow: Foreign Languages Publishing House, 1945), pp. 324–27, 346–48, 360.

tories, and commit acts of wrecking in collective and state farms, with the object of undoing the achievements of the workers and collective farmers and evoking popular discontent against the Soviet Government. And in order, while doing so, to shield their puny group from exposure and destruction, they simulated loyalty to the Party, fawned upon it, eulogized it, cringed before it more and more, while in reality continuing their underhand, subversive activities against the workers and peasants.

At the Seventeenth Party Congress [in 1934], Bukharin, Rykov and Tomsky made repentant speeches praising the Party and extolling its achievements to the skies. But the congress detected a ring of insincerity and duplicity in their speeches; for what the Party expects from its members is not eulogies and rhapsodies over its achievements, but conscientious work on the Socialist front. And this was what the Bukharinites had showed no signs of for a long time. The Party saw that the hollow speeches of these gentry were in reality meant for their supporters outside the congress, to serve as a lesson to them in duplicity, and a call to them not to lay down their arms.

Speeches were also made at the Seventeenth Congress by the Trotskyites Zinoviev and Kamenev, who lashed themselves extravagantly for their mistakes, and eulogized the Party no less extravagantly for its achievements. But the congress could not help seeing that both their nauseating self-castigation and their fulsome praise of the Party were only meant to hide an uneasy and unclean conscience. However, the Party did not yet know or suspect that while these gentry were making their cloying speeches at the congress they were hatching a villainous plot against the life of S. M. Kirov.

On December 1, 1934, S. M. Kirov was foully murdered in the Smolny, in Leningrad, by a shot from a revolver.

The assassin was caught red-handed and turned out to be a member of a secret counter-revolutionary group made up of members of an anti-Soviet group of Zinovievites in Leningrad.

S. M. Kirov was loved by the Party and the working class, and his murder stirred the people profoundly, sending a wave of wrath and deep sorrow through the country.

The investigation established that in 1933 and 1934 an underground counter-revolutionary terrorist group had been formed in Leningrad consisting of former members of the Zinoviev opposition and headed by a so-called "Leningrad Centre." The purpose of this group was to murder leaders of the Communist Party. S. M. Kirov was chosen as the first victim. The testimony of the members of this counter-revolutionary group showed that they were connected with representatives of foreign capitalist states and were receiving funds from them.

The exposed members of this organization were sentenced by the Military Collegium of the Supreme Court of the U.S.S.R. to the supreme penalty—to be shot.

Soon afterwards the existence of an underground counter-revolutionary organization called the "Moscow Centre" was discovered. The preliminary investigation and the trial revealed the villainous part played by Zinoviev, Kamenev, Yevdokimov and other leaders of this organization in cultivating the terrorist mentality among their followers, and in plotting the murder of members of the Party Central Committee and of the Soviet Government.

To such depths of duplicity and villainy had these people sunk that Zinoviev, who was one of the organizers and instigators of the assassination of S. M. Kirov, and who had urged the murderer to hasten the crime, wrote an obituary of Kirov speaking of him in terms of eulogy, and demanded that it be published.

The Zinovievites simulated remorse in court; but they persisted in their duplicity even in the dock. They concealed their connection with Trotsky. They concealed the fact that together with the Trotskyites they had sold themselves to fascist espionage services. They concealed their spying and wrecking activities. They concealed from the court their connections with the Bukharinites, and the existence of a united Trotsky-Bukharin gang of fascist hirelings.

As it later transpired, the murder of Comrade Kirov was the work of this united Trotsky-Bukharin gang.

Even then, in 1935, it had become clear that the Zinoviev group was a camouflaged Whiteguard organization whose members fully deserved to be treated as White guards.

A year later it became known that the actual, real and direct organizers of the murder of Kirov were Trotsky, Zinoviev, Kamenev and their accomplices, and that they had also made preparations for the assassination of other members of the Central Committee. Zinoviev, Kamenev, . . . and others were committed for trial. Confronted by direct evidence, they had to admit publicly, in open court, that they had not only organized the assassination of Kirov, but had been planning to murder all the other leaders of the Party and the Government. Later investigation established the fact that these villains had been engaged in espionage and in organizing acts of diversion. The full extent of the monstrous moral and political depravity of these men, their despicable vallainy and treachery, concealed by hypocritical professions of loyalty to the Party, were revealed at a trial held in Moscow in 1936.

The chief instigator and ringleader of this gang of assassins and spies was Judas Trotsky. Trotsky's assistants and agents in carrying out his counter-revolutionary instructions were Zinoviev, Kamenev and their Trotskyite underlings. They were preparing to bring about the defeat of the U.S.S.R. in the event of attack by imperialist countries; they had become defeatists with regard to the workers' and peasants' state; they had become despicable tools and agents of the German and Japanese fascists.

The main lesson which the Party organizations had to draw from the trials of the persons implicated in the foul murder of S. M. Kirov was that they must put an end to their own political blindness and political heedlessness, and must increase their vigilance and the vigilance of all Party members. . . .

In 1937, new facts came to light regarding the fiendish crimes of the Bukharin-

Trotsky gang. The trial of Pyatakov, Radek and others, the trial of Tu-khachevsky, Yakir and others, and lastly the trial of Bukharin, Rykov, Krestin-sky, Rosengoltz and others, all showed that the Bukharinites and Trotskyites had long ago joined to form a common band of enemies of the people, operating as the "Bloc of Rights and Trotskyites."

The trials showed that these dregs of humanity, in conjunction with the enemies of the people, Trotsky, Zinoviev and Kamenev, had been in con-spiracy against Lenin, the Party and the Soviet State ever since the early days of the October Socialist Revolution. The insidious attempts to thwart the peace of Brest-Litovsk at the beginning of 1918, the plot against Lenin and the con-spiracy with the "Left" Socialist Revolutionaries for the arrest and murder of Lenin, Stalin and Sverdlov in the spring of 1918, the villainous shot that wounded Lenin in the summer of 1918, the revolt of the "Left" Socialist-Revolutionaries in the summer of 1918, the deliberate aggravation of dif-ferences in the Party in 1921 with the object of undermining and overthrowing Lenin's leadership from within, the attempts to overthrow the Party leadership during Lenin's illness and after his death, the betrayal of state secrets and the supply of information of an espionage character, to foreign espionage services, the vile assassination of Kirov, the acts of wrecking, diversion and explosions, the dastardly murder of Menzhinsky, Kuibyshev and Gorky—all these and similar villainies over a period of twenty years were committed, it transpired, with the participation or under the direction of Trotsky, Zinoviev, Kamenev, Bukharin, Rykov and their henchmen, at the behest of espionage services of bourgeois states.

The trials brought to light the fact that the Trotsky-Bukharin fiends, in obedience to the wishes of their masters—the espionage services of foreign states—had set out to destroy the Party and the Soviet state, to undermine the defensive power of the country, to assist foreign military intervention, to pre-pare the way for the defeat of the Red Army, to bring about the dismember-ment of the U.S.S.R., to hand over the Soviet Maritime Region to the Japanese, Soviet Byelorussia to the Poles, and the Soviet Ukraine to the Germans, to de-stroy the gains of the workers and collective farmers, and to restore capitalist slavery in the U.S.S.R.

These Whiteguard pigmies, whose strength was no more than that of a gnat, apparently flattered themselves that they were the masters of the country, and imagined that it was really in their power to sell or give away the Ukraine, Byelorussia, and the Maritime Region.

These Whiteguard insects forgot that the real masters of the Soviet country were the Soviet people, and that the rykovs, bukharins, zinovievs and kamenevs were only temporary employees of the state, which could at any moment sweep them out from its offices as so much useless rubbish.

These contemptible lackeys of the fascists forgot that the Soviet people had only to move a finger, and not a trace of them would be left.

The Soviet court sentenced the Bukharin-Trotsky fiends to be shot.

The People's Commissariat of Internal Affairs carried out the sentence.

The Soviet people approved the annihilation of the Bukharin-Trotsky gang and passed on to the next business. . . .

If we had not defeated the Trotskyites and Bukharinites, we could not have brought about the conditions that are essential for the building of Socialism.

If we had not defeated the nationalist deviators of all shades and colours, we could not have educated the people in the spirit of internationalism, we could not have safeguarded the banner of the great amity of the nations of the U.S.S.R., and we could not have built up the Union of Soviet Socialist Republics.

It may seem to some that the Bolsheviks devoted far too much time to this struggle against the opportunist elements within the Party, that they over-rated their importance. But that is altogether wrong. Opportunism in our midst is like an ulcer in a healthy organism, and must not be tolerated. The Party is the leading detachment of the working class, its advanced fortress, its General Staff. Sceptics, opportunists, capitulators and traitors cannot be tolerated on the directing staff of the working class. If, while it is carrying on a life and death fight against the bourgeoisie, there are capitulators and traitors on its own staff, within its own fortress, the working class will be caught between two fires, from the front and the rear. Clearly, such a struggle can only end in defeat. The easiest way to capture a fortress is from within. To attain victory, the Party of the working class, its directing staff, its advanced fortress, must first be purged of capitulators, deserters, scabs and traitors.

It cannot be regarded as an accident that the Trotskyites, Bukharinites and nationalist deviators who fought Lenin and the Party ended just as the Menshevik and Socialist-Revolutionary parties did, namely, by becoming agents of fascist espionage services, by turning spies, wreckers, assassins, diversionists and traitors to the country. . . .

2.

In January 1956, Nikita Khrushchev appeared before the twentieth party congress in Moscow to denounce the misdeeds of the late Josef Stalin. His speech, probably the most startling political oration of the twentieth century, was intended to be secret; it has never been published in the Soviet Union. But the text promptly found its way into the hands of foreign critics, and was widely publicized; and several years later, at the twenty-second party congress in 1961, Khrushchev came into the open with his denunciation of Stalin.

Why the Soviet leadership thought it necessary to adopt such drastic tactics is still a subject of controversy. Some observers have concluded that the Khrushchev faction might more easily change Stalin's methods of government if it could first repudiate Stalin himself; others think that the new Soviet leaders may have been seeking a long-postponed revenge against their domineering ex-master; still others guess that the episode may have been related to factionalism within the Kremlin or within the world communist movement. There was indeed some evidence that certain high Soviet leaders had vigorously opposed the downgrading of Stalin.

Whatever the true explanation may be, the new orthodoxy about Stalin's role in Soviet history represents an almost total reversal of the old. One of the lengthiest sections of Khrushchev's speech dealt with the Great Purge; it attributed virtually complete responsibility for it to the "sickly suspicious" Stalin. Notably absent from the speech was any reference to the role of the Khrushchev faction during the purge years, even though most of its members were rising rapidly in the Soviet hierarchy at the time.

KHRUSHCHEV: The Crimes of the Stalin Era *

In December 1922, in a letter to the Party Congress, Vladimir Ilyich [Lenin] wrote: "After taking over the position of Secretary General, Comrade Stalin accumulated in his hands immeasurable power and I am not certain whether he will be always able to use this power with the required care."

This letter—a political document of tremendous importance, known in the party history as Lenin's "testament"—was distributed among the delegates to the 20th Party Congress. You have read it and will undoubtedly read it again more than once. You might reflect on Lenin's plain words, in which expression is given to Vladimir Ilyich's anxiety concerning the party, the people, the state, and the future direction of party policy.

Vladimir Ilyich said: "Stalin is excessively rude, and this defect, which can be freely tolerated in our midst and in contacts among us Communists, becomes a defect which cannot be tolerated in one holding the position of the Secretary General. Because of this, I propose that the comrades consider the method by which Stalin would be removed from this position and by which another man would be selected for it, a man who, above all, would differ from Stalin in only one quality, namely, greater tolerance, greater loyalty, greater kindness and more considerate attitude toward the comrades, a less capricious temper, etc. . . ."

When we analyze the practice of Stalin in regard to the direction of the party and of the country, when we pause to consider everything which Stalin perpetrated, we must be convinced that Lenin's fears were justified. The negative characteristics of Stalin, which, in Lenin's time, were only incipient, transformed themselves during the last years into a grave abuse of power by Stalin, which caused untold harm to our party. . . .

Stalin acted not through persuasion, explanation and patient cooperation with people, but by imposing his concepts and demanding absolute submission to his opinion. Whoever opposed this concept or tried to prove his viewpoint and the correctness of his position was doomed to removal from the leading collective and to subsequent moral and physical annihilation. This was especially true during the period following the 17th Party Congress, when many prominent party leaders and rank-and-file party workers, honest and dedicated to the

* From *The Crimes of the Stalin Era: Special Report to the 20th Congress of the Communist Party of the Soviet Union* by Nikita S. Khrushchev. Edited by Boris I. Nicolaevsky. (New York: *The New Leader*, 1956), pp. 9, 12–14, 17, 24–27, 32–34. Reprinted by permission of the editors of *The New Leader*.

cause of Communism, fell victim to Stalin's despotism.

We must affirm that the party had fought a serious fight against the Trotsky-ites, rightists and bourgeois nationalists, and that it disarmed ideologically all the enemies of Leninism. This ideological fight was carried on successfully, as a result of which the party became strengthened and tempered. Here Stalin played a positive role.

The party led a great political-ideological struggle against those in its own ranks who proposed anti-Leninist theses, who represented a political line hostile to the party and to the cause of socialism. This was a stubborn and a difficult fight but a necessary one, because the political line of both the Trotsky-ite-Zinovievite bloc and of the Bukharinites led actually toward the restoration of capitalism and capitulation to the world bourgeoisie. Let us consider for a moment what would have happened if in 1928–1929 the political line of right deviation had prevailed among us, or orientation toward "cotton-dress indus-trialization," or toward the kulak, etc. We would not now have a powerful heavy industry, we would not have the *kolkhozes,* we would find ourselves dis-armed and weak in a capitalist encirclement.

It was for this reason that the party led an inexorable ideological fight and explained to all party members and to the non-party masses the harm and the danger of the anti-Leninist proposals of the Trotskyites and the rightist oppor-tunists. And this great work of explaining the party line bore fruit; both the Trotskyites and the rightist opportunists were politically isolated; the over-whelming party majority supported the Leninist line and the party was able to awaken and organize the working masses to apply the Leninist party line and to build socialism.

Worth noting is the fact that, even during the progress of the furious ideo-logical fight against the Trotskyites, the Zinovievites, the Bukharinites and others, extreme repressive measures were not used against them. The fight was on ideological grounds. But some years later, when socialism in our country was fundamentally constructed, when the exploiting classes were generally liq-uidated, when the Soviet social structure had radically changed, when the social basis for political movements and groups hostile to the party had vio-lently contracted, when the ideological opponents of the party were long since defeated politically—then the repression directed against them began.

It was precisely during this period (1935–1937–1938) that the practice of mass repression through the Government apparatus was born, first against the ene-mies of Leninism—Trotskyites, Zinovievites, Bukharinites, long since politically defeated by the party—and subsequently also against many honest Commu-nists, against those party cadres who had borne the heavy load of the Civil War and the first and most difficult years of industrialization and collectivization, who actively fought against the Trotskyites and the rightists for the Leninist party line.

Stalin originated the concept "enemy of the people." This term automatically rendered it unnecessary that the ideological errors of a man or men engaged in a controversy be proven; this term made possible the usage of the most cruel repression, violating all norms of revolutionary legality, against anyone who in any way disagreed with Stalin, against those who were only suspected of hostile intent, against those who had bad reputations. This concept "enemy of the people" actually eliminated the possibility of any kind of ideological fight or the making of one's views known on this or that issue, even those of a practical character. In the main, and in actuality, the only proof of guilt used, against all norms of current legal science, was the "confession" of the accused himself; and, as subsequent probing proved, "confessions" were acquired through physical pressures against the accused. This led to glaring violations of revolutionary legality and to the fact that many entirely innocent persons, who in the past had defended the party line, became victims.

We must assert that, in regard to those persons who in their time had opposed the party line, there were often no sufficiently serious reasons for their physical annihilation. The formula "enemy of the people" was specifically introduced for the purpose of physically annihilating such individuals.

It is a fact that many persons who were later annihilated as enemies of the party and people had worked with Lenin during his life. Some of these persons had made errors during Lenin's life, but, despite this, Lenin benefited by their work; he corrected them and he did everything possible to retain them in the ranks of the party; he induced them to follow him. . . .

Can it be said that Lenin did not decide to use even the most severe means against enemies of the Revolution when this was actually necessary? No; no one can say this. Vladimir Ilyich demanded uncompromising dealings with the enemies of the Revolution and of the working class and when necessary resorted ruthlessly to such methods. You will recall only V. I. Lenin's fight with the Socialist Revolutionary organizers of the anti-Soviet uprising, with the counterrevolutionary kulaks in 1918 and with others, when Lenin without hesitation used the most extreme methods against the enemies. Lenin used such methods, however, only against actual class enemies and not against those who blunder, who err, and whom it was possible to lead through ideological influence and even retain in the leadership. Lenin used severe methods only in the most necessary cases, when the exploiting classes were still in existence and were vigorously opposing the Revolution, when the struggle for survival was decidedly assuming the sharpest forms, even including a civil war.

Stalin, on the other hand, used extreme methods and mass repressions at a time when the Revolution was already victorious, when the Soviet state was strengthened, when the exploiting classes were already liquidated and socialist relations were rooted solidly in all phases of national economy, when our party was politically consolidated and had strengthened itself both numerically and ideologically.

It is clear that here Stalin showed in a whole series of cases his intolerance, his brutality and his abuse of power. Instead of proving his political correctness and mobilizing the masses, he often chose the path of repression and physical annihilation, not only against actual enemies, but also against individuals who had not committed any crimes against the party and the Soviet Government.

Here we see no wisdom but only a demonstration of the brutal force which had once so alarmed V. I. Lenin. . . .

Lenin taught that the application of revolutionary violence is necessitated by the resistance of the exploiting classes, and this referred to the era when the exploiting classes existed and were powerful. As soon as the nation's political situation had improved, when in January 1920 the Red Army took Rostov and thus won a most important victory over [White commander Anton] Denikin, Lenin instructed [Cheka chief Felix] Dzerzhinsky to stop mass terror and to ablish the death penalty. Lenin justified this important political move of the Soviet state in the following manner in his report at the session of the All-Union Central Executive Committee on February 2, 1920: "We were forced to use terror because of the terror practiced by the Entente, when strong world powers threw their hordes against us, not avoiding any type of conduct. We would not have lasted two days had we not answered these attempts of officers and White Guardists in a merciless fashion; this meant the use of terror, but this was forced upon us by the terrorist methods of the Entente.

"But as soon as we attained a decisive victory, even before the end of the war, immediately after taking Rostov, we gave up the use of the death penalty and thus proved that we intend to execute our own program in the manner that we promised. We say that the application of violence flows out of the decision to smother the exploiters, the big landowners and the capitalists; as soon as this was accomplished we gave up the use of all extraordinary methods. We have proved this in practice."

Stalin deviated from these clear and plain precepts of Lenin. Stalin put the party and the NKVD up to the use of mass terror when the exploiting classes had been liquidated in our country and when there were no serious reasons for the use of extraordinary mass terror.

This terror was actually directed not at the remnants of the defeated exploiting classes but against the honest workers of the party and of the Soviet state; against them were made lying, slanderous and absurd accusations concerning "two-facedness," "espionage," "sabotage," preparation of fictitious "plots," etc. At the February–March Central Committee plenum in 1937 many members actually questioned the rightness of the established course regarding mass repressions under the pretext of combatting "two-facedness."

Comrade Postyshev most ably expressed these doubts. He said:

"I have philosophized that the severe years of fighting have passed. Party members who have lost their backbones have broken down or have joined the camp of the enemy; healthy elements have fought for the party. These were the years of industrialization and collectivization. I never thought it possible that after this severe era had passed Karpov and people like him would find themselves in the camp of the enemy. (Karpov was a worker in the Ukrainian Central Committee whom Postyshev knew well.) And now, according to the testimony, it appears that Karpov was recruited in 1934 by the Trotskyites. I personally do not believe that in 1934 an honest party member who had trod the long road of unrelenting fight against enemies for the party and for socialism would now be in the camp of the enemies. I do not believe it. . . . I cannot imagine how it would be possible to travel with the party during the difficult years and then, in 1934, join the Trotskyites. It is an odd thing. . . ." (Movement in the hall)

Using Stalin's formulation, namely, that the closer we are to socialism the more enemies we will have, and using the resolution of the February–March Central Committee plenum passed on the basis of [NKVD chief] Yezhov's report, the *provocateurs* who had infiltrated the state security organs together with conscienceless careerists began to protect with the party name the mass terror against party cadres, cadres of the Soviet state and the ordinary Soviet citizens. It should suffice to say that the number of arrests based on charges of counterrevolutionary crimes had grown ten times between 1936 and 1937.

It is known that brutal willfulness was practiced against leading party workers. The party statute, approved at the 17th Party Congress, was based on Leninist principles expressed at the 10th Party Congress. It stated that, in order to apply an extreme method such as exclusion from the party against a Central Committee member, against a Central Committee candidate and against a members and all members of the Party Control Commission"; only if two-Committee plenum and to invite to the plenum all Central Committee candidate members and all members of the Party Control Commission"; only if two thirds of the members of such a general assembly of responsible party leaders find it necessary, only then can a Central Committee member or candidate be expelled.

The majority of the Central Committee members and candidates elected at the 17th Congress and arrested in 1937–1938 were expelled from the party illegally through the brutal abuse of the party statute, because the question of their expulsion was never studied at the Central Committee plenum.

Now, when the cases of some of these so-called "spies" and "saboteurs" were examined, it was found that all their cases were fabricated. Confessions of guilt of many arrested and charged with enemy activity were gained with the help of cruel and inhuman torture.

At the same time, Stalin, as we have been informed by members of the Political Bureau of that time, did not show them the statements of many accused political activists when they retracted their confessions before the military tribunal and asked for an objective examination of their cases. There were many such declarations, and Stalin doubtless knew of them.

The Central Committee considers it absolutely necessary to inform the Congress of many such fabricated "cases" against the members of the party's Central Committee elected at the 17th Party Congress. . . .

Many thousands of honest and innocent Communists have died as a result of this monstrous falsification of such "cases," as a result of the fact that all kinds of slanderous "confessions" were accepted, and as a result of the practice of forcing accusations against oneself and others. In the same manner were fabricated the "cases" against eminent party and state workers. . . .

The vicious practice was condoned of having the NKVD prepare lists of persons whose cases were under the jurisdiction of the Military Collegium and whose sentences were prepared in advance. Yezhov would send these lists to Stalin personally for his approval of the proposed punishment. In 1937-1938, 383 such lists containing the names of many thousands of party, Soviet, Komsomol, Army and economic workers were sent to Stalin. He approved these lists.

A large part of these cases are being reviewed now and a great part of them are being voided because they were baseless and falsified. Suffice it to say that from 1954 to the present time the Military Collegium of the Supreme Court has rehabilitated 7,679 persons, many of whom were rehabilitated posthumously.

Mass arrests of party, Soviet, economic and military workers caused tremendous harm to our country and to the cause of socialist advancement.

Mass repressions had a negative influence on the moral-political condition of the party, created a situation of uncertainty, contributed to the spreading of unhealthy suspicion, and sowed distrust among Communists. All sorts of slanderers and careerists were active. . . .

Only because our party has at its disposal such great moral-political strength was it possible for it to survive the difficult events in 1937-1938 and to educate new cadres. There is, however, no doubt that our march forward toward socialism and toward the preparation of the country's defense would have been much more successful were it not for the tremendous loss in the cadres suffered as a result of the baseless and false mass repressions in 1937-1938.

We are justly accusing Yezhov for the degenerate practices of 1937. But we have to answer these questions:

Could Yezhov have arrested Kossior, for instance, without the knowledge of Stalin? Was there an exchange of opinions or a Political Bureau decision concerning this?

No, there was not, as there was none regarding other cases of this type.

Could Yezhov have decided such important matters as the fate of such eminent party figures?

No, it would be a display of naiveté to consider this the work of Yezhov alone. It is clear that these matters were decided by Stalin, and that without his orders and his sanction Yezhov could not have done this. . . .

Facts prove that many abuses were made on Stalin's orders without reckoning with any norms of party and Soviet legality. Stalin was a very distrustful man, sickly suspicious; we know this from our work with him. He could look at a man and say: "Why are your eyes so shifty today?" or "Why are you turning so much today and avoiding to look me directly in the eyes?" The sickly suspicion created in him a general distrust even toward eminent party workers whom he had known for years. Everywhere and in everything he saw "enemies," "two-facers" and "spies." Possessing unlimited power, he indulged in great willfulness and choked a person morally and physically. A situation was created where one could not express one's own will.

When Stalin said that one or another should be arrested, it was necessary to accept on faith that he was an "enemy of the people." Meanwhile, Beria's gang, which ran the organs of state security, outdid itself in proving the guilt of the arrested and the truth of materials which it falsified. And what proofs were offered? The confessions of the arrested, and the investigative judges accepted these "confessions." And how is it possible that a person confesses to crimes which he has not committed? Only in one way—because of application of physical methods of pressuring him, tortures, bringing him to a state of unconsciousness, deprivation of his judgment, taking away of his human dignity. In this manner were "confessions" acquired. . . .

3.

The Polish-born ex-Communist Isaac Deutscher, writing prior to the revelations of Nikita Khrushchev, was forced to reconstruct the story of the Great Purge in rather impressionistic fashion. Although an anti-Stalinist, Deutscher offers a hypothesis that might almost be called sympathetic to Stalin. He links the purge to the impending threat of war; and he finds that Stalin's destructive fury was counterbalanced by important constructive achievements. Indeed, in his conclusion to the book Deutscher describes Stalin as the leader of ". . . a tragic, self-contradictory but creative revolution," and adds that ". . . the better part of Stalin's work is as certain to outlast Stalin himself as the better parts of the work of Cromwell and Napoleon have outlasted them."

DEUTSCHER: Stalin: A Political Biography *

But why did Stalin need the abominable spectacle? It has been suggested that he sent the men of the old guard to their death as scapegoats for his economic failures. There is a grain of truth in this, but not more. For one thing, there was a very marked improvement in the economic condition of the country in the years of the trials. He certainly had no need for so many scapegoats; and, if he had needed them, penal servitude would have been enough, as was the case in the earlier trials of the so-called Industrial Party and the Mensheviks. Some of the people convicted in those earlier trials re-emerged in the forties as celebrated personalities and bearers of high honours (e.g. Professor Ramsin). Stalin's real and much wider motive was to destroy the men who represented the potentiality of alternative government, perhaps not of one but of several alternative governments. It is, naturally enough, impossible to quote chapter and verse from Stalin's own speeches and writings for this. It is in the whole preceding story, in the setting of the trials and in their consequences, that the motivation for his deeds is found. From the outset he had identified any attempt at creating an alternative government, and even the thought of this, with counter-revolution. The destruction of all political centres from which such an attempt might, in certain circumstances, have emanated, was the direct and undeniable consequence of the trials.

* Isaac Deutscher, *Stalin: A Political Biography* (New York: Oxford University Press, 1949), pp. 375–78, 382–84. Copyright 1949 by Oxford University Press, Inc., and reprinted by permission.

The question that must now be answered is why he set out to reach this objective in 1936. Considerations of domestic policy can hardly explain his timing. Widespread though popular dissatisfaction may have been, it was too amorphous to constitute any immediate threat to his position. The opposition was pulverized, downtrodden, incapable of action. Only some sudden shock, some convulsive disorder involving the whole machine of power, might have enabled it to rally its scattered and disheartened troops. A danger of that kind was just then taking shape; and it threatened from abroad. The first of the great trials, that of Zinoviev and Kamenev, took place a few months after Hitler's army had marched into the Rhineland; the last, that of Bukharin and Rykov, ended to the accompaniment of the trumpets that announced the Nazi occupation of Austria. German imperialism was rearming and testing its strength. . . . [Stalin] had no illusions that war could be altogether avoided; and he pondered the alternative courses—agreement with Hitler or war against him—that were open to him. In 1936 the chances of agreement looked very slender indeed. Western appeasement filled Stalin with forebodings. He suspected that the west was not only acquiescing in the revival of German militarism but instigating it against Russia.

The prospect of a single-handed fight between Russia and Germany seemed grim. In the First World War the strength of the German military machine, involved as it was then in a struggle on two fronts, sufficed to deal a shattering blow to Russia and to sap Tsardom. The shadow of the last Tsar must have more than once appeared before Stalin, as he viewed Hitler's preliminaries to war. One might sketch an imaginary conversation between the living man and the ghost. "Your end is approaching," the phantom whispers; "exploiting the chaos of war, you destroyed my throne. Now the chaos of another war is going to engulf you." "You dethroned monarchs, you really learn nothing," the living man replies. "Surely you were defeated not by the war itself, but by the Bolshevik party. To be sure, we used the conditions created by war to our advantage, but. . . ." "Are you quite sure," the ghost interrupts, "that no opposition is going to use a new war for its advantage? Remember the terrible turmoil in Petersburg when the news came that the Germans had captured Riga? What if the Germans appear in Riga again, or in Kiev, in the Caucasus or at the gates of Moscow?" "I am telling you, you had the formidable Bolshevik party against you, while I have exiled Trotsky and crushed all my other opponents." The phantom roars with laughter: "In 1914–17 did not I keep you in Siberia and were not Lenin and Trotsky in exile? . . ."

In the supreme crisis of war, the leaders of the opposition, if they had been alive, might indeed have been driven to action by a conviction, right or wrong, that Stalin's conduct of the war was incompetent and ruinous. At an earlier stage they might have been opposed to his deal with Hitler. Did not Trotsky foreshadow this sort of action against Stalin in his famous "Clemenceau thesis?" Let us imagine for a moment that the leaders of the opposition lived to witness the terrible defeats of the Red Army in 1941 and 1942, to see Hitler at the gates of Moscow, millions of Russian soldiers in German captivity, a dangerous crisis in the morale of the people such as had developed by the autumn of 1941, when the whole future of the Soviets hung by a thread and Stalin's moral authority was at its nadir. It is possible that they would have then attempted to overthrow Stalin. Stalin was determined not to allow things to come to this.

His charges against them were, of course, shameless inventions. But they were based on a perverted "psychological truth," on a grotesquely brutalized and distorting anticipation of possible developments. His reasoning probably developed along the following lines: they may want to overthrow me in a crisis —I shall charge them with having already made the attempt. They certainly believe themselves to be better fitted for the conduct of war, which is absurd. A change of government may weaken Russia's fighting capacity; and if they succeed, they may be compelled to sign a truce with Hitler, and perhaps even agree to a cession of territory as we once did at Brest Litovsk. I shall accuse them of having entered already into a treacherous alliance with Germany (and Japan) and ceded Soviet territory to those states.

No milder pretext for the slaughter of the old guard would have sufficed. Had they been executed merely as men opposed to Stalin or even as conspirators who had tried to remove him from power, many might still have regarded them as martyrs for a good cause. They had to die as traitors, as perpetrators of crimes beyond the reach of reason, as leaders of a monstrous fifth column. Only then could Stalin be sure that their execution would provoke no dangerous revulsion; and that, on the contrary, he himself would be looked upon, especially by the young and uninformed generation, as the saviour of the country. It is not necessary to assume that he acted from sheer cruelty or lust for power. He may be given the dubious credit of the sincere conviction that what he did served the interests of the revolution and that he alone interpreted those interests aright. . . .

While the guillotine was in motion, it seemed to many that in the end Stalin, too, would be caught by it. He was destroying the old guard; yet he himself had been one of them. On whom could he rely for support once that prop of the Bolshevik regime was gone? "Stalin is nearing the completion of his tragic mission," Trotsky wrote in September 1937; "the more it seems to him that he needs nobody any longer, the nearer is the hour when he himself will be needed by nobody. If the bureaucracy succeeds in changing the forms of property and if a new possessing class crystallizes from its ranks, the latter will find new leaders without a revolutionary past and more educated ones. Stalin will hardly hear a word of thanks for the job he has accomplished. The open counter-revolution will settle accounts with him, very probably charging him with Trotskyism." A few months later Trotsky made a different forecast: "Stalin is preparing his 'coronation' on the ruins of the revolution and the corpses of revolutionaries. Stalin's Bonapartist coronation will coincide with his political death for the labour movement." None of these prophecies came true; and, as to Stalin's "coronation," it took place before and not after the trials. The truly astonishing aspect of the purges, astonishing in view of their scope and vehemence, is how little they changed the surface of Soviet Russia, how little the structure of the regime seemed, after all, to be affected by the heavy axe that had cut into it. After as before the trials, Russian society seemed to be on the one hand feverishly intent over its economic pursuits and on the other languishing in a condition of moral and political torpor. Before and after, Stalin was hailed as the father of the peoples, and the beloved leader. . . .

The deeper reason for Stalin's triumph lay in that, unlike Robespierre, he offered his nation a positive and new programme of social organization which, though it spelt privation and suffering to many, also created undreamt-of openings for many others. These latter had a vested interest in his rule. This, in the last resort, explains why, after the slaughter of the old guard, Stalin did not find himself left in a vacuum. For nearly three years his iron broom had furiously swept every office in state and party. Not more than a handful of that mass of administrators who had held office in 1936 could be found there in 1938. The purges created numberless vacancies in every field of public activity. In the five years from 1933 to 1938 about a million administrators, technicians, economists, and men of other professions had graduated from the high schools, an enormous number for a country whose educated classes had previously formed a very thin layer of society. This was the new intelligentsia whose ranks filled the purged and emptied offices. Its members, brought up in the Stalinist cult from childhood, were either hostile to the men of the old guard or indifferent to their fate. They threw themselves into their work with a zeal and enthusiasm undimmed by recent events. Their qualifications, it is true, were very modest. They had almost no practical experience. The nation had still to pay an exorbitant price for the practical apprenticeship of its civil servants, industrial managers, and military commanders; and that apprenticeship was to last well into the Second World War. . . .

4.

Professor Merle Fainsod, who has taught political science at Harvard for the past thirty years, is the author of a classic analysis of *How Russia Is Ruled*. After sketching the chain of events of the Great Purge, Mr. Fainsod seeks to provide a theoretical base for the episode, and finds it in "the manipulation of terror as a system of power." He elucidates both the advantages and the dangers of such a control device, which he describes as essential to any totalitarian dictator.

FAINSOD: How Russia Is Ruled *

The crescendo of the Great Purge was reached in the . . . period which extended from late September 1937, when Yezhov was appointed head of the NKVD, until the end of July 1938, when Lavrenti Beria was designated as

* From Merle Fainsod, *How Russia Is Ruled* (Cambridge: Harvard University Press, 1953), pp. 371–74, 375–76. Copyright 1953 by the President and Fellows of Harvard College. Reprinted by permission of the Harvard University Press.

Yezhov's deputy and eventual successor. The announcement of Yezhov's removal did not come until December, but meanwhile Beria assumed *de facto* command of the NKVD organization, and early in 1939 Yezhov disappeared and was probably liquidated.

The period of the Yezhovshchina [Soviet term for the Yezhov purge era] involved a reign of terror without parallel in Soviet history. Among those arrested, imprisoned, and executed were a substantial proportion of the leading figures in the Party and governmental hierarchy. The Bolshevik Old Guard was destroyed. The roll of Yezhov's victims included not only former oppositionists but many of the most stalwart supporters of Stalin in his protracted struggle with the opposition. No sphere of Soviet life, however lofty, was left untouched. Among the purged Stalinists were three former members of the Politburo . . . and three candidate members. . . . An overwhelming majority of the members and candidates of the Party Central Committee disappeared. The senior officer corps of the armed forces suffered severely. According to one sober account, "two of five marshals of the Soviet Union escaped arrest, two of fifteen army commanders, twenty-eight of fifty-eight corps commanders, eighty-five of a hundred and ninety-five divisional commanders, and a hundred and ninety-five of four hundred and six regimental commanders." The havoc wrought by the purge among naval commanding personnel was equally great. The removal of Yagoda from the NKVD was accompanied by the arrest of his leading collaborators. . . . The Commissariat of Foreign Affairs and the diplomatic service were hard hit. Among the Old Guard, only Litvinov, Maisky, Troyanovsky, and a few lesser lights survived. Almost every commissariat was deeply affected.

The purge swept out in ever-widening circles and resulted in wholesale removals and arrests of leading officials in the union republics, secretaries of the Party, Komsomol, and trade-union apparatus, heads of industrial trusts and enterprises, Comintern functionaries and foreign Communists, and leading writers, scholars, engineers and scientists. The arrest of an important figure was followed by the seizure of the entourage which surrounded him. The apprehension of members of the entourage led to the imprisonment of their friends and acquaintances. The endless chain of involvements and associations threatened to encompass entire strata of Soviet society. Fear of arrest, exhortations to vigilance, and perverted ambition unleashed new floods of denunciations, which generated their own avalanche of cumulative interrogations and detentions. Whole categories of Soviet citizens found themselves singled out for arrest because of their "objective characteristics." Old Bolsheviks, Red Partisans, foreign Communists of German, Austrian, and Polish extraction, Soviet citizens who had been abroad or had relations with foreign countries or foreigners, and "repressed elements" were automatically caught up in the NKVD web of wholesale imprisonment. The arrests mounted into the millions; the testimony of the survivors is unanimous regarding crowded prison cells and teeming forced labor camps. Most of the prisoners were utterly bewildered by the fate which had befallen them. The vast resources of the NKVD were concentrated on one objective—to document the existence of a huge conspiracy to undermine Soviet power. The extraction of real confessions to imaginary crimes became a major industry. Under the zealous and ruthless ministrations of NKVD examiners, millions of innocents were transformed into traitors, terrorists, and enemies of the people.

How explain the Yezhovshchina? What motives impelled Stalin to organize a blood bath of such frightening proportions? In the absence of revealing testimony from the source, one can only venture hypotheses. Stalin's desire to consolidate his own personal power appears to have been a driving force. The slaughter of the Bolshevik Old Guard may be viewed partly as a drastic reprisal for past insubordination; it was more probably intended as a preventive measure to end once and for all any possibility of resistance or challenge from this direction. The extension of the purge to the Stalinist stalwarts in the Party and governmental apparatus is much more difficult to fathom. It is possible that many fell victim to the system of denunciations in the course of which their loyalty to Stalin was put in question, that a number were still involved in official or personal relationships with former oppositionists, that some were liquidated because they displayed traces of independence in their dealings with the Supreme Leader, that others were merely suspected of harboring aspirations toward personal power, and that still others simply furnished convenient scapegoats to demonstrate the existence of a conspiracy that reached into the highest circles.

Implicit in any understanding of the Yezhovshchina is a theory of the role of terror in Stalin's formula of government. The consolidation of personal rule in a totalitarian system depends on the constant elimination of all actual or potential competitors for supreme power. The insecurity of the masses must be supplemented by the insecurity of the governing elite who surround the Supreme Dictator. The too strongly entrenched official with an independent base of power is by definition a threat to the dictator's total sway. The individuals or groups who go uncontrolled and undirected are regarded as fertile soil for the growth of conspiratorial intrigue. The function of terror thus assumes a two-fold aspect. As prophylactic and preventive, it is designed to nip any possible resistance or opposition in the bud. As an instrument for the reinforcement of the personal power of the dictator, it is directed toward ensuring perpetual circulation in the ranks of officeholders in order to forestall the crystallization of autonomous islands of countervailing force.

The manipulation of terror as a system of power is a delicate art. A dictator in command of modern armaments and a secret police can transform his subjects into robots and automatons, but if he succeeds too well, he runs the risk of destroying the sources of creative initiative on which the survival of his own regime depends. When terror runs rampant, as it did at the height of the Yezhovshchina, unintended consequences follow. Fear becomes contagious and paralyzing. Officials at all levels seek to shirk responsibility. The endless belt of irresponsible denunciations begins to destroy the nation's treasury of needed skills. The terror apparatus grows on the stuff on which it feeds and magnifies in importance until it overshadows and depresses all the constructive enterprises of the state. The dictator finds himself caught up in a whirlwind of his own making which threatens to break completely out of control.

As the fury of the Yezhovshchina mounted, Stalin and his intimates finally became alarmed. Evidence accumulated that the purge was overreaching itself and that much talent sorely needed by the regime was being irretrievably lost. The first signal of a change of policy was given in a resolution of the January 1938 plenum of the Party Central Committee entitled "Concerning the Mistakes of Party Organizations in Excluding Communists from the Party, Concerning Formal-Bureaucratic Attitudes toward the Appeals of Excluding Members of the VKP(b), and Concerning Measures to Eliminate these Deficiencies." The resolution identified a new culprit, the Communist-careerists, who sought to make capital out of the purge by securing promotions through provocatory denunciations of their superiors. It was these careerists, the resolution charged, who were primarily responsible for sowing suspicion and insecurity within Party ranks and for decimating the Party cadres. The resolution concluded with a ten-point program designed to put an end to mass expulsions and to secure the rehabilitation of former members who had been expelled as the result of slanders. The immediate effect of this resolution was to produce a new purge of so-called Communist-careerists. At the same time, the Party press began to carry stories of the reinstatements of honest Communists who had been the unfortunate victims of unjustified denunciations. . . .

The full circle of the Great Purge offers a remarkable case study in the use of terror. Arrests ran into the millions. The gruesome and harrowing experiences of the victims blackened the face of Stalinist Russia. The havoc wrought in leading circles appeared irreparable. Yet despite the damage and the hatred engendered, the dynamic momentum of the industrialization program was maintained. The arrests of responsible technicians and officials frequently produced serious setbacks in production, but as their replacements acquired experience, order was restored, and production began to climb again. While many functionaries reacted to the purge by shunning all responsibility, others responded to the fear of arrest by working as they had never worked before. Terror functioned as prod as well as brake. The acceleration in the circulation of the elite brought a new generation of Soviet-trained intelligentsia into positions of responsibility, and Stalin anchored his power on their support. Meanwhile, Stalin emerged from the purge with his own position consolidated. The major purpose of decapitating the Bolshevik Old Guard had been accomplished. Every rival for supreme power who was visible on the horizon had been eliminated. The Party and the nation were thoroughly intimidated. The purgers had been purged and the scapegoats identified. The ancient formula of protecting the infallibility of the Leader by punishing subordinates for their excessive ardor was impressively resurrected.

The moving equilibrium on which Stalin balanced his power structure entered a new phase. The temporary lifting of the blanket of fear was designed to restore morale, to revive hope and initiative, and to reforge the bonds between regime and people which the purge had dangerously strained. But the mitigation of the terror involved no abandonment of the system. For the totalitarian dictator, terror is an indispensable necessity, and its invocation is a guarantee that no organized force will rise to challenge his undisputed rule. The Stalinist refinement on the use of terror as a system of power involved oscillating phases of pressure and relaxation which varied with the dictator's conception of the dangers which he confronted. The essence of control was never abandoned. At the same time, when the pressure became too great, a mirage of security and stability was held out in order to enlist the energy and devotion of the oncoming generations. It is a system which devours many of its servants, but as in games of chance, since the winners and survivors are highly rewarded and cannot be identified in advance, the ambitions of the players are periodically renewed, and the regime bases its strength on their sacrifices. . . .

5.

In an earlier chapter of this book, Leonard Schapiro of the University of London argued that Lenin was chiefly responsible for the emergence of Soviet totalitarianism. In his most recent book, Mr. Schapiro suggests that Stalin, like Lenin, faced a possible choice between moderation and increased repression. But he contends that the choice was less real in Stalin's case, and that the Great Purge developed, by "a certain inexorable logic," out of what had gone before.

SCHAPIRO: The Communist Party of the Soviet Union *

From Stalin's point of view the trials served an important purpose. By focussing attention on an enemy outside—Trotsky, in alliance with Germany and Japan— they helped to divert attention from discontent at home. They provided an explanation for the economic hardships and industrial shortcomings. Above all, they painted a picture, in colours sufficiently lurid for the simplest mind to understand, in which any opposition to Stalin was clearly identified with treason. Much of the credit for this achievement must go to [State Prosecutor] Vyshinsky. For he succeeded in keeping out of the trial any suggestion which any defendant tried to make that his opposition had been in any way ideological, or that there was any mass support behind the opposition. The defendants were portrayed as traitors and common criminals, not as ideological opponents.

The only disadvantage which Stalin faced as the result of the trials was the risk of antagonizing Western opinion, especially socialist opinion, at a time when he was intent upon cementing a "popular front" of all left-wing parties

* From Leonard Schapiro, *The Communist Party of the Soviet Union* (New York: Random House, 1960), pp. 427-31. © Copyright 1960 by Leonard Schapiro. Reprinted by permission of Random House, Inc. New York.

as an insurance against the possibility of an attack by Germany. But the risk was worth taking, since he could be sure of two powerful allies; ignorance of Soviet conditions and hatred of Hitler, which readily led even some non-communists in the West to treat the trials as genuine. Even so sober an observer of the Russian scene as Sir Bernard Pares could regard the wrecking activities as "proved up to the hilt," and the rest of the evidence as "convincing. . . ."

The three show trials were only the most dramatic aspect of the greater process of Stalin's two-year assault on the party and on the population at large—the *Ezhovshchina* as the Russians called it, after its main executant, Ezhov [Yezhov]. The question must be posed why Stalin found it necessary to inflict this blow. Explanations which seek the answer in parallels with the more degenerate Roman emperors and in Stalin's mental derangement do not convince—except to the extent that any man who is ready to sacrifice millions of lives in order to execute his policy should be regarded as insane. Stalin was certainly of a vengeful nature, and vain to the point of unbalance. But the assault on the party showed too much careful preparation, planning and system for madness to be the explanation. It is easy, perhaps tempting, to blame the cruelties and injustices of those years upon the aberrations of one man—this, for example, was to be the explanation put forward by the party leaders in 1956, when Stalin's death was eventually followed by a reassessment of his reputation. But it is an explanation which neither makes allowance for the circumstances in which that man found himself nor illuminates the reasons which enabled one man to impose his will on so many millions. Viewed from Stalin's point of view, there was a certain inexorable logic which led to the holocausts of the late 30's.

It was not ambition alone which had led Stalin in the 20's to amass his great power over the party. The survival in power of the party was at stake during those years, and few communists ever doubted that for the party to retain its monopoly of power was the first and foremost aim of all policy. But this survival required centralized discipline inside the party, and Stalin was probably the only man who could ensure it. The backing which he received during his conflict with the left opposition was primarily due to the realization of this fact. Even Trotsky himself wavered in his opposition for fear of upsetting the whole structure of party rule. But the control over the party which Stalin built up in the 20's was only a prelude to the social revolution which he effected in the early 30's. Leaving aside the question whether the timing of this revolution was wise or the methods used for effecting it necessary, there is no doubt that in carrying it through Stalin had a considerable measure of support from the party. But since this revolution meant an all-out war by the communist party against the majority of the population, the peasants, it was unavoidable that Stalin's personal power over the party should have increased in the process: the reasons which had helped his power to grow in the 20's were increased an hundredfold when the campaign against the peasants began.

By 1934 Stalin's revolution had been successfully accomplished, at any rate to the extent that the point of no return had been reached. The collectivization of agriculture was a fact, and industrial development was at last beginning to show signs of an upward trend. Two courses were now open to the party. One was peace, a halt to purges, a relaxation of discipline, a resting upon the laurels of success. Something of this kind may have inspired those (if there were such) who looked to Kirov as the embodiment of a new outlook. To Stalin such a course may well have appeared disastrous. He may have feared that the end of the corybantic drive which had so far carried the party to victory would bring a dangerous relaxation which would also spell the end of the party's monopoly of rule. He may also, and rightly, have foreseen that in conditions of peace within the party there would be no room for him. For it is seldom that the man who has ruled by terror can himself survive when once that terror comes to an end. Too many passions and hatreds have been aroused, too many voices are raised calling for vengeance for past wrongs. The Riutin programme in 1932, if accounts of it are authentic, placed the removal of Stalin in the fore-front of its demands—a fact which Stalin is not likely to have forgotten in 1936. Thus Stalin was led to choose the second course, terror. But terror is use-less, indeed dangerous to those who apply it, if it stops halfway and does not render harmless all who might, if left alive or at liberty, harbour thoughts of revenge. With the thoroughness which always characterized him Stalin did not stop half-way: he carried out a complete renovation of the party by the elimi-nation of the generation which had made the revolution and won the civil war, and the raising up of new men who owed everything to him. Thus, Stalin's revolution in agriculture and industry and his assault on the party which con-summated this revolution must be seen as integrated parts of one and the same process.

The question whether Stalin's achievement in transforming the country out-weighs the loss and suffering he inflicted upon it is meaningless: it depends in turn on another question, to which no answer is possible, whether the same, or better, results might not have been achieved by different men with different methods. But for Stalin his success and his personal despotism were one and the same, and it was to the consolidation of this personal despotism that the terror made an essential contribution. Its main effects were three. It was first of all prophylactic, since it eliminated all who might conceivably be expected to rival or oppose him. It was secondly constructive, since it restocked the entire elite of the country with men who owed everything to Stalin and who knew that their continued survival depended on conformity to his wishes. Third, and perhaps most important, both inside the ranks of the party and outside them, it broke up, effectively and for a long time to come, all possibility of cohesion or solidarity. For the purge of the party was accompanied by a much more exten-sive terror against all important sections of society. No one, in any walk of life, who had for some time past become entrenched in a position of authority and had surrounded himself with compliant subordinates or congenial colleagues remained unscathed. In the wave of panic, denunciation, hypocrisy and intrigue which was unleashed, no one could trust his fellow or feel secure in the pro-tection of any institution or individual on whom he had hitherto relied. The

"atomization" of society, which some have seen as the most characteristic feature
of totalitarian rule, was completed in the years of the terror. . . .

6.

One of the techniques of totalitarian rule, according to some authorities, is
a process of alternation between intense pressure (or even terror) and relaxation. Too much terror may produce a kind of hopeless apathy; too much
relaxation may lead to stabilization and crystallization, permitting some
privileged groups to dig themselves in and thus to limit the authority of the
power elite. One version of this general thesis is advanced by Zbigniew
Brzezinski, a Polish-born and Canadian-educated political scientist who has
taught since 1955 at Harvard. Mr. Brzezinski explains, in this context, the
need for a Soviet purge in the 1930's and the reasons why it got out of hand;
and he contends that totalitarian systems cannot endure without a "permanent
purge."

BRZEZINSKI: The Permanent Purge *

Between the years 1936 and 1938 the Soviet Union was subjected to terror and
purges on a scale unprecedented in modern history. Terror, applied on a vast
scope and embracing the entire society paralleled and supplemented the purges,
which themselves were collecting their toll in the Party and in the state administration. Indeed, at the height of this massive operation, the all-pervading
terror and the accentuated purge merged into one gigantic operation in which
to be purged meant to be subjected to terroristic procedures and to be terrorized
meant for many to live in the dread of the purge.

The new blood bath followed immediately after the purge of 1933–1935
(officially declared over by the decree of the Central Committee of the Party
on December 25, 1935), which was both a prelude to and an integral part of
what was to come. . . .

The need for continued purging of Party members, as well as of individuals
outside the Party, grew also out of the growing stability of the regime itself.
In almost all aspects of Soviet life efforts were being directed towards the attainment of two objectives; the stabilization of the system, and greater efficiency in
the controls exercised over it by the government. In education the so-called
progressive methods, stressing absence of discipline and freedom of expression,
were replaced by more traditional pedagogical techniques, emphasizing obedience and authority. The school system was no longer to train individuals capable
of handling themselves once the state "withers away," but to mass-produce
citizens able and willing to submit and adjust themselves to the state, which
controlled their entire existence. The existing limitations on scientific discussions
were further tightened, and strict adherence to the philosophical interpretations

* From Zbigniew K. Brzezinski, *The Permanent Purge: Politics in Soviet Totalitarianism* (Cambridge: Harvard Universty Press, 1956), pp. 65–68, 168–70. Copyrght 1956 by the President and
Fellows of Harvard College. Reprinted by permission of the Harvard University Press.

of the system was enjoined. In a characteristic development, the view that the individual citizen is responsible for his actions and behavior replaced the former deterministic views with respect to the role of the environment on the development of individual personality. The individual thus became personally accountable for his inability to adjust to the totalitarian pattern, and responsibility for maladjustment could be laid squarely on the shoulders of the person directly concerned.

In almost all aspects of Soviet life, the increasing political stability of the regime and the gradual re-emergence of more traditional social patterns (admittedly closely controlled by the regime) demanded the replacement of the old Bolsheviks, as well as the earlier products of the Bolshevik education, by the "new Soviet man." Without this, echoes of the earlier ideological conflicts would continue to linger among the lower echelons, and the "monolithic" unity of the system would not be attained. This situation was as true of the Party as of industry, of the army as of the state functionaries. The revolution, having changed its demeanor, now needed not revolutionaries but disciplined workers, willing and determined to strive for the goals of the state and not for its withering away. The old revolutionaries were to be replaced by rulers; the theorists and visionaries by administrators and bureaucrats. . . .

The regime was now in a somewhat paradoxical position. Its power was apparently secure. The first stage of its program for the reshaping of Soviet society had been successfully concluded with the completion of the collectivization and the first Five Year Plan. In brief, the initial period of revolution and transition was slowly being replaced by internal stability. Similar trends were visible on the international plane—the policy of revolution was, at least officially, abandoned, and collective security and cooperation against the Fascist danger became the standard motifs of Soviet foreign policy pronunciamentos. But the regime could not yet permit this stability to develop into inactivity, into a complacent satisfaction with the present. The totalitarian nature of the system demanded further goals, further gigantic operations, further social and economic plans. And analogous drives had also to be maintained on the political plane, through political means, to insure the revival of revolutionary fervor and to prevent the degeneration of the Party and the state. . . .

Totalitarianism needs the purge. Disloyal and potentially deviant individuals or groups must be unmasked and their followers liquidated. The tensions, the conflicts, and the struggles within the totalitarian system must somehow be released or absorbed lest they erupt into disintegrating violence. The problems of promotion and circulation of the elite must be solved within the monolithic framework of a system which eliminates freedom of choice and free competition. Corrupt and careerist elements must be weeded out periodically in order to maintain revolutionary fervor. The purposes of the purge are accordingly many and varied, and the need for it ever present. The purge thus becomes permanent. . . .

At one time in recent Soviet history the purge did cease to be a mere process of government and instrument of power consolidation to become a mass phenomenon, threatening the unity of the Soviet state. The mass purges of the Yezhov period, although admittedly initiated by the regime for the express purpose of eliminating considerable numbers of people, developed a forward motion of their own and tended to involve indiscriminately all the segments of the Soviet population. The *Yezhovshchina* thus indicated once again that a rationally conceived operation of liquidation can easily become irrational when operating within a framework which has very few restraints on political power. In such a system all sorts of aberrations and abuses allow authority-hungry and ruthless individuals to come to the fore and exploit the situation to their advantage. This generic weakness of the system was fully revealed during the Great Purge.

Until then Soviet leaders had been extremely careful to balance the system's coercive aspects with simultaneous concessions. For example, the violence of the collectivization was balanced by the opening of Party ranks to thousands of new members, hitherto kept out. The screening of the Party during the Kirov era was accompanied by economic concessions to the consumers and farmers. A similar balance was effected during the twenties, although the more relaxed nature of the system then made it less necessary. The mass purge of the late thirties, however, threatened this delicate "golden mean" and tended to deprive the regime of all its sources of support, leaving it dependent almost entirely on its police apparatus. The leadership of the Communist Party, however, . . . succeeded in overcoming this growing danger; and the mass purge reverted to the normal process of periodic accentuations.

The need for the purge will not diminish with the growing stability of the totalitarian regime. Instability is not its primary cause. Measures to eliminate stagnation and corruption will always be needed. Channels for drawing new members into the system will have to be kept open. The problem of succession, for instance, will remain a source of constant friction; and its solution, either before or after a dictator's demise, is bound to change the alignments within the power structure. It may be assumed that such struggles will result in purges of increased intensity.

X.

THE SECOND APPEASEMENT ERA: MUNICH

The Munich agreement has given the word "appeasement" a new and disagreeable meaning. No longer is "soothing or pacifying" an adequate definition; appeasement now implies moral inadequacy and a lack of determination to defend one's rights against aggression. Thus Munich has "come to stand in the English language as a symbol for national humiliation and betrayal," [1] and today many people find it hard to realize that there are still those who strongly defend the actions of the western powers in their dealings with Hitler in 1938, and that the conclusion of the Munich pact was exceedingly popular at the time, even with some of those who, today, would be the first to emphasize the horror of anything approaching "appeasement."

The easiest defense of Munich is the one which avoids any defense of the principle of appeasement itself: Neville Chamberlain and Daladier had no choice but to do as they did; the pact was the best that could have been gotten under the circumstances, and, since the West, especially Britain, was in no position to fight in 1938, "the criticism directed against Munich could have been directed with more accuracy against Britain's tardiness in rearming rather than against the pact itself." [2] This is essentially the argument of a prominent British Tory in his recent biography of Chamberlain, which also emphasizes that, psychologically as well as militarily, the British were unprepared for war in 1938 and that Chamberlain's policy reflected the desires of his people. [3] This theme, of Chamberlain as the friend of the peace-loving, "little" man, is a common one: ". . . was it not to his credit that he tried to save the simple people from the catastrophe of war and the devastating effects of an immediate invasion?" [4] It is around these and similar points that most of the dispute concentrates today: how strong were the Czech defenses; how well would

[1] P. A. Reynolds, *British Foreign Policy in the Inter-War Years* (London: Longmans, Green, 1954), p. 149.

[2] John F. Kennedy, *Why England Slept* (Garden City: Doubleday, 1962), p. 160. See also Lord Strang, *Britain in World Affairs* (London: Faber & Faber and André Deutsch, 1961), pp. 320–25. For a detailed survey of Munich, one should consult J. W. Wheeler-Bennett, *Munich: Prologue to Tragedy* (New York: Duell, Sloan and Pierce, 1948).

[3] Iain Macleod, *Neville Chamberlain* (London: Frederick Muller, 1961), Chapter 15.

[4] Viscount Templewood, *Nine Troubled Years* (London: Collins, 1954), p. 323.

the Czech army, supported by the Skoda armaments works but weakened by the acrimony between Czechs and Slovaks, have fought? Could Britain and France have furnished any effective aid if Czechoslovakia had been attacked in 1938? Did not the British gain more than the Germans from the year's delay in the outbreak of war, since during that post-Munich year their rearmament made much progress, and the R.A.F. was equipped with the Hurricanes and the Spitfires that won the Battle of Britain? If that was so, does it explain why Hitler was supposedly in such a vile mood at Munich, feeling cheated out of a war he badly wanted?[5] Or was it the Germans, rather, who gained most by the postponement, as they managed in that year to eliminate or isolate the eastern European allies of France? Had war come at the time of Munich, would the German armies have been able to reach the Channel Coast and to secure the bases from which to threaten Britain with invasion? Had there been a chance of a coup by the German military against the Nazi regime in 1938—a coup which was thwarted by Hitler's success at Munich? And what of the psychological consequences of Munich? Surely the British, simple and sophisticated alike, were a more united and determined people in 1939 than in 1938, with the Commonwealth behind them, and with Hitler's determination to dominate all Europe, German and non-German alike, clearly established for the first time by his seizure of Prague? How did the year's delay affect the morale of the French and the fighting capability of the French army?

However, many of the more interesting questions, which open the way to more profitable speculation, take a broader view. Was Munich a great turning point in European history, when the West voluntarily surrendered influence over eastern Europe—a surrender not reversed, but reconfirmed, by the second world war?[6] Or, might it not be argued that Chamberlain and Daladier were not "taken in" by Hitler, but were rather masters of the modern art of psychological warfare; that they forced Hitler to conduct his future aggressions over the shambles of his pledged word, given in a solemn pact—a pact which, unlike Versailles, was no *diktat,* and which, unlike Locarno, bore his own signature? Perhaps Chamberlain, far from being a simple, trusting businessman, nothing but a good Lord Mayor for Birmingham in a lean year, was playing a supremely cunning game, and was attempting to do what so many have since maintained should have been done—that is, turn Germany to the east, where it would become involved in a war with the Soviet Union, a war which would have eliminated both of the major totalitarian powers of the world. This hypothesis opens a wide field for speculation, ranging from the Soviet Union's willingness and ability to fight in 1938, and from the legacy of Munich to the era of the Cold War,[7] to the validity of the belief that a life and death struggle between two totalitarian monsters must result in death for both.

When Daladier returned to Paris from Munich he feared that there would be exceedingly hostile demonstrations at the airport; yet he, like Chamberlain, was greeted with great enthusiasm, and the appeasement policy turned out to be very popular at first with both the British and the French people. An inquiry into the reasons for this public reaction is one of the most valuable aspects of a consideration

---

[5] See Ivone Kirkpatrick, *The Inner Circle* (London: Macmillan, 1959), p. 128. See also pp. 131–34.

[6] Hajo Holborn, *The Political Collapse of Europe* (New York: Knopf, 1954), p. 158.

[7] See *ibid.,* p. 157, where it is claimed that the Russians saw Munich as an attempt on the part of the West to turn German ambitions eastward; Chamberlain's dislike and distrust of the Soviet Union (see Keith Feiling, *Neville Chamberlain* [London: Macmillan, 1947], p. 403, for an indication of this antipathy) are often cited as evidence that such was the plan; but compare the view of Stephen Borsody, *The Triumph of Tyranny* (New York: Macmillan, 1960), p. 102.

of the Munich pact. Was the impact of the Popular Front, which in certain elements of French society resulted in the belief that Hitler was preferable to Blum, partly responsible for Daladier's warm reception, and for the fact that "the French . . . were resolved to reach agreement at all cost" at Munich? [8] And in England, how can the truly spontaneous joy with which Chamberlain was greeted be explained? Was it simply relief that a war, until then expected at any moment, had been averted, that caused *The Times* to assert that "no conqueror returning from a victory on the battlefield has come home adorned with nobler laurels," or the *Sunday Dispatch* to say that "the gratitude of millions of mothers, wives, sweethearts, pours out to feed a flood which will sweep Mr. Neville Chamberlain to a high pinnacle in history," or the *Birmingham Daily Gazette* to maintain that "Birmingham is proud that the peace of Europe, when all but lost, has been saved by a cool-brained and determined Birmingham man?" [9] A few men felt otherwise. Duff Cooper argued that if the Czechs were to be deserted or even advised to surrender, "we should be guilty of one of the basest betrayals in history." [10] Winston Churchill vigorously denounced Munich in Parliament: "£1 was demanded at the pistol's point. When it was given, £2 were demanded at the pistol's point. Finally, the dictator consented to take £1 17s. 6d. and the rest in promises of good will for the future." [11] But Chamberlain remained the hero of the moment.

Some historians have argued that the appeasement mood in Britain can be explained by a decline in the quality of statesmanship—a decline illustrated by the Chamberlain group's failure to distinguish between the interests of their social order and those of their country. "[They] were essentially middle-class, not aristocrats. They did not have the hereditary sense of the security of the state, unlike Churchill, Eden, the Cecils." [12] Other critics suggest that sympathy for Nazism in certain restricted but important circles played a part in determining British policy; [13] or that foreign policy was being influenced by men who lacked understanding of history and diplomacy, and who suffered from the often-noticed British lack of interest in eastern Europe. "How horrible, fantastic, incredible it is [cried Chamberlain at the time] that we should be digging trenches and trying on gas-masks here because of a quarrel in a far-away country between people of whom we know nothing." [14] Or can an explanation for the British attitude be found in the fact that Britain, unlike France, owed nothing to Czechoslovakia? In fact, were many influential Englishmen convinced that Germans—even Nazis—were a basically reasonable people, like themselves; were many of these same Englishmen still suffering from feelings of guilt over the Versailles Treaty? No less a figure that Barrington-Ward, deputy editor of *The Times,* possessed this complex: "That the mistakes of Versailles had to be paid for by the Allies, remained one of B-W's deepest convictions." [15]

[8] Kirkpatrick, *op. cit.,* p. 128. See also Charles A. Micaud, *The French Right and Nazi Germany 1933–1939* (Durham: Duke University Press, 1943).
[9] Quoted in Macleod, *op. cit.,* p. 268.
[10] Duff Cooper, *Old Men Forget* (London: Rupert Hart-Davis, 1957), p. 239.
[11] Charles Eade, editor, *The War Speeches of the Rt Hon Winston S. Churchill* (London: Cassell, 1951), I, 25.
[12] A. L. Rowse, *Appeasement: a Study in Political Decline 1933–1939* (New York: W. W. Norton, 1961), p. 117.
[13] See, for an example of this sympathy, Nevile Henderson, *Failure of a Mission* (New York: G. P. Putnam's Sons, 1940), esp. pp. 12–13.
[14] Quoted in Feiling, *op. cit.,* p. 372.
[15] *The History of The Times* (London: Printing House Square, 1952), IV, Part 2, p. 950.

At any rate, a once very important man, who had good reason to regret a former conflict between Germany and England, was exceedingly pleased by the outcome of the Munich Conference: "I have not the slightest doubt," wrote ex-Kaiser William II to Britain's Queen Mary, "that Mr. N. Chamberlain was inspired by Heaven & guided by God who took pity on his children on Earth by crowning his mission with such relieving success."[16] But disillusion came quickly, and a noted scholar has recently characterized Munich as "the nadir of diplomacy—a personal deal between two men at the expense of a third party."[17] In fact, by the Christmas of 1938 the following verse appeared, which now represents, whether justly or unjustly, what has come to be the dominant view of Munich:

> Peace on earth are fighting words
> And the milk of human kindness curds,
> So let us on this festive date
> Arise and reaffirm our hate
> For Adolf Hitler, the Nazi thug
> Mussolini, the Fascist mugg,
> And each and every moral eunuch
> That had a hand in the Pact of Munich.
> The rhyme is bad but the Pact was worse—
> Neville's plane may be Europe's Hearse.[18]

1.

Sir Lewis Namier was one of Britain's most distinguished scholars. Born in the Polish provinces of the old Austro-Hungarian empire, he became professor of modern history at Manchester University, and an Honorary Fellow of Balliol College, Oxford. His most famous work is *The Structure of Politics at the Accession of George III*, which revolutionized the study of eighteenth-century England. But Sir Lewis was not the least hesitant about venturing into twentieth-century diplomatic history, and the book from which the following selection is taken has become one of the classic statements of the antiappeasement point of view.

NAMIER: Europe in Decay *

Mr. Churchill's considered judgment on Munich is summed up in two sentences: "There is no merit in putting off a war for a year if, when it comes, it is a far worse war or one harder to win" and "I remain convinced . . . that it would have been better . . . to fight Hitler in 1938 than it was when we finally had to do so in September, 1939." Mr. Churchill touches upon the question "whether decisive action by Britain and France would have forced Hitler to recede or have led to his overthrow by a military conspiracy," and further quotes some of the opinions of German generals about the military chances at

---

[16] Quoted in James Pope-Hennessy, *Queen Mary* (London: George Allen and Unwin, 1959), p. 592.

[17] Charles L. Mowat, *Britain Between the Wars* (London: Methuen, 1955), p. 615.

[18] Frank Sullivan, "Greetings, Friends!" *The New Yorker*, 24 December 1938, p. 19.

* From Sir Lewis Namier, *Europe in Decay* (London: Macmillan, 1950), pp. 161–63. Reprinted by permission of Lady Namier.

the time. But while German "conspiracies" had a peculiar way of not coming
off, and German military opinions repeatedly proved wrong, there are indisputable facts to support Mr. Churchill's thesis. The Czechs had thirty-five
divisions, better equipped than any other allied army; an excellent defensive
system covering most of their frontier; and a powerful armaments industry.
The Skoda works was "the second most important arsenal in Central Europe,"
and its production alone was in 1938–1939 nearly equal to the output of the
British arms factories: Munich made it "change sides adversely." Lastly, Czechoslovakia was a potential Russian air base wedged between Berlin, Vienna,
and Munich. The liquidation of Czechoslovakia was a disastrous loss to the
allies.

Further, the as yet unripened German army had a great deal to gain by the
additional year. Had the Germans attacked Czechoslovakia in September 1938,
only five effective and eight reserve divisions would have been available to
hold their western front against a hundred French divisions. In armaments, the
advance of the Western Powers was "petty" during the year compared with
that of the Germans. "Munition production on a nation-wide plan is a four
years' task. The first year yields nothing; the second very little; the third a lot,
and the fourth a flood." In 1938 Germany had reached the third or fourth year
of most intense preparation, while Britain was merely starting, with a much
weaker impulse. In the air alone Britain began to improve her position. But
though in 1938 there might have been air raids on London, "for which we
were lamentably unprepared," there could have been no "decisive Air Battle of
Britain" until the Germans obtained the necessary bases in France and the Low
Countries: and in 1938 the Germans had not the tanks with which they broke
the French front. "For all the above reasons, the year's breathing-space said to
be 'gained' by Munich left Britain and France in a much worse position . . .
than they had been at the Munich crisis."

One more argument could be adduced in support of Mr. Churchill's thesis.
He uses some harsh expressions about the men who then ruled Poland; and few
would choose to defend their very mean action in Teschen. There was a streak
of the gangster in Colonel Beck, and a passion for power-display and booty.
But even he would have preferred to practise these against, rather than in the
company of, the Germans. In March and October 1933 Pilsudski had proposed
preventive military action against Hitler; and when Hitler entered the Rhineland on March 7, 1936, no one urged an immediate armed riposte as strongly
as Beck. Had the Western Powers shown firmness in the summer of 1938, they
might have had Poland with them; but Beck was not to be impressed or convinced by a Runciman mission or by propitiatory flights to Berchtesgaden and
Godesberg.

About the moral side of Munich Mr. Churchill's judgment is equally clear.
Responsible French statesmen had repeatedly declared that France's engagements toward Czechoslovakia "are sacred and cannot be evaded." Here was a
solemn obligation. "For the French Government to leave her faithful ally,
Czechoslovakia, to her fate was a melancholy lapse . . . and it must be recorded

with regret that the British Government not only acquiesced but encouraged the French Government in a fatal course." "The British and French Cabinets at this time presented a front of two over-ripe melons crushed together; whereas what was needed was a gleam of steel."

2.

In the following selection Robert Sencourt provides a standard defense of Neville Chamberlain's foreign policy. Mr. Sencourt has written widely, especially in the fields of Spanish and Church history; he has also been professor of English literature at the University of Egypt. Among his many books is an exceedingly sympathetic biography of Winston Churchill, published in 1940, in which, as one might expect, his treatment of Sir Winston's opposition to the Munich Pact is brief and muted.

SENCOURT: The Foreign Policy of Neville Chamberlain *

The problem [which Neville Chamberlain faced in 1938] . . . was to strengthen a Britain, much weakened in the last few years, against the danger from Hitler's combination of perfidy, outrage, and roaring armaments, when it had to be recognized that there was no such thing as collective security, when America stood aloof, and when Russia had announced her intention of working for the destruction of the capitalist system. If the Western powers sought to solve their problem by war—so Stalin warned them in 1934—they would see an enormous increase of the Soviet power which the previous war had engendered. As events have proved, those were not idle words. None considered them more carefully than the leader of the Conservative party. He moulded his policy accordingly: it was to control Germany in the West and to allow her *Lebensraum* by extending her economic domain in the East. There she would menace no British interest; there, if she found an enemy, it would be not the West, but the Russia of that Stalin who had sounded the warning against war.

But in this plan there was a complication: France was bound to the Petite Entente of Prague, Bucharest, and Belgrade. And this complication contained yet another of which Neville Chamberlain's piercing gaze had soon to take full cognisance: it was that no more in 1938 than in 1936 did the French intend to fight except in defence of their own frontier. The French Staff had decided that to risk their resources and reserves in an attempt to repair the gimcrack contrivances of disparate nationality that had been temporarily tied together after the fatal crack up of the Austro-Hungarian Empire would be for France neither practical nor prudent. Tacitly, but unmistakably, Paris had let go the Petite Entente. And Hitler knew it.

It was at this point that there arose a certain tension between the Prime

* From Robert Sencourt, "The Foreign Policy of Neville Chamberlain," in *The Quarterly Review*, Vol. 292 (1954), pp. 147-51, 155. Reprinted by permission of the author and of the publisher, Sir John Murray.

Minister and certain diplomats left by Mr. Eden in high positions at the Foreign Office. Those diplomats lived on the tradition on which they had been brought up, that of the Anglo-French Entente, which, victorious in 1919, had made its plans, now proved abortive, for Europe. Neville Chamberlain with his business mind saw that if he were to engage against Germany he could not count on the practical support of the army of which Gamelin was commander-in-chief.

The issue was soon put to the test with regard to Prague. Three months after the rape of Vienna, in February 1938, Hitler began to menace it; in May he withdrew; in August and September he returned to the fray with a demand for those 3,000,000 German-speaking peoples who neighboured his frontier at Eger, Marienbad, and Karlsbad. When he announced that he was prepared to launch a war to free them, there was no air force in France. The British Ambassador in Paris reported that there all but a small, noisy and corrupt section were against war. The French Premier Daladier, as early as September 13th, turned to Chamberlain, begging him to intervene with Hitler, and prevent a war.

We now come to that expisode in Neville Chamberlain's career where attack has been sustained and venomous. Sir Winston and all his henchmen urge that war should have been declared: that if Britain had then declared war, Hitler would have given in. Mr. Wheeler-Bennett, the most persistent in making out the case, has now undermined it. In his latest book, "The Nemesis of Power," he proves that the German generals had neither the courage nor the means to revolt against Hitler. The last recruit to this platoon—and not the least forgetful —was Lord Norwich [Duff Cooper].

Many facts need to be remembered. Russia had refused her support, so had large portions of the British Empire; France had no air force, our own was very weak, so was that of Prague. Her neighbours, Poland and Hungary, were prepared to invade to redeem territories they deemed to be rightly theirs. The country had no defence whatever along her extended Austrian border. Her three million Sudetens were against her, within their mountain frontier. From Prague came despatches that important elements sought to eliminate Benes. And the only possible strength was in some tanks which were not put to the test. It is hardly likely that they could have done much against those German forces which a year later smashed up in a fortnight Poland with its army three times that of Prague. If these points have been forgotten by Lord Norwich, he still had little reason to argue that the British Government should go to war in such a cause if its ally, who alone had written obligations, asked it not to do so, and when Roosevelt was doing all he could to prevent a war beginning. If on one side we have the books of Sir Winston Churchill, Lord Norwich, Sir Lewis Namier, and Mr. Wheeler-Bennett, on the other we have those of W. W. Hadley of the "Sunday Times," and M. Fabre-Luce, those of Lord Maugham and Lord Simon. We have the speeches made at the time by Lord Halifax and by Lord Chatfield, then Minister for the Coordination of Defence. We have the expressed approbation of Roosevelt. We have the impassioned adherence of the French Government and the enthusiasm of the French and British peoples. These acclaimed Chamberlain as a hero for the skill with which he avoided war on this issue. He received a far greater ovation than had ever been given to a Prime Minister.

To attack Neville Chamberlain's foreign policy over that issue is to say that against the advice of his service chiefs and in defiance of the trust placed in him by the French Government, on an issue that would disrupt the Empire, he should have plunged Europe into a war which diplomacy could and did avoid. On that issue Lord Simon has expressed a judicial opinion once and for all. To join with Lord Norwich in attacking Neville Chamberlain on the issue of Munich is to indulge a wild hypothesis; and the only thing to be adduced in its favour is that a few Czech tanks would have been more effective against him than the whole weight of the French, Belgian, Dutch, and British armies banded together after another twenty months of preparation. The daring conceit that German generals, who in Hitler's most fatal moves still followed him, would in this case have turned against him is gone for ever.

It is true that after Munich Neville Chamberlain did make a *faux pas*. He made an impromptu speech in which he used the phrase "peace in our time." But he did this at a moment when he was carried away to share an emotion with the crowds who had been cheering him for hours in the most tremendous ovation, when he was exhausted at his age of seventy after his first flights in an aeroplane, and after weeks of tense council and strained negotiation, when one after another had thanked him for restoring peace to a world threatened with the most cruel havoc.

But that phrase, which voiced too much of the hope in men's hearts before they were driven over the verge of ruin, must not be confused with Chamberlain's view of Hitler or with his foreign policy. His reaction to Hitler had been disgust. He saw in him from the first a man who was willing to hurl Europe into war rather than make wise negotiation, he saw in him a vulgar and dangerous man even though he had immense talents of both exposition and argument. He recognised in Hitler a portentous force of evil, and came back with the strongest feelings of revulsion. But he would not have saved Britain if he had spoken publicly of these; his only hope was to speak in public as though Hitler could be held to his promises. And he did speak so. But he pushed on the orders to rearm; he gained time and with his work on the Air Force, as air marshals have attested, made those decisive changes which when the time came saved Britain in the Battle of Britain. Even if there had been nothing more to Munich than gaining time while the Air Force was built up, then it must be admitted that Neville Chamberlain gained that time,—he saved England. It was admittedly at a high cost, for he lost the services of Lord Norwich at the Admiralty.

So much for Munich. Hitler soon broke his guarantees. Having received the necessary assurances from Stalin that Russia would not interfere, he drove his tanks and machine guns into Prague and reduced it, though nominally independent, to a vassal state. Then and only then did it become clear that Hitler's plans went beyond the German-speaking elements of Europe to dominance of the Continent as a whole. . . .

If Britain is now ruined and imperilled, if the whole world is disrupted, it is certainly not because of the foreign policy of Neville Chamberlain; it is because he was not able to apply his sagacity to the confusion of Europe till too late. In his reasonableness and common sense, his coordination of the will for peace with the firm grasp of decision and principle, he incarnated the tradition of leadership in the Conservative Party. It is the best we can have now: and we will be stronger against the great perils of to-day when we recognise that it was the best *we could have then*. The foreign policy of sound Conservatives to-day is still that of Neville Chamberlain founded on the fact that "war gains nothing, ends nothing and cures nothing."

3.

Many Americans find it hard to believe that any Englishman could ever have harbored a doubt about the virtues of Sir Winston Churchill. It is well, therefore, to remember that Churchill has been one of the most controversial figures in British politics for well over sixty years; he was first elected to the House of Commons in the last year of Queen Victoria's reign, and by the time of the first world war was one of the most important politicians in Britain. Yet he did not become prime minister until 1940, when, at the age of 65—an age considered appropriate for retirement in many circles—he assumed the leadership of Britain in the second world war. During this career of nearly two-thirds of a century many Englishmen have regarded him as brilliant but dangerously erratic. As a young and a very well-connected correspondent in the Boer War he made a great reputation, and entered Parliament as a Tory; in 1904 he went over to the Liberals and rose to become Home Secretary, First Lord of the Admiralty, and, with Lloyd George, the principal target of the conservative elements of Britain—"a traitor to his class"; with the decline of the Liberals after the first world war he returned to the Tories, was made Chancellor of the Exchequer, and managed by his conduct during the General Strike of 1926 to alienate the labor movement; in the 1930's he strongly disagreed with the leaders of his party, first over the government of India and then over the threat of German rearmament, not to mention his burst of knight-errantry in the matter of Edward VIII's abdication. By 1938, therefore, Churchill was regarded as an outsider, was distrusted and disliked by a wide range of people, and was too flamboyant to suit the tastes of many Englishmen. The reputation which he enjoys today is, it can be seen, something relatively new; yet even within the last decade certain aspects of his past career, from the Gallipoli campaign of 1915 to his long-standing mistrust of socialism, have been brought up to embarrass him. Certainly his views of Munich, which are widely accepted today, only served to anger his fellow Tories in 1938 and to confirm them in their belief that he, like many of his ancestors, was not "a good party man."

Sir Winston, in the passage below, opens his argument by asserting that, had the West stood firm in 1938, Hitler might well have backed down from his determination to go to war, if necessary, to gain the Sudetenland. Does Marshal Keitel's testimony, given at the Nuremberg Trials, provide convincing evidence in this regard?

CHURCHILL: The Gathering Storm *

We have now also Marshal Keitel's answer to the specific question put to him by the Czech representative at the Nuremberg Trials:

Colonel Eger, representing Czechoslovakia, asked Marshal Keitel: "Would the Reich have attacked Czechoslovakia in 1938 if the Western Powers had stood by Prague?"

Marshall Keitel answered: "Certainly not. We were not strong enough militarily. The object of Munich (i.e., reaching an agreement at Munich) was to get Russia out of Europe, to gain time, and to complete the German armaments."

Hitler's judgment had been once more decisively vindicated. The German General Staff was utterly abashed. Once again the Fuehrer had been right, after all. He with his genius and intuition alone had truly measured all the circumstances, military and political. Once again, as in the Rhineland, the Fuehrer's leadership had triumphed over the obstruction of the German military chiefs. All these generals were patriotic men. They longed to see the Fatherland regain its position in the world. They were devoting themselves night and day to every process that could strengthen the German forces. They, therefore, felt smitten in their hearts at having been found so much below the level of the event, and in many cases their dislike and their distrust of Hitler were overpowered by admiration for his commanding gifts and miraculous luck. Surely here was a star to follow, surely here was a guide to obey. Thus did Hitler finally become the undisputed master of Germany, and the path was clear for the great design. The conspirators lay low, and were not betrayed by their military comrades.

It may be well here to set down some principles of morals and action which may be a guide in the future. No case of this kind can be judged apart from its circumstances. The facts may be unknown at the time and estimates of them must be largely guesswork, coloured by the general feelings and aims of whoever is trying to pronounce. Those who are prone by temperament and character to seek sharp and clear-cut solutions of difficult and obscure problems, who are ready to fight whenever some challenge comes from a foreign Power, have not always been right. On the other hand, those whose inclination is to bow their heads, to seek patiently and faithfully for peaceful compromise, are not always wrong. On the contrary, in the majority of instances they may be right, not only morally but from a practical standpoint. How many wars have been averted by patience and persisting good will! Religion and virtue alike lend their sanctions to meekness and humility not only between men but between

* From Winston S. Churchill, *The Gathering Storm* (Boston: Houghton Mifflin, 1948), pp. 318–21. Reprinted by permission of the publishers.

nations. How many wars have been precipitated by firebrands! How many mis-understandings which led to wars could have been removed by temporising! How often have countries fought cruel wars and then after a few years of peace found themselves not only friends but allies!

The Sermon on the Mount is the last word in Christian ethics. Everyone respects the Quakers. Still, it is not on these terms that Ministers assume their responsibilities of guiding states. Their duty is first so to deal with other nations as to avoid strife and war and to eschew aggression in all its forms, whether for nationalistic or ideological objects. But the safety of the State, the lives and freedom of their own fellow countrymen, to whom they owe their position, make it right and imperative in the last resort, or when a final and definite conviction has been reached, that the use of force should not be excluded. If the circumstances are such as to warrant it, force may be used. And if this be so, it should be used under the conditions which are most favourable. There is no merit in putting off a war for a year if, when it comes, it is a far worse war or one much harder to win. These are the tormenting dilemmas upon which mankind has throughout its history been so frequently impaled. Final judgment upon them can only be recorded by history in relation to the facts of the case as known to the parties at the time, and also as subsequently proved.

There is, however, one helpful guide, namely, for a nation to keep its word and to act in accordance with its treaty obligations to allies. This guide is called *honour*. It is baffling to reflect that what men call honour does not correspond always to Christian ethics. Honour is often influenced by that element of pride which plays so large a part in its inspiration. An exaggerated code of honour leading to the performance of utterly vain and unreasonable deeds could not be defended, however fine it might look. Here, however, the moment came when Honour pointed the path of Duty, and when also the right judgment of the facts at that time would have reinforced its dictates.

For the French Government to leave her faithful ally, Czechoslovakia, to her fate was a melancholy lapse from which flowed terrible consequences. Not only wise and fair policy, but chivalry, honour, and sympathy for a small threatened people made an overwhelming concentration. Great Britain, who would certainly have fought if bound by treaty obligations, was nevertheless now deeply involved, and it must be recorded with regret that the British Government not only acquiesced but encouraged the French Government in a fatal course. . . .

4.

The late Lord Halifax was one of Britain's most prominent public servants. During a long career he not only served as Neville Chamberlain's foreign secretary, but also as a viceroy of India and as British ambassador to the United States. As he was a man of undoubted integrity, his retrospective defense of Munich deserves serious examination; is it as effective as Sencourt's?

HALIFAX: Fullness of Days *

The criticism excited by Munich never caused me the least surprise. I should very possibly indeed have been among the critics myself, if I had not happened to be in a position of responsibility. But there were two or three considerations to which those same critics ought to have had regard. One was that in criticising the settlement of Munich, they were criticising the wrong thing and the wrong date. They ought to have criticised the failure of successive Governments, and of all parties, to foresee the necessity of re-arming in the light of what was going on in Germany; and the right date on which criticism ought to have fastened was 1936, which had seen the German re-occupation of the Rhineland in defiance of treaty provisions. I have little doubt that if we had then told Hitler bluntly to go back, his power for future and larger mischief would have been broken. But, leaving entirely aside the French, there was no section of British public opinion that would not have been directly opposed to such action in 1936. To go to war with Germany for walking into their own back-yard, which was how the British people saw it, at a time moreover when you were actually discussing with them the dates and conditions of their right to resume occupation, was not the sort of thing people could understand. So that moment which, I would guess, offered the last effective chance of securing peace without war, went by.

Nor were the critics disposed to weigh either political or strategic facts which were in conflict with natural emotions. They either did not know or greatly care that there was grave doubt whether the Commonwealth would be at one in supporting the United Kingdom in a policy of active intervention on behalf of Czechoslovakia in 1938; and once the Austrian Anschluss had taken place, whether you liked it or not, Czechoslovakia was no longer a defensible proposition. But with those who were to be the critics, for motives entirely honorable and deserving of all respect, these practical facts were submerged beneath generous resentment at seeing a small people coerced and victimised by a large bully, while those standing by appeared unwilling to put themselves to any personal risk to help. This reaction was strongly reinforced by two other elements. One was the unhappy attempt made by some of those defending Chamberlain's Government to represent what had happened as something which was in the long run going to be of advantage to Czechoslovakia by ridding her of a German population that would never be easy of assimilation and which was therefore bound to give recurring trouble. Such argument sounded in the last degree hypocritical, and the only possible defence of Munich, which was the genuine defence, was that it was a horrible and wretched business, but the lesser of two evils.

The other element that gave fuel to the fires of criticism was the unhappy

* From Lord Halifax, *Fullness of Days* (New York: Dodd, Mead, 1957), pp. 199–202. Copyright 1956, 1957 by Edward Frederick Lindley Wood, 1st Earl of Halifax. Reprinted by permission of Dodd, Mead & Co.

phrases which Neville Chamberlain under the stress of great emotion allowed himself to use. "Peace with honour"; "Peace for our time"—such sentences grated harshly on the ear and thought of even those closest to him. And almost immediately afterwards, as his biographer reminds us, he was begging the House of Commons not to read too much into words used under conditions of strain so exhausting and so profound. But when all has been said, one fact remains dominant and unchallengeable. When war did come a year later it found a country and Commonwealth wholly united within itself, convinced to the foundation of soul and conscience that every conceivable effort had been made to find the way of sparing Europe the ordeal of war, and that no alternative remained. And that was the big thing that Chamberlain did.

In this connexion Churchill did Chamberlain less than justice in his War history. He says: "Chamberlain returned to England. . . . He waved the joint Declaration which he had got Hitler to sign. . . . As his car drove through cheering crowds . . . he said to Halifax . . . 'all this will be over in three months'; *but* from the windows of Downing Street he waved his piece of paper again and used these words . . . 'I believe it is peace for our time.'"

The implication of that sentence can hardly be other than that Chamberlain was concerned to mislead the public into the acceptance of a belief which he did not himself share; whereas of course in fact his two remarks referred to two totally different things. I was the only person with him when he made the first observation and was instrumental in giving the information to Professor Feiling, from whose biography Churchill has quoted the words. I am therefore in the best position to know what Chamberlain meant by it. When he said "All this will be over in three months" he was referring to the popular enthusiasm of the moment; when he spoke about "Peace for our time," he was concerned with the spirit in which he believed Hitler to have signed the declaration and which at that moment he was disposed to trust. Chamberlain no doubt had his faults, and the words that he used about Hitler as he spoke to the crowd in Downing Street were soon to be roughly denied by the event. But no one could fairly charge him with lack of frankness. . . .

5.

Georges Bonnet was foreign minister of France from April 1938 to September 1939. The following letter, which he addressed to *The New York Times,* is another illustration of the eagerness with which many of the participants in the Munich pact are still ready to leap to its defense. At the time of Munich, however, M. Bonnet was not highly regarded by some of his fellow appeasers: Neville Chamberlain remarked privately that "Bonnet . . . is clever, but ambitious and an intriguer. The French are not very fortunate in their foreign secretaries." [1] As for the antiappeasers, Bonnet has always been one of their favorite targets. Sir Lewis Namier, perhaps the most savage critic, wrote in retrospect that "it is difficult to define M. Bonnet's policy; first, he

[1] Keith Feiling, *Neville Chamberlain* (London: Macmillan, 1947), p. 353.

would give way to pressure in a ready, complacent manner; next, he would reassert himself, and try to regain detachment and independence; and he would then change colour, till he seemed to have none of his own." [2]

BONNET: Letter to the editor of *The New York Times* *

To the Editor of The New York Times:

I have been reading C. L. Sulzberger's article on Berlin and Munich in your issue of Sept. 30. As Mr. Sulzberger taxes the French Government with "cowardice" (this Government was unanimously backed up by Parliament) and as I was a member of that Government as Foreign Affairs Minister, I would be grateful if you would bring to the notice of your readers the following comments:

Mr. Sulzberger contends that as a result of the Munich agreement "the chance of any potentially strong stand on Germany's eastern border was removed, France's alliance scheme dissolved"; and that in 1938 World War II would have come "earlier and under circumstances less favorable to Hitler."

I would draw your attention to the following facts: In 1938 our military authorities stated that defeat was a certainty. "Within a fortnight there will be nothing left of the French Air Force," the chief of our air staff declared, while the artillery chief stated "there would be no modern guns available before a year." Statements by our Allies were equally disappointing. Great Britain said: "For the first year of war, a hundred aircraft and two divisions without any modern equipment." "Not one man, not one cent" was Roosevelt's reply to our Ambassador's request for assistance.

The U.S.S.R. demanded free passage for their troops through Poland and Rumania, which both nations refused with fierce deliberation. Finally, the Czech military authorities informed us they were in no position to resist an attack by the German army and that their own forces would have to seek refuge in the mountains. It was unanimously felt that the military and diplomatic situation was disastrous.

By 1939 our international relations had improved. Since Munich we had signed agreements with Rumania and Turkey. Also, Poland, which at the time of Munich was against Czechoslovakia, eventually fought on our side.

This lapse of time was on our side. Due to the progress achieved in the two years between 1938 and 1940 the Royal Air Force won the air battle over London, which proved a vital factor in bringing victory to the Allies. This fact had been recognized by United Kingdom experts as also on Nov. 19, 1946 by the Prime Minister, Clement Attlee.

Iain MacLeod, the new leader of the House of Commons and Chairman of the Conservative party in the Oct. 15 issue of The Sunday Times of London, confirmed this fact in the following words: "Some things seem completely clear to me. First neither Britain nor the Empire could have or would have gone to

---

[2] L. B. Namier, *Europe in Decay* (London: Macmillan, 1950), p. 66.

* Copyright by *The New York Times*. Reprinted by permission of *The New York Times* and Georges Bonnet.

war in 1938. The gain of a year from Munich to September, 1939, was, on balance, of far more advantage to Britain than to the Axis Powers."

And Hitler stated before his death: "We should have gone to war in 1938."

Georges Bonnet,
Paris, Oct. 25, 1961

6.

The opinions of the Oxford historian A. J. P. Taylor are as firm on the subject of Munich as on the merits of the Locarno pact. Here, as in Chapter VI, one should consider whether Mr. Taylor plays favorites in the writing of history: is he unduly cynical about the foreign policies of the European nations in 1938; is his comparison of British and French moral attitudes justified; is he too easy, or too hard, on Adolf Hitler? Whatever one may say of Mr. Taylor's judgments, no one can deny that they are provocative and well-expressed.

TAYLOR: The Origins of the Second World War *

The conference at Munich was meant to mark the beginning of an epoch in European affairs. "Versailles"—the system of 1919—was not only dead, but buried. A new system, based on equality and mutual confidence between the four great European Powers was to take its place. Chamberlain said: "I believe that it is peace for our time"; Hitler declared: "I have no more territorial demands to make in Europe." There were still great questions to be settled in international affairs. The Spanish civil war was not over. Germany had not recovered her colonies. More remotely, agreements would have to be reached over economic policy and over armaments, before stability was restored in Europe. None of these questions threatened to provoke a general war. The demonstration had been given that Germany could attain by peaceful negotiation the position in Europe to which her resources entitled her. The great hurdle had been successfully surmounted: the system, directed against Germany, had been dismantled by agreement, without a war. Yet, within six months, a new system was being constructed against Germany. Within a year, Great Britain, France, and Germany were at war. Was "Munich" a fraud from the start—for Germany merely a stage in the march towards world conquest, or, on the side of Great Britain and France, merely a device to buy time until their re-armament was more advanced? So it appeared in retrospect. When the policy of Munich failed, everyone announced that he had expected it to fail; and the participants not only accused the others of cheating, but boasted that they had been cheating themselves. In fact, no one was as clear-sighted as he later claimed to have been; and the four men of Munich were all in their different ways sincere, though each had reserves which he concealed from the others.

* From A. J. P. Taylor, *The Origins of the Second World War* (New York: Atheneum, 1962). pp. 187–92. Copyright 1961 by A. J. P. Taylor. Reprinted by permission of Atheneum Publishers.

The French yielded most, and with least hope for the future. They surrendered the position of paramount European power which they had appeared to enjoy since 1919. But what they surrendered was artificial. They yielded to reality rather than to force. They had supposed all along that the advantages won in 1919 and subsequently—the restrictions on Germany and the alliances with East European states—were assets which they could supinely enjoy, not gains which they must fiercely defend. They did not lift a finger to assert the system of Versailles after the occupation of the Ruhr in 1923. They abandoned reparations; they acquiesced in the re-armament of Germany; they allowed the German re-occupation of the Rhineland; they did nothing to protect the independence of Austria. They kept up their alliances in Eastern Europe only from a belief that these would bring them aid if ever they were themselves attacked by Germany. They abandoned their ally, Czechoslovakia, the moment she threatened to bring them risk instead of security. Munich was the logical culmination of French policy, not its reversal. The French recognised that they had lost their predominance in Eastern Europe, and knew that it could not be restored. This is far from saying that they feared for themselves. On the contrary, they accepted the British thesis, preached ever since Locarno, that they were in less danger of war if they withdrew behind the Rhine. They had preferred safety to grandeur—an ignoble policy perhaps, but not a dangerous one. Even in 1938, though they feared air bombardment, they did not fear defeat if war were thrust upon them. Gamelin was always emphatic that the democratic powers would win; and the politicians believed him. But what would be the point of war? This was the argument which had prevented French action since 1923, and which prevented it now. Germany, even if defeated, would still be there, great, powerful, determined on redress. War might stop the clock. It could not put it back; and afterwards events would move forward to the same end. The French were therefore willing to surrender everything except their own security, and they did not believe that they had surrendered this at Munich. They had a firm and, as it turned out a well-founded, faith that the Maginot line was impregnable—so much so that they regarded the Siegfried line, less correctly, as impregnable also. They assumed that a stalemate had been established in Western Europe. They could not impede the advance of German power in Eastern Europe; equally Germany could not invade France. The French were humiliated by Munich, not—as they supposed—endangered.

The British position was more complicated. Morality did not enter French calculations, or entered only to be discarded. The French recognised that it was their duty to assist Czechoslovakia; they rejected this duty as either too dangerous or too difficult. Léon Blum expressed French feeling best when he welcomed the agreement of Munich with a mixture of shame and relief. With the British, on the other hand, morality counted for a great deal. The British statesmen used practical arguments: the danger from air attack; the backwardness of their re-armament; the impossibility, even if adequately armed, of helping Czechoslovakia. But these arguments were used to reinforce morality, not to silence it. British policy over Czechoslovakia originated in the belief that

Germany had a moral right to the Sudeten German territory, on grounds of national principle; and it drew the further corollary that this victory for self-determination would provide a stabler, more permanent peace in Europe. The British government were not driven to acknowledge the dismemberment of Czechoslovakia solely from fear of war. They deliberately set out to impose this cession of territory on the Czechs before the threat of war raised its head. The settlement at Munich was a triumph for British policy, which had worked precisely to this end; not a triumph for Hitler, who had started with no such clear intention. Nor was it merely a triumph for selfish or cynical British statesmen, indifferent to the fate of far-off peoples or calculating that Hitler might be launched into war against Soviet Russia. It was a triumph for all that was best and most enlightened in British life; a triumph for those who had preached equal justice between peoples; a triumph for those who had courageously denounced the harshness and short-sightedness of Versailles. Brailsford, the leading Socialist authority on foreign affairs, wrote in 1920 of the peace settlement: "The worst offence was the subjection of over three million Germans to Czech rule." This was the offence redressed at Munich. Idealists could claim that British policy had been tardy and hesitant. In 1938 it atoned for these failings. With skill and persistence, Chamberlain brought first the French, and then the Czechs to follow the moral line.

There was a case against ceding Sudeten territory to Germany—the case that economic and geographic ties are more important than those of nationality. This had been the case against breaking up the Habsburg Monarchy; the Czechs who had taken the lead in breaking up the Monarchy could not use this argument, nor could their advocates in Western Europe. The dispute had to be transferred from the field of morality to that of practical considerations—to what is disapprovingly called *realpolitik*. The most outspoken opponents of Munich, such as Winston Churchill, asserted quite simply that Germany was becoming too powerful in Europe and that she must be stopped by the threat of a great coalition or, if necessary, by force of arms. Self-determination—the principle to which Czechoslovakia owed her existence—was dismissed as a sham. The only moral argument used was that the frontiers of existing states were sacred and that each state could behave as it liked within its own borders. This was the argument of legitimacy; the argument of Metternich and the Congress of Vienna. If accepted, it would have forbidden not only the break-up of the Habsburg Monarchy, but even the winning of independence by the British colonies in America. It was a strange argument for the British Left to use in 1938; and it sat uneasily upon them—hence the hesitations and ineffectiveness of their criticism. Duff Cooper, First Lord of the Admiralty, had no such doubts when he resigned in protest against the Munich settlement. As became an admiring biographer of Talleyrand, he was concerned with the Balance of Power and British honour, not with self-determination or the injustices of Versailles. For him, Czechoslovakia had no more been the real issue in 1938 than Belgium had been in 1914. This argument destroyed the moral validity of the British position in the first World war, but it had an appeal for the Conservative majority in the House of Commons. Chamberlain had to answer it in its own terms of power. He could not stress the unwillingness of the French to fight, which had been the really decisive weakness on the Western side. Therefore he had to make out that Great Britain herself was in no position to fight Germany.

Chamberlain was caught by his own argument. If Great Britain had been too weak to fight, then the government must speed rearmament; and this involved doubt in Hitler's good faith, whether avowed or not. In this way, Chamberlain did more than anyone else to destroy the case for his own policy. Moreover, one suspicion breeds another. It is doubtful whether Hitler ever took Chamberlain's sincerity seriously before Munich; it is certain that he did not do so a few days afterwards. What was meant as appeasement had turned into capitulation, on Chamberlain's own showing. Hitler drew the lesson that threats were his most potent weapon. The temptation to boast of Munich as a triumph of force was too great to be resisted. Hitler no longer expected to make gains by parading his grievances against Versailles; he expected to make them by playing on British and French fears. Thus he confirmed the suspicions of those who attacked Munich as a craven surrender. International morality was at a discount. Paradoxically, Benes was the true victor of Munich in the long run. For, while Czechoslovakia lost territory and later her independence also, Hitler lost the moral advantage which had hitherto made him irresistible. Munich became an emotive word, a symbol of shame, about which men can still not speak dispassionately. What was done at Munich mattered less than the way in which it was done; and what was said about it afterwards on both sides counted for still more.

There had been two empty chairs at Munich, or rather chairs were not provided for two Great Powers, though each had claims to an invitation. President Roosevelt, at the height of the crisis, urged a meeting in some neutral capital. He did not indicate whether an American representative would attend; and in any case "the Government of the United States . . . will assume no obligations in the conduct of the present negotiations." Roosevelt applauded Chamberlain on the news of the Munich conference: "Good man." Afterwards, when appeasement turned sour, the Americans rejoiced that they had not been at Munich. They could condemn the British and the French for doing what they themselves would have done in their place. Lack of American support had helped towards making the "democratic" powers give way. Yet Americans drew from Munich the moral that they should support these feeble powers still less. Roosevelt, entangled in troubles over domestic policy, had no mind to add to his difficulties by provoking controversy over foreign affairs. Europe could go on its way without America.

The Russians had been more precise in their plan for a conference. They had wanted a meeting of the "peace-loving Powers" to co-ordinate resistance against the aggressor. They, too, could assume an attitude of moral superiority. Parading their own loyalty to treaty obligations, they laid all the blame on French weakness. One Soviet diplomatist said on 30 September: "We nearly put our foot on a rotten plank. Now we are going elsewhere." Potyomkin, the assistant commissar, made the meaning of this clear when he said to Coulondre: "My poor friend, what have you done? For us I see no other way out than a fourth partition of Poland." The Russians professed to have no fears for their own security. Litvinov told Coulondre: "Hitler will be able to attack Great Britain or the U.S.S.R. He will choose the first solution, . . . and to carry this enterprise through successfully he will prefer to reach an understanding with U.S.S.R." Inwardly the Russians were less confident. No approach came from Hitler; instead the claim that he had saved Europe from Bolshevism. Ingenious observers expected Hitler's next move to be into the Ukraine—a move expected by Western statesmen with some pleasure, by Soviet statesmen with dread. The Soviet rulers would have liked to isolate themselves from Europe; but they were by no means sure that Europe would isolate itself from them. Hence, after a short period of recrimination, they had to renew the call for a Popular Front and for collective security against aggression. It is hard to believe that they expected this policy to succeed. . . .

7.

The following selection is representative of the "official" Soviet attitude toward the Munich pact. In reading it, one should be careful to sift the propaganda from the history, and to consider whether the Soviet position is entirely without merit. Can one blame the Russians for having been distrustful of the policy of Chamberlain and Daladier in 1938; could the Munich pact be responsible, at least in part, for the postwar Soviet mistrust of the West? Or, on the other hand, is this nothing more than an example of the Soviet practice of using history as an effective political weapon?

POTEMKIN ET AL.: Istoriia Diplomatii *

During the discussion of the Czechoslovak question at Munich, Hitler angrily told Daladier and Chamberlain that Czechoslovakia was "Bolshevism's outpost in Europe." Czechoslovakia (he asserted) is bound to the Soviet Union by a mutual-assistance pact. The government of the U.S.S.R. is inciting it to war against Germany; the purpose is not merely to deal a blow to Hitler, but also to start a world war, the consequence of which might be a Bolshevik revolution. Therefore those who demand that Czechoslovakia be defended are contributing to the destruction of the existing order in Europe.

Urgent warnings arrived in Prague from Paris and London: Czechoslovakia must not rest its hopes on the Soviet Union, for the latter country is too far away, has no common frontier with Czechoslovakia, and has no desire to enter

* From V. Potemkin et al., Istoriia Diplomatii, Vol. III (Moscow, 1945), pp. 643–46. Translated by the editors.

a war in spite of its contractual obligation to help Czechoslovakia. Thus the diplomacy of the French and English governments sought to discourage the Czechoslovak people and to degrade the Soviet Union in the eyes of democrats throughout the world.

Another motive of bourgeois diplomacy also emerged. The idea of common action with the Soviet Union against Hitler had no greater appeal to these bourgeois leaders. General Faucher, former head of the French military mission in Czechoslovakia, expresses this viewpoint with a soldier's frankness in the course of a conversation with certain political figures in Prague.

General Faucher declared that it would not be desirable for France to crush Hitler with the aid of the Soviet Union. Above all, world public opinion might give credit for the victory to the Red Army, thus painfully affecting France's national honor. But another thing was even more important. To crush Hitler with the collaboration of the Soviet Union might produce a wave of intense sympathy for the Soviet Union. This in turn would contribute to a dangerous growth of the revolutionary workers' movement. Such a perspective had no appeal whatsoever to the French government. "In short," concluded General Faucher, "we don't want to intervene against Hitler with the Bolsheviks for allies." The facts that were known to everyone contradicted these slanderous inventions of anti-Soviet diplomacy. The whole world knew that the Soviet government considered itself honor-bound to carry out its contractual agreements, and that it was striving tirelessly for the cause of collective security and for the kind of mutual aid that would unite the democratic countries against the warmongers.

The Soviet Union found itself to be the only state that remained faithful to its international obligations toward Czechoslovakia.

"Being bound to Czechoslovakia by a mutual-assistance pact," declared the Soviet representative in the League of Nations Assembly on September 21, 1938, "the Soviet Union has abstained from intervening in the Czechoslovak government's negotiations with the Sudeten Germans; it regards these negotiations as a domestic affair that concerns the Czechoslovak government alone. We have refrained from giving any advice to the Czechoslovak government, for we have considered it inadmissible that this government grant concessions to the Germans, to the detriment of its own national interests, simply to spare us the necessity of carrying out the commitments contained in the pact. Likewise, we have given no advice to the contrary."

Early in September 1938, the French government addressed an inquiry to the Soviet government concerning the attitude of the latter in case Czechoslovakia should be attacked.

The Soviet government's reply was clear and direct: it called for an immediate meeting of representatives of the USSR, England, and France; an open declaration by these powers affirming that they would aid Czechoslovakia in case the latter were attacked by Germany without provocation; the submision of the question to the League of Nations, which would study means of defense; finally, technical consultation between representatives of the general staff of the USSR, France and Czechoslovakia, with a view to working out a plan of joint military operations. Such was the proposal of the Soviet government. Furthermore, it was stressed that the USSR would aid Czechoslovakia in every possible way if, in accordance with France's pact with Czechoslovakia, France were to intervene to defend the latter.

In mid-September, the Czechoslovak government itself asked the government of the USSR if the latter was prepared, in accordance with the Czech-Soviet pact, to give immediate and effective aid to Czechoslovakia in case the latter were to get similar assistance from France. The Soviet government replied to this question without delay and in an affirmative manner. As is known, the Czech-Soviet pact provided that the USSR would lend assistance to Czechoslovakia only in case France also were to aid the latter. Everybody could understand that in forcing Czechoslovakia to accept the German-English-French ultimatum, France was in fact violating its obligation to help Czechoslovakia as provided by the Franco-Czech pact.

For that reason, the Soviet government was formally freed of its obligation to help Czechoslovakia, as established by the Czech-Soviet pact. Nevertheless, the government of the Soviet Union did not take advantage of its right to abandon Czechoslovakia to its fate. The Czech-Soviet pact was not declared to be inoperative. The USSR was ready as before to lend its support to Czechoslovakia, if the latter government so desired. On the critical days of September 27 and 28, when the president of the United States proposed to mediate in order to solve the German-Czech conflict in peaceful fashion, the United States representative in the Soviet Union, Kirk, was informed that the Soviet government favored the convocation of an international conference that would consider extending collective assistance to Czechoslovakia and that would decide on practical measures to maintain peace.

That was not all. When the Polish press announced that Polish troops were concentrated on the Czechoslovak frontier, the chargé d'affaires of the Polish republic was summoned to the people's commissariat on foreign affairs on the evening of September 23. He was told, in the name of the Soviet government, that according to reports not denied by the Polish government, Polish troops were concentrated on the Czechoslovak frontier; these troops were apparently about to be hurled against Czechoslovak territory. The government of the Soviet Union hoped that these reports would be immediately denied by Poland. If this were not done and if Polish troops should in fact invade Czechoslovakia, the government of the USSR would recognize these facts as constituting an act of unprovoked aggression. For these reasons, it would be obliged to denounce the Polish-Soviet non-aggression pact of July 25, 1932.

In the evening of this same day, the Polish government gave its reply. The tone was excessively insolent. At bottom, however, the Polish government sought to vindicate itself: it explained that it was taking certain military measures for purely defensive purposes. Soon the foreign press announced that part of the Polish troops had been withdrawn from the Czechoslovak frontier.

Obviously, the Soviet Union's firm warning had produced its effect.

Meanwhile, the reactionary press of England and France actively spread the completely fabricated report that the USSR had not decided to carry out its agreed commitments to Czechoslovakia.

The machinations of the slanderers were exposed; the Soviet government's reply to the inquiries of France and Czechoslovakia were revealed at Geneva, in the League of Nations Assembly. The provocationist scheme of the reactionaries was thus unmasked. Indeed, the USSR stood before the world as the only country which, in the moment of general panic, desertion, and treason, had kept calm, had proved its unshakeable fidelity to its contractual promises, had shown firm determination to defend international peace and democracy against the warmongers.

8.

Soviet accounts of the Munich episode always insist that the Soviet Union was prepared to come to the aid of Czechoslovakia, especially if French aid had been forthcoming also. Many western historians and statesmen—Churchill included—have accepted this point of view. If the claim is valid, then this fact must weigh heavily in any assessment of the merits or faults of the Munich settlement. Some serious questions about Soviet intentions have been raised, however, by certain scholars—and notably by George F. Kennan. Mr. Kennan is one of this country's most eminent diplomats; he has served as ambassador to both the Soviet Union and Yugoslavia. During his temporary separation from the Foreign Service in the 1950's, he turned to the writing of history, and won a Pulitzer prize for his multivolume work on Soviet-American relations. During the Munich period he was stationed at the United States embassy in Moscow; and it is on the basis of his intimate acquaintance with Soviet foreign policy aims and methods that he questions the orthodox Soviet thesis.

KENNAN: Russia and the West Under Lenin and Stalin *

The Munich agreement was a tragically misconceived and desperate act of appeasement at the cost of the Czechoslovak state, performed by Chamberlain and the French premier, Daladier, in the vain hope that it would satisfy Hitler's stormy ambition, and thus secure for Europe a peaceful future. We know today that it was unnecessary—unnecessary because the Czech defenses were very strong, and had the Czechs decided to fight they could have put up considerable resistance; even more unnecessary because the German generals, conscious of Germany's relative weakness at that moment, were actually prepared to attempt the removal of Hitler then and there, had he persisted in driving things to the point of war. It was the fact that the Western powers and the Czechoslovak government did yield at the last moment, and that Hitler once again achieved a bloodless triumph, which deprived the generals of any excuse for such a move. One sees, as so often in the record of history, that it sometimes

* From George F. Kennan, *Russia and the West Under Lenin and Stalin* (Boston: Atlantic-Little, Brown, 1961), pp. 322–24. Reprinted by permission of Little, Brown and Co.–Atlantic Monthly Press.

pays to stand up manfully to one's problems, even when no certain victory is in sight.

The great issue at stake in the Munich crisis was, of course, the validity of Czechoslovakia's treaties of alliance with France and with Soviet Russia. The Soviet treaty with Czechoslovakia provided that Russia was obliged to come to Czechoslovakia's assistance *only if France did the same.* As the crisis developed just before Munich, the Soviet government reiterated, with impeccable correctness, its readiness to meet its treaty obligations to Czechoslovakia, if France would do likewise. This confirmed many people in the West in the belief that only Russia had remained true to her engagements at that crucial moment— that Russia had been prepared to assume the full burden of a war with Hitler over the issue of Czechoslovakia, had the Western powers only played their part.

This was substantially accurate in the juridical sense; but things were not exactly this way in practice. You must remember a basic geographic reality which underlay the entire chapter of Soviet participation in the policy of collective security, and particularly the pacts with the French and the Czechs. This was the fact that whereas the Western powers had, in effect, a common border with Germany, the Soviet Union did not; it was separated from Germany and from Czechoslovakia by two countries, Poland and Rumania, both of which feared any movement of Russian troops onto their territory as much as they feared a similar movement of the troops of Hitler, and neither of which was at any time willing to say that it would permit Soviet troops to cross its territory in the implementation of Russia's obligations to Czechoslovakia or to France. This meant that no military planning for a passage of Russian troops across these countries was possible; and in the event of a war with Germany in which all three countries—France, Czechoslovakia, and Russia—might have been involved, the Western powers and Czechoslovakia could expect to become immediately engaged, whereas any Russian action would still have to await clarification of the Soviet right of passage across these intervening countries. In the reluctance of the Polish and Rumanian governments to permit transit of Soviet troops, the Soviet government had a ready-made excuse for delay in meeting its obligations of mutual assistance. This impediment was apparent at the time of Munich: the Rumanian government, in particular, was heavily pressed by the Czechs and the Western powers to declare its readiness to permit Soviet troops to pass; but I cannot find that it ever clearly did so. In any case, I myself had it from no less an authority than the German military attaché in Prague, whose task it had been to study this problem for the German High Command, that the physical characteristics of the Rumanian railroad network were such that, even had the Rumanians permitted the passage, it would have taken the Soviet command approximately three months to move a division into Slovakia over this primitive and indirect route. The implications of this state of affairs are obvious. The Russian expression of readiness to assist Czechoslovakia if France did likewise was a gesture that cost Moscow very little. It is fair to say that had the Czechs decided to resist, there was, for various reasons, a good chance that they might have been saved. It is hardly fair to say that they would have been saved by the troops of the Soviet Union.

XI.

YALTA AND THE FATE OF EASTERN EUROPE

The second world war has provided no peace treaty to criticize, but it has provided a conference—Yalta—which, in many ways, has taken the place of a Versailles as an object of controversy, especially in the United States, where the very word "Yalta" has been used freely in party politics. As a result, many Americans find it hard to examine the Yalta conference dispassionately.

Today, in the midst of a cold war, the need for scapegoats is felt by many who are politicians, and by many who are merely frustrated. Yalta, it has been claimed, was another Munich, another attempt to appease dictators whose only desire was world conquest, and whose every move was designed to facilitate that end. Had the United States been firm in its dealings with the Soviet Union, had it yielded nothing, had it made counterdemands, and had it used the vast power which it had assembled in Germany and central Europe to back up those demands, there would have been no cold war, for Stalin, a practical if an evil man, would have understood that we "meant business." Confronted with the willingness of the United States to move its armies eastward against his own forces, Stalin would have retreated behind his own frontiers and stayed there, and the security of the western world would not be in such peril today.

Those who take an entirely opposite view of postwar Soviet policy also find much to criticize in the Yalta agreements. The foundations of the cold war, it is argued, were laid by America's and by Britain's undue mistrust of Soviet aims; the object should have been to make the Soviet Union abandon its suspicions of the West, suspicions which, after the Allied intervention in Russia in 1917–20 and the Munich pact, were not wholly unjustified. But by doing all possible to thwart the natural Soviet desire for the establishment of friendly governments in the states of eastern Europe the Allies increased Soviet suspicions and weakened any faith the Russian leaders may have built up in Western goodwill. Critics of this sort contend that the only way to make Soviet Russia trustworthy was to trust it completely, rather than to deny it the fruits of its victory.

Still others think that Yalta, and the other wartime conferences, did go a long way in trusting the Russians, as long a way as was consistent with national safety. To do so was necessary, they argue, for today our consciences are clear in the knowledge that we did everything possible to avoid the cold war. As for the concessions made, they were few, at least in Europe. Russian troops were already occupying most of eastern Europe, and if the Soviet Union was determined to establish satellite governments in the countries occupied by its armies there was little we could do about it, short of the use of force—something which American and British public opinion would not have tolerated, and which, in the long run, would have reacted disastrously against us. However, by means of the Yalta pact, we put the Russians in the position of having to violate solemn agreements in order to establish their satellites; accordingly we gained a moral advantage over the Soviet Union, which, if not much, was better than nothing.

The tendency to choose a side in a historical debate because of its political attraction, rather than because of its merits, appears in the discussions concerning western strategy during the second world war as well as in debates over the merits of Yalta. In fact, in many instances the two subjects tend to become linked. It is often argued that in 1944 Churchill wanted to invade the Balkans to prevent Soviet hegemony in eastern Europe—but that the United States insisted on concentrating on the invasion of Normandy, thus ruining Churchill's scheme and helping Stalin, just as the Americans were soon to help Stalin again at Yalta. But it might be well to consider whether Churchill ever did advocate what he is alleged to have advocated, and if he did, whether his advice was militarily feasible. Perhaps the quickest way to eastern Europe for the American and British armies was through Normandy, and not through the Ljubljana Gap, as the position of our forces in the spring of 1945 showed. Perhaps our failure to counteract Soviet influence in eastern Europe came from our rejection of Churchill's advice against halting our armies outside Berlin and Prague just before the Nazi collapse, rather than from failure to follow his advice about the Balkans a year earlier. Would the sending of western forces further into what was to become the Soviet zone of Germany have given us the "leverage" by which we could have compelled the Soviet Union to hold what we would have called free elections in Poland and in the other areas occupied by their armies, or would it have brought the cold war to a dangerous climax then and there, and have made the United States and Britain appear before the world as aggressors or potential aggressors? Did the United States suffer from the inability to see that the miilitary aspect of war is only the immediate aspect, and, once victory is assured, not even the most important aspect? Did we understand that victory means little if it is not achieved in the right political context? Did we display lamentable naïveté, or shrewd realism, in refusing to invade the eastern Mediterranean island of Rhodes, in insisting on invading southern France rather than striking north from the head of the Adriatic, and in refusing to race the Russians to Berlin, because we were suspicious of projects which were basically political rather than purely military?

So it will be seen that a consideration of the agreements reached at Yalta will probably concern not only the agreements themselves, but will also bear upon the wider issues of military and diplomatic coordination, of the working of a wartime alliance between nations of widely differing social structures, and of the difficulties of negotiation when one does not hold all the cards—issues sadly relevant today.[1]

[1] In this chapter, discussion of the Far Eastern aspects of the Yalta conference has been excluded

1.

Chester Wilmot was born in Australia; he served as a war correspondent in the second world war, and later became a BBC commentator. He wrote one of the volumes of the Australian official history of the war, and achieved considerable prominence when his remarkable book *The Struggle for Europe* was published. He died in a plane crash in 1954. In the following passage Mr. Wilmot provides a challenging criticism of the alleged American failure to appreciate what was really at stake in February 1945. Not only do his views provide a provocative beginning for any discussion of the merits of the Yalta conference, but they should also cause one to ponder the degree to which personal prejudice and temperament ought to be taken into account by the historian.

WILMOT: The Struggle for Europe *

En route to the Crimea, Roosevelt and Churchill held a brief preliminary conference at Malta, where they discussed the Yalta agenda and those issues which had introduced a certain acrimony into their relationship since their last meeting at Quebec in September. From these discussions Churchill hoped that there would emerge a common policy which he and the President could then present to Stalin and by their unity offset the advantage of his strength. It was apparent, however, that Roosevelt was as anxious as ever to avoid making commitments or giving the Russians any reason to think that they were dealing with an Anglo-American alliance. He saw himself as "the Good Neighbour of the World," the independent arbiter whose task it was to preserve harmony between Churchill and Stalin and to prevent Anglo-Soviet rivalry from causing a breach in "Big Three Unity." In the course of the Malta meeting the British delegation were dismayed to find that their American colleagues were less suspicious of Russia's post-war intentions than they were of Britain's. The appreciation of this fact—astonishing though it may seem at this distance—is essential to the understanding of what happened at Yalta.

The roots of this suspicion lay deep in history. Ever since 1776 Americans have nurtured a profound prejudice against "colonialism," and have tended to presume that the independence which brought them such benefits must likewise transform the lives of peoples less fortunate than themselves. With little regard for the merits, or the difficulties, of particular cases, they have consistently favoured the early grant of self-government to all dependent peoples, and particularly to those still under the dominion of the British Crown, for to Americans—by virtue of their past—Britain has remained the symbol of all Imperialism. Although ready to concede that British colonial policies were more progressive and more humane than those of any other country, they persisted in

* From Chester Wilmot, *The Struggle for Europe* (New York: Harper and Brothers, 1952), pp. 632, 635–38, 639–40. Copyright 1952 by Chester Wilmot. Reprinted by permission of Harper and Row.

the belief that Imperial rule contained such inherent evils that even good empires must be bad. . . .

Roosevelt's vision of the peace included not only the ending of the colonial system, but the abandonment of what he regarded as its essential concomitants, spheres of influence and regional balances of power. He expected, as Hull told Congress, that when the United Nations organisation was established there would "no longer be any need for spheres of influence, for alliances, for balance of power, or any other of the special arrangements through which, in the unhappy past, nations strove to safeguard their security or promote their interests."

This idealistic vision was not shared by Churchill who knew from long experience of European history that nations are less likely to succumb to the temptation of aggrandisement if their ambitions are restrained by a reasonable balance of power, and that such a balance could be preserved only by alliances and other "special arrangements." Churchill was by no means anti-Russian, but as early as October 1942 he had set down the view that "it would be a measureless disaster if Russian barbarism were to overlay the culture and independence of the ancient states of Europe." After Teheran, while continuing to work for Hitler's defeat and Stalin's friendship, he had become alive to the danger that the war would leave the Soviet Union in a position of overwhelming power which could be counter-balanced only by a strong British Empire, a firm Anglo-American alliance and a United States of Europe.

The prospect of a Russian advance deep into Central and South-Eastern Europe dismayed Churchill, and was one of the main reasons for his unflagging advocacy of those Balkan operations which Roosevelt and the American Chiefs of Staff so persistently vetoed. Thwarted in his desire to forestall Russia militarily, Churchill endeavoured to restrain her by striking a political bargain direct with the Kremlin. In the early summer of 1944, before the Red Army had made any serious inroad on the Balkans, the Prime Minister proposed to Stalin (without the President's knowledge) that the "controlling interest" in Rumania and Bulgaria should be exercised by the Soviet Union, and in Greece and Yugoslavia by Britain. When news of this proposal reached Washington the secretive British approach to Moscow was resented, and the plan was condemned by Hull on the ground that it amounted to "the division of the Balkans into spheres of influence." In reply Churchill argued that he was not proposing to carve up the Balkans, but that in the re-establishment of civil government "someone must play the hand" and that this should be done by the power responsible for military operations in each country. Roosevelt was not altogether satisfied, but he agreed to give the arrangement a three months' trial on the understanding that it would apply only to immediate problems and would not prejudice the post-war settlement. Nevertheless, the plan remained suspect in Washington, particularly as the President gave his consent to it without consulting, or even advising, his Secretary of State!

American suspicions were sharpened when Churchill, during his visit to Moscow in October 1944, "extended the arrangement still further, even reducing to percentages the relative degree of influence which Britain and Russia individually should have in specified Balkan countries." Each of the major powers placed its own interpretation on this agreement. The Russians regarded it as a formal acknowledgment of their predominant role and interest in the Danube Basin. The British saw it as the recognition of the *fait accompli* in that region and were thankful to have preserved even a small voice in the affairs of the Danubian states and to have kept Russia out of Greece. In Churchill's opinion it was not a matter of dividing the Balkans between Britain and Russia, but of preventing the Soviet Union extending its sphere of influence over the whole peninsula. The Americans, on the other hand, considered the agreement a betrayal of the Atlantic Charter, a sinister scheme to further Britain's Imperial ambitions. In the State Department it was denounced as "Churchiavellian."

Before the close of the year a more severe strain was imposed on Anglo-American relations by developments in the Mediterranean, where, by Allied agreement, the chief political responsibility rested on Britain. In Italy, when the Bonomi Cabinet resigned at the end of November, the British Government let it be known that it could not endorse any new administration which included Count Sforza either as Prime Minister or Foreign Secretary. Although regarded by Churchill—with some justification—as an untrustworthy intriguer, Sforza had a long record of opposition to Fascism and was greatly respected in the United States where he had lived in exile throughout Mussolini's reign. When Churchill's disapproval of Sforza became known in Washington, there was a storm of protest in the press, and Edward Stettinius, who had just succeeded Hull as Secretary of State, felt obliged to dissociate himself publicly from the British policy. On December 5th he issued a statement in which he declared that "the composition of the Italian Government" was "purely an Italian affair" and should be settled "along democratic lines without influence from the outside."

Churchill . . . was particularly irate at the criticism implied in Stettinius's statement that the principle of non-interference "would apply in an even more pronounced degree with regard to governments of the United Nations in their liberated territories." In London this was rightly taken as a thinly-veiled reference to Greece, where a most ugly situation had arisen following the employment of British troops to prevent the recognized government being overthrown by Communist partisans who had "invaded" Athens. Since the British in Greece were there, as Churchill reminded Parliament, "with American and Russian consent [and] at the invitation of the Government of all parties," they could not "leave Athens to anarchy and misery, followed by tyranny established on murder."

Nevertheless, the use of British forces against Greek Communists, who so recently had been fighting the Germans, caused a grave heart-burning on both sides of the Atlantic, and Churchill came under the fiercest criticism, at home and abroad, that was directed at him during the entire war. It was assumed, even by men of goodwill, that his strictures on the Communists were unjustifiably severe, and he was accused of exploiting the crisis so that he could maintain in power a reactionary regime bent upon restoring an unpopular monarchy.

In Washington feeling ran so high that Admiral King—never a man to miss an opportunity of embarrassing his country's principal ally—gave orders to the commander of the U.S. naval forces in the Mediterranean that he was "not to permit any American LSTs to be used to transfer supplies to Greece." Fortunately Hopkins intervened to have the order countermanded, but not before it had come to Churchill's knowledge and roused him to a fresh pitch of righteous indignation. Further sharp exchanges passed across the Atlantic with the result, as Sherwood says, that "relations between the White House and Downing Street were more strained than they had ever been before." It was considered in Washington that "Churchill's well-known predilection for constitutional monarchy was dictating policies which were against the people's will," and that, in defiance of the Atlantic Charter, he was determined to restore the "unsavory status quo ante in Europe." . . .

Roosevelt was not alone in thinking that Diplomacy by Friendship would bring a sympathetic response from Stalin. The most influential of his advisers—military and political alike—were agreed, as Hull says, that they "must and could get along with the Soviet Government," and that this would be possible if they were "patient and forbearing." The idea that they could "get along with" the Russians came more easily to the American leaders than to the British, for the United States is the great melting pot and the American people have shown an unparalleled capacity for absorbing into their own society a multitude of nationalities.

Perhaps the best exposition of Roosevelt's idea is to be found in a memorandum which Hopkins wrote six months after Yalta. "We know or believe," he said, "that Russia's interests, so far as we can anticipate them, do not afford an opportunity for a major difference with us in foreign affairs. We believe we are mutually dependent upon each other for economic reasons. We find the Russians as individuals easy to deal with. The Russians undoubtedly like the American people. They like the United States. They trust the United States more than they trust any other power in the world . . . above all, they want to maintain friendly relations with us. . . . They are a tenacious, determined people who think and act just like you and I do."

Eisenhower endorsed this view of the Russian people when he wrote, "In his generous instincts, in his love of laughter, in his devotion to a comrade, and in his healthy, direct outlook on the affairs of workaday life, the ordinary Russian seems to me to bear a marked similarity to what we call an 'average American.'" Eisenhower believed too that there was a special bond between the United States and the Soviet Union, a bond that was inevitably lacking in the Anglo-American association. He felt, he says, that "in the past relations of America and Russia there was no cause to regard the future with pessimism." On the one hand, "the two peoples had maintained an unbroken friendship that dated back to the birth of the United States as an independent republic"; on the other, "both were free from the stigma of colonial empire building by force."

This remarkable statement stems straight from the Founding Fathers. It was the American way of saying that politically both peoples were free from original sin. That this was not true of either was irrelevant; it was believed, not merely by Eisenhower but also by many Americans who should have been better acquainted with their own history. This belief was implicit in Roosevelt's approach to the problems which were to be discussed at Yalta. In his eyes, Britain was an Imperial Power, bearing the "colonial stigma"; Russia was not. That assessment of his allies was a decisive factor in Roosevelt's readiness to make concessions to the Soviet Union both in Europe and Asia in order to ensure Stalin's entry into the Pacific War. . . .

2.

George N. Crocker, a California lawyer and a former Assistant United States Attorney, has been described as a "profound student of history." His book on Roosevelt's foreign policy during the second world war has proved tremendously popular in many circles, and has run through several printings in a short time. Mr. Crocker, obviously a believer in the role of the individual in history, traces the blame for what he sees as the shortcomings of American policy in 1945 to the follies and the misconceptions of Roosevelt and of some of his immediate advisers, and maintains that they could not, or did not, properly gauge the relative threats to the United States of the great totalitarian systems of the mid-twentieth century. Whether or not one agrees with Mr. Crocker's interpretation and treatment of the facts, it is important to read his opinions with care, for they represent a widely held view of the Crimean conference of 1945.

CROCKER: Roosevelt's Road to Russia *

Franklin D. Roosevelt's fourth inauguration was held on January 20, 1945. Three days later, the President boarded the cruiser *Quincy*. For several months his fondest dream, next to his re-election, had been another love feast with "Uncle Joe" Stalin, but now the Russian dictator had made it plain that if the President of the United States wanted to see him, he would have to trek to Russia to do it. The conference would be on the soil of the Soviet Union or nowhere.

General John R. Deane, head of the American Military Mission in Moscow, had seen Americans, under White House policy, licking the Russians' boots *ad nauseam* for three years, but this troubled him more than anything. "No single event of the war irritated me more," he wrote in *The Strange Alliance*, "than seeing the President of the United States lifted from wheel chair to automobile,

* From George N. Crocker, *Roosevelt's Road to Russia* (Chicago: Regnery, 1959), pp. 241–62. Reprinted by permission of the Henry Regnery Company.

to ship, to shore, and to aircraft, in order to go halfway around the world as the only possible means of meeting J. V. Stalin."

All of the President's advisers except Harry Hopkins opposed his going. Cocksure, ill-prepared, and, as at Teheran, with no strategy beyond his old obsession that the important thing was for Stalin to "like" him, he ignored them and went across the world to engage in an ostentatious spectacle of personal vanity and power which was to be his last. The Crimean, or Yalta, Conference was held in February. On April 12, Roosevelt died. . . .

Millions of words have been written about Yalta. In a sense, the Teheran Conference was more critical, for there, Stalin and Roosevelt stacked the deck with which the game was played out at Yalta. But when they came together on the Russian shore of the Black Sea in February of 1945, they finalized decisions so malodorous—for slave labor, forcible repatriation of refugees, the uprooting of millions of human beings from their homes and lands, the breaking of pledges of the right of self-determination, and similar brutalities—that Yalta has become, more and more as each year passes, a symbol of international immorality. The reams of apologetics which the Roosevelt cultists have poured forth in an attempt to prevent the damage to their hero's reputation from becoming too devastating have had only a sparse and ephemeral success. Too much is known. The verdict of history is inevitable. . . .

It has been said, with some truth, that when Woodrow Wilson entered the cockpit of the peace conference at Versailles after World War I, he was a sheep among wolves. But if Wilson was sometimes naive, he was a meticulous scholar and was never casual. Roosevelt approached Yalta as if he were on a vacation. In fact, the Hopkins notes are frank enough to say: "I was sure the President would wind up by going to the Crimea, the primary reason being that it was a part of the world he had never visited and his adventurous spirit was forever leading him to go to unusual places and, on his part, the election being over, he would no longer be disturbed about it for political reasons." He rested much of the time on the *Quincy*'s voyage across the Atlantic. James F. Byrnes, who was on board, was amazed at his lack of preparation for the forthcoming conference, although stacks of pertinent reports and data were on the ship. This worried Byrnes.

Illness may have played a part. According to Stettinius, the President was in a bad state when he made his inaugural address on the porch of the White House on January 20. "That day he had seemed to tremble all over. It was not just his hands that shook, but his whole body as well." Stettinius found him "cheerful, calm, and quite rested" when the ship arrived at the island of Malta on February 2, or so he says in his book. But Admiral King later told Harry Hopkins that when he went aboard the *Quincy* that day and saw the President, he was "alarmed" at the state of his health and noted a deterioration since the inauguration. Even so, Sherwood assures us that Mr. Roosevelt was "as always buoyant and excited at the prospect of new adventures as he left the *Quincy* to make the rest of his journey by air. . . ."

President Roosevelt, and, of course, Harry Hopkins, too, cherished an implacable fixation that the Bolsheviks who ruled Russia were men of good will and that their expansionist aspirations, which were plainly evident, boded no evil for Europe and the world. Whether this was a sincere conviction based on a rational process, or a "peculiar aberration," as Wilmot calls it, or sheer hypocrisy, may be a Freudian puzzle. However, that these two men knew that the Soviet Union was winning its battle to become the "dominant" power in Europe and that they embraced this concept with complete equanimity is not open to question. . . .

Throughout the war period, Roosevelt deliberately put on blinders when any fact derogatory to the Russians turned up. Thus in April, 1943, he had scoffed when John Franklin Carter presented him with a special intelligence report casting upon the Russians the guilt for the massacre of fifteen thousand Polish officers in the Katyn Forest, and he had shown acid displeasure in May, 1944, when former Governor of Pennsylvania George H. Earle, who had been Minister to Austria and Bulgaria and Special Envoy to Turkey, brought to the White House documents and photographs attesting Russian guilt in that cold-blooded atrocity. On March 24, 1945, two weeks before he died, Roosevelt wrote a letter to Earle, then a commander in the Navy, expressly forbidding him to publish an article contending that Russia was a greater menace than Nazi Germany. He suppressed the article and had Earle shipped off to Samoa.

The pro-Russian atmosphere in Washington—so hard to combat because the President himself, his wife, and his most intimate friend were at the center of it—was galling to many, including the frustrated Secretary of the Navy, James Forrestal. His diaries reveal that in September, 1944, he had written to a friend that "if any American suggests that we act in accord with our own interests, he is apt to be called a . . . Fascist or imperialist, while if Uncle Joe suggests that he needs the Baltic provinces, half of Poland, all of Bessarabia and access to the Mediterranean, all hands in Washington agree that he is a fine, frank, candid and generally delightful fellow." Such was the frame of mind Roosevelt took to Yalta. . . .

Yalta, of course, was Stalin's show. He was the star. At the conference table, he was at once the most blunt and the most subtle. As a host, he overwhelmed his impressionable guests with lavish care, so that Churchill telegraphed home that the Russians' "prodigality exceeds belief." On one occasion somebody said casually that there was no lemon peel in the cocktails. The next day, a lemon tree, loaded with fruit, was in the hall, brought from far away by air. Mesmerized from the start, Roosevelt presented a spectacle that can only be described as pitiful—this fading President, floating slowly out of this life, outmatched and outwitted at every point, mouthing meaningless cliches, and dripping with flummery in the presence of the dictator.

How did the host of Yalta look in the flesh? "He has got an unpleasantly cold, crafty, cruel face," wrote Alanbrooke in his diary, "and whenever I look at him I can imagine his sending off people to their doom without turning a hair. On the other hand, there is no doubt he has a quick brain."

To call the Yalta Conference "one of the biggest drunken brawls I ever saw," as did one of the American interpreters, who observed more than one participant helped out, in a stupor, from the banquet table, is no doubt an extravagance. To say that an alcoholic atmosphere pervaded it is more felicitous. Stalin, and even Molotov, and the square-faced, stubble-topped generals and commissars in the Russian contingent could be genial when it served their purpose, even to the British, about whom they always had some reservations. Certainly they were more accomplished consumers of vodka and champagne than their British and American guests, who, by all accounts, brought to the festivities of this eight-day Saturnalia a do-or-die spirit, if inadequate preparation for such rugged competition. . . .

[According to the final report and communiqué], the German nation was to be dismembered. The details were referred to a committee, but this much was settled: a huge chunk was to be torn off and given to Poland as a sop for the mayhem to be performed on that unhappy country; some choice morsels, such as the city of Königsberg, were to be donated to the Soviet Union outright; and the rest of eastern Germany was to be spread-eagled for forced Communization by Russian masters, since occupation by the Red Army meant nothing less than that. How and when this nightmare would ever end was too unpleasant a subject to be faced at Yalta. Technically, the exact western Polish boundary was to be fixed at "the Peace Conference." This was a way of deferring the blame. Actually, the present Oder-Neisse line was, roughly, the demarcation contemplated at Yalta.

Ten million Germans were doomed to be turned out of their homes and set out on the roads to flee westward, for all of the territories to be detached were ethnically German. East Prussia, Pomerania, and Brandenburg had never in six hundred years even been under dispute. . . . It is not extravagant to say that Königsberg and Breslau had been Germanic cities almost as long as London had been English.

What followed Yalta was a mass expulsion which Churchill himself was impelled to allude to as "tragedy on a prodigious scale." Actually, never in history, even in the worst of pagan times, has there been such a millionfold uprooting of human beings. By the fall of 1945 shocked voices in England were heard to say that it was the most enormous official atrocity in all of the world's history, and Churchill admitted in the House of Commons in August that the land grab, "comprising as it does one-quarter of the arable land of Germany, is not a good augury for the future of Europe."

Reparations were to be exacted from the rest of Germany "in kind," said the communiqué. This meant factories, locomotives, goods, etc. The secret protocol added that reparations were to include human labor. This was, as Byrnes said when he learned of it, an authorization for forced or slave labor, which it was known the Russians intended to impose but which was, of course, abhorrent to the American people. Franklin D. Roosevelt had always taken pains to pose as a humanitarian, so it is not surprising that no inkling of this item of the Yalta agreements was allowed to creep into the public announcements.

Poland also was to be dismembered. Some eleven million people who lived east of the so-called Curzon Line in prewar Poland were to be surrendered to the Soviet Union without any semblance of a plebiscite. Thus Roosevelt, Stalin, and Churchill decreed Soviet annexation of almost half of Poland's territory and about one-third of her population. Roosevelt weakly proposed that Stalin allow Poland to keep Lwow and the nearby oil fields. He was as aware as Stalin was that the Drohobycz oil region was essential to the Polish economy, but he showed his hand too quickly. "He pointed out," says Stettinius, "that he was merely suggesting this for consideration rather than insisting on it." Naturally, the dictator scooped up all the chips.

The Polish government-in-exile, under which whole regiments of Poles were fighting valiantly for the Western powers in Italy and on the western front, was now betrayed, and the Lublin Committee, a group of Polish Communists domiciled for years in Moscow, where they had been trained in Stalin's tough school for the task of administering Poland, was described in the communiqué as "the present Provisional Government of Poland." This meant the surrender of Poland to Communism. For four days Churchill fought against this faithlessness, but his American colleague would not stick to his guns with him. Sharp differences between Churchill and Stalin came to the surface on the first day this subject was discussed. That evening, the President made a fatal move. He compromised his independence by sending a letter to Stalin in which he announced: "I am determined there shall be no breach between ourselves and the Soviet Union." With that statement he admitted that if Stalin made an issue of Poland, the United States would give way.

Thus fortified, Stalin tossed to the Prime Minister and the President only some high-sounding words to take home. He agreed that the puppet provisional government would be "reorganized" by the inclusion of "democratic leaders from Poland itself and from Poles abroad," but he refused to mention names. Since in Communist diction Communists were "democratic," this was a hollow promise. He also agreed that "free and unfettered elections" would be held. If, as we suspect, the men at the conference table—who were, surely, not insensitive to the incongruous—found it necessary to suppress smiles at this, the fact is not recorded; yet the scene is not without humor. Such elections had never been held by the Communists in Russia or elsewhere, and it could not have been seriously expected that they were about to be held in Poland under Stalin's hand-picked cabal and the occupying Red Army, particularly since it was specified that only "democratic and anti-Nazi parties" would have the right to put up candidates, and, in the Marx-Lenin-Stalin tradition of interpretation, only pro-Russian, pro-Communist, anti-capitalist political elements could possibly merit that description.

The British demanded that the elections be under the supervision of the American, British, and Soviet Ambassadors. Stalin bluntly rejected this, arguing that it would be an affront to the pride and sovereignty of the Poles! When, at the end, Eden, knowing that an unsupervised election would be a mockery, endeavored to insist upon this safeguard, Stettinius announced that Roosevelt was willing to eliminate it, saying "the President was anxious to reach agreement and that to expedite matters he was willing to make this concession." Freedom in Poland was doomed. Admiral Leahy quickly recognized the loosely worded Polish formula as a "phony." He spoke up before it was signed. "Mr. President," said Leahy, "this is so elastic that the Russians can stretch it all the way from Yalta to Washington without ever technically breaking it." Roosevelt said he knew that. . . .

[In the so-called "Declaration on Liberated Europe"] there followed some unctuous phrases about assisting the "liberated" states to hold free elections and establish democratic governments, but these things were to be done in "concert" and "jointly" and only when "in the opinion of the three governments" (U.S., U.K., and U.S.S.R.) conditions "make such action necessary." The loophole nullified the whole Declaration, as far as it might ever circumscribe the Russian "liberators." In effect, the Western Powers were agreeing not to lift a finger for freedom in eastern Europe without the consent of the Soviet Union.

It was also arranged that the permanent "United Nations" body would be impotent to interfere effectually with the incipient Communist empire. At Yalta the veto was agreed upon, and Roosevelt acceded to Stalin's preposterous demand that the Soviet Union have three votes in the General Assembly. The State Department's "specialist" on setting up the United Nations was none other than Alger Hiss. In fact, he was slated to become the sparkplug and presiding officer at its organizing convention in April. To a man of Stalin's foresight, the potentialities which this new polyglot conglomeration of nationalisms and basically disunited world factions would furnish to Soviet tacticians for propaganda and mischief were obvious. . . .

A dark moral blot upon the Yalta record was the promise to Stalin that the Russian nationals rounded up by the Americans and British in Germany, France, and Italy would be deported to Russia, by force if necessary. There were about two million of these. Some had been captured by the Germans; others had voluntarily fled from Communism early in the war. Many were found in German uniforms, but others were civilian escapees who wanted only to find freedom. Most of them begged not to be sent back to Russia, knowing their fate would be the firing squad or Siberian slave camps.

The State Department had decided to disallow forcible repatriation and abide by the provisions of the Geneva Convention on the treatment of prisoners of war, but a message was dispatched to Washington from Yalta overruling this decision. As a consequence, when the war ended, a sickening drama was enacted. All the Russians were herded indiscriminately—screaming, in tears, at bayonet point or dragged bodily—into boxcars and sent to Russia. Not the slightest attention was paid to the Geneva Convention, the doctrine of asylum, or the humane regard for individual choice which had ameliorated man's cruelty in less barbarous years. The gruesome spectacle was singed in memory, but not until ten years later, when the State Department published the so-called "Yalta Papers," was it known for sure that this unholy crime against humanity had been connived at Yalta. The contemporary publicity was silent about it.

It was also silent about any furtive promise by Roosevelt to Stalin to let the Russian army reach Berlin and Prague first. Yet . . . President Beneš of Czechoslovakia was convinced there was one. So was General George S. Patton, who was ordered to halt his troops only a dash from the Czech capital to allow the Russian army time to "liberate" the city and seize two of the biggest prizes in Europe: the vast Skoda munitions works and the uranium deposits at Jachymov.

Patton's deductions were not likely to be erroneous on a point so tender to him. However, the full details of the humiliating checkrein put on Patton at Pilsen and Bradley's strange sit-down at the lightly defended Elbe River, with Berlin only fifty-three miles away and his own American patrols in its suburbs, remain obscure to this day. Eisenhower's utterances on the subject have been guarded and divergent. It is definitely known that Churchill considered the capture of Berlin and Prague by the Western Allies to be a matter of transcendent postwar importance and that his stern pleas struck no spark in Roosevelt. Eisenhower's final battle plans were drawn up in March, the month after Yalta. They left Berlin and Prague to the Russians. Without getting British approval or even mentioning the subject to Air Chief Marshal Tedder, his deputy, he sent his plans by a direct telegram to Stalin for clearance on March 28. Naturally, Stalin approved them with alacrity. It is hardly plausible that Eisenhower would have followed such a course and made such a decision without word from the highest level. Churchill was furious and protested at once to both Eisenhower and the President, but in vain. Churchill's messages to Roosevelt on April 1 and April 5 were pathetic entreaties, serious warnings. It was "a pity," he said, that Eisenhower had sent the telegram to Stalin. "I say quite frankly that Berlin remains of high strategic importance." He might as well have been shouting at a tree.

Of this period, Churchill writes in his memoirs: "The United States stood on the scene of victory, master of world fortunes, but without a true and coherent design. Britain, though still very powerful, could not act decisively alone. I could at this stage only warn and plead. Thus this . . . was to me a most unhappy time. I moved amid cheering crowds . . . with an aching heart and a mind oppressed by forebodings."

Churchill knew the secret, too—the secret in the White House closet, the face of reality which Roosevelt and Hopkins had kept in murky banishment through three years of artifice and propaganda. Three wars were raging, not one. One of them was the expansionist onslaught of Communist imperialism, the Juggernaut of the twentieth century, the rapacious destroyer which Selwyn Lloyd has described as "a horse of strange parentage, by Karl Marx out of Catherine the Great." It was in this war that Roosevelt refused to man the ramparts, leaving Churchill a lonely figure, impotent to act alone. Thus the paradox: the moment of "victory" was for Churchill "a most unhappy time." Veiled by the temperance of his words is a branding accusation which history will not overlook. The discretion of a statesman permitted him to say no more at the time.

3.

Rudolph A. Winnacker, after having taught history at the Universities of Michigan and Nebraska, entered government service, and today is the chief historian in the Office of the Secretary of Defense. In the following article he provides an interpretation of the Yalta conference quite different from that which has just been read. Not only must one consider the merits of Mr. Winnacker's argument, but one should also try to determine whether he is a better historian than Mr. Crocker: is his view narrower or broader; does he seem to have a better "feel" for the time or is he prone to regard issues from an "ivory tower"; does he take more factors into account, or is he misled by superficial issues; does his article suffer from having been written too soon after the event, or does immediacy give him greater understanding of it?

WINNACKER: Yalta—Another Munich? *

We are a peace-loving people, though we do not shirk a fight which is forced upon us. We do not want war, but all around us we hear talk about war. The tone is sometimes resentful, often surprised, sometimes fearful, never enthusiastic. Most of us feel no personal responsibility for the current sad state of international relations, and with a clear conscience we look for a scapegoat. For many people the decisions reached at the Yalta Conference hold the most prominent place among the causes of the current crisis.

Scapegoat hunting is a difficult indoor sport. The best of historians after a lifetime of careful and painstaking research and with the best techniques of historical scholarship have often agreed to disagree on their analysis of the same historical problem. For amateurs the rules are usually not so strict. Amateurs may state their prejudices much more blatantly. They may freely ignore evidence without loss of reputation. They may resort to partial quotations and misquotations, or cite newspaper items as expressions of official policy. They may do all this, because their basic aim is to obtain converts for a cause, not to promote the understanding of human affairs. But it does not pay to point this out to them. . . .

The criticisms of American policy at the Yalta Conference have been of two types: criticism of the procedures employed in reaching decisions and criticism of the decisions themselves. The first problem need not detain us long. It is true that President Roosevelt's assistants, official and unofficial, found it often difficult, in the absence of clear directives, to discharge their duties efficiently. Many decisions were made off the cuff. In the formulation of some of the most important policies, the people most responsible for their execution were consulted only casually and were finally faced by a firm decision about which they had grave misgivings. At the conferences of the heads of governments

* From Rudolph A. Winnacker, "Yalta—Another Munich?" in *The Virginia Quarterly Review*, XXIV (1948), pp. 521–25, 531–37. Reprinted by permission of the author and of the editors of *The Virginia Quarterly Review*.

lly hectic for conscientious advisers. Sometimes civilians, some-
ry were ignored. The recollections of Mr. Stimson, Mr. Hull,
figures are full of evidence supporting this thesis.

mplied by the criticisms made that a more systematic and
ration of problems of state during the Roosevelt Administra-
... would have changed to any great extent the decisions reached, the argument appears of doubtful validity. President Roosevelt had firm, though often
not very specific, ideas on basic policy problems that none of his advisers could
have combated successfully. He listened to ideas from private as well as official sources, but he kept his own counsel. He was quick to adopt suggestions which fitted his own pattern of thought. He used conferences with his
advisers to elaborate his ideas, not to change them. He seldom would sharply
disagree with opinions advanced, but inopportune proposals were buried by
failure of action on the White House level. In other words, the experience
of the entire Roosevelt era argues against the thesis that, if the President had
only consulted Mr. "X" or General "Y" at Yalta, the course of history would
have been changed. The Yalta Conference dealt with basic policy problems
and on these the President had firm and well-established convictions. The
time for revision had not yet come.

The second criticism, that the decisions reached at Yalta during the week
from February 4 to 11, 1945, are largely responsible for the disadvantageous
political and military situation which we face, requires more detailed examination. In general, the criticism runs as follows: At the Yalta Conference
President Roosevelt, already a very sick man, unnecessarily presented the
Russian Communists with control over Europe as well as Asia. By the vague
agreements on the political future of Eastern European countries he threw
the whole of this area into Soviet hands. And even worse, the agreements
on the occupation zones of Germany and Austria moved the Russian colossus
into Central Europe, where it gained a strategic position from which to
threaten, infiltrate, and even control what was left of Western European
civilization. All this was without proper regard for or consultation with the
peoples involved. . . . A much stronger attitude should have been taken toward the Soviet Union. Much better conditions would have been obtained by
telling the Soviets that the Western allies would keep on advancing until
concrete evidence of Soviet good faith in carrying out its obligations were
forthcoming.

The fact that as a result of World War II one hundred million people in
Eastern Europe are under Soviet domination, the vast majority against their
will, is not debatable. The effect of the misery created and the hopes shattered
cannot even approximately be measured. Nor can it be disputed that in a world
of power politics the Soviet Union has gained tremendous strategic advantages
in Europe and the Far East that have enabled her to exert most effective
pressure against the Western powers.

Disagreements arise when the discussion turns to the alternative courses of
action advocated and their possible consequences, especially when the his-

toric. circumstances surrounding Yalta are completely ignored. It is at this point that the greatest caution is advisable. No wishful thinking and no "I said in 1945 . . ." will lessen the seriousness of the problems that were raised at Yalta. Judgments cannot be based on what individuals would have done as individuals; all policies should be evaluated as proposed by a President of the United States, carrying the wide responsibilities this office represents, and answerable to the people for the decisions taken. It is from this point of view that the Yalta Conference must be analyzed.

First, a matter of definition: to make Yalta solely responsible for our so-called surrender to the Soviet Union is, strictly speaking, not correct. Some of the decisions to which the critics object were reached at other times. The zonal occupation of Germany dates back to Teheran in December, 1943, and was worked out during 1944 by the European Advisory Commission sitting in London, closely watched, directed, and stymied by the home governments. Much of the future policy toward Germany is implied in the "unconditional surrender" formula announced at Casablanca in January, 1943, and spelled out in the Anglo-American agreement on "pastoral Germany" signed at Quebec in September, 1944. These policies were in general confirmed by the decisions reached at Yalta and later at Potsdam. The future status of the Western Slavs was discussed at Teheran, where support to Tito was agreed upon, and was a recurring theme in the long debates between the allies regarding the Mediterranean or the Channel as the major road of invasion. Still, the Yalta Conference represents the logical culmination of our war policy. It was the last conference of the major allied war leaders, Roosevelt, Churchill, and Stalin. Its agenda included the problem of a United Nations organization, the fate of liberated Europe, and the treatment of Germany as well as of Japan. For these reasons Yalta may serve as a convenient symbol of American war and postwar policy and will be considered as such in this discussion. . . .

Strong arguments of a political nature support the policy followed at Yalta. The Soviet Union had gained immense prestige in the United States and in Europe by her successful resistance to the Nazis. Regardless of the official policy pursued, this prestige could not be eradicated overnight. An announcement stating that agreement with the Soviet Union was impossible would have been followed by indignant accusations from millions of sincere citizens, claiming that reactionary elements in the government were preparing, if not provoking, war against our former ally. Even after three years of Soviet violations of the agreements reached at Yalta and other conferences, defenders of the Soviet Union's foreign policy have been able to found a political party in the United States with the main objective of surrendering Europe and Asia to Soviet domination in the hope of starting a new era of good will on earth. It might be regrettable, but it is not disputable, that any less conciliatory policy than that practiced by our government would have divided us much more deeply. In a democracy basic attitudes cannot be changed overnight. The formulation of public opinion on foreign policy requires not only time but also indisputable facts to make an impression on the large number of idealists who refuse to believe that evil can exist in this world.

In less idealistic Europe the effect of a break between the allies would probably have been equally disastrous. Communist arguments about American
imperialism and neo-Fascism would have obtained a sympathetic hearing
from many more millions of ordinary war-weary citizens. Despite the recent
sad experience with popular-front governments, left-wing parties of all types,
dreading war and reactionary rule more than the dictatorship of the proletariat,
would have preferred alliance with the Communists to co-operation with the
Right. Throughout the world the Soviet Union would have had increased opportunities to accomplish her aims by conquest from within, rather than by
war from without. As a result of a policy of patience and a prolonged attempt to find a basis for agreement, the Soviet Union now faces an aroused
Western world, where only a minority is not convinced that Communism
is at least as much of a danger as Nazism ever was. These considerations cannot be lightly tossed aside in a discussion of our national policy during World
War II.

There are those who claim that a showdown with the Soviets would not
have been necessary. A firm stand at Yalta for the rights of the majority in
Eastern European countries, for the integrity of China, and for a reasonable
settlement in Germany would have made the Soviet Union yield to our demands. This opinion is usually concluded with the terse statement: "I know
the Russians!" Most of the listeners, not knowing the Russians intimately, are
at a disadvantage in combating such well-documented opinions. Still, if it is
true that the Soviets understand only force and are realistic judges of their
opponents' strength, it appears extremely doubtful that a mere bluff at Yalta
would have worked. It is a fact that the Soviet Union could probably not
have faced a war with the Western powers at the time, but at least she was
not handicapped by public opinion on this issue. Above all, she was either
already in possession of the areas in dispute or prepared to occupy them before the Western powers. Only an aroused United States might have made
an impression on the realists in the Kremlin. Even then the probable division
among the Western powers and the existence of thousands of Communist-led
Partisans along the American lines of communication might have encouraged
the Soviet Union to await developments. Nobody can say with certainty that
a bluff would or would not have worked, but the painful experience gained
since Yalta argues strongly against the success of such a policy.

Some of the critics admit that at Yalta the United States was not in a position to enforce better terms. By that time, it is said, it was too late to remedy
the defects of a policy which was wrong from the beginning. The less virulent
exponents of this thesis insist that by adopting a Balkan rather than a Channel
strategy we would have been in a position to contain the Soviet Union within
her 1939 boundaries. Prime Minister Churchill is usually mentioned in this
connection as a reference and praised for his farsightedness. Unlike our statesmen, he thought of winning the peace as well as the war. There are no reasons why we could not have undertaken such an offensive, but it would have

been at the expense of other operations and its final outcome might not have justified the necessary investments. The first price to be paid would have been the abandonment of the invasion of France. As it turned out, this operation was undertaken just in time to prevent a serious dislocation of the British war effort by the Nazi V-bomb attack, launched from sites on the Channel coast. In addition, the Balkan operation itself could hardly be considered very sound strategically. Balkan terrain has been for centuries a nightmare to military strategists. Rugged mountains would have had to be crossed through difficult passes before reaching the Danube plain, and additional mountain ranges protected Germany proper. To accomplish the proposed political objective of liberating the border states in Eastern Europe, final success would have had to be achieved before October, 1944. At that time Soviet troops were outside Warsaw and in control of most of Roumania and Bulgaria. It is doubtful that the Western powers could have met this time schedule. Moreover, the most serious military and political problems would have been raised by such an operation if it had been successful. With the most tenuous lines of communications, we would be facing hostile Soviet forces and giving to the whole world the appearance of protecting the Nazis against the justified vengeance of the Russian people and their allies. The principles of singleness of objective and concentration of force are seldom violated with impunity in war or in diplomacy.

The most outspoken critics of our war policy imply that the Communists were always a greater menace to the values we live for than the Nazis and that aid to the Soviet Union was our greatest blunder. Most people find it difficult to make a choice between these two exponents of ruthlessness and persecution. To them a Europe dominated by the Nazis is as great a threat to our security as a Europe under Soviet domination. It happened that in 1941 and 1942 the Nazis were the greatest menace of the two. Their own blunders kept them from achieving their conquest of Russia. The possibility of such a victory cannot be written off as of no consequence to the United States on the assumption that the Nazis would have been unable to organize and develop the resources which they had gained. Such arguments have doubtful validity in the twentieth century with its effective methods of communication and transportation.

Perhaps we should have changed our policy after the Soviet victory at Stalingrad and the first effective Soviet counteroffensives in early 1943. By coming to terms with the Germans, if not the Nazis, we could conceivably have employed their manpower and industrial resources in containing the Soviet Union. Aside from the obvious difficulties in executing such a tortuous policy, it would have been the surest way of alienating essential friends and losing whatever moral prestige we possess. Neither the French nor the Italians, neither the Poles nor the Roumanians, neither the Belgians nor the Dutch love the Russians, but neither do they like the Germans. The deep and justified hatred for the Nazis and their supporters existing in Europe is the greatest asset the Soviet Union has. An Anglo–American–German alliance would have thrown even the most conservative European patriot into the Soviet camp. In the United States, the commotion caused by the Darlan incident would have been a minor rehearsal for the popular revulsion against such an amoral reversal of alliances. Even full knowledge of what the future held for us would not have justified or made feasible such a policy.

Our war policy, and especially the Yalta Conference, can be criticized for many errors of omission and commission. Most of these criticisms are fully justified, but their bearing on the postwar relations between the United States and the Soviet Union is debatable. Few will deny that Lend-Lease to the Soviet Union was loosely administered. Detailed documentation on actual shortages and production rates, as required from other countries, was never obtained. A more business-like attitude toward the Soviets might have improved the morale of our Moscow representatives, produced some savings in Lend-Lease shipments, and led to a favorable action on American requests for the use of airfields and the travel of military observers. It would probably not, however, have achieved a change in the Soviet attitude toward the West.

Similarly, the Yalta procedure hardly fitted into the Wilsonian tradition of open covenants, openly arrived at; though the desirability of this principle cannot be challenged, its effectiveness is another matter. . . . It is also contradictory, to put it mildly, to affirm your faith in the Atlantic Charter, including a renunciation of any "territorial changes that do not accord with the freely expressed wishes of the people concerned," and agree at the same time to the annexation of the Kurile Islands by the Soviet Union and to vast changes in the boundaries of Poland. It will always be one of the greatest tragedies in history that the hopes and rights of the Eastern European countries could not have been supported by more substantial guarantees at Yalta, but to hold the United States, and not the Soviet Union, responsible for this failure might be considered effective propaganda, but hardly a product of rational analysis. The disapproval felt for these and other decisions reached at Yalta is probably fully justified. The moral prestige of the United States was not increased by our participation. Still, the critics face the formidable task of showing that any other course of action would have produced more favorable results.

Whatever alternative policies are suggested, they should not be brushed off by a casual remark that they are based on hindsight. It is a statesman's responsibility to analyze a situation correctly and at no time to make any agreements which, if his estimate was mistaken, would jeopardize the security of his country. It is clear now that our wartime analysis of Soviet intentions was incorrect. How great the chances for the success of our policy were will probably never be known. It might be that as we are divided between isolationists and internationalists, so the ruling group at Moscow is divided between Russian Communists and World Revolutionaries. The fact remains that the latter group is in control. In carrying out a policy whose basic assumption was not realized, we did not, however, surrender any significant card which it was within our power to withhold. At the same time, we concluded definite agreements whose violation by the Soviet Union made it clear that the Soviets were embarked upon a policy of aggression. Unity at home is the first prerequisite of national security.

It happened that within one decade we encountered two threats to our way of life. We were incapable of meeting both of them simultaneously. We did, however, destroy one, the more dangerous one at the time. We are making progress in containing the other threat. Despite the grave danger to the nation in the recent past and at the present time, we have maintained our basic democratic principles and procedures. This fact is perhaps the scapegoat people are looking for. More arbitrary methods might have provided greater efficiency, flexibility, and possibly even success. But such gains would have been paid for by the destruction of the very values we were and are defending. Fortunately, most of us are unwilling to pay this price.

4.

William H. McNeill, who teaches history at the University of Chicago, provides an interpretation of the Yalta conference which some readers may not find to their liking, but which others will probably find remarkably well-balanced, broad, and dispassionate. In attributing the fundamental failure at Yalta to a failure of intellectual understanding, is Mr. McNeill avoiding issues, and refusing to perform the necessary task of apportioning blame, by plunging into the never-never land of "ideas"? Or has he, rather, freed himself from the distorting tendency of many observers to see history as the catalog of individual error? Does Mr. McNeill's position vary in any fundamental way from that of Rudolph Winnacker?

McNEILL: America, Britain, and Russia: Their Cooperation and Conflict 1941–1946 *

The Yalta Conference, 4–11 February 1945, was probably the most important war-time meeting of the Big Three. It came at the time of transition from war planning to peace planning, at a critical moment when the mould of post-war relations between the great Allies was still malleable by words. At Teheran, military strategy had dominated the discussion; by the time of the Potsdam Conference, on the other hand, the relations between the Russians and the West had so hardened that there was little to be done but ratify the existing fact by agreeing to disagree. At Yalta, on the other hand, the Big Three seemed (though the seeming may have been illusory) to have a wider margin of choice. They met at a time when each country's post-war role was yet to be clearly formulated; at a time when it seemed possible to turn their respective policies either towards agreement or towards conflict with one another. For the first time, Roosevelt, Churchill, and Stalin met with a full

* From William H. McNeill, *America, Britain, and Russia: Their Cooperation and Conflict 1941–1946* (vol. III of A. Toynbee [ed.], *Survey of International Affairs 1939–1946*) (London: Royal Institute of International Affairs, 1953), pp. 531–36, 564–66. Reprinted by permission of the Institute and the Oxford University Press.

retinue of political and military advisers; and the atmosphere as well as the organization of the conference was that of a full-dress international gathering. By comparison, Teheran had been an informal, personal encounter between the three chiefs of government, supplemented by military staff conversations.

The United States, Britain, and Russia each approached the Yalta Conference with definite goals in view. For the Americans, two aims took precedence over all others. First, Roosevelt and his advisers wished to smooth out the obstacles to agreement with the Russians which had arisen at Dumbarton Oaks in order to assure the speedy establishment of a United Nations organization. Secondly, the Americans hoped to settle future strategy in both Europe and the Far East. The strategic problem in Europe hinged upon the dispute between British and American Chiefs of Staff as to how best invade Germany; in the Far East it centred upon Russia's part in the war against Japan.

In comparison, local European political problems took second rank. The Americans still looked forward to a rapid withdrawal of their troops from Europe as soon as Germany had been beaten. Roosevelt told Stalin and Churchill at Yalta that it would be impossible for the American Government to keep any troops in Europe for more than two years after Hitler's overthrow; and, long before that, plans called for the transfer of combat units to the Pacific as fast as ships could be found to carry them. Moreover, many of Roosevelt's most trusted advisers did not expect that public opinion would support an active American policy in Europe after the end of the war. Roosevelt certainly had no desire to repeat President Wilson's fiasco of 1918–20. The spectacle of a new American arbiter of Europe repudiated by his own country could only lead to confusion and misunderstanding. It would be much better if Europeans settled their own affairs to suit themselves, so long as they did so within the general world framework envisaged by the proposals of Dumbarton Oaks, and paid more or less respectful attention to the principles of the United Nations Declaration and the Atlantic Charter.

According to this line of reasoning, the first thing Americans should try to achieve was to secure an agreement with the Russians about the United Nations organization. That done, European disputes could be left to the Europeans, with a little helpful advice and perhaps some prodding from the United States. It is true that the experts of the State Department came to Yalta with some definite ideas as to how the outstanding disputes in Europe should be solved, but Roosevelt was not inclined to take their advice very seriously. In the debates at the Conference, the President in general preferred not to act as champion of any particular formula. Instead he assumed the role of mediator between Churchill and Stalin whenever he could, leaving the positive initiative for settlement of the tangled affairs of Europe largely to the British and Russians.

On the military side, the British were as anxious as the Americans to settle the dispute over European strategy which had arisen between the two countries; and as usual they were prepared to leave to the Americans the problems of war in the Pacific. But the facts of geography, if nothing else, reversed in British eyes the priority among the political issues to be solved. The problem of Allied policy towards Germany and Poland; the role of France in the postwar balance of power on the Continent; the future of British influence in the Balkans and Persia—these were pressing and important matters, and only after they had been amicably settled by the Great Powers did it seem sensible to go ahead with the formation of a world-wide United Nations organization. High principles and professions of friendship would, after all, mean next to nothing if they could not be translated into detailed agreements about the future fate of particular countries and regions.

Stalin approached the Yalta Conference in a somewhat similar spirit. It seems reasonable to impute to him three general aims. He wanted what help he could get for the economic reconstruction of the Soviet Union. This meant reparations from Germany and, if possible, loans from the United States. Secondly, in return for his intervention against Japan in Manchuria, Stalin wished to acquire the territories and special rights which the Tsarist Government had lost in the Far East after the Russo-Japanese war of 1904–5. Thirdly, and this was by all odds the most important of his aims, Stalin wished to lay the basis for the future security of his country against Germany. This, he probably believed, required the continuation of the general understanding which the war had brought about among the Big Three. To maintain that understanding he was prepared to make concessions, and he did make several that must have seemed to him very great indeed.

But Stalin also believed that the future security of the Soviet Union required the establishment of governments friendly to Russia in the East European countries that lay between Russia and Germany. It is possible, even probable, that Stalin had not yet come fully to realize the dilemma which this very natural wish created for him. As later events were to show, a government which satisfied the Soviet definition of friendliness could hardly at the same time satisfy the Western Powers' definition of a democracy. But the forcible imposition of "friendly" governments in countries like Poland or Rumania was likely to offend, even antagonize Britain and America. Thus the two basic requirements for Soviet security as Stalin saw them in February 1945 were to prove mutually incompatible in the long run.

In February 1945, however, this dilemma had not become clear. Stalin seems to have hoped that it would be possible to create "people's democracies" in the states of Eastern Europe whose governments would, in effect, perpetuate the "popular fronts" which local Communist Parties had created during the war. In such governments, the Communist Parties would, of course, play an important though not an exclusive role; and "fascists" and "collaborators" would be legally excluded from political activity. By extending the definition of these terms to include anyone actively anti-Russian or anti-Communist, it might prove possible to assure the establishment of friendly governments which at the same time would not offend the democratic shibboleths of the West. Who, after all, in Britain or America, would care to defend the right of a "fascist" to make trouble in Russia's zone of influence, especially if Stalin took steps to restrain Communists from embarrassing Britain and America in Western Europe and in the other parts of the world where Anglo-American influence predominated? How far he was prepared to go in this direction had been recently and dramatically proved in Greece, and Churchill was both aware of and grateful for Stalin's extraordinary restraint.

It thus appears probable that at the time of the Yalta Conference Stalin felt that if he refrained from interfering in British and American zones of influence he could expect the Western nations to do the same in the Russian zone in Eastern Europe. The problem was merely to fix amicably the limits of the Russian zone; and the recent agreement reached by the European Advisory Commission which defined the Russian zone of occupation in Germany, combined with the agreements which he had made with Churchill at Moscow in October 1944 with respect to the Balkans and Danubian Europe, seemed already to have solved a large part of that problem. There remained the Far East and, most difficult of all, Poland.

In each area Stalin had what must have seemed to him good bargaining counters. In the Far East he could offer the help of the Red Army against Japan and an agreement to recognize the Government of Chiang Kai-shek at the expense of the Chinese Communists. As for Poland, there were hints that he considered France a sort of equivalent. The bargain he hoped to make was simple. In return for his recognition of and support for de Gaulle's Provisional Government (sealed by the Treaty concluded in December 1944) he felt he could demand British and American recognition of and support for the new Provisional Government of Poland.

But neither Britain nor America saw things in such a light. Churchill was anxious to rescue Poland from Russian domination; and what seemed to Stalin a friendly Polish Government seemed to Churchill to promise a mere puppet show. Roosevelt, for his part, hoped that the whole problem of spheres of influence could be transcended by basic agreement upon the principles of international relations—an agreement which would obviate the need for unilateral intervention by any one of the Great Powers in any part of Europe. For practical purposes, his view coincided with Churchill's: Poland, he felt, should be genuinely free to run her own affairs and the Polish people should be permitted to elect whatever sort of government they preferred.

Neither Roosevelt nor Churchill seems frankly to have faced the fact that, in Poland at least, genuinely free democratic elections would return governments unfriendly to Russia—certainly by Stalin's definition, and, indeed, by any definition of international friendliness. Stalin's dilemma—his wish at once to maintain harmony with the Western Powers and to create a belt of friendly governments between himself and Germany—was matched by a similar dilemma in the policy of the West. The democratic process upon which so many eulogies were expended could not produce governments in Eastern Europe (or in many other parts of the world) that would further the harmony of the Great Powers and prove acceptable to all of them.

Men were not so uniform, so rational, nor possessed of such good will, as the democratic theory presupposed; and in talking of East European governments which would be both democratic and friendly to Russia the Western Powers were in large part deluding themselves.

In February 1945, however, these truths had yet to be demonstrated by the progress of events. Stalin, as much as Roosevelt, and Churchill, as much as Stalin, talked of the importance of free democratic elections to determine as soon as possible the future form of government in the various countries of Europe which had been liberated from the Nazis; and the identity of their phrases disguised the divergence of their hopes and intentions. It was because the Big Three failed to cut through the smoke-screen of words and face frankly the differences that existed among them that the agreements reached at Yalta in so many cases were no more than verbal and did not long endure the test of practice. In the course of the long discussions over the formation of a Polish government—the topic which took more time than anything else at Yalta—the real differences between Russia and the West were often very near the surface, but neither side dared to grasp the nettle.

Reading the record in retrospect one is tempted to scorn the pious phrases which were used so freely on all sides; but it is perhaps over-hasty to do so. War-time propaganda and military co-operation had obscured the great differences between Russian and Western ideas of democracy; and it seemed imperative to many good, honest, and intelligent men to retain the common slogans in the hope that the reality of agreement might gradually grow up under the shelter of an identity of verbal formulae. Deliberately to uncover the disagreements which a common profession of faith in democracy hid might have made things worse, might even have fractured the Grand Alliance before Germany and Japan had been defeated. With a war yet to win, such an alternative was rejected out of hand by all the participants in the Yalta Conference. Hence the persistence with which they refuse to examine the real hopes and fears which they attached to phrases like "free democratic elections" . . . .

In view of subsequent disillusionment, it is hard to recapture the mood of the days that followed the publication of the Yalta communiqué. Within a short time hesitation and doubts about the agreements reached in the Crimea began to assert themselves. The reversal of feeling which followed upon the inability of the Great Powers to make the Yalta agreements work brought the virtues of the agreements themselves into dispute. Yet at the time there was little hesitation or doubt, and it is in the light of the immediate situation of February 1945 that the agreements must in fairness be judged. Certainly there had been compromise on all sides. Stalin had conceded to Roosevelt a limitation on the Soviet veto power on the Security Council; Roosevelt had conceded territory and special rights in the Far East to Stalin. Stalin had conceded something to the British in Yugoslavia; and Churchill had yielded a good deal in Poland.

In trying to estimate whether Roosevelt and Churchill made a good bargain, one fact must always be borne in mind: the Red Army was already in possession of most of Eastern Europe, in a position to defy the West if Stalin chose to do so. And in Manchuria, the Russians would surely have been able to take all or more than all that Roosevelt had conceded as soon as Japanese power collapsed. Thus, unless one argues that the Western Powers should have prepared to fight Russia as soon as Germany collapsed, or to break off their battles against the Nazis and Japanese short of victory—both of which would have been inconceivable at the time—it seems only fair to say that the concessions made at Yalta to Stalin were no more than recognition (and, in the case of Poland, only partial recognition) of the existing military balance of power.

Yet Yalta was for the Western Powers, and particularly for Roosevelt, a sort of Waterloo. The generous ideals which Roosevelt proclaimed and cherished accorded ill with Stalin's actions in Poland and Eastern Europe generally; and the deal over the Far East was surely a contradiction of Roosevelt's own principles. But having compromised his ideals to satisfy Stalin Roosevelt failed to win the Soviet dictator's support for what remained of them. Rooseveltian principles, even blunted and twisted to accommodate Russian interests, did not appeal to Stalin. What he wanted was an alliance against Germany, not a brave new world. If Stalin ever found time to try to unravel the intellectual and personal puzzle that Roosevelt put before him he may well have felt a sort of amused scorn for the President's vision of humanity saved from its own evil passions by bath-tubs and democracy. As a Marxist, Stalin presumably believed that such a panacea overlooked the prime root of all social evil—capitalism; but this proposition, so axiomatic to a Marxist, was one that very likely never even crossed Roosevelt's mind. He was a reformer, not a revolutionary; a humanitarian, not an ideologue; a politician, not a political scientist. Yet in Stalin's imagination capitalism was an ever present threat to his party and country, a threat which he could never entirely overlook nor long forget in any dealing with its leading representatives, whether Hitler, or Churchill, or Roosevelt.

The fundamental failure at Yalta was not Roosevelt's resort to compromise but a failure of intellectual understanding. To be sure, Roosevelt did not cling consistently to his ideal world of the future. But practical compromise between principle and expediency, between the ideal and the possible, had been the keynote of Roosevelt's whole career in domestic American politics, and with the combination he had worked wonders. When he attempted to apply similar methods to international relations, however, his wonder-working power abruptly vanished. The reason was that Roosevelt failed to take adequately into account the enormous intellectual and moral gulf which divided him and the West generally from Stalin and Russia. Without a more extensive adherence to similar moral principles, without a common acceptance of conventional limits to the use of force, without a greater sympathy, a firmer consensus, and a more genuine community of mind, workable compromise was impossible. Only by accepting Stalin on his own terms, only by unreservedly espousing the amorality of power could more durable agreements have been reached. But that would have seemed to Roosevelt (and to the American and British publics as well) a cynical betrayal of the best hope of humanity.

At Yalta neither side fully recognized the difference in intellectual and moral climate which so divided them. Yet the difference made their most honest efforts to reach agreement no more than a fumbling at cross purposes. Under the circumstances it is not strange that the Yalta agreements did not long endure, and that after Yalta the Grand Alliance, despite various ups and downs, showed ever increasing signs of rupture.

5.

Stephen Borsody, whose analysis of the Locarno treaties appeared in Chapter VI, surveys the Yalta agreements with the perspective of fifteen years and with the advantage of having spent most of his life in eastern Europe. He examines many of the theories which have been elaborated concerning American military and diplomatic failures in the closing years of the war, and offers an interpretation which stands in interesting contrast to many of those which have already been quoted. Does Mr. Borsody's position put him at the opposite extreme from Chester Wilmot—is he Roosevelt's advocate in the debate between partisans of Roosevelt and Churchill? Does he display more, or less, realism than George N. Crocker in his treatment of the problems faced by western leaders in 1945?

BORSODY: The Triumph of Tyranny *

The Yalta agreements were based on several broad principles upon which the peace in Europe was supposed to rest. First of all, peace in Europe was to be guaranteed by the global co-operation of the United States, Britain and Russia within the framework of the United Nations. Furthermore there were three specific policies according to which the peaceful reorganization of Europe was to proceed: friendship with Russia, hostility to Germany, restoration of the pre-war nation-state system. Or at least, Western diplomacy took for granted that these would be the principles of European peace-making. As far as Soviet Russia went, if tactics are distinguished from policy, it is obvious in retrospect that Soviet diplomacy had never emancipated itself from the fundamental principle of Bolshevik foreign policy: hostility to the West.

Since the breakdown of the Yalta agreements, several theories have been advanced to explain the causes of the failure. The most popular among them was perhaps the one least instructive. This was what Henry Steele Commager aptly called the "conspiracy theory of Yalta." According to this theory President Roosevelt, naive and senile, sold out half of Europe to Stalin at Yalta as a result of some Communist, or leftist, conspiratorial work in the State Department. The "conspiracy theory" was popularized by Senator Joseph R.

* From Stephen Borsody, *The Triumph of Tyranny* (New York: The Macmillan Company, 1960), pp. 183–91. Reprinted by permission of The Macmillan Company.

McCarthy, chief promoter of the "Red Scare" in the United States after the Second World War. But post-war American party struggles also added much fuel to the demagogic interpretation of the Yalta agreements. The Republicans, who had been out of power for almost a generation, indulged in some irresponsible criticism of Yalta in order to discredit both the foreign and the domestic policies of the Democratic Administration.

Following General Eisenhower's electoral victory in 1952, the Republican-administered State Department made public (March 1955) the American documents concerning the Big Three agreements (*The Conferences at Malta and Yalta, 1945*). The release added little or nothing to what was already known about Yalta. The Yalta Papers paid special attention to Alger Hiss, former State Department official, target of the advocates of the "conspiracy theory," who was convicted of perjury for denying that he had passed official documents to a confessed Soviet spy. But it was clear from the documents that Hiss participated in the Yalta negotiations as a reporter rather than as a policy maker. This fact did not prevent Republican Senator Karl Mundt, for instance, from contending after the publication of the Yalta Papers that the Russians were able to obtain concessions from the United States at the Yalta conference because "at that time Alger Hiss was acting in an espionage capacity." The conspiracy theory was far from dead ten years after Yalta.

This theory was as unrealistic as the once flourishing leftist suspicion which sensed some reactionary conspiracy precipitated by Roosevelt's death in April 1945, behind the breakdown of the East-West alliance. After the war, many Western liberals believed unity between the Western Powers and Soviet Russia broke down because one of its chief architects and a leading Western liberal, President Roosevelt, died. This belief was echoed by the President's son, Elliot, in the mythical suggestion that "Franklin Roosevelt's ideals and statesmanship would have been sufficient to keep the unity a vital entity during the post-war period. . . ." And long after Roosevelt's death, the belief lingered on among liberals that East-West co-operation had broken down mainly because of reactionary intrigues. So, for instance, Rexford G. Tugwell, one-time member of President Roosevelt's Brain Trust, in a book published in 1957 hinted at "a reversal of the dead President's intentions" and "the intransigence towards Russia of the reactionaries in the Cabinet, the Department of State and the embassies everywhere," as having been the cause of the cold war. The theory of reactionary conspiracy, it seems, had its diehard believers as did the theory of leftist conspiracy.

Pro-Soviet sympathies of the Left were, no doubt, responsible to a great extent for the naive Western views on Russia and communism, but much more conducive to Western friendliness for the Soviet Union was the fact that East and West were united in a life and death struggle against a common enemy, Hitler's Germany. Many Western progressives committed a grave mistake by portraying communists as essentially "social reformers." But their influence in shaping the West's pro-Russian policy was greatly exaggerated and their motives grossly distorted.

The pro-Soviet Left in the West during the war advocated friendship with the Soviet Union primarily for military reasons, as did everybody else. As a rule, they favoured co-operation with the Soviet Union in the interest of their respective nations, rather than in the interest of Russia or communism. The worst they did was to make co-operation with the Russians an ideological issue, hailing East-West unity as a triumph for liberalism and suspecting as reactionaries all who did not commit themselves wholly to friendship with the Soviet Union. Prominent in their thinking was the shame of Munich. They fostered what Beneš liked to call the West's "bad conscience" regarding Munich. This could have been a real service, had they not also, in the meantime, spread the naive belief that co-operation with Russia would undo past crimes and mistakes and introduce a new millennium. They thus weakened the sense of realism that the West so greatly needed. But in no way did they make Western policy, either at Yalta or at any other place where the crucial decisions were made.

Another theory, propounded most elaborately by Chester Wilmot in his book *The Struggle for Europe*, explained Yalta mainly in terms of alleged Anglo-American antagonism. In order to represent Americans as entertaining strong anti-British and pro-Russian biases, Wilmot quoted statements by General Eisenhower and others, such as: "The ordinary Russian seems to me to bear a marked similarity to what we call an 'average American,'" "special bond between the U.S.A. and the U.S.S.R.," "unbroken friendship [with the U.S.S.R.] that dated back to the birth of the United States," "both were free from the stigma of colonial empire building by force"—only to come to the following conclusion: "This belief was implicit in Roosevelt's approach to the problems which were to be discussed at Yalta. In his eyes, Britain was an imperial power, bearing the 'colonial stigma'; Russia was not. That assessment of his allies was a decisive factor in Roosevelt's readiness to make concessions to the Soviet Union both in Europe and Asia in order to ensure Stalin's entry into the Pacific war."

The consequence of this alleged anti-British and pro-Russian bias was that the Americans opposed Churchill's strategy. Regarding Churchill's strategy —and motives—Wilmot claimed that in 1943 Churchill favoured military operations in the Balkans in order to achieve "the restoration of democratic influence in Central and South-Eastern Europe." As Arthur Schlesinger, Jr., pointed out while refuting these theories: "Not a fragment of evidence is presented to support the confident assertion that Churchill ever had these political motives at that time. . . ." But it is easier to start than to stop a myth.

Believers in the Balkan invasion myth pretended to know that, at the Teheran meeting of the Big Three in 1943, the aim of Churchill's strategy was the defence of Europe against communism. Furthermore they were convinced that had Churchill's plan been carried out the post-war bolshevization of Eastern Europe could have been prevented. That such political motives, if they had existed and shaped Allied strategy, could have ruined East-West co-operation and could even have led to a separate peace between Germany and Russia, did not bother the makers of this myth. Nor did they care to explore the military complications of such strategy, automatically taking its success for granted. And of course they disregarded the simple fact that Churchill in 1943 did not advocate Balkan invasion plans on the scale or with the motives that the believers of the myth said he did.

In his memoirs, Churchill clearly stated the nature and motives of his Balkan invasion plans of 1943. Said he, in defence against the makers of myths: "It has become a legend in America that I strove to prevent the Cross-Channel enterprise called 'Overlord,' and that I tried vainly to lure the Allies into some mass invasion of the Balkans, or a large-scale campaign in the eastern Mediterranean, which would effectively kill it. Much of this nonsense has already in previous chapters been exposed and refuted." Especially refuted in Churchill's memoirs is the contention that the strategy which he urged in 1943 in the Balkans and the eastern Mediterranean had something to do with efforts alleged against him to forestall the Red Army in Central Europe. It is clear from Churchill's narrative that what he sought was to speed up the common victory. He was eager to employ the large forces already assembled in the Mediterranean most efficiently, and wanted "to use otherwise unemployable forces to bring Turkey into the war." "The object," he wrote, "of all the operations in the Mediterranean which I had contemplated was to take the weight off Russia and give the best possible chance to 'Overlord.'"

It is true that in 1944—but assuredly not in 1943, as Wilmot claimed— Churchill became suspicious of Russia's intentions and tried at that time "to forestall the Russians in certain areas of Central Europe." However, at Yalta he seemed to regain his confidence in Russia, and it was only afterwards, in the spring of 1945, when the Soviets trampled down indiscriminately (not only in Rumania and Bulgaria) the Big Three Yalta agreements, that he definitely lost that confidence, and began to advocate both diplomatic and military resistance.

During the spring of 1945 Churchill's views on Soviet Russia began to differ fundamentally from those maintained by the American State Department, and in the light of subsequent events it is clear that Churchill was right and the United States policy-makers were wrong. Wilmot's "colonial stigma" theory may perhaps partly explain why at this particular juncture the United States brushed aside Churchill's prophetic warnings. The American policy-makers suspected an anti-communist bias in Churchill; and in some instances they acted as if they were more fearful of the bogey of British imperialism than aware of the obvious facts of Soviet imperialism. However, there is no evidence that at any time during the earlier phases of the war, any anti-British sentiments could have been "a decisive factor" in the pro-Russian policy of the United States.

Certainly Roosevelt was especially anxious to dispel the suspicion of the Russians that they were facing an Anglo-American front, and he therefore often played the role of mediator between Stalin and Churchill. But this was a tactical position, which cannot prove that Roosevelt sought the friendship of Soviet Russia more ardently than did Churchill. Both Western leaders sought it, although, apart from their common conviction that the friendship of Russia was essential in winning the war and in building the peace, their underlying motives may have been somewhat different.

Roosevelt had a better grasp than Churchill of the forces propelling the modern world towards social change; also, he was in sympathy with them. He was convinced that capitalism and communism, by different methods, could both serve human progress. Or at least, Roosevelt seemed to hold this conviction during the period of East-West co-operation. He did not believe this in 1940, at the time of the Russo-Finnish war, when he told an American Youth Congress that the Soviet dictatorship was "as absolute as any other dictatorship in the world." A highly pragmatic man, he adopted, tried and discarded many hypotheses in his life. Had he lived after the Second World War, doubtless he would have been able again to change his views on the democratic potentialities of Soviet tyranny. During the war, at any rate, fashionable leftist doctrines about the synthesis of democracy and communism made a greater impression on Roosevelt than on Churchill, although the Conservative Churchill was not entirely immune to them. In a letter of October 11th, 1944 which he never dispatched but did publish in his memoirs, Churchill wrote to Stalin: "We feel we were right in interpreting your dissolution of the Comintern as a decision by the Soviet Government not to interfere in the internal political affairs of other countries. . . . We have the feeling that, viewed from afar and on a grand scale, the differences between our systems will tend to get smaller. . . ."

Such ideological speculations did not impress Churchill too deeply. On the other hand, up until the spring of 1945, he was more ready than Roosevelt to accept the Soviet Union as a partner in power politics; his percentage agreements with Stalin clearly proved this. Churchill viewed the post-war world more in the perspective of balance of power, whereas Roosevelt viewed it more in the perspective of global co-operation; nevertheless, both Churchill and Roosevelt seemed to assume that after Germany's defeat the Western democracies, by recognizing Russia's legitimate security interest in Eastern Europe, would be able to co-operate successfully and to coexist peacefully with the Soviet Union.

The critics of Yalta were particularly prone to forget what the military situation had been at the time of the Crimean conference. The defenders of Yalta therefore were anxious to stress that, under the then existing military situation, the Yalta agreements were the very best the Western negotiators could obtain from the Russians. This argument was forcefully stated by Secretary of State Stettinius. He reminded the critics of Yalta that "while President Roosevelt was meeting with Prime Minister Winston Churchill and Marshal Stalin in the Crimea, American and British troops had just recovered the ground lost by the Battle of the Bulge. The Allies had not yet bridged the Rhine. In Italy our advance had bogged down in the Apennines. Soviet troops, on the other hand, had just swept through almost all of Poland and East Prussia, and at some points had reached the Oder River in Germany. Most of Hungary had been captured, and the Yugoslav Partisans had recaptured Belgrade in November 1944. By February 1945, therefore, Poland and all of Eastern Europe, except for most of Czechoslovakia, was in the hands of the Red Army. As a result of this military situation, it was not a question of what Great Britain and the United States would permit Russia to do . . . but what the two countries could persuade the Soviet Union to accept."

And at a time when, in the McCarthyite phase of post-war American politics, Yalta became the symbol of "treason," George F. Kennan helped to set the record straight by pointing out: "The establishment of Soviet military power in Eastern Europe . . . was not the result of these talks; it was the result of the military operations during the concluding phases of the war. There was nothing the western democracies could have done to prevent the Russians from entering those areas except to get there first, and this they were not in a position to do."

Several military analysts questioned the inevitability of Eastern Europe's control by the Red Army. Their arguments, however, were far from convincing. They either maintained without benefit of evidence, like Chester Wilmot, that no heed had been given to the right military counsel which allegedly had been available; or else, in hindsight counsel, they recommended such moves as would seem, even today, of doubtful military value for achieving victory over Nazi Germany. Opinion in the latter category was voiced by Hanson W. Baldwin, who suggested it was a great mistake not to let Hitler and Stalin fight each other "to a frazzle," because it would have placed the democracies in supreme power in the world, instead of elevating one totalitarianism at the expense of another and of the democracies.

It cannot be denied that supreme world power for the democracies would have been the ideal result of the war. Past experience should prove, however, that to attempt to achieve this by pitting Germany against Russia can more easily create a bond of union between those two powers (as, for example, at Rapallo and in the Nazi-Soviet pact) than secure a Western victory over both. The defenders of Yalta profited by the experiences of the past to the extent of recognizing Big Three unity as the indispensable prerequisite of military victory. On the other hand their political arguments in support of the Yalta agreements were less than convincing. They put all the blame for failure to carry out the Yalta agreements on the Russians. They claimed in effect that the agreements were good, if the Russians had only kept them. This was also the essence of a most elaborate defensive thesis presented by W. Averell Harriman, one of President Roosevelt's advisers at Yalta, before the United States Senate Committee on Foreign Relations on July 13th, 1951. In brief, this defensive thesis maintained that not only did the West not sell out East Europe to the Communists, as reckless critics of Yalta charged, but on the contrary Yalta provided for the liberated nations of Eastern Europe to have democratic governments, established through free elections.

This argument was sound inasmuch as the Kremlin was to be called to task for violating the Yalta agreements. On the other hand, it is questionable whether Soviet readiness to co-operate in holding "free and unfettered" elections in the countries of Eastern Europe was ever considered to be as much of a possibility as was later claimed, rather naively, by the defenders of Yalta. After all, Soviet Russia's poor record, as well as the Middle Zone countries', in practising free elections was well known. Moreover, the Western Powers never pressed too hard the issue of supervising the elections in the Soviet sphere. From the Yalta agreements the conclusion could have been drawn, above all by the Russians, that some allowance had been made for the Russian interpretation of "free" elections—though of course not as much allowance as the Russians themselves took the liberty of making.

XII.

THE NUREMBERG TRIALS

The kinds of disputes which arise from a consideration of the Nuremberg Trials [1] usually fall into one of two categories: the technical and legal, of the type usually found in law journals; and the more emotional and dramatic, of the type usually found in the popular press. In this chapter, it is hoped that some important issues, representative of both categories, will be raised, and that the student will try to decide which are relevant for the historian. Here, four possible starting points for discussion will be indicated.

At the outset, it should be considered whether the trials set an exceedingly good or an exceedingly bad precedent. In any future war, will "war guilt," as a matter of course, be attributed to the losing side? Has international law, which has always recognized war itself as legitimate, established an unrealistic distinction by trying to differentiate between legal, or defensive, war, and illegal, or aggressive, war? It may be argued that the punishment of "war criminals" will inevitably degenerate into nothing more than "victor's justice," into an opportunity for revenge. It could also be maintained that this type of reaction to war is a natural outgrowth of the modern age, and started, as so many features of our times have started, with the French Revolution, and with the whole concept of ideological war—the modern equivalent of the earlier religious struggles. Were Napoleon's journeys to Elba and St. Helena the first steps on the road to Nuremberg—the first steps toward a world of revenge and of total war fought to the bitter end, or were they the beginnings of a long struggle toward a world ruled by law, justice, and concepts of humanity?

Secondly, one might consider the role of the Soviet Union as one of the judging powers at Nuremberg. Were the Soviet officials so involved in violations of international law themselves that the entire moral basis of the trials was undermined by their presence? Did the lack of "clean hands" on the part of the Russians, to use the expression common in Anglo-American equity, preclude them from "recovering" against the Germans? Or, should it be argued that the past "crimes" of the Russians were irrelevant; that the Nazis alone were on trial, and were being tried for specific violations of international law, and that therefore the moral character

---

[1] It should be kept in mind that the United States was involved in two types of trials at Nuremberg: those of the International Military Tribunal and those of the United States Military Tribunal; the former is the Tribunal considered in this chapter; the second is especially vulnerable to attack on a purely legal basis—see August von Knieriem, *The Nuremberg Trials,* translated from the German by Elizabeth D. Schmidt (Chicago: Regnery, 1959).

of one of the judges is of no account? After all, if one is on trial for theft, the fact that the judge himself has committed theft is no defense; one is before the "bar of justice," and the judge is but the executor of the law. To argue otherwise, might one not be forced to deny the "body" of international law, and thus to deny the principle of the rule of law rather than the rule of men in international juridical proceedings, and thereby compromise the whole basis of the trials? Or might one maintain that the enormity of the Russian "crimes," and especially the collusion of the Russians with the Nazis in the execution of those "crimes," creates a special case, and that the failure to recognize this would inevitably imperil the future healthy development of international law, which, in the final analysis, like all other law, ultimately rests on moral judgments?

It is also argued that the trials were a "good thing" for the Germans, as the horrors of Nazi rule were laid before them, documented and detailed, and thus the possibility of a recurrence of the post–World War I myth of complete innocence was foreclosed. But, on the other hand, one might consider whether, in conducting the Nuremberg Trials, we ran the risk of creating a new "Versailles," with all the bitterness this might have entailed. Furthermore, was there not some danger of providing the Germans with convenient scapegoats, onto whose shoulders could be shifted all the blame for the Nazi atrocities, some of which, at least, belonged to the nation as a whole?

Finally, and this is a particularly rich field of discussion for those with a leaning toward law or political science, it is well to ponder whether the nature of international law itself inevitably rendered the trials nothing but a "victor's justice," for is there, can there be, any such thing as international *law* under which "war criminals" can be called to account? Surely *law* implies the existence of a sovereign, which will back up, with the bayonet if necessary, the decisions of its courts? Even the Anglo-American common law, founded on precedent and built up empirically, is, as Oliver Wendell Holmes emphasized, "not a brooding omnipresence in the sky but the articulate voice of some sovereign or quasi-sovereign that can be identified." [2] It should be asked: who is the sovereign or quasi-sovereign in the case of international law, under whom an equitable legal system can be built? Was not international law at Nuremberg just the sugar coating on vigilante justice, on the justice of individuals—even if they were individual nations—acting directly, rather than under a sovereign and through law?

It is probable that even the most detailed consideration of the above points will lead to no firm conclusions, but that fact in itself may illustrate that there are no final answers to many of the problems of life, and that the best avenues open to man will never be free of doubt or of compromise with the undesirable. These compromises, a great man once pointed out, are common even in the realm of law: "The life of the law has not been logic: it has been experience. The felt necessities of time, the prevalent moral and political theories, intuitions of public policy, avowed or unconscious, even the prejudices which judges share with their fellow-men, have had a good deal more to do than the syllogism in determining the rules by which men should be governed. The law . . . cannot be dealt with as if it contained only the axioms and corollaries of a book of mathematics." [3] Those words shocked many in the noon of the positivist age; today, lawyers, and even historians and politicians, may take comfort in them.

[2] *Southern Pacific v. Jensen*, 244 U.S. 205, 222 (1917).
[3] Oliver Wendell Holmes, *The Common Law* (Boston: Little, Brown, 1881), p. 1.

1.

One of the problems often encountered in a discussion of the Nuremberg Trials is the danger of becoming involved in legal technicalities. Yet in the following selection that danger is avoided, and a happy balance is achieved between the legal and the more general political and historical aspects of the trials. Mr. Wechsler is a professor of law at Columbia University, a leading authority on constitutional law, and a former assistant attorney general of both the state of New York and the United States. Moreover, he is well qualified to discuss the trials, as he was a technical adviser to the American members of the International Military Tribunal.

WECHSLER: The Issues of the Nuremberg Trial *

One may say without impertinence to historians that the judgment that history will render upon a legal proceeding is not usually a matter of acute concern either to counsel or to the court. In this respect, at least, the Nuremberg trial was a highly exceptional affair; for the perspective of most of the participants, and even that of the defendants, was focused very much on the future, distant and problematical as it is. The dominant mood was put in words by Justice Jackson in opening the case for the prosecution: "We must never forget that the record on which we judge these defendants to-day is the record on which history will judge us tomorrow."

The verdict of history will not be rendered for a long time, but we may be certain that the process of deliberation will be active and that the debate has already begun. The trial is extolled as a crucial achievement in the development of international law, a triumph of reason and justice in the bitter wake of the war. But voices have been raised from the beginning to proclaim the battle cry of the attack: novelty and confusion, error and pretense, a peril to essential liberties safeguarded by domestic law. What are the issues that challenge examination as this active critique unfolds? What are the factors to be weighed in the balance by those who will record for the judgment of posterity the history of our turbulent time?

It is a lawyer's habit, that I would not resist if I could, to begin with a statement of the case.

Credible information received in the course of the war reported cruelties and atrocities perpetuated by the Germans, especially in the occupied countries, that no conception of military necessity could sustain. Impotent to render physical assistance, the heads of state of the principal Allies responded with warnings, jointly and severally repeated, that the guilty would be apprehended and punished. The triumph of arms brought with it the physical custody of thousands of persons suspected of complicity in the conduct to which these

* From Herbert Wechsler, "The Issues of the Nuremberg Trial," *Political Science Quarterly*, vol. 62 (1947), pp. vii–13, 14–16, 23–26. Reprinted by permission of the editors of the *Political Science Quarterly*.

warnings had been addressed. It brought the custody of the survivors among the principal enemy personalities believed, upon probable cause, to be responsible for the initiation of the war. Most of these persons had, indeed, made frantic efforts to surrender to the forces advancing from the west; and by far the largest number when the firing ceased were in American hands. Within Germany no governmental authority survived the unconditional surrender, save that which the Potsdam Powers themselves exercised by the military occupation. It took no great foresight in the last days to anticipate that these conditions would obtain. It was essential that a policy be formulated for dealing with the individuals in question when the fighting should finally come to an end.

The problem thus presented was answered by the principal Allies in the Agreement executed in London on August 8, 1945 . . . It is no secret that this protocol represented, in its major content, the proposals put forward by Justice Jackson on behalf of the United States. It provided for the creation of a Tribunal, deemed to exercise military powers and therefore entitled the "International Military Tribunal"; each of the four signatories was to designate one member and an alternate. The Tribunal was accorded jurisdiction "to try and punish persons who, acting in the interests of the European Axis countries," might be charged and convicted of any of the conduct which the Charter defined as a crime. The crimes thus defined were called "crimes against peace," "war crimes" and "crimes against humanity." Crimes against peace comprehended in substance the "planning, preparation, initiation or waging of a war of aggression, or a war in violation of international treaties . . . or assurances" or conspiring so to do. War crimes comprehended generally "violations of the laws or customs of war" with some specification of the behavior, such as the murder or ill-treatment of prisoners of war, deemed to constitute such violations. The definition of crimes against humanity supplemented that of crimes of war—but the concept was accorded very little scope because of the requirement that the acts of inhumanity included be committed "in execution of or in connection with" some other crime within the jurisdiction of the Tribunal, that is, a crime against peace or a war crime.

For such conduct the Charter declared that "there shall be individual responsibility"; that "leaders, organizers, instigators and accomplices" conspiring to commit such offenses shall be mutually responsible for the actions perpetrated in the execution of their common plan; that official position shall be neither an excuse nor a mitigation; and that superior orders may be a mitigation if justice so requires, but not a defense.

In addition, the Charter provided that in the trial of any individual and in connection with any act of which he might be convicted, the Tribunal might declare that "the group or organization of which the individual was a member was a criminal organization." The point of such a declaration was that thereafter the members of the organization might be prosecuted for their membership in "national, military or occupation courts" of the signatories—in which event the Charter provided that "the criminal nature of the group or organization is considered proved and shall not be questioned." . . .

Twenty-two of the twenty-four individual defendants were brought to trial, one of them, Martin Bormann, *in absentia*. After a trial lasting the better part of a year, on a record exceeding 17,000 pages depicting horrors never before recorded in a court, Schacht, Von Papen and Fritsche were acquitted; the declaration of criminality was denied in the case of the Cabinet, the General Staff and the S.A., and granted, but in highly qualified and limiting terms, with respect to the Leadership Corps, the Gestapo and the S.S. Nineteen individuals were convicted, of whom eleven, including Bormann, were sentenced to death, the others to imprisonment for terms ranging from ten years to life. All of those sentenced to death were convicted of war crimes or crimes against humanity; all but four, Kaltenbrunner, Frank, Sauckel and Bormann, were also convicted of crimes against peace.

History will ask whether these men and these organizations were justly condemned or acquitted. The inquiry will involve many phases not all of which can be examined here. I shall attempt no more than to direct attention to the general issues.

Should the United States—and the question may be put with equal validity for each of the victors—have cast its influence against any punitive proceedings, declining to participate and refusing to surrender the persons of its prisoners to other countries clamoring to proceed? Such a course would have forsaken the pledges and the warnings issued as an instrument of war and would have responded with a blanket *nolumus* [we are unwilling] to the demand for retribution that rose like a plaintive chant from all the desolated lands. Certainly only the firmest conviction that punishment in this situation could serve no adequate temporal purpose would have sanctioned dismissal of the millions of complainants with the admonition that "vengeance belongs to God." In truth, the volume of accumulated passion sufficed in itself to establish such a temporal purpose—for who can doubt that indiscriminate violence, a blood bath beyond power of control, would have followed an announcement by the responsible governments that they were unwilling to proceed? If nothing else was to be accomplished, it was essential that some institutional mechanism be provided that would reserve the application of violence to the public force, to cases in which punishment might serve a constructive purpose and in which reason would conclude that it was deserved.

It is not to be conceded, however, that this negative function, whatever its importance, is the only purpose that was to be served. The assumption of domestic society that punishment is a preventive weapon is not as irrelevant to international behavior as some persons seem disposed to affirm. In so far as the penalty eliminates a danger presented by the particular individual—hardly an objective of indifference to a military occupation—the function is no less plain in this situation than it is in municipal affairs. But the dominant justification of punishment, especially of the punishment of death, is usually felt to be the deterrence of others; and here it has been asserted that the justification must fail because victory carries immunity whether or not the victor was the aggressor and whatever the measures by which victory was attained.

The argument has a degree of validity but it does not prove enough to prevail. Treason, too, is punishable only when it is abortive; when "it prospers," as the old verse goes, "none dare call it treason"; it is the traitors who call the turn. With respect to war and the manner in which it is conducted, as with respect to treason, there are men who, valuing personal survival, will take account of the contingency of failure. It is to them that the threats are addressed. Moreover, the threat of punishment is not limited in the mode of its operation to the weight that it carries as a factor in decision at the climactic moment of choice. It also operates, and perhaps more significantly, at anterior stages in the patterns of conduct, the dark shadow of organized disapproval eliminating from the ambit of consideration alternatives that might otherwise present themselves in the final competition of choice. These considerations point to some deterrent efficacy; that, and not the assurance of prevention, is all that we can claim for punishment as an instrument of domestic law. It is deemed to be sufficient in municipal affairs, not because of a mathematical calculation of its efficiency, but rather because society, so desperately in need of instrumentalities of prevention, cannot dispense with such potency as condemnation and punishment have. . . .

It will be said that I have spoken of the Nuremberg trial in terms that ignore the entire controversy and, in a genuine sense, my critic will be right. I have not addressed myself to whether a tribunal of the victors could be impartial, to whether the law of the Charter is *ex post facto* or whether it is "law" at all. These are, indeed, the issues that are currently mooted. But these are elements in the debate that should lead us to be suspicious of the issues as they are drawn in these terms. For, most of those who mount the attack on one or another of these contentions hasten to assure us that their plea is not one of immunity for the defendants; they argue only that they should have been disposed of politically, that is, dispatched out of hand. This is a curious position indeed. A punitive enterprise launched on the basis of general rules, administered in an adversary proceeding under a separation of prosecutive and adjudicative powers is, in the name of law and justice, asserted to be less desirable than an *ex parte* execution list or a drumhead court-martial constituted in the immediate aftermath of the war. I state my view reservedly when I say that history will accept no conception of law, politics or justice that supports a submission in these terms. Those who choose to do so may view the Nuremberg proceeding as "political" rather than "legal"—a program calling for the judicial application of principles of liability politically defined. They cannot view it as less civilized an institution than a program of organized violence against prisoners, whether directed from the respective capitals or by military commanders in the field.

I will go further, however, and assert that history would have granted short shrift to a program of summary execution, for such a program is intrinsically unreasonable and could not have been carried out without mistake. Moreover, despite the controversy as to whether the Geneva Convention survives unconditional surrender, when no army remains in the field, I cannot conceive for myself that such a program comports with the Convention's demands. If the execution of prisoners without trial is a war crime while hostilities are in progress, I do not see why it is in any better position when hostilities have come to an end. In my view, Justice Jackson was wrong in arguing that the defendants could point to no other law than the London Charter to assure them any hearing at all. They could point to the Geneva Convention. But the substance of his argument was right. Those who relied upon a treaty for their protection could not argue that treaties were without significance as a basis of liability, if their punishment was otherwise just.

No one who examines the record and the judgment, as most of the commentators have not, will question the disinterestedness of the Tribunal; and those who argue that disinterestedness is inherently impossible in this situation may ask themselves why nations that can produce such impartial critics should be intrinsically incapable of producing equally impartial judges. The fact is that the judgment of the Tribunal was mainly a judgment of limitation, its principal operation more significantly that of protecting innocence than that of declaring and punishing guilt. When I speak of "innocence" I mean not only a technical freedom from responsibility under the rules laid down; I mean, more deeply, the exculpation of those who could not justly be declared to be guilty under rules of liability that we would be prepared to apply to ourselves.

No one who is satisfied that the conditions of punishment laid down by the Charter and the Tribunal are essentially just and constructive, in the terms I have previously advanced, will in the end deny them his endorsement on the ground that they are retroactively defined. There is, indeed, too large a disposition among the defenders of Nuremberg to look for stray tags of international pronouncements and reason therefrom that the law of Nuremberg was previously fully laid down. If the Kellogg-Briand Pact or a general conception of international obligation sufficed to authorize England, and would have authorized us, to declare war on Germany in defense of Poland—and in this enterprise to kill countless thousands of German soldiers and civilians— can it be possible that it failed to authorize punitive action against individual Germans judicially determined to be responsible for the Polish attack? To be sure, we would demand a more explicit authorization for punishment in domestic law, for we have adopted for the protection of individuals a prophylactic principle absolutely forbidding retroactivity that we can afford to carry to that extreme. International society, being less stable, can afford less luxury. We admit that in other respects. Why should we deny it here?

There is, however, one point in the current debate that we cannot summarily dismiss. It is the point that the punitive enterprise we have undertaken applies only to the enemy. My concern on this score is not with the contention that sanctions must for this reason be ineffective, a point that I have previously met. Nor is it with the argument that we have established a precedent that some future victor may invoke against us. If we are guilty of aggression we shall merit its invocation; if we are not, we can ask for no more—not alone for ourselves but for our cause—than the opportunity to establish our innocence that the Nuremberg defendants received. My concern is with the point of equality itself, so important an element of justice—equality in the sense that the sanctions do not apply either to our allies or to ourselves. The Russians cannot be put to their defense in relation to Finland or to Poland. We are obliged to present to no Tribunal the considerations we would advance to justify the manner in which we exhibited to Japan the power of the atom bomb. This is a genuine difficulty—to which the Tribunal indicates its sensitivity in various ways, such as refusing to assess a penalty against Doenitz for submarine violations that did not differ significantly from our own practice in the Pacific, as attested by Admiral Nimitz. To be sure, the depravity of our enemies and the fact that theirs was the aggression accord us such large leeway in this connection that our relative moral position is secure. But this is a mitigation rather than a defense to the inequality that Nuremberg involves.

I do not think that the difficulty argues that we should have abstained from the Nuremberg venture and accorded immunity to the guilty defendants, the only terms on which abstinence would have been real. It argues rather that Nuremberg, far more than San Francisco, was the assumption of an irrevocable obligation—to build a world of just law that shall apply to all, with institutions strong enough to carry it into effect. It is, moreover, as Justice Jackson has so properly reiterated, an obligation assumed as well by those of our allies who participated in the trial or gave it their sanction by adhering to the Charter. If we succeed in that great venture—and no nation can succeed alone—Nuremberg will stand as a cornerstone in the house of peace. If we fail, we shall hear from the German ruins an attack on the Nuremberg judgment as the second "diktat" of Versailles; and, notwithstanding the goodness of our intentions, we may have no sufficient answer.

2.

Lord Hankey is one of Great Britain's most prominent public servants. Although never very well known to the public at large, he has been in the center of governmental affairs for over a half century. He became assistant secretary of the Committee of Imperial Defence in 1908, and was its secretary from 1912 to 1938. He was secretary to the War Cabinet in 1916, to the Imperial War Cabinet in 1917–18, and to the Cabinet from 1919 to 1938. He was clerk of the Privy Council from 1923 to 1938, and served in Winston Churchill's coalition government during the second world war. He has written extensively, many of his books being of fundamental importance to anyone interested in twentieth-century British history. Noted for his tact and disinterestedness, Lord Hankey is nevertheless an impassioned advocate in the following selection.

HANKEY: Politics, Trials and Errors *

What are the "advantages" claimed for the trials by their defenders? . . .

One of the most comprehensive lists of the advantages claimed is given in a Report on the Nuremberg Trials sent by the American Chief Prosecutor to the President of the United States of America on October 7, 1945. First in the list of accomplishments is put the Charter [of the International Military Tribunal] itself, and its adoption by adherence of nineteen nations. No one will grudge praise to those who reached agreement in such difficult conditions. . . . Yet, can the reader of these proceedings . . . escape misgivings? The Chief Prosecutors Designate at the coming trial were then acting as a drafting Committee to settle the rules of the Tribunal. There is no doubt that the Charter is popular in some high judicial circles; but some distinguished legal authorities, both in England and America, are not enamored by these trials at all, and among them are even prosecutors at some of the lesser trials both in Germany and Japan. . . . There is very little, then, in the first claim.

The Chief Prosecutor's second advantage claimed is the incorporation in the principles of the Charter of the "power of the precedent." If that means such precedents as trials of the Vanquished by the Victors, and the making—by the prosecutors designated for the trial—of new crimes *ex post facto,* and of rules to enable important evidence to be excluded, then a great many people will differ as to its being anything like a precedent of which we ought to be proud. If the "precedent" is set with a view to a universal practice by the Victor in every future war of setting up his own Tribunal with his own list of crimes to try and punish the leading politicians and Generals and thousands of the citizens of the vanquished as war criminals, then the outlook is stupefying.

The third claim—"a workable procedure for the trial of crimes surmounting international difficulties"—is a matter of opinion depending on the meaning of the word "workable." The system does not appear to have proved very "workable" at the Tokyo trials to judge from the dissenting judgments. . . .

The fourth claim is that in a world torn with hatreds "the Four Powers have given the example of submitting their grievances against these men to a dispassionate inquiry on legal evidence." Not everyone will agree that an inquiry undertaken exclusively by Victors can be described as "dispassionate."

The Chief Prosecutor's fifth claim is that Nazi aggressions, persecution, and other nefarious activities have, as the result of these trials, been so carefully docketed and documented that "there can be no responsible denial of their crimes in the future and no tradition of martyrdom of the Nazi leaders can arise among informed people." That might be worth something if the mass of the people were well informed. But they are not. After a generation has passed away who can say that the Germans will not be as gullible as they

* From Lord Hankey, *Politics, Trials and Errors* (Chicago: Henry Regnery, 1950), pp. 127–31, 139–43. Reprinted by permission of the Henry Regnery Co.

were in the nineteen-thirties? It is unlikely that their history books will tell the school children what we think they ought to know, and it will be extremely difficult to get the Chief Prosecutor's lesson home to them. I wonder whether some such words were not said of Joan of Arc in May, 1431, when she was burned as a witch! But her crimes have been refuted and she is now a Saint and a Martyr. Moreover, the mistakes of the trials themselves have been "docketed and documented" in this book and others.

In Britain a frequent claim is that the trials have uprooted National Socialism and all its works. That is doubtful. For the Nazi system was based on that militarism that we thought to have destroyed by the victory of 1918, and the Versailles Treaty of 1919. Suppression, however, only forced it underground, and fifteen years later Germany was rearming and militarism was more rampant than ever. With Europe now divided into two camps, both striving for the body and soul of Germany no one can predict the result. But German civilization and culture are nearer to western than to eastern ideals, and one day her much decried militarism may become the pivot of western defence. Before then the Victor Powers should do their utmost to mitigate the results of unconditional surrender and war crimes trials, in the latter case by such methods as remission or reduction of sentences, provisional release and additional amenities. In Japan a review of sentences is long overdue.

Another advantage frequently claimed is that we have made it impossible for the Germans to say, as they said after the first world war, that "we were never beaten, we were starved" or, as some preferred "we were stabbed in the back," or again "the Generals let the army down." It would not have been worth while to incur all the casualties and losses of the last two years of the war to gain a safeguard against a similar excuse now. Such claims are something that can never be countered except by the nation itself. After the German Commander-in-Chief had himself proposed an armistice in 1918 and the Germans had had to submit to so harsh a Treaty one would hardly have thought that they could make such claims. And yet they did—and they will do it again. Already some Germans are saying: "Hitler and the Nazis let Germany down" and others that "the Generals let Hitler down"!

To these lists of advantages wrongly claimed as having been gained at the War Crimes Trials there must be added some which are much more popular with lawyers, and especially British lawyers, than with laymen.

The first and most important of these is the establishment of a Rule of Law to do for nations what national systems of law have done for individuals throughout the world by providing for the punishment and prevention of crime and the maintenance of order.

No doubt that is a very high ideal and it is provided for by the structure of the Charter of the United Nations with the International Court of Justice at the Hague as its principal judicial organ, which *in theory* should even be able to clear up the legal aftermath of a war. *In practice,* however, if Victor States have committed the same crimes as those of which they accuse the enemy, if they have so much to hide that by one expedient or another they

have to keep their misdeeds out of the jurisdiction of the Court, if they wish
to dictate the list of crimes beforehand and to create them *ex post facto,* then
that system becomes unusable. The United Nations simply cannot create a
Tribunal or a system of Tribunals, as did the four principal Allies, to work
on those lines. They would have to be fair to the two parties. In deciding on
aggressions, for example, they would have to investigate the allegations and
elicit the facts from both sides. Their Courts could not use captured documents of the Vanquished, even great documents of State, without obtaining
the corresponding documents of the Victors. They would have to pay much
more attention than did the Nuremberg and Tokyo Tribunals to "international custom, as evidence of a general practice accepted as law." For example, they could not ignore the Universal Declaration of Human Rights approved by the General Assembly of the United Nations on December 10,
1948, and especially the following Articles:—

Article 10

Everyone is entitled in full equality to a fair and public hearing by *an independent
and impartial Tribunal* in the determination of his rights and obligations and of
any criminal charge against him.

Article 11

1. Everyone charged with a penal offence has *the right to be presumed innocent
until proved guilty* according to law in a public trial at which he has had all the
guarantees necessary for his defence.

2. *No one shall be held guilty of any penal offence on account of any act or
omission which did not constitute a penal offence, under national or international
law, at the time when it was committed.* Nor shall a heavier penalty be imposed
than the one that was applicable at the time the penal offence was committed.

It is inconceivable that the United Nations would consider a Tribunal
composed exclusively of Victor judges to be "an independent and impartial
tribunal" for the trial of the Vanquished as insisted upon by Article 10. Similarly, Article 1 of the Charter of the Nuremberg Tribunal establishing it "for
the just and prompt trial and punishment of the major war criminals of the
European Axis" is hardly consistent with the principle enunciated in Article
11, 1. And the *ex post facto* creation of crimes for the Nuremberg and Tokyo
Tribunals is utterly incompatible with Article 11, 2.

In these circumstances the value of the Nuremberg and Tokyo trials for
the establishment of a Rule of Law appears negligible. Rather have they given
it a grave setback. . . .

We must recall the dates which tell the story of the first German and
Russian aggressions in 1939-40. The Russo-German Pact of Neutrality and
non-Aggression was signed on August 23, 1939, behind the back of an Anglo-
French Military Mission, which was trying to negotiate a military pact with
Marshal Voroshilov. The secret Protocol affirming *inter alia* Russia's special
interest in Bessarabia was signed on the same day. The German aggression
on Poland began on September 1, 1939, and the Russian aggression on
September 17, 1939, after most of the Polish troops had been drawn off

to oppose the German invasion. On September 27 a second secret protocol was signed allowing the Soviet to take over Lithuania and settling the partition of Poland. On November 30, 1939, the Russians, notwithstanding their pact of non-aggression and neutrality of January, 1932, invaded Finland, and on December 13, 1939, the League of Nations Assembly denounced the invasion as a breach of the Kellogg Pact. In June, 1940, Russia occupied, and in August, 1940, she annexed, the Baltic states with all of whom she had concluded many Pacts of neutrality and non-aggression in the 20's and 30's, right up to 1939. Meanwhile, Germany had attacked Norway and Denmark, April 9, 1940, Holland, Belgium, and Luxemburg, May 10, 1940, and France a few days later, and Great Britain had mined the Norway Leads, April 8, 1940, and had landed forces in Norway (about April 15). Broadly then the Russian aggressions in the east were proceeding more or less simultaneously with the German aggressions and the counter-operations of the Allies in the West.

The fruits of the earlier Russian aggressions were fully harvested in 1947, after the Nuremberg trials were over, and are still not widely appreciated in Western Europe. To quote Dr. F. W. Pick:—

Russia has gained a common frontier with Norway and robbed Finland of its only northern outlet, thus throwing her fully back on to the Baltic. . . . Finland, through the Peace Treaty of 1947, is burdened with heavy reparations and serious losses of national territory. Estonia, Latvia, Lithuania, and half of former East Prussia have been declared Russian territory, thus making Pillau the Western naval fortress of the Soviet Union. In addition, as long as Poland—now with its broad access to the sea, a major Baltic power—is under Soviet influence that sea has almost become a Russian lake. . . . Are we then back—say in the eighteenth century?

This is the complete replica, in the case of Russia, of the Nazi acts of aggression—the plot and schemes, principles, and policy, preparations, strategy, tactics, and actual execution, most of it planned long before the Nazi movement was born or thought of, carried out before the beginning of the Nuremberg and Tokyo Trials, and continued concurrently with the trials and ever since to this very day!

How was it that the . . . [Soviet Union was] allowed to participate in the prosecution of Germany on charges of aggression when the League had denounced her as an aggressor? Why was it that the Nazi defence at Nuremberg was not allowed to refer to these acts of Russian aggression? Had they been permitted to do so, had the Tribunal not worked in intellectual quarantine, it must have seen that in the sphere of aggression the Nazis had only been doing what Russia had done with complete impunity. Surely none of the prisoners could have been condemned on the political charges if the Tribunal had been able to take official cognizance of these contemporary Russian Aggressions.

Mr. John Wheeler-Bennett in his *Munich: Prologue to Tragedy,* writing of the Russo-German Agreement of August 23, 1939, gives the explanation: "*In deference to Soviet susceptibilities the protocols were not introduced as evidence* before the International Military Tribunal at Nuremberg, but Baron von Weizsacker, the former State Secretary to the German Foreign Ministry, was permitted to refer to their contents under cross-examination on May 21, 1946," though only from memory.

The phrase "deference to Soviet susceptibilities" accounts for a great deal. It explains why the London Charter-making Conference in 1945 was so anxious to prevent the defendants from putting forward the kind of defence which it was known from captured documents was their one chance, and which would have been so terribly inconvenient to the Allies. It explains why it was impossible to have a neutral tribunal, or even to include a few neutrals to sit with the victor judges. It explains why the Tribunals had to work in quarantine and to rule out as irrelevant anything that might incriminate an allied subject, or indeed anything not bearing directly on the selected, immediate charges. It explains why they had to dodge the fact that acts of aggression—as committed by Russia after the Kellogg Pact had supposedly created a new law—had remained as they have always been, the practice of mankind. However reprehensible, it had never been charged as a crime against any individual. It explains why so many people are saying to-day that there is only one war crime—and that is, to be on the losing side! "Deference to Soviet susceptibilities" perhaps explains why at the Tokyo trial Mr. Shigemitsu, who had been struck out by the Chief Prosecutor from the list of persons to be charged, was reinstated in the list shortly after the arrival of the Russian judge. Perhaps it also explains the following passages in a progress report presented by the Chief Prosecutor to the American President on June 6, 1945:—

These hearings, however, must not be regarded in the same light as a trial under our system, where defence is a matter of constitutional right. Fair hearings for the accused are, of course, required to make sure that we punish only the right men for the right reasons. But the procedure of these hearings may properly bar obstruction and dilatory tactics resorted to by defendants in our ordinary criminal trials.

The balance, then, may be struck. On the one hand, we have to set whatever we think remains of the advantages claimed for the War Crimes Trials after the criticism to which they have been exposed, *viz.*—the framing of the Charter; the Power of the Precedent; a workable Precedent for International Trials; Compilation of a documentation of Nazi activities to stop Nazi hero-worship and martyrdoms; Uprooting of National Socialism; the Germans can never say "We were not beaten"; the creation of new crimes *ex post facto,* including Aggression.

On the other side, we have the counter-claims, *viz.*:—War Crimes Trials were part of a most unfortunate policy of threats, which exacerbated the war; forced a fight to a finish; gave the enemy the courage of despair; strengthened Hitler and the propaganda of Goebbels; rendered impossible peace overtures or negotiations; lengthened the war; rendered Treaty-making and German reconstruction after the war almost impossible; bled the whole world white; and weakened the moral position of the allies. To these political criticisms must be added: misgivings about the London Conference of June, 1945, to draft the Charter; the exclusion from the trials of subjects important to the defence such as the Russian aggressions; indefensibility of trials by the Victors of the Vanquished; also of new *ex post facto* crimes including Aggression; the handicap to the defendants of the unavoidable "deference to Soviet susceptibilities"; the points advanced in the protest of American Counsel for defence against the unfairness of the Tokyo trials; the absence of British Counsel for the defence from both trials; the inordinate length of the indictments.

Every reader can judge for himself whether the War Crimes Trials in these circumstances could possibly have reached the standard of justice and fairness fit and proper for the judgement of statesmen of the highest rank, Admirals, Generals, Air Marshals, or their equivalent, diplomats, high civil servants, and other national leaders—or anyone else! Remembering that it was a Victors' trial does anyone think that the results are likely to be accepted as fair by the British, allied, neutral, and ex-enemy peoples now and down the ages? And, finally, would anybody, even if confident of innocence, if placed in the position of a defeated enemy, feel that a fair deal could be counted on from a similar Court created by an enemy after a victorious war? Would anyone entrust to such a Court, with a Charter laid down for it by the victorious enemy, with power to create and interpret new *ex post facto* crimes, the fate of himself or herself, of a husband or wife, or sweetheart, son or daughter, parent, near relation, or friend?

3.

The Communists have a tendency, one often suspects, to see all issues in black and white. The Nuremberg Trials are no exception. In the brief passage which follows, an attack is made on what is alleged to be the lukewarm, or even hostile, attitude of many Americans toward what was done in Nuremberg after the last war. But, though filled with propaganda, the Soviet article does illustrate the moral difficulties into which the trials have plunged many people in this country: if a man like the late Senator Taft criticized the acts of the International Military Tribunal, he left himself open to attack as a defender of some of the most dreadful crimes of history; if he refrained from criticism, he failed to express his concern that others might misuse the Nuremberg precedent. The fundamental questions thus arise: do legal scruples permit one to be shocked by the fate of the Nazis; if so, and if one *is* shocked, is there any way to counter the Soviet contentions?

POLTORAK: History's Verdict *

The International Military Tribunal passed sentence on the chief German war criminals—Goering, Ribbentrop and the others—five years ago, Oct. 1, 1946,

* From an article in the Soviet periodical *Literaturnaya gazeta* for Oct. 2, 1951, translated in *Current Digest of the Soviet Press*, III, no. 40 (1951), pp. 8–9. Reprinted by permission of the editors of the *Current Digest of the Soviet Press*, published weekly at Columbia University by the Committee on Slavic Studies appointed by the American Council of Learned Societies and the Social Science Research Council.

in a small hall of the building of the former Nuremberg District Court.

World public opinion hailed the sentencing of the criminal Hitlerite ring-leaders as an act of just punishment. But quite a different view was taken by international and particularly American reaction which was hostile to the trial and even more so to the sentence. Former Hitlerite Foreign Minister von Ribbentrop arrogantly declared that "a few years from now the jurists of the whole world will condemn this trial." Jurists in the service of reaction did their best to make this "prediction" come true even sooner.

U.S. Senator Taft was "shocked" by the fate of Goering, Ribbentrop and other war criminals. In a burst of frankness he said: "The United States will long regret carrying out the Nuremberg sentence." The greater part of the reactionary newspapers and magazines of both the U.S.A. and Britain expressed wonder that the governments of these countries had even consented to hold the trial, which was totally inconsistent with the post-war policy of the Anglo-American ruling circles.

"You must agree that if an ordinary man [sic] had dropped from the moon and landed in Nuremberg he would have concluded that utter idiocy reigned there." These were the words addressed to readers by Montgomery Belgion, one of the Anglo-American apologists for fascism, who wrote a book on the trial of the Hitlerite ringleaders. Throughout Belgion's book runs the thread that the Nuremberg trial was a harmful, incomprehensible undertaking.

From the very start the idea of holding an international trial of the ring-leaders in the German war crimes was not to the liking of the American-British ruling circles. They feared that much which had been guarded as secret would be disclosed. The trial might have revealed, for example, the criminal part that ruling circles of the U.S.A., Britain and France had played in backing Hitlerism.

But the desire is one thing and the opportunity another; the pictures of the monstrous crimes committed by the Hitlerites were too fresh in the memories of the people. In these circumstances the American-British reactionaries at that time, in 1945, could not refuse outright to hold the trial or to sentence the chief war criminals.

Let us try to imagine the following scene. On trial is a criminal accused of systematic robbery and murder, of forming entire gangs for these purposes and of inciting others to commit murders, etc. After a court investigation the defense lawyer, in his speech, does not dispute the facts of murder and robbery, but seeks to prove that murder has never been considered a crime, that robbery is an ordinary human matter, and so on. On this basis he regards his client's trial as a complete misunderstanding.

The history of jurisprudence has never recorded such a case.

But the conduct of the Nazi lawyers and of the transoceanic patrons of fascism at Nuremberg may justly be compared with the defense counsel's speech in the above scene, with the mere difference that Goering and the others were tried not for individual murders but for wiping out millions of people and not for robbing two or three apartments but for laying waste entire countries and nations.

Indeed, what most disturbed American reaction during the trial?

The necessity of recognizing fascist aggression as an international crime.

The German lawyers hardly had voiced their views when from across the ocean came voices crying out against recognition of aggressive warfare as an international crime. How can one proclaim a crime what the American imperialists have been doing for decades and for which they have been so energetically preparing ever since the second world war?

In the people's desire to condemn aggressive war and to proclaim it an international crime the American reactionaries saw a blow to the basic principles of imperialist policy. In the very early days of the trial the American magazine The Nation declared the Nuremberg trial was undermining "the bases of *our* public life."

It is not surprising, therefore, that when the verdict was handed down the imperialist press in the U.S.A. set up an incredible howl. The magazine Fortune carried an article under the significant title "Nuremberg Confusion," stating: "Yesterday the chief German war criminals were on trial. Today, however, the tribunal itself stands before the court of public (?) opinion."

Most of those who in the U.S.A. are termed professors of international law found it necessary to toss mud at the Nuremberg verdict. And, of course their greatest indignation was aroused by that part of the verdict which speaks of aggressive war as an international crime. . . .

Recently Hudson, chairman of the U.N. committee on international law, . . . expressed the fears of U.S. and British ruling circles of the possibility of a "new Nuremberg." Hudson said that he had "had occasion to come into contact with numerous military people who expressed anxiety over the text of Article 6(a) of the charter of the Nuremberg tribunal (dealing with responsibility for aggression). These people are afraid that they may eventually be accused of waging an aggressive war, although the definition of an aggressive war has not yet been given."

Let us note, incidentally, that in 1945, when the Nuremberg trial was going on, one American magazine declared that ". . . on the basis of this theory of law the graduates of West Point might some day be executed as war criminals . . . and, of course, the members of the general staff . . . if the U.S.A. ever, Lord forbid, lost a war." Here is what the American military fear! Let us say frankly it is quite a well-grounded fear!

History has condemned aggression as an international crime. The peoples passed their verdict five years ago when they condemned Hitlerite aggression.

The significance of the Nuremberg verdict consists not only in that it punished the worst criminals against peace. It is a menacing warning to warmongers of all kinds who may wish to plunge the world into the abyss of new bloody trials.

4.

Montgomery Belgion, who is attacked in the preceding article, here presents his side of the case. A journalist, Mr. Belgion was editor in charge of the European edition of the *New York Herald* in 1915, and later served on the editorial staffs of the London *Daily Mail* and the *New York World.* He argues that no good will come of the punishment of the vanquished by the victors. Such a point of view has a sportsmanlike ring about it, and it may be the very point of view needed amid the horrors of the twentieth century. Or, on the other hand, is such sportsmanship somewhat misplaced when one's foe is not Robert E. Lee, but Adolf Hitler?

BELGION: Victors' Justice *

It cannot be seriously pretended that those trials, whether of so-called "war criminals," of "organizers" or "accomplices," or of members of former "organizations" pronounced to have been "criminal," were not political trials exactly as the trials of so-called "quislings" were. It cannot be seriously pretended that the eagerness with which the prosecutions were undertaken and the pertinacity with which they were pursued did not derive from a spirit of revenge. For although the foe was now prostrate, he had come near to triumph, and especially in the countries which he had occupied on the Continent, the people who were borne aloft by his downfall were the very people he in his triumph would have kept at arm's length from power.

But nobody among the victorious peoples of the West wished to be thought nakedly revengeful. Still less did any one want to admit to himself that he was being impelled to demand the trials by a desire for vicarious vengeance. The influence of twenty centuries of a Christian tradition was still too strong to allow that. Instead there was the self-deception that the clamour for the punishment of Germans was inspired, not by a desire for vengeance, but by a desire for justice. As there had certainly been guilt, it was tempting to imagine that the guilt was wholly and exclusively German. On the strength of a wealth of atrocity stories, of the reports of the condition of concentration camps, and of all sorts of fact and rumour, it was easy to feel that justice was called for and that justice could be done.

There must often have been the same self-deception when a man was lynched. In California in the old days, when courts of law were few and far between, it was common to lynch desperadoes and to imagine that, as the victims had usually done that of which they were accused and for which they were executed, lynching was justice. But that was a self-deception none the less. Lynching cannot be justice on account of those very features in which the Nuremberg Trial was akin to lynching. A court is constituted, even if it is self-constituted. The accused is invited to try to exculpate himself, even

* From Montgomery Belgion, *Victors' Justice* (Hinsdale, Illinois: Henry Regnery, 1949), pp. 171–73, 185–87. Reprinted by permission of the Henry Regnery Company.

though he will not be heeded. Usually, too, the delusion of righteousness is strong in the executioner-judges. But the guilt of the apprehended person or persons is presumed in advance, the judges have no properly constituted body of law to administer, they do not observe the rules of evidence, and the sentence pronounced is arbitrary. Hence lynching is never justice. And the Nuremberg Trial was not justice.

We can understand how natural it was for the unreasoning and warm-hearted multitude in the victorious West to fall into the self-deception that vengeance could also be justice. It is more difficult to understand how their rulers and governors were able to fancy that the prosecution and punishment of so-called "war criminals" would be an undertaking that contributed to the future stability of peace. That self-deception was, you would have thought, too transparent. As the French Protestant pastor, Jacques Ellul, wrote in a weekly paper in the week following the delivery of the sentences: "We did not wreak vengeance: that would have made us wicked! but we manufactured a special and entirely novel law designed to enable us to sentence to death." How could it have been imagined that, first the Germans, and then the world, would not realize this?

Already in November 1947 a German lecturer at Heidelberg was predicting that in Germany every detail of the Trial, and details of some of the later trials too, would become the topic of interminable discussion down the years, and that the Trial was destined to engender a German literature as vast as that provoked by Article 231 of the Treaty of Versailles. After all, the prediction was not surprising. The circumstances of the Trial, far from putting it beyond challenge, simply invited challenge. But what will be the sequel? . . .

In 1919 the western victors wished to levy reparations on the vanquished, and they felt that they must have a title to do so. This title they conferred on themselves by means of an assertion of "war guilt" which they inserted in their peace treaty. A second war having broken out in 1939, the same western victors assumed that its cause must again lie in the "war guilt" of the vanquished. They supposed that there had been only one error after 1918: the punishment inflicted on the vanquished was not sufficiently severe. In order to inflict even more drastic punishment this time, they again felt the need of a title. It was the same title, namely, the "war guilt" of the vanquished. But this time they wished to render it, as they must have supposed, unchallengeable. They delivered it to themselves by means of the verdict of a tribunal.

That verdict was, however, worthless. To some extent the holding of the Trial at which it was rendered had been dictated by a desire for vengeance. In addition, the penalties upon individuals which the tribunal inflicted as a result of the verdict were as much punishment of the vanquished as any of the more general punitive treatment which the verdict was held to warrant. That is to say, the conveyance of the title was itself of a kind with that which it was held to render permissible.

Furthermore, the prosecution and punishment of individuals among the vanquished at the hands of the victors after the war had ended were an undertaking fraught with grave menace for the future of civil manners. The prosecution and punishment were carried out according to a totalitarian notion of justice which neither England nor "kingless commonwealths on the other shore of the Atlantic Ocean" had ever known, and which the Continent of Europe had discarded at the French Revolution. In the principal Trial there was a sinister pretension to administer international law. That meant in effect that this Trial was an attempt to degrade the law of nations from a set of moral rules to a criminal code, an attempt which, if it could ever succeed, would abolish the law of nations altogether.

Against those grave judicial and moral abuses, can there be set anything that was achieved for the cause of peace? On the contrary, it now seems more probable . . . that nothing is to be gained after a war by the punishment of the vanquished by the victors, even if the vanquished have been to blame for the war itself. It now seems more probable than ever that for victors to assert after a war the "war guilt" of the vanquished serves but to disguise the real sources of international disturbance.

Possibly it is because the western victors in 1919 did not recognize the moral basis of international relations that war returned to Europe and to the world in 1939. Possibly it is because the western victors again in 1945 did not recognize the moral basis of those relations that the world was treated to the spectacle of victors' justice, and one more great war had ended without leading men's feet into the way of peace.

5.

As is stressed in the following article, which was written while the trials were still in progress, no very effective case can be made out against Nuremberg until at least one suitable alternative is presented. Mr. Phleger, a strong supporter of the International Military Tribunal, argues forcefully that there was no suitable alternative, and obviously feels that the trials are the beginning of what could be, with good luck and good will, a valid and stable system of international law and justice. Like Mr. Wechsler, Herman Phleger is a distinguished lawyer; after having been in private practice for many years, he was legal adviser to the Department of State from 1953 to 1957, and served as a member of the American delegations to the Inter-American Conference at Caracas in 1954 and the Geneva Summit Conference in 1955. He has also been a United States member of the Permanent Court of Arbitration under The Hague Treaties, and United States representative to the 13th Session of the General Assembly of the United Nations.

PHLEGER: Nuremberg—a Fair Trial? *

Why do I believe the defendants are having a fair trial? Because, in the first place, they are fully informed of the law which they are charged with violating (the claim that it is *ex post facto* I shall consider in a moment); they were

*From Herman Phleger, "Nuremberg—a Fair Trial?" *Atlantic Monthly*, vol. 177 (April 1946), pp. 62–65. Reprinted by permission of the author and of the editors of the *Atlantic Monthly*.

served with a specification of the offenses charged, in their own language, well in advance of trial; they are represented by counsel acceptable to them, including some of the most eminent lawyers in Germany. Dr. Dix, Schacht's counsel, is one of the most prominent lawyers in Berlin; Ribbentrop's counsel is Dr. Fritz Sauter, long a leader of the German bar; all give an impression of competence and courage. The defendants have the right to introduce evidence, to cross-examine witnesses, to testify, and to address the court. The proceedings are in, or are translated into, a language understood by them.

The proceedings are public. The press of the world is represented, and within the limits of available space, visitors are admitted. Every word of testimony is recorded and preserved, both in the original and translation, and daily transcripts are made available. Exhibits are furnished the defendants in advance.

The whole atmosphere of the proceeding is dignified and orderly. The Tribunal displays a high regard for the defendants' rights. The law to be applied is fixed by the Charter, not the Tribunal. Its function is to decide, under the law prescribed, whether the evidence produced proves the charges of the indictment. This duty I am sure the court will discharge with courage and scrupulous fairness. The defendants will be deemed innocent unless and until proved guilty by evidence produced in open court, responsive to the charges of the indictment. Any judgment will be in writing and will state the reasons on which it is based.

It has been observed that the victors are here sitting in judgment on the vanquished; that the accusers are trying the accused. But in the trial of any crime, the state is the aggrieved party; and it declares the law, establishes the court, and appoints the judge. Here, as in other criminal cases, everything possible has been done to surround the proceeding with the traditional safeguards that experience has shown will most surely result in a fair trial, including the appointment, as judges, of men of high character, who no one can doubt will fairly, conscientiously, and courageously perform the duties of their office. Theoretically, it seems desirable that the Charter and the Tribunal should include neutral nations and neutral judges. But in a world where there are few, if any, genuine neutrals, and where the feeling was general that no nation should remain neutral with such issues at stake, this end was obviously not possible of attainment.

Having in mind that this Tribunal is the joint institution of four nations, plus fifteen others, all with varying legal procedures, and with differing conceptions of justice and law, I take it as a remarkable display of international cooperation that agreement should have been reached on a matter so close to the national prejudices of all, and that the resulting procedure, both in theory and fact, should conform so closely to our own ideas of justice.

Turning now to the legal basis for the trial, the question most often asked is whether the defendants are being tried under an *ex post facto* law—that is, whether the Charter makes criminal, acts which were innocent when done. *Ex post facto* laws are prohibited by our Constitution and are rightfully considered contrary to good morals and natural law.

The only charge in the indictment which can be claimed to be *ex post facto* is the one involving the waging of aggressive wars. All the other accusations, including those of mistreatment of prisoners and other violations of the laws of war, as well as those of wholesale murder and other crimes against humanity, relate to acts which have been recognized universally as criminal and punishable under the laws of all civilized communities.

Every legal principle of general application, such as the prohibition against *ex post facto* laws, is founded on reason. Does the reason apply here?

Blackstone in his Commentaries makes it clear that the reason for the rule is that law, to be valid, must be prescribed; it must be notified to the people who are to obey it, "not like Caligula, who (according to Dio Cassius) wrote his laws in a very small character, and hung them upon high pillars, the more effectively to ensnare the people," but in the most public and conspicuous manner. And Blackstone continues, "There is a still more unreasonable method than this, which is called making of laws *ex post facto* (after the fact); when after an action (indifferent in itself) is committed, the legislator then for the first time declares it to have been a crime, and inflicts a punishment upon the person who has committed it. Here it is impossible that the party could foresee that an action, innocent when it was done, should be afterward converted to guilt by a subsequent law; he had therefore no cause to abstain from it; and all punishment for not abstaining must of consequence be cruel and unjust."

Apply the principle here. Do we find that the planning and waging of aggressive war by these defendants was an act "indifferent in itself" at the time; or that these defendants could have believed their conduct was "innocent when . . . done" and would not be subsequently punished, and "had therefore no cause to abstain from it"?

It seems clear from what follows that these defendants not only knew that aggressive wars were outlawed and unlawful when they planned them, but they also knew they would be individually punished if they were not successful. They did not rely upon any principle of international law; indeed they had no respect for international law, and only used its forms to make more complete the surprise attendant upon its later violation. These defendants were not entrapped or taken by surprise.

The doctrine that aggressive warfare is an international wrong is not an invention of the London Charter; it was established by a series of agreements in the interval between the two world wars. The Treaty of Versailles arraigned the former German Emperor for violating international morality and the sanctity of treaties, and he was saved from trial only by the failure of the Netherlands government to surrender his person. By the Treaty of Locarno, to which Germany was a party, it was stipulated in 1925 that the signatories would "in no case invade or resort to war against each other." In 1927 forty-eight members of the League of Nations, including Germany, agreed through their representatives that a war of aggression constitutes an international crime. By the Briand-Kellogg Pact of 1928, practically all the nations of the world, including Germany, Italy, and Japan, agreed to renounce war as an instrument of national policy and to settle disputes by pacific means. This succession of solemn international agreements established a common world-wide understanding that wars of aggression were illegal, and rendered obsolete the nineteenth-century view that the law would not inquire into the justice of a war between sovereign powers.

International law is not embodied in any fixed code; its principles are to be found in established custom, treaties, conventions, the works of writers, court decisions, and like pronouncements. If it is to grow and progress in the future as it has in the past, changes in legal conceptions which have occurred must be recognized and applied. The absence of judicial precedent for the Charter provision on crimes against peace does not prevent its being an accurate declaration of existing law.

"International law, or the law that governs between states, has, at times, like the common law within states, a twilight existence during which it is hardly distinguishable from morality or justice, till at length the *imprimatur* of a court attests its jural quality." So said Mr. Justice Cardozo in *New Jersey v. Delaware*. The Charter, joined in by nineteen nations, declaring, recognizing, and defining the crime of aggressive war, would seem to be a sufficient *imprimatur* to attest the outlawry which had earlier been openly declared against wars of aggression. Its application to the individuals who are being tried by the Tribunal does not have the quality, either in principle or in form, of an *ex post facto* law.

No principle of international law requires that we shall stultify the Briand-Kellogg Pact by accepting the proposition that an illegal war is a legal cloak under which its perpetrators are shielded from responsibility for its inevitable consequences. To those who believe it does so in some technical sense, it may be said that a refusal to execute the Charter on that ground would have been to grasp at the shadow of the past, and to sacrifice the substance of the present and the future.

The Charter provides that there shall be individual responsibility for the specified crimes, that the position of an individual as a head of state shall not be a defense, and that the fact that an individual acted under orders shall not free him from responsibility but may be considered in mitigation. . . .

Collective responsibility under international law, by which the innocent are made to suffer with the guilty, has not proved effective in the past as a deterrent to war. There is certainly no universal principle that prohibits the punishment of individuals, both high and low, for breaches of international law, and the definite declaration of nineteen nations that such responsibility exists and will be enforced, is a distinct step forward and is to be commended.

The defense of superior orders is a complex subject, and the precedents are not harmonious. Most military codes require obedience to lawful orders only, from which it would follow that a superior's order to commit a crime is no defense. On the other hand, a common soldier ordered to shoot by his superior, has no choice, and at least where the order is not plainly illegal, the soldier should be protected. This, I feel sure, is what the result will be under the rule declared by the Charter.

But in the present case the admirals and the generals were not obeying superior orders: they were giving orders. They are charged, not with having executed the order of a superior, but with being Nazi conspirators, who, equally with the others, actively joined in the rise of the Party, its seizure of power, and its subsequent career of aggressive war, murder, and oppression. They are not being tried because they are soldiers, but because they are politicians.

Certainly it does not seem that the provisions of the Charter declaring individual responsibility, making former chiefs of state subject to the same law as are lesser figures, and making obedience to superior orders in the commission of a crime matter in mitigation rather than an absolute defense, are subject to valid criticism either on the ground that they are new law, or that they are bad law. It would indeed be an anomaly if these defendants were all to escape on pleas that some acted under superior orders, and that all who did not so act were immune from punishment as chiefs of state.

It has been suggested that the parties to the Charter had no power to provide for the punishment of crimes committed in Germany by Germans against other Germans, in some cases before the war began.

The indictment charges in detail that the defendants planned and perpetrated, deliberately and systematically, a multitude of crimes against their own fellow citizens. In executing these plans, hundreds of thousands of utterly harmless men, women, and children were tortured, murdered, and subjected to inhuman treatment unknown to the Western world for centuries. In effect, this provision of the Charter declares that the community of nations may, and must, assume responsibility for the punishment of such crimes. The decision of the Powers to assume this responsibility is understandable. There is room for the conviction that the civilized world simply cannot afford to condone, by inaction, this wholesale negation of the very foundation of Christian morality.

But aside from these considerations, the fact is that so far as concerns the present defendants, there is adequate legal basis for their prosecution by this Tribunal. In the first place, the murders and other crimes committed under their direction were criminal under the law of all civilized states, including the law of Germany, and in the words of an authoritative writer, "principles of criminal law generally accepted among the different nations are a proper source of international law." In the second place, the declared purposes of these crimes were an integral part of the Nazi plan of international aggression. The fact that these defendants, because of their absolute control over the German state, were factually immune from punishment does not deprive their acts of their criminal character. As a result of the unconditional surrender of the German armies, the occupation by the military forces of the Allies, and the collapse of the German government, the Allies are now the government of Germany.

The Declaration of Berlin of June 5, 1945, promulgated by the governments of the United States, Great Britain, the U.S.S.R., and France, declares that these governments assume supreme authority with respect to Germany, "including all the powers possessed by the German government, the high command and any State, municipal or local government or authority." The occupying powers, therefore, have not only the power but the duty to punish crimes against German law, including crimes committed before they assumed the powers of government. These defendants have committed crimes against German law, for which they were not prosecuted prior to the occupation, and are therefore subject to prosecution now. The practical inefficacy of trial by Germany courts in such a situation was demonstrated after the First World War.

On the other hand it is asserted by some that the defendants are obviously guilty, and should be summarily executed; that a trial is but a form to cloak what is clearly justified as an act of retribution. This sounds strangely like Nazi doctrine. Under our conception of justice, every man is presumed innocent until proved guilty. These defendants have entered pleas of not guilty, and the maintenance of our standards of justice, not to mention our self-respect, requires that they be given a full and fair opportunity to meet the charges brought against them, whether their defenses be legal, factual, or both. It will indeed be a salutary example to the German people, inured to the summary judgment of the People's Court or imprisonment in a concentration camp without hearing, to witness a fair trial accorded men charged with such revolting crimes.

But in addition to the desirable objective of punishing those responsible for the war and its atrocities, other ends are attainable as a result of the trial. One is that of furthering the cause of future peace through actual enforcement of rules of international law by imposing effective sanctions against those who wage aggressive war. Another is the making of a true record of the facts of the war that will be available to all, for all time.

The desirability of developing international law to provide effective punishment for its breach is obvious. The deterrent effect on prospective violators seems clear. The trial is a step in the right direction. One nation cannot have its own way in international matters. The United States could not write the specifications alone. The fact that the four great nations and fifteen others have, despite their varying conceptions of law and procedure, agreed upon a common formula is a remarkable victory for international cooperation. Only at times such as this, when world conditions and relationships are fluid, are such results attainable.

The relationship built by the necessity of fighting a common enemy provided an opportunity which, to judge by the last war, might not be of indefinite duration. The relinquishment of this opportunity merely because of hope that at some future time something better might be developed would be wholly unjustified. Those who have an uneasy feeling that some of the participating nations may not have a perfect record on the score of aggressive war should comfort themselves with the thought that having joined in a solemn international definition of the crime, and in the conduct of a trial for its violation, the participants have all made a commitment on the subject that might otherwise be difficult or impossible to obtain.

Experience after World War I demonstrates that unless a full record, one that will command public acceptance, is made of the facts surrounding the war, there will arise in a short time two schools of thought concerning almost every aspect of what occurred, and German historians and politicians will soon be asserting that no atrocities were committed, that all the wars they commenced were defensive wars, justified by the acts of their enemies, and that only another war can redress the injustices done them in this.

The defendants may, and no doubt will, controvert and explain much of the evidence produced by the prosecution. The resultant record of the causes and events of the war, tested by the procedure of actual trial, will be unique in the history of the world. What would we give for such a record of the last war, or of some of the great trials of history? This will be no "white paper," written *ex parte* in some nation's Foreign Office. The public is entitled to know the facts; this trial will supply them.

In the final analysis, the effect of the Charter and the trial on the future course of international law and on the attainment of peace is what is important, not the punishment of twenty or a thousand men. On balance, the score is overwhelmingly in favor of the Tribunal. There were only three alternatives: to let the defendants go free; to punish them summarily; or to try them. Only the last alternative held any hope for the future. The trial, authorized by the Charter, will be conducted by the Tribunal with scrupulous fairness; of that we may be sure, considering the character of its members and of counsel for the prosecution, all of whom realize that while the defendants are being tried by the record in this proceeding, the court and its officers will be subject to the verdict of history.

This verdict may be confidently awaited; moreover, if this trial shall have established for all time the rule of law that any person who commits the acts of which these defendants are accused shall be subject to individual accountability under international law, then out of the miseries and sacrifices of this war, some good will have come, and the millions of innocent men, women, and children for whose torture and murder these men are being tried will not have died in vain.

XIII.

THE IMPACT OF
FREUDIAN THOUGHT

Occasionally in human history, a single creative thinker puts his mark upon an entire era and gives historians an excuse for attaching his name to that whole age. Thus we often speak of the Age of Socrates, of the Age of Newton, of the Age of Darwin; and we begin to hear our own times described as the Freudian Age. It is easy enough to criticize such shorthand labels, and to point out how oversimplified and even misleading they can be. It is quite proper to quibble over the real relationship between the man and his time, and to ask whether a thinker does not simply reflect or symbolize the mood of an era, rather than create or reshape that mood. Perhaps the late nineteenth century would have been "Darwinian" in spirit even without Darwin; perhaps the twentieth would be "Freudian" even without Freud.

Such speculation, though relevant, is probably not very profitable. Sigmund Freud did exist, and his ideas did gradually permeate western thought—aided, no doubt, by the chronic tensions and upheaval of the age. Prior to 1914, the impact was relatively slight, even though Freud had worked out most of his ideas and his techniques during the 1890's and the early 1900's. He had attracted a small coterie of dedicated disciples, some of whom (notably C. G. Jung and Alfred Adler) were eventually to break with the master and were to found heretical schools. The full flood of Freudian influence came after the first world war, both in Europe and in the United States; by the time the second postwar period arrived, Freudian terminology had become part of everyday language, and Freudian or neo-Freudian conceptions of man and society had penetrated not only literature and the arts, but political and social theorizing as well. Often, no doubt, the penetration was not very deep, and was confined to the slipshod use of a few Freudian catchwords; many users of Freudian phrases had never read a page of Freud. But the influence of a thinker, or the pervasive character of his ideas, is not always measured by his rating on the best-seller lists, or by the number of man-hours that have been devoted to reading him in the original. Not every Darwinian had read *The Origin of Species;* not every Marxian has read *Das Kapital.*

Freud is often viewed as the protagonist of an irrationalist revolt. His defenders have an easy time refuting such a charge; they can show that he was a man of the positivist age, that he intended (though perhaps not always successfully) to cling to the most rigorous scientific method, to "the basic tenets of controlled in-

389

quiry." Orthodox Freudians can point out that if the master's views were later distorted by some of his disciples and by the general public, no one ought to blame Freud himself for the distortion. They can also contend that Freud never set himself up as a philosopher who presumed to provide a new *Weltanschauung* for the age. Yet in his later years, Freud did go well beyond the role of the mere clinician seeking a therapy for mental illness; in such essays as *Civilization and its Discontents* (1930), he advanced some broader conceptions of man and society, and even suggested that entire systems or epochs of civilization may at times become neurotic. If Darwin made no direct contribution to the "social Darwinism" created by his followers, Freud surely bears some responsibility for what one might call "social Freudianism."

Although Freud himself contended that man's most basic drives (the love instinct and the death instinct) are antisocial in nature, and that the repression of these drives produces frustration and neurosis, he probably never believed that man and society are totally irreconcilable. Yet it is not surprising that some of his disciples arrived at that conclusion. "It is a shattering experience," writes one American scholar, "for anyone seriously committed to the Western traditions of morality and rationality to take a steadfast, unflinching look at what Freud has to say." For ". . . it begins to be apparent that mankind, in all its restless striving and progress, has no idea of what it really wants." [1] Neo-Freudians, on the other hand, have softened the pessimistic mood of the orthodox doctrine, and have sought to argue that man and society can be reconciled through some sort of "social adjustment"— through a reorganization of society that would permit the spontaneous development of the "integrated personality." But such a conclusion, the orthodox Freudians argue, is a tender-minded perversion of the master's thought; it pushes aside Freud's "dark vision of the embattled self" in favor of "cheery platitudes"; it abandons all that is challenging and serious in the Freudian insights.[2]

It may be argued that any serious discussion of the Freudian impact in the twentieth century ought to be preceded by extended study of the Freudian doctrines themselves, both through his own writings and through the commentaries of trained psychoanalysts. Yet the broader impact of Freudianism on our age is conveyed through the works of nonprofessionals: writers, artists, behavioral scientists, essayists, historians. The selections that follow are nonspecialized in nature; they provide a variety of views about the Freudian impact, most of them from literate and perceptive observers of the contemporary scene. If Americans outnumber Europeans among them, that does not mean that the Freudian impact has been a purely American phenomenon, but only that public debate about it has been more vigorous in this country.

The authors represented below include both defenders of Freud and critics of various kinds, ranging from the Communists to the Catholics. After reading them, it may be useful to discuss the probable motivations of both critics and defenders (Freudianism, after all, has taught us always to look for hidden motivations!). It may be relevant to ask whether Freud's new perceptions about the basic drives of man knock all the props from under the older Enlightenment view of man as an essentially rational being, capable of self-government and of self-improvement. Or can the Freudian insights be integrated somehow with the Enlightenment view, in order to produce a sounder and more workable doctrine that may serve as the

[1] Norman O. Brown, *Life Against Death: the Psychoanalytic Meaning of History* (New York: Random House, 1959), pp. xi–xii.

[2] Philip Rieff, *Freud: the Mind of the Moralist* (New York: Viking Press, 1959), p. 56.

base for a functioning society? Freud's bitterest critics (and some of his more extreme defenders as well) will reject that possibility. But if it is true that "the nuggets of philosophical wisdom . . . mined from Freud's writings have long been commonplaces in an ethical tradition that stems from Socrates to John Dewey . . . ," [3] then perhaps it may be possible to reconcile Freud's findings with that long humanistic tradition, even though the immediate impact of Freudianism may seem to be so disruptive as to portend a kind of ethical and social disintegration.

1.

Like most anniversaries, the centenary of Sigmund Freud's birth brought a rash of articles and books to commemorate or analyze his work. One of the best of these—sympathetic and perceptive, with an occasional touch of irony —was a brief essay by Alfred Kazin, the noted author, teacher, and literary critic. Mr. Kazin, who was born and educated in New York City, taught in several American universities before becoming professor of American studies at Amherst College. He has written a number of essays on psychoanalysis, and is one of the few laymen who has been invited to lecture to audiences of analysts.

KAZIN: The Freudian Revolution Analyzed *

It is hard to believe that Sigmund Freud was born over a century ago. Although Freud has long been a household name (and, in fact, dominates many a household one could mention), his theories still seem too "advanced," they touch too bluntly on the most intimate side of human relations, for us to picture Freud himself coming out of a world that in all other respects now seems so quaint.

Although Freud has influenced even people who have never heard of him, not all his theories have been accepted even by his most orthodox followers, while a great many of his essential ideas are rejected even by many psychoanalysts. In one sense Freud himself is still battling for recognition, for because of the tabooed nature of the materials in which he worked and the unusually speculative quality of his mind, Freud still seems to many people more an irritant than a classic.

On the other hand, Freud's influence, which started from the growing skepticism about civilization and morality after the First World War, is now beyond description. Freudianism gave sanction to the increasing exasperation with public standards as opposed to private feelings; it upheld the truths of human nature as against the hypocrisies and cruelties of conventional morality; it stressed the enormous role that sex plays in man's imaginative life, in his relations to his parents, in the symbolism of language.

It is impossible to think of the greatest names in modern literature and art— Thomas Mann, James Joyce, Franz Kafka, T. S. Eliot, Ernest Hemingway,

---

[3] Sidney Hook, in *The New York Times Book Review*, June 24, 1962, p. 7.

* From Alfred Kazin, "The Freudian Revolution Analyzed," in *The New York Times Magazine*, May 6, 1956. Reprinted by permission of the author and of the editors of *The New York Times*.

William Faulkner, Pablo Picasso, Paul Klee—without realizing our debt to Freud's exploration of dreams, myths, symbols and the imaginative profundity of man's inner life. Even those who believe that original sin is a safer guide to the nature of man than any other can find support in Freud's gloomy doubts about man's capacity for progress. For quite other reasons, Freud has found followers even among Catholic psychiatrists, who believe that Freud offers a believable explanation of neurosis and a possible cure, and so leaves the sufferer cured to practice his faith in a rational way.

Many psychologists who disagree with Freud's own materialism have gratefully adopted many of Freud's diagnoses, and although he himself was chary about the psychoanalytical technique in serious mental illness, more and more psychiatrists now follow his technique, or some adaptation of it. For no other system of thought in modern times, except the great religions, has been adopted by so many people as a systematic interpretation of individual behavior. Consequently, to those who have no other belief, Freudianism sometimes serves as a philosophy of life.

Freud, a tough old humanist with a profoundly skeptical mind, would have been shocked or amused by the degree to which everything is sometimes explained by "Freudian" doctrines. He offered us not something that applies dogmatically to all occasions, but something useful, a principle of inquiry into those unconscious forces that are constantly pulling people apart, both in themselves and from each other.

Freud's extraordinary achievement was to show us, in scientific terms, the primacy of natural desire, the secret wishes we proclaim in our dreams, the mixture of love and shame and jealousy in our relations to our parents, the child as father to the man, the deeply buried instincts that make us natural beings and that go back to the forgotten struggles of the human race. Until Freud, novelists and dramatists had never dared to think that science would back up their belief that personal passion is a stronger force in people's lives than socially accepted morality. Thanks to Freud, these insights now form a widely shared body of knowledge.

In short, Freud had the ability, such as is given to very few individuals, to introduce a wholly new factor into human knowledge; to impress it upon people's minds as something for which there was evidence. He revealed a part of reality that many people before him had guessed at, but which no one before him was able to describe as systematically and convincingly as he did. In the same way that one associates the discovery of certain fundamentals with Copernicus, Newton, Darwin, Einstein, so one identifies many of one's deepest motivations with Freud. His name is no longer the name of a man; like "Darwin," it is now synonymous with a part of nature.

This is the very greatest kind of influence that a man can have. It means that people use his name to signify something in the world of nature which, they believe, actually exists. A man's name has become identical with a phenomenon in nature, with a cause in nature, with a "reality" that we accept— even when we don't want to accept it. Every hour of every day now, and especially in America, there are people who cannot forget a name, or make a slip of the tongue, or feel depressed; who cannot begin a love affair, or end a marriage, without wondering what the "Freudian" reason may be.

No one can count the number of people who now think of any crisis as a personal failure, and who turn to a psychoanalyst or to psychoanalytical literature for an explanation of their suffering where once they would have turned to a minister or to the Bible for consolation. Freudian terms are now part of our thought. There are innumerable people who will never admit that they believe a word of his writings, who nevertheless, "unconsciously," as they would say, have learned to look for "motivations," to detect "compensations," to withold a purely moralistic judgment in favor of individual understanding, to prize sexual satisfaction as a key to individual happiness, and to characterize people by the depth and urgency of their passions rather than by the nobility of their professions.

For much of this "Freudian" revolution, Freud himself is not responsible. And in evaluating the general effect of Freud's doctrines on the modern scene, especially in America, it is important to distinguish between the hard, biological, fundamentally classical thought of Freud, who was a determinist, a pessimist, and a genius, from the thousands of little cultural symptoms and "psychological" theories, the pretensions and self-indulgences, which are often found these days in the prosperous middle-class culture that has responded most enthusiastically to Freud.

There is, for example, the increasing tendency to think that all problems are "psychological," to ignore the real conflicts in society that underlie politics and to interpret politicians and candidates—especially those you don't like— in terms of "sexual" motives. There is the cunning use of "Freudian" terms in advertising, which has gone so far that nowadays there's a pretty clear suggestion that the girl comes with the car. There are all the psychologists who study "motivations," and sometimes invent them, so as to get you to buy two boxes of cereal where one would have done before.

There are the horrendous movies and slick plays which not only evade the writer's need to explain characters honestly, but, by attributing to everybody what one can only call the Freudian nightmare, have imposed upon a credulous public the belief that it may not be art but that it is "true"—that is, sex—and so must be taken seriously. And, since this is endless but had better stop somewhere, there are all the people who have confused their "urges" with art, have learned in all moral crises to blame their upbringing rather than themselves, and tend to worship the psychoanalyst as God.

The worst of the "Freudian revolution" is the increasing tendency to attribute all criticism of our society to personal "sickness." The rebel is looked on as neurotic rather than someone making a valid protest. Orthodox Freudians tend to support the status quo as a matter of course and to blame the individual for departing from it. Freud himself never made such a mistake, and no one would have been able to convince him that the Viennese world around him was "normal."

The identification of a military group, or a class, or a culture, with an absolute to which we must all be adjusted at any price is a dangerous trend. And the worst of it is that to many people psychoanalysts now signify "authority," so that people believe them on any and all subjects.

On the other hand, the greatest and most beautiful effect of Freudianism is the increasing awareness of childhood as the most important single influence on personal development. This profound cherishing of childhood has opened up wholly new relationships between husbands and wives, as well as between parents and children, and it represents—though often absurdly overanxious—a peculiar new tenderness in modern life. Similarly, though Freud's psychology is weakest on women, there can be no doubt that, again in America, the increasing acknowledgment of the importance of sexual satisfaction has given to women an increasing sense of their individual dignity and their specific needs.

But the greatest revolution of all, and one that really explains the overwhelming success of Freudianism in America, lies in the general insistence on individual fulfillment, satisfaction and happiness. Odd as it may seem to us, who take our striving toward these things for granted, the insistence on personal happiness represents the most revolutionary force in modern times. And it is precisely because our own tradition works toward individual self-realization, because private happiness does seem to us to be both an important ideal and a practical goal, that Freudianism has found so many recruits in this country. . . .

Freud's work appealed to the increasing regard for individual experience that is one of the great themes of modern literature and art. The sensitiveness to each individual as a significant register of the consciousness in general, the artistic interest in carrying human consciousness to its farthest limits—it was this essential side of modern art that Freud's researches encouraged and deepened. He brought, as it were, the authority of science to the inner promptings of art, and thus helped writers and artists to feel that their interest in myths, in symbols, in dreams was on the side of "reality," of science, itself, when it shows the fabulousness of the natural world.

Even if we regret, as we must, the fact that Freud's influence has been identified with a great many shallow and commercially slick ideas, the fact remains that if Freud's ideas appealed generally to the inwardness which is so important to modern writers and artists, it was because Freud thoroughly won his case against many aggressive but less intelligent opponents. . . .

Civilization as we know it, Freud said, had been built up on man's heroic sacrifice of instinct. Only, Freud issued the warning that more and more men would resent this sacrifice, would wonder if civilization was worth the price. And how profoundly right he was in this can be seen not only in the Nazi madness that drove him as an old man out of Vienna, that almost cost him his life, but in the increasing disdain for culture, in the secret lawlessness that has become, under the conformist surface, a sign of increasing personal irritation and rebelliousness in our society. More and more, the sexual freedom of our time seems to be a way of mentally getting even, of confused protest, and not the pagan enjoyment of instinct that writers like D. H. Lawrence upheld against Freud's gloomy forebodings.

For Freud the continuous sacrifice of "nature" that is demanded by "civilization" meant that it was only through rationality and conscious awareness that maturity could be achieved. Far from counseling license, his most famous formula became—"Where id was, ego shall be"—the id representing the unconscious, the ego our dominant and purposive sense of ourselves. However, consciousness meant for Freud an unyielding insistence on the importance of sexuality. And it was just on this issue that, even before the first World War, his movement broke apart.

Jung went astray, as Freud thought, because he was lulled by the "mystical" side of religion; Adler, through his insistence that not sex but power feelings were primary. Later, Harry Stack Sullivan and Erich Fromm tended to emphasize, as against sex, the importance of personal relatedness to others, and nowadays many psychoanalysts tend to value religion much more highly than Freud ever could. But the root of the dissidence was always Freud's forthright insistence on the importance of sexuality and his old-fashioned, mid-nineteenth century positivism. For Freud always emphasized the organic and the physical rather than the social and the "cultural."

In fact, it is now possible to say that it is precisely Freud's old-fashioned scientific rationalism, his need to think of man as a physical being rather than a "psychological" one, that explains the primacy of Freud's discoveries. Psychoanalysis, especially in America, has become more interested in making cures than in making discoveries, and it is significant that there has been very little original thought in the field since Freud.

Freudianism has become a big business, and a very smooth one. The modern Freudian analyst, who is over-busy and who rather complacently uses his theory to explain everything, stands in rather sad contrast to that extraordinary thinker, Sigmund Freud.

Perhaps it is because Freud was born a century ago that he had the old-fashioned belief that nothing—not even a lot of patients—is so important as carrying your ideas beyond the point at which everybody already agrees with you. Nowadays everybody is something of a Freudian, and to many Freudians, the truth is in their keeping, the system is complete. But what mattered most to Freud was relentlessly carrying on the revolution of human thought.

2.

Another centenary essay comes from the pen of Crane Brinton, professor of history at Harvard University. Mr. Brinton, who was educated at Harvard and Oxford, is one of the most provocative and prolific of American historians of this generation; he is currently president-elect of the American Historical Association. It is natural, therefore, that he should try to "locate" and to assess Freud's place in the stream of modern intellectual history.

BRINTON: Freud and Human History *

I should like to attempt a brief description of the world-view (there really is no substitute for that blessed German word *Weltanschauung*) most congruous with Freud's place in Western thought. Now in spite of the romanticists' attempt to unseat eighteenth-century Right Reason with appeals to the Oversoul, to *Vernunft*—the transcendental in us all— no one had yet really shown ordinary educated men in 1900 that conscious analytical thought is under many circumstances impossible. This Freud really did achieve, building on the work of his predecessors as a scientist must and summarizing the familiar sequence of purely hysterical symptoms, hypnosis, Charcot, Breuer, and so on to the famous tripartite map of the mind as Id, Ego, and Superego. Freud convinced many, as the romanticists had failed to do, that straight thinking of the sort Condorcet and his eighteenth-century peers held would solve all our problems was not an activity natural and easy for men, not even after the evils of Church and State had been eliminated. For Freud concluded that what really kept men from straight thinking was not, to use awkward but clear terms, the macro-environment of Church, State, Society, but the micro-environment of nursery, family, peer-group, school, neighborhood. Reform of these last was clearly, even to the most convinced environmentalist, a formidable task.

It came to seem to Freud a very hard task indeed, an impossible one in terms of a human lifetime. But it did not seem an impossible task to free certain individuals from these deeply-rooted environmental evils. Freud was at bottom a good child of the eighteenth century. He was no optimist, but neither was that misplaced Jansenist the Marquis de Condorcet. Freud did believe that the individual under psychoanalysis and with due guidance could *think* his way out of a bad environment and into happiness here on earth. The process was longer, harder, and above all more expensive than Condorcet had dreamed. But the neurotic patient whose analysis has been successful has learned the truth, and the truth has made him free.

Freud is then at bottom one of ours. He is, to use Disraeli's famous phrase quite without irony, on the side of the angels—somewhat Unitarian if not actually positivist angels, it is true, but still angels. He does not urge us—nor did he urge his patients—to think with our blood, to follow our Id, libido, or Unconscious as the true guide, to kick over the traces. He was not even very romantic, as scientists go. His pessimism, which was very real and very profound, had a kind of folk background of common sense and even good humor. It was nothing like the pessimism of a Kierkegaard or a Kafka, both of which psychotics the good doctor would have thought of as almost too far gone for psychoanalytical saving. Freud wanted the decencies, the nineteenth-century decencies.

It is true that at the Hollywood B level Freud sometimes appears as a man

* From Crane Brinton, "Freud and Human History," in the *Saturday Review*, May 5, 1956, pp. 8–36. Reprinted by permission of the author and of the editors of the *Saturday Review*.

who urged us all to go the Tahitians and the Balinese one better, if possible. It is also true that at higher levels he is held up as one of those who, along with Dewey and Mr. Justice Holmes, have led men away from the old certainties of natural law and classic reason into the hellish uncertainties of relativity. But these off-center accusations are a normal part of the American intellectual arena, and need not worry us. It is more important to note that Freud's whole work has played an important part in the growth of a twentieth-century distrust of eighteenth- and nineteenth-century "intellectualism," a distrust incorporated, certainly, into such anti-democratic world-views as the many fascisms, German, Italian, Spanish, and the rest.

For the pure orthodox of the tradition of the Enlightenment any attempt to question the dogma of the natural goodness and reasonableness of man is of course heresy. And, in a narrow way, the orthodox here is not without some logical justification. Anti-democrats and anti-parliamentarians have now for years been able to get ammunition from William James, Bergson, Graham Wallas, Walter Bagehot, who were basically "liberals," as well as from ambivalent thinkers like Nietzsche and Mosca and from firm anti-democrats like Carlyle, Wagner, Pareto—and Mussolini and Hitler themselves. In fact, one may risk the statement that some of their best ammunition came from some of the liberals. Freud, for whom the rationalist and associationist psychology of the Enlightenment was simply wrong, as Ptolemy was for Copernicus and Galileo simply wrong, has also provided ammunition to those who want to do away with democracy.

Yet I do not think that in the long run the purely orthodox democrat in the tradition of the Enlightenment has a leg to stand on here. If democracy cannot adapt itself to the implications of Freud's scientific achievements then by the standards of its own basic sources it has failed. This is the real paradox: that Freud the real scientist (this does not mean he was infallibly right), whose findings seem to challenge basic democratic beliefs in the nature of man, is a far better guide for us than, say, Marx the pseudoscientist (this does not mean he was always wrong), whose life was honestly dedicated to an attempt to gain for all men the democratic decencies so far denied to so many.

For though the Freudian ways of the mind—Id, Ego, Superego—may one day seem quite absurd, though much of the particulars of his science may be—indeed almost certainly will be—quite out of date quite quickly, what may with some exaggeration be called his "discovery" of the unconscious mind is a genuine scientific achievement on a par, say, with Harvey's discovery that the heart is a pump. We can never go back to mind as Descartes, the philosopher, or even Locke and Condillac, understood mind. We can of course always go back to mind as St. Thomas Aquinas or Descartes the theologian understood it, but that has nothing directly to do with the physiological and psychological sciences.

Democracy has from the beginning insisted that it is not transcendental; it must adapt itself to the facts of life, in the long run, even if the facts are unpleasant. It must adapt itself to the facts of life even if these facts are filtered through that strange instrument the mind of the scientist. What Freud and many other twentieth-century thinkers have confronted democracy with may well be its most serious challenge. But the challenge will have to be met.

It can be met, indeed in a democracy must be met, in many different ways. It can be met as a Reinhold Niebuhr has met it, or as many another Christian has met it; it is not quite true, but near enough true, that Freud taught Original Sin. It can be met, as more and more good social scientists are meeting it, by a willingness to see their role as more like that of the physician, who is grateful for any slight gain against disease, but does not expect to eliminate it, than like that of the prophet, who will have heaven here on earth, tomorrow.

But it cannot be met by democrats who continue to believe that Something Went Wrong, something pretty big and simple, something that can be preached or legislated out of the way, Capitalism, Wall Street, Hollywood, the American Business Man, the Roman Catholic Church, Science and Technology, Colonialism—the list is long. It cannot even be met by social engineering. For perhaps the deepest layer in the Freudian attitude is the belief that the individual must summon from within himself the energies and the wisdom that will free him; the therapist can help, can guide, but he cannot "engineer," he cannot rig a miracle.

3.

The impact of Freudian ideas has been particularly strong upon the so-called behavioral sciences (though perhaps it was reflected more immediately and profoundly in literature and the fine arts). Not all behavioral scientists, however, have welcomed this Freudian intrusion. One of the most vigorous and sustained attacks upon the broader consequences of Freudianism may be found in Richard LaPiere's *The Freudian Ethic*. Mr. LaPiere, professor of sociology at Stanford University, builds his case around a contrast between the Protestant ethic—which, he believes, was the code of values that dominated western culture until the twentieth century—and the "Freudian ethic"— which has rapidly been smothering what is left of the older values. He focuses primarily upon the American scene, and finds evidence to support his case in child-rearing practices, educational theory, the treatment of criminals, the downgrading of private enterprise, the growth of "political maternalism," and so on. All of these changes, Mr. LaPiere contends, are "malfunctional," and constitute "our unrecognized road to disaster." Although his book has the one-sidedness of a tract, it provides us with a challenging statement of the anti-Freudian case.

LaPiere: The Freudian Ethic *

The premise upon which the Protestant ethic evolved was the secular supplement to Luther's insistence that the individual human being has a conscience,

* From Richard LaPiere, *The Freudian Ethic* (New York: Duell, Sloan and Pearce, 1959), pp. 59–65, 81–82, 183–84, 247, 284–86. Copyright 1959, by Richard LaPiere. Reprinted by permission of Duell, Sloan & Pearce, an affiliate of Meredith Press

which can and should be his guide to conduct—the idea that he is capable of independent, rational conduct. This idea was embodied, nearly three centuries later, in the Declaration of Independence as the self-evident truths "that all men are created equal; that they are endowed by their Creator with certain inalienable rights; that among these are life, liberty, and the pursuit of happiness." That Declaration and the political Constitution that was designed to implement it were devised by men of enterprise in order to free men of enterprise from the constraints of a government that still had its roots in the authoritarian tradition of the Middle Ages. These documents, like the Mayflower Compact that had so long preceded them, were attempts to give political sanction to the Protestant ethic. And for a century and a half many, but far from all, of the changes that were worked in American society were in accord with the spirit if not the letter of these testaments to the value and validity of the Protestant ethic.

The rise of Freudian doctrine as the prevailing concept of the nature of man is at once a measure of the decline of the Protestant ethic and a denial of the idea that man is a creature of reason. Freud's idea of man is one that in many respects resembles that which prevailed through the Middle Ages and which was sanctioned by the medieval Church. In the Freudian concept, man is not born free with the right to pursue life, liberty, and happiness; he is shackled by biological urges that can never be freely expressed and that set him in constant and grievous conflict with his society. Life for him must be an unhappy and unending struggle to reconcile, both within himself and between himself and others, forces that are inherently antagonistic. Freud does not say, in the theological manner, that man fell from Grace and must therefore suffer in this life. But he does come to much the same concept of man: that man is by nature (or at least by virtue of the inevitable conflict between man's nature and society) a weak and irresolute creature without the stamina to endure the stresses and strains of living, and who cannot therefore hope to enjoy life on this earth.

There has been interminable debate concerning why Freud devised the particular doctrine that goes under his name. His disciples take the understandable but scientifically untenable position that Freud simply discovered by scientific means the truth about man; his opponents lean to the view that the Freudian doctrine of man is at best a delusion of Freud's and may have been a calculated method of winning him enduring prestige as the founder of a metaphysical cult. Far more tenable, if still unprovable, is the hypothesis that Freud, proceeding in accordance with the intellectual standards of the late nineteenth century, simply invented the various concepts—libido, id, ego, superego, Oedipus complex, etc.—that together make up his doctrine in an honest endeavor to comprehend the still largely incomprehensible behavior of neurotic people. At any event, it does seem evident that his idea of the nature and capabilities of man was derived directly from too long and unmitigated exposure to people, his patients, who were incapable of managing their personal affairs, people who did not, for whatever reasons, conform even in outline to the Protestant ethic.

In a sense, Freud's major error lay in assuming that the people who came to him for treatment were representative of mankind in general. For the very fact that his patients came to him for "mental" treatment is *ipso facto* evidence that they were not—unless, indeed, we wish to assume that all men are at all times in need of psychiatric aid. Had Freud been content to accept his explanatory system as a therapeutic rationale for use in the treatment of neurotics, and had his converts also adhered to this view, a quite different result might have obtained. But almost from the outset of his work, Freud insisted that he was interested in developing—or "discovering"—the laws governing all human conduct, not just those that govern, or fail to govern, the conduct of psychologically abnormal individuals.

The atypical character of the people from whom Freud derived his doctrine of man would seem to explain his conviction that men are inherently unstable; and one must assume that his preoccupation with sex, a fixation that is close to monomaniacal, was a function either of his own personality or of those of the patients who came under his observation. The latter assumption is most acceptable, for even the most ardent anti-Freudian must admit that Freud's treatment of sex was aseptic rather than pornographic; and there is some factual basis for this assumption. Most of Freud's patients were not only neurotic but also neurotic middle- and upper-middle-class Viennese Jews. They were not, therefore, even a representative sample of neurotics.

Vienna in the time of Freud, if not since, was the pretentious, cosmopolitan center of an empire that had all but vanished. It was a once-great city in reduced circumstances, a city that had lost many of its economic and political functions and was—to some extent at least—living on its glamorous past. In sociological terms, it was a highly disorganized and demoralized community; in lay terms, it was a city of sin. Apparently the fashion in Vienna at that time was for men and women of means to engage in elaborate, perhaps even highly ritualized, extramarital sexual play. And while keeping up with this fashion may not have bothered greatly the moral consciences of Catholic Austro-Hungarians, who had long been noted for their adaptability, it undoubtedly ran counter to the strict and rigid moral code of bourgeois Jews. It may well be, therefore, that Freud's patients were atypical neurotics, *i.e.,* their mental distress was commonly occasioned by the opposition between their training in sexual morality and the social pressures that demanded violation of that morality. This interpretation of Freud's preoccupation with sex is not, of course, acceptable to Freudians; but it has the dual virtues, over alternative interpretations, of having some factual basis and of shifting the onus for that preoccupation from Freud to his patients. . . .

The Freudian ethic, as it will be termed hereafter, is not a code of licentiousness. It does not, in fact, grant to the individual the ability or right to *do* anything. As a code of conduct the Freudian ethic is entirely negative. It is composed of sentiments and attitudes regarding man's capabilities that, if literally applied, would keep him from attempting anything positive, to say nothing of attempting to devise anything new. For it makes the world about him a hostile and inhospitable place, and it makes him a terrified (unconsciously, of course) and reluctant inhabitant of that world. It even goes further; not only is his external world inimical to his psychic welfare, but this world has been "internalized" to the end that a part of himself intimidates the rest. There is therefore no escaping psychic agony. Should he withdraw from the external world, he will still be at odds with himself.

Philosophically, the Freudian ethic is related not only to that of medieval Europe but also to the ethical ideal of the Greek-Roman stoics. It is like the medieval in that it reduces man to a passive state and unlike it in that it does not provide a higher authority—the Church—to assume responsibility for the individual and guide him in the ways of righteousness. It is like stoic philosophy in that it is contemptuous of the world of external realities and unlike it in that it does not provide a hope that the individual can ignore the world and thereby achieve peace of mind.

Since the Freudian ethic is still undergoing development and since, further, it is negative rather than positive in character, the ethic is at present more a state of mind than an actual ideal of individual conduct. Some appreciation of this state of mind can, perhaps, be gained from the terminology used by those who subscribe to it. In their discourse there is recurrent reference to guilt feeling, personal insecurity, unstructured personality, instability, "internalization" (of hate, envy, and other destructive emotions), "projection" (of anything from hate to love), frustration, aggressive tendencies, trauma, and the all-inclusive term "tensions." Such terms are used in reference not only to recognizably abnormal individuals but to everyone. Still more revealing is the total absence in the Freudian discourse of such terms, prominent in the Protestant ethic, as self-confidence, personal integrity, self-reliance, responsibility, or such very earthy terms as "moral courage," "intestinal fortitude," or, more vulgarly, "guts."

The elements of the Protestant ethic are fairly easy to describe. For one thing, our language abounds in character-designating terms that reflect this ethic; for another, the ethic is structured and positive, rather than amorphous and negative. What the Freudians hold as ideal is adjustment of the individual to his life circumstances—*i.e.,* the maintenance of a precarious balance between his id, ego, and superego, and between all three of these and external circumstances. This adjustment ideal may, in turn, be designated in a variety of positive terms—contentment, complacency, sense of security, and perhaps even apathy. But when an attempt is made to indicate the personal qualities that contribute to the achievement of this ideal state, it is necessary to resort to description by negation. Thus the Freudian ethic comes out something as follows: absence of strong social motivations (the inescapable urges of the libido are, of course, anti-social drives), lack of constraining or inhibiting social principles, lack of supernaturalistic or other fixed faiths (except, of course, faith in the Freudian version of the self), lack of set goals, lack of any rigorous system of personal-social values and sentiments, and complete absence of any sense of obligation toward others.

The Freudians do not deny that men may possess positive personality attributes of the sort incorporated in the Protestant ethic. But to them, such positive characteristics are either the product of the inevitable clash between the individual and society or the consequence of traumatic experiences that have befallen the individual in the course of that conflict. Whatever their source, they are inimical to the individual's psychic welfare; where they exist, they should be exorcised by psychoanalysis; and to prevent their development, society should be remodeled to accord with the Freudian idea of man. No society can really be good, for everything social is contrary to the psychic welfare of the individual. To this end it should avoid inculcating in him any socially prescribed personality attributes—motivations, goals, values, sentiments, or feeling of personal obligation. The individual should not be required or even expected to submit to social authority whatever its character, to accept responsibility for his own or anyone else's welfare, or to be concerned with anything except the preservation of his precarious psychic balance.

In the harsh, unsympathetic terms of the Protestant ethic, the individual who even approximated the Freudian ideal would be a selfish egocentric, an incompetent, a wastrel, an irresponsible, and in general a social parasite unwelcome in the company of respectable men. In the days when men who conformed more or less to the Protestant ethic tended to dominate our society, such an individual would surely have failed in competition with more sturdy men and as an incompetent would have been treated with contempt. But in this age of Freudian enlightenment, such an individual seems to represent the emerging ideal type of man. . . .

Although the Freudian doctrine is a revolutionary one, it is not a doctrine of revolution. Unlike Marxianism, it has not given ideological sanction to direct and violent assault upon the social *status quo*. It does not, in fact, provide a logical basis for any kind of effort to remodel society. Freud was himself disinterested in society as such, and he treated it as a miserable but inescapable and presumably for the most part unchangeable context that the individual must endure as best he can—with, of course, aid from psychoanalysis. Freud was, for example, as antagonistic to religion, whatever its form, as was Marx; but, unlike Marx, he did not suggest that it might be dispensed with. For Freud there was no good society, past, present, or future.

Freud's disciples have, however, ignored the logical implications of his doctrine and have advocated modification of society to the end that the conflict between the individual and society would be lessened, if not resolved. Such advocacy has not been organized, as was that of Marxianism, and has been neither systematic nor consistent. It has, rather, been "spontaneous" and individualistic, with the result that the attacks upon the social *status quo* have been both segmental and insidious. And for this reason, if no other, the attempts to remodel our society to fit the Freudian image of man have aroused only limited and scattered resistance. It is far too early to say whether these attempts will have enduring consequences; but it does seem likely that the current acceptance of the Freudian doctrine and the current efforts to validate the Freudian ethic profit from the fact that their attack on existing society is only in limited areas and by indirection. For it is clear that social change is always fragmentary, unsystematic, and for the most part inadvertent. Social revolutions and revolutionary mass movements may dramatize the desire for change, but they do not of themselves work significant changes in the existing social system. Those changes, when they come, are produced slowly and piecemeal. . . .

The Protestant ethic evolved, gained advocates, and became in time the prevailing ethic of Western Europeans only because it reflected and in turn implemented changes that were already in process. Among these changes was the growth in number and social significance of independent business entrepreneurs, who operated outside the restrictive sphere of the medieval guilds and could therefore apply enterprise to the discovery and exploitation of new markets for goods and to the use of new techniques in processing, fabricating, and distributing goods. Allied with these independent entrepreneurs in a community of interest against the Church and other agencies of traditionalism were the early scientists, explorers, and political opportunists—all men of enterprise in their various ways. These were the men who in the sixteenth century gave their considerable support to the Reformation, and it was their values and sentiments that in time became codified in the Protestant ethic. As their efforts brought more and more changes to Western society, their numbers increased, and the new ethic came to prevail; and by the opening of the eighteenth century they constituted a clearly defined and powerful class, the *bourgeoisie*. It was this class that honored the Protestant ethic; and because they did so, they formed a class unique in human experience, a class that served as the driving force for the many innovations and developments that have brought Western peoples to their present social state.

The emergence of the Freudian ethic and its invasion of various aspects of current American society similarly reflect, and in turn implement, changes that are occuring elsewhere in our society. Among the more significant of these changes has been the incipient decline of the *bourgeoisie,* with their attachment to the values and sentiments of the Protestant ethic, and their replacement—still only partial—by a new class that is operating in terms of the values and sentiments that are sanctioned by Freudianism. It is of course too much to say that Freud and his disciples have brought this new class into being, and thereby jeopardized the *bourgeoisie;* but there is certainly a historical concordance between the rise of the Freudian ethic and the rise of this new class, and currently each depends for its growth on the other. . . .

There is no real reason to think that man is inherently weak and incompetent, that he is individually incapable of assuming responsibility for his own welfare, that his organizations are thus by nature fragile and in constant need of protection, or that only through constant and indulgent political ministrations can a society be kept operating effectively. This idea of man, so ardently propagated by the Freudians, has, however, during the past few decades been given political validation; and as governments have assumed maternal responsibility for maintaining society, the individual citizen and his organizations have tended to acquire a dependence upon a political maternalism that differs only in form and degree from the maternal love, affection, and permissive care which the Freudians believe are essential to the psychic welfare of every child. . . .

It is the thesis of this study that many of the changes that have been of late years occurring in our society are malfunctional and that they will, if they continue uncorrected, constitute our unrecognized road to disaster. The particular changes that have been analyzed here involve quite different aspects of our society—ideological, procedural, and organizational; and they take such dissimilar forms as a growing preference for the permissive mode of child rearing and the growth of political maternalism. These changes are being wrought by men of many kinds and various functions—by psychiatrists and child psychologists of the Freudian persuasion, by permissive parents and progressive teachers, by welfare workers and impressionable judges, by managers of business and industry and leaders of labor and academic life, and by politicians and political administrators of many sorts. Moreover, they are being demanded or welcomed, or at least passively accepted, by almost everyone.

All these changes, varied as they are in source, in form, and in purpose, seem to be converging in such a way as to constitute a general social drift—a movement of many parts to produce one common and unintended consequence. That consequence is a slowing down of the rates of change in our society, a progressive reduction in its dynamism, a trend toward social stability. Every one of the changes that have been here discussed has as its recognized and avowed objective the provision of more security for some kind or class of individual—the protection of the infant from stressful experience; the school child from competition and strain to achievement; the college youth from the need to excel; the young hoodlum from the pangs of punishment; the employer from competition with other employers; the workingman from competition with his fellows; and the nonworkingman from the normal consequences of the fact that he does not work.

To a considerable extent these changes are actually increasing the security of various classes of individuals in our society. But every change is also reducing the range of permissible individual variation, for it demands, no doubt as the necessary price of security, increasing conformity by the individual to socially imposed standards of conduct. Thus every change is to some extent destroying those social conditions that have been conducive to the perpetuation of the Protestant ethic, to the generation of men of enterprise, and so to the continuation of the age of enterprise.

On the positive side, these various changes may be seen as contributing in one way or another to the emergence, the social sanction, and the social maintenance of a new ethic, an ethic that translates into action as apathy and indifference. This new ethic presupposes that man is by inherent nature weak, uncertain, and incapable of self-reliance and that he must, therefore, be provided by society with the security that is his greatest need. Since the most outstanding and most popular proponent of this view of man has been Sigmund Freud, the newly emerging ethic has been designated by his name.

It is perhaps possible to conceive a society in which the Freudian ethic prevails and in which, therefore, the members tend to demand much each of the others and to give little each to the others in return. It is perhaps possible that, in view of the many nonhuman agents of production that are presently at our command, the level of life in such a society could be acceptably high. That society would, necessarily, be a stable one—a self-maintaining and unchanging system; if we were to achieve this condition, we would, in our own particular way, have reached the goal of all utopianists—a society in which every member lives the calm and complacent life and drifts from birth to death without excessive effort, without strain, and entirely free from fear in any form. If we were to achieve this blissful social state, it would be only just to acclaim Freud as our Messiah. He hated and despised society as he knew it, but he would no doubt have approved a society so admirably suited to the Freudian man.

There is, however, slight likelihood that Freud will be honored as the savior of mankind, although there is some possibility that he may be remembered as the prophet of doom.

4.

Critics of the Freudian impact on our era do not all agree that the shortcomings of Freudianism require a return to the Protestant ethic. O. Hobart Mowrer, research professor of psychology at the University of Illinois and former president of the American Psychological Association, contends that both the Protestant ethic and the Freudian revolution had disastrous consequences. An alternative to Freudianism is needed, and is beginning to emerge as non-Freudian psychology moves beyond primitive behaviorism to a more sophisticated understanding of man's mental and emotional makeup. This process, he believes, involves a rediscovery of reason and a reassertion of the role of a modernized religion.

MOWRER: Psychiatry and Religion *

As we move forward, with ever-accelerating tempo, into what we are pleased to call the Age of Science, we are faced by an awesome paradox. As man, through science, acquires more and more control over the external world, he has come to feel less and less capable of controlling himself, less and less the master of his own soul and destiny. In the same decade in which we produced the atomic submarine and started probing interstellar space, we have also seen, significantly, the emergence of the Beatnik; personality disintegration has become endemic; and society itself is commonly said to be "sick." We remain optimistic about what man can continue to do through science by way of deal-

* From O. Hobart Mowrer, "Psychiatry and Religion," in *The Atlantic Monthly* (July, 1961), pp. 88–91. Reprinted by permission of the author and of the editors of *The Atlantic Monthly*.

ing with his environment, but we have become extremely pessimistic about man.

This reciprocal relationship is not accidental: the same presuppositions and intellectual operations that have given us such unprecedented power over nature when extended to ourselves produce a pervasive feeling of helplessness, confusion, resignation, desperation. We seem to be the hapless pawns of a great mechanical, impersonal juggernaut called the cosmos. By the very principles and premises that have led to the conquest of the outer world, we ourselves lose our autonomy, dignity, self-mastery, responsibility, indeed, our very identity. Little wonder, then, that we feel weak, lost, fearful, "beat." Being part of nature, we, too, apparently obey strict cause-and-effect principles; and if this be true, if our own experience and conduct are as rigidly determined and predetermined as is the rest of nature, the whole notion of purpose, responsibility, meaning seems to vanish. . . . At the same time, some highly pertinent developments are quietly and unobtrusively occurring in psychological and sociological thought which hold promise of delivering us from our current predicament, both philosophically and practically.

Pre-Reformation Catholicism held man "doubly responsible," which is to say, capable of both good and evil. When, in this context, one behaved badly, is was to his discredit; and when one behaved well, it was decidedly to his credit. There was thus for the individual a sort of moral balance sheet, as it has been called, and ultimate salvation or damnation depended, quite simply and directly, on the number and magnitude of the entries on the two sides of this fateful ledger. . . .

The essence of Luther's position, particularly as it has filtered down to us through John Calvin and other Protestant expositors, is that man is responsible, so to say, in only one direction: capable of choosing the wrong and fully accountable for having done so, he is, however, supposedly unable to do anything whatever toward his own redemption and must wait, helplessly, upon the unpredictable favor, or "grace," of God. . . . We are no doubt justified in looking back upon the Reformation as representing, in many ways, a magnificent achievement. But we have been slow to appreciate, it seems, how dearly it has cost us. Protestantism, whatever its virtues and strengths, has also had the tragic consequence of leaving us without clear and effective means of dealing with personal guilt. And it is this fact, I submit, more than any other that is responsible for what Paul Tillich has aptly called "the psychic disintegration of the masses" in modern times.

By the turn of the century, the influence of religion and moral suasion had so far declined that the medical profession was being inundated by a new type of illness. Purely functional in origin but often expressed somatically, the new malady was characterized by a pervasive "loss of nerve," which, as a matter of medical convenience, was dubbed "neurosis." . . .

In this era of confusion and crisis, psychoanalysis had its inception and spectacular proliferation. Religion had disqualified itself for dealing honestly and effectively with man's deepest moral and spiritual anguish. Freud's discoveries purported to rescue man from the perplexities of the Protestant ethic and the ravages of unresolved guilt, not by restoring him to full ethical responsibility, but by relieving him of all responsibility. In short, the notion was that one should not feel guilty about anything. . . . This was all to be achieved not by a return to the outmoded principle of double responsibility but by adoption of a new and radical doctrine of double *irresponsibility.* . . .

But as the clock of history has ticked off the decades of this century, we have gradually discovered that Freud's great postulate, not of total depravity but of total determinism, has liberated us only in the sense of dumping us from the frying pan into the fire. At long last we seem to be waking up to the fact that to be "free" in the sense of embracing the doctrine of double irresponsibility is not to be free at all, humanly speaking, but lost.

Within the past five years there has been a growing realization, at least in the disciplines most intimately concerned with such matters, of the futility, the deadly peril of this general trend. After an extensive study of the therapeutic claims and accomplishments of psychoanalysis, the English psychologist Dr. Hans Eysenck has recently summed up the situation with this laconic statement: "The success of the Freudian revolution seemed complete. Only one thing went wrong: *the patients did not get any better."* And this verdict has been amply borne out by numerous other inquiries of a similar kind. . . .

While psychoanalysis was developing as a predominantly medical enterprise, a parallel movement with similar philosophic and practical implications was also taking form and gaining momentum in academic circles. I refer to the radical repudiation, in the first two or three decades of this century, of all that was inward, subjective, and personal, known as behaviorism, with its new and exclusive emphasis upon that form of cause-effect relationship implied by the so-called stimulus-response, or S-R, formula. Here determinism, although couched in somewhat different terms, was no less absolute than in psychoanalysis, and the individual was again relieved—or should we say deprived?—of all semblance of accountability. Behavior or action or conduct was the inevitable consequence of "antecedent stimulus conditions" (causes), and moral accountability became, in this context, a meaningless and, indeed, opprobrious concept. The conditioned and unconditioned reflex, in the language of Pavlov and Watson, was the "functional unit" of all behavior; and Thorndike, in his slightly different theory of habit, likewise spoke of stimulus-response "connections" or "bonds." All of which had at least the incidental effect, if not intent, of obliterating the whole notion of freedom, choice, responsibility by reducing behavior, absolutely and completely, to S-R connections and reflexes. . . .

The behavioristic doctrine of total determinism manifestly does not deliver us from the one-sided determinism of Luther and Calvin any more effectively than does that brand of complete irresponsibility adduced by Freud. If the doctrines of Luther and Calvin disposed the Western world to "Christian despair," those of Freud and Watson have, it seems, engulfed us in a despair that is infinitely deeper and more absolute.

It is only within the last decade or so that we have begun to see a way out. The existentialists, in their very legitimate protests against the general abrogation of responsibilty—first one-sidedly, in Protestant theology, and then more systematically, in psychoanalysis and behaviorism—have recently been attracting some well-deserved attention. But when they go on to reject the scientific approach, totally and inherently, they are on dangerous ground and may shortly find themselves, in this regard, discredited.

Having denounced Protestant predestination and psychological determinism alike, what do the existentialists offer, alternatively? Only a counsel of brave despair, an admonition to have the courage to be, on the assumption that being (existence) *is* an ironic joke and ultimate tragedy. Just how do we come by this courage? By lifting ourselves by our own bootstraps? In practice, it seems that this philosophy leaves us quite as helpless and hopeless as does the Protestant principle, with its emphasis upon man's inevitable guilt and God's uncertain grace.

If one takes the time to examine contemporary behavior theory, one finds that scientific developments in psychology have moved a long way from the naive and primitive assumptions of behaviorism. Now it is generally agreed that there is by no means a reflexive or ineluctable connection between stimulation and response. Now we are quite certain that the coupling between our sensory receptors and our muscles is much looser and infinitely more complicated than the earlier theories implied. According to present views, stimulation may suggest a given response or course of action, but whether we "give consent" as Catholic theologians would say, to the suggestion, thought, or image is dependent upon the hopes and fears which we weigh and ponder in deciding whether to act or refrain from acting. In other words, given a stimulus, a particular and predetermined response does not automatically pop out of the organism, as our earlier, push-button psychology seemed to demand. Response—and responsibility—in this new frame of reference is crucially dependent upon the anticipated consequences of our actions. In short, we have rediscovered reason. Instead of being merely stimulated (the Latin term for "goaded"), living organisms become goal-directed, purposive, deliberate, or, if you will, free and responsible.

Beginning with the naive and oversimplified behaviorism of Watson, academic psychology in this century has thus achieved a relatively advanced degree of sophistication; whereas psychoanalysis, which started with Freud's highly elaborated and ingenious speculations, has rather steadily involuted, regressed. The original emphasis on unconscious (irresponsible) motivation has, of late years, given way to a new accent on "ego psychology," which involves frequent reference to "ego strength" and "ego weakness" in a manner unmistakably reminiscent of the older notions of character and will power; and with the ink hardly dry on this ego-psychology literature, psychoanalysts are now beginning to show a new respect for and interest in the superego, or conscience.

These developments, I say, are retrogressive as far as Freud's original formulations go, but in terms of common sense they are decidedly in the right direction. However, they are suicidal as far as psychoanalysis itself is concerned, which was conceived and laid its claim to recognition as an independent discipline along very different lines.

All the developments just reviewed thus strike a new note, or at least one that has considerable novelty for contemporary men and women. Once more we are coming to perceive man as pre-eminently a social creature, whose greatest and most devastating anguish is experienced not in physical pain or biological deprivation but when he feels alienated, disgraced, guilty, debased as a person. And the thrust of much current therapeutic effort is in the direction of trying to help such individuals recover their sociality, relatedness, community, identity.

Here, surely, is a promising meeting ground for psychology, psychiatry, and sociology and for much that is common to both classical Judaism and authentic Christianity. But, logically and programmatically, it strikes at the heart of the Protestant principle. Yesterday, as a Presbyterian, I attended church and heard the minister quote Reinhold Niebuhr, with approval, to the effect that "Christian faith is more profound than mere moral idealism," thus echoing the contempt which Protestantism has always had for the "merely moral man." And the preceding Sunday I heard another minister preach a fine "Reformation" sermon on the theme that "the fruit of grace is responsibility for action in the world"; that is, the theme that we are good because—and if—we are saved, not the reverse. Scientific and humanistic thought can never, I believe, come to terms with such hyperbole. The fact that Protestant theologians keep reverting in their sermons to the question of just what it means to be "saved by grace," rather than by works, suggests that they themselves are not quite certain.

As a psychologist, I have no competence to judge the effectiveness of religion in saving men's immortal souls, and, I confess, this is not my major interest. But I do maintain that religion has great potential for serving, and saving, men and women in this world which is not now being at all adequately realized. If, in the secular sciences, we have rediscovered something of the logic and conditions of responsible action, perhaps this will be an encouragement to the theologians themselves to take a more courageous and responsible position and quit hiding behind a preposterous piece of medieval sophistry.

5.

Rudolf Allers took a medical degree at the University of Vienna in 1906, and held posts in various institutes of psychiatry (Prague, Munich, Vienna) during most of the period 1906–38. In the mid-twenties he turned also to metaphysics, and earned a doctorate in philosophy at the University of Milan. He emigrated to the United States in 1938, served for ten years as professor of philosophy at the Catholic University of America, and then transferred to a similar post at Georgetown University. His unique background and training make him one of the best-informed Catholic students of Freudianism

The following passage from one of his essays appeared in the liberal Catholic weekly *The Commonweal*.

ALLERS: Psychoanalysis and Religion *

The attitude of the average psychoanalyst is to view everything which does not fit into his preconceived world as a "symptom." That someone should be concerned with his fate in eternity, or that he think of eternity at all, that he trust or fear God, that he feel obligated to conform to the commands of his religion, all this is "symptomatic."

Freud's theories have achieved an enormous influence. There is hardly any area of human life and activity that has not been penetrated by psychoanalytic notions. This penetration is particularly evident in the fields of literary criticism, sociology, and education. One reason for this amazingly general acceptance of psychoanalytic views has been indicated above. Psychoanalysis claims to be "scientific." But it is that only insofar as it claims to apply the principles of science to the study of human affairs. However, this claim is in accord with a widely diffused tendency; many people believe that the procedures of science are the only ones by which reliable knowledge can be attained. They never conceive of the possibility that there may be aspects of reality which do not lend themselves to this approach and where the results of such methods must be erroneous. One cannot reproach the psychoanalysts for harboring the same idea; in this, too, they are children of their age.

But one can hold them responsible for consistently disregarding all objections. Freud never answered any criticism, nor do his pupils. They have a very easy way out of such difficulties. Since they are convinced of the absolute truth of their doctrine, criticism or rejection must be explained in terms of this doctrine. If the critic had been analyzed, so they argue, he would realize the truth of the Freudian teaching; if he refuses to recognize the doctrine, it is because his views are determined by some unconscious factors which analysis would bring to the fore. This is, in fact, an attitude which has no parallel in the history of human thought. Neither will one easily find another example of such disregard for factual evidence as is common among the psychoanalysts.

This is true also in their way of dealing with questions of religion. They have, of course, to recognize the fact that religion plays a great role in the lives of many people, who, for the rest, cannot be considered as neurotic or abnormal in any sense. Some psychoanalysts are willing to admit that religion may possess a definite value for men. But if they admit this, they make at the same time certain restrictions. The beliefs men cherish should be such that the psychoanalyst can approve of them.

Now, the psychoanalyst is essentially a positivist. Only that is true which can be observed and verified. If he concedes the relevance of religious beliefs, he can do so only from a pragmatic viewpoint. Religion may be all right inas-

* From Rudolf Allers, "Psychoanalysis and Religion," in *The Commonweal*, vol. 54 (1951), p. 262. Reprinted by permission of the author.

much as it proves helpful to the individual in carving out for himself a place in reality, finding satisfaction, and achieving "adjustment." . . . Psychoanalysis is, in fact, fundamentally a system which does not recognize anything above man. . . .

Freud's doctrine had to be anti-religious and atheistic. It had to explain religion in the terms of its fundamental assumptions, just as it had to deal in the same manner with many other aspects of human existence.

In the face of the almost general recognition of psychoanalysis, one is confronted with the question of what attitude to assume in regard to this doctrine. We are concerned here with the problem whether or not psychoanalysis is as such a tenable theory, though it can be shown that it is not, because it rests on arbitrary and unproven suppositions and is in open conflict with ascertainable facts. That this is the case obviously renders easy the answer whether psychoanalysis ought to be considered as a scientific achievement. It is not and cannot be regarded as such.

Some, however, believe that certain propositions of psychoanalysis can be disengaged from the context in which they appear in Freud's doctrine. These people believe especially that one can detach Freud's method from his basic conceptions. This, too, is a standpoint as dangerous as it is untenable, for practice and theory are intimately connected with each other. The method presupposes the theory. The method, indeed, consists to a considerable extent in interpretation, and this interpretation must be made in terms of the theory. Freud's doctrine is not one on psychology and, besides this, or above it, also a philosophy. It is a complete and indissoluble synthesis of both of these constituents. To accept parts of Freud's system is logically impossible. If anything, Freud was a consistent thinker; his work is truly a system in which every part is related to and dependent on the whole. To accept certain segments and to reject others can be done only if one either misunderstands Freud or the ideas with which the psychoanalytic theory conflicts.

Psychoanalysis cannot but be atheistic. It must be that because it is rooted in a perfectly naturalistic and materialistic philosophy. It is the clearest statement of an absolutist humanism, of a view which is unwilling to recognize that there may be something higher than man.

6.

Not all of Europe has succumbed to the Freudian impact. In 1958, the Academy of Medical Sciences of the Soviet Union organized a "Scientific and Theoretical Conference on Questions of the Ideological Struggle with Contemporary Freudianism." Neutralism or compromise in this struggle, the conference decided, would be not only impossible but contemptible. This violent rejection of Freudianism as "one of the most reactionary and pseudo-scientific manifestations of bourgeois ideology" is one aspect of Soviet doctrine that has not been altered by Stalin's death and posthumous disgrace. Toward the end of the Stalin era, a Soviet medical journal published the following representative philippic.

BANSHCHIKOV AND PORTNOV: Freudianism in the Service
of Bourgeois Reaction *

The teaching of Sigmund Freud occupies by no means the last place among
the doctrines which American imperialism has put to its use. Together with
the "philosophy" of pragmatism and with spiritualism and astrology, Freudianism tries to provide grounds for renouncing the attempt to reach a rational scientific understanding of the laws of nature and endeavors to divert minds into
the dark depths of mysticism. . . .

As the inevitable downfall of capitalism nears, the representatives of reactionary science work all the more furiously and shamelessly. . . .

Freudianism is one of the dark forces which the bosses of Wall Street stub-
bornly support. It has proved to be a convenient weapon for militant bourgeois
reaction and has been used as such for a long time already in the struggle
against materialist theory and true science. All followers of this reactionary idealist school in bourgeois medicine are now busy "debunking" and denying the
materialist teaching of the great Russian physiologist I. P. Pavlov.

Freudianism traces its origin to idealist philosophy. The German idealist
Eduard Hartmann was the immediate inspirer of these ideas; back in the middle of the last century he opposed to Darwinism his "philosophy of the unconscious." . . .

The Freudian doctrine, exported from Europe, has struck deep roots in
American sociology, art criticism, psychology, anthropology and particularly
medicine. Freud's book "The Interpretation of Dreams," in which he de-
velops the "theory" of the role of sexual experience in psychic life and formu-
lates the "doctrine" of the unconscious, has proved handy for the gangsters of
science and the corrupters of human souls. . . .

Freudianism denies the objective character of the world and the interrelated-
ness of phenomena. It asserts that economic factors play no part whatever in
human relations and that only the "unconscious" can imperiously determine
these relations. The Freudians even undertake to "remove" all class, national
and religious antagonisms by means of psychoanalysis.

These maniacal ideas have been just as convenient as could be to the instigators
of war. That is why the contemporary followers of Freud have accepted them
with such rapture.

The British philosopher Bertrand Russell, who founded his world concept on
Freudianism and Weismannism, contends that human conduct is determined
by the hereditary and unchanging instincts of hunger, sex and aggression. In
his opinion, a war of conquest—that terrible product of the capitalist system—

* From The Current Digest of the Soviet Press, IV (1952), no. 43, p. 11 (translated from an
article in the Soviet periodical The Medical Worker). Reprinted by permission of The Current
Digest of the Soviet Press, published weekly at Columbia University by The Joint Committee of
Slavic Studies appointed by the American Council of Learned Societies and the Social Science Research Council.

fosters satisfaction of the aggressive instinct and should therefore be assessed as a positive phenomenon.

The doctrine of the unconscious, of complexes and of the repression of unsatisfied sexual drives into the subconscious, has made a deep imprint on America and many other bourgeois countries, and not only in many branches of psychiatry. With the full support and encouragement of the ruling circles, Freudianism has become in the U.S.A. the dominant methodology of the entire field of so-called psychosomatic medicine. . . .

One has only to look through the journal Psychosomatic Medicine in recent years to see to what depths of degeneracy American medicine has sunk.

M. Sperling, in the article "The Role of the Mother in Psychosomatic Disorders in Children," printed in No. 6, 1949, sententiously declares, for example, that various children's diseases are based upon an unresolved emotional conflict which finds expression in the child's unconscious hatred of his relatives or parents. . . .

The Freudians try at all cost to substantiate the permanency and legitimacy of the imperialist system, the exploitation of the working people and wars of conquest. . . .

The question arises involuntarily: "What has Freudianism given to medical science and practice proper?" What "accomplishments" have occurred in medicine as a result of this development of Freud's teachings?

In the first place, Freudianism has destroyed the nosological system of medicine. This is particularly vivid in the concepts of "psychosis" and "neurosis." In the clinical picture of many neuropsychiatric diseases, they distinguish only vestigial phenomena: manifestations of the disease process and attempts at restitution. And the attempts at restitution are looked upon as manifestations which lead to conflict with the environment and qualify as diseases.

The Freudians have injected incredible confusion, chaos and scholasticism in this most intricate question.

The capitalist system, with its cruel exploitation, the misery of the working people, prostitution, trampling on human dignity and "war psychoses," is what generates the high incidence of disease and the high mortality rate. The main source of illness is the corrupting influence of capitalism.

The clearer this ineluctable truth becomes to the people, the more strenuously do the Freudians seek the causes of pathology in the debris of the subconscious, in conflicts allegedly linked with the battle between the subconscious and the conscious, or, to put it briefly, in the sick man himself rather than in his environment.

The Freudians have repudiated the laboratory methods built up by science (clinical diagnosis, biochemical and bacteriological methods), attaching no importance whatever to them.

The psychoanalytic study of psychosis and many somatic illnesses, which has introduced nothing but confusion and distortions into diagnosis, could not lead and has not led to effective therapy. Freudian therapy reduces to the notorious "laying bare" by psychoanalysis of ungratified instincts and drives "latent in the subconscious."

Present-day psychoanalysts deny the principles of a causal and pathogenic therapy founded on a scientific understanding of processes in the human organism and fiercely gang up against progressive physiology. For example, Psychosomatic Medicine systematically opposes idealist Freudian views to the materialist teaching of I. P. Pavlov.

The great Russian physiologist called the principle of determinism the first principle of every exact scientific investigation. . . .

I. P. Pavlov's teaching affirms the material conditioning of psychic processes and shows that mind, which is a function of the brain, does not exist without matter. All psychic processes, no matter how intricate they may be, are conditioned by the effect upon the brain of multiform influences emanating from the external and internal environment. Psychic processes cannot be understood apart from this necessary condition, which has found brilliant expression in the Pavlovian doctrine of temporary connections and the reflex mechanism upon which they are based.

It is common knowledge that I. P. Pavlov commented with great sarcasm on the notorious Freudian psychoanalysis and the psychoanalysts who dig "in the debris of the unconscious."

In a conversation with one of the followers of the Freudian school, the great Russian physiologist states with glowing conviction that ultimately physiology will penetrate even the realm of the subconscious and will succeed in correctly describing all the processes taking place in the brain.

"In studying the phenomena of irradiation," he said, "we are already able to determine the pattern of development in the neural process of the conscious or the subconscious, while Freud merely tried to divine the internal states of a human being. The future will show whose path is right."

This prediction has been borne out. Life has confirmed the all-conquering strength of the materialist ideas of the Pavlovian physiology.

7.

A somewhat more restrained and scholarly statement of the current Marxian position on Freud may be found in Harry K. Wells's dual study, *Pavlov and Freud*. Mr. Wells, an American social scientist, repudiates Freud as a speculative, antiscientific myth-maker whose "obscurantist" tendencies have reinforced the reactionary prejudices of western peoples, notably in the United States. Pavlov rather than Freud, he argues, ought to be the culture-hero of the twentieth century.

WELLS: Pavlov and Freud *

The Freudian rocket was built in Vienna but launched in the United States. Psychoanalysis never gained the broad foothold in other countries that it did in

* From Harry K. Wells, *Pavlov and Freud*, vol. II (*Sigmund Freud: A Pavlovian Critique*) (New York: International Publishers, 1960), pp. 235–37. Reprinted by permission of International Publishers.

ours. France had its own Pierre Janet; Germany remained largely within the experimental traditions of Helmholtz and Wundt and medically oriented psychiatry; Austria never really took its own to its bosom; and Great Britain and Russia, though subjected to the influence, never succumbed as did the United States. Our country not only launched psychoanalysis, but became its world-center and dissemination point.

Just as a particular transitory set of conditions in cerebral physiology, psychology and psychiatry gave rise to Freud, so a set of ideological and historical conditions in the United States insured his influence.

It can be said, in the most general terms, that Freud's success in America was in large part due to the fact that his philosophy was entirely consonant with the predominant national outlook. The dualistic, subjective idealism of his approach to the human mind posed little scientific danger to the semi-official ideology. On the contrary, it by and large enhanced that ideology by giving obscurantism a broader base in the mind and culture of the American people.

The exact contrary, of course, was true of Pavlov's philosophy. The consistent and militant monistic materialism of the science of higher nervous activity was, and is, in the sharpest possible opposition to the prevailing manner of thought. This in itself is sufficient to account for the relatively slow rate of recognition of Pavlov's science. But there was, and is, at least one more powerful influence at work.

For literally thousands of years mankind has been taught to view the human mind or soul as some kind of extraordinary and miraculous phenomenon requiring an extra-mundane, extra-scientific explanation. This mysterious and mystical approach to mind is deeply imbedded in all of us, and is not easily uprooted.

During the last three thousand years of this tenacious belief, there have been materialist philosophers who have insisted that mind is a natural phenomenon dependent on the body and particularly the brain. With the development of modern science, and particularly with progress in cerebral physiology, nineteenth century materialist philosophers and scientists insisted that mind is a *function* of matter highly organized in the form of the human brain, specifically the cerebral hemispheres. But so long as it was as yet unknown just how the hemispheres could give rise to mental life, the materialist position was almost in the position of a *counter-belief,* in spite of the fact that the inference was inherent in all science. Only when science could *demonstrate* first, that the cerebral hemispheres constitute the specific organ or seat of mind—which was done by the method of extirpation in the 1870's—and second, that there are specific mechanisms of cortical functioning underlying mental activity, only then could materialism be *fully* transformed from a philosophical doctrine into an established *scientific* principle derived from experimentation. This final demonstration that mind is a function of the brain, is the greatest contribution of the science of higher nervous activity. At the same time it is a bitter pill to swallow for it eliminates the last refuge of human exceptionalism to the pervading order of natural law.

Full acceptance of the science of higher nervous activity would entail the transformation not only of psychology and psychiatry into mature sciences, but also eventually of the thinking of each and every human being.

Pavlov went a long way toward taking the mystery out of mind, while Freud in effect deepened and complicated that mystery.

In these terms we can begin to understand the philosophical, scientific and historical significance of the two men.

Philosophically, Freud was an exponent of an anti-scientific subjective idealist world outlook and method; *scientifically,* he was an exponent of speculative, instinct-psychology, perpetuating the myth of the mysterious human mind; *historically,* he tried to leap rather than fill a major gap in human knowledge and therefore can have little bearing on the future of psychology and psychiatry, save as an impediment.

The significance of Pavlov is quite another matter. *Philosophically,* he was not only an exponent of monistic materialism and the scientific method, but in fact made significant contributions which strengthen the outlook and method of science in the unending struggle against ignorance, superstition and pseudo-science, and against their exploitation in reactionary ideology. *Scientifically,* he in essence eliminates the hiatus in cerebral physiology, which in turn puts psychology and functional psychiatry in a position to become fully mature, experimental sciences. The future of psychology will undoubtedly be closely intermeshed with the science of higher nervous activity—and the same holds for functional psychiatry. *Historically,* Pavlov has already won a permanent place of honor in the pantheon of science. As time goes on, he may be recognized the world over as sharing the kind of significance assigned to a Copernicus, a Darwin, a Marx—marking great turning points in human knowledge.

8.

Of all recent studies of Freud, probably the most brilliant and penetrating is that of Philip Rieff, professor of sociology at the University of Pennsylvania. Mr. Rieff is an unrepentant admirer of Freud, whom he defends both against his critics and against his heretical successors, the neo-Freudians. Freud's work he describes as "perhaps the most important body of thought committed to paper in the twentieth century"; Freud himself he calls "a statesman of the inner life, aiming at shrewd compromises with the human condition, not at its basic transformation . . . , a moralist without even a moralizing message." Rieff's admiration, however, never becomes blind adulation; his analysis is tough-minded and sometimes critical, and it hides none of the disturbing aspects of Freudian thought. Like Freud, he foresees no cure for man's "chronic illness," and no real reconciliation between man and society. Instead, in an age of generalized neurosis, the psychoanalytic patient must seek only to reconcile himself to his own inner depths; "his newly acquired health entails a self-concern that takes precedence over social concern and encourages an attitude of ironic insight on the part of the self toward all that is not self." If the dominant character type of the twentieth century is really what Rieff calls "psychological man," the consequences for western society are quite incalculable.

RIEFF: Freud, the Mind of the Moralist *

Freud was not hopeful; nor was he nostalgic. Retrospectively, he treasured no pagan or primitive past. He looked forward to no radically different future. Pagan antiquity had encouraged too much sensual pride and demonstrated the erotic illusion no less fully than Christianity, by encouraging spiritual pride, had demonstrated the ascetic illusion. Freud disdained permissiveness as much as asceticism; both falsely resolved the essential dualism in human experience, that very dualism between mind and flesh that produces the misery of the human condition. What man suffers from finally is no more the supremacy of spirit over flesh than of flesh over spirit; it is the dualism that hurts. Freud's own attitude toward a variety of historical dualisms, including Christianity, was always respectful, for he considered that they were but versions of a more fundamental dualism in the nature of man and in the cosmos. For this reason he never seriously entertained any utopian aspiration. Indeed, his own theory "had always been strictly dualistic and had at no time failed to recognize, alongside the sexual instincts, others to which it ascribed force enough to suppress the sexual instincts." This dualism Freud described as between "sexuality" and the "ego instincts"; later he distinguished two polar instincts, love and death. Whatever the terminology, it is important to see that—unlike the Christian or rationalist consciousness—Freud denies any permanent healing of the "derangement of communal life," of the struggle between individual interest and the economy of social demands, of the antagonism between binding and destructive forces in individual and group life. The most one can win against the eternal dualisms is a rational knowledge of their effects upon one's own life.

Perhaps it might be more accurate to see depth psychology not as an emancipation of sex but as an enfranchisement. Freud recognized that in fact the silent vote of the psychic world never had been silent. He is the Bentham of the unenfranchised unconscious; what he brought into the realm of legitimacy, he also brought to responsibility. If one cannot educate the ruled, then one must educate the rulers. This very aim, to educate the ruling ego, is a sure mark of Freud's classical liberalism. By enfranchising the ineducable populace of sexuality, Freud seeks to bring it into responsible relations with the ruling power. To the liberal political tradition, with its belief that the "two nations" could be brought together, Freud offered a supporting parallel in psychological and moral theory, for he desired, as far as possible, to bring the instinctual unconscious into the rational community. For this new art of compromise a new kind of specialist is needed, one who can take a destiny apart and put it back together again in a slightly more endurable shape. . . .

* From Philip Rieff, *Freud, the Mind of the Moralist* (New York: The Viking Press, 1959), pp. 344–45, 353. Copyright 1959 by Philip Rieff. Reprinted by permission of The Viking Press, Inc.

On the cultural significance of the neurotic character, Freud is entirely explicit. Neurotics are rebels out of weakness rather than strength; they witness to the inadequacies of cultural restraint. But they are unsuccessful rebels, for they pay too high a price for their revolt, and ultimately fail, turning their aggressions against themselves. Instead of being repressed and turning inward as the neurotic is, the normal personality is active and outgoing. Expedient normal attitudes lead to some active achievement in the outer world. The brisk managerial ego of the normal personality devotes itself to aggression against the environment, to the practical use of objects; it does not fixate upon them. As Freud put it elsewhere: neurotic anxiety comes from a libido which has "found no employment"; therefore, the dream, like work, has a "moralizing purpose." Again, the economic metaphor discloses Freud's ideal of health as well: a fully employed libido.

In a brilliant passage Freud describes the normal attitude toward reality as one combining the best features of neurotic and psychotic attitudes: "Neurosis does not deny the existence of reality, it merely tries to ignore it; psychosis denies it and tries to substitute something else for it. A reaction which combines features of both these is the one we call normal or 'healthy'; it denies reality as little as neurosis, but then, like a psychosis, is concerned with effecting a change in it." Thus the neurotic character is the unsuccessful protestant of the emotional life; in him inwardness becomes incapacity. The normal character continues to protest, Freud implies, but is "not content . . . with establishing the alternation within itself." Thus, in Freud's conception of the normal man, there is a certain echo of the Romantic idea of genius—the ideal man who attains to the self-expression that other men, intimidated by convention, weakly forgo.

As the passage just quoted suggests, Freud did not draw a sharp line between the concepts of normal and neurotic. His dictum that "we are all somewhat hysterical," that the difference between so-called normalcy and neurosis is only a matter of degree, is one of the key statements in his writings. Its meaning is threefold.

First, it declassifies human society, creating an essential democracy within the human condition. Even the Greek tragedy—the most aristocratic context —was leveled out by Freud; the unique crime of the tragic hero becomes an intention in every heart, and in the most ordinary of plots, the history of every family. Misfortune is not an exceptional possibility, occasioned by rare circumstances or monstrous characters, but is the lot of every person, something he has to pass through in his journey from infancy to old age. The aristocratic bias of the "heroic" myth is replaced, in Freud, by the democratic bias of the "scientific" myth: Oedipus *Rex* becomes Oedipus Complex, which all men live through. It is because of the suppressed tragedies of everyday life that men respond so fully to the more explicit tragedies on the stage. But this does not mean that Freud proposed a genuinely tragic view of life; he was much too realistic for that. Ordinary men compromise with their instinctual longings and become neurotic; the tragic hero, because he suffers and dies, must be presumed to have carried out his wishes in a way forbidden to most men.

Secondly, to say that all men are neurotic means to imply an injunction to tolerance. At least Freud's discovery that the commonplace is saturated with the abnormal, the pathological—that psychopathology no longer deals with the exception but with the ordinary man—does something to alter established habits of moral judgment. It lightens the heavier burdens of guilt and responsibility, for many offenses can be made to appear smaller if perceived in sufficient depth.

Third, and more important, this conception of neurosis reveals the essentially ethical nature of Freud's idea of normality. Normality is not a statistical conception, for the majority is no longer normal. Normality is an ethical ideal, pitted against the actual abnormal. By another name, normality is the negative ideal of "overcoming"—whatever it is that ought to be overcome. Being essentially negative, normality is an ever-retreating ideal. An attitude of stoic claim is required for its pursuit. No one catches the normal; everyone must act as if it can be caught. Nor can the psychological man forget himself in pursuit of the normal, for his normality consists of a certain kind of self-awareness. Not least of all, the analysts themselves, Freud thought, needed to return to analysis every few years to renew their knowledge of themselves.

The psychological ideal of normality has a rather unheroic aspect. Think of a whole society dominated by psychotherapeutic ideals. Considered not from the individual's but from a sociological point of view, psychoanalysis is an expression of a popular tyranny such as not even de Tocqueville adequately imagined. Ideally, the democratic tyranny which is the typical social form of our era will not have a hierarchy of confessors and confessants. Rather . . . everyone must be a confessant, everyone must aspire to be a confessor. This is the meaning of the psychoanalytic re-education Freud speaks of. In the emergent democracy of the sick, everyone can to some extent play doctor to others, and none is allowed the temerity to claim that he can definitively cure or be cured. The hospital is succeeding the church and the parliament as the archetypal institution of Western culture.

What has caused this tyranny of psychology, legitimating self-concern as the highest science? In part, no doubt, it is the individual's failure to find anything else to affirm except the self. Having lost faith in the world, knowing himself too well to treat himself as an object of faith, modern man cannot be self-confident; this, in a negative way, justifies his science of self-concern. Though the world is indifferent to him, the lonely ego may here and there win something from it. For the rectitude and energetic naiveté of the man who was the ideal type during the middle-class, Protestant phase of American culture, we have substituted the character traits of husbanded energy and finessed self-consciousness. The Frank Merriwell of a psychological culture will not, like the moral athlete of Protestant culture, turn his reveries into realities. Rather, he will be mindful to keep realities from turning into reveries.

In this age, in which technics is invading and conquering the last enemy— man's inner life, the psyche itself—a suitable new character type has arrived on the scene: the psychological man. Three character ideals have successively dominated Western civilization: first, the ideal of the political man, formed and handed down to us from classical antiquity; second, the ideal of the religious man, formed and handed down to us from Judaism through Christianity, and dominant in the civilization of authority that preceded the Enlightenment; third, the ideal of the economic man, the very model of our liberal civilization, formed and handed down to us in the Enlightenment. This last has turned out to be a transitional type, with the shortest life-expectancy of all; out of his tenure has emerged the psychological man of the twentieth century, a child not of nature but of technology. He is not the pagan ideal, political man, for he is not committed to the public life. He is most unlike the religious man. We will recognize in the case history of psychological man the nervous habits of his father, economic man: he is anti-heroic, shrewd, carefully counting his satisfactions and dissatisfactions, studying unprofitable commitments as the sins most to be avoided. From this immediate ancestor, psychological man has constituted his own careful economy of the inner life.

The psychological man lives neither by the ideal of might nor by the ideal of right which confused his ancestors, political man and religious man. Psychological man lives by the ideal of insight—practical, experimental insight leading to the mastery of his own personality. The psychological man has withdrawn into a world always at war, where the ego is an armed force capable of achieving armistices but not peace. The prophetic egoist of Western politics and Protestant Christianity who, through the model with which he provided us, also laid down the lines along which the world was to be transformed, has been replaced by the sage, intent upon the conquest of his inner life, and, at most, like Freud, laying down the lines along which those that follow him can salvage something of their own. Turning away from the Occidental ideal of action leading toward the salvation of others besides ourselves, the psychological man has espoused the Oriental ideal of salvation through self-contemplative manipulation. Ironically, this is happening just at the historic moment when the Orient, whose westernmost outpost is Russia, has adopted the Occidental ideal of saving activity in the world. The West has attempted many successive transformations of the enemy, the world. It now chooses to move against its last enemy, the self, in an attempt to conquer it and assimilate it to the world as it is. For it is from the self that the troublesome, world-rejecting ideal of the religious man came forth.

Freudianism closes off the long-established quarrel of Western man with his own spirit. It marks the archaism of the classical legacy of political man, for the new man must live beyond reason—reason having proved no adequate guide to his safe conduct through the meaningless experience of life. It marks the repudiation of the Christian legacy of the religious man, for the new man is taught to live a little beyond conscience—conscience having proved no adequate guide to his safe conduct through life, and furthermore to have added absurd burdens of meaning to the experience of life. Finally, psychoanalysis marks the exhaustion of the liberal legacy represented historically in economic man, for now man must live with the knowledge that their dreams are by function optimistic and cannot be fulfilled. Aware at last that he is chronically ill, psychological man may nevertheless end the ancient quest of his predecessors for a healing doctrine. His experience with the latest one, Freud's, may finally teach him that every cure must expose him to a new illness.

XIV.

DEMOCRATIC SOCIALISM AT MID-CENTURY: TRANSITION OR DECAY?

The nineteenth century was the triumphant age of liberalism; the twentieth was destined to be that of socialism. Or so it seemed, at least, to many Europeans as the nineteenth century neared its close. Social Democratic parties had been established in virtually every country of Europe, and in many places they seemed to be on the march toward power. By 1914, Social Democracy was the strongest single party in Germany, the second-strongest in France; in Great Britain, Italy, Belgium, Scandinavia, socialism was growing more rapidly than any rival. Lenin's victory in Russia in 1917 brought a temporary setback, for it split the Marxian movement in most countries; the revolutionary left wing broke away to join the Third International. But the Social Democratic movement recovered rapidly in the 1920's, and became a major factor in European politics between the wars. Socialists governed Great Britain for a time; they participated in coalition cabinets in Germany, Belgium, the Scandinavian countries, the Spanish republic (after 1931), and France (after 1936); in Austria, they steadily dominated the municipality of Vienna until 1934.

Although the rise of totalitarian movements and the outbreak of the second world war disrupted European Social Democracy, it emerged in 1945 with brighter prospects than ever. Few other political groups had a better record of resistance to fascism; no rival seemed so well equipped to clear away the wreckage of the war and to use state power for purposes of progress and social justice. Almost everywhere in Free Europe, socialist parties participated in, or led, the postliberation governments: in Great Britain, France, Belgium, The Netherlands, Norway, Sweden, Denmark, Finland, Italy, Austria—even in Hungary and Czechoslovakia for a time.

Germany was expected to join the list as soon as the allied occupation authorities should deem the Germans ready to govern themselves once again.

Disillusionment was not long in coming. By 1950, a powerful reverse tide had set in; by 1960 it had swept the Socialists out of a share of power almost everywhere. Only in Scandinavia were they still in control—in part, perhaps, because the Scandinavian Socialists' principles had never been very orthodox in the first place. In most of the major countries of Free Europe, the Socialists were gloomily becoming accustomed to a role as permanent outsiders, while Christian Democrats or various kinds of liberal-conservatives held the reins of power.

This relatively dismal record, especially after such high hopes, quite naturally led to a great deal of soul-searching among European Socialists during the mid-century decade. The socialist movement, being rather rigorously doctrinaire in spirit, had always been riven by internal controversy; sectarian feuds and splits are natural to any group that takes its ideology seriously, especially when the group has to play a pragmatic political role at the same time. But the kind of self-examination that set in after 1950 struck deeper, for it posed the question of socialism's very survival as a significant political force.

To some degree, the debate involved a retrospective analysis of socialism's record over the past fifty years. Did the root of the trouble go back to errors committed in the past, to false steps that had gotten the movement onto the wrong track? Between the wars, had the Socialists clung too rigidly to Marxian dogmas about class conflict, about the historic role of the proletariat, thus sacrificing their chance of building a broadly based party cutting across all classes? Or had they, on the contrary, failed to be doctrinaire enough; had they grown flabby and reformist and petty-bourgeois in spirit, so that class-conscious proletarians and revolutionary activists abandoned the party in disgust? Or was the trouble, rather, their failure to harmonize doctrine and action; had they talked like revolutionaries while behaving like opportunistic reformers? Or did the real trouble lie in socialism's refusal to adapt itself to changing times? Had it tended to become bureaucraticized and ossified by its emphasis on loyalty and seniority, so that socialist parties had come to be dominated by ageing and unimaginative party hacks, incapable of attracting the younger generation? Had socialism, through its dogged adherence to outmoded conceptions, failed to recognize the true nature of the totalitarian movements, and the strength of those nonrational drives that move masses of men?

The alleged mistakes of the interwar generation, however, did not provide the only possible explanation for socialism's sad state at mid-century. Some alternative theories were more comforting, if not more conducive to hope of a quick revival. Such, for example, was the theory that socialism had done its work almost too well; that by instituting drastic reforms just after the second world war, and by forcing other parties to borrow much of its reform program, the Socialists had virtually worked themselves out of a job. Socialists could point out that when they fell from power, their successors rarely repealed any of their fundamental reforms. Britain and France, for example, continued as mixed economies, operated in part by the state and in part by private enterprise; and the welfare state measures of the socialist era were uninfringed. Likewise in Sweden: when a Conservative party leader in the late 1950's was asked what kind of Sweden he wanted to conserve, his reply was "the Sweden of today"—a society shaped by a quarter-century of socialist rule.

But whether the explanation of socialism's crisis was damning or flattering for its leaders, the problem remained the same: was there any future for Social Democracy in Europe? Were fundamental changes in party structure and doctrine the key to survival and renewal? If so, what might Socialists offer to replace their old appeals? Or would the abandonment of traditional dogmas destroy socialism's very *raison d'être,* and condemn it to more rapid disintegration? The bitterest and most sustained debate over these issues occurred in Great Britain, where the Labour party engaged in a running controversy that almost produced an outright schism in 1960. The German Social Democrats, on the other hand, chose to act rather than argue: at their party congress in 1959, they adopted a new manifesto that swept away virtually all of the traditional dogmas. Into the discard went antimilitarism, anticlericalism, even anticapitalism. Party chairman Erich Ollenhauer told the congress: "The demand that the political program of Karl Marx and Friedrich Engels be made the basis of a Social Democratic program in the year 1959 is so un-Marxist as to be unthinkable. If we were able to follow this line of thought, we would be reduced to a sect."

No other major Socialist party in Europe (except those of Scandinavia, which had always been led by men of pragmatic rather than doctrinaire spirit) has yet chosen to risk drastic overhaul on the German pattern. But the issue confronts them all, and even a refusal to decide will constitute some kind of decision. Democratic Socialism is by no means the only important political force in free Europe at mid-century: but the outcome of its current crisis will go far to shape the nature of democratic politics there during the next generation.

1.

Kurt L. Shell is an Austrian-born political scientist who has taught at Columbia University and Harpur College. In the review article that follows, he examines a series of books published in the early 1950's by European socialist authors. In the process of commenting on their arguments, he provides us with a thoughtful analysis of the complexity of modern socialism, and an account of its chronic difficulties. His conclusions, though cautious, are essentially pessimistic.

SHELL: The Crisis of Modern Socialism *

It would be a mistake to view the intellectual and political movement of socialism as a clearly identifiable and neatly circumscribed historical structure. Out of the many strands which have gone into the making of "socialism" it is possible, by simplifying the complexity of the process, to select at least four broad sources of socialist inspiration and thus four different versions of the socialist goal. These different concepts of socialism are not to be identified with specific historical figures or groups or movements, but represent rather the basic social and psychological elements which combined in varying degree to

* Kurt L. Shell, "The Crisis of Modern Socialism," in *World Politics,* IX (1957), pp. 295–305. Reprinted by permission of the editors of *World Politics.* Mr. Shell's essay comments on the following books: Joseph Buttinger, *In the Twilight of Socialism* (New York, 1953); R. H. S. Crossman (ed.), *New Fabian Essays* (London, 1952); Paul Sering, *Jenseits des Kapitalismus* (Vienna, 1948); and the Socialist Union, *Socialism: a New Statement of Principles* (London, 1952).

form the socialist movements known to us. The crisis of modern socialism—as exhibited in the books under consideration—is due to the fact that each of these concepts, for different reasons, has reached a dead-end from which advance toward any one goal means retreat from others also previously embraced.

The authors whose views have given rise to the following reflections provide a representative sample of the diverse strands of socialism at mid-century, unified by their common compulsion to reevaluate the premises and policies of the movement. Joseph Buttinger, former chairman of the underground organization, Revolutionary Socialists (formed after the dissolution of the Austrian Social Democratic Party by Dollfuss in 1934), most poignantly reflects the loss of faith in the Marxist theory of historical progress and the potentialities of human nature for infinite improvement. His disillusionment —which led him to adopt a position of political quietism (for which the present book represents a detailed apologia vis-à-vis his more "engaged" friends)—is a measure of the depth of his previous emotional commitment to the socialist vision of a radically transformed society. Paul Sering, member of the German Socialist Party prior to Hitler's coming to power and of the German socialist *émigré* organization subsequently, attempts to salvage Marxist theory from the blows dealt to it by Keynesian economics and the bitter Soviet experiment. Socialist Union—a group of intellectuals in the British Labour Party dedicated to "re-thinking"—is consciously anti-Marxist, stressing a humanist and ethical approach to socialism which, however, frequently leads to distressingly platitudinous and indecisive conclusions. The contributors to the *New Fabian Essays* (running from ex-Communist John Strachey to right-winger C. A. R. Crosland) point up many of the problems facing contemporary British socialists (and socialists elsewhere) as a result of the partial success achieved by the Labour Party during its tenure of office, without, however, being able to contribute much to the solution of these problems; a solution which they recognize to be prerequisite to the resumption by socialist parties of their traditional role as parties of movement and inspiration. The failure, common to these diverse spokesmen of European socialism, to reconstruct a socialist edifice matching that erected by their predecessors of the nineteenth century leads to the conclusion that—to use some convenient Marxist terms—"inevitable historical forces" and/or "inherent contradictions" have caught up with socialism itself.

The first of the four tributaries to socialism referred to had its origin in the subjective experience of the industrial proletariat of nineteenth-century Europe, in its experience of economic privation and insecurity, its lack of power vis-à-vis the "boss class," and its inability to extract a "just wage" from the employing class. The mass of industrial workers, rendered capable of organized political effort by the new factory civilization, were drawn into struggles whose foremost aim was the alleviation of these most pressing hardships. The second source, which might be termed that of "humanitarian socialism," aimed at the political and economic emancipation of the working class primarily for ethical reasons. The postulate of individual self-development and of the inherent equality of men appeared to be denied by a class system in which economic and political power were monopolized by one class and used to circumscribe the chances of the members of the industrial working class. Equality of opportunity was an intrinsic part of this faith. And equality of opportunity was deemed incompatible with gross economic inequalities. Adherents of this position, though they accepted collective means and rediscovered the worth of community and the state, shared instincts and values which were individualist, libertarian, essentially middle class.

The most characteristic feature of the third approach, that of Marxist "scientific socialism," was the combination of egoistical and ethical aspirations—expressed by and on behalf of the proletariat—in a system closely related to the historical process. It put responsibility for the attack on the existing system squarely on the working class itself, endowing the aims of that class with historical (and therefore, to Marxists, ethical) justification; and linked it to a promise of an otherwise undefined future of social justice in which "the last shall be first." The political effectiveness of Marxist doctrine lay in its ability to concentrate resentment and to inspire it by a message of historic mission. The theory of "scientific socialism," though in essence a working hypothesis about the relation between economic institutions and social organization, was put forth—and widely received—as the prophecy of inevitable developments deducible from the definition of existing class relations. The deceptive clarity lent to the theory by its use of lapidary definitions and of dialectical dichotomies corresponded to a fighting mood engendered by the misery and turmoil of emerging industrial capitalism. In the Marxist forecast of the future socialist order only the negatives stand out clearly: capitalism will *collapse;* exploitation of man by man will *cease;* the state will *wither away.* For Marxists the war was more important than its aims. Speculation about the concrete outlines of the future society was discouraged, in part because it was assumed that a profound change in economic relations would create its own forms of social life inconceivable to men raised and confined in bourgeois society; in part because preoccupation with the shape of the future society would detract from the proletariat's concentration on the present struggle and create divisions where hatred of the existing systems had created a feeling of solidarity. Three tacit assumptions underlay the Marxist theory: that the future society, being proletarian—or, more correctly, classless—would inevitably represent an improvement, materially and spiritually, over the existing bourgeois one; that the correct ordering of the economic relations of society would inevitably free mankind from the problems of power as well as want; and that man, free for the first time in history, would use this freedom rationally and beneficially in the service of his own happiness and spiritual growth.

The gap which "scientific socialism" refused to fill could not, however, remain unfilled. For some socialists, at least, the negative stimulus of class antagonism had to be supplemented by a more definite vision of a just society. The vague hints put forth by Marx and Engels needed amplification if men were to give of their generous best. Socialism, for these visionaries, became a "new Jerusalem," where abolition of private property was a means to the transvaluation of all values, to the release of all that was highest in human nature. With the elimination of material self-aggrandizement, all the dross of human selfishness would be discarded. Honesty instead of hypocrisy; co-operation instead of selfishness; spirituality instead of materialism; rationality instead of irrationality—these qualities would distinguish socialist man and socialist society from their present-day models. Spontaneity and equality would replace the hierarchy and alienation characteristic of capitalist industrialism. In every instance, the features of the envisioned socialist society contrasted with those of the existing one. As the institutions and values of bourgeois capitalism were those of individualism, socialist utopianism was frequently linked to the contrasting notion of a collectivist order. Class and party, fulfillment of the individual through his submergence in the collectivity, these came to be viewed as worthy of replacing the existing bourgeois values. Out of this emphasis arose the insistence on "socialist honor," on *Haltung* [attitude, deportment] in socialist ranks. The demand for ruthless frankness and unselfishness in the relations of party members toward each other, and for a—seemingly irrelevant—abstinence from nicotine and alcohol represented a protest against the "corrupt" bourgeois way of life.

In the nineteenth century the industrial proletariat had been assigned the role of economic, political, and social pariah. The revolt against this status gave energy to the working-class movements of Europe, a revolt simultaneously directed against the power of the ruling class and the economic misery which was deemed to flow from class domination. Any explanation of the slackening of socialist energy must take into account, above all, the emancipation of the working class from its former pariah position.

The physical environment in which the worker moves—the factory, his home, his community—has now been transformed. The taint of social inferiority has been largely removed and equality of opportunity realized to a considerable degree. The voice of industrial labor, organized in massive trade unions and large political parties, is heard loudly in the land. The improvement in working-class living standards—reflected not only or even primarily in higher wages, but in shorter work weeks, longer paid vacations, and an extensive system of social security—has done more than merely alleviate the most pressing miseries of the past. It has, in many instances, progressed far enough to create a problem novel to the working class: how to dispose meaningfully of the surplus of time and money accruing to it. As Roy Jenkins points out in his contribution to the *New Fabian Essays,* incomes have been equalized (under the impact of working-class power) to the point where admittedly further measures in the same direction would have no significant redistributive effect. And social services have been extended to the point where they, too, are ceasing to act as an equalizing element and have come to resemble merely a collective self-insurance system or a means of securing the aid of more fortunate *individuals* (as distinct from classes) for their less fortunate fellows. And in response to the widespread demand for economic security—a demand made effective by the power of political organization—the autonomy of the economic sphere, the market's claim to self-regulation, has been superseded by the acknowledgment of the community's right to judge the economy in terms of its results for the nation's welfare and to regulate it accordingly. This process of transformation has led many socialists—to the evident disgust of their more radical comrades—to speak of the present as the "age of socialist fulfillment."

The growing working-class satisfaction with the development of contemporary society has been accompanied by disappointment about a number of prophecies based on socialist (particularly Marxist) theory. Capitalist economies have failed to collapse as inevitably and rapidly as anticipated, and socialists like Strachey or Sering have had to come to terms with an awareness that Keynes may have provided the tools for the permanent stabilization of an essentially capitalist order. The polarization of the social structure into a mass of exploited proletarians and a small minority of exploiting capitalists has not taken place; and consequently the subjective feeling of class consciousness has failed to emerge as predicted. Lastly, where capitalism was severely modified or superseded, as in Nazi Germany and the Soviet Union, the emergent system did not exhibit the features anticipated by socialists. These developments undermined socialist theory at three fundamental points: they destroyed the clear-cut concept of the working class as the bearer of historical destiny; they raised a question as to the inevitability of historical progress toward socialism; and, most significantly, they exposed as a fallacy the assumption shared by socialists of all hues that the subordination of private economic power automatically brought in its train a society of free and happy men.

The strength of socialist theory had been that it contained specific assumptions about the relation between economic organization, social power, and human freedom—as well as between human freedom and human happiness. The confusion of present-day socialists is the result of their loss of confidence in the correctness of these assumptions. Socialism, engaged in *exploring* these relations instead of *assuming* them, is, for the first time, forced to become truly "scientific" instead of merely ideological; but thereby it also commits itself to the judgment of empirical evidence. It is forced to surrender a theory providing it with clear-cut signposts (at least to the major goals) and is left with only a set of values, idiosyncrasies, and verbal and organizational commitments.

These "socialist" ideals may be summarized as "freedom," "equality," and "participation." However, the appropriation of these values and their implementation by socialists raise several obvious and fundamental problems.

Socialists have habitually linked freedom to economic security. With the realization of a full employment economy and growing output, the framework for individual freedom has been established. What specific socialist measures are required beyond these economic achievements? Does the concept of freedom have a distinctly socialist meaning which sets it apart from its traditional, liberal, individualistic connotations? Is the intermediate goal of efficient planning compatible with an increase of individual liberty? If socialists today have come to see in the managerial society rather than in capitalism the most dangerous enemy of human freedom, can socialists commit themselves to measures involving the extension of state power? There is a dim awareness among socialists that "freedom to develop one's personality fully" as conceived by socialists must differ from the bourgeois "freedom to develop one's personality fully," whose results are by no means approved by socialists. To be "socialist freedom" it must possess a social dimension. But an answer beyond the vague assertion of the necessity for "fellowship"—the fulfillment of an individual through his identification with others—is lacking. By increasingly stressing consumer freedom—expenditure of economic surplus by means of putting higher wages in the hands of individual wage earners rather than on the basis of collective priorities—socialists avoid the taint of potential totalitarianism inherent in the collective determination of private wants. But they simultaneously abdicate their insistence on "remaking" man through a new set of economic institutions. In the past, socialists had few doubts that in the "new Jerusalem" social and collective values would rank above "petty personal and material ones." Yet the simplicity, the self-sufficiency, the self-abnegation, and even the Puritanism which characterized the traditional socialist *Haltung* are unlikely to resist corrosion by a greatly increased capacity to spend funds for personal purposes; and socialist purists already note and denounce the growing *embourgeoisement* of present-day leaders and members alike.

The difficulties that socialists have encountered in implementing the goal of equality—perhaps the most characteristically socialist of all goals—spring from their failure to resolve the contradiction between equality defined as equality of opportunity—with its implication of rewards as widely divergent as the differences in the "marketable" qualities possessed by individuals—and equality conceived as a true community of equals. Forced to apply themselves to the practical task of maintaining and increasing industrial production, socialists have generally accepted the permanent need for material incentives, and assume that differential wages, like prices, will have to be retained as a means of allocating labor in a complex industrial civilization. Under the pressure of the need for administrative efficiency, as well as the traditional, liberal, individualistic strain representing one aspect of the socialist intellectual tradition, socialists today generally restrict the meaning of equality to "equality of opportunity." Yet, the utopian spark, the vision of a non-competitive society of equals in which men are not valued and rewarded according to their economic usefulness, has not been completely extinguished. A feeling of uneasiness remains at the thought of identifying with socialism the type of society in which each individual is rewarded strictly according to his deserts. The urge for social justice is not exhausted by the distributive concept which in its crudest form is expressed by the slogan: he who does not work shall not eat. The concept of the "equal dignity and worth of all men" which socialism shares with Christianity has radical implications. But the noble ideal of brotherhood is in conflict with the equally noble ideals of striving for perfection (which depends on the recognition of a hierarchy of values) and efficient performance. Thus the ideal of a brotherhood of equals remains in contemporary socialist thought merely as a vague aspiration, a weak trace. It still finds expression in the socialist—though by no means exclusively socialist—insistence on maintaining at a decent level the weak, the ineffectual, and the useless; in a tendency to diminish the span between top and bottom incomes; in the demand for simple and unostentatious living by party leaders; and in the continued quest for a meaning which would carry equality of opportunity beyond that of a race in which all are encouraged "to scramble up the ladder of ambition, with the strongest and most unscrupulous winning all the prizes." Where large accumulations of wealth have survived war, inflation, and inheritance taxes, or where—as in Britain—strong remnants of a social caste system exist, the socialist demand for equality of opportunity and parity of esteem still expresses itself in concrete policies. But on the Continent an extensive system of general public education, coupled with a leveling of incomes, has largely met the demand for an order in which careers are open to the talented and has thus exhausted the socialist impetus toward an egalitarian society.

The third of the socialist goals, the insistence on participation as giving concrete meaning to democracy and overcoming the "alienation" suffered by modern man in a mass society, was expected to find expression in socialist implementation of "industrial democracy." Here, too, socialists appear to have reached the limit of what they deem compatible with the efficiency of a productive economic system and are generally unwilling to accept the notion—propounded by rare mavericks like R. H. S. Crossman—that socialism demands maximum distribution of responsibility and participation even at the price of sacrificing economic efficiency. On the contrary, the distance between the managerial elite and the mass of workers is increasing through the integration of the trade unions into the management stratum, the development of a group of "socialist managers," and the corresponding growth of a feeling on the part of the workers that they are subject to manipulation by distant and irresponsible powers.

The growing uncertainty about the fundamental principles of socialism has been accompanied, naturally enough, by an abandonment of the traditional sharp dichotomy between capitalism and socialism and thus also of the anticipation of a sudden transformation—peaceful or violent—of the one system into the other. The welfare state, characterized by full employment, planning, controls, housing programs, social security, health services, and progressive taxation, is recognized as a structure *sui generis,* neither capitalist nor socialist. But if it is a transitional structure, do socialists know the boundary which divides the transitional stage from the socialist one? The slowness of change, no longer resented as a source of frustration, is now extolled by many socialists as an integral part of the goal itself, as a guarantee of its values and durability. The definition of "class" has become fuzzy and the state has ceased to be viewed merely as an instrument of class rule. If society is no longer divided into two irreconcilable camps but is conceived of as a multiplicity of partly competing, partly cooperating social groups, a case for compromise and coalition has been established. The atmosphere of the political struggle has been transformed; the class enemy whose elimination was once viewed as the condition of socialist triumph has become the political opponent, and co-existence with him is accepted as a prerequisite of political democracy. Socialist parties become parties "like all the others," forced into continuous political compromises, attempting to gain new members and voters from various strata unacquainted with socialist values and traditions. This has brought with it an erosion of the former insistence on socialist *Haltung,* of the view that socialism implies cultural as well as economic changes, and that there are or should be specifically "socialist forms of living."

In this "period of fulfillment" the enthusiasm and idealism which used to be expended in the service of the cause—on occasion, indiscriminately and intolerantly—are today without an objective and even without encouragement. Socialist leaders tend to be embarrassed, even frightened, by "enthusiasm." They stress that the present is not the time for prophets, teachers, dreamers or fighters, but for prudent and realistic planners and administrators. Where they are members of government coalitions or exercise power and influence, they necessarily accept responsibility for the existing system and defend its achievements as a justification of their exercise of power. Dissatisfaction with these achievements, comparison of reality with anticipation, inquiry into the reasons for disappointment, these are frequently felt by leaders to be criticisms directed against themselves and their policies. Independent efforts at "re-thinking" are more often frowned upon than encouraged from above.

Having abandoned past attachment to a more or less rigid ideology and refusing to undertake or encourage serious reexamination of socialist theories and policies, the parties' responses have become increasingly tactical, rhetorical, opportunist and, as a result, haphazard and unintegrated. The lack of direction flowing from the uncertainty as to basic principles has largely emasculated socialist parties as parties of fundamental reform. The most practical questions of everyday politics, as R. H. S. Crossman has pointed out, cannot be resolved intelligently unless the party realizes clearly where its ultimate goals lie: "Are food subsidies and price controls temporary war-time expedients to be dispensed with as soon as we can return to the price system; or are they part of the structure of a socialist state? Does democratic socialism involve the permanence of a mixed economy and, if so, should profit-making in the private sector be encouraged or limited? Should wages be left to find their own level through collective bargaining, or is it the function of a Labour Government to modify the wages structure in the light of national interests and social justice? Is a centralized public corporation a more socialist method of running a public utility than municipal or co-operative ownership? Does socialist principle demand that we should receive our spectacles and dentures free, but pay for travelling on nationalized railways?"

Once a welfare state has been created in which the goals of full employment and equal opportunity have been broadly accepted and realized, socialist parties apparently lose their drive for further significant changes. Their primary concern becomes to consolidate and round out these gains rather than to move toward a fundamentally different social order. Formulating actions increasingly in response to internal and external pressures, socialist parties have largely exhausted their capacity to provide creative solutions to basic problems and have ceased, therefore, to be a source of inspiration to their followers.

2.

The thesis that twentieth-century socialism has been the victim of an outmoded and petrified ideology is forcefully advanced by the Yugoslav-born scholar Milorad M. Drachkovitch. After studying at the University of Geneva, Mr. Drachkovitch taught at the College of Europe in Bruges and at several American universities. He is presently a staff member of the Hoover Institution and a lecturer in political science at Stanford University. In the following selection, Mr. Drachkovitch briefly recapitulates his views on the origins and development of socialism, on the sociological changes of the twentieth century that have allegedly made nonsense of Marx's predictions, and on the reasons for socialism's failure to adapt to these changes.

DRACHKOVITCH: De Karl Marx à Léon Blum *

Socialism is intimately linked to the existence and to the consequences of the great revolutions, industrial and political, that have disrupted European society since the second half of the 18th century. "By the middle of the 18th century the fundamental industrial revolution, that which transformed our mode of thinking, our means of production, our manner of living, had been accomplished." Along with the development of its "paleotechnic phase," which reached the peak of its curve about 1870 and began its accelerated decline about 1900, went the growth of the capitalist system in its pure form, and on the other hand, as though in response, that of the labor and socialist movements.

At the same time, however, socialism "was an outgrowth of revolutionary individualism, just as the ideas of the 19th century were the outgrowth of those of the 18th, and consequently it cannot fail to bear the marks of its origins." Thus, if the revolution of 1789 was inspired by physiocratic concepts which may be described as a kind of agrarian capitalism, that revolution nevertheless opened a triple path to socialism: through the violence with which it broke up the whole structure of the old regime . . . ; through the system of social inequalities that it established so that most socialists could view themselves as the continuers of the unfinished work of 1789; through the extremist movement of Babeuf, whose genuinely proletarian revolutionary equalitarianism would inspire many later collectivist demands of socialism and communism.

Two other essential facts characterize this "paleotechnic" phase of European socialism. First of all, it can be divided into two periods: that of socialist "prehistory," which corresponds to the development of utopian docrines . . . ,

* From Milorad M. Drachkovitch, *De Karl Marx à Léon Blum: la crise de la social-démocratie* (Geneva: Librairie E. Droz, 1954), pp. 138–44. Translated by the editors. Reprinted by permission of the author and of Mlle. Eugénie Droz.

[and then] another, characterized by the triumphant doctrine of Marx and Engels: "Struggle becomes the watchword of this tough and ferocious proletarian generation that matures in the second half of our century: not peace, not conciliation, not universal brotherhood, but struggle." This socialism was characterized both by its eschatological belief in the early downfall of the capitalist order and by its narrowly restricted capacities for action.

The other essential fact complicating this situation was the set of deep differences in concept, mentality, and structure that marked the socialist movements of the major European countries, where the English, French, and German varieties of labor and socialist movements, with their disparate natures, made the doctrinal demand for proletarian revolutionary unity quite illusory.

The ideological triumph of Marxism within European socialism meanwhile brought on the long latent crisis which was to erupt for the first time in 1914, for the equivocations and contradictions of both doctrine and movement . . . simply had to end in rupture. If Marxism corresponded to the general, technical and spiritual conditions of a given epoch—notably the third quarter of the 19th century in western Europe—, the changes in those conditions at the end of the century confused the socialist movement. Marx's thought, despite the genius of the man and the pretensions to scientific prophecy in his doctrine, was conditioned by its time. [The Belgian Socialist] Henri de Man has explained Marx's doctrine in relation to the historical epoch in which he lived and has noted that Marx conceived of "historical development as the working out of a principle of causality whose logic corresponded to that of mechanical operations." The great Marxian theories, particularly in their catastrophic and therefore mechanistic aspect, could influence and inspire militant followers, but could not foreshadow historical and social facts.

In fact, the course of industrial and political evolution, far from obeying doctrinal imperatives, was to impose its own imperatives upon the socialist movement. The end of the paleotechnic phase—that is, the beginnings of the neotechnic phase, with all the revolutionary changes produced by the introduction of electrical energy into industrial life—was to have a dual and unforeseeable result: "The growth of the middle classes, and the survival of small industry." This sociological phenomenon, which prevented a dichotomy of social classes, was to be accompanied in the political sphere by a general democratizing of public life, through which the working class was increasingly integrated into the structure of the national states. Thus: ". . . in place of the Revolution that would expropriate property, the labor movement was born. And with the labor movement came broader political liberties, social legislation, and mass parties." In this situation the revolutionary idea faded, and the concrete task that remained was to try to improve the economic and social conditions of the working class through daily parliamentary and syndical effort. Socialism entered upon a period of *"attentisme"*: this meant a reconciling of "the reformist practice of the present moment with a revolutionary perspective transferred to the future." As early as 1904 Rosa Luxembourg formulated this insoluble dilemma of socialism, forced to tack unceasingly between these two reefs: "on the one hand, the loss of its mass character, on the other, a renunciation of the final goal; either to fall back into the status of a sect or to be transformed into a movement of bourgeois reform." International peace made it possible to conceal this and many other aspects of the crisis of socialism. The war of 1914 brought on its resounding failure, with incalculable results.

The first world war, from every point of view, was decisive. "The age of tyrannies dates from August 1914," declared Elie Halévy, who listed as its immediate results: "from the economic viewpoint, a greatly broadened state control of all means of production, distribution and exchange. . . . From the intellectual viewpoint, state control of thought. . . ." In this respect Karl Kautsky fell into step with Halévy, for in Kautsky's opinion "the war was the principal cause for this transformation of humanitarian tendencies into a tendency to brutality."

The Bolshevik revolution dealt the *coup de grâce* to the emergent Russian democracy, bourgeois as well as socialist, and established the first model of the totalitarian state. In Italy, the former socialist Mussolini followed the example of Lenin's voluntarism to establish his right-wing dictatorship. Germany remained in complete chaos for a number of years, then its democracy recovered for a time, but it was Hitler who profited by the weaknesses of his political rivals, by the disintegration of social structures, by the economic crisis. The western democracies put up a better resistance because their foundations were deeper and because the ravages of the war (notably those of a psychological nature) affected them less profoundly. But the League of Nations, which was primarily their creation, could not preserve peace, for it had no resources to prevent the irrepressibly bellicose tendency of the totalitarian regime from producing the catastrophe of 1939.

European socialism, dislocated by the war of 1914, torn by internal conflict, recovered several years after the end of hostilities and participated with varying success . . . in the political life of all the states. In Russia, Italy, and Germany, it experienced catastrophes, in other countries—such as Poland, Austria, and Spain—serious setbacks, in still others—France, England—less severe defeats; finally, in a few—the Scandinavian countries—relative successes. Two essential phenomena were fatal to the socialists of these countries: either their inability to put up an effective opposition to the totalitarian movements, or their incapacity to utilize political power in the interests of their cause. In this second case, the reformists could do no more than contribute to improvements in the workers' condition, without managing to further and to shape a socialist society; the radicals (*i.e.*, left-wing socialists) utilized an extremist vocabulary without ever being able to achieve the conquest of power called for in their programs.

In general, this negative balance-sheet of the interwar period, this "chain of failures," can be explained by the following facts: (1) the general weakness of European democracy, of which socialism constituted an integral part between the two wars; (2) the profound transformations of social classes; (3) special conditions in the different countries, which made a unified international socialist action illusory; (4) the phenomenon of left- and right-wing totalitarianisms, the intrinsic nature of which was not understood by democratic socialism; (5) the absence of proper and constructive solutions to remedy the crisis of capitalism; (6) doctrinal inadequacy, which meant a lack of ideological guideposts.

From among these elements . . . we would like to emphasize certain aspects, both in order to understand the past and to provide orientation in the future. We have already sketched out some of the social consequences of technical progress in the early "neotechnic" period. The second industrial revolution produced a new social stratification, different from that of the paleotechnic phase studied by Marx. While the trend of the 19th century was toward the expansion of the secondary sector (industry) . . . at the expense of the primary sector (agriculture), thus justifying to a certain extent the prediction that society would be polarized into two antagonistic classes, the growing tendency since the beginning of the 20th century has been quite different. It is characterized by profound social and professional mutations in the active population since the beginning of the century. Referring to the studies of Colin Clark on the general evolution of the industrial countries between 1906 and 1950, Michel Collinet writes: "The primary sector (agriculture) has been declining steadily, to the advantage of the tertiary (transportation, trade, services), while the secondary (industry) grew in proper ratio to the growth of industrial production until 1931, then levelled off. . . . Even before the war [of 1939], the 'social tertiary' amounted to one-third of the population and clearly outnumbered the industrial proletariat. . . ."

Technical progress thus engendered the growth of this large, varied and heterogeneous salaried middle class ("social tertiary"), distinct, especially in the psychological realm, from the working class; while within this latter group, a special metamorphosis occurred. According to Max Adler, a rigorously orthodox socialist, "The events of recent decades have caused within the proletariat itself certain changes that have destroyed its characteristic and uniform traits and that have, therefore, altered its role and its revolutionary capacity in the class struggle in a way quite different from that indicated by Marx's analysis." While Marx distinguished within the proletariat these three strata: active proletariat (participating in the productive process); unemployed (the industrial reserve army) and "Lumpenproletariat" (which does not participate in production), Max Adler analyzed a profoundly altered situation and listed five strata within the working class: career officials of socialist parties, unions, and cooperatives; workers living in a "superior" position; and then the three strata described by Marx. The most important factor in this situation is the tendency of those workers belonging to the most skilled categories to become a kind of "workers' aristocracy," sharply separated from the rest of the proletariat both in way of life and in general outlook. In addition to this tendency toward *embourgeoisement* or toward bureaucratization, strengthened by the growth of workers' organizations which bring an unfortunate moral separation between hierarchical levels, Adler stressed the modern character of certain categories of unemployed persons—lacking work experience, lacking discipline, lacking any Marxist education, easy prey for fascist movements whose paramilitary organizations could resolve the problems of material existence and of moral surrender.

The consequence of all this was that in an especially disturbed period of history—the interwar years—when technical progress was dislocating the old structures of production and of capitalist society, at the same time favoring new and unanticipated realignments of social classes, the socialist movement remained helpless. Official Marxist phraseology no longer got a hearing in the working class "aristocracy," it irritated and alienated the various strata of the new middle classes, the older cadres of bourgeois society were hostile to it by definition; even a part of the proletariat and of the unemployed were attracted by the violent movements of "the era of tyrannies." Nevertheless, the socialist movement still grouped the masses, and in spite of setbacks in Russia and Italy, seemed to be advancing until 1929. The great economic crisis for which it could find no remedies, the dazzling rise of Hitlerism against which it failed to take a vigorous stand, and finally, the Blum experiment, which promised much and accomplished so little, showed socialism's inability to replace the faltering established order whose funeral oration it kept on delivering. If the economic debacle of 1929 accentuated the crisis of capitalism, socialism's failure to come up with its own effective solutions to avert economic and political chaos was especially ominous. The totalitarian movements offered their solutions and scored some successes. In the Europe of 1939, socialism, save in Great Britain, was no more than a negligible force.

This fact was reflected, furthermore, in the doctrinal evolution of socialism between the two wars. On the one hand, the Austrian socialists, who gave the International its tone, remained faithful to Marxist orthodoxy in its deterministic and mechanistic form. After the debacle of 1934, Otto Bauer defined his "integral socialism," and it represented a capitulation (with some amendments) to Communism. In the center, Karl Kautsky, unalterably opposed to Bolshevism, remained theoretically at the stage of his pre-1914 writings. On the other wing, the "neo-socialists"—above all Henri de Man—properly saw the need to go "beyond" Marxism, to rejuvenate socialism and to adapt it to the new structures of society. But the international situation pushed them toward the fascist systems, whose warlike assaults reduced their efforts to naught. Only the Communists remained effective, but their strength sprang not from their theory but from the possession of power or, better still, from the existence of a powerful empire.

The end of the second world war offered western socialism a new and third chance to act freely. A resolutely democratic and reformist movement in most countries of western Europe, a parliamentary factor of the first rank, socialism at the present moment must study the crises of its past, the realities of the present-day world, the activities of its adversaries or partners of left and right, if it wants to recover the ambitious role which it claimed in the past. This is all the more true since the phenomenon of historical acceleration signifies that after every failure, a great human movement must pay more dearly for its redemption. To better understand the redoubtable challenges that presently confront socialism, let us raise three questions:

Without rethinking its doctrine and without modernizing its program, will socialism be capable of resolving the economic, political, and social problems of that "tertiary civilization" which is now in course of development?

Will socialism know how to stand up effectively, either defensively or offensively, to Communism, which represents both a universal secular order at total war with present-day society, and a group of militarized states, directed by technicians of politics and by technocrats?

In the human realm—of essential importance, given man's eschatological need—will socialism be capable of founding, as Ignazio Silone hopes and believes, "a culture, a civilization, a new type of harmonious life among men?"

It is not for us to reply to these questions. One thing, however, is certain: it is only by learning the lessons of its crises and its past failures that socialism can again play a great role in the future. Marxian socialism has been able to push a long way in its criticism of the established order, because Marx "was a penetrating analyst of the bad side of human nature," and because capitalist society has left itself open to criticism. But the best founded criticism does not suffice to build a new society, just as the noblest abstract aspirations will remain utopian so long as men will not learn to harmonize them with the imperatives of particular epochs and will refuse to fight vigorously for their victory. The social structures of present-day Europe, its moral and psychological climate and its need for reorganization demand above all that it free itself from certain outmoded ideological clichés. Marxism, notably in the form advocated by Marx's disciples, no longer corresponds to the social, economic, political, ideological and psychological infrastructures of our times, just as capitalism of the Manchester school will never again be resuscitated. In consequence, if it is to recover its constructive role in a Europe that can only be pluralistic, socialism must rid itself of the monistic myths of the past.

3.

For a half-century before his death in 1959, G. D. H. Cole taught at Oxford and took a leading role in the British socialist movement. During the last two decades he served as chairman or president of the Fabian Society, that peculiarly British movement of intellectual Socialists dedicated to gradualism. An incredibly prolific author, he wrote almost a hundred books, many of which dealt with socialist history or theory; among them was a multivolume *History of Socialist Thought,* one of the classics in the field. In 1955 Mr. Cole took a hard look at the movement to which he had devoted so much of his life, and found it in a precarious state. Socialism, he argued, had abandoned its international character, and had degenerated into a series of national movements interested only in creating a set of rival welfare states. Such conduct, he insisted, must be futile and self-defeating; as a substitute, he called for a new crusade to be conducted by a minority of dedicated internationalists who would rise above national loyalties and would aim at influence rather than power. Only thus, he contended, would it be possible to rescue socialism, and to restore "the quintessence of Socialist faith."

COLE: The Future of Socialism *

Is Socialism, as it exists today, a nationalistic or an internationalist movement? A generation ago most active Socialists would have been shocked at the very posing of such a question. All the Socialist Parties of the Second International, except the British, professed to be followers of Marx; and Marxism was beyond all question an internationalist doctrine, based on the conception of the primacy of the class-struggle and on a rejection of that of national solidarity under capitalism. Doubtless, the Socialist Parties of the West qualified their Marxism in various ways. The French, under Jean Jaurès, agreed with the Germans under August Bebel in affirming the right and duty of national defence against an aggressor; and the French, or most of them, also recognised the duty of rallying to the defence of the Republic against internal reaction. But, though it was accepted that each national party had to adapt its policy to the conditions prevailing in its own country, they also regarded it as a duty to frame their several policies within the general requirements of a common struggle against capitalism and imperialism, and felt themselves to be engaged, not in a number of separate and independent movements, but in an international contest for the establishment of a new kind of society.

In Western Europe, this type of internationalist Socialism underwent a drastic eclipse in August, 1914, when in each of the belligerent countries the Socialist Party rallied to the support of the national State and it was made plain that the famous Stuttgart resolution of the International signified nothing when the time came for translating it into action. In retrospect, it is easy to see that there could hardly have been any other outcome. In Russia, where the autocracy had no thought of invoking the help of the Socialists in the war effort and there was no effective parliamentary machine, it was relatively easy for the Social Democrats to maintain their hostility to Czardom—though, even then, Lenin's revolutionary defeatism was much too strong meat for many of them to swallow. In the Western countries, with their growing parliamentary parties and their hopes of winning over a majority of the electors to their side, the situation was entirely different. The Socialist parties had to reckon with the certainty that to oppose the war effort of their States would cost them, not merely votes—very many votes—but the very possibility of carrying on the constitutional parliamentary propaganda which had become their principal activity, and would involve the destruction of the imposing organisations they had built up over so many years.

* G. D. H. Cole, "The Future of Socialism," *New Statesman and Nation,* vol. 49 (1955), pp. 60–62 and 92–93. Reprinted by permission of the editors of *New Statesman and Nation.*

Even if they had continued to speak of a coming "revolution," they had come to think of this "revolution," not as any sort of rising or rebellion in arms, but as the sequel to a parliamentary victory; so that they would be defending and not attacking the constitution and would have the verdict of the democracy on their side. This kind of "revolution" demanded that they must at all costs be united among themselves in a single party and that this party must do nothing to antagonise any substantial body of voters who could be won over to support it. A party which set out to win and to hold an electoral majority could afford to do nothing that would prejudice its electoral chances; and this meant, not only that its general policy had to be moderate in order to bring in the waverers, but also that it had to be nationalistic to the extent of bowing to nationalist feeling whenever it was seriously stirred by the course of international events.

These tendencies had revealed themselves long before 1914 to those who were prepared to look facts straight in the face. But most of the Socialist politicians were not prepared to do this, and preferred to accept an underlying contradiction between their doctrines and their readiness to act. After 1914, the contradiction could no longer be ignored; but there was more than one way of resolving it. After 1917 there were two plain ways. One, taken by the founders of the Third International, was to accept the consequences of ostracising all who would not subordinate parliamentary success to the cause of world revolution. This was the basis of the famous Twenty-one Conditions on which the Comintern insisted for admission; and it involved, as soon as became plain, renunciation of all hopes of early conquest of political power in the Western countries. The other was to renounce internationalism as a method of action, and to fall back on the policy of working for parliamentary majorities in the various States, at the price of offering to each electorate what it wanted, or could be induced to accept. This was the course followed by the parties of the revived Second International and accepted, after a period of hesitation, by those parties which attempted for a time to steer a middle course.

At this stage, Russia and the Comintern stood clearly for internationalism, and Western Social Democracy for national policies of social reform adapted to the conditions of each separate country. But before long the situation drastically changed, as the Russians had to give up their hopes of speedy revolution in the West and to settle down to making what they could of their own survival in face of foreign intervention and civil war. Stalin became the apostle of "Socialism in One Country"; and the Comintern, for as long as it was allowed to continue, ceased to be truly international and became an agency for the promotion of Russian interests, basing its activities on the dogma that whatever was good for Communist Russia must be good for the proletariat of the whole world. In the Communist camp, Russia came first and the rest nowhere—until, after 1945, the arrival of Communist China compelled the Russians to begin thinking again. Meanwhile, in the West, the rise of substantial Communist Parties in Weimar Germany and in France and Italy, and to a less extent elsewhere, destroyed the working-class unity which had been a postulate of

Social Democratic policy and therewith removed all hope of the constitutional Socialist "revolution" through electoral victory. Only Great Britain and the Scandinavian countries avoided this outcome through the weakness of their Communist movements. Elsewhere, the most that could be hoped for was that the Socialists would be able to play some effective part in parliamentary conditions that would yield, not Socialism, but some instalments of the Welfare State. In these circumstances Socialism, even nationally, had to take a back seat, and internationalism was virtually ruled out altogether in most of Europe.

There remained the Scandinavian countries and Great Britain, in which the Socialists were still in a position to hope for electoral success that would give them the power to put a moderate Socialist policy into effect. The chance came first to the Swedes, then in the other Scandinavian countries, and latest of all, in 1945, in Great Britain. In all these countries Labour or Social Democratic Governments were able to carry through considerable developments of social welfare, within the limits set by the need to do nothing that would interfere seriously with the continued functioning of capitalist business. They were able to tax their wealthy classes, to establish a large measure of social security, and to extend in some degree the intervention of the State in the planning of economic development.

These were real achievements, much more notable in their effects than the limited measures of nationalisation which accompanied them. But in each case where the Socialists won political power by constitutional means, an *impasse* was reached when they had put their immediate programmes into effect. The improvements which they had brought about in social conditions, far from making the majority of the electorate eager to advance to full Socialism, made a large section of their more lukewarm supporters, among the workers as well as in other classes, less discontented with things as they were and less disposed to face the risks involved in supporting thorough-going Socialist policies. Moreover, in Great Britain especially, but also in Scandinavia, the sense of international insecurity, which measures of domestic social security could not remove, and that of dependence on the immensely powerful capitalist economy and military potential of the United States, put venturesome policies at a very serious discount.

It became an axiom among Socialist as well as other politicians that there must be no breach with the Americans, for both economic and political reasons; and the belief in the indispensability of the Atlantic alliance came to be an important factor in the modification of Socialist policies and in the conversion of trade union leaders to a "pressure-group" conception of working-class action based on imitation of the non-Socialist Trade Unions of the United States. These tendencies were aggravated by the presence of Communism, even where it was not a strong political force; for the pro-Russian activities of the Communists had the effect of exposing every sort of militant activity to a Communist taint and of driving the Social Democratic and trade union leaders further Rightwards than they would have wished to go, had they not been forced into an alliance with anti-Socialists on the international political front.

These things happened even where democratic Socialism was strongest. Where the Communist Parties were stronger, the effects were even worse. The Socialist Parties—what was left of them—having no hope of winning power on their own, were either driven into coalitions in which they had little influence, or stood impotently aside in the hope of avoiding responsibility for a situation they could not control. In several countries their sense of helplessness drove them into the arms of the anti-Socialist advocates of European Union, among whom the Catholics were the dominant factor; and they became desperately anxious to make up for their own weakness by dragging the British Labour Party into the same camp.

In this situation, how much of Socialism survives in Western Europe? In France, in Belgium, and in Holland, hardly anything; for Socialist Parties which are supported by only a fraction of the working-class and show no sign of increasing their influence are clearly helpless in the matter of changing the basis of the social order. Social Democracy is stronger in Western Germany; but even there it does not seem likely to win a majority of the electors to its side. The Scandinavians are better placed; but even when they win elections they show but little sign of a desire to use their success as a means to establishing Socialism, or even to narrowing the scope for capitalist enterprise. Scandinavian achievement, like British, has stopped short at the Welfare State; and there seems to be no great wish to go further. As for Great Britain, the contents of recent Labour Programmes furnish enough evidence that the Labour Party has very little notion of what it wants to do next and is basing its hopes of electoral victory much more on its opponents' mistakes, or on the mere swing of the pendulum, than on any constructive projects of its own.

All this is clearly no accident. It is not that the Socialist leaders have wantonly and without cause abandoned their Socialist aspirations, or at any rate postponed them to an indefinite future. They have realised that not enough of the electors want Socialism to return a really Socialist Government to power; and, with this, many of them have ceased themselves to want Socialism. How can they, as good democrats, want what they feel a majority of the voters will refuse to support? They are professedly democrats first and Socialists only afterwards, and subject to democratic consent. Their task as politicians, as they see it, is not to design Utopias or plot revolutionary *coups,* but to beat the Tories by rallying a progressive majority behind them.

In order to win such a majority, they must combine the promise of more social welfare with reassurance to the fearful that they will neither dislocate the economy (by making capitalism unworkable) nor risk upsetting the Atlantic alliance (by offending the United States). They can, indeed, try to exert a restraining influence on American anti-Communist policy; but in the last resort, when the Americans insist, they must give way. Moreover, even in home affairs, they must limit themselves to measures that do not cost a great deal, because there is not very much more that can be extracted from the rich without knocking away the foundations of capitalist enterprise—and this can be risked only if it can be immediately replaced by Socialist institutions they have no prospect of getting an electoral mandate to set up, even if they knew how to do so.

The politicians clearly cannot be expected to state these unhappy truths; for to admit that they are truths would involve a confession of their own bankruptcy. But they cannot escape a growing recognition by electors that they have but little to offer and that Socialism forms no part of their immediate plans. In terms of immediate electoral prospects, no doubt, the present policy of "No Socialism" probably pays better than a Socialist policy would pay; but I doubt if it will pay well enough to put the Labour Party back in office unless the Tories do something outrageously silly. Moreover, even if it did put the Labour Party back, what could a Labour Government do except so disappoint the electors as to ensure a speedy return to opposition?

What . . . are those of us who still believe in Socialism to do? By "believing in Socialism," I mean believing in social equality, rejecting the solution of a Welfare State still based mainly on capitalist profit-making, and holding this faith in equality as applying, not to one country, but to all—that is, as an international gospel of humanism. I do not delude myself that such a gospel is ever likely to be popular, to the extent of commanding the allegiance of a majority, except in a society that is already Socialist. I therefore dismiss the possibility of arriving at Socialism—in the sense here given to the word—by convincing a majority of any popular electorate to support it. It is no doubt possible—though I think pretty difficult—that a majority may be persuaded to vote for a policy of *national* Socialism—that is, for social equality within a single country; but I can see no possibility of a majority vote in any advanced country in favour of an equal sharing of resources among all the peoples of the earth. A majority might be induced to vote for a policy from which that majority would derive a clear benefit for itself; but it is simply not on the cards that in any of the more advanced countries a majority should favour equality of treatment for all mankind, with no preference for its own national group. Men are not like that, not so much because they are consciously selfish as because they are mostly not imaginative enough to think altruistically on so grand a scale.

I assume, then, that Socialists, in the sense I have given to the word, are bound to remain a small minority in every country. What ought these small minorities to do? Ought they to rest content with helping the "national Socialists" to win majorities, in the hope that a sequence of national victories for "Socialism" will somehow add up to, or promote the cause of, international Socialism, or is there a duty resting on them to do something positive to assert their international faith?

Broadly speaking, the Socialist movements in the various countries were built up largely by idealists who did believe in the brotherhood of men and hoped to advance towards it by promoting a more limited social justice within their own societies, while collaborating to the best of their power with similar movements elsewhere. In order to win support, they had to appeal to much larger numbers to whom the brotherhood of men meant nothing and who were mainly moved by the prospect of advantage to themselves and to others who were near enough and similarly enough placed to themselves to arouse their imaginative sympathy—which meant, in practice, that they had to identify their cause with that of the national working-class movements of their own countries. Such an attitude made sense as long as there seemed to be a real hope that it would lead to the victory in each country of "national Socialism"— that is, of publicly planned production of wealth with a view to its distribution as equally as possible among the whole people. If, however, . . . success in the earlier stages of this campaign, instead of leading on to Socialism, tends in fact rather to put obstacles in the way of achieving it, then the case is completely altered.

For a series of Welfare States, each trying to distribute as high incomes as it can for the benefit of its own citizens, but each compelled to do this only within the limits set by the continuance of a profit-making economy, is clearly calculated, not to promote a fairer sharing-out of the world's resources, but rather to aggravate national selfishness as the politicians vie one with another in promising benefits to the peoples. For example, who supposes that a British Labour Government would venture to give for the proposed "world war upon want" help that would seriously diminish its power to improve living standards in Great Britain, or that, in any country, a Government depending on popular support could successfully call on the electorate to reduce its own standards in order to raise those of the poorer peoples?

Mass parties cannot do such things. Socialism of a more than national essence is not a practicable basis for such parties. All that the small groups of international idealists can hope to do is to influence them to behave rather less nationalistically than they would otherwise do. The practical question is whether this influence can best be exercised by working entirely within each national party or by attempting also to establish links across national frontiers, so as to make possible a concerted crusade by the internationalists in all countries. I believe that we have reached a point at which there is no prospect of rescuing Socialism from its imprisonment within national frontiers—which in fact stultify it even on the national plane—except by re-creating an international Socialist movement, not as a federation of national parties, but rather as a crusade of a devoted minority in every country. Such a crusade would, no doubt, need to be carried on by organised groups within each country; but these groups would have to put themselves in a position to act together in pursuance of a common programme. This they could not do unless their members were pledged to stand together without being bound by a final loyalty to their national Socialist Parties—which they would have to defy whenever these parties' national policies ran counter to the practical requirements of international Socialism.

I am suggesting, then, the establishment of a World Order of Socialists individually pledged to put first their duty to Socialism as a world-wide cause, and offering to the working-class and Socialist movements of their own countries no more than a secondary loyalty. This involves a concerted refusal to accept any kind of party discipline that requires the individual to accept the majority verdict of his fellow-nationals against that of the proposed Order. It might accordingly involve expulsion from a national party which insisted on obedience to majority rule; and those who pledged themselves to the World Order would run the risk of finding themselves in the political wilderness in their own countries. To many, this will probably seem a fatal objection; but I can see no alternative except that of renouncing the quintessence of the Socialist faith. Nor need the expulsions occur: that would depend on the good sense of the Socialist parties and on the strength of the sense among their members of having reached a dead end from which they need to be retrieved by some force which they are unable themselves to provide.

Inevitably, in the present state of the world, the Order of Socialists would take its stand for the cause of international peace. It is an intolerable situation that the profession of pacifism should have come to be so suspect, because of its Communist associations, as to alienate the support of great masses of ordinary, decent people who stand aghast at the thought of war. The World Order I have in mind would stand not merely for co-existence but for the fullest possible resumption of friendly international intercourse across both national and "cold war" frontiers, and against every policy that divides the peoples of the world into two great opposing camps. It could not be Communist, or even communistic, because it is of the essence of Communism to reject the idealistic outlook on which it would be bound to rest. But it could not be anti-Communist either, in any sense that involves taking sides with capitalism, or with capitalist powers, against the countries that are under Communist rule. If Communists wished to join it, on its own terms, they would be as welcome as anybody else. It would be a crusade and not a political party.

From this it follows that the World Order would have no ambition to form Governments, or to carry its programme into effect by assuming power in any shape. Its purpose would be to influence, not to execute. It would seek to influence mass-opinion by speech and writing and, most of all, by personal contacts in every country; and it would also need to influence leaders to bring their policies into harmony with its ideas, as far as they could do so within the limits of their own national requirements. It would be in one sense like a Fabian Society for the whole world, in that its method would be essentially that of permeation. But it would be unlike the Fabian Society in that its aim would be, not to persuade the peoples of the world to go slow, but to make them understand that merely national Socialism involves not so much going slow as ceasing to move at all; that there can be no escape from the existing impasse, save through swift and decisive action. Such action must transcend national limits and be designed to end the isolation of the contending power blocs by creating a consciousness of world unity in Socialism as the compelling need of our times.

Frankly, I do not know how to set about the creation of this World Order. There seem to be two possibilities. One is to begin by founding a group of like-minded individuals within a single country and then to appeal to Socialists in other countries to join hands in a common movement. The other is to begin by appealing to individuals one knows of in a number of countries, and to establish at the outset a small international group whose members would then attempt to draw up an agreed policy in very broad terms and, with this as a basis, would seek to promote national groups in their own countries. In such a programme, peace and international friendship, and therewith international "war on want," and a wide toleration of varying democratic "ways of life," would obviously have to take the leading place.

For the rest, the crusaders themselves would need to define it, keeping it broad and simple and rejecting every attempt to impose a rigid dogmatism, either of ideology or of positive prescription of method. The first course is obviously the easier—though even it is difficult enough: the second would be greatly preferable, if it were practicable to bring the pioneers together to work out the basic programme. In either course of action I am too old to play more than a very minor part. Such tasks are mainly for the young, who can think more freely and act more boldly than disillusioned seniors. Even for the jaded, what joy it would be to have their faith in Socialism reinvigorated by an international band of crusaders who would get Socialist thought and action out of the ruts in which they have become bogged! There used to be a vision, which put heart into our earlier struggles, of a world made alive by the sense of human fellowship—a world in which fellowship would be the first great lesson taught at school and the first principle of men's daily intercourse. If that vision has been irrevocably lost, Socialism is lost with it; for Socialism, in its essence, is a thing of the spirit, and not a mere machinery of social control. But I cannot believe men so changed in spirit that they cannot be stirred afresh by the Socialist gospel if only a few of them can get together across national frontiers to redefine it in modern terms and to offer it the devotion of their lives.

4.

In 1960 the influential British monthly *Encounter* published a series of articles that brought into sharp focus the controversy that was threatening to split the Labour party into two warring camps. Stating the case for a fundamental renovation of the party's doctrine and action was C. A. R. Crosland, a member of the House of Commons in 1950–55 and again since 1959. Mr. Crosland was educated at Oxford, and after war service, taught economics there for a time before entering politics. His book *The Future of Socialism* (1956) was a kind of revisionist manifesto, and it aroused a storm of criticism within the Labour party. One of his critics charged that "what Crosland is trying to do is to make people's mouth water at the prospect of an omelette without jangling their nerves with the sound of broken egg-shells. . . ." Crosland forcefully summarized his case in the article reprinted below. He contended that British socialism was lagging behind its continental sister parties because it had failed to adapt itself to social change; and he concluded by setting forth a series of new goals that would provide new inspiration for Socialists without blurring the differences between left and right in politics.

CROSLAND: The Future of the Left *

It is sometimes said that there is now a world-wide trend to the Right, of which the recent British election was only the inevitable local manifestation. Can such a trend be demonstrated?

The answer depends on the time-span which is being considered. We can easily detect the reversal of the swing to the Left which occurred in the 1930's and culminated in most countries in 1945. Such a reversal began over a decade ago, and was inevitable; for all the pre-war Left-ward pressures on the electorate shifted their direction after the war. In the 1930's, the Great Depression combined with mass unemployment convinced the voters that capitalism evidently could not solve its inner contradictions, and should be replaced by Socialism. It stimulated radicalism and the politics of revolt, and encouraged a general antipathy to big business. Abroad, the main enemy, Fascism, was on the Right. All these factors, and later the war itself, pulled people to the Left. By 1946 the majority of democratic countries (Britain, the U.S.A., France, Belgium, Holland, Norway, Sweden, Australia, New Zealand) were governed by Left-wing parties or Left-oriented coalitions.

In the subsequent years, however, all these influences went into reverse. Post-war full employment appeared to demonstrate that capitalism had solved its inner contradictions. The alleviation of poverty weakened the mood of radical revolt. Inflation replaced unemployment as the main domestic threat; and it came to be associated in the public mind, not with big business, but with Left-wing Governments and the Trade Unions. Abroad, the main enemy now was on the Left: Communism. Above all, the governments of the Left became identified with the high taxation, rationing, controls, austerity and inflation which inevitably characterised the post-war period and in some cases recurred after Korea. All these factors pulled people to the Right; and by 1952 Left-wing parties or coalitions had fallen from governmental power in Britain, the U.S.A., France, Belgium, Denmark, Australia, and New Zealand.

But has this trend been accentuated since? Are we now faced, not merely with a "natural" swing of the pendulum which might be reversed for all manner of reasons, but with a long-term secular trend to the Right? Many people think that we are, and that (to quote Professor D. W. Brogan . . .) "in 1959 the prospects of what is now the traditional Left look bleaker than they did in 1919 or 1945 . . ."

Generally, this is because the Left has gained so much of what it sought;

* C. A. R. Crosland, "The Future of the Left," *Encounter*, XIV (March 1960), 3–12. Reprinted by permission of the author and of the editors of *Encounter*. Mr. Crosland's article will also be reprinted in a forthcoming volume of his essays, *The Conservative Enemy*, to be published by Schocken Books (New York, 1963).

the reformed, full-employment, welfare-state "capitalism" of to-day obviously evokes much less antagonism than its predecessor of the 1930's. More particularly, the trend is attributed to certain familiar social and economic changes. The strength of the Left, it is said, is being eroded by the changing age-structure of most Western populations and the relative decline of the traditionally Labour older age-groups; the growing political emancipation of women, who allegedly lean more to the Right than do their mates; the decline of the older basic industries such as coal, railways, and textiles in which Socialist loyalties were always strongest; the housing migration from the solidly working-class slum areas into socially more fluid suburban estates and new towns; the changing character of the labour-force and the decline of the blue-collar relative to the white-collar working class; the cultural effect of the new mass media; and above all the sudden irruption of the upper working class into the world of automobiles, gadgets, and consumer durables.

All these changes, it is said, are weakening the traditional class loyalties of the workers and encouraging the spread of a middle-class psychology; and this is reflected politically in a trend to the Right. As a result "the parties of the Right have been growing in electoral strength and parliamentary support for a whole decade," and will continue to grow for the foreseeable future.

Election results, however, do not provide wholly conclusive evidence for this view. Left-wing governments or coalitions remained in power throughout the decade in Sweden and Norway. The Left regained power in Denmark in 1953 and in New Zealand in 1957. In Congressional elections, the U.S. Democrats won more seats in 1958 than in 1950 or 1952. On the other hand, Right-wing governments replaced Left-wing governments during the latter part of the decade in Belgium, Holland, and (if the terms have meaning there) Canada, and had no difficulty in maintaining themselves in power almost throughout the decade in Britain, Germany, and Italy.

If we look at the matter in terms of votes, and compare the first post-Korean election with the most recent election in each country, we find that the proportion of votes cast for Left-wing parties increased in Germany, Austria, Italy, Norway, U.S.A. (Congressional elections), Australia, and New Zealand, and decreased in Britain, Belgium, Denmark, Holland, Sweden, Canada, and France. The evidence is thus not at all clear. Certainly those Right-wing governments which were fortunate enough to preside over the great European boom of the 1950's—in Britain, Germany, and Italy—have easily maintained their position. But in terms of votes the figures show seven countries with a rising, and seven countries with a declining Left-wing vote. In two of the latter, moreover, special factors were operating—the change of régime in France and a long-run swing of the pendulum in Canada; while in Holland and Sweden the Left lost less than 2 per cent of the total vote. This leaves Britain as one of only three countries where, without special explanation, the Left-wing vote has suffered a serious decline.

There is thus no world-wide trend to the Right so strong that it can be used by the Labour Party as an escapist excuse for recent setbacks; on the contrary, the persistent decline in the British Labour vote goes, if anything, against the international trend. Yet the underlying social and economic factors mentioned above are unquestionably operating. One must provisionally conclude that their political effect varies according to the adaptability of the party of the Left—that they handicap not all parties of the Left automatically, but particularly those which (like the British Labour Party) are identified in the public mind with a sectional, traditional, class appeal. There is, indeed, a great deal of impressionistic evidence from the recent election to suggest that this is the case.

The task of the Labour Party, then, seems abundantly clear. First, it should initiate detailed social surveys to elicit the motives for recent voting behaviour. If these show, as in Britain they probably will, that social trends are now operating against it, then the Party should have one overriding aim over the next three years: to adapt itself, without in any way surrendering basic principles, to the realities of social change, and to present itself to the electorate in a mid–20th-century guise.

Instead, it is caught up in a confused and irritable debate on nationalisation. An outsider might easily be forgiven for not knowing what this was all about. It appears to revolve mainly around Mr. Hugh Gaitskell's Blackpool speech. But all that Mr. Gaitskell said was this. First, the Labour Party now accepts a mixed economy, and is no longer committed to the complete public ownership of all the means of production, distribution and exchange. Secondly, to the extent that the Party still wishes to enlarge the public sector, it should normally do so not by the creation of more and more state monopolies, but by other and more flexible forms of social ownership.

But were not both these propositions accepted years ago? "It is clear to the serious student of modern politics," wrote Mr. Aneurin Bevan in 1952,

that a mixed economy is what most people of the West would prefer. The victory of Socialism need not be universal to be decisive. I have no patience with those Socialists, so-called, who in practice would socialise nothing, while in theory they threaten the whole of private property. They are purists and therefore barren. It is neither prudent, nor does it accord with our conception of the future, that all forms of private property should live under perpetual threat. In almost all types of human society, different forms of property have lived side by side. . . . Where the frontier between the public and private sector should be fixed, is a question that will be answered differently in different nations.

The Labour Party itself, in *Labour and the New Society* (described as "a statement of the policy and principles of British democratic Socialism"), officially declared in 1950 that "private enterprise has a proper place in the economy." The Socialist International, in its famous Frankfurt declaration of 1952, stated that Socialist planning "does not presuppose public ownership of all the means of production. . . . [It] is compatible with the existence of private ownership in important fields." Almost every major social-democratic party in the world has now committed itself to accepting a mixed economy.

. . . . Then what is all the furore about? One would have hoped now for a calm discussion, in the light of the public's manifestly clear views on future nationalisation, of exactly how far it should be carried, exactly what forms it should take, and exactly how it should be presented to the public. No doubt some heat would have been engendered even then, as people argued about where the frontier should be drawn. But the present tumult and shouting, although confined to a militant minority, goes far beyond this, and needs some special explanation.

It is to be explained, first, by the paradox that Mr. Gaitskell's speech came as a great surprise to many of the rank-and-file, who had not grasped what the leadership had been saying for the past ten years. This was partly because the leadership, both Left and Right, tended to speak with two voices—one for the electors and another for the Party militants; it never, for example, sought to amend the Party constitution with its apparent commitment to 100 per cent public ownership. The Left-wing leaders, especially, were schizophrenic on the subject of nationalisation; intellectually they accepted a mixed economy, emotionally they still clung to the dogma of wholesale public ownership. The result was a series of very confused noises.

Consequently, although successive election manifestos faithfully reflected the growing moderation of the leadership, some Party activists continued to believe . . . that Labour was still committed to the long-term goal of total public ownership. As with the pre-Hitler German Social Democrats, the extremist phraseology of the Party's formal aims bore no relation to the moderate, practical content of its short-term programme. And as with the German Social Democrats, the blurred image and the confusion which resulted did nothing but harm (except psychologically to the militants, who could still retain, whatever practical concessions they had to make to-day, the expectation of millennial triumph in the future). It was this confusion which Mr. Gaitskell sought to dissipate by his Blackpool speech. But the revelation of what the leadership actually thought came as a fearful shock to those militants who still interpreted the Party's formal constitution to mean 100 per cent public ownership.

Further hostility was aroused by the feeling that the "revisionists" were proposing a cynical surrender of principle for the sake of electoral advantage. In fact a political party is not behaving immorally in studying the wishes of the voters, provided that it wants power not for reasons of personal ambition or prestige, but in order to put a programme into effect. Indeed the traditionalist Left has often advocated its policies precisely on electoral grounds. There is much talk (though rather more in Chelsea and Oxford than in Stepney or Nyasaland) of the dangers of sacrificing principle; what is forgotten is the sacrifice of Socialist objectives, not to mention human freedom and welfare, involved in a long period of impotent opposition. In any event, there is a profound difference between short-run attempts at vote-catching in the next election, and a long-run attempt to adapt the Party's attitudes in the light of wholly changed conditions. Revisionism, which after all was being preached in Britain long before the last election, is a long-term effort to enable the Labour Party to survive in mid–20th-century conditions.

It is, nevertheless, certain to be resented, for natural psychological reasons. The older party stalwart, brought up in the inter-war years to equate Socialism with the nationalisation of the means of production, feels lost and bewildered if deprived of this familiar mental sheet-anchor. The dogma of nationalisation informed and symbolised his early years of struggle; if he is asked to give it up, he feels that he is being asked to say that his whole political life, to which he sacrificed so much, was pointless and wasted. This feeling is wrong but natural. Again, some middle-class Socialists, to whom (as to converts in other fields) militancy and attachment to dogma are psychologically necessary, react to any suggestion of heterodoxy in a highly emotional and over-determined manner. Revisionism destroys the simplicity, the certainty, and the unquestioning conviction that come from having clear-cut crusading objectives to fight for, and a hated, easily-identified enemy to fight against. It makes everything complicated and ambiguous; it is an explicit admission that many of the old dreams are either realised or dead. No wonder it is resented—especially in the moment of defeat. Some of the more recent revisionists might have displayed a greater understanding of these inevitable human reactions.

Anti-revisionism is fortified in Britain by two special factors. The first is the dogged persistence of an underlying class antagonism. To the militant minority of British workers, much more than to German or Scandinavian or American workers, the employer is still, even if only subconsciously, "the class enemy"; and nationalisation, much more than high taxation or government controls or the strength of the Unions, symbolises the determination to defeat or extirpate him. To suggest that it is no longer the ultimate aim seems, to the militant worker, simply a betrayal of the class struggle; and matters are not improved when at the same time middle-class revisionists, by cavilling at the allegedly harmful working-class "image" of the Party, appear also to threaten his own social status and the validity of his instinctive class loyalties.

The other special factor is the extreme conservatism, common, alas, to most elements in British life, of the British working-class movement. The resistance to change (as I also found when trying to propagate radical reforms inside the Co-operative Movement) is sometimes stupendous. It is surely depressing, and would be true of no other country in the world, that a proposal to re-write a forty-year-old constitution should arouse such acute suspicion and resentment, even amongst some who like to think of themselves as radical. Traditionalism in Britain is no monopoly of the Right.

These are some of the reasons why Mr. Gaitskell, saying at Blackpool nothing more than Eduard Bernstein had said sixty years ago, found so many angry Kautskys in his audience. It was a curious irony; for, in the days of the original Revisionist controversy, Bernstein, suspected of having been seduced by the non-doctrinal anti-Marxist approach of the early Fabians, was accused by his traditionalist opponents of seeing the world "through English glasses."

"You have decided to be an Englishman—take the consequences and be·

come an Englishman [Karl Kautsky wrote to him in 1898]. The development which you have undergone . . . heads away from German Social Democracy, although not from Socialism. Try to achieve a place in the English movement and to become a representative of English Socialism." The wheel has turned full circle. Bernstein, were he alive to-day, would come under heavier fire in the British than in the German Socialist Movement; for the former, from being the most flexible and empirical, has become (at least if we were to judge by the vocal minority) the most conservative and fundamentalist in the world.

The most rational criticism of the "new" doctrine is as follows. Mr. Gaitskell, declaring at Blackpool that nationalisation was only a means and not a "Socialist first principle," attempted (correctly) to define Socialism in terms of certain social and ethical values. This attempt is criticised, generally on the grounds that many Liberals or "Bow-Group" Tories might assent to some of these ideals, and specifically on the grounds that to relegate nationalisation to a lower status is to destroy the most fundamental distinction between Socialists and their opponents.

The latter criticism, even if correct, seems rather belated. It implies that before the Blackpool speech the Labour Party was accustomed to making public ownership the primary issue at elections.

. . . . It is perfectly well known to anyone in touch with affairs that for many years past the Labour Party has not fought elections primarily on the issue of nationalisation. It has fought them rather on housing, education, social services, planning, the distribution of income, and foreign and colonial policy; and it has found no difficulty whatever in differentiating itself from the Conservatives.

However, it might still be objected (though most unplausibly) that these are only short-term issues of immediate popular concern. A Socialist party also needs to have clearly distinctive long-term aims; and the aims expressed by Mr. Gaitskell do not fulfil this condition since some of them would be acceptable to progressive opinion in other parties.

This criticism shows some forgetfulness of history. It has always been the case that an idealistic or forward-looking minority of non-Socialists has sympathised with, and even sought to further, some of the aims of the Socialist or militant working-class movements.

. . . . Indeed, some past definitions of Socialism, unlike Mr. Gaitskell's, have been so vague that almost anyone could have accepted them *in toto*. Who, for example, could decently reject Socialism if it consisted, as Sidney Webb maintained, of "the economic side of the democratic ideal"? Or if, as Shaw asserted in *Everybody's Political What's What*, "Socialism is . . . the economist's hatred of waste and disorder, the aesthete's hatred of ugliness and dirt, the lawyer's hatred of injustice, the saint's hatred of the seven deadly sins"? The same is true of many of the ethical formulations of Socialism. Keir Hardie, for example, wrote of Socialism as being "a form of social economy

very closely akin to the principles set forth in the Sermon on the Mount";
while Bruce Glasier, whose militancy was never in doubt, wrote that "Socialism is religion—that part of it that concerns the right state of our present
lives, the right state of our relations to our fellows, the right moral health of
our souls. Yet it may be better simply to say with William Morris that Socialism is fellowship." Such quotations, despite the distinction of their authors,
can no doubt be dismissed as being altogether too vague. But the fact remains
that even more explicit formulations of Socialist aims have always elicited
some sympathy from *some* non-Socialists. Indeed this must be the case. Socialism denotes a belief in the pre-eminence of certain values, such as equality
or co-operation or collective welfare or internationalism. But such values are
not absolute. They cannot be held rigidly and uncompromisingly, any more
than can the opposite conservative values of hierarchy or competition or individualism or patriotism. No normal Socialist is completely and exclusively
an egalitarian, denying all validity to all arguments for inequality; no normal
Conservative is completely and exclusively an individualist, denying all validity
to all arguments for collective action. The beliefs of each of us are a com-
pound, in proportions which vary along a spectrum from extreme Left to
extreme Right, of opposing sets of principles; and we are labelled Socialist or
Conservative according to which set predominates.

A Socialist, then, will seldom totally repudiate the theoretical validity of
all Conservative principles, or *vice versa;* but each will rate the other's values
much lower than his own, and hence will choose and act quite differently in
any given situation. It follows, however, and indeed is evident from the
historical examples quoted above, that there must inevitably be *some* common
ground between a statement of Socialist and one of progressive Conservative
beliefs.

The area of common ground, moreover, is likely to be greater to-day than
in the past. Opposing values are held in a more uncompromising form, the
more sharply society is divided into antagonistic social classes. A Marxist-type
class struggle polarises not only persons, but also personal beliefs; and everyone takes up the most extreme ideological position.

But of course class-conflict is not of this character in Britain to-day. The
lines of class-division are certainly more sharply etched than in many other
countries; but they are more blurred than they were a century ago. Outbursts
of class resentment still occur; but they no longer take the same prolonged,
embittered form. Economic prosperity and social security have softened the
acerbities of political conflict. Under the impact of democratic pressure and a
changing climate of opinion, Conservatives have come to accept a large measure
of liberal reform; and much of what the Left preached forty years ago is now
non-controversial. Under these circumstances, the militant language of class-
war, the terminology of revolt and counter-revolt, is (slowly) passing out of
usage. It would surely be incredible, in this more human society, if all the
items in a formulation of Socialist objectives aroused the total hostility of

every Liberal or progressive Tory. Most people would judge it a thoroughly good thing that they do not.

But it does not follow that because politics are now less bitter, therefore they are wholly drained of content: or because fisticuffs are now less common, therefore there is nothing left to fight about. The average Conservative (who is after all what matters), though he no longer harks back to mid-Victorian capitalism, still does not want the same sort of society as a Socialist does. He still gives an overwhelmingly high priority to his Right-wing principles; and he still has excellent reasons for wanting to see a Conservative Government returned. It is thus absurd to say that a moderate statement of Socialist aims, such as Mr. Gaitskell made at Blackpool, removes all fundamental differences between Left and Right: or that "there is nothing left of socialism" because nationalisation is demoted to a lower status. We need only consider some of the formulated aims to see how unlikely it is that the average Conservative would accept their implications.

First, the emphasis on social welfare. No one supposes that the Conservatives will suddenly dismantle the Welfare State, or utterly neglect the claims of the socially under-privileged groups. But equally one can hardly deny that a deep difference exists between the two parties about the priority to be accorded to social welfare. This is not because Conservatives are necessarily less humanitarian, but because they hold particular views as to the proper rôle of the State, the desirable level of taxation, and the importance of private as opposed to collective responsibility. Their willingness for social expenditure is circumscribed by these views; and the consequence is a quite different order of priorities.

Secondly, the aim of "an equitable distribution of wealth," related not to the accidents of birth but to individual effort and ability. This might sound an innocuous principle, to which anyone could say amen. In fact it has, in Britain, the most radical implications. This is because inherited property is an exceptionally important influence in Britain on the distribution of wealth. The application of this apparently non-controversial principle would therefore require a determined attack on large-scale inheritance. This a Conservative, though he is willing somewhat to mitigate existing inequalities, cannot countenance; for it offends against his views of the rôle of the family, the proper level of taxation, the rights of property, the need for large personal savings, and the importance of tradition and continuity in our national life. And quite apart from inheritance, there are, and always will be, deep differences between Right and Left as to what constitutes a desirable distribution of wealth.

Thirdly, the ideal of the "classless society." I do not discuss here what meaning can properly be attached to this concept, as I have done so at length elsewhere. It suffices to say that Britain could be made a great deal more "classless" than it is to-day, but that this would entail a major reform of the private sector of education (and notably of the "public" schools). This again most Conservatives would not countenance; for it would offend against their beliefs about the rights of the moneyed individual, the importance of social hierarchy, and the value of a national élite. Generally, it seems absurd to maintain that most Conservatives favour the same pattern of class-relations as most Socialists.

Fourthly, "the fundamental equality of all races and all peoples." This is no doubt an ambiguous phrase, to which some (though by no means all) Conservatives might pay lip-service. But anyone who thinks there is no reality behind it, and that debates about Suez and Nyasaland reflect only day-to-day tactical disagreements and not profound differences of feeling and principle, must be living in a rather remote world. A belief in racial equality and the rule of law runs deep in the blood of active Socialists (though not of all their working-class supporters). The typical Conservative, by contrast, if he holds such beliefs at all, will constantly subordinate them to deeply-felt emotions about national prestige or the British Empire or the rights of white settlers.

Fifthly, there are contrasting views, though they were not very clearly expressed in Mr. Gaitskell's speech, about the proper dividing-line between the public and private spheres of responsibility. This difference, which runs like a thread through much of our political debate, manifests itself in innumerable ways—over the proportion of the national income to be devoted to communal services, over the division between private and public capital expenditure, and increasingly in the field of what is loosely called town and country planning. This latter subject may well become the dominant issue of the 1960's. We are gradually waking up to the fact that both our cities and our countryside are horribly threatened—by the growth of traffic, by speculative metropolitan office-building, by the steady encroachment of suburban housing on the countryside, and aesthetically by the low architectural standard of most new building. Whether we stave off the threat, or succumb to it, will depend on how far the country is willing to sacrifice private interests and unregulated liberty to social control and Government initiative. There will be only too much to divide the Socialist from the Conservative in this field.

But at this point Socialists must beware. They may justly attack the vulgar bias towards unregulated private interest which is one of the characteristics of our prosperous society. They must not, however, attack this society root and branch. Simply to dismiss it as "evil" and "rotten," as some Left-wing speakers did at Blackpool, is not only electorally imbecile; it betrays an arrogant indifference, possible only amongst bourgeois Chelsea *literati,* to the lives and fears and hopes of ordinary people.

Surprisingly enough, ordinary people like to be materially well-off. And any normal Socialist will wholeheartedly rejoice at the spread of material affluence—on grounds of personal freedom, since rising standards widen the area of choice and opportunity; on grounds of social justice, which surely requires that the masses should now also be admitted to the world of material ease which others have so long enjoyed: on general egalitarian grounds, since rising consumption increases both the fact and consciousness of social equality: and on grounds of democratic anti-paternalism, since this is clearly what the workers want. And anyone who tells them they are wrong, and that they are simply becoming vulgarised or Americanised, will rightly be given short shrift. Generally, people enjoying an above-average standard of living should be chary of admonishing the masses on the perils of material wealth.

A Socialist should never be distinguished as one who thus admonishes. He should, however, certainly be distinguished as one who deplores the present division between public and private spending, the present balance between public interest and pursuit of private profit, and generally the cultural values presently being disseminated by commercial television and the Beaverbrook press. On this last point, some Labour politicians are perhaps open to criticism; no doubt from a laudable desire to dissociate themselves from the doctrines both of puritanism and the class-war, they are in danger of adjusting rather too completely to the social and cultural values ruling to-day.

One could list still other major Left-Right issues: aid to the under-developed areas, protection of the consumer against large-scale producing interests, the achievement (still far away) of real equality of educational opportunity, the degree of planning, and the liberty of the subject—in addition, of course, to the rôle of public ownership. But it is surely already obvious that Mr. Gaitskell, when he defined Socialism in terms other than the nationalisation of all the means of production, did not somehow spirit away all differences between Socialists and their opponents. These differences are, happily, mitigated as compared with half-a-century ago; and one should not exaggerate them merely to stage a mock political battle or create a Parliamentary fracas. But no one who examines the real implications of Mr. Gaitskell's formulation, or even sits through an average sample of Parliamentary debates, could possibly suppose that nothing except public ownership divides the two political parties.

If British Socialism succeeds in adapting itself and its doctrines to the mid–20th-century, it will still find plenty of genuine battles left to fight. Besides, it might even get back into power, and have a chance to win them.

5.

A sharp rebuttal to Mr. Crosland's article was promptly delivered by one of the leading figures in the Labour party's left wing, Richard Crossman. Like his rival, Mr. Crossman was educated at Oxford and taught there for several years before the war. He has been a member of the House of Commons since 1945, and was for almost two decades on the editorial staff of the left-wing Labourite weekly *The New Statesman and Nation*. He has written a number of books on philosophy and politics. In the article reprinted below, Mr. Crossman insists that socialism must cling to its ancient birthright if it is to retain its meaning and identity.

CROSSMAN: The Spectre of Revisionism *

> A spectre is haunting Europe—the spectre
> of Revisionism. Mr. Gaitskell is not alone.

How characteristic that Mr. Anthony Crosland should start his pronunciamento in last month's *Encounter* by a facetious comparison with Karl Marx! His bantering allusion to the *Communist Manifesto* expresses pretty faithfully the mixture of Bohemian flippancy and economic punditry with which he has been conducting his campaign for modernising the Labour Party. Mr. Crosland concluded his book, *The Future of Socialism,* with a plea that British Socialists should cease to be drab and should cultivate gaiety and liveliness. It is ironical that the effect of his Revisionist Manifesto has been to plunge us back into a dreary doctrinal argument which is depressing the Labour Party and boring the general public to distraction.

The most recent definition of Revisionism was given by Mr. Crosland in last month's *Encounter*. "The Labour Party should have one overriding aim over the next three years: to adapt itself, without in any way surrendering basic principles, to the realities of social change, and to present itself to the electorate in a mid–20th-century guise."

But what form should the adaptation take and what should be the guise— or disguise—in which the Labour Party should represent itself in the 1960's? I have read and re-read *The Future of the Left* and can only discover one concrete proposal, a revision of the Party Constitution in order to remove any suggestion that it is committed either to wholesale nationalisation or to further nationalisation of whole industries. Mr. Crosland has no difficulty in showing that practically the whole leadership of the Labour Party—including Mr. Bevan, Mrs. Castle, Mr. Mikardo, and myself—has long since avowedly abandoned wholesale nationalisation as an objective. But he believes that the Party militants still blindly adhere to it, largely owing to the influence of "the Left-wing leaders who intellectually accept a mixed economy but still cling to the dogma of wholesale public ownership." These Left-wing leaders, according to Mr. Crosland, can rely on the wording of the Party Constitution because "the extremist phraseology of the Party's formal aims bears no relation to the moderate practical content of its short-term programme." And so he reaches his conclusion that the Constitution must be re-written and that anyone who opposes this is suffering from "schizophrenia."

Alas! The "fact" on which his whole argument depends is an un-fact. The "extremist phraseology" of the Party Constitution quite simply does not exist. Here is the actual wording of the relevant clause.

Clause IV—Party Objects

(4) To secure for the workers by hand or by brain the full fruits of their industry and the most equitable distribution thereof that may be possible, upon the basis of

* Richard H. S. Crossman, "The Spectre of Revisionism," *Encounter*, XIV (April 1960), 24–28. Reprinted by permission of the author and of the editors of *Encounter*.

the common ownership of the means of production, distribution, and exchange, and the best obtainable system of popular administration and control of each industry or service.

The more I study this formula, the more admiration I feel for Sidney Webb and Arthur Henderson, who drafted it in 1918. At the Blackpool Conference Mr. Gaitskell urged us to distinguish Socialist ends from Socialist means and to recognise nationalisation as a means. This is just what Clause 4 does. First it distinguishes the Socialist end—the end of exploitation and the most equitable distribution of the fruits of our labours—from the organisation of the economy through which this can best be accomplished. Next it defines the two essential features of the Socialist economy which alone can achieve the Socialist end of equitable distribution. The first of these features is not nationalisation but common ownership, and to this is added a second—"the best obtainable system of popular administration and control"—a rather vague phrase, which at least rejects as non-Socialist the kind of nationalised Board, responsible neither to Parliament nor to its workers, which was set up by the Attlee Government. I can see that Mr. Herbert Morrison, whose brainchild these Boards were, could object to Clause 4 as it stands. But Mr. Crosland's case for re-writing it falls, for the conclusive reason that this clause does not commit Labour either to wholesale nationalisation or to further nationalisation of whole industries and contains none of the "extremist phraseology" which he strangely attributes to it.

Must we be content, therefore, with the Party's present attitude to nationalisation? On the contrary, we should find a new and radical approach to this topic, based on a ruthless critique of the nationalisation undertaken by the Attlee Government. For the public discredit into which public ownership has fallen is very largely due to the disregard of Socialist principle with which whole industries have been subjected to management by remote, centralised Boards, which Parliament is expressly forbidden to investigate or control. Unfortunately, before 1945, the Labour Party had done very little advanced planning and there were no blueprints ready, showing how the industries due for nationalisation were to be organised. Since the detailed job of applying Socialism to the coalmines, the railways, etc., was left to the civil servants in the Ministries, it is hardly surprising that what we got were not socialised industries but centralised, bureaucratic State monopolies. The nationalised Board—neither a public enterprise responsible to Parliament nor yet an efficient profit-making monopoly—is a hybrid, neither fish nor fowl. It can be made to work fairly satisfactorily in certain public services, such as gas, electricity, and atomic energy. But it is a monstrous burden on most productive industries. So the proper way to counter public hostility to nationalisation is not to re-write Clause 4 but to admit frankly the dreadful mistakes made by the Attlee Government and then to work out precise proposals for nationalising the nationalised industries, decentralising their oligarchies and subjecting them to full public control.

It would be silly to imagine, however, that, having disposed of the case for revising Clause 4, one has finished with Revisionism. The influence Mr. Crosland wields—far greater outside than inside the Labour Party—derives less from his particular proposals than from his new philosophy of Socialism—or, if you prefer it, his revised "Social Democratic" outlook. This has been received enthusiastically by the whole press, including the Top People who write *The Times, The Guardian,* and *The Economist.* Among non-Socialists, indeed, there is virtual unanimity that, unless his ideas are accepted by the Labour leadership—not so much as a specific body of concrete proposals but as a general philosophy of life—the outlook for the Labour Party is dim.

What exactly is Mr. Crosland's up-to-date Socialism? The attempt to summarise a view with which one disagrees is always dangerous. I have tried, however, to be scrupulously fair in listing what seem to me the essential features of his Revisionism.

(1) *Economic.* Since full employment can now be maintained by regulating a free-enterprise system, the old-fashioned Socialist analysis of the contradictions of capitalism is no longer valid. Socialists must now admit the Government won the election because they successfully maintained both full employment and stable prices, as well as achieving a rapid increase in living standards, contrasted with the austerity of life under the Labour Government. The only safe assumption is that the next election will be fought under at least as favorable, if not more favorable, economic conditions.

(2) *Social.* Rising living standards are rapidly undermining the class-conscious solidarity which used to cement the Labour Movement. More and more workers dislike business-men less than they dislike trade union leaders, and vote Conservative because they don't want to feel themselves members of the working class.

(3) *Electoral.* One result of increasing prosperity is to reduce the real differences between the two big parties and so to make it even more important to present the right image to the electorate. To regain working-class votes, Labour must remove the image of austerity and the fear that a Labour Government would upset the prosperity people are now enjoying. With these obstacles out of the way, the swing of the pendulum should bring it to office.

(4) *International.* Socialist doubts about revisionism should be removed by the knowledge that most members of the Socalist International, including the Dutch, Swedes, Swiss, Austrians, and Germans—not to mention the Australians, New Zealanders, and the CCF in Canada—have all accepted the new philosophy. It is a sign of insularity that the British Labour Party is "a bit to the rear of the column."

Let me admit at once that Revisionism faithfully reflects the political mood of Britain during the last eight years. But is it an adequate Socialist philosophy for the decade which lies ahead? Mr. Crosland is impatient of anyone who even asks the question. He is sure that we must dismiss the idea of the coming crisis, accept the Affluent Society, and try to make it more just and equitable. It is here that we part company. I believe that we must give warning of the crisis ahead and condemn the Affluent Society as incapable of coping with it. I also believe that, by preaching this austere doctrine now, when its apparent irrelevance makes us unpopular, we shall win public confidence as history goes our way.

There are two reasons why I hold this view. One is practical and concerned with electoral tactics. The other is theoretical and concerned with the shape of things to come.

Assume for the moment that the Revisionist predictions are correct—by 1964 people will be even more prosperous and contented than they are to-day. In these circumstances Mr. Crosland expects Labour to win, if only it will remove from its image those distasteful features—including the commitment to further nationalisation—which prevent the swing of the pendulum. This hope seems to me to be based on a misjudgment of the electorate and a mis-reading of history. What we have seen since the beginning of the century has not been an in-and-out of two big parties, as the pendulum swings to and fro, but long periods of Right-wing rule, with an occasional swing to the Left when something goes badly wrong. As a nation, we normally accept the Tory Establishment and only put the Left into power when it is time for a big change. Mr. Crosland assumes this condemns us to "impotent op-position." Oh dear! how can he fail to see that in a period of complacent prosperity, a vigorous Socialist Opposition will have far more power for good than a weak Labour Government with a small majority.

There is another factor to be considered. Leaders seek to change the inmost nature of their parties at dire peril. The Labour Party was founded as a movement of moral protest, which denounced the capitalist *status quo* and preached the need for a Socialist transformation of society. To tell our party workers that the need for a Socialist transformation has been eliminated, and that the leadership must now show it can manage a mixed economy as well as the Tories, will destroy the morale of the rank-and-file without regain-ing the confidence of the electorate. Those who believe that what the country needs is an alternative Government, as distinct from a radical Opposition, should found a new party or revive Liberalism.

One of the curious features of the present controversy is that the leading Revisionists—Mr. Crosland, Mr. Roy Jenkins, and Mr. Douglas Jay—are all professional economists of note. Yet the expert advice they have proffered since last October has been almost exclusively concerned with mass psychology, electoral tactics, and propaganda techniques. This at least disproves the accusa-tion that economists are "desiccated calculating machines!" As an old-time professional propagandist, however, I am scared stiff by the obsession they reveal with the techniques of "winning friends and influencing people." Mr. Crosland, for example, tells us that the "one overriding aim of the Labour Party over the next three years should be to adapt itself . . . and to present itself in a mid–20th-century guise." *"The one overriding aim."* If there is one thing I learnt from five years of psychological warfare, it is that the best propaganda consists in apparently doing no propaganda at all. An Opposition which spent three years in dolling itself up to woo the electorate would condemn itself to certain defeat. The voters would learn to despise it and its members would lose their last shred of self-respect. What makes Revisionism a vote-loser is its obsession with winning votes.

How, then, should the Opposition conduct itself in these next four years? The best way to regain the confidence of the British people is, first of all, to regain our own self-respect. Instead of veering with every gust of popular opinion; instead of watering down policies in order to paper over differences inside the Party or avoid offending an important interest; instead of pulling punches for fear of upsetting the Establishment; instead of behaving as the public contemptuously expects every politician to behave—instead of all this, we should make ourselves thoroughly unpopular by harrying the Establishment, warning the country of the troubles that lie ahead, and showing how they can only be overcome by a further advance towards Socialism. The best way for an Opposition to survive a period of unpopularity is to stand by its principles—in the confidence that history will prove it right.

Having dealt with the practical objections to Revisionism, I must now turn to consider its theoretical inadequacies. If we were to see the world through Mr. Crosland's eyes, would this help us to understand the post-war era and anticipate the shape of things to come?

In order to adapt our Socialism to the mid–20th-century, we need first and foremost a new critique—a successor to *Das Kapital*—which expounds the working of the new, regulated capitalist economies and exposes their new inadequacies and contradictions. Naturally, anyone who undertakes this task will be attacked, as Karl Marx was, by every banker and economic pundit. Nevertheless, the job has been started—in this country by Thomas Balogh and in America by John Kenneth Galbraith, author of *The Affluent Society*. What saddens me about Mr. Crosland is that, instead of joining in the assault on economic orthodoxy, he seems to be advising the Labour Party to come to terms with it. Whereas, for example, *The Affluent Society* mercilessly exposes the vulgarity, the wastefulness, the incompetence, and the inherent contradictions of Western capitalism, Mr. Crosland's *The Future of Socialism* is chiefly concerned to emphasise its stability and strength. He also seems strangely unaware of the threat to freedom presented by the irresponsible concentrations of power which characterise the modern oligopoly.

My second criticism of Mr. Crosland's outlook is that, although he dubs the rest of us "insular," he himself displays a most curious provincialism. In the whole of *The Future of the Left* there is no mention of what is happening outside the North Atlantic area, apart from vague references to aid for underdeveloped areas and colonial equality. He talks a great deal about the stability of the post-war economy and the increase in national wealth under the Tories since 1951, but does not mention that this latter has been mainly caused by a fortunate improvement of our terms of trade. As a result of these gaps in his analysis, he sees only the negative factors which have caused public ownership to become increasingly unpopular since 1945, and completely overlooks the new factors which may completely change that attitude in the next ten years. Mr. Crosland urges the Labour Party to follow the example of the Dutch, Swedish, Swiss, Austrian, and West German Socialists. What he does not mention is that the Swedish Socialist Party—after a long bout of Revisionism—faces the gravest crisis in its history and that the Austrians have for fifteen years shared power quite happily with their anti-Socialist opponents, while the Dutch, the Swedes, the Swiss, and the Germans are minority parties, without any real hope of ever carrying out a Socialist programme.

What strikes me is Mr. Crosland's failure to observe the terrifying contrast between the drive and missionary energy displayed by the Communist bloc and the lethargic, comfortable indolence of the Western democracies. Revisionism assumes that the expansion of our Affluent Society will continue at a comfortable pace, until gradually the whole world, including Soviet Russia, has accepted its values and admitted that a nation's greatness is measured by the number of washing-machines and motor-cars per head of population. I suggest we should make a very different assumption—that the whole Western world will face a grave crisis as the balance of power shifts and the countries which rely on planning and nationalisation catch up on our rich and easy-going economies.

Mr. Crosland rightly sees that this crisis is unlikely to take the old-fashioned form of mass unemployment—and wrongly concludes that there will be no crisis at all. Thus he fails to observe both the new conflict and the new solutions, such as have already emerged under de Gaulle since the collapse of the Fourth Republic and such as may well recur in India when Nehru dies.

At present the American Administration and the British Government are nearly as complacent and blind to these new factors as Mr. Crosland himself. But history will force them on our attention, as the Communist countries demonstrate with ever increasing force the efficiency of nationalisation. Progressively year by year we shall see that, judged in terms of national security, scientific and technological development, popular education, and, finally, even of mass living standards, free enterprise is losing out in the peaceful competition between East and West. It would be strange indeed for the Labour Party to abandon its belief in the central importance of public ownership at the precise moment when the superiority of socialised economies is being triumphantly vindicated in world affairs.

The Tories have an obvious reply. They say that the Kremlin's brutal power derives not from public ownership but from the one-party State. A dictator can boost defence and welfare services at the cost of personal consumption. But this is an excuse which no Socialist can accept. To concede that dictatorship is intrinsically more efficient than democracy is to admit defeat before the race begins. Indeed, our whole Democratic Socialist case is surely based on the contention that those who combine planning *and* free choice, social discipline *and* civil liberty, a strong Executive *and* independent justice, are not only better but stronger than their totalitarian adversaries. I fully realise that, for some time to come, abandonment of public ownership will be urged upon the Labour Party by all the best people; and that those who predict a crisis of Western democracy and warn that it can only be cured by a radical advance towards Socialism will make many enemies in a political climate as complacent and short-sighted as that of the 1930's. But they are the kind of enemies the Labour Party needs to make if it is to become once again a fighting Opposition.

A few words, in conclusion, about the background and the probable outcome of the Revisionist controversy. When Mr. Hugh Gaitskell took over from Mr. Clement Attlee, the Labour Party had been tearing itself to pieces for several years. So the new Leader decided to staunch its wounds with twelve wads of Socialist re-thinking, each packed into a bulky policy document. We all agreed to stop the abstract Left-Right argument about public ownership and instead to seek agreement on practical measures which a Labour Government could carry out if elected to power. Both Gaitskellites and Bevanites showed a surprising readiness to make concessions of abstract principle and accept practical compromises in order to achieve a workable agreement.

The result of this cessation of doctrinal feuding was highly beneficial. We not only evolved a policy for the next Labour Government and a programme for the general election; we also began to heal those personal hatreds and clique rivalries which had been turning the word "comrade" into a term of abuse. To the surprise of its friends as well as its opponents, the Labour Party last autumn went into the election campaign with a united leadership and a volunteer organisation more numerous and more enthusiastic than at any time since 1945. Even the unexpected extent of the Tory victory did not impair either the prestige Mr. Gaitskell had richly earned during the campaign or the renewed fervour of those who had flocked to support him.

It is against this background that we must view the decision of the Revisionists that the morrow of defeat was the right moment to call for a retreat from nationalisation. Mr. Crosland is either very innocent or a little disingenuous when he expresses surprise that his own, Mr. Jay's, and Mr. Jenkins' declarations caused such a furore. Did they really believe that steel nationalisation would be joyfully jettisoned by rank-and-file Socialists as soon as Mr. Jay gave the word? Did they seriously assume that, by applying shock tactics in the moment of defeat, they could jerk the wheels of the party machine into Revisionist ruts? If they did, they must be sadly disconcerted by what happened. The Labour Party was shocked not into an acceptance of their proposals but into a cold, frustrated anger at the prospect of another long, dreary period of doctrinal feuding. Since then the Revisionists have been hastily retreating towards orthodoxy. In their flight they have jettisoned nearly all their concrete proposals, until, as we have seen, all that remains of their programme is the single proposition that Clause 4 of the Constitution should be revised.

If Mr. Crosland is right and Revisionism is indeed "a spectre haunting Europe," it looks as though in Britain it is a ghost that will be laid without too much trouble.

6.

The *Encounter* debate over socialism's prospects quickly became international in scope. The American sociologist Daniel Bell came to the support of Mr. Crosland's revisionist position, but suggested that the argument ought to be pushed a step further. He called attention to the growing importance of questions of economic growth and planning, as distinct from mere distribution, and underlined the sociological changes of the contemporary era that are altering class relationships. Mr. Bell, born and educated in New York City, spent ten years as labor editor of *Fortune* magazine, and is presently professor of sociology at Columbia University.

BELL: The Future of the Left *

Socialist theory, in its analysis of contemporary society, has usually been relatively hard-headed and complex, even when wrong, but in its vision of the future simplistic and naïve. "The government of persons is replaced by the administration of things." This was Engels' "magical" formula for the meaning of socialism. "To organise the whole national economy like the postal system . . . this is our immediate aim," wrote Lenin in *State and Revolution*. And, continuing, he portrayed the problem of running the State as simply one of "registering, filing, and checking . . . so simplified and reduced . . . [as] to be quite within the reach of every literate person." And so the fates of millions were committed to utopian fantasies.

It is to Mr. Crosland's enormous credit that in his studies of the "future" of Socialism and of the Left he tries to be more hard-headed and realistic. But Mr. Crosland is not only a student, but a politician, and sometimes the political constraints bind too tightly, which is the case, I think, in his *Encounter* article. He does not go far enough with the implications of his case. Let me try and push the argument.

Socialism has been singularly a *distributivist* doctrine. It presumed (the texts are overwhelming and need not be cited) that capitalism had solved all problems of production (at least the "forces" of production) and the remaining issues were ones of social justice. Its emphasis was, therefore, on "equality." Mr. Crosland continues that tradition, and rightly so, in his pleas for greater social and educational equality in British life. But there remains, to confound Marx and the early Keynes, the problem of *growth*. The economic questions are no longer those of the thirties—how to maintain *effective demand*. We know now how to do it. The key questions are how to maintain and speed economic growth—within the framework of personal freedom and without incurring inflation.

That problem, unfortunately, runs the risk of being obscured by new sloganising. Mr. Michael Foot, in addressing himself to that issue, in a recent

* Daniel Bell, "The Future of the Left," *Encounter*, XIV (May 1960), 59–61. Reprinted by permission of the author and of the editors of *Encounter*.

number of *Spectator,* says simply that the Russians have shown the way—by *planning.* But that is not really true. The Russians, until recently, have not planned, but *mobilised,* which is a very different thing. Their techniques were quite primitive and often quite wasteful. What they did was no different from the mobilisation techniques of the British Ministry of Supply during World War II, or the U.S. War Production Board from 1943 to 1945. By concentrating on a few key objectives, and by pouring large investment sums into a few areas, the Soviet Union was able to mobilise its natural resources and manpower to build a large industrial base. But the so-called "Method of Balances" which the Soviets presumably used for allocation purposes was simply a statement of over-all outputs and inputs with no specific details about the simultaneous balancing of thousands of different products. And enormous waste did result from such procedures. Only now, when consumers are able to demand *wide varieties* of goods, and when shifts of resources may have to be made to accommodate *different* demands, will the Russians confront the kind of economic problems that Western countries have faced in the last decades.

The questions of planning and growth are, thus, still before us; and the answers are still open ones. It may be that the technical sophistication of post-Keynesian economics—the "input-output" models of Leontieff and similar theoretical advances—does provide us with more viable tools. But these can only be employed, as tools, within a framework of policy, and this, so far as Labour is concerned, is largely undefined. Or rather the definitions apply to other problems: Mr. Crosland, in his essay, was seeking to differentiate "left" from "right" along the axis of "equality"; and this may be a valid differentiation. But the problems of the "future" of the "Left," as well as the "future" of Britain (or America, or Russia) have to be specified in other terms: the nature of economic incentives, of social motivations ("meaning" in work), of restrictionist practices (in part, the habits of trade unions), and a range of similar concerns.

The key social group in all these matters is the rising class of technicians, engineers, administrative, and managerial employees, who while not a numerical (or electoral) majority are the "ginger" group of the technical society. Just as the industrial worker (although not the majority of the early capitalist society) created the social problems of the past hundred years, so the new technical classes will set the problems of the new decades. Their recruitment, their education, their culture, their élan, their desires, become crucial for the health and growth of the society. And inevitably the social politics of a country (although not always the electoral issues) will revolve about them. I think that Mr. Crosland, in his *Encounter* essay, neglects these structural changes in the character of modern society, and their consequences.

There is, I think, one other, political-ideological change which Mr. Crosland inadequately confronts: the fact that the socialist movements of Western Europe (or more narrowly, Scandinavia, Germany, Austria, the Low countries and Britain, the countries of "revisionism") have become since World War II a part of the fabric of their societies in a way which was never true before 1939. Orthodox socialist theory never could really conceive the possibility of tinkering with and transforming the social structure of their countries, particularly through economic techniques, or more specifically through fiscal policy. Marxian dogmatics was posed in "all-or-none" terms: capitalism or socialism. The consequence was that when Labour governments took power in England (Ramsay MacDonald) and Germany (Muller and Hilferding) because of the social and political collapses in these countries, the Socialist governments had no concrete *economic* policies to meet the crises. Both Hilferding and Mac-Donald resorted to the most orthodox and conservative economic policies (budget-cutting, gold-hoarding, etc.) with disastrous deflationary consequences. To this extent, Keynes was not only the reformer of capitalism but the transformer of socialism. The consequences of this are most apparent in Scandinavia where the Social Democratic governments have gone furthest in the utilisation of fiscal techniques for social purposes. But this has produced not only a change in the politico-ideological atmosphere, but in the social structure as well. The traditions, once so strong (and in Britain as well), that the working-class boy does not seek to rise out of and "desert his class" are fading. The changes in the educational structure, produced by the need for new technical education and by the breakdown of old class-feeling, begin to transform the society as well. Recently the Copenhagen labour press changed its name from *Social Demokraten* to *Aktuelt* (The News), in order to hold its circulation. With the growth in productivity rather than collective bargaining setting the limits of further material improvement, the trade union has begun to lose most of its old functions. These are now "immanent" tendencies in Western society, and Britain is not wholly exempt from these.

7.

The startling decision of the German Socialist party to burn most if its old idols and to risk a new kind of appeal to the voters has been incisively ana- lyzed by one of the ablest foreign correspondents in Germany, F. R. Allemann. Formerly a Swiss journalist in Bonn, Mr. Allemann has more recently become editor of the Berlin periodical *Der Monat*. In the article reprinted below, Mr. Allemann explains the complex motives behind this doctrinal revolution, and the long intraparty struggle that preceded the victory of the revisionists. Although his reaction is sympathetic, he raises a crucial question: will the new line deprive German socialism of its emotional appeal?

ALLEMANN: Farewell to Marx *

The point about party programmes is that they are rarely taken seriously. The electors do not take them seriously because they never read such ponderous documents anyway; the politicians, once they are in power, usually base their policies more on solid concrete interests than ideological maxims.

* F. R. Allemann, "Farewell to Marx," *Encounter* (March 1960), 67–69. Reprinted by permission of the author and of the editors of *Encounter*.

But there are exceptions to every rule. The German social-democracy is a "programme party" of the first water: in its history of nearly a hundred years it has always attached the greatest importance to basing its policy on a solid system of principles laid down in a fixed programme rather than merely on the urgent issues of the moment. In this respect at least it has remained true to its Marxist tradition: in its view any political action that is intended to influence and transform society must be based on an analysis of that society. But since social conditions are never static but subject to constant change, Social Democrats are repeatedly compelled to re-interpret a new reality in their programme.

It is only in this context that it is possible to understand their new "programme of principles" which was recently adopted in Bad Godesberg by an overwhelming majority at a specially convened Party Congress. It marks the final break of the great German opposition party with the fundamental tenets of Marxism. It is not only that the name of Karl Marx and the concept of Marxism are missing from the declaration of principles which has now become binding on the party; words like "class" and "class struggle" are also carefully avoided in the document. The notion that the working class acts as the "grave-digger of capitalism" and that it is destined, by overthrowing capitalist class-society, to bring about the classless society—this optimistic basic idea of the theory that pretentiously described itself as "scientific socialism" has now been thrown by the German Social Democrats on to the scrap-heap of utopias.

At the same time, the transfer of the means of production to common ownership, which has hitherto represented the essence of every socialist programme, has been stripped of its overriding importance. It is true that common ownership will continue to be recognised as a "legitimate form of public control," but the analysis no longer centres on property as such but on "economic power" which must be restrained by subjection to "public control."

The consequences which follow from this new outlook are very far-reaching. It is probably the first time that a socialist party has admitted explicitly that the private ownership of the means of production is entitled to "protection and promotion"—"insofar as it does not hinder the construction of an equitable social order." This means that the SPD has dropped the idea that socialism requires the nationalisation of the whole of industry, not only "for the time being" but as a matter of principle.

And it has abandoned just as deliberately the aim of subjecting the whole economy to strict central planning: the Social Democratic Party, we are now told, "accepts the free market, where-ever there is real competition." The basic formula is now "as much competition as possible—as much planning as necessary" and the SPD now not only describes free consumer-choice and the free choice of place of employment as "all-important foundations" but also regards free competition and the entrepreneurial initiative as "important elements of social democratic economic policy."

This does not mean that the German Left has made its peace with the existing social order. But it does mean that it has given up the attempt to organise the extremely complicated texture of a modern industrial society on the basis of a single uniform principle. The economic pattern of the future which it now has in mind is a balanced economy in which the private-profit motive is assigned its due place but in which the State is set the task of preventing, by a variety of methods, of which the nationalisation of large industrial complexes is one, the private-profit motive leading to the accumulation of tremendous profits in private hands and the consequent concentration of economic power which is capable of influencing the political sphere. "The control of great economic power is . . . the central task of a libertarian economic policy" are the words used in the section on "Property and Power" which really constitutes the essence of the new programme.

At the same time, however, the events of recent decades have made the German Social Democrats realise that this problem of economic power cannot be disposed of by simply transferring power from private hands into the hands of the State. They have come to see that being dependent on an uncontrollable state bureaucracy is not necessarily better than being dependent on a private capitalist. They therefore maintain that "there are dangers in all concentrations of economic power, even in the hands of the State." The conclusions drawn from this consideration have, however, been laid down in very general and somewhat vague terms: common ownership is to be "organised according to the principles of self-government and decentralisation"; in the organisations by which it is administered "the interests of the workers and employees must be represented just as much as the public interest and that of the consumers." Furthermore, the SPD declares that it is its aim to create conditions "in which everyone can as a free agent make his own fortune from a rising income"; eventually, the Party regards such fortune-making as a certain—though necessarily limited—counterpoise to the individual's increasing dependence on anonymous social forces. Here—and not only here—the Social Democrat programme has points of contact with certain ideas of a reformed, socially disciplined liberalism. That is probably inevitable if the basic problem is seen as the establishment of a free society which is neither dominated by large-scale capitalism nor one in which the individual is degraded to the position of a mere cog in a coercive state machine. This libertarian approach leads to the wholesale rejection of any idea of coming to terms with the communists. The attitude to democracy has also undergone a corresponding change. The SPD has always been a democratic party—and often enough *the* democratic party in Germany. But whereas it formerly regarded democracy merely as a stage to socialism, it has now come to consider the democratic form of government as having value in itself, as an end in itself and not merely a means to an end. For anyone who lived through the Hitler period or is now engaged in unremitting altercation with the communism which has established its rule in a part of his own country, can no longer regard the democratic state as a merely "transitional" stage.

But the belief in a plural society cannot of course be restricted to economics and politics on their own; those who assent to the activity of various and even contrary forces in economic and political life, will be bound to fight all forms of regimentation and co-ordination in the cultural sphere. Hence the programme deliberately refrains from proclaiming "ultimate truths": neither the state nor a political party should have any power in the field of religious and philosophical principles. Here again we see the same basic characteristic which informs the whole programme: deliberate modesty and restraint. Marxism set out both "to interpret" and "to change the world." The German Social Democrats of today make no claim to provide a universally valid philosophy nor do they believe any longer that their policy is in accord with irrevocable laws of social dynamics. There are probably still many conscious (and even more unconscious) Marxists in their ranks. But they form a minority. The majority are wholly concerned with the problem of so continuing to develop this society that it can be called "wholly of man." The German Left still has a strong conviction that it is on the side of progress, but it is tempered by an unmistakable feeling of scepticism towards all exaggerated, and therefore dangerous, schemes of utopia.

It would certainly be wrong to see nothing but sturdy electoral opportunism behind the new programme. No doubt, three lost elections in which the conservative forces of the Federal Republic have become increasingly strong, have greatly contributed to this change of outlook. Like the British Labour Party, the SPD has had to face the fact that the traditional mythos of the Labour movement has lost its force in modern affluent society.

In fact, the discussion which for the time being the Godesberg Programme has brought to an end, was already begun in 1953. In the general elections of that year Dr. Adenauer's Christian Democratic Union, which four years previously had only eked out a bare plurality over the Social Democrats, gained an absolute majority in Parliament, thereby becoming the first party to do so in German history (a feat which even the Nazis failed to achieve, at least in free elections). The shock set the forces in motion which have now gained the upper hand in the SPD; the discussion lasted six years.

But the fact that the debate, sometimes conducted in public, sometimes behind the scenes, has lasted so long shows the strength of the opposition with which the zealous party-reformers had to contend. It needed the renewed electoral defeat of 1957 to secure their final victory. This was due above all to the fact that the central core of German Social Democracy is incomparably more "conservative" and more closely connected with the old traditions of the working-class movement than is its fringe: the 600,000 Party members find it incomparably more difficult to free themselves from traditional formulae and ideas than do the millions of voters; above all, the official cadre on whose ardour and devotion the solid strength of the Party really depends, is distinguished from the mass of the membership by a special brand of ingrained Left-conservatism. When, therefore, in 1953 for the first time leading figures from the ranks of Socialist Parliamentarians came forward with the idea that the Party should cast the "old ballast" overboard and turn itself from a party of the working class into a more broadly-based *"Volkspartei,"* it did not look as if their attack had the slightest chance of succeeding. At the Berlin Party Conference of 1954 the Left-wing (consisting of Marxist, pacifist, anti-militaristic elements) was still counter-attacking successfully and the leading spokesman of the "Reform Group," Professor Carlo Schmid (the Deputy Speaker of the Bundestag and a powerful orator), Fritz Erler (the brilliant defence and foreign policy expert), and Willy Brandt (later to become Lord Mayor of Berlin), seemed to be in the position of hopeless outsiders. But it was from this initial setback that the intellectual leaders of the "Reformers" learnt their lesson. When they renewed their offensive in 1957 they no longer attacked on a broad front, but concentrated first within the organisation on securing the Party leadership; for a time, ideological conflicts were shelved. At the Stuttgart Party Conference of 1958, they were successful: the influence of the salaried party officials was seriously checked and the Party Executive was streamlined by the creation of a seven-man Praesidium. That is to say: reform of personnel was given priority over reform of policy, and the overhauling of the party machine over that of party doctrine. It was only because the leadership of the Party had passed into the hands of personalities who were open to the new ideas that it was possible to win the Party over in a comparatively short time; the dead-weight of a clumsy bureaucratic *Apparat* having been disposed of, a fresh team of leaders consisting of some of the best minds in the Party succeeded in tackling the reconstruction of the intellectual formulation of Social Democratic policy. Even now, however, the opposition was still considerable. It is true that when it came to the final vote in Bad Godesberg the new programme was adopted with only 16 delegates "against." But this figure is misleading since it was evident in the preceding discussion that a very much stronger and more vocal majority was opposed to certain formulations which were, in their opinion, aimed "too far" in the direction of what has in the classical Socialist discussions been labelled "Revisionism."

Finally, one thing must not be forgotten: not all the supporters of the new programme will interpret the document in the same way. There is an influential group who look at it from the tactical, or, to use the expression that is so popular in post-war Germany, the "optical" point of view: not as a break with a policy that has failed but rather as a new and more intelligible, more elastic formulation of the old policy.

The leading exponent of this group is the Deputy Party Leader Herbert Wehner: he is certainly one of the strongest political influences in German Socialism, at the same time one of the most controversial, a kind of Nye Bevan, with all Bevan's passion if without his oratorical brilliance. It is only their alliance with Wehner that has enabled the reformers to get their ideas accepted; it was only the burning sincerity with which this former leading Communist attacked the radicalism of some of the Left-wingers that persuaded many delegates to overcome their doubts in Bad Godesberg. But Wehner himself sees in the programme above all a politically necessary attempt to clothe old Socialist ideas in a more attractive garb, more in accordance with present-day German mentality, without violating their essential nature. He is too much a true believer of the old Socialist school to jettison any fundamental tenets of Marxism, but he is also too astute a politician not to realise that at present the important thing for the Social Democrats is to abandon their rôle as a "permanent minority," and that they can succeed in this only if they speak a language which takes into account the present idiosyncrasies of a prosperous middle-class Germany. Wehner went all-out on behalf of a programme about which he feels differently than some of his more adaptable comrades who take the view that the failures of Socialism in the continental country that was once its stronghold must be interpreted as a sign that "the old theories no longer fit the new reality."

But the failures of socialism in the continental country that was once its stronghold must be interpreted as a sign that the old theories no longer fit the new reality. Nevertheless, the Godesberg programme is a very serious and very consistent attempt to take this fact into account and, to use Marxist phraseology, to bring "consciousness" more in harmony with "social reality." The German Social Democrats have given up Marxism not because it has become "un-popular" but because their defeats have made them realise that it is utterly impossible to tackle the world of to-day and the tasks of to-morrow with an intellectual instrument of yesterday.

One key-question remains. However "realistic" the new programme may be —will it have anything of the "fire and passion" that emanated from Marxian utopianism and chiliasm? If the differences between Socialist and bourgeois politics become only a matter of degree, Socialism may look forward to re-cruiting new friends and voters and to take up the struggle for power with greater hope of success—but will it not have to pay for this victory with a loss of impetus and militancy? The Godesberg Programme "demythologises" the ideology of German Socialism so thoroughly that one cannot help wondering whether it will be able to mobilise the emotional forces by which the old Socialist movement was sustained and developed and from which it drew a good deal of its inner strength. Only the next few years will show whether the new "popular breadth" (so hoped for and so necessary for success) which the German Left now promises itself will be able to compensate for the possible loss of old-style emotional depth.

XV.

A HALF-CENTURY
IN PERSPECTIVE

Students of history—those, at least, who make a career of studying it—are normally reluctant to look into the future. Their reluctance is probably both natural and healthy, for attempts to discover "lessons" in history, and to extrapolate from the past into the future, lead one onto very thin ice indeed.

Historians are almost as chary about general judgments on the immediate present, or even on the very recent past. To examine the individual events of yesterday may be acceptable, but to seek the meaning of yesterday, the broad trends and dominant currents of recent times, the *Zeitgeist* of the twentieth century, strikes most historians as at best premature, and at worst irresponsible. There are occasional exceptions, nevertheless; and these few bold scholars are joined by a more considerable number of nonhistorians, less inclined to be cautious about attempting to identify the spirit of our times.

This volume began with several selections on the transition to the twentieth century; those selections were designed to provide a kind of backdrop for the study of contemporary European history, and to analyze the intellectual currents that were beginning, from 1890 to 1914, to break down the nineteenth-century world-view. The selections in Chapter XV will, in a sense, pick up where those in Chapter I left off; they will offer some reflective commentaries on those trends of thought that were to become influential or dominant during the two generations after 1914.

Once again, many of these essays are the work of Americans rather than Europeans, and some of them may seem to focus their attention too narrowly on the American mood. Yet when one deals with twentieth-century intellectual history (as with the history of diplomacy and war), one finds it increasingly difficult to separate the American from the European experience. A common intellectual climate, a common set of world problems, have tended to erode many of the old differences between the two shores of the Atlantic. Insofar as we can identify the twentieth century's *Zeitgeist*, it is likely to belong to Americans and Europeans alike.

A number of labels have been suggested for our era: the Freudian age, the age of irrationalism, the Counter-Enlightenment, the age of anxiety, the neurotic age. Most of these labels reflect a mood of pessimism, doubt, even despair; and one can find reinforcement for these gloomy inclinations in much of modern literature, political and social thought, and philosophy. Existentialism has by no means been the only philosophical system (if it *is* a system) of the mid-century generation; yet for a time at least its stoical response to a disordered and "absurd" world seemed to be the most representative expression of a widespread European mood.

It may be that the selections reprinted below are weighted too heavily in the direction of that pessimistic mood. By the end of the 1950's, one could detect some signs of a changing temper in the western world—a temper of cautious confidence and restrained hope. Despite a decade of severe tension, the threat of nuclear war remained potential rather than real; despite the ominous warnings of Marxians, no recurrence of the great depression seemed to be in sight. But the reasons for the change in Europe's mood were not only negative in nature; there were some positive explanations as well. The idea of western European unification, which had long seemed to be little more than a phantom pursued by a few well-intentioned idealists, suddenly began to take on solid consistency as the six-nation Common Market emerged triumphantly from its trial stage, and found itself besieged by new applicants for admission. At the same time, the monolithic unity of the Soviet-dominated bloc showed signs of disintegration as post-Stalinist trends brought some relaxation of totalitarian controls, and as the heretical theory of "polycentrism" began to find vocal advocates in the communist world. Meanwhile, Europe had managed to survive the painful process of disengagement from the ex-colonial areas of Africa and Asia without experiencing the kind of uncontrollable emotional backlash that sometimes results from a humiliating retreat.

Perhaps, in the light of these newer developments, the mid-century temper is already outmoded. Yet even if continuing trends should prove this to be so, the dominant outlook of the mid-century generation (deeply rooted in that of the interwar years) will continue to have its interest for the student of history, concerned as he must be to detect and to explain the prevailing world-view of each successive age.

1.

Peter Viereck, noted essayist and Pulitzer-prize-winning poet, was trained as a historian at Harvard, and has taught modern history at Mount Holyoke College since 1948. In the essay that follows, he sketches a somber portrait of Europe in our age, and traces much of the trouble to the "ethical revolution" that occurred after 1870. He points up the destructive impact of the first world war ("the worst single catastrophe in human history"), and the unintentionally disintegrative effects of relativist liberalism. His argument is that of a conservative who calls for a reassertion of traditional western values.

VIERECK: The Revolution in Values: Roots of the European Catastrophe *

The revolution in values has almost annihilated the European heritage. Nourished over the centuries by the teachings of Christ and Saint Paul, by Socrates and Pericles, by Aristotle and Erasmus, the European heritage is built on reverence for the precious uniqueness of the individual soul. This heritage,

* From Peter Viereck, "The Revolution in Values: Roots of the European Catastrophe, 1870–1952," in *Political Science Quarterly*, vol. 67 (1952), pp. 343–345, 348–349. Reprinted by permission of the editors of the *Political Science Quarterly*.

which has absorbed so many social and political changes, is compatible with democratic capitalism or with democratic socialism or with democratic national-ism. It is incompatible with the new totalitarian blood-and-iron nationalism and socialism, the extremes of which are fascism and bolshevism. Both are neces-sarily against the Christian ethic and the democratic polity. Both liquidate the concept of "Europe" and "the West."

The European heritage, expressed in some of the freest and most creative cultures of mankind, is an amalgam of the four traditional ancestries of West-ern man: the stern moral commandments and social justice of Judaism; the love of the free Hellenic mind for beauty and for untrammeled intellectual speculation; the Roman Empire's universalism and its exaltation of objective impersonal rule of law; and the Golden Rule and international, interracial brotherhood of Christianity.

These four ancestries were often mutually conflicting and, still more often, hypocritically evaded. Nevertheless, their ever-shifting amalgam has for some two thousand years given Europeanism its society-building spark, its creative imagination, its urge to discover new continents—new Americas—of the earth and of the mind. Never attained, often betrayed, less often practiced than preached, yet never wholly extinguished, these traditional values are what goaded Western man to greatness.

The history of Europe after 1870 relates the decline—not necessarily fall—of Europe. It is the history of how a heritage of two thousand years was smashed in three generations of state worship, power worship, world depressions, and world wars. As a result, the historian of Nazi Europe and Communist Europe observes that the typical institutions are no longer the parliament, the university, and the cathedral, but the secret police, the gas chamber, and the forced-labor camp.

At first the value-system known as "Europe" did seem to tame the two revolutionary forces of nationalism and socialism, extracting from them what was valuable, changing national frontiers and social frontiers without sacrificing personal liberties. It was a good example of "challenge and response." A seem-ingly successful absorption of the challenge, a case of practical evolutionary conservatism, marked the history of Europe from 1870 up to World War I. Reactionary tsars and kaisers and revolutionary socialists and nationalists were all making ever handsomer concessions (no matter how grudgingly) to reasonableness and to parliamentary processes.

By 1914, socialism and nationalism seemed "house-broken." Marxist socialist parties had relaxed into "Social Democrats"; most nationalistic hotheads were calming down into national democrats; for a while, there was more talk of the Hague Peace Conferences than of the approaching war. To a great extent, the leading parties of socialism and likewise of nationalism had been assimilated into the European parliamentary system, working in lawful, gradual, parliamen-tary fashion for the changes they demanded.

That is why World War I was a tragedy so irrevocable. It cut suddenly short the slow, patient taming-process. World War I is the worst single catastrophe in human history. Even worse than World War II, though it killed less millions: for by the time of World War II there was much less freedom and decency left to destroy than in 1914; by 1939 Europe's decline into totalitarianism was already far advanced.

World War I smashed both the moral and economic fabric of European civilization. This is why its advent at the time was hailed so ecstatically by its two chief beneficiaries, Hitler (1889–1945) and Lenin (1870–1924). These two men between them, and what they stood for, brought about the terrible European crisis threatening America's very existence today. Hitler reduced blood-and-iron nationalism and racism to its ultimate, logical absurdity, just as Lenin was the ultimate extreme of the blood-and-iron socialism of the 1870's. . . .

Militarist nationalism and class-war socialism intentionally undermined the values of the West and intentionally fulfilled the ethical revolution of 1871–1951. Liberalism, though often slandered far too glibly by conservatives, does also have a partial guilt in this. It is a far lesser guilt than that of nationalism and socialism. Relativist liberalism unintentionally, not intentionally, served the ethical revolt against European values.

"Pragmatic" and "positivist" liberalism was so eager to prove all values "relative" that it undermined the ethical heritage and Christian restraints of the West, as well as the organic traditional institutions that served as a unifying social cement. Thereby liberalism unintentionally paved the way for Hitlerism and Stalinism. Liberalism always begins attractively by liberating men from absurd old prejudices and aristocratic excesses. It ends tragically by putting all men in the position of those few illuminati who, when initiated into the seventh circle of Syria's medieval Order of Assassins, were told the Order's secret of secrets: *"There is no truth; everything is permitted."* Or, to cite an unconscious Broadway jazz echo of the Assassins: "Anything goes." No wonder that Fascist and Communist mass-murder, based on the assumption that every means is permitted to achieve one's ends, followed a century of relativist liberalism and of the most modern "scientific" enlightenment.

To this indictment, most contemporary intellectual leaders in the sciences and in the humanities would react vigorously. Their reply would stress intellectual honesty, no matter at what cost to social unity and no matter at what cost to the sanction and alleged sugar-coating of religion still needed to enhance ethical behavior. Indeed they would see, as man's supreme ethic, that respect for reason and scientific method, no matter where it may lead, on which the decline of ethics and spirituality and the rise of materialism are sometimes blamed.

Their reply (to sum up very superficially the main intellectual trend in current secular culture) would run somewhat like this: For modern man, the answer to relativism and chaos in truth and ethics is not and cannot be a system of absolute codes of truth and absolute codes of behavior based on bigotry, superstition, and contempt for reason. The "modern" would, as a source of truth, disregard intuition and disregard religious inspiration. To him these are an emotional self-deception. Moreover, intuition and inspiration are "too hot to handle." They simply do not lend themselves to the scientific method of analysis.

Aside from this, the "modern" position does have great cogency in so far as it reminds outraged, antimaterialistic moralists that the answer to "Anything goes" is not some political or ideological Inquisition saying: "Nothing goes."

2.

Although it is fashionable for intellectuals to view our era with either despondency or contempt, there are occasional exceptions. James Joll, one of the ablest of the postwar generation of Oxford historians, takes the position that an era ought to be measured by its cultural vitality and creativity, and that by any test of originality and achievement, the first quarter of the twentieth century deserves to rank as a kind of golden age. Unlike many Europeans, he even argues that this modern Renaissance may be carried forward under American leadership during the second half of the century.

JOLL: When Was the Golden Age? *

Empires fade; technological advances are absorbed or outstripped; political harmony, even on the rare occasions it has been attained, does not last. It is the permanent products of periods of high civilization that determine our view of them. Pheidias, Plato and Aeschylus, Shakespeare and the host of poets who were his contemporaries, Galileo, Michelangelo and Bramante are the people who have left a physical mark on our world, or who can affect our experience directly. . . . It is artistic and intellectual achievement and not political or economic growth that finally earns a period the title of "great," whatever the conditions which produced that achievement. And it follows that, in the hierarchy of historical sciences . . . art, history and the history of ideas must have a high place; and their omission from the study of any period is bound to lead to bad history.

We can now turn to the . . . interesting question: What are the chances of the twentieth century being regarded as a "great" period in this sense? It may be a silly question; for it is not clear that subsequent ages will in fact be left with anything tangible to judge us by. For the scientific progress of our time— on which part of our possible "greatness" rests—may very well produce a physical destruction that could make Hobbes's famous passage a precise description of the end of our civilization:

There is no place for industry because the fruit thereof is uncertain: and consequently no Culture of the Earth, no navigation nor use of the commodities that may be imported by sea; no commodious Building; no Instruments of moving and removing such things as require much force; no Knowledge of the face of the Earth; no account of Time; no Arts; no Letters; no Society: and, what is worst of

* From James Joll, "When Was the Golden Age?" in *The Twentieth Century*, vol. 161 (1957), pp. 521–25. Reprinted by permission of the editors of *The Twentieth Century*.

all, continual fear and danger of violent death; And the life of man solitary, poor, nasty, brutish and short.

The items the absence of which Hobbes enumerates might well serve as a list of the essentials in anything we can call civilization.

In the sense, therefore, that any survival at all may depend on our being able to solve the problems of international relations satisfactorily, it may be that this is the only test by which the twentieth century should be judged, and, accordingly, the study of international relations should be our main preoccupation. By this standard, Eden is more important than Einstein, Pineau than Picasso, however odd this may sound. Yet to abandon all hope of the twentieth century leaving lasting influences of a kind left by previous generations seems to be an act of self-conscious nihilism that is not warranted by the facts, so it is perhaps worth while to see how far Western civilization in the first half of the twentieth century compares with previous epochs, and how far it seems likely to leave enduring traces that will widen the experience of future ages as the great cultures of the past have done.

"It is a time when everything cracks, when everything is destroyed, everything isolates itself, it is a more splendid thing than a period when everything follows itself." This was Gertrude Stein's judgment on the twentieth century; and certainly during its early years it produced a complete and conscious revolution in the arts and in science on which its claim to be considered a "great age" rests. The period from, say, 1880 to 1920 can, as far as intellectual and artistic achievement is concerned, hold its own in any competition of this kind. The most striking feature, and this perhaps distinguishes it from the other periods discussed, is the completeness and consciousness of its break with the past. While the Renaissance began with a conscious rediscovery of a tradition, the twentieth century began with a conscious rejection of tradition. In the arts there was a feeling that both the traditional techniques and the traditional subject matter had been exhausted, and that new developments were possible that would open a wider range of experience and expression and enable the artist to penetrate more deeply than ever before into the nature of the world. And so, in music, Schoenberg declared that traditional tonality was exhausted and instituted a completely new system, based on a twelve-note scale instead of an eight-note one, with new rules of composition and new aesthetic principles which have transformed the art of composition in our day and have influenced even those composers who have never formally adhered to the dodecaphonic school; and, if the works of Schoenberg himself occasionally seem to suffer from a too pedantic preoccupation with his own system, the works of his disciple, Alban Berg, are among the greatest of our time. The twelve-tone system was only one, even if the most complete and intellectual, of the breaks in musical tradition: Stravinsky's use of primitive rhythms in his early works (one is irresistibly reminded of the parallel in the visual arts— Picasso's discovery of negro art two or three years earlier) or Bartok's absorption of living folk music into a completely new and original style, all marked a conscious and complete rejection of the past. In painting there was a reaction against the whole traditional conception of art. The Cubism of Picasso and Braque showed how different views of the same object could be combined into a single vision and how a new, illuminating analysis could be made of the object itself and its relations to the space around it. These painters, too (and others, in a frenzy of destruction of all accepted forms of art, carried the idea to fantastic extremes), showed how a work of art need not be constructed from conventional materials, and used sand, tin or pieces of cut-out paper to produce a new and exciting vision of the world.

In literature the first twenty years of the twentieth century produced perhaps fewer startling revolutions in technique; there is no serious literary equivalent of Cubism even in the work of James Joyce or of Gertrude Stein. Where literature participated in the general intellectual ferment of the early twentieth century was in its absorption of the philosophical and psychological discoveries of the period. Proust's exploration of time or James Joyce's evocation of the stream of consciousness would only have been possible in a civilization that also included Bergson, Freud and Einstein. These writers succeeded in giving the effect of a new dimension in their work, and of thus widening our experience through art in a way that is comparable to the impact of Cubism or the extended range of sounds in contemporary music. All these revolutionary changes in the arts, indeed, must be seen against the changing background of general beliefs. The battle between religion and science that had tortured so many nineteenth-century intellectuals had died down, and with it much of the crude materialism that had passed for progressive thought in the middle of the last century. In its place a new and more subtle view of the world was being developed by psychologists, physicists and philosophers. Einstein and others were, rightly or wrongly, popularly supposed to have demonstrated the relativity and indeterminacy of much that had hitherto been thought immutable; Freud had transformed the view of human nature even more radically than the physicists had that of the physical universe; and the work of the logicians and mathematicians was starting a philosophical revolution whose results are still being worked out and ever more widely applied.

Thus the first quarter of the twentieth century, quite apart from the political and economic revolutions it produced, has many of the features which entitle it to be called a great creative period. It was a period of bold experiment when people were aware of new possibilities in all directions; it inspired the sensation, at least among small groups of people, that they were taking part in an exciting and fruitful movement of an entirely new kind. It produced works of art and intellectual discoveries of the highest quality and of permanent importance. It was essentially a European movement. Its centres were Paris and Vienna—the Paris of Picasso, Proust and Bergson, and the Vienna of Freud, Mahler and Wittgenstein. It was a movement that flourished on the eve of a period of political and economic decline; its critics have called it degenerate art or *Kulturbolshevismus* and held it responsible for that decline in one or other of its aspects, associating it with whatever form of political belief they disapprove of most. But, although Europe is no longer the centre of the world and although the creative impetus has diminished except in giant figures like Picasso or Stravinsky, who survive from the earlier part of the century, European culture of the first quarter of the twentieth century will leave a mark on the future as powerful as that left by the Renaissance.

There is indeed a danger that Europeans are living too much in elegiac or embittered contemplation of their lost ascendancy, and are unwilling to assess the cultural developments that are going on elsewhere. For if one looks at American civilization today there are perhaps grounds for optimism; and perhaps America will have her first great age in the second half of the twentieth century. Once European intellectuals can get over their distaste for the more obviously disagreeable or embarrassing features of American life, their patronizing attitude often turns to admiration. Since the end of the Second World War the decline of Europe and its general disillusionment and disorientation have perhaps begun to make America lose its sense of inferiority towards European culture; and Americans have acquired a new self-confidence. The most obvious way in which this expresses itself is in the size, beauty and boldness of American architecture to-day, which has absorbed what was best in the modern architectural movement in Europe, adapted it to American needs and scenery, and produced something new and exciting. But everywhere there are signs of originality and vitality. Enormous sums are spent on academic activities; science flourishes—even if the association of physics and politics occasionally produces its Oppenheimer case. There is almost universally a career open to the talents. There are better performances of more music than anywhere else. American writers are no longer provincial English writers, but have an energy and a polish that make them immediately recognizable. A new school of self-confident painters has emerged since the war and, in turn, produced yet another revolution in European painting in imitation of it. Even those who dislike it are forced to admit the fervour with which this new art is being pursued, and to recognize the artists' conviction that they are doing something new and important. And one could continue the list and enlarge the grounds for optimism. Of course it is a minority culture (and one is more conscious of the majority in America than anywhere else); but so were the great cultures of the past. And, of course, I should dislike living there—but not so much as in fifth-century Athens, Renaissance Italy or Elizabethan England.

3.

Even more passionately than Peter Viereck, John H. Hallowell argues the conservative thesis that nineteenth-century liberalism and materialism prepared the way for the "moral and spiritual crisis" of our times. The twentieth century's predominating mood of anxiety and despair, its generalized tendency to dehumanize man, are (in Mr. Hallowell's opinion) the logical consequences of the reversal of traditional western values by the liberal positivists. Mr. Hallowell, who was educated at Harvard and Princeton, has taught political theory at Duke University since 1942. The passage reprinted below is taken from the concluding chapters of his textbook on the history of modern political thought.

HALLOWELL: Main Currents in Modern Political Thought *

It requires no great seer or prophet to discern today the signs of decadence that are everywhere manifest. Only the most stubborn and obtuse would venture optimistic predictions for the future of the world and its civilization. The complacent optimism of the last century has given way to a deep-rooted despair and men everywhere are gripped by fear and insecurity. Anxiety gnaws at their vitals. Everywhere men tremble, whether they are yet conscious of the cause of their fears, before the judgment of God.

The sickness of the modern world is the sickness of moral confusion, intellectual anarchy, and spiritual despair. The revolution of nihilism, born of this confusion and despair, is peculiar not alone to any one country or people but in varying degrees is taking place everywhere. With almost frantic zeal we search for the political or economic panacea that will save us and the world from disaster, not seeing, apparently, that the disaster is already upon us and that for the cure we must examine the state of our own souls. The political and economic crises from which the world suffers are not causes but symptoms of a crisis that is even more profound—a spiritual crisis within the soul of man. Having alienated himself from God, having discredited the reason with which he was endowed by God, unable or unwilling to identify the evil with which the world of man is infected—modern man oscillates between extravagant optimism and hopeless despair. As his optimism is shattered more and more by the force of events he sinks lower and lower into the slough of despondency. In his despondency he is tempted to strike out against the enemy he cannot identify, whose name he does not know, in desperate action. In his anxiety to escape from utter futility and meaningless existence he is tempted to give up his most priceless heritage—his freedom—to any man who even promises deliverance from insecurity. He is tempted to put his faith in the most absurd doctrine, to submit his will to the most brutal dictator, if only in such a way he can find that for which he longs with all the passion of his being —a meaningful existence, a life worth living, a life worth dying to preserve.

Modern man's great lack is lack of conviction, particularly the conviction that good and evil are real. Mistaking indifference for tolerance he refuses to become convinced of anything for fear that his convictions may lead him to be intolerant. . . .

Genuine humility is a virtue but indifference disguised as humility is a corrosive poison. Despair disguised as humility and indifference parading as

* From John H. Hallowell, *Main Currents in Modern Political Thought* (New York: Henry Holt, 1950), pp. 618–29. Copyright 1950, Holt, Rinehart and Winston, Inc. Reprinted by permission of the publishers.

tolerance are manifestations of the sickness of the modern world. Good and evil, truth and falsehood, have no positive dimensions.

Lulled into complacent self-satisfaction by the liberal positivistic doctrine of the nineteenth century modern man became a blind devotee of the Goddess Progress who, he believed, bestowed her blessings upon man in the form of increased knowledge and control over nature through an automatic and impersonal process, in which man, at best, was but a passive tool of Nature or of History. Where formerly men looked to God for the salvation of their souls, they now looked to science and technology for the gratification of their desires. Paradise on earth was substituted for eternal spiritual salvation as an aspiration worthy of men's efforts. The method for bringing about this paradise, moreover, had been found to lie within the power of man: paradise on earth waited only upon the proper execution of a plan to be discovered in the truths and with the methods of the natural sciences. It required no sacrifice on the part of man, no change in his behavior, no moderation of his appetites—it required simply the application of intelligence, directed by science, to social problems. Progress was conceived as automatic, irreversible, and inevitable. Time alone would heal all wounds, cure all evil and solve all problems. In his search for bodily well being and comfort, in his search for economic security and political utopia, modern man appears not simply to have lost his soul but to have forgotten that he has a soul to lose. Everyday in every way, until very recently at least, modern man believed, the world is getting better and better. Through increased knowledge of and control over nature, through education and technology, man through science would overcome all the evil with which the world is infected and live in perpetual peace and harmony with his neighbor. This, at least, was his fervent hope and his faith.

The optimism that characterized the nineteenth century has given way in the twentieth to a deep-rooted despair. The very Science upon which the nineteenth century pinned its hopes for the realization of Utopia has led many individuals in the twentieth century to the brink of meaninglessness. Man is but a chance product of the earth, his aspirations and his ideals products of vain imagination—only a kind of desperate bravado serves to keep him afloat in a sea of meaningless existence. . . .

Most men today no longer believe that progress is automatic, irreversible, and inevitable though many still cling, if with much less assurance than formerly, to a belief in education, science and technology as the way out of our difficulties. With the invention of the atom bomb modern man realizes that the blessings of science are not unmixed, that science can be used for evil purposes as well as good and that science itself is silent on the question as to what purposes its knowledge should be put. Man's technical knowledge and capacity has outstripped his moral capacity. Evil has manifested itself so unmistakably in the twentieth century that modern man finds it increasingly difficult to deny its reality, even if he still has considerable difficulty calling it by name.

The liberals of the last century ascribed evil to men's ignorance and to their faulty political institutions. Evil was to be overcome by education and political reform. Equating evil with intellectual error the liberals were led, as Lewis Mumford points out, "to the flattering conclusion that the intelligent cannot sin and that the mentally adult can do no evil." The inability or unwillingness of the liberal to recognize the reality of evil lulled him into a false sense of security. . . .

While the liberals denied the reality of evil and ascribed the appearance of evil in the world to faulty political institutions and lack of "enlightenment," the Marxians explained the appearance of evil in the world to the prevailing capitalistic mode of production, to the institution of private property and to the class conflict engendered by that institution. Evil would disappear, they predicted, inevitably and automatically, with the establishment of a classless society through the medium of revolution and the dictatorship of the proletariat. With the distribution of material goods in accordance with men's needs, men would no longer be frustrated in their search for material satisfaction and all evil would disappear.

However profoundly liberalism may differ from Marxism in details and in conclusions both start from the assumption that human nature is essentially good and ascribe whatever evil there is in the world to bad or faulty institutions. But why these institutions, political and economic, should be so bad, and so much in need of reform, if men are essentially good is a question to which neither has a very satisfactory answer. Or why men should believe that they will be able to do in the future what they have never succeeded in doing in the past, namely, to establish a perfect political and economic system, is never explained.

In recent years one of America's most astute thinkers, Reinhold Niebuhr, has recalled to our consciousness a fact which both liberalism and Marxism have ignored with almost fatal consequences to our civilization. Evil, he points out, is something real and the name for it is sin. Its locus is not in institutions, which are but a reflection of human purposes, but in human nature itself. . . .

The crisis of our times stems from this inability or unwillingness to recognize the evil in the world for what it is, the sin of man. What describes more accurately the evil that is rampant in the world to-day if it be not the perversion of men's wills? What describes more realistically the evils we must seek to overcome by God's grace if not pride, self-righteousness, greed, envy, hatred, and sloth? What has for centuries brought man to catastrophe if it has not been their attempt to create a god in their own image rather than seeking to make their own image more like that of God? What is the root of all evil if it is not that man seeks to make himself God? . . .

But if modern man has lost sight of the sinfulness of man he has also lost sight, in his despair, of the image of God in man; and man has become progressively dehumanized. The inhumanity of man to man has manifested itself in varying degrees throughout the ages man has lived but not until modern times has man's inhumanity to man been pursued as a matter of principle. . . .

This dehumanization of man is made manifest in all spheres of life. In the factory it is not the individual personality that is the important factor in production but the machine and if the machine is to operate with the maximum efficiency for which it is designed, the individual man must become more and more like a cog in the machine, an adjunct to it. The individual may falter, the machine cannot and the individual who cannot keep up with the pace of the machine must give way to one who can. For the producer of goods man is primarily a consumer. If his appetite lags it must be stimulated artificially, he must be stimulated to buy if for no other reason than envy of others who buy. It is not a question of how much or what kind is good for him as a human being but how much he must buy if the producers are to go on producing. Capitalism, Professor Tillich declares, aims "to provide the greatest possible number of men with the greatest possible amount of economic goods" and "seeks to arouse and to satisfy ever-increasing demands without raising the question as to the meaning of the process which claims the service of all the spiritual and physical human abilities." Few question *why* men should have more and more goods or whether it is good or necessary for them to have as many as they do. Material comfort and the accumulation of wealth are considered to be self-sufficient ends. From an aspect and means of life, economic activity has increasingly become, an end in itself, an end to which the spiritual nature of man is subordinated if not obliterated.

The dehumanization of man in modern art is so obvious as hardly to require mention. The artist today who paints an individual in such a way that he clearly resembles a human being is regarded not only as outmoded but as lacking in "artistic" talent. The more abstract the art, the more morbid its subject matter, the further it is removed from human values, the "better" it is thought to be as "art" by many moderns. And what is true of art is true also of modern literature. . . . The outstanding characteristic of modern culture is its fragmentarianism and discontinuity. It is a chaos not an order. No single thread binds it together. Man as an integral being, physical and spiritual, rational and passionate, has been analyzed out of existence—some one part of his nature is taken as his essential characteristic. Man as such has been dissolved into one of his component parts.

An English writer and publisher, Victor Gollancz, believes that we are experiencing something quite new in the history of Western civilization, not simply the rejection of the values traditionally associated with that civilization but something even more ominous—the complete reversal of those values and the glorification of their opposites. This reversal of the values traditionally associated with Western civilization finds its most characteristic expression in the twentieth century in contempt for human personality, in the denial of "the *essential* spiritual equality of all human beings." Having lost sight of the fact that God created all men in His image, that God is the Father of all men and that consequently all men are brothers, the modern world has no basis for believing that men *are* equal. Where individuals still cling to the belief in individual equality it is often without any understanding of the basis for that belief and consequently without any rational means of defending it. . . . The choice the Western world faces, Mr. Gollancz believes, is not essentially between rival economic or political systems (though some are better than others) but between the re-affirmation of the values traditionally associated with Western civilization and their negation. The crisis we are experiencing is not essentially a political or economic one, but a moral and spiritual one.

4.

When historians seek to characterize any age, they are inclined to point out both its unique aspects and its similarity to some past era. A. L. Rowse, Fellow of All Souls College at Oxford and one of the most distinguished of contemporary British historians, argues that certain aspects of the twentieth century do seem to be quite unprecedented: the development of nuclear power, for example, and the emergence of Asia and Africa into the forefront of world affairs. Yet he concludes also that our era may have a great deal in common with the later Renaissance, when Europe's resurgence was taking on a predominantly scientific and technical tinge. Although that age was shaken by severe ideological and political conflict, it stands out in retrospect as a time of notable achievement and advance. Mr. Rowse suggests that the twentieth century may, in longer perspective, be viewed in somewhat the same way.*

ROWSE: Is Our Age Unique? *

It is becoming a commonplace—at least in Western thinking—to assume that our time in history is a unique one. How far we are justified perhaps only a historian can tell, and he must be careful to give a balanced answer. . . .

If we look back over history for some guidance as to the character of our epoch, most historians would agree that the later Renaissance, rather than the earlier, offers a fruitful parallel—the period just before and after 1600 when the Renaissance impulse, after being dominantly scholarly and artistic, became noticeably scientific and technical: the age of Bacon and Galileo, of William Harvey, Kepler, and Descartes.

We have evidence of a disturbance to men's minds similar to that of our own time in the work of so intellectually responsive a writer as the poet Donne. There are such famous lines as:

> And new philosophy calls all in doubt,
> The element of fire is quite put out. . . .

Or, for the effect on the mind:

> The sun is lost, and the earth, and no man's wit
> Can well direct him where to look for it.
> And freely men confess that this world's spent,
> When in the planets and the firmament
> They seek so many new.

* From A. L. Rowse, "Is Our Age Unique?" in the *Saturday Review*, vol. 45 (June 2, 1962), 11–13. Reprinted by permission of the author and of the editors of the *Saturday Review*.

This is a direct reaction to the discovery that there are innumerably more stars in the universe than anyone had ever been able to observe until the time of Galileo's telescope. It is also a delayed reaction to the acceptance of the Copernican system.

The revelation of the "aweful vastness" of the universe, in Pascal's phrase, was profoundly disturbing. It is natural that we should be no less disturbed today by the revelation of its infinite complexity, its terrible potentialities, and —more strictly intellectually—by the difficulty of making sense of it, of making out what Whitehead calls "the final order of things." We stand before the new world uneasily, with mingled excitement and apprehension. It is like another lunge forward of the Renaissance impulse into the uncharted and unforeseeable.

Whitehead characterized that earlier period, in his "Science and the Modern World," in terms of a revolt against medieval authority—where the acceptance of intellectual authority is the essence of medievalism—of an effort to revise men's view of the nature of knowledge and to discover the ultimate grounds of truth. Along with such an effort went a respect for the concrete fact such as the Middle Ages rarely exemplified. . . .

This new attitude, which has been described as a revival of naturalism, implied a fundamental confidence that there was a final order of things which might be described in terms of cause and effect and which was rationally explicable. When Newton came along, it was thought that this order had been made clear, and men relapsed upon a cushion of intellectual contentment. One sees this in the spiritual comfort and in the note of complacency in the eighteenth century. It is to be discerned all through the age's literature and art; and even in—or perhaps most obviously in—its architecture, which is all classical composure and decorum, at ease with itself.

There is nothing of that in today's architecture—and architecture is an art very revealing, externally, of the nature of a society. Ours is all unrest, confusion, ambitious exploration—the Age of Anxiety, indeed. And to achieve any comparable rational explication of the order of things is infinitely more difficult. We still await our Newton.

It is an accepted point that the medievals inhabited a God-centered universe, whereas the post-Renaissance age has been increasingly centered upon man. (From another point of view, what we are face to face with now is the Nature of Man.) But one wonders whether the center of interest may not now be moving outward again from man to technology, his creature; or beyond that to the phenomena of physics, the analysis of the elemental constitution of the universe. In any event man is in some danger, if not of displacement by the machines he has created, at least of depersonalization. But that is as much a product of mass civilization with its mass standards, as of technology.

Mass civilization is certainly a characteristic of our time. In fact, some elect persons inhabiting ivory towers think of the modern world as a return to the Dark Ages—with a spreading of barbarism, a lowering of standards, an erosion of quality, and of distinction and the outstanding; in exchange for equality, sameness, and the submergence of the individual in the cult of mere quantity. . . .

Nevertheless, it is not necessarily a relapse into barbarism, a return to another Dark Ages. However poor a view we take of popular education, it provides a basis for some kind of culture—except that the culture will be different, predominantly scientific and technological in tone.

In that, we shall be carrying forward the original impulses of Bacon and Galileo in the later Renaissance period. Perhaps most of all Bacon, with his emphasis on the utility of science and his immense intellectual optimism in believing that by way of inductive experiment more and more scientific knowledge would be opened to us. It would not be inappropriate to take that most worldly of men for a patron saint of our period in time.

Something of the impetus of the later phase of the Renaissance was lost in the religious wars that devastated northern Europe in the late sixteenth and early seventeenth centuries. It is a commonplace that Germany never recovered the ground lost in the Thirty Years War. One sees something of spiritual desolation no less than physical ravages reflected in a masterpiece like Grimmelshausen's "Simplicissimus." Even in England the hateful experience of the Civil War brought about a change of spirit.

As the fires of fanaticism based on mutually exclusive faiths burned down, men began to see the silliness of it all.

> When civil fury first grew high,
> And men fell out they knew not why

Such was the reflection after it was over. Men began to return to sense, and even to the investigation of the phenomena of the senses. With that the Royal Society was on its way, with its cool spirit of natural observation, weighing and charting and experimenting; its encouragement of a simple prose in place of high flights of fancy, indeed of what was really a "prose spirit," a scientific attitude towards life and the world.

As a historian my hope is that after the fires of ideological conflict, of political and economic dogmas, in our time have burned themselves out, or at least burned down, they may be succeeded by an age of prose and sense, of cool investigation and rational enjoyment. In short, we might have something of the spirit of the later seventeenth and early eighteenth century rather than of the earlier period, something of the age of Newton and Locke rather than that of Milton and Oliver Cromwell.

The beginning of such an age can already be seen in the amount of scientific cooperation that exists today. There is of course nothing new, let alone unique, in international cooperation in science, except the scale on which it is now practiced, a scale that could be enlarged even further if political conditions allowed. But my point is, rather, the historical one that the scientific mentality is a more peaceable and cooperative one in essence. It lives by exploring things and fitting them together, not—as ideologies do—by accentuating differences.

Meanwhile there is the enormous positive achievement of modern science on the human side—and no visible end to its growth—in meeting the material needs of the world, in terms of food, resources, and health and treatment. It is indeed a tragic absurdity—which played its part in exacerbating social and political conflict, too—that as recently as the 1930s men were throwing away and destroying the superfluity of some areas of the world while other areas were in want. The 1950s notably reversed this situation, and we have found a direction in which politics and science can go hand in hand doing good work for the human race as one.

I see one future limitation upon this good work, and again science offers the only alleviation. A marked feature of our time, though again not a unique one, is the immense growth of world population. Sir Charles Darwin, in a somewhat gloomy Malthusian book, "The Next Million Years," called attention to the ultimate danger of an unrestricted increase in world population outrunning the growth of food resources. The basis of his argument was the assumption that man could not control human reproduction.

Science is already giving the lie to this assumption; for although there certainly is a grave latent danger if man does not control the increase, such control is now within the power of particular societies. But for world control, cooperation among societies is indispensable.

Everything, then, enforces the conclusion that, given all the various circumstances of our time, cooperation is now essential to survival. And that *is* something unique in history.

5.

Among the descriptive labels that have been proposed for the twentieth century is "the Counter-Enlightenment." The phrase suggests a total reversal of that mood of optimism and hope, that confidence in man's ability to understand and improve himself through reason, that marked the thought of so many eighteenth-century *philosophes*. Judith Shklar, an assistant professor of government at Harvard University, argues that the revolt against the Enlightenment has been carried on uninterruptedly ever since the French Revolution, and that both the "romantics" and the "Christian fatalists" of the twentieth century represent its culmination. These two anti-Enlightenment factions, though different in many ways, share a common sense of despair, of alienation from society. Just as striking as the growth of these doctrines, Miss Shklar contends, is the "withering" of the Enlightenment tradition—the total failure of its heirs to offer any kind of effective rebuttal. Liberalism, socialism, radicalism, she asserts, are no more than desiccated remnants of once-vigorous ideologies; they can provide no challenge to the dominant theorists of social despair. "A reasoned skepticism," she concludes, "is consequently the sanest attitude for the present."

SHKLAR: After Utopia *

"In the beginning was the Enlightenment." Any study of contemporary social thought might well begin with these words. Yet nothing is quite so dead today as the spirit of optimism that the very word Enlightenment evokes. Indeed, we are faced not with the mere end of the Enlightenment but with the prevalence of theories that arose in opposition to it. If the Enlightenment still figures in the realm of ideas it is as a foil for attack, not as an inspiration to new ideas. Romanticism, the earliest and most successful antagonist of the Enlightenment, has numerous successors today, especially in existentialism and in the various philosophies of the absurd. The revival of social thought that was almost forced upon Christians by the French Revolution is still active today. But the gradual decay of the radical aspirations of liberalism and the evaporation of socialist thought have left the Enlightenment without intellectual heirs. The Enlightenment is the historical and intellectual starting point of contemporary social theory, but only because a great part of our thinking today is based on ideas, romantic and Christian, that were from the first consciously directed against it.

In retrospect the Enlightenment stands out as the high point of social optimism from which we have gradually, but steadily, descended, at least philosophically. . . .

Romanticism was the revolt of aesthetic sensibility against the philosophic spirit. Eventually, moreover, this aesthetic difference implied a break with the Enlightenment as a whole, and the birth of a new attitude toward nature and society as well. . . . The aesthetic revolt of romanticism was . . . only part of a more general dissatisfaction with the entire age. If we look deeper, beyond even the conscious expressions of romantic thought, we discover a specific consciousness. What appeared in the republic of letters at that time was very early, and with unrivalled subtlety, described by Hegel as the "unhappy consciousness." This is the "alienated soul" that has lost all faith in the beliefs of the past, having been disillusioned by skepticism, but is unable to find a new home for its spiritual longings in the present or future. Hopelessly tossed back and forth between memory and yearning, it can neither accept the present nor face the new world. This is essentially a religious phenomenon, what Miguel de Unamuno was later to call the "tragic sense of life," a longing for immortality which is constantly harrowed by doubts of its possibility. However, this consciousness did not express itself in religious terms in the early years of romanticism. It was not only that "God is dead," but that culture had perished. The "unending yearning" was felt primarily as culture longing. It was a yearning for Greece, first, then for the world of Ossian and for the colorful Middle Ages, and later for the Renaissance as well—indeed for any time more blessed than the present.

* From Judith Shklar, *After Utopia: the Decline of Political Faith* (Princeton: Princeton University Press, 1957), pp. 3, 12, 15–16, 17–18, 21–22, 23–24, 218–221. Reprinted by permission of the Princeton University Press.

This sense of lostness in the "real" world that marks the unhappy conscious-ness, and that lies at the root of the romantic revival, is also what gives the movement its continuity. It is this which allows us to speak of romanticism as prevalent throughout the last century and today, in spite of the inner dissen-sions, the changes in modes of expression and in literary subject matter. The refusal to accept a world of nature in which all must die, or a social universe in which "the whole" counts more than each person, marks the entire course of romantic thought. The Enlightenment was able to rationalize and live at peace with these conditions; the romantic rebelled against them. . . .

When we speak of romanticism here, we mean primarily the manifestations of the unhappy consciousness, for today it is no longer the implicit basis of a new literature, it is a conscious attitude. Existentialism and the less systematic philosophies of the absurd regard themselves openly as the awareness that "God is dead." While the early romantics showed considerable combative vigor, and really believed that the spirit of poetry might yet conquer the world of prose, the contemporary romantic cherishes no such hope—indeed, no hope of any sort. Instead of dramatic energy there is now only a feeling of futility. Romanticism now expresses itself in a denial of the very possibility of our knowing—much less controlling—history, nature, or society. It asserts our freedom from God and social determination, but this implies only an absence of permanent attachments. Man has become a foreigner wandering aimlessly around unknown territory; the world, both historical and natural, has become meaningless. The relevance of all social thought and action becomes doubtful in the face of a human situation in which nothing is certain but the individual's reactions to the external world and his need to give expression to his inner condition. As seen with the inner eye, the world appears as a strange and hos-tile prison which one cannot either understand or alter; at best it can be evaded. The great tragedy of the present age is that history, society, and politics, for all their insignificance to our real self, press upon us unavoidably. The outer world is crushing the unique individual. Society is depriving us of our selfhood. The entire social universe today is totalitarian, not just some political movements and some states. Technology and the masses are the conditions of life everywhere today, and these, forming the very essence of totalitarianism, are the epitome of all the forces in society that have always threatened the individual personality. This is the romanticism of defeat, the ultimate stage of alienation. It is also the very farthest point from the spirit of the Enlighten-ment. Romanticism began by denying the facile optimism of the men of reason, but under the stress of the social enormities of the present age it has come to reject the entire modern world, and implicitly, the very possibility of social knowledge and amelioration. . . .

Many Christian thinkers, both Catholic and Protestant, today subscribe to the idea that civilizations live and die with their traditional religious faiths, and that ultimately all social events are the expression of some religious at-titude. As for the Enlightenment, the English Catholic historian, Christopher Dawson, who is perhaps the most perfect representative of the school of Christian fatalists today, can still speak of it as "the last of the great European heresies." Moreover, it is the historical fatalism implicit in a theory that makes cultural life dependent upon one factor—religious faith—that unites so many Christian social theorists today. War, totalitarianism, in short, the decline of European civilization—all are inevitable results of the absence of a religious faith in the modern age. Since a real renewal of Christianity is unlikely, the end of Western culture is more than likely. In this, Protestant theologians like the Swiss Emil Brunner and the English Nicholas Micklem, Anglo-Catholics like V. A. Demant and T. S. Eliot, and such Roman Catholic thinkers as Hilaire Belloc, Christopher Dawson, Romano Guardini, and Erich Voegelin quite agree. Here the democratic Maritain is at one with the authoritarian monarchist Henri Massis.

The relation of this type of religious thought to romanticism is not obvious. To be sure, both dislike much in common. But even if they shared a common distaste for the Enlightenment, it was for different reasons. It is one thing to reject neo-stoicism as a rationalist disregard for revelation; it is quite another thing to despise it as lifeless and unpoetic. Again today the Christian in revolt against the present age is no less in a state of cultural alienation than the romantic. The external aspects that arouse his indignation—rootless city life, technology, the prevalence of modes of thought that derive from the natural sciences, the popularity of totalitarian parties and ideologies—also offend the romantic. However, for the romantic, cultural alienation involves an absolute estrangement, whereas the believer can still rest securely in his faith. To long for such a haven without being able to find it is the essential condition of the unhappy consciousness. For the Christian thinker it is only the lack of faith among those about him that is terrifying, not the emptiness within himself. . . . There is thus no real affinity between romanticism and Christianity. The romantic and the Christian fatalist are alike only in a negative sense: in their common alienation from the age of the Enlightenment first; then from the entire world of science, industry, commerce; and now from a culture apparently doomed to war and totalitarianism.

Romantic and Christian despair in the realm of social thought are different, then, and would be more so if the end of European culture did not for the Christian have an even deeper religious meaning. However, the end of the West may very well mean the disappearance of Christianity in the world, and this possibility has aroused many Christians to a new and dramatic awareness of the old prophecy of the end of the world. The eschatological consciousness, already present in Maistre and in Lamennais, before his apostasy, is today the Christian equivalent of the unhappy consciousness. For the sense of doom is extended from the merely cultural level to the supernatural, and all mankind is faced with its final hour—a finality that for the romantic is already accomplished in the end of civilization. Thus recently Josef Pieper, a German Catholic thinker, in a brief but complete statement of the doctrine of the last things, foresees the apocalypse in the events of recent years. In specific political events, especially in totalitarianism, he discerns a foretaste of the rule of Anti-Christ.

Totalitarian ideologies represent the devil's counter-religions. The martyrdom of Christians in totalitarian states is a prelude to that heightening of tensions between the forces of Christ and Anti-Christ that precedes the end of time. Implicitly or explicitly the apocalypse has haunted all those Christian thinkers who since the French Revolution could see nothing but decadence and decline in the life of the modern age. It is difficult to imagine anything farther removed from the spirit of the Enlightenment than this. . . .

What answers can be offered to these counsels of social despair? Romanticism refuses to analyze the social world with any degree of thoroughness, and Christian fatalism subjects modern history to an excess of simplification in order to satisfy its sense of outrage. But to have noted all these shortcomings is not a reply. In fact, no reply is forthcoming. The spirit of rational optimism which alone could furnish a reply does not flourish at present. The Enlightenment was not killed by its opponents; even its most natural followers found its leading conceptions inadequate in an age that has proved all their hopes false. There are, of course, traces of survival. Sartre, very characteristically, notes that the conformism of Americans is really due to their universal rationalism and optimism. But even in America this spirit is no longer encountered among social philosophers. There are few serious people who really believe today that the advantages of democratic government are so self-evident that once it is established it must appeal to all. Probably President Wilson's Fourteen Points were the last great document to testify to that faith. By now it is only too well known that democracy is not inevitable, that it may be destroyed from within, and that even the most successful constitutional democracies are not the models of social perfection that the Enlightenment had dreamed about. This disenchantment—perhaps it is realism—even among the most consistent advocates of democratic government is the real measure of the decline of social optimism.

What has happened is not only that the Enlightenment has no heirs but that radicalism in general has gone totally out of fashion. Radicalism is not the readiness to indulge in revolutionary violence; it is the belief that people can control and improve themselves and, collectively, their social environment. Without this minimum of utopian faith no radicalism is meaningful. At present, however, even those who regard themselves as adherents of the "spirit of 1789" seem to lack it. For instance, Stuart Hampshire, the Oxford philosopher, recently deploring the absence of radicalism today, defined it as the wish to expand the personal liberty of as many people everywhere as possible. Quite rightly he notes that the mere defense of existing liberties is not enough, that this indeed is conservative. One cannot but agree with him that the necessary effort to ward off the dangers of fascism and communism has reduced libertarian efforts to just that. However, even he never explains why liberty is so valuable, what social ends it is to serve. Unlike the radicals of the 18th century, he does not promise that liberty will bring harmony, or that it will necessarily involve any moral elevation. It is, in fact, liberty for its own sake. It is good will, but not genuine radicalism.

If this were an isolated example, it would matter but little. However, it is just among the most obvious heirs of the Enlightenment, among liberals and democratic socialists, that the spirit of radicalism has most conspicuously disappeared. And it is this which prevents either one from offering anything like a complete answer to the theories of social despair. Ever since the French Revolution, liberalism has become increasingly uncertain of itself, so that at present there flourishes a conservative liberalism that is just as cheerless as Christian fatalism. Democratic socialism, on the other hand, if it exists at all as a systematic theory, has become purely defensive. Certainly neither liberals nor socialists today believe in inevitable progress or in the ability of free, rational men to live without coercion in a perfectly harmonious society. The conservative school of liberalism has indeed turned against all rationalism as a destructive force. Its disdain for intellectuals and for rational political action is such as to amount to a rejection of political theory in general.

Socialism, even the democratic variety, has always occupied an equivocal position toward the Enlightenment. After all, the Webbs, no less than Marx, made the rejection of 18th-century utopianism the very basis of their thought. Moreover, the "scientist" pretensions of both are inherently opposed to the spirit of radicalism. In their view progress was impersonal, the inevitable course of supra-personal development, and human choice was limited to getting on or off the historical bandwagon. It was not man who made history, but history that propelled man. As has often been observed, such a philosophy owes far more to conservatism than to the Enlightenment. To be sure, there were socialists who tried to throw off the yoke of historicism and to create a socialist philosophy akin to that of the Enlightenment, but very few were able to abandon the tactical advantage of claiming that they were also in tune with the march of "history" or, rather, the inevitable course of economic and technological development. The cost of inevitabilism has been high. For when totalitarianism and war proved its "scientific" claims to be utterly false, socialists were left without a philosophy. There are, of course, other reasons for the virtual absence of socialist theory today. For years the need to be "anti-fascist," and now to resist communism, has consumed all its energies. These attitudes have become a substitute for theory. Moreover, the close alliance of socialist theory and the demands of the "movement" have always been an intellectual liability. But, above all, the evaporation of radicalism has affected socialism just as much as every other type of political theory.

As one looks back to the last century, the decline of radical hope seems like a steady process, especially in the case of liberalism, for the French Revolution dealt a blow to liberal radicalism from which it never recovered. The generations of liberals that followed that event were never able to regain the social self-confidence that had reigned during the 18th century, nor were they able to stand up to the challenge of the newly developed conservative philosophy. On the contrary, with the years liberalism absorbed more and more of its spirit. Two wars and totalitarianism have only completed the rout.

6.

Anxiety, says the poet W. H. Auden, is the hallmark of our age. In pre-Freudian days, the anxious person might have been dismissed as a victim of something called "neurasthenia," a nervous disorder to be cured by a long and restful ocean voyage. The idea that anxiety may be a widely generalized human trait, and even a necessary and useful one, is surely a quite unprecedented conception. To turn anxiety into an asset may be a classic case of making a virtue of necessity; yet the case is persuasively argued by Margaret Mead, associate curator of ethnology at the American Museum of Natural History. Dr. Mead, one of America's most distinguished anthropologists and a lecturer of wide renown, has written extensively on both primitive and advanced cultures of the twentieth century.

MEAD: One Vote for This Age of Anxiety *

When critics wish to repudiate the world in which we live today, one of their familiar ways of doing it is to castigate modern man because anxiety is his chief problem. This, they say, in W. H. Auden's phrase, is the age of anxiety. This is what we have arrived at with all our vaunted progress, our great techno-logical advances, our great wealth—everyone goes about with a burden of anxiety so enormous that, in the end, our stomachs and our arteries and our skins express the tension under which we live. Americans who have lived in Europe come back to comment on our favorite farewell which, instead of the old goodbye (God be with you), is now "Take it easy," each American ad-monishing the other not to break down from the tension and strain of modern life.

Whenever an age is characterized by a phrase, it is presumably in contrast to other ages. If we are the age of anxiety, what were other ages? And here the critics and carpers do a very amusing thing. First, they give us lists of the op-posites of anxiety: security, trust, self-confidence, self-direction. Then, without much further discussion, they let us assume that other ages, other periods of history, were somehow the ages of trust or confident direction.

The savage who, on his South Sea island, simply sat and let bread fruit fall into his lap, the simple peasant, at one with the fields he ploughed and the beasts he tended, the craftsman busy with his tools and lost in the fulfillment of the instinct of workmanship—these are the counter-images conjured up by descriptions of the strain under which men live today. But no one who lived in those days has returned to testify how paradisiacal they really were.

Certainly if we observe and question the savages or simple peasants in the world today, we find something quite different. The untouched savage in the middle of New Guinea isn't anxious; he is seriously and continually frightened

* Margaret Mead, "One Vote for This Age of Anxiety," in *The New York Times Magazine*, May 20, 1956, pp. 13, 56–58. Reprinted by permission of the author and of the editors of *The New York Times*.

—of black magic, of enemies with spears who may kill him or his wives and children at any moment, while they stoop to drink from a spring, or climb a palm tree for a coconut. He goes warily, day and night, taut and fearful.

As for the peasant populations of a great part of the world, they aren't so much anxious as hungry. They aren't anxious about whether they will get a salary raise, or which of the three colleges of their choice they will be admitted to, or whether to buy a Ford or Cadillac, or whether the kind of TV set they want is too expensive. They are hungry, cold and, in many parts of the world, they dread that local warfare, bandits, political coups may endanger their homes, their meager livelihoods and their lives. But surely they are not anxious.

For anxiety, as we have come to use it to describe our characteristic state of mind, can be contrasted with the active fear of hunger, loss, violence and death. Anxiety is the appropriate emotion when the immediate personal terror—of a volcano, an arrow, the sorcerer's spell, a stab in the back and other calamities, all directed against one's self—disappears.

This is not to say that there isn't plenty to worry about in our world of today. The explosion of a bomb in the streets of a city whose name no one had ever heard of before may set in motion forces which end up by ruining one's carefully planned education in law school, half a world away. But there is still not the personal, immediate, active sense of impending disaster that the savage knows. There is rather the vague anxiety, the sense that the future is unmanageable.

The kind of world that produces anxiety is actually a world of relative safety, a world in which no one feels that he himself is facing sudden death. Possibly sudden death may strike a certain number of unidentified other people —but not him. The anxiety exists as an uneasy state of mind, in which one has a feeling that something unspecified and undeterminable may go wrong. If the world seems to be going well, this produces anxiety—for good times may end. If the world is going badly—it may get worse. Anxiety tends to be without locus; the anxious person doesn't know whether to blame himself or other people. He isn't sure whether it is 1956 or the Administration or a change in climate or the atom bomb that is to blame for this undefined sense of unease.

It is clear that we have developed a society which depends on having the right amount of anxiety to make it work. Psychiatrists have been heard to say, "He didn't have enough anxiety to get well," indicating that, while we agree that too much anxiety is inimical to mental health, we have come to rely on anxiety to push and prod us into seeing a doctor about a symptom which may indicate cancer, into checking up on that old life insurance policy which may have out-of-date clauses in it, into having a conference with Billy's teacher even though his report card looks all right.

People who are anxious enough keep their car insurance up, have the brakes checked, don't take a second drink when they have to drive, are careful where they go and with whom they drive on holidays. People who are too anxious either refuse to go into cars at all—and so complicate the ordinary course of life—or drive so tensely and overcautiously that they help cause accidents. People who aren't anxious enough take chance after chance, which increases the terrible death toll on the roads.

On balance, our age of anxiety represents a large advance over savage and peasant cultures. Out of a productive system of technology drawing upon enormous resources, we have created a nation in which anxiety has replaced terror and despair, for all except the severely disturbed. The specter of hunger means something only to those Americans who can identify themselves with the millions of hungry people on other continents. The specter of terror may still be roused in some by a knock at the door in a few parts of the South, or in those who have just escaped from a totalitarian regime or who have kin still behind the Curtains.

But in this twilight world which is neither at peace nor at war, and where there is insurance against certain immediate, downright personal disasters, for most Americans there remains only anxiety over what may happen, might happen, could happen.

This is the world out of which grows the hope, for the first time in history, of a society where there will be freedom from want and freedom from fear. Our very anxiety is born of our knowledge of what is now possible for each and for all. The number of people who consult psychiatrists today is not, as is sometimes felt, a symptom of increasing mental ill health, but rather the precursor of a world in which the hope of genuine mental health will be open to everyone, a world in which no individual feels that he need be hopelessly brokenhearted, a failure, a menace to others or a traitor to himself.

But if, then, our anxieties are actually signs of hope, why is there such a voice of discontent abroad in the land? I think this comes perhaps because our anxiety exists without an accompanying recognition of the tragedy which will always be inherent in human life, however well we build our world. We may banish hunger, and fear of sorcery, violence or secret police; we may bring up children who have learned to trust life and who have the spontaneity and curiosity necessary to devise ways of making trips to the moon; we cannot—as we have tried to do—banish death itself.

Americans who stem from generations which left their old people behind and never closed their parents' eyelids in death, and who have experienced the additional distance from death provided by two world wars fought far from our shores are today pushing away from them both a recognition of death and a recognition of the tremendous significance—for the future—of the way we live our lives. Acceptance of the inevitability of death, which, when faced, can give dignity to life, and acceptance of our inescapable role in the modern world, might transmute our anxiety about making the right choices, taking the right precautions, and the right risks into the sterner stuff of responsibility, which ennobles the whole face rather than furrowing the forehead with the little anxious wrinkles of worry.

Worry in an empty context means that men die daily little deaths. But good anxiety—not about the things that were left undone long ago, that return to haunt and harry men's minds, but active, vivid anxiety about what must be done and that quickly—binds men to life with an intense concern.

There is still a world in which too many of the wrong things happen somewhere. But this is a world in which we now have the means to make a great many more of the right things happen everywhere. For Americans, the generalization which a Swedish social scientist made about our attitudes on race relations is true in many other fields: anticipated change which we feel is right and necessary but difficult makes us unduly anxious and apprehensive, but such change, once consummated, brings a glow of relief. We are still a people who—in the literal sense—believe in making good.

7.

The distinctive trait of the mid–twentieth century, says the sociologist Daniel Bell, is the exhaustion of ideologies—that is, of ideas seen as levers for social action—in the western world. The inspiration that once moved intellectuals to passionate belief and action has evaporated, leaving only a sense of alienation to take its place. Only in Africa and Asia are new ideologies emerging, and those are distorted and misguided ones. Writing from an anti-ideological position, Mr. Bell argues that the new alienation of western intellectuals is not necessarily a disastrous thing. Alienation, he tells us, is not synonymous with nihilism, but rather suggests ". . . a positive role, a detachment, which guards one against being submerged in any cause, or accepting any particular embodiment of community as final." In his conclusion he holds out at least a cautious hope that the end of ideology may lead twentieth-century intellectuals to a different and healthier kind of revolutionary wisdom.

BELL: The End of Ideology *

There have been few periods in history when man felt his world to be durable, suspended surely, as in Christian allegory, between chaos and heaven. In an Egyptian papyrus of more than four thousand years ago, one finds: ". . . impudence is rife . . . the country is spinning round and round like a potter's wheel . . . the masses are like timid sheep without a shepherd . . . one who yesterday was indigent is now wealthy and the sometime rich overwhelm him with adulation." The Hellenistic period as described by Gilbert Murray was one of a "failure of nerve"; there was "the rise of pessimism, a loss of self-confidence, of hope in this life and of faith in normal human effort." And the old scoundrel Talleyrand claimed that only those who lived before 1789 could have tasted life in all its sweetness.

This age, too, can add appropriate citations—made all the more wry and bitter by the long period of bright hope that preceded it—for the two decades between 1930 and 1950 have an intensity peculiar in written history: world-wide economic depression and sharp class struggles; the rise of fascism and racial imperialism in a country that had stood at an advanced stage of human

* From Daniel Bell, *The End of Ideology* (Glencoe, Illinois: The Free Press, 1960), pp. 369–75. Copyright 1960 by The Free Press, a corporation. Reprinted by permission of the publishers.

culture; the tragic self-immolation of a revolutionary generation that had proclaimed the finer ideals of man; destructive war of a breadth and scale hitherto unknown; the bureaucratized murder of millions in concentration camps and death chambers.

For the radical intellectual who had articulated the revolutionary impulses of the past cenury and a half, all this has meant an end to chiliastic hopes, to millenarianism, to apocalyptic thinking—and to ideology. For ideology, which once was a road to action, has come to be a dead end. . . .

Ideology is the conversion of ideas into social levers. . . . It is more. It is the commitment to the consequences of ideas. . . .

What gives ideology its force is its passion. Abstract philosophical inquiry has always sought to eliminate passion, and the person, to rationalize all ideas. For the ideologue, truth arises in action, and meaning is given to experience by the "transforming moment." He comes alive not in contemplation, but in "the deed." One might say, in fact, that the most important, latent, function of ideology is to tap emotion. Other than religion (and war and nationalism), there have been few forms of channelizing emotional energy. Religion symbolized, drained away, dispersed emotional energy from the world onto the litany, the liturgy, the sacraments, the edifices, the arts. Ideology fuses these energies and channels them into politics.

But religion, at its most effective, was more. It was a way for people to cope with the problem of death. The fear of death—forceful and inevitable— and more, the fear of violent death, shatters the glittering, imposing, momentary dream of man's power. The fear of death, as Hobbes pointed out, is the source of conscience; the effort to avoid violent death is the source of law. When it was possible for people to believe, really believe, in heaven and hell, then some of the fear of death could be tempered or controlled; without such belief, there is only the total annihilation of the self.

It may well be that with the decline in religious *faith* in the last century and more, this fear of death as total annihilation, unconsciously expressed, has probably increased. One may hypothesize, in fact, that here is a cause of the breakthrough of the irrational, which is such a marked feature of the changed moral temper of our time. Fanaticism, violence, and cruelty are not, of course, unique in human history. But there was a time when such frenzies and mass emotions could be displaced, symbolized, drained away, and dispersed through religious devotion and practice. Now there is only this life, and the assertion of self becomes possible—for some even necessary—in the domination over others. One can challenge death by emphasizing the omnipotence of a movement (as in the "inevitable" victory of communism), or overcome death (as did the "immortality" of Captain Ahab) by bending others to one's will. Both paths are taken, but politics, because it can institutionalize power, in the way that religion once did, becomes the ready avenue for domination. The modern effort to transform the world chiefly or solely through politics (as contrasted with the religious transformation of the self) has meant that all other institutional ways of mobilizing emotional energy would necessarily atrophy

In effect, sect and church become party and social movement.

A social movement can rouse people when it can do three things: simplify ideas, establish a claim to truth, and, in the union of the two, demand a commitment to action. Thus, not only does ideology transform ideas, it transforms people as well. The nineteenth-century ideologies, by emphasizing inevitability and by infusing passion into their followers, could compete with religion. By identifying inevitability with progress, they linked up with the positive values of science. But more important, these ideologies were linked, too, with the rising class of intellectuals, which was seeking to assert a place in society.

The differences between the intellectual and the scholar, without being invidious, are important to understand. The scholar has a bounded field of knowledge, a tradition, and seeks to find his place in it, adding to the accumulated, tested knowledge of the past as to a mosaic. The scholar, qua scholar, is less involved with his "self." The intellectual begins with *his* experience, *his* individual perceptions of the world, *his* privileges and deprivations, and judges the world by these sensibilities. Since his own status is of high value, his judgments of the society reflect the treatment accorded him. In a business civilization, the intellectual felt that the wrong values were being honored, and rejected the society. Thus there was a "built-in" compulsion for the free-floating intellectual to become political. The ideologies, therefore, which emerged from the nineteenth century had the force of the intellectuals behind them. They embarked upon what William James called "the faith ladder," which in its vision of the future cannot distinguish possibilities from probabilities, and converts the latter into certainties.

Today, these ideologies are exhausted. The events behind this important sociological change are complex and varied. Such calamities as the Moscow Trials, the Nazi-Soviet pact, the concentration camps, the suppression of the Hungarian workers, form one chain; such social changes as the modification of capitalism, the rise of the Welfare State, another. In philosophy, one can trace the decline of simplistic, rationalistic beliefs and the emergence of new stoic-theological images of man, e.g. Freud, Tillich, Jaspers, etc. This is not to say that such ideologies as communism in France and Italy do not have a political weight, or a driving momentum from other sources. But out of all this history, one simple fact emerges: for the radical intelligentzia, the old ideologies have lost their "truth" and their power to persuade.

Few serious minds believe any longer that one can set down "blueprints" and through "social engineering" bring about a new utopia of social harmony. At the same time, the older "counter-beliefs" have lost their intellectual force as well. Few "classic" liberals insist that the State should play no role in the economy, and few serious conservatives, at least in England and on the Continent, believe that the Welfare State is "the road to serfdom." In the Western world, therefore, there is today a rough consensus among intellectuals on political issues: the acceptance of a Welfare State; the desirability of decentralized power; a system of mixed economy and of political pluralism. In that sense, too, the ideological age has ended.

And yet, the extraordinary fact is that while the old nineteenth-century ideologies and intellectual debates have become exhausted, the rising states of Asia and Africa are fashioning new ideologies with a different appeal for their own people. These are the ideologies of industrialization, modernization, Pan-Arabism, color, and nationalism. In the distinctive difference between the two kinds of ideologies lie the great political and social problems of the second half of the twentieth century. The ideologies of the nineteenth century were universalistic, humanistic, and fashioned by intellectuals. The mass ideologies of Asia and Africa are parochial, instrumental, and created by political leaders. The driving forces of the old ideologies were social equality and, in the largest sense, freedom. The impulsions of the new ideologies are economic development and national power.

And in this appeal, Russia and China have become models. The fascination these countries exert is no longer the old idea of the free society, but the new one of economic growth. And if this involves the wholesale coercion of the population and the rise of new elites to drive the people, the new repressions are justified on the ground that without such coercions economic advance cannot take place rapidly enough. And even for some of the liberals of the West, "economic development" has become a new ideology that washes away the memory of old disillusionments.

It is hard to quarrel with an appeal for rapid economic growth and modernization, and few can dispute the goal, as few could ever dispute an appeal for equality and freedom. But in this powerful surge—and its swiftness is amazing—any movement that instates such goals risks the sacrifice of the present generation for a future that may see only a new exploitation by a new elite. For the newly-risen countries, the debate is not over the merits of Communism—the content of that doctrine has long been forgotten by friends and foes alike. The question is an older one: whether new societies can grow by building democratic institutions and allowing people to make choices—and sacrifices—voluntarily, or whether the new elites, heady with power, will impose totalitarian means to transform their countries. Certainly in these traditional and old colonial societies where the masses are apathetic and easily manipulated, the answer lies with the intellectual classes and their conceptions of the future.

Thus one finds, at the end of the fifties, a disconcerting caesura. In the West, among the intellectuals, the old passions are spent. The new generation, with no meaningful memory of these old debates, and no secure tradition to build upon, finds itself seeking new purposes within a framework of political society that has rejected, intellectually speaking, the old apocalyptic and chiliastic visions. In the search for a "cause," there is a deep, desperate, almost pathetic anger. . . . The irony . . . for those who seek "causes" is that the workers, whose grievances were once the driving energy for social change, are more satisfied with the society than the intellectuals. The workers have not achieved utopia, but their expectations were less than those of the intellectuals, and the gains correspondingly larger.

The young intellectual is unhappy because the "middle way" is for the middle-aged, not for him; it is without passion and is deadening. Ideology, which by its nature is an all-or-none affair, and temperamentally the thing he wants, is intellectually devitalized, and few issues can be formulated any more, intellectually, in ideological terms. The emotional energies—and needs—exist, and the question of how one mobilizes these energies is a difficult one. Politics offers little excitement. Some of the younger intellectuals have found an outlet in science or university pursuits, but often at the expense of narrowing their talent into mere technique; others have sought self-expression in the arts, but in the wasteland the lack of content has meant, too, the lack of the necessary tension that creates new forms and styles.

Whether the intellectuals in the West can find passions outside of politics is moot. Unfortunately, social reform does not have any unifying appeal, nor does it give a younger generation the outlet for "self-expression" and "self-definition" that it wants. The trajectory of enthusiasm has curved East, where, in the new ecstasies for economic utopia, the "future" is all that counts.

And yet, if the intellectual history of the past hundred years has any meaning—and lesson—it is to reassert Jefferson's wisdom (aimed at removing the dead hand of the past, but which can serve as a warning against the heavy hand of the future as well), that "the present belongs to the living." This is the wisdom that revolutionists, old and new, who are sensitive to the fate of their fellow men, rediscover in every generation. "I will never believe," says a protagonist in a poignant dialogue written by the gallant Polish philosopher Leszek Kolakowski, "that the moral and intellectual life of mankind follows the law of economics, that is by saving today we can have more tomorrow; that we should use lives now so that truth will triumph or that we should profit by crime to pave the way for nobility."

And these words, written during the Polish "thaw," when the intellectuals had asserted, from their experience with the "future," the claims of humanism, echo the protest of the Russian writer Alexander Herzen, who, in a dialogue a hundred years ago, reproached an earlier revolutionist who would sacrifice the present mankind for a promised tomorrow: "Do you truly wish to condemn all human beings alive today to the sad role of caryatids . . . supporting a floor for others some day to dance on? . . . This alone should serve as a warning to people: an end that is infinitely remote is not an end, but, if you like, a trap; an end must be nearer—it ought to be, at the very least, the labourer's wage or pleasure in the work done. Each age, each generation, each life has its own fullness. . . ."

8.

In the opening chapter of this book, a passage from Gerhard Masur's *Prophets of Yesterday* summed up the dominant characteristics of the period 1890–1914, seen as an epoch in European intellectual history. At the end of his study, Mr. Masur attempts to assess the consequences of that epoch, and of the Great War of 1914–18, for the course of European development since 1914. While recognizing the disastrous effect of the war on Europe's political and economic supremacy, and on certain illusions about the essential rationality of man, Mr. Masur argues that it also speeded the Europeanization of the world, and may have opened the way to "an era of global awareness and interdependence."

MASUR: Prophets of Yesterday *

The historian has sometimes been called a prophet in retrospect. Surveying the past from the vantage point of the present, he may indeed find little difficulty in fitting together the scattered pieces of his puzzle in such a form that they give a rational picture of time past and time present. Is this, however, the end of his task? He tells us what happened, even why it happened, but if asked for the underlying significance of events, the historian who is only a "prophet in retrospect" will be unable or unwilling to answer.

Without doubt, the historian who searches for meaning in history is conditioned by his own position in space and time. His efforts to ascertain the sense of past events will include value-judgments. The closer the event, the truer this becomes. But the historian should not be intimidated by these considerations. If his search for the meaning of historical events leads him beyond the confines of objective evidence, he must accept the challenge, unless he is content to be a mere chronicler in the Crocean sense.

I do not imply that the historian has a passkey to history, or that his judgment should be guided by his own hopes or fears. I mean only that, speaking for myself, I have tried to ascertain the significance of the events forming the background of this book by taking into consideration the implications that were present, albeit obscured, in the cultural history of the period.

From this perspective, what was the meaning of the great change that came over the world in 1914? Obviously the war was more than a diplomatic accident of gigantic proportions. No one can believe that the handful of old men who controlled Europe's foreign affairs were ultimately responsible for the holocaust, or that the mechanics of a superannuated alliance system dragged the Old World against its will into the war. Few of the leaders welcomed the conflict. Some, like Sir Edward Grey, had a foreboding of the darkness that was settling over the Continent. But the number of those who contemplated the dimensions the war might assume or had any idea of its length or its consequences was small.

If we review the interpretations of the war put forth while the conflict was still in progress, we meet likewise with an astonishing myopia. The nationalistic aims of France, Germany, Italy, or Russia, which were served up as justifications, may be passed over in silence. Some, like Bernard Shaw, maintained that the war was only another example of the struggle that had been

* From Gerhard Masur, *Prophets of Yesterday* (New York: Macmillan, 1961), pp. 411–19. Copyright 1961 by Gerhard Masur. Reprinted by permission of The Macmillan Company.

carried on for so long under the balance-of-power system. And there were the idealists, like H. G. Wells and Woodrow Wilson, who proclaimed that this was the war to end international anarchy, a hope that was recognized as futile even while the war was raging. Finally, there was Lenin's interpretation of the war as the end-phase of imperialism which would open the gate to world revolution. This vision, too, was soon scorned by everyone who did not wear the blinkers of dialectic materialism.

Contemporary historians, like Hajo Holborn, have maintained that the First World War initiated the political collapse of Europe which the Second World War consummated. In our perspective, it would seem that the First World War did something more and something less than usher in the political collapse of Europe. Stated positively, it generated an awareness of the global interdependence of all countries and all nations. Lest this be construed as a voice for One World, let me add that no such hopes are implied by recognizing that World War I demolished some of the barriers which have, in the past, separated one civilization from another.

From inside Europe the war looked like collective suicide; from outside it took on a different aspect. Like many that preceded it, this war was "an express train of history." It speeded up developments already envisaged by prewar writers. Europe's triumph over the world had been, as we stated earlier, the result of an ecumenic civilization. Nineteenth century Europe continued to believe that the fruits of such a civilization would remain the privilege of Western man. His political and economic position before 1914 was indeed unique, but ultimately untenable.

Positions of power, however, are not lightly surrendered. The First World War exposed the inherent contradiction in the European situation. By an ironic dialectic, it encouraged the non-European to adopt the ideals which Europe had for many years claimed as her own, but which she seemed to have forsaken during the carnage. Dostoevski prophesied that "we arrive all or none," and had proclaimed the coming of a pan-human consciousness. It is my belief that the twentieth century is on the way to an acknowledgment of pan-humanism as one of its important commitments.

The term "pan-humanism" stands in need of clarification. It is both a fact and an assignment still to be realized. It implies a recognition of universal interdependence, and it is by no means limited to the fields of politics or economics. In the arts, Malraux has described its significance in the phrase, "museum without walls." It can be noted in religion, in philosophy, literature, anthropology, and last but not least, in history. Those who assert that in a world torn by strife and global competition there seems little room for pan-human consciousness, must still admit that it is already used as a potent weapon for propaganda. Even where it is employed only as an ideological decoy to conceal the struggle for power, it bespeaks a new stage of global awareness.

The European preeminence that drew to a close in 1914 prepared the world for this new consciousness; herein lies the greatness and the tragedy of this phase of European history. To give it birth, the shell that had enclosed nineteenth century European civilization had to be shattered. It was in this perspective that the war of 1914 became a World War.

Let us summarize briefly the contributions to this process made by philosophers, scientists, and artists. First, there were the efforts of those who wanted to understand the world exclusively in terms of immanence or, as we might also say, in materialistic terms. From Marx to Darwin, from Nietzsche to Freud, man had been deprived of his claim to appraise human existence in terms of values. The new vistas did not replace the old transcendental ones outright, nor did they necessarily make them obsolete. But they did create tensions that ranged all the way from nature to history and from society to the individual. The Europeans who were exposed to these ideas became involved in conflicting arguments and antinomic motivations which deprived them of the naive confidence that had once guided their lives. As a result, the belief in European superiority was gradually impaired in religion, in race, and in culture.

The human personality had not been spared in the process of re-evaluation, or devaluation. This great force, which since the days of the Renaissance and the Reformation, had supplied so many of the creative impulses by which European civilization had advanced, seemed now reduced to a shadow of its former self. Remote indeed were the days when Locke and Adam Smith had seen in the competitive power of the individual a fertile source for harmonic progress. Even the individualism of Goethe, the ideal of personal fulfillment, seemed no longer achievable in the societal setting of an industrial age. All that was left was the esthetic individualism which replaced the categorical imperative of Kant by an esthetic imperative. But the esthetic attitude was reserved for "the happy few," for the privileged members of the bourgeoisie. It would have been ludicrous to recommend it to the working class. Moreover, it left a large part of human existence unfulfilled; it did not quench the longing to be a sharer in the human community. In this way, it led some leaders, such as George, d'Annunzio, and Barrès, to embrace nationalism as a remedy for loneliness and isolation.

As we have seen, the idea of the free and self-determining national community appeared on the European scene at the same time that political individualism scored its first great triumphs in 1789. However, at the end of the nineteenth century the national community, with its ideological corollary, nationalism, had all but overpowered individualism.

By and large, it may be said that in 1914 the Europeans considered the nation-state to be the highest and most desirable form of communal living. Consequently it should command the greatest sacrifices. And the war surpassed all expectations as to the sacrifices that could be demanded. Of course, competition and strife between political communities were nothing new. They had existed in all times and had often led to merciless action. But the scale on which the Europeans were fighting from 1914 to 1918 was novel. Whereas populations had been enslaved and cities erased during the period of antiquity and in the Middle Ages, it was now the fate of an entire civilization that lay in the balance. The ferocity with which the Europeans threw themselves into the struggle, the fact that peace by compromise was ruled out, seems to prove the point.

But while Europe bled white, the majority of non-Europeans looked on. Realizing that the power of Western man was crumbling as a result of his own acts, they nevertheless did not hesitate to take into their own hands the tools of his fate: industrialism for one, nationalism for another. Here, then, is the legacy that Europe bequeathed to the world at the very moment when the days of her supremacy were numbered. From the disintegration of colonial empires in Asia and Africa (begun in 1914), an amazing array of nationalities has arisen, each claiming the right of self-determination. Even the Russian Revolution, marching behind the shield of international solidarity, has drawn its real strength from national forces and from the desire of its leaders to make Russia the most powerful nation. Hence, it may be argued that the world took up Europe's battle. If history is, as Hegel says, the progress in the consciousness of liberty, a new phase of this development began in 1914. If Europe was forced to relinquish her eminence, it was by means of weapons forged in her own arsenal, and the white man may derive what comfort he can from such reflections.

The change in class and society that came after 1914 is not limited to the Western world, but few would deny that it originated here. The battlefields of the Great War produced a democracy of death, and from it survivors should have learned a single lesson: the democracy of the living. But they were slow to see the light. The war brought dynastic rule to an end in the four great Eastern empires: Russia, Austria, Germany, and Turkey. In turn, the removal of dynasties brought about the elimination of feudal remnants in central and eastern Europe, although the liquidation of the land-holding class and its influence on the government was, in some instances, delayed until 1945.

Wherever dynastic rule was preserved, it was stripped of its quasi-religious splendor, of the belief in the magic qualities inherent in royal blood, a relic of medievalism. In general, one might say that the old horizontal order of society gave way to a vertical structure. A hierarchy of talent and work replaced the old hierarchy of blood, property, and church membership. The integration of the working class into the body politic, well under way by 1914, was greatly speeded up by the war. In Western Europe the teachings of evolutionary socialism were adopted in large measure. In Russia the "fourth estate" took over and destroyed the older classes. But if we examine the picture a little more closely, we must admit that the shaping of society was not determined by one theory or another, nor by the dynamics of the masses themselves, but by the process of rationalization in its multifaceted aspects. In this respect Max Weber has proved most clairvoyant.

Weber's formula, "the disenchantment of the world," would, however, seem too simple to describe the complicated process of rationalization. The rationalism of the twentieth century bears little resemblance to that of the Enlighten-

ment. It knows its own limitations; it knows that man is only partially susceptible to rational analysis. It is, therefore, much less confident of its potentialities.

In the realm of history and of sociology Western man has lost the feeling
of superiority, the narcissistic concern with Europe. As other civilizations came
within the range of his curiosity, he admitted, not without regret, to historicism
and relativism. The impact of these theories, esoteric as they were, on the
masses may have been negligible, but it did influence the outlook of the European intelligentsia, and contributed in large measure to the new awareness of
which I have spoken.

The natural sciences, on the other hand, found themselves in their spectacular
advances confronted with revolutionary aspects of the universe which resisted
a unifying explanation. The world of science, which had for so long inspired
the European claim to superiority, was without a common bond. Where once
a great cognitive effort had spread out fanwise, there were now only divergent
labors lacking a common philosophical foundation. The antimetaphysical attitude of Marx and Darwin found its consummation in Weber, Dilthey, and
Freud, and the countercurrents of Bergson and Croce were not strong enough
to turn the tide. By 1914 an impasse had been reached which had important
consequences. Since man cannot long survive in an atmosphere of general
skepticism, the European turned to other sources for justification. If science
could no longer furnish the support needed, and if religion had lost its unifying
power, there seemed nothing to do but look for an ersatz solution. Of such,
Europe produced a large supply after 1914. The manufacturers of myths had
a field day; state, class, race, and sex were set up on the altars to which man
brought the sacrifice of his intellect and often of his conscience.

Strangely enough, the process of rationalization was not thereby deprived of
its momentum. The impact of technology on European life continued. Throughout the nineteenth century there had been an expansion of the practical intellect at the expense of creativity and moral consciousness which had produced
an undisciplined monster groping blindly in all directions. Premonitions of this
state of affairs can be noted in Kierkegaard, Baudelaire, Burckhardt, and Bergson, but it was left for the Great War to drive the lesson home.

Obviously the war itself was an irrational happening which seemed to
refute all the claims of the rationalists. Nevertheless, it was conducted by the
most advanced technology: poison gas, airplanes, tanks, submarines. An irrational undertaking was carried out by rational means. The war was ultimately
decided by the industrial potential of the United States. We have seen
Lenin's grasp of the lessons to be drawn from scientific management, and his
advocacy of their application in the new Soviet society. If I may be forgiven an
overstatement, I would say that he and his successor followed Taylor's advice
in their deliberate effort to industrialize Russia.

We are led logically into another aspect of the problem of rationalization and
its impact on the European scene. To what extent did Europe try to rebuild
society according to rational principles? Here we must depend on the answer
to a second question. Does Russia belong to Europe, to the West? Only in

Russia was society reconstructed according to preconceived notions and blue-prints. Lenin erased the old society and erected a new one. It has often been said that in doing so he turned Russia's face away from the West. Yet the in-spiration for this experiment came from Karl Marx and his belief that the age of social justice was about to begin. That this appeal has inflamed the imagina-tion of millions of non-Europeans is, therefore, one more triumph of the European mind. One is inclined to think that Khrushchev is closer to Western leaders than to Ivan the Terrible.

In the meantime, the West followed its old habit of counter-balancing revolu-tionary principles by evoking traditions and customs heavily weighted with emotional appeal. In other words, the progress of rationalism was not uncon-ditional. The institutions with which Europe emerged from the First World War were substantially the same as those by which the Old World had lived before the cataclysm. This fact in itself should caution us against too far-reaching an interpretation of the effects that the war had on Europe. However, there can be no hesitation in asserting that Europe had lost her supremacy. Her own self-confidence was shaken and the world had learned that the prin-ciples on which the European position rested could be emulated without great difficulty.

The consequences of Europe's deposition were not well understood by the Europeans; it took the Second World War to make the meaning of the first apparent. However, the joint result has been the advent of a new con-sciousness, though its manifestations may be dim, confused, misguided, and often contradictory. Submerged as we are in the day-to-day struggle between two competing ideologies and systems of power, we often fail to see the similarity between the leading figures of the twentieth century, regardless of the camp to which they belong. I feel certain that future historians will, how-ever, discern this resemblance. Such an assertion returns us to our original thesis: that the meaning of the First World War lies in the destruction of European supremacy and the consequent dawn of an era of global awareness and interdependence.

It would be folly to pretend that the whole of European culture before 1914 had pointed toward such a transformation. There were broad strata that were not at all affected by the schismatic trends we have found it necessary to stress. In the novel, the drama, the opera, there is much that should warn us against hasty generalizations. The names of Arnold Bennett, Yeats, Puccini, Chekov, come to mind. There is always more in any given era that a schematically con-structed Zeitgeist is able to account for. I neither wish to belittle the impor-tance of these men, nor do I claim that the picture of European culture given in these pages is all-encompassing. Yet the conclusion remains that the Euro-pean mind had reached a deadlock, that its most representative productions had become schizophrenic and self-contradictory.

Such an observation should not, however, lead us to adopt catchwords like "decline of the West." The decline of the West became a certainty only in the fields of politics and economics. In the realm of culture the seeds sown by Western man have survived. There was in 1914 no other literature, no other art, science, or philosophy that was comparable to the European production in those fields. And when the world adopted Europe's legacy it naturally fell under its spell and continued to interpret human existence in terms derived from Darwin and Marx, from Nietzsche and Freud, from Einstein and Planck.

That the "world of yesterday" in its particular form was destined to vanish was a foregone conclusion. Europe has never tried to fossilize its own creations; it has always allowed new impulses to assert themselves. That these impulses in 1914 broke through barriers and frontiers which had until then checked their force, would seem preordained.

Historical consciousness, as the West developed it, implies the knowledge that all forms and structures built by the human mind are finite and destined to be superseded. Yet this same resignation to which modern man is constrained assures him of an asset of which he cannot be deprived, his spiritual self-determination. Einstein said once that the most incomprehensible thing about the universe was the fact that it is comprehensible. In regard to man, one is tempted to rephrase this comment by saying that the most incomprehensible thing about him is his determination to comprehend himself. Born with the sickness unto death, victim of folly and pride, he maintains the single distinction to dare fate by his thought.

Of such daring there is ample evidence in the period that has occupied our minds. To many, the age that preceded the First World War is remote and clouded. For some it was a fool's paradise maintained by prejudice and self-indulgence. For others it was an Eden of security. Neither interpretation does justice to its particular importance at the threshold of a new era. The words "progress" and "decline" have meaning only for those who belong to a given society, to a given civilization. The transformation of European culture which took place between 1890 and 1914 makes it apparent that historical developments do not lose their significance once we realize that mankind does not move upward, but onward.